BMW 520i & 525e Owners Workshop Manual

A K Legg T Eng MIMI

Models covered
BMW 520i & 520i Lux; 1990 cc
BMW 525e & 525e Lux; 2693 cc

Does not cover 525i or revised range introduced June 1988

ABCDE
FGHIJ
KLMNO
PQRST

Haynes Publishing Group
Sparkford Nr Yeovil
Somerset BA22 7JJ. England

Haynes Publications, Inc
861 Lawrence Drive
Newbury Park
California 91320 USA

Acknowledgements
Thanks are due to the Champion Sparking Plug Company Limited, who supplied the illustrations showing spark plug conditions, to Holt Lloyd Limited who supplied the illustrations showing bodywork repair and to Duckhams Oils, who provided lubrication data. Thanks are also due to Sykes-Pickavant Limited who provided some of the workshop tools, and to all those people at Sparkford who assisted in the production of this manual.

A book in the **Haynes Owners Workshop Manual Series**

Printed by J. H. Haynes & Co. Ltd., Sparkford, Nr Yeovil, Somerset BA22 7JJ, England

ISBN 1 85010 560 X

British Library Cataloguing in Publication Data
Legg, A. K. (Andrew K.) *1942 –*
BMW 520i & 525e owners workshop manual.
1. Cars. Maintenance & repair
I. Title
629.28722
ISBN 1-85010-560-X

Contents

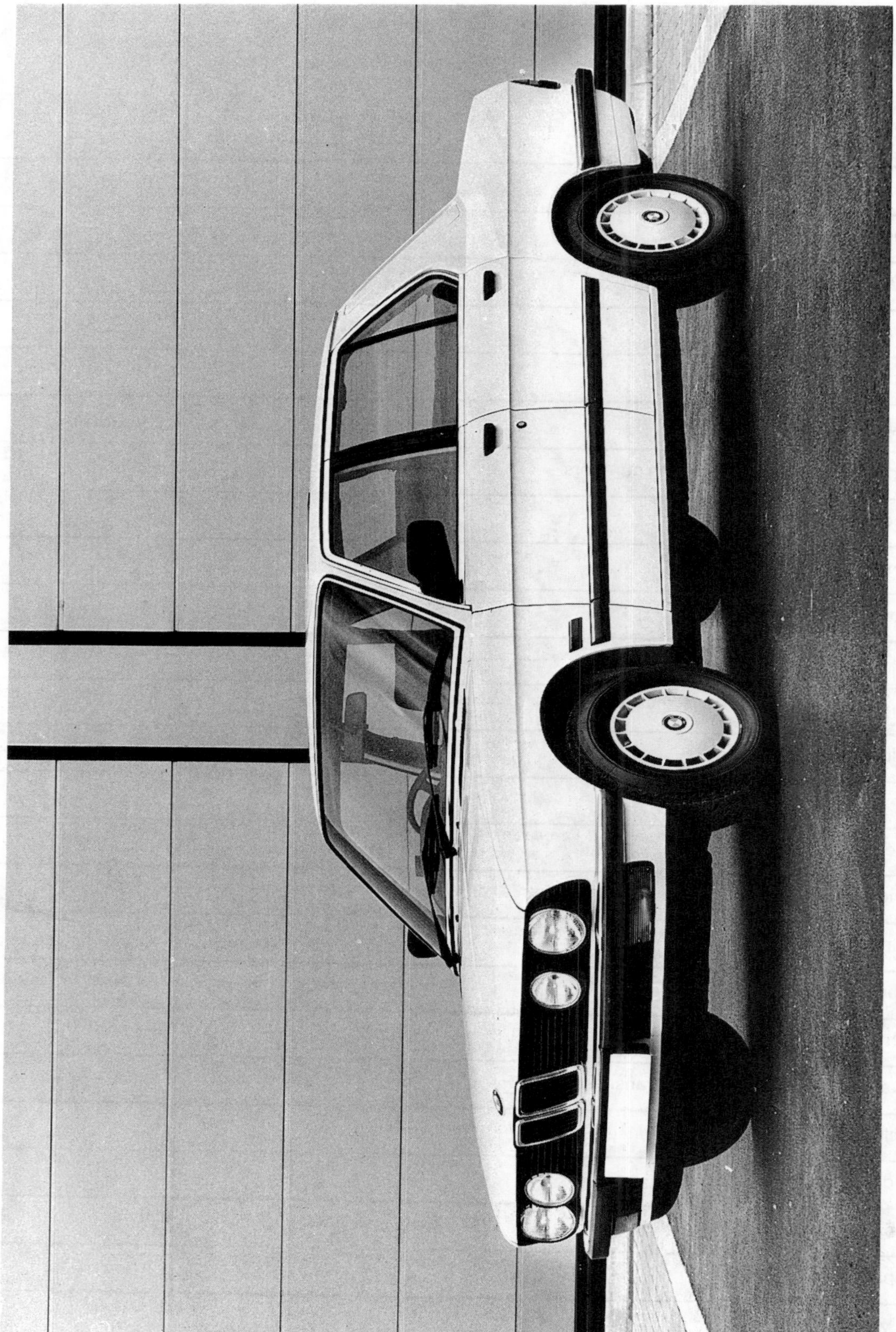

BMW 520i

About this manual

Its aim

The aim of this manual is to help you get the best value from your vehicle. It can do so in several ways. It can help you decide what work must be done (even should you choose to get it done by a garage), provide information on routine maintenance and servicing, and give a logical course of action and diagnosis when random faults occur. However, it is hoped that you will use the manual by tackling the work yourself. On simpler jobs it may even be quicker than booking the car into a garage and going there twice, to leave and collect it. Perhaps most important, a lot of money can be saved by avoiding the costs a garage must charge to cover its labour and overheads.

The manual has drawings and descriptions to show the function of the various components so that their layout can be understood. Then the tasks are described and photographed in a step-by-step sequence so that even a novice can do the work.

Its arrangement

The manual is divided into twelve Chapters, each covering a logical sub-division of the vehicle. The Chapters are each divided into Sections, numbered with single figures, eg 5; and the Sections into paragraphs (or sub-sections), with decimal numbers following on from the Section they are in, eg 5.1, 5.2, 5.3 etc.

It is freely illustrated, especially in those parts where there is a detailed sequence of operations to be carried out. There are two forms of illustration: figures and photographs. The figures are numbered in sequence with decimal numbers, according to their position in the Chapter – eg Fig. 6.4 is the fourth drawing/illustration in Chapter 6. Photographs carry the same number (either individually or in related groups) as the Section or sub-section to which they relate.

There is an alphabetical index at the back of the manual as well as a contents list at the front. Each Chapter is also preceded by its own individual contents list.

References to the 'left' or 'right' of the vehicle are in the sense of a person in the driver's seat facing forwards.

Unless otherwise stated, nuts and bolts are removed by turning anti-clockwise, and tightened by turning clockwise.

Vehicle manufacturers continually make changes to specifications and recommendations, and these, when notified, are incorporated into our manuals at the earliest opportunity.

Whilst every care is taken to ensure that the information in this manual is correct, no liability can be accepted by the authors or publishers for loss, damage or injury caused by any errors in, or omissions from, the information given.

Project vehicles

The main project vehicle used in the preparation of this manual, and appearing in many of the photographic sequences was a 1987 BMW 525e Lux.

Introduction to the BMW 520i and 525e

The BMW 520i was introduced in October 1981 and the 525e in June 1983. Both models are manufactured to fine limits and live up to the BMW reputation of quality workmanship.

The 520i is fitted with a 1990 cc six cylinder engine and the 525e with a 2693 cc six cylinder engine. Both engines are of single overhead camshaft, in-line type with a light alloy cylinder head and cast iron cylinder block. The camshaft is driven by a toothed belt. The 520i is fitted with either a manual gearbox or automatic transmission, whereas the 525e is only fitted with an automatic transmission.

Both models are absolutely conventional in design and should present no problems to the home mechanic. The only area where some extra caution is advisable is in the electronic engine management system and fuel control system.

General dimensions, weights and capacities

Dimensions

Overall length	4620 mm (181.9 in)
Overall width	1700 mm (66.9 in)
Overall height	1415 mm (55.7 in)
Wheelbase	2625 mm (103.3 in)
Front track	1430 mm (56.3 in)
Rear track:	
520i	1470 mm (57.9 in)
525e	1460 mm (57.5 in)
Turning circle	10.9 m (35 ft 9 in)

Weights

Kerb weight:	
520i with manual transmission	1260 kg (2778 lb)
520i with automatic transmission	1260 kg (2822 lb)
525e	1300 kg (2866 lb)
Maximum gross vehicle weight:	
520i with manual transmission	1770 kg (3902 lb)
520i with automatic transmission	1790 kg (3946 lb)
525e	1810 kg (3990 lb)
Maximum roof rack load	75 kg (165 lb)
Minimum towing weight:	
Braked trailer:	
520i with manual transmission	1400 kg (3086 lb)
520i with automatic transmission	1500 kg (3307 lb)
525e	1500 kg (3307 lb)
Unbraked trailer	500 kg (1102 lb)
Maximum towing hitch downward load	50 kg (110 lb)

Capacities

Engine oil (including filter)	4.5 litres (7.9 pints)
Cooling system:	
520i models	10.5 litres (9.2 pints)
525e models	11.0 litres (9.7 pints)
Fuel tank	70 litres (15.4 gal)
Manual gearbox:	
240	1.05 litres (1.8 pints)
242	1.0 litres (1.7 pints)
245	1.5 litres (2.6 pints)
ZF	1.15 litres (2.0 pints)
Automatic transmission:	
Fluid capacity (fluid change):	
ZF-3HP-22	2.0 litres (3.5 pints)
ZF-4HP-22	3.0 litres (5.3 pints)
Refill from dry:	
ZF-3HP-22	5.7 to 6.1 litres (10.0 to 10.7 pints)
ZF-4HP-22	6.4 to 7.5 litres (11.3 to 13.2 pints)
Final drive capacity (drain and refill):	
520i:	
To 1985	1.5 litres (2.6 pints)
1986 on	1.7 litres (3.0 pints)
525e	1.7 litres (3.0 pints)
Power steering system	1.2 litres (2.1 pints)

Jacking, towing and wheel changing

Jacking

The jack supplied with the car should only be used for wheel changing, as described later. When raising the vehicle for repair or maintenance, preferably use a trolley or hydraulic jack, with a wooden block as an insulator, to prevent damage to the underbody. Place the jack under the jacking points, which are located behind the front wheels and in front of the rear wheels. Position the axle stands under the jacking points or alternatively beneath the main underbody channels.

Towing

Towing eyes are provided at the front and rear of the car – the front eye is behind a small hinged panel (photos). When being towed, turn the ignition key to position 1 so that the brake lights, direction indicators, horn and wipers are operational. The hazard lights should also be switched on. Note that with the engine stopped, more effort will be required to stop the car, as the brake servo will be inoperative. In addition the power steering pump will not be operating so more effort will be required to turn the steering wheel.

The gear lever should be in neutral on manual gearbox models, or position 'N' on automatic transmission models. Automatic transmission models should not be towed further than 30 miles (50 km) or faster than 30 mph (50 km/h). To tow the car for greater distances, add 1 litre (1.8 pints) of automatic transmission fluid to the transmission, but remember to drain the excess fluid before driving the car on the road again. If these conditions cannot be met, or if transmission damage has occurred, remove the propeller shaft.

Wheel changing

To change a roadwheel, first park on a firm level surface if possible. Chock the wheel opposite the one being removed. Apply the handbrake, and engage first or reverse gear on manual gearbox models, or 'P' on automatic transmission models.

Lift the floor mat in the luggage compartment, then unscrew the wing nut and remove the spare wheel. Remove the jack from the left-hand side of the luggage compartment.

Where fitted, unlock and remove the wheel bolt lock. Remove the trim from the roadwheel and use the brace to slacken the wheel bolts. Pull out the small cover and engage the jack with the jacking point nearest the roadwheel. Make sure that the jack is located squarely on the ground. Raise the jack until the roadwheel is just clear of the ground. Unscrew and remove the wheel bolts and take off the roadwheel.

Where necessary remove the hub cap from the spare wheel by releasing the spring. Fit the centering pin from the toolkit which is located on the underside of the boot lid (photo), into one of the tapped holes in the wheel hub. Locate the spare wheel on the centering pin and screw in three of the wheel bolts. Remove the centering pin and screw in the last wheel bolt. Lightly tighten the bolts with the brace. Lower the car to the ground and remove the jack, then tighten the wheel bolts in diagonal sequence. Tighten the bolts as hard as possible using the brace from the toolkit, but have their tightness checked as soon as possible with a torque wrench. When fitting the spare wheel for the first time, it must be checked for tightness after 1000 km (600 miles).

Refit the wheel trim, making sure that the valve hole is located over the valve. Tap the trim into position with the palm of the hand.

Front towing eye

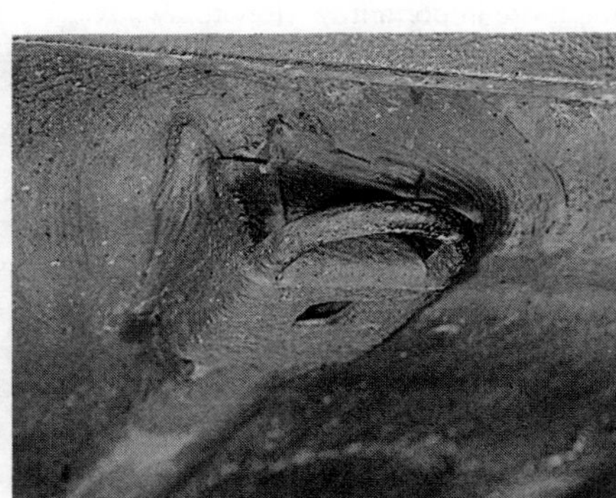

Rear towing eye

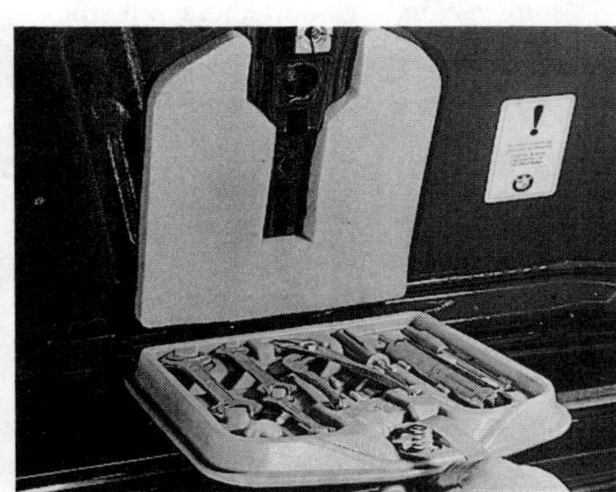

Toolkit located on the underside of the boot lid

Buying spare parts and vehicle identification numbers

Buying spare parts

Spare parts are available from many sources, for example: BMW garages, other garages and accessory shops, and motor factors. Our advice regarding spare part sources is as follows.

Officially appointed BMW garages – This is the best source for parts which are peculiar to your vehicle and are not generally available (eg complete cylinder heads, internal gearbox components, badges, interior trim etc). It is also the only place at which you should buy parts if the vehicle is still under warranty. To be sure of obtaining the correct parts, it will be necessary to give the storeman your car's vehicle identification number, and if possible, take the old parts along for positive identification. Many parts are available under a factory exchange scheme – any parts returned should always be clean. It obviously makes good sense to go straight to the specialists on your car for this type of part, as they are best equipped to supply you.

Other garages and accessory shops – These are often very good places to buy materials and components needed for the maintenance of your car (eg oil filters, spark plugs, bulbs, drivebelts, oils, and greases, touch-up paint, filler paste, etc). They also sell general accessories, usually have convenient opening hours, charge lower prices and can often be found not far from home.

Motor factors – Good factors will stock all of the more important components which wear out relatively quickly (eg exhaust systems, brake pads, seals and hydraulic parts, clutch components, bearing shells, pistons, valves etc). Motor factors will often provide new or reconditioned components on a part exchange basis – this can save a considerable amount of money.

Vehicle identification numbers

Modifications are a continuing and unpublicised process in vehicle manufacture, quite apart from major model changes. Spare parts manuals and lists are compiled upon a numerical basis, the individual vehicle identification numbers being essential to correct identification of the component required.

When ordering spare parts, always give as much information as possible. Quote the car model, year of manufacture, body and engine numbers as appropriate.

The Vehicle Identification Number is located on the right-hand front wheel arch next to the front suspension strut upper mounting (photo).

The body number is located on the seam between the left-hand front wing and inner panel (photo).

The engine number is stamped on a machined face on the left-hand side of the cylinder block near the base of the oil level dipstick tube (photo).

Vehicle Identification number (VIN)

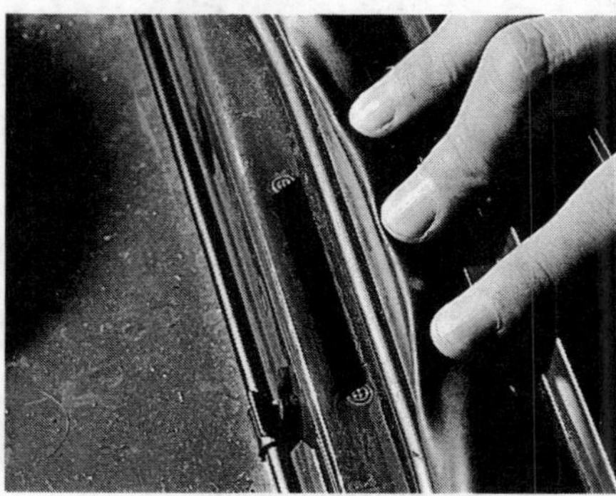
Body number location

Engine number

General repair procedures

Whenever servicing, repair or overhaul work is carried out on the car or its components, it is necessary to observe the following procedures and instructions. This will assist in carrying out the operation efficiently and to a professional standard of workmanship.

Joint mating faces and gaskets

Where a gasket is used between the mating faces of two components, ensure that it is renewed on reassembly, and fit it dry unless otherwise stated in the repair procedure. Make sure that the mating faces are clean and dry with all traces of old gasket removed. When cleaning a joint face, use a tool which is not likely to score or damage the face, and remove any burrs or nicks with an oilstone or fine file.

Make sure that tapped holes are cleaned with a pipe cleaner, and keep them free of jointing compound if this is being used unless specifically instructed otherwise.

Ensure that all orifices, channels or pipes are clear and blow through them, preferably using compressed air.

Oil seals

Whenever an oil seal is removed from its working location, either individually or as part of an assembly, it should be renewed.

The very fine sealing lip of the seal is easily damaged and will not seal if the surface it contacts is not completely clean and free from scratches, nicks or grooves. If the original sealing surface of the component cannot be restored, the component should be renewed.

Protect the lips of the seal from any surface which may damage them in the course of fitting. Use tape or a conical sleeve where possible. Lubricate the seal lips with oil before fitting and, on dual lipped seals, fill the space between the lips with grease.

Unless otherwise stated, oil seals must be fitted with their sealing lips toward the lubricant to be sealed.

Use a tubular drift or block of wood of the appropriate size to install the seal and, if the seal housing is shouldered, drive the seal down to the shoulder. If the seal housing is unshouldered, the seal should be fitted with its face flush with the housing top face.

Screw threads and fastenings

Always ensure that a blind tapped hole is completely free from oil, grease, water or other fluid before installing the bolt or stud. Failure to do this could cause the housing to crack due to the hydraulic action of the bolt or stud as it is screwed in.

When tightening a castellated nut to accept a split pin, tighten the nut to the specified torque, where applicable, and then tighten further to the next split pin hole. Never slacken the nut to align a split pin hole unless stated in the repair procedure.

When checking or retightening a nut or bolt to a specified torque setting, slacken the nut or bolt by a quarter of a turn, and then retighten to the specified setting.

Locknuts, locktabs and washers

Any fastening which will rotate against a component or housing in the course of tightening should always have a washer between it and the relevant component or housing.

Spring or split washers should always be renewed when they are used to lock a critical component such as a big-end bearing retaining nut or bolt.

Locktabs which are folded over to retain a nut or bolt should always be renewed.

Self-locking nuts can be reused in non-critical areas, providing resistance can be felt when the locking portion passes over the bolt or stud thread.

Split pins must always be replaced with new ones of the correct size for the hole.

Special tools

Some repair procedures in this manual entail the use of special tools such as a press, two or three-legged pullers, spring compressors etc. Wherever possible, suitable readily available alternatives to the manufacturer's special tools are described, and are shown in use. In some instances, where no alternative is possible, it has been necessary to resort to the use of a manufacturer's tool and this has been done for reasons of safety as well as the efficient completion of the repair operation. Unless you are highly skilled and have a thorough understanding of the procedure described, never attempt to bypass the use of any special tool when the procedure described specifies its use. Not only is there a very great risk of personal injury, but expensive damage could be caused to the components involved.

Tools and working facilities

Introduction

A selection of good tools is a fundamental requirement for anyone contemplating the maintenance and repair of a motor vehicle. For the owner who does not possess any, their purchase will prove a considerable expense, offsetting some of the savings made by doing-it-yourself. However, provided that the tools purchased meet the relevant national safety standards and are of good quality, they will last for many years and prove an extremely worthwhile investment.

To help the average owner to decide which tools are needed to carry out the various tasks detailed in this manual, we have compiled three lists of tools under the following headings: *Maintenance and minor repair, Repair and overhaul,* and *Special.* The newcomer to practical mechanics should start off with the *Maintenance and minor repair* tool kit and confine himself to the simpler jobs around the vehicle. Then, as his confidence and experience grow, he can undertake more difficult tasks, buying extra tools as, and when, they are needed. In this way, a *Maintenance and minor repair* tool kit can be built-up into a *Repair and overhaul* tool kit over a considerable period of time without any major cash outlays. The experienced do-it-yourselfer will have a tool kit good enough for most repair and overhaul procedures and will add tools from the *Special* category when he feels the expense is justified by the amount of use to which these tools will be put.

It is obviously not possible to cover the subject of tools fully here. For those who wish to learn more about tools and their use there is a book entitled *How to Choose and Use Car Tools* available from the publishers of this manual.

Maintenance and minor repair tool kit

The tools given in this list should be considered as a minimum requirement if routine maintenance, servicing and minor repair operations are to be undertaken. We recommend the purchase of combination spanners (ring one end, open-ended the other); although more expensive than open-ended ones, they do give the advantages of both types of spanner.

Combination spanners – 10, 11, 12, 13, 14 & 17 mm
Combination spanners – $\frac{7}{16}$, $\frac{1}{2}$, $\frac{9}{16}$, $\frac{5}{8}$, $\frac{11}{16}$, $\frac{3}{4}$ & $\frac{13}{16}$ in AF
Adjustable spanner – 9 inch
Gearbox/rear axle drain plug key
Spark plug spanner (with rubber insert)
Spark plug gap adjustment tool
Set of feeler gauges
Brake bleed nipple spanner
Screwdriver – 4 in long x $\frac{1}{4}$ in dia (flat blade)
Screwdriver – 4 in long x $\frac{1}{4}$ in dia (cross blade)
Combination pliers – 6 inch
Hacksaw (junior)
Tyre pump
Tyre pressure gauge
Oil can
Oil filter removal tool
Fine emery cloth (1 sheet)
Wire brush (small)
Funnel (medium size)

Repair and overhaul tool kit

These tools are virtually essential for anyone undertaking any major repairs to a motor vehicle, and are additional to those given in the *Maintenance and minor repair* list. Included in this list is a comprehensive set of sockets. Although these are expensive they will be found invaluable as they are so versatile – particularly if various drives are included in the set. We recommend the $\frac{1}{2}$ in square-drive type, as this can be used with most proprietary torque wrenches. If you cannot afford a socket set, even bought piecemeal, then inexpensive tubular box spanners are a useful alternative.

The tools in this list will occasionally need to be supplemented by tools from the *Special* list.

Sockets (or box spanners) to cover range in previous list
Reversible ratchet drive (for use with sockets)
Extension piece, 10 inch (for use with sockets)
Universal joint (for use with sockets)
Torque wrench (for use with sockets)
Self-locking grips
Ball pein hammer
Soft-faced hammer, plastic or rubber
Screwdriver – 6 in long x $\frac{5}{16}$in dia (flat blade)
Screwdriver – 2 in long x $\frac{5}{16}$in square (flat blade)
Screwdriver – $1\frac{1}{2}$ in long x $\frac{1}{4}$ in dia (cross blade)
Screwdriver – 3 in long x $\frac{1}{8}$ in dia (electricians)
Pliers – electricians side cutters
Pliers – needle-nosed
Pliers – circlip (internal and external)
Cold chisel – $\frac{1}{2}$ inch
Scriber
Scraper
Centre punch
Pin punch
Hacksaw
Brake hose clamp
Brake/clutch bleeding kit
Selection of twist drills
Steel rule/straight-edge
Allen keys (inc. splined/Torx type if necessary)
Selection of files
Wire brush (large)
Axle-stands
Jack (strong trolley or hydraulic type)
Light with extension lead

Special tools

The tools in this list are those which are not used regularly, are expensive to buy, or which need to be used in accordance with their manufacturers' instructions. Unless relatively difficult mechanical jobs are undertaken frequently, it will not be economic to buy many of these tools. Where this is the case, you could consider clubbing together with friends (or joining a motorists' club) to make a joint purchase, or borrowing the tools against a deposit from a local garage or tool hire specialist.

The following list contains only those tools and instruments freely available to the public, and not those special tools produced by the vehicle manufacturer specifically for its dealer network. You will find occasional references to these manufacturers' special tools in the text of this manual. Generally, an alternative method of doing the job without the vehicle manufacturers' special tool is given. However, sometimes, there is no alternative to using them. Where this is the case and the relevant tool cannot be bought or borrowed, you will have to entrust the work to a franchised garage.

Valve spring compressor
Coil spring compressors
Piston ring compressor
Balljoint separator
Universal hub/bearing puller
Impact screwdriver
Micrometer and/or vernier gauge
Dial gauge
Stroboscopic timing light
Dwell angle meter/tachometer
Universal electrical multi-meter
Cylinder compression gauge
Lifting tackle
Trolley jack

Buying tools

For practically all tools, a tool factor is the best source since he will have a very comprehensive range compared with the average garage or accessory shop. Having said that, accessory shops often offer excellent quality tools at discount prices, so it pays to shop around.

There are plenty of good tools around at reasonable prices, but always aim to purchase items which meet the relevant national safety standards. If in doubt, ask the proprietor or manager of the shop for advice before making a purchase.

Care and maintenance of tools

Having purchased a reasonable tool kit, it is necessary to keep the tools in a clean serviceable condition. After use, always wipe off any dirt, grease and metal particles using a clean, dry cloth, before putting the tools away. Never leave them lying around after they have been used. A simple tool rack on the garage or workshop wall, for items such as screwdrivers and pliers is a good idea. Store all normal wrenches and sockets in a metal box. Any measuring instruments, gauges, meters, etc, must be carefully stored where they cannot be damaged or become rusty.

Take a little care when tools are used. Hammer heads inevitably become marked and screwdrivers lose the keen edge on their blades from time to time. A little timely attention with emery cloth or a file will soon restore items like this to a good serviceable finish.

Working facilities

Not to be forgotten when discussing tools, is the workshop itself. If anything more than routine maintenance is to be carried out, some form of suitable working area becomes essential.

It is appreciated that many an owner mechanic is forced by circumstances to remove an engine or similar item, without the benefit of a garage or workshop. Having done this, any repairs should always be done under the cover of a roof.

Wherever possible, any dismantling should be done on a clean, flat workbench or table at a suitable working height.

Any workbench needs a vice: one with a jaw opening of 4 in (100 mm) is suitable for most jobs. As mentioned previously, some clean dry storage space is also required for tools, as well as for lubricants, cleaning fluids, touch-up paints and so on, which become necessary.

Another item which may be required, and which has a much more general usage, is an electric drill with a chuck capacity of at least $\frac{5}{16}$ in (8 mm). This, together with a good range of twist drills, is virtually essential for fitting accessories such as mirrors and reversing lights.

Last, but not least, always keep a supply of old newspapers and clean, lint-free rags available, and try to keep any working area as clean as possible.

Spanner jaw gap comparison table

Jaw gap (in)	Spanner size
0.250	$\frac{1}{4}$ in AF
0.276	7 mm
0.313	$\frac{5}{16}$ in AF
0.315	8 mm
0.344	$\frac{11}{32}$ in AF; $\frac{1}{8}$ in Whitworth
0.354	9 mm
0.375	$\frac{3}{8}$ in AF
0.394	10 mm
0.433	11 mm
0.438	$\frac{7}{16}$ in AF
0.445	$\frac{3}{16}$ in Whitworth; $\frac{1}{4}$ in BSF
0.472	12 mm
0.500	$\frac{1}{2}$ in AF
0.512	13 mm
0.525	$\frac{1}{4}$ in Whitworth; $\frac{5}{16}$ in BSF
0.551	14 mm
0.563	$\frac{9}{16}$ in AF
0.591	15 mm
0.600	$\frac{5}{16}$ in Whitworth; $\frac{3}{8}$ in BSF
0.625	$\frac{5}{8}$ in AF
0.630	16 mm
0.669	17 mm
0.686	$\frac{11}{16}$ in AF
0.709	18 mm
0.710	$\frac{3}{8}$ in Whitworth; $\frac{7}{16}$ in BSF
0.748	19 mm
0.750	$\frac{3}{4}$ in AF
0.813	$\frac{13}{16}$ in AF
0.820	$\frac{7}{16}$ in Whitworth; $\frac{1}{2}$ in BSF
0.866	22 mm
0.875	$\frac{7}{8}$ in AF
0.920	$\frac{1}{2}$ in Whitworth; $\frac{9}{16}$ in BSF
0.938	$\frac{15}{16}$ in AF
0.945	24 mm
1.000	1 in AF
1.010	$\frac{9}{16}$ in Whitworth; $\frac{5}{8}$ in BSF
1.024	26 mm
1.063	$1\frac{1}{16}$ in AF; 27 mm
1.100	$\frac{5}{8}$ in Whitworth; $\frac{11}{16}$ in BSF
1.125	$1\frac{1}{8}$ in AF
1.181	30 mm
1.200	$\frac{11}{16}$ in Whitworth; $\frac{3}{4}$ in BSF
1.250	$1\frac{1}{4}$ in AF
1.260	32 mm
1.300	$\frac{3}{4}$ in Whitworth; $\frac{7}{8}$ in BSF
1.313	$1\frac{5}{16}$ in AF
1.390	$\frac{13}{16}$ in Whitworth; $\frac{15}{16}$ in BSF
1.417	36 mm
1.438	$1\frac{7}{16}$ in AF
1.480	$\frac{7}{8}$ in Whitworth; 1 in BSF
1.500	$1\frac{1}{2}$ in AF
1.575	40 mm; $\frac{15}{16}$ in Whitworth
1.614	41 mm
1.625	$1\frac{5}{8}$ in AF
1.670	1 in Whitworth; $1\frac{1}{8}$ in BSF
1.688	$1\frac{11}{16}$ in AF
1.811	46 mm
1.813	$1\frac{13}{16}$ in AF
1.860	$1\frac{1}{8}$ in Whitworth; $1\frac{1}{4}$ in BSF
1.875	$1\frac{7}{8}$ in AF
1.969	50 mm
2.000	2 in AF
2.050	$1\frac{1}{4}$ in Whitworth; $1\frac{3}{8}$ in BSF
2.165	55 mm
2.362	60 mm

Conversion factors

Length (distance)

Inches (in)	X	25.4	= Millimetres (mm)	X	0.0394	= Inches (in)
Feet (ft)	X	0.305	= Metres (m)	X	3.281	= Feet (ft)
Miles	X	1.609	= Kilometres (km)	X	0.621	= Miles

Volume (capacity)

Cubic inches (cu in; in^3)	X	16.387	= Cubic centimetres (cc; cm^3)	X	0.061	= Cubic inches (cu in; in^3)
Imperial pints (Imp pt)	X	0.568	= Litres (l)	X	1.76	= Imperial pints (Imp pt)
Imperial quarts (Imp qt)	X	1.137	= Litres (l)	X	0.88	= Imperial quarts (Imp qt)
Imperial quarts (Imp qt)	X	1.201	= US quarts (US qt)	X	0.833	= Imperial quarts (Imp qt)
US quarts (US qt)	X	0.946	= Litres (l)	X	1.057	= US quarts (US qt)
Imperial gallons (Imp gal)	X	4.546	= Litres (l)	X	0.22	= Imperial gallons (Imp gal)
Imperial gallons (Imp gal)	X	1.201	= US gallons (US gal)	X	0.833	= Imperial gallons (Imp gal)
US gallons (US gal)	X	3.785	= Litres (l)	X	0.264	= US gallons (US gal)

Mass (weight)

Ounces (oz)	X	28.35	= Grams (g)	X	0.035	= Ounces (oz)
Pounds (lb)	X	0.454	= Kilograms (kg)	X	2.205	= Pounds (lb)

Force

Ounces-force (ozf; oz)	X	0.278	= Newtons (N)	X	3.6	= Ounces-force (ozf; oz)
Pounds-force (lbf; lb)	X	4.448	= Newtons (N)	X	0.225	= Pounds-force (lbf; lb)
Newtons (N)	X	0.1	= Kilograms-force (kgf; kg)	X	9.81	= Newtons (N)

Pressure

Pounds-force per square inch (psi; lbf/in^2; lb/in^2)	X	0.070	= Kilograms-force per square centimetre (kgf/cm^2; kg/cm^2)	X	14.223	= Pounds-force per square inch (psi; lbf/in^2; lb/in^2)
Pounds-force per square inch (psi; lbf/in^2; lb/in^2)	X	0.068	= Atmospheres (atm)	X	14.696	= Pounds-force per square inch (psi; lbf/in^2; lb/in^2)
Pounds-force per square inch (psi; lbf/in^2; lb/in^2)	X	0.069	= Bars	X	14.5	= Pounds-force per square inch (psi; lbf/in^2; lb/in^2)
Pounds-force per square inch (psi; lbf/in^2; lb/in^2)	X	6.895	= Kilopascals (kPa)	X	0.145	= Pounds-force per square inch (psi; lbf/in^2; lb/in^2)
Kilopascals (kPa)	X	0.01	= Kilograms-force per square centimetre (kgf/cm^2; kg/cm^2)	X	98.1	= Kilopascals (kPa)
Millibar (mbar)	X	100	= Pascals (Pa)	X	0.01	= Millibar (mbar)
Millibar (mbar)	X	0.0145	= Pounds-force per square inch (psi; lbf/in^2; lb/in^2)	X	68.947	= Millibar (mbar)
Millibar (mbar)	X	0.75	= Millimetres of mercury (mmHg)	X	1.333	= Millibar (mbar)
Millibar (mbar)	X	0.401	= Inches of water (inH$_2$O)	X	2.491	= Millibar (mbar)
Millimetres of mercury (mmHg)	X	0.535	= Inches of water (inH$_2$O)	X	1.868	= Millimetres of mercury (mmHg)
Inches of water (inH$_2$O)	X	0.036	= Pounds-force per square inch (psi; lbf/in^2; lb/in^2)	X	27.68	= Inches of water (inH$_2$O)

Torque (moment of force)

Pounds-force inches (lbf in; lb in)	X	1.152	= Kilograms-force centimetre (kgf cm; kg cm)	X	0.868	= Pounds-force inches (lbf in; lb in)
Pounds-force inches (lbf in; lb in)	X	0.113	= Newton metres (Nm)	X	8.85	= Pounds-force inches (lbf in; lb in)
Pounds-force inches (lbf in; lb in)	X	0.083	= Pounds-force feet (lbf ft; lb ft)	X	12	= Pounds-force inches (lbf in; lb in)
Pounds-force feet (lbf ft; lb ft)	X	0.138	= Kilograms-force metres (kgf m; kg m)	X	7.233	= Pounds-force feet (lbf ft; lb ft)
Pounds-force feet (lbf ft; lb ft)	X	1.356	= Newton metres (Nm)	X	0.738	= Pounds-force feet (lbf ft; lb ft)
Newton metres (Nm)	X	0.102	= Kilograms-force metres (kgf m; kg m)	X	9.804	= Newton metres (Nm)

Power

Horsepower (hp)	X	745.7	= Watts (W)	X	0.0013	= Horsepower (hp)

Velocity (speed)

Miles per hour (miles/hr; mph)	X	1.609	= Kilometres per hour (km/hr; kph)	X	0.621	= Miles per hour (miles/hr; mph)

*Fuel consumption**

Miles per gallon, Imperial (mpg)	X	0.354	= Kilometres per litre (km/l)	X	2.825	= Miles per gallon, Imperial (mpg)
Miles per gallon, US (mpg)	X	0.425	= Kilometres per litre (km/l)	X	2.352	= Miles per gallon, US (mpg)

Temperature

Degrees Fahrenheit = (°C x 1.8) + 32

Degrees Celsius (Degrees Centigrade; °C) = (°F - 32) x 0.56

**It is common practice to convert from miles per gallon (mpg) to litres/100 kilometres (l/100km), where mpg (Imperial) x l/100 km = 282 and mpg (US) x l/100 km = 235*

Safety first!

Professional motor mechanics are trained in safe working procedures. However enthusiastic you may be about getting on with the job in hand, do take the time to ensure that your safety is not put at risk. A moment's lack of attention can result in an accident, as can failure to observe certain elementary precautions.

There will always be new ways of having accidents, and the following points do not pretend to be a comprehensive list of all dangers; they are intended rather to make you aware of the risks and to encourage a safety-conscious approach to all work you carry out on your vehicle.

Essential DOs and DON'Ts

DON'T rely on a single jack when working underneath the vehicle. Always use reliable additional means of support, such as axle stands, securely placed under a part of the vehicle that you know will not give way.
DON'T attempt to loosen or tighten high-torque nuts (e.g. wheel hub nuts) while the vehicle is on a jack; it may be pulled off.
DON'T start the engine without first ascertaining that the transmission is in neutral (or 'Park' where applicable) and the parking brake applied.
DON'T suddenly remove the filler cap from a hot cooling system – cover it with a cloth and release the pressure gradually first, or you may get scalded by escaping coolant.
DON'T attempt to drain oil until you are sure it has cooled sufficiently to avoid scalding you.
DON'T grasp any part of the engine, exhaust or catalytic converter without first ascertaining that it is sufficiently cool to avoid burning you.
DON'T allow brake fluid or antifreeze to contact vehicle paintwork.
DON'T syphon toxic liquids such as fuel, brake fluid or antifreeze by mouth, or allow them to remain on your skin.
DON'T inhale dust – it may be injurious to health (see *Asbestos* below).
DON'T allow any spilt oil or grease to remain on the floor – wipe it up straight away, before someone slips on it.
DON'T use ill-fitting spanners or other tools which may slip and cause injury.
DON'T attempt to lift a heavy component which may be beyond your capability – get assistance.
DON'T rush to finish a job, or take unverified short cuts.
DON'T allow children or animals in or around an unattended vehicle.
DO wear eye protection when using power tools such as drill, sander, bench grinder etc, and when working under the vehicle.
DO use a barrier cream on your hands prior to undertaking dirty jobs – it will protect your skin from infection as well as making the dirt easier to remove afterwards; but make sure your hands aren't left slippery. Note that long-term contact with used engine oil can be a health hazard.
DO keep loose clothing (cuffs, tie etc) and long hair well out of the way of moving mechanical parts.
DO remove rings, wristwatch etc, before working on the vehicle – especially the electrical system.
DO ensure that any lifting tackle used has a safe working load rating adequate for the job.
DO keep your work area tidy – it is only too easy to fall over articles left lying around.
DO get someone to check periodically that all is well, when working alone on the vehicle.
DO carry out work in a logical sequence and check that everything is correctly assembled and tightened afterwards.
DO remember that your vehicle's safety affects that of yourself and others. If in doubt on any point, get specialist advice.
IF, in spite of following these precautions, you are unfortunate enough to injure yourself, seek medical attention as soon as possible.

Asbestos

Certain friction, insulating, sealing, and other products – such as brake linings, brake bands, clutch linings, torque converters, gaskets, etc – contain asbestos. *Extreme care must be taken to avoid inhalation of dust from such products since it is hazardous to health.* If in doubt, assume that they *do* contain asbestos.

Fire

Remember at all times that petrol (gasoline) is highly flammable. Never smoke, or have any kind of naked flame around, when working on the vehicle. But the risk does not end there – a spark caused by an electrical short-circuit, by two metal surfaces contacting each other, by careless use of tools, or even by static electricity built up in your body under certain conditions, can ignite petrol vapour, which in a confined space is highly explosive.

Always disconnect the battery earth (ground) terminal before working on any part of the fuel or electrical system, and never risk spilling fuel on to a hot engine or exhaust.

It is recommended that a fire extinguisher of a type suitable for fuel and electrical fires is kept handy in the garage or workplace at all times. Never try to extinguish a fuel or electrical fire with water.

Note: *Any reference to a 'torch' appearing in this manual should always be taken to mean a hand-held battery-operated electric lamp or flashlight. It does NOT mean a welding/gas torch or blowlamp.*

Fumes

Certain fumes are highly toxic and can quickly cause unconsciousness and even death if inhaled to any extent. Petrol (gasoline) vapour comes into this category, as do the vapours from certain solvents such as trichloroethylene. Any draining or pouring of such volatile fluids should be done in a well ventilated area.

When using cleaning fluids and solvents, read the instructions carefully. Never use materials from unmarked containers – they may give off poisonous vapours.

Never run the engine of a motor vehicle in an enclosed space such as a garage. Exhaust fumes contain carbon monoxide which is extremely poisonous; if you need to run the engine, always do so in the open air or at least have the rear of the vehicle outside the workplace.

If you are fortunate enough to have the use of an inspection pit, never drain or pour petrol, and never run the engine, while the vehicle is standing over it; the fumes, being heavier than air, will concentrate in the pit with possibly lethal results.

The battery

Never cause a spark, or allow a naked light, near the vehicle's battery. It will normally be giving off a certain amount of hydrogen gas, which is highly explosive.

Always disconnect the battery earth (ground) terminal before working on the fuel or electrical systems.

If possible, loosen the filler plugs or cover when charging the battery from an external source. Do not charge at an excessive rate or the battery may burst.

Take care when topping up and when carrying the battery. The acid electrolyte, even when diluted, is very corrosive and should not be allowed to contact the eyes or skin.

If you ever need to prepare electrolyte yourself, always add the acid slowly to the water, and never the other way round. Protect against splashes by wearing rubber gloves and goggles.

When jump starting a car using a booster battery, for negative earth (ground) vehicles, connect the jump leads in the following sequence: First connect one jump lead between the positive (+) terminals of the two batteries. Then connect the other jump lead first to the negative (–) terminal of the booster battery, and then to a good earthing (ground) point on the vehicle to be started, at least 18 in (45 cm) from the battery if possible. Ensure that hands and jump leads are clear of any moving parts, and that the two vehicles do not touch. Disconnect the leads in the reverse order.

Mains electricity and electrical equipment

When using an electric power tool, inspection light etc, always ensure that the appliance is correctly connected to its plug and that, where necessary, it is properly earthed (grounded). Do not use such appliances in damp conditions and, again, beware of creating a spark or applying excessive heat in the vicinity of fuel or fuel vapour. Also ensure that the appliances meet the relevant national safety standards.

Ignition HT voltage

A severe electric shock can result from touching certain parts of the ignition system, such as the HT leads, when the engine is running or being cranked, particularly if components are damp or the insulation is defective. Where an electronic ignition system is fitted, the HT voltage is much higher and could prove fatal.

Routine maintenance

Maintenance is essential for ensuring safety, and desirable for the purpose of getting the best in terms of performance and economy from your vehicle. Over the years, the need for periodic lubrication has been greatly reduced, if not totally eliminated. This has unfortunately tended to lead some owners to think that because no action is required, the items either no longer exist, or will last forever. This is certainly not the case; it is essential to carry out regular visual examination as comprehensively as possible, in order to spot any potential defects at an early stage before they develop into major expensive repairs.

Both 520i and 525e models are equipped with a service indicator system which is described in detail in Chapter 12. The system indicates the servicing requirements according to time, distance covered and number of starts made, and therefore this will vary from driver to driver and will not be in relation to set mileages and periods as is the usual convention. The service indicator has three different service warnings – 'oil service', 'annual check', and 'inspection', and these are lit together with the yellow warning light to advise the driver that servicing is required immediately. The driver will have been aware that a service was imminent since the number of green warning lights on display would have been reduced to one just prior to the yellow light coming on. If the service is not carried out and the car is still operated, the red warning light will be illuminated and the car must then be immediately taken off the road. This is in the interests of safety and to avoid excessive wear to the mechanical components of the car.

Although not instigated by BMW, it is recommended that a weekly check is made in addition to the servicing from the service indicator. A print-out of the items requiring service together with the remaining time and distance of other items can be obtained by visiting your BMW garage, although some charge will obviously be made for this. There is no BMW recommended alternative mileage – only related servicing for the models covered in this manual, but if the service indicator becomes faulty on a car which has covered a high mileage, the owner may decide to carry out servicing at 10 000 mile (15 000 km) intervals entirely at his own risk. This action would of course nullify any warranty and may well work out to be more expensive in the long run than purchasing a new service indicator.

The following service schedules are a list of the maintenance requirements and are recommended by the manufacturers with the exception of the weekly service. Where applicable, these procedures are covered in greater detail throughout this manual, usually in the *Routine maintenance* section near the beginning of each Chapter. After completing the service requirements, the service indicator should be reset using the special tool described in Chapter 12.

Every week

Engine, cooling system and brakes

Check the engine oil level and top up if necessary (Chapter 1)
Check the coolant level and top up if necessary (Chapter 2)
Check the brake fluid level in the master cylinder and top up if necessary (Chapter 9)

Lights and wipers

Check the operation of all lights, wipers and washers
Check and if necessary top up the washer reservoir

Tyres

Check the tyre pressures (including the spare) – Chapter 10
Visually examine the tyres for wear or damage (Chapter 10)

BMW Inspection 1

Engine compartment

Renew the spark plugs (Chapter 4)
Check the valve clearances (Chapter 1)
Renew the air cleaner element (Chapter 3)
Check the cooling system hoses (Chapter 2)
Check the coolant antifreeze concentration (Chapter 2)
Check the power steering fluid level (Chapter 10)
Check the clutch hydraulic fluid level (Chapter 5)
Check the brake fluid level (Chapter 9)
Check the windscreen washer system and fluid level (Chapter 12)
Check the battery electrolyte level (Chapter 12)
Check the water pump/alternator drivebelt (Chapter 2)
Check the power steering pump drivebelt (Chapter 10)
Check the air conditioning compressor drivebelt (Chapter 11)
Lubricate the accelerator linkages
Check and adjust the ignition timing (520i models only) – Chapter 4
Check the idle speed and CO (Chapter 3)

Running gear (ie car raised from the ground)

Change the engine oil and oil filter (Chapter 1)
Check the gearbox oil level (Chapter 6)
Check the automatic transmission fluid level (Chapter 6)
Check the final drive unit oil level (Chapter 8)
Check the fuel lines, fuel tank and hoses (Chapter 3)
Renew the fuel filter (Chapter 3)
Check the exhaust system (Chapter 3)
Check the steering (Chapter 10)
Check all brake linings (Chapter 9)
Grease roadwheel centres and hubs (Chapter 10)
Check the brake hydraulic circuit (Chapter 9)
Check the handbrake adjustment (Chapter 9)
Check the tyres and pressures (Chapter 10)

Body/electrical

Check the lights
Check the horn
Check the wipers and washers
Check the seat belts (Chapter 11)
Lubricate all locks and the sunroof (Chapter 11)

BMW Inspection 2

Inspection 1 plus the following:

Engine compartment

Renew all drivebelts every alternate Inspection 2, or every 4 years

Under-bonnet view of a BMW 525e

1 *Accelerator cable connection to the top of the accelerator pedal*
2 *Right-hand brake pedal linkage arm*
3 *Inlet manifold*
4 *Automatic transmission kickdown cable*
5 *Throttle housing*
6 *Accelerator cable*
7 *Heater control valve*
8 *Brake vacuum servo*
9 *Brake hydraulic fluid reservoir and master cylinder*
10 *Vacuum servo hose to the inlet manifold*
11 *Power steering gear fluid reservoir*
12 *Idle control valve*
13 *Airflow sensor*
14 *Fusebox*
15 *Air cleaner*
16 *Battery*
17 *Left-hand bonnet lock*
18 *Engine oil level dipstick*
19 *Bottom hose*
20 *Alternator*
21 *Diagnostic socket*
22 *Fanbelt*
23 *Thermostat housing*
24 *Fuel pressure regulator*
25 *Radiator*
26 *Viscous cooling fan*
27 *Top hose*
28 *Engine lifting eye*
29 *Engine oil filler cap*
30 *By-pass hose*
31 *Right-hand bonnet lock*
32 *Ignition coil and HT lead*
33 *Washer fluid reservoir*
34 *Coolant expansion tank filler cap*
35 *Front suspension strut upper mounting*

Front underbody view of a BMW 525e

1. *Fuel feed and return lines*
2. *Brake hydraulic lines*
3. *Automatic transmission fluid hoses for the cooler in the radiator*
4. *Automatic transmission fluid dipstick tube*
5. *Steering centre tie-rod*
6. *Automatic transmission fluid sump*
7. *Torque converter housing*
8. *Front anti-roll bar*
9. *Exhaust front downpipes*
10. *Underbody strengthening bar*
11. *Front suspension crossmember*
12. *Front track control arm*
13. *Right-hand engine mounting*
14. *Coolant expansion tank hose to water pump*
15. *Radiator*
16. *Oil filter*
17. *Viscous cooling fan*
18. *Engine oil drain plug*
19. *Engine sump*
20. *Power steering pump drivebelt*
21. *Power steering pump*
22. *Left-hand engine mounting*
23. *Front anti-roll bar link*
24. *Steering outer tie-rod*
25. *Rear track control arm*

Rear underbody view of a BMW 525e

1 *Rear anti-roll bar*
2 *Final drive unit rear mounting*
3 *Rear exhaust silencer*
4 *Fuel tank drain plug*
5 *Rear brake disc caliper*
6 *Rear semi-trailing arm*
7 *Rear brake flexible hydraulic hose*
8 *Rear suspension crossmember mounting*
9 *Propeller shaft rear universal joint*
10 *Exhaust system mounting*
11 *Driveshaft*

Running gear (ie car raised from the ground)

Change the manual gearbox oil (where applicable) – Chapter 6
Change the automatic transmission fluid (where applicable) – Chapter 6
Change the final drive unit (Chapter 8)
Clean the automatic transmission filter screen (Chapter 6)
Check the clutch disc wear
Check the handbrake linings (Chapter 9)
Check the driveshaft rubber gaiters (Chapter 7)
Check the suspension (Chapter 10)

Every 12 months

Change the brake fluid (Chapter 9)
Check the underbody (Chapter 11)
Check the headlight beam alignment (Chapter 12)

Every 2 years

Change the coolant (Chapter 2)

BMW oil service

Change the engine oil and oil filter (Chapter 1)

BMW Safety test (optional with oil service)

Check the steering (Chapter 10)
Check the brake linings (Chapter 9)
Check the brake hydraulic circuit (Chapter 9)
Check the brake fluid level (Chapter 9)
Check the handbrake linings (Chapter 9)
Check the handbrake adjustment (Chapter 9)
Check the tyres and pressures (Chapter 10)
Check the operation of all lights, wipers and washers
Check the seat belts (Chapter 11)
Check the horn

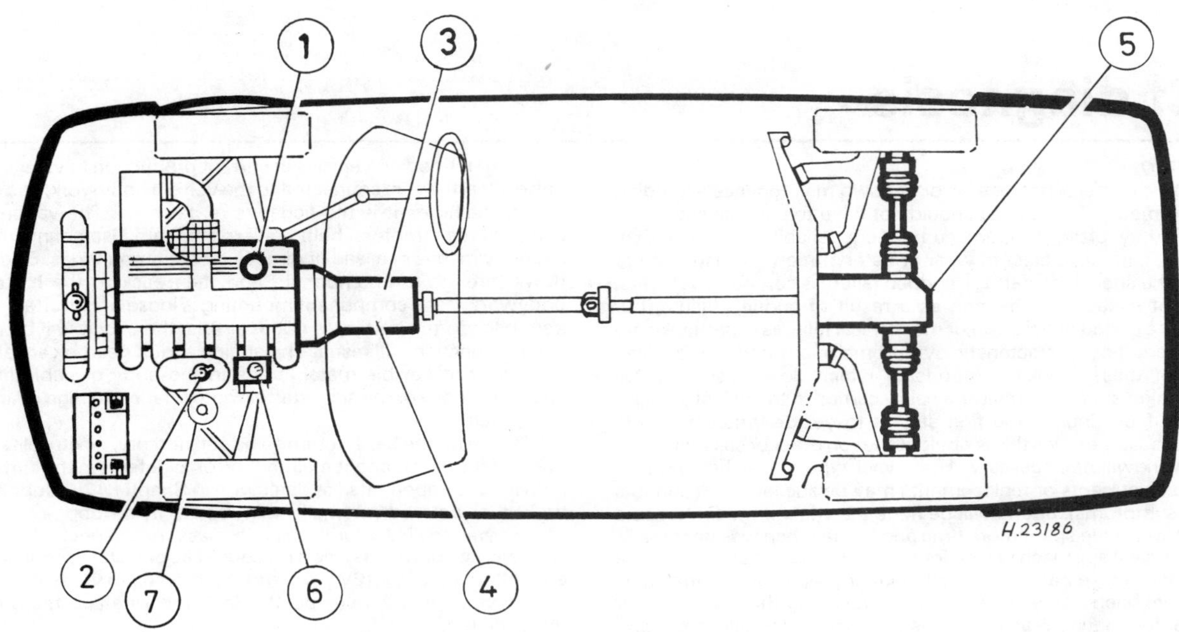

Recommended lubricants and fluids

Component or system	Lubricant type/specification	Duckhams recommendation
Engine (1)	Multigrade engine oil, viscosity SAE 10W/40 to 20W/50, to API SG	Duckhams QXR or Hypergrade
Cooling system (2)	Ethylene glycol based antifreeze with corrosion inhibitor	Duckhams Universal Antifreeze and Summer Coolant
Manual gearbox (3)	Gear oil, viscosity SAE 80 to API GL4, or single-grade mineral-based engine oil, viscosity SAE 20, 30 or 40 to API SG	Duckhams Hypoid 80
Automatic transmission (4)	Dexron II type ATF	Duckhams D-Matic
Final drive (5)	BMW-approved hypoid gear oil, viscosity SAE 90	Duckhams D12001*
Brake and clutch hydraulic systems (6)	Hydraulic brake fluid to SAE J 1703 or DOT 4	Duckhams Universal Brake and Clutch Fluid
Power steering (7)	Dexron II type ATF	Duckhams D-Matic

** Only available to the motor trade; refer to your BMW dealer*

Fault diagnosis

Introduction

The vehicle owner who does his or her own maintenance according to the recommended schedules should not have to use this section of the manual very often. Modern component reliability is such that, provided those items subject to wear or deterioration are inspected or renewed at the specified intervals, sudden failure is comparatively rare. Faults do not usually just happen as a result of sudden failure, but develop over a period of time. Major mechanical failures in particular are usually preceded by characteristic symptoms over hundreds or even thousands of miles. Those components which do occasionally fail without warning are often small and easily carried in the vehicle.

With any fault finding, the first step is to decide where to begin investigations. Sometimes this is obvious, but on other occasions a little detective work will be necessary. The owner who makes half a dozen haphazard adjustments or replacements may be successful in curing a fault (or its symptoms), but he will be none the wiser if the fault recurs and he may well have spent more time and money than was necessary. A calm and logical approach will be found to be more satisfactory in the long run. Always take into account any warning signs or abnormalities that may have been noticed in the period preceding the fault – power loss, high or low gauge readings, unusual noises or smells, etc – and remember that failure of components such as fuses or spark plugs may only be pointers to some underlying fault.

The pages which follow here are intended to help in cases of failure to start or breakdown on the road. There is also a Fault Diagnosis Section at the end of each Chapter which should be consulted if the preliminary checks prove unfruitful. Whatever the fault, certain basic principles apply. These are as follows:

Verify the fault. This is simply a matter of being sure that you know what the symptoms are before starting work. This is particularly important if you are investigating a fault for someone else who may not have described it very accurately.

Don't overlook the obvious. For example, if the vehicle won't start, is there petrol in the tank? (Don't take anyone else's word on this particular point, and don't trust the fuel gauge either!) If an electrical fault is indicated, look for loose or broken wires before digging out the test gear.

Cure the disease, not the symptom. Substituting a flat battery with a fully charged one will get you off the hard shoulder, but if the underlying cause is not attended to, the new battery will go the same way. Similarly, changing oil-fouled spark plugs for a new set will get you moving again, but remember that the reason for the fouling (if it wasn't simply an incorrect grade of plug) will have to be established and corrected.

Don't take anything for granted. Particularly, don't forget that a 'new' component may itself be defective (especially if it's been rattling round in the boot for months), and don't leave components out of a fault diagnosis sequence just because they are new or recently fitted. When you do finally diagnose a difficult fault, you'll probably realise that all the evidence was there from the start.

Electrical faults

Electrical faults can be more puzzling than straightforward mechanical failures, but they are no less susceptible to logical analysis if the basic principles of operation are understood. Vehicle electrical wiring exists in extremely unfavourable conditions – heat, vibration and chemical attack – and the first things to look for are loose or corroded connections and broken or chafed wires, especially where the wires pass through holes in the bodywork or are subject to vibration.

All metal-bodied vehicles in current production have one pole of the battery 'earthed', ie connected to the vehicle bodywork, and in nearly all modern vehicles it is the negative (–) terminal. The various electrical components – motors, bulb holders etc – are also connected to earth, either by means of a lead or directly by their mountings. Electric current flows through the component and then back to the battery via the bodywork. If the component mounting is loose or corroded, or if a good path back to the battery is not available, the circuit will be incomplete and malfunction will result. The engine and/or gearbox are also earthed by means of flexible metal straps to the body or subframe; if these straps are loose or missing, starter motor, generator and ignition trouble may result.

Assuming the earth return to be satisfactory, electrical faults will be due either to component malfunction or to defects in the current supply. Individual components are dealt with in Chapter 12. If supply wires are broken or cracked internally this results in an open-circuit, and the easiest way to check for this is to bypass the suspect wire temporarily with a length of wire having a crocodile clip or suitable connector at each end. Alternatively, a 12V test lamp can be used to verify the presence of supply voltage at various points along the wire and the break can be thus isolated.

If a bare portion of a live wire touches the bodywork or other earthed metal part, the electricity will take the low-resistance path thus formed back to the battery: this is known as a short-circuit. Hopefully a short-circuit will blow a fuse, but otherwise it may cause burning of the insulation (and possibly further short-circuits) or even a fire. This is why it is inadvisable to bypass persistently blowing fuses with silver foil or wire.

Spares and tool kit

Most vehicles are supplied only with sufficient tools for wheel changing; the *Maintenance and minor repair* tool kit detailed in *Tools and working facilities,* with the addition of a hammer, is probably sufficient for those repairs that most motorists would consider attempting at the roadside. In addition a few items which can be fitted without too much trouble in the event of a breakdown should be carried. Experience and available space will modify the list below, but the following may save having to call on professional assistance:

Spark plugs, clean and correctly gapped
HT lead and plug cap – long enough to reach the plug furthest from the distributor
Distributor rotor
Drivebelt(s) – emergency type may suffice
Spare fuses
Set of principal light bulbs
Tin of radiator sealer and hose bandage
Exhaust bandage
Roll of insulating tape
Length of soft iron wire
Length of electrical flex
Torch or inspection lamp (can double as test lamp)
Battery jump leads
Tow-rope
Ignition water dispersant aerosol
Litre of engine oil
Sealed can of hydraulic fluid
Emergency windscreen
Worm drive clips

If spare fuel is carried, a can designed for the purpose should be used

Carrying a few spares can save a long walk

to minimise risks of leakage and collision damage. A first aid kit and a warning triangle, whilst not at present compulsory in the UK, are obviously sensible items to carry in addition to the above.

When touring abroad it may be advisable to carry additional spares which, even if you cannot fit them yourself, could save having to wait while parts are obtained. The items below may be worth considering:

Cylinder head gasket
Alternator brushes
Tyre valve core

One of the motoring organisations will be able to advise on availability of fuel etc in foreign countries.

Engine will not start

Engine fails to turn when starter operated

Flat battery (recharge, use jump leads, or push start)
Battery terminals loose or corroded
Battery earth to body defective
Engine earth strap loose or broken
Starter motor (or solenoid) wiring loose or broken
Automatic transmission selector in wrong position, or inhibitor switch faulty
Ignition/starter switch faulty
Major mechanical failure (seizure)
Starter or solenoid internal fault (see Chapter 12)

Starter motor turns engine slowly

Partially discharged battery (recharge, use jump leads, or push start)
Battery terminals loose or corroded
Battery earth to body defective
Engine earth strap loose
Starter motor (or solenoid) wiring loose
Starter motor internal fault (see Chapter 12)

Starter motor spins without turning engine

Flat battery
Starter motor sticking on sleeve
Flywheel gear teeth damaged or worn
Starter motor mounting bolts loose

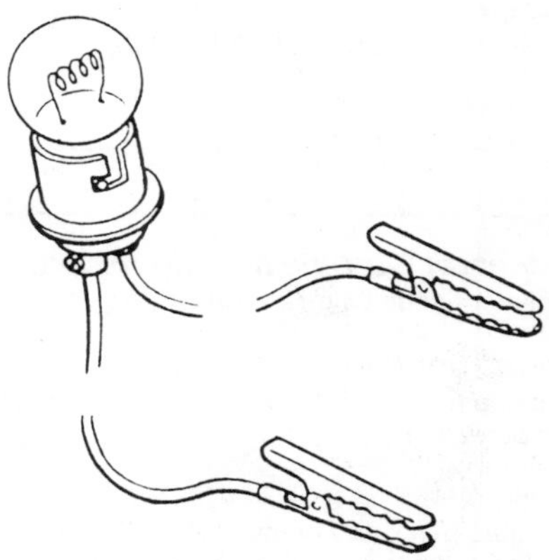

A simple test lamp is useful for checking electrical faults

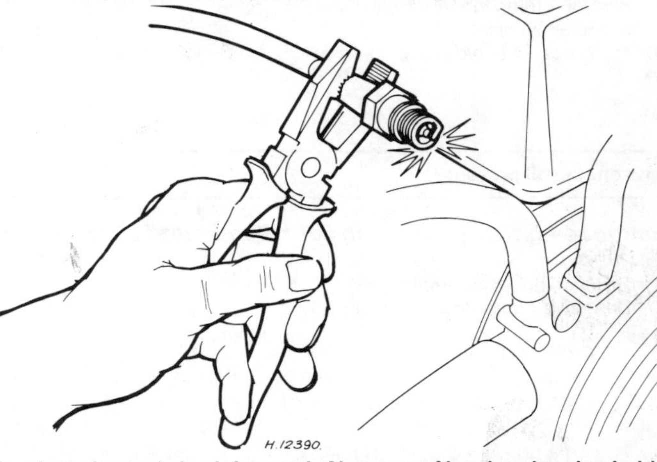

Crank engine and check for spark. Note use of insulated tool to hold plug lead. Use a spare plug, not one removed from engine (fire risk)

Engine turns normally but fails to start

Damp or dirty HT leads and distributor cap (crank engine and check for spark) – try moisture dispersant such as Holts Wet Start
No fuel in tank
Excessive choke (hot engine) or insufficient choke (cold engine)
Fouled or incorrectly gapped spark plugs (renew or regap)
Other ignition system fault (see Chapter 4)
Other fuel system fault (see Chapter 3)
Poor compression (see Chapter 1)
Major mechanical failure (eg camshaft drive)

Engine fires but will not run

Air leaks at inlet manifold
Fuel starvation (see Chapter 3)
Ballast resistor defective, or other ignition fault (see Chapter 4)
Other fuel system fault (see Chapter 3)

Engine cuts out and will not restart

Engine cuts out suddenly – ignition fault

Loose or disconnected LT wires
Wet HT leads or distributor cap (after traversing water splash)
Coil or condenser failure (check for spark)
Other ignition fault (see Chapter 4)

Engine misfires before cutting out – fuel fault

Fuel tank empty!
Fuel pump defective or filter blocked (check for delivery)
Fuel tank filler vent blocked (suction will be evident on releasing cap)
Other fuel system fault (see Chapter 3)

Engine cuts out – other causes

Serious overheating
Major mechanical failure (eg camshaft drive)

Engine overheats

Ignition (no-charge) warning light illuminated

Slack or broken drivebelt – retension or renew (see Chapter 2)

Ignition warning light not illuminated

Coolant loss due to internal or external leakage (see Chapter 2)
Thermostat defective
Low oil level
Brakes binding
Radiator clogged externally or internally
Viscous cooling fan not operating correctly
Engine waterways clogged
Ignition timing incorrect
Mixture too weak

Note: *Do not add cold water to an overheated engine or damage may result*

Low engine oil pressure

Gauge reads low or warning light illuminated with engine running

Oil level low or incorrect grade
Defective gauge or sender unit

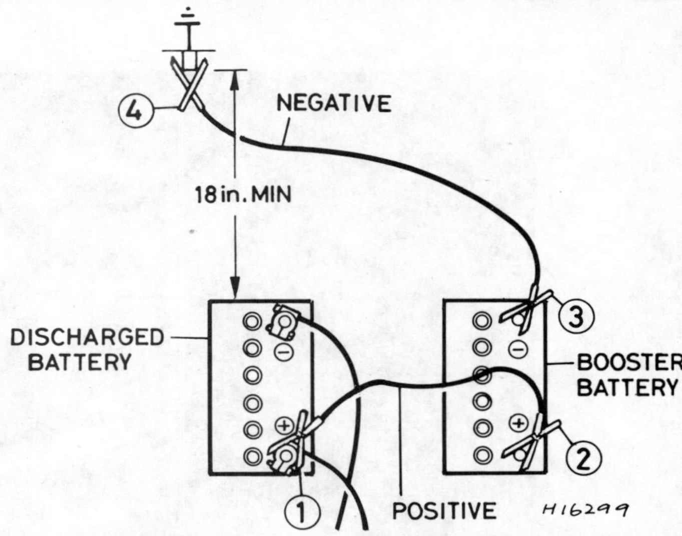

Jump start lead connections for negative earth – connect leads in order shown

Wire to sender unit earthed
Engine overheating
Oil filter clogged or bypass valve defective
Oil pressure relief valve defective
Oil pick-up strainer clogged
Oil pump worn or mountings loose
Worn main or big-end bearings

Note: *Low oil pressure in a high-mileage engine at tickover is not necessarily a cause for concern. Sudden pressure loss at speed is far more significant. In any event, check the gauge or warning light sender before condemning the engine.*

Engine noises

Pre-ignition (pinking) on acceleration

Incorrect grade of fuel
Ignition timing incorrect
Excessive carbon build-up in engine

Whistling or wheezing noises

Leaking vacuum hose
Leaking manifold gasket
Blowing head gasket

Tapping or rattling

Incorrect valve clearances
Worn valve gear
Broken piston ring (ticking noise)

Knocking or thumping

Unintentional mechanical contact (eg fan blades)
Worn drivebelt
Peripheral component fault (generator, water pump etc)
Worn big-end bearings (regular heavy knocking, perhaps less under load)
Worn main bearings (rumbling and knocking, perhaps worsening under load)
Piston slap (most noticeable when cold)

Chapter 1 Engine

Contents

Specifications

General

Type	Six-cylinder in-line, single overhead camshaft (ohc) with fuel injection	
Designation	M20 series	
Code:		
1990 cc	B20	
2693 cc	B27	
	1990 cc	**2693 cc**
Bore	80 mm	84 mm
Stroke	66 mm	81 mm
Capacity	1990 cc	2693 cc
Firing order	1-5-3-6-2-4 (No 1 cylinder at front of engine)	
Direction of crankshaft rotation	Clockwise	
Compression ratio:		
520i	9.8:1	
525e:		
Up to 1986	11.0:1	
From 1986	10.2:1	
Compression pressure (min)	10 to 11 bar	
Power output:		
520i up to 1986	92 kW at 5800 rpm	
520i 1986 on	95 kW at 6000 rpm	
525e up to 1986	92 kW at 4250 rpm	
525e 1986 on	95 kW at 4250 rpm	

Cylinder block

Material	Cast iron
Cylinder bore diameter:	
B20 engine:	
Standard	80.00 + 0.01 mm
Intermediate size	80.08 + 0.01 mm
1st oversize	80.25 + 0.01 mm
2nd oversize	80.50 + 0.01 mm
B27 engine:	
Standard	84.00 + 0.01 mm
Intermediate size	84.08 + 0.01 mm
1st oversize	84.25 + 0.01 mm
2nd oversize	84.50 + 0.01 mm

Cylinder block (continued)

Maximum cylinder bore ovality:	
B20 engine	0.02 mm
B27 engine	0.03 mm
Maximum cylinder bore taper (all engines)	0.02 mm

Crankshaft

Number of main bearings	Seven
Main bearing journal diameter (double classification):	
Standard:	
Red	$60.00^{-0.010}_{-0.020}$ mm
Blue	$60.00^{-0.020}_{-0.029}$ mm
1st undersize:	
Red	$59.75^{-0.010}_{-0.020}$ mm
Blue	$59.75^{-0.020}_{-0.029}$ mm
2nd undersize:	
Red	$59.50^{-0.010}_{-0.020}$ mm
Blue	$59.50^{-0.020}_{-0.029}$ mm
Main bearing running clearance	0.03 to 0.07 mm
Main bearing journal diameter (triple classification):	
Standard:	
Yellow	59.984 to 59.990 mm
Green	59.977 to 59.983 mm
White	59.971 to 59.976 mm
1st undersize (0.25 mm):	
Yellow	59.734 to 59.740 mm
Green	59.727 to 59.733 mm
White	59.721 to 59.726 mm
2nd undersize (0.50 mm):	
Yellow	59.484 to 59.490 mm
Green	59.477 to 59.483 mm
White	59.471 to 59.476 mm
Main bearing running clearance	0.020 to 0.046 mm
Crankshaft endfloat	0.08 to 0.163 mm
Crankpin journal diameter:	
Standard	$45.00^{-0.009}_{-0.025}$ mm
1st undersize	$44.75^{-0.009}_{-0.025}$ mm
2nd undersize	$44.50^{-0.009}_{-0.025}$ mm
Crankpin journal running clearance	0.03 to 0.07 mm
Crankpin journal diameter (double classification):	
Standard	44.975 to 44.991 mm
1st undersize (0.25 mm)	44.725 to 44.741 mm
2nd undersize (0.50 mm)	44.475 to 44.491 mm
Crankpin journal running clearance	0.020 to 0.055 mm

Flywheel

Maximum run-out (measured on outer diameter)	0.1 mm
Minimum thickness:	
B20	25.1 – 0.1 mm
B27	32.1 – 0.1 mm

Pistons and piston rings

Maximum deviation in weight	± 10 grams	
Piston diameter	**B20**	**B27**
Standard	79.98 mm	83.98 mm
Intermediate	80.06 mm	84.06 mm
1st oversize	80.23 mm	84.23 mm
2nd oversize	80.48 mm	84.48 mm
Piston-to-bore clearance (max)	0.15 mm	0.12 mm
Number of piston rings	Two compression, one oil control	
Piston ring end gaps	0.20 to 0.50 mm	
Piston ring-to-groove clearance:		
Top compression ring	0.04 to 0.08 mm	
Second compression ring	0.03 to 0.07 mm	
Oil control ring	0.02 to 0.05 mm	

Connecting rods

Maximum deviation from parallel of conrod bores with bearing shells at distance of 150 mm	0.04 mm
Maximum deviation in weight	± 4 grams

Cylinder head

Material	Light alloy
Minimum acceptable height after machining	124.7 mm
Valve guide protrusion	14.5 mm
Valve seat angle	45°
Valve seat width	1.65 ± 0.35 mm
Valve seat correction angles	15°/75°

Camshaft

Endfloat	0.2 mm
Running clearance	0.016 to 0.052 mm

Valves

Valve clearance:	**Cold**	**Hot**
B20 (up to 1985 models)	0.25mm (0.010 in)	0.30 mm (0.012 in)
B20 (1985 on models)	0.20 mm (0.008 in)	0.25 mm (0.010 in)
B27	0.25 mm (0.010 in)	0.30 mm (0.012 in)
Valve timing:	**B20**	**B27**
Inlet opens	24° BTDC	–
Inlet closes	56° ABDC	–
Exhaust opens	64° BBDC	–
Exhaust closes	16° ATDC	–
Minimum valve head thickness:		
Inlet	1.3 mm	
Exhaust	2.0 mm	
Maximum tilt wear of valve in guide	0.8 mm	
Rocker arm radial clearance	0.016 to 0.052 mm	
Valve guide protrusion	14.0 to 15.0 mm	

Lubrication system

System pressure:	
Idling	0.5 to 2.0 bar
Maximum speed	4.0 to 6.0 bar
Engine oil type/specification	Multigrade engine oil, viscosity SAE 10W/40 to 20W/50, to API SG (Duckhams QXR or Hypergrade)
Oil filter type	Champion C101
Engine oil capacity (including oil filter)	4.5 litres (7.9 pints)
Difference between MIN and MAX marks on dipstick	1 litre (1.8 pints)
Oil pump clearances:	
Gear teeth to pump body	0.016 to 0.054 mm
Gear endfloat	0.11 mm
Gear backlash	0.24 mm
Pressure relief valve (in pump) free spring length	43.8 to 44.2 mm

Torque wrench settings

	Nm	lbf ft
Main bearing caps	58 to 63	42 to 45
Cylinder head bolts:		
Stage 1	40 to 45	29 to 33
Stage 2	Wait 15 minutes	
Stage 3	60 to 65	43 to 47
Stage 4	Run the engine for 25 minutes	
Stage 5	Angle tighten 20° to 30°	
Front engine lifting eye	20 to 24	15 to 17
Oil drain plug:		
17 mm	30 to 36	22 to 26
19 mm	59 to 64	43 to 46
Sump	9 to 11	7 to 8
Front and rear oil seal housings:		
M6	9 ± 1	6.5 ± 0.5
M8	22 ± 2	16 ± 1
Flywheel	105 ± 7	76 ± 1
Crankshaft pulley bolt	410 ± 20	296 ± 14
Crankshaft pulley/vibration damper	20 to 24	15 to 17
Big-end caps:		
Stage 1	20	14.5
Stage 2	Angle tighten 70°	
Camshaft adaptor plate	60 ± 5	63 ± 3.5

Torque wrench settings (continued)

	Nm	lbf ft
Camshaft sprocket	65 to 70	47 to 50
Timing belt tensioner	20 to 24	15 to 17
Rocker arm clamp screw	10 ± 1	7 ± 0.5
Intermediate shaft sprocket	60 ± 5	63 ± 3.5
Oil pressure switch	30 to 40	22 to 29
Oil pressure safety valve	25 to 30	18 to 22
Oil pump	20 to 24	15 to 17
Oil pump cover	9 ± 1	6.5 ± 0.5
Oil filter housing	40 ± 5	30 ± 3.5
Camshaft lubrication pipe	6 to 8	4.5 to 6.0

1 General description

The engine is of six-cylinder, in-line type, with an overhead camshaft driven by a toothed belt. The cylinder block is of cast iron while the cross-flow type cylinder head is of light alloy and incorporates spherical combustion chambers. The crankshaft is of cast steel and runs in seven main bearings. The connecting rods are of forged steel construction with light alloy pistons and chromium plated compression rings. On the B27 engine (fitted to 525e models) the piston crowns are slightly raised to achieve a higher compression ratio, and cut-outs are provided for clearance of the inlet valves (photo).

The valve clearances are adjusted by means of eccentric cams on the rocker arms. The camshaft is supported in seven bearings on the 520i and in four bearings on the 525e.

The lubrication system is of pressurised type with an oil pump located within the sump and driven from a gear on the rear end of the intermediate shaft. The lubrication circuit incorporates a pressure control valve. The oil dipstick guide tube is designed for automatic oil draining.

The crankcase ventilation system is of positive type, whereby gases, which accumulate in the engine crankcase, are drawn out through a spring-loaded tube into the inlet manifold. The gases are then drawn into the engine combustion chambers, where they are burned during the normal combustion cycle.

1.0 Piston crown on the B27 engine fitted to the 525e model

2 Routine maintenance

Carry out the following at the intervals given in *Routine maintenance* at the front of this manual

Check valve clearances

1 Refer to Section 12.

Check engine oil level

2 The engine oil level should be checked with the car on level ground and the engine cold.

3 Withdraw the dipstick, wipe it clean on a non-fluffy rag and reinsert it. Where applicable the loop on the dipstick should be pointing towards the left-hand side of the car.

4 Withdraw the dipstick again and check that the oil is between the min and max marks (photo).

5 If necessary, unscrew the filler cap from the valve cover and top up to the upper mark with oil of the specified grade. The space between the max and min marks represents approximately 1 litre (1.8 pints).

6 Refit the filler cap and dipstick.

Change engine oil and filter

7 The engine oil should be changed with the engine hot.

8 Remove the oil filler cap and then unscrew the drain plug and drain the oil into a suitable container (photo), taking precautions against scalding, as the oil will be hot.

9 When disposing of the used engine oil, **do not** pour it down the drain - this is illegal and causes pollution. Your dealer or Local Authority may be able to dispose of it safely.

10 With all the oil drained, check the drain plug washer and renew if necessary, then refit and tighten the plug.

11 Using an oil filter removal strap, unscrew the oil filter and discard it. There will be some spillage of oil, so position the container beneath the filter.

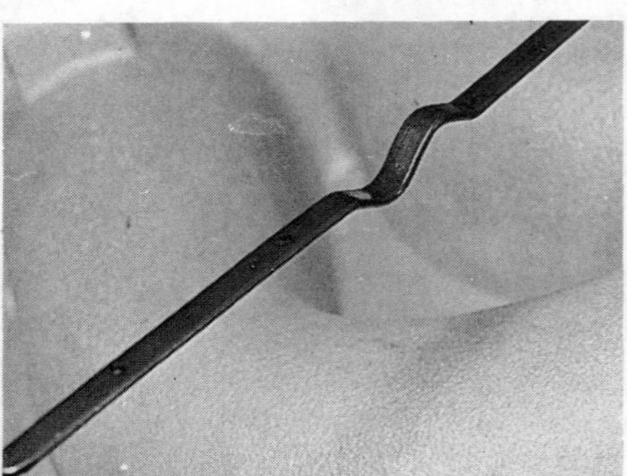

2.4 Engine oil level dipstick markings

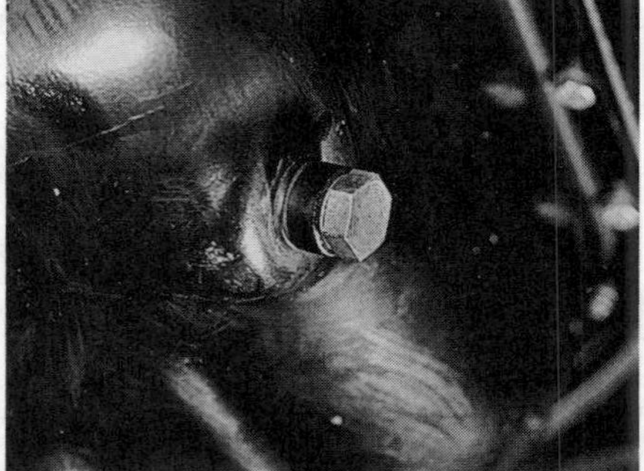

2.8 Engine oil drain plug on the sump

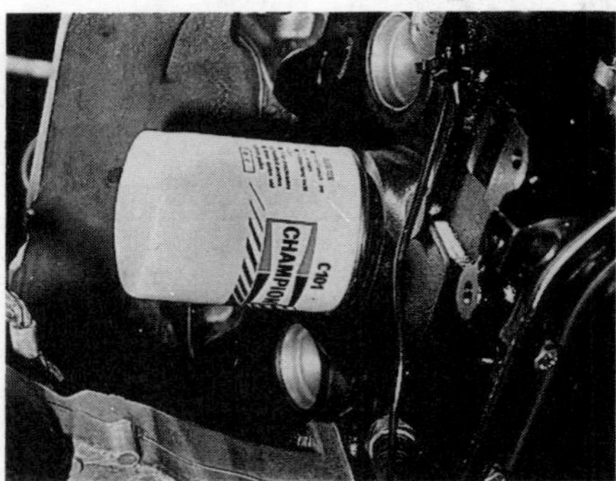

2.13 New oil filter fitted to engine

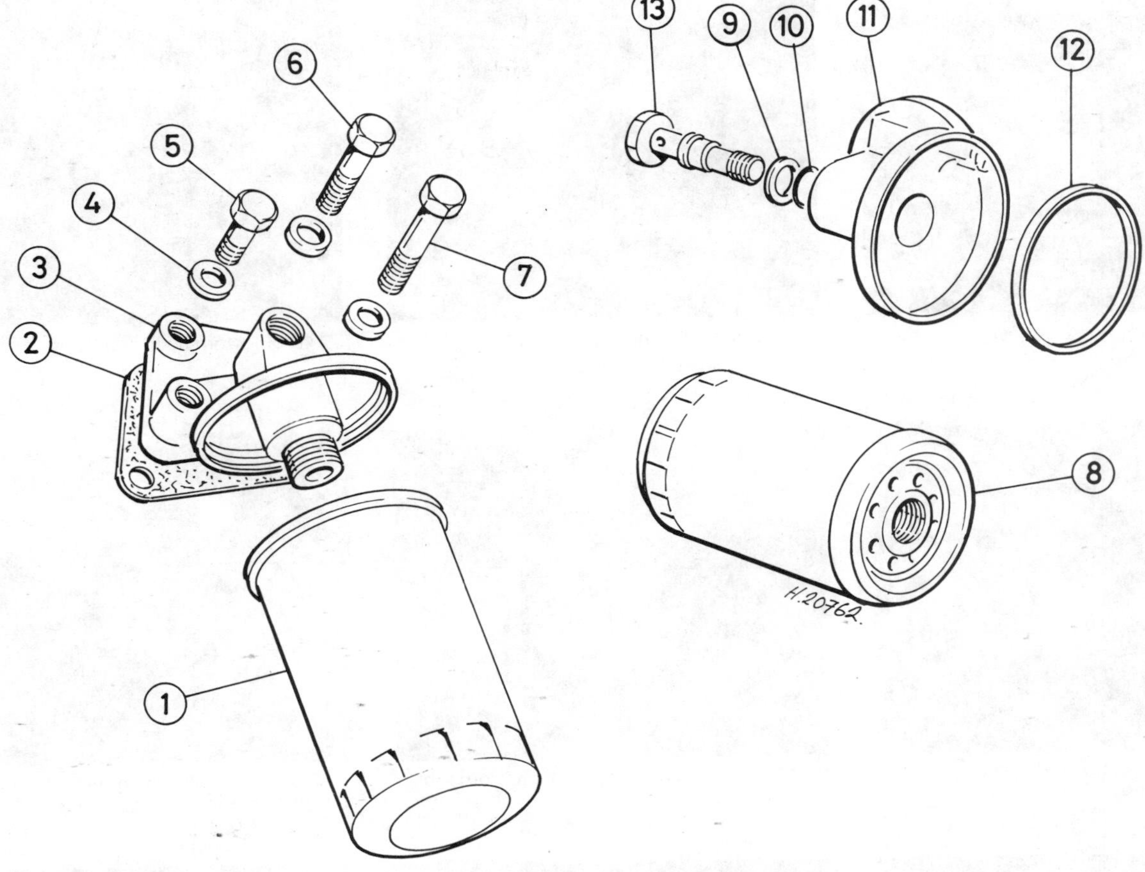

Fig. 1.1 Oil filter and housing components (Sec 2)

1 *Oil filter (non-air conditioning models)*
2 *Gasket*
3 *Head*
4 *Washer*
5 *Bolt*
6 *Bolt*
7 *Bolt*
8 *Oil filter (air conditioning models)*
9 *Gasket*
10 *O-ring*
11 *Housing*
12 *O-ring*
13 *Hollow bolt*

12 To remove the filter on cars equipped with air conditioning, unscrew the adaptor hollow bolt, remove the assembly and then unscrew the filter cartridge from the adaptor.
13 Wipe clean the sealing face on the cylinder block. Smear a little engine oil on the sealing rubber of the new filter, then screw it into position using hand pressure only (photo). On cars with air conditioning always renew the filter aluminium seal and bolt seal.
14 Fill the engine with the correct grade and quantity of oil.
15 Start the engine and run it for a few minutes. Check that the oil pressure warning light goes out, and check around the oil filter for leaks.
16 Switch off the engine, wait for a few minutes for the oil to drain into the sump, then check the oil level again and finally top up as necessary.

3 Major operations possible with the engine in the car

The following operations may be carried out with the engine in position in the car:

(a) *Timing belt renewal*
(b) *Cylinder head removal and refitting*
(c) *Intermediate shaft removal and refitting*
(d) *Sump and oil pump removal and refitting*
(e) *Front end cover oil seals renewal*
(f) *Crankshaft rear oil seal renewal (after removal of the transmission and flywheel)*
(g) *Engine mountings*

4 Major operations requiring engine removal

The following operations are only possible after removal of the engine from the car:

(a) *Pistons and connecting rods removal and refitting*
(b) *Crankshaft and main bearings removal and refitting*

5 Engine – removal and refitting

1 There are two methods of removing the engine – either the transmission can be removed first, or the engine can be removed leaving the transmission in position. With manual transmission models, the transmission should be removed first as described in Chapter 6. With automatic transmission models, the transmission may be removed first or alternatively may be left in position. However, to use the latter method it is necessary to have a long socket extension in order to reach the upper bolts securing the transmission to the engine.
2 Chock the rear wheels, then jack up the front of the car and support on axle stands. Alternatively, position the car over an inspection pit.
3 Unscrew the drain plug then drain the engine oil into a suitable container, taking precautions against scalding if the oil is hot.
4 Unscrew the plastic nuts and bolts and remove the engine splash guard.
5 Drain the cooling system as described in Chapter 2. Unscrew the drain plug located on the right-hand side of the cylinder block, and drain the coolant from the block.

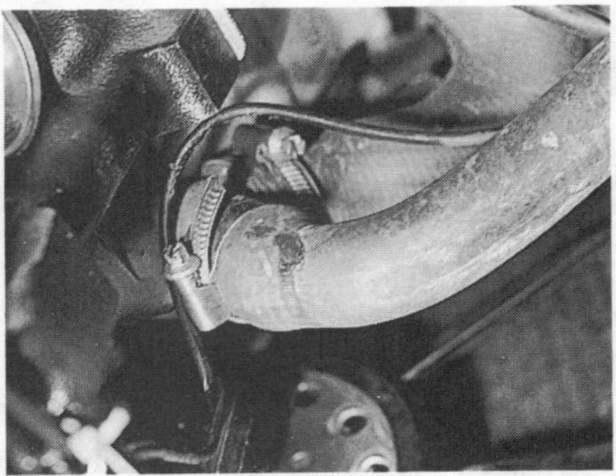
5.13 Expansion tank hose connection to the water pump

5.14A Disconnecting the top hose ...

5.14B ... bottom hose ...

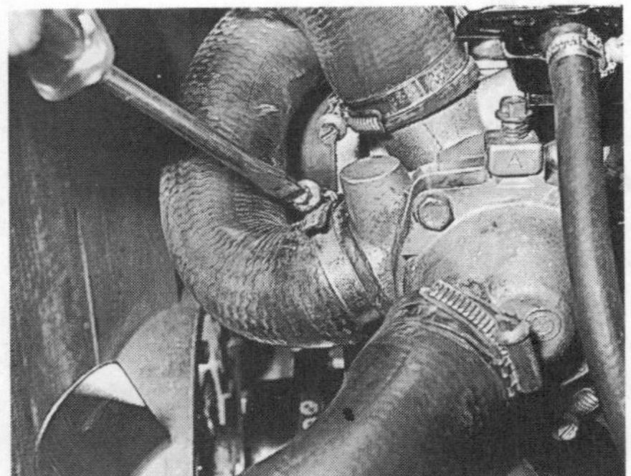
5.14C ... and by-pass hose from the thermostat housing

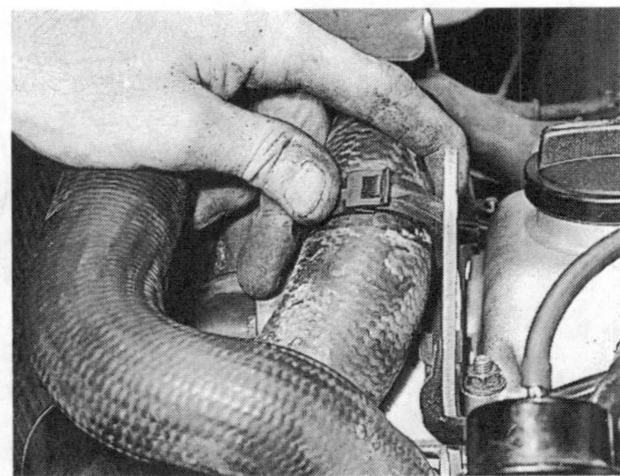
5.14D Releasing the by-pass hose from the plastic clip

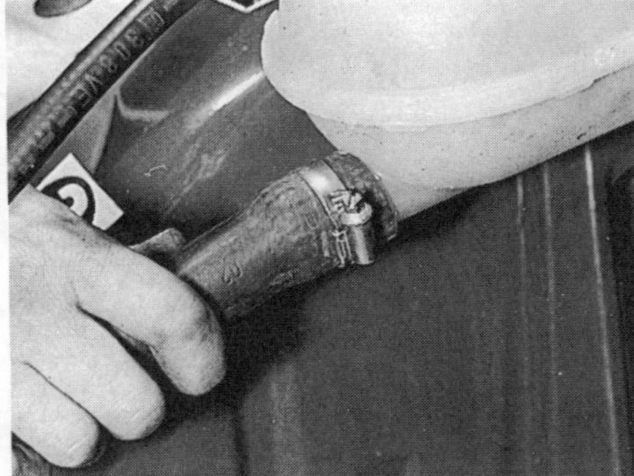
5.15 Disconnecting the outlet hose from the expansion tank

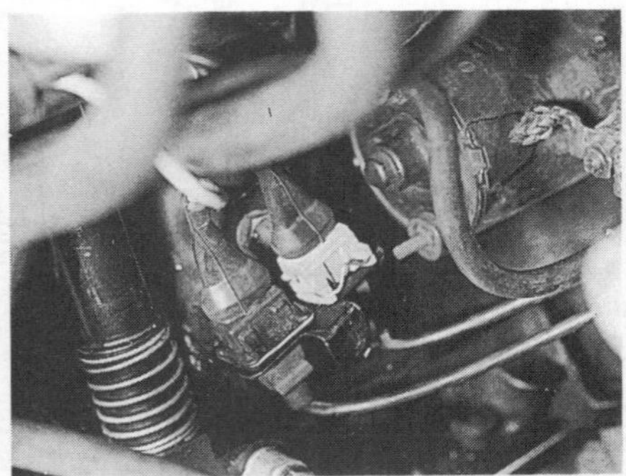
5.19 Ignition reference and speed transmitter sensor plugs

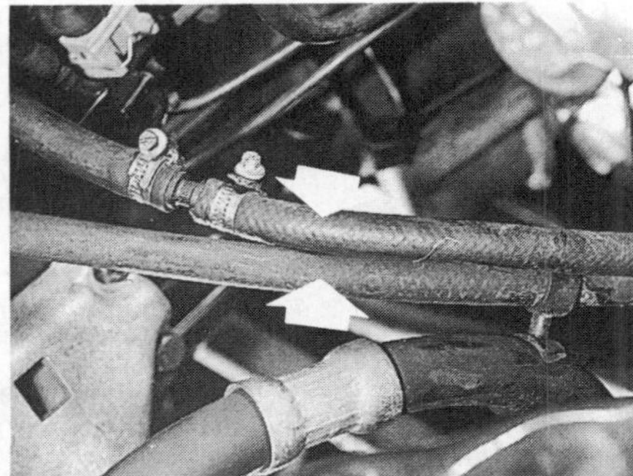
5.20 Fuel supply and return hoses (arrowed)

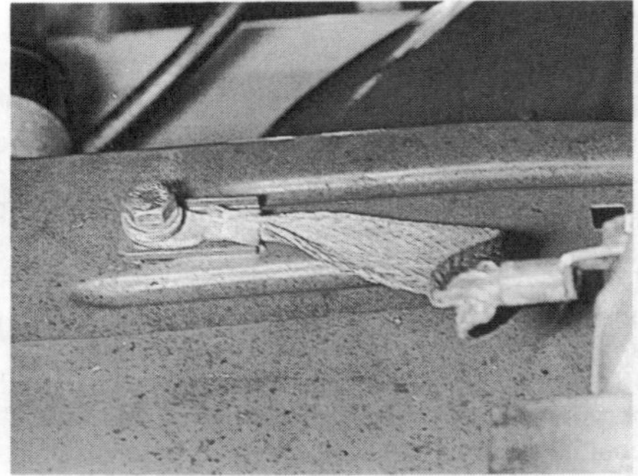
5.23 Engine earth strap located on the underbody

6 Remove the exhaust front downpipes with reference to Chapter 3.

7 Remove the radiator and viscous cooling fan with reference to Chapter 2. Cap the fluid cooler pipes to prevent dust and dirt entering the system.

8 Remove the bonnet with reference to Chapter 11.

9 Disconnect the battery negative and positive leads. The positive lead may be temporarily attached to the engine.

10 Remove the air cleaner and ducting. On models with K-Jetronic fuel injection, remove the mixture regulator/fuel distributor with reference to Chapter 3. On models with L-Jetronic or Motronic fuel injection, remove the airflow sensor and idle control valve with reference to Chapter 3.

11 On models with air conditioning, detach the compressor leaving the hoses still connected and tie the compressor to one side.

12 Disconnect the main HT lead and LT leads from the ignition coil.

13 Disconnect the expansion tank hose from the water pump (photo).

14 Loosen the clips and disconnect the top and bottom coolant hoses from the engine. Also disconnect the by-pass hose from the water pump and thermostat housing and release the plastic clip (photos).

15 Disconnect the hose from the expansion tank on the right-hand side of the engine compartment (photo).

16 Disconnect the accelerator cable, cruise control cable and automatic transmission kickdown cable with reference to Chapters 3 and 6. The cable support brackets may be unbolted and the cables left attached if necessary.

17 Where applicable, disconnect the ECU vacuum hose from the inlet manifold.

18 Disconnect the brake vacuum servo hoses from the inlet manifold.

19 On models with Motronic fuel injection, disconnect the ignition reference and speed transmitter sensor plugs from the bracket on the left-hand side of the engine (photo). Note the location of each plug. Unbolt the bracket from the cylinder block. Also remove the sensors from the transmission with reference to Chapter 4.

20 Disconnect the fuel supply and return hoses, and where necessary release the hoses from their brackets (photo).

21 Disconnect the heater hoses from the control valve and bulkhead noting their fitted positions.

22 Remove the power steering pump with reference to Chapter 10

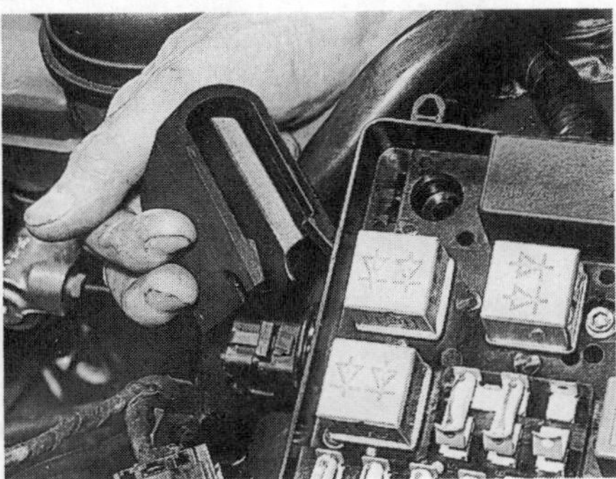
5.24A Removing the fusebox side cover

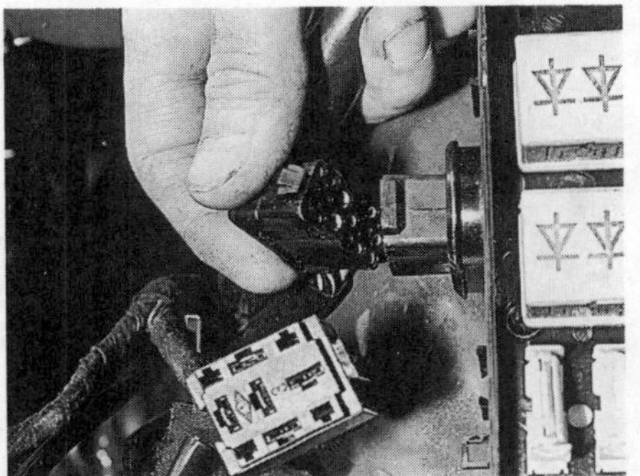
5.24B Disconnecting the wiring harness from the fusebox

5.25 Electronic control unit (ECU) and support

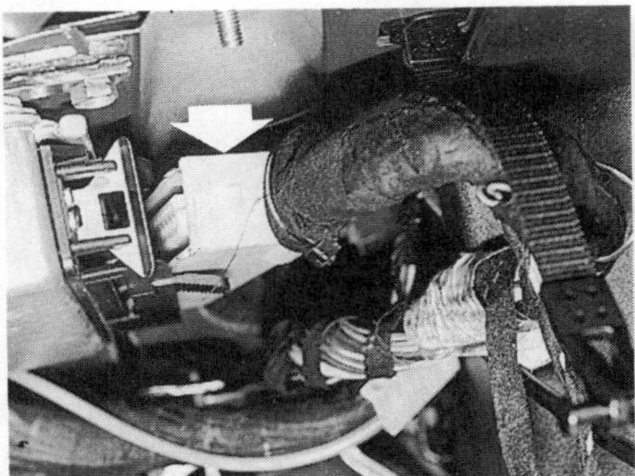
5.26A Disconnect the ECU multi-plug ...

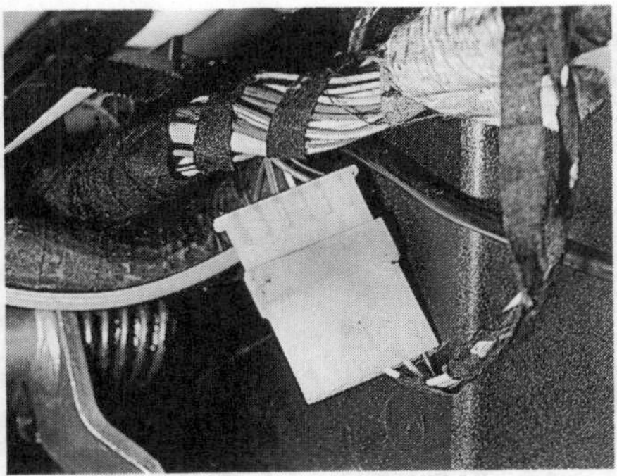
5.26B ... and the wiring harness multi-plug

5.28A ECU wiring harness routing through the bulkhead panels

5.28B Removing the ECU multi-plug through the inner panel ...

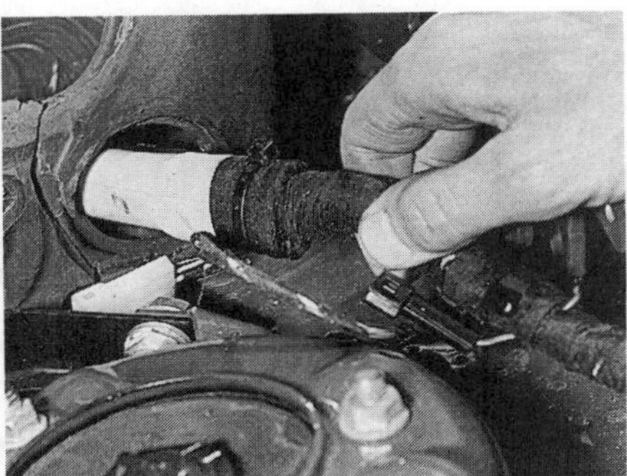
5.28C ... and outer panel

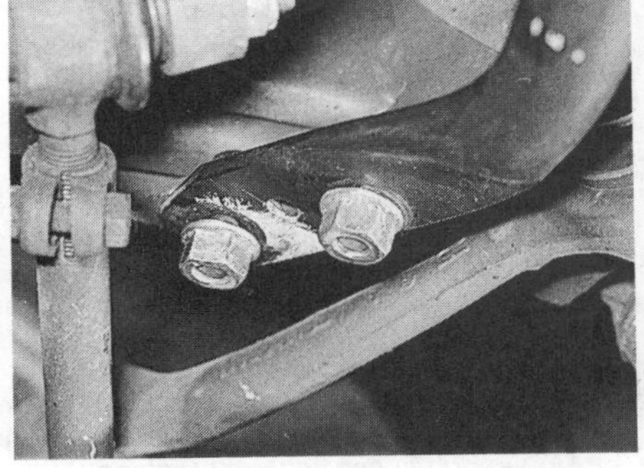
5.36 Underbody strengthening bar mounting nuts

but leave the hoses connected. Tie the pump to one side.

23 Unbolt the engine earth strap from the right-hand side underbody (photo).

Models with L-Jetronic or Motronic fuel injection

24 Remove the cover from the fusebox on the left-hand side of the engine compartment. Slide up the plastic cover and disconnect the wiring harness plug from the fusebox (photos). Also remove the relays located outside the fusebox.

25 Working inside the car, open the glovebox and disconnect the straps by pushing out the pins. Remove the rear cover and release the support to expose the ECU (photo).

26 Disconnect the multi-plug from the ECU by pulling out the rear end and unhooking the front end. Also disconnect the wiring harness multi-plug (photos).

27 Cut free the wiring harness retaining straps in the engine compartment.

28 Carefully feed the wiring harness and multi-plugs through the bulkhead and into the engine compartment. Use a screwdriver to release the grommets (photos). Tie the harness to the engine.

Models with K-Jetronic fuel injection

29 Disconnect the wiring harness from the fusebox on the left-hand side of the engine compartment and tie it to the engine.

Method with automatic transmission left in position

30 Remove the starter motor with reference to Chapter 12.

31 Support the transmission on a trolley jack.

32 Unbolt the transmission rear mounting crossmember from the underbody.

33 Place a piece of wood over the front anti-roll bar. Use a plastic tie to keep it in position.

34 Unscrew and remove the bolts which connect the torque converter to the driveplate. Turn the crankshaft while doing this to bring each bolt into view. Mark the driveplate and torque converter in relation to each other to ensure correct reassembly.

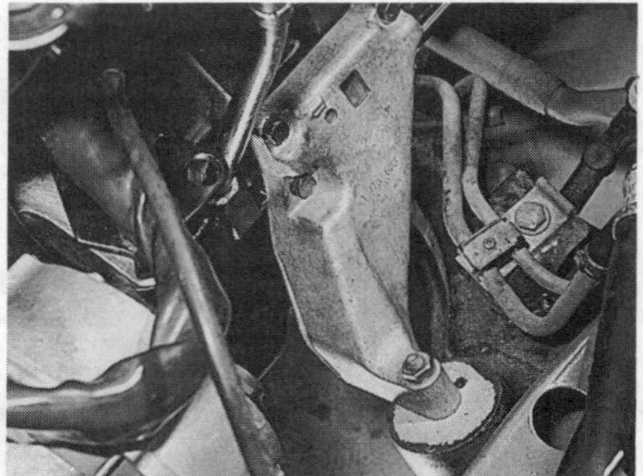
5.43A Upper view of the left-hand side engine mounting

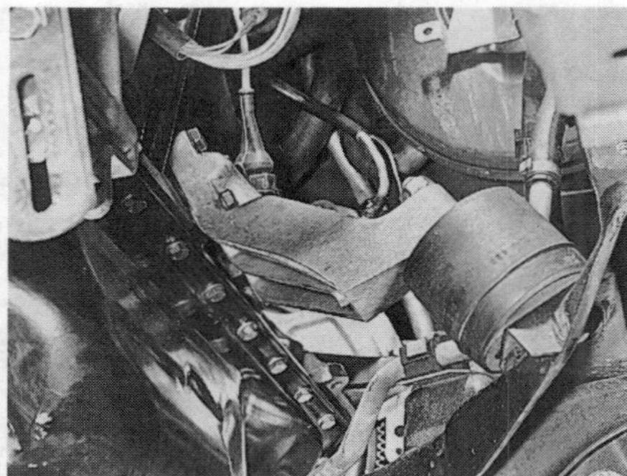
5.43B Lower view of the left-hand side engine mounting

5.43C Upper view of the right-hand side engine mounting

5.43D Lower view of the right-hand side engine mounting

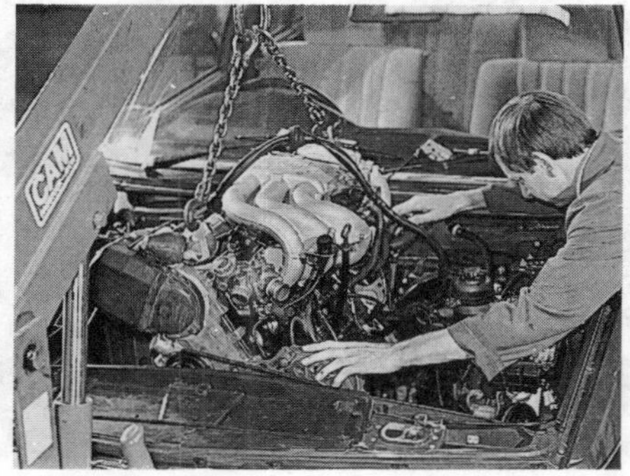

5.47 Lifting the engine from the engine compartment

35 Unbolt and remove the cover plate/housing from the bottom front of the transmission. Also where applicable unscrew the single bolt securing the engine rear plate to the transmission.
36 Unscrew the nuts and remove the underbody strengthening bar from under the rear of the engine (photo).
37 Lower the transmission and engine until they are just resting on the front crossmember and anti-roll bar but make sure that the selector cable is not strained – disconnect it if necessary. If required, the anti-roll bar may be unbolted from the underbody to provide additional working room.
38 Unscrew and remove the transmission-to-engine bolts which may be of Torx type. A double extension will be required to reach the upper bolts and it will be necessary to lever the transmission to one side. Leave one lower bolt finger-tight at this stage.
39 Raise the transmission to its normal position and support with two trolley jacks to ensure that it is kept level.
40 Prise out the plastic grille from the bottom of the transmission.
41 Attach a hoist to the engine, so that it will be kept horizontal during the removal procedure, and just take its weight. Lifting eyes are provided at the front and rear of the engine.
42 Remove the final lower bolt from the transmission.
43 Unscrew the engine mounting lower nuts from the underbody, then unbolt the mountings from the cylinder block and remove them (photos). Remove the oil filter for better access to the right-hand mounting.
44 Withdraw the engine forward from the transmission keeping it horizontal, and at the same time have an assistant insert a lever through the grille opening in the transmission and hold the torque converter in place. Do not allow the torque converter to move forwards otherwise fluid will be lost.

Method with transmission removed

45 Attach a hoist to the engine, so that it will be kept horizontal during the removal procedure, and just take its weight. Lifting eyes are provided at the front and rear of the engine.
46 Unscrew the engine mounting lower nuts from the underbody, then unbolt the mountings from the cylinder block and remove them. Remove the oil filter for better access to the right-hand mounting.

Both methods

47 Lift the engine from the engine compartment, taking care not to damage the components on the inner wings and bulkhead (photo).
48 If a factory exchange engine is to be fitted, transfer the ancillary components from the old engine and also fit the new oil dipstick tube supplied. Apply suitable sealant to the base of the tube before driving it into the crankcase. Remove the spigot bearing from the rear of the crankshaft if the exchange engine is to be fitted to an automatic transmission.
49 Refitting is a reversal of removal, but before starting the engine, check that it has been filled with oil, and also that the cooling system has been filled with coolant (Chapter 2). Before tightening the engine and transmission mountings, rock the engine by hand to ensure correct alignment. Tighten all nuts and bolts to the specified torque. Adjust the power steering pump drivebelt with reference to Chapter 10, and the air conditioning compressor drivebelt with reference to Chapter 11. Adjust the accelerator cable, cruise control cable and automatic transmission kickdown cable with reference to Chapters 3 and 6.

6 Engine dismantling – general

1 If possible, position the engine on a bench or strong table for the dismantling procedure. Two or three blocks of wood will be necessary to support the engine in an upright position.
2 Cleanliness is most important, and if the engine is dirty, it should be cleaned with paraffin before commencing work.
3 Avoid working with the engine directly on a concrete floor, as grit presents a real source of trouble.
4 As parts are removed, clean them in a paraffin bath. However, do not immerse parts with internal oilways in paraffin, as it is difficult to remove.
5 It is advisable to have suitable containers to hold small items

according to their use, as this will help when reassembling the engine and also prevent possible losses.

6 Always obtain complete sets of gaskets when the engine is being dismantled, but retain the old gaskets with a view to using them as patterns to make replacements if new ones are not available.

7 When possible, refit nuts, bolts, and washers in their location after being removed, as this helps to protect the threads, and will also be helpful when reassembling the engine.

8 Retain unserviceable components in order to compare them with the new parts supplied.

7 Ancillary components – removal and refitting

With the engine removed from the car, the externally mounted ancillary components given in the following list may be removed. The removal sequence need not necessarily follow the order given:

(a) *Throttle housing (Chapter 3)*
(b) *Distributor (Chapter 4)*
(c) *Thermostat (Chapter 2)*
(d) *Oil filter (Chapter 1)*
(e) *Clutch (Chapter 5)*

8 Engine – complete dismantling

1 Mark the flywheel in relation to the rear of the crankshaft.

2 Hold the flywheel stationary using a screwdriver against a bolt inserted into the rear of the cylinder block, or by using a piece of bent metal engaged with the teeth of the flywheel and in contact with the bolt.

3 Unscrew the flywheel bolts, then remove the driveplate (automatic transmission models) and flange plate (photos).

4 Remove the flywheel from the rear of the crankshaft. Also remove the rear engine plate (photos).

5 If an engine stand is available, fit the engine to the stand at this stage.

6 Remove the engine oil level dipstick (photo).

7 Loosen the clips and disconnect the coolant hoses from the rear left-hand side of the cylinder head and cylinder block. If preferred, the rear outlet may be unbolted from the cylinder head and the gasket removed (photos).

8 Loosen the clips and disconnect the hoses from the thermostat housing on the front of the head. Also disconnect the small hose for the throttle housing from the rear left-hand side of the cylinder block (photos).

9 Remove the HT leads, spark plugs, distributor cap, rotor arm and dust cover with reference to Chapter 4. Unscrew the valve cover nuts and remove the HT lead conduit (photo).

10 Disconnect the wire from the oil pressure switch located on the right-hand side of the engine, and release the wire from the plastic tie (photos).

11 Make a careful note of the location and routing of the engine wiring harness, then disconnect it from the engine. Cut any plastic ties as necessary. The harness is routed through the inlet manifold centre branches (photo). When disconnecting the temperature sensors from the thermostat housing on models with L-Jetronic or Motronic fuel injection, note that the brown multi-plug is the one to the temperature gauge and is connected to the socket with the single terminal. The blue multi-plug is for the temperature time switch.

12 Remove the inlet manifold with reference to Chapter 3.

13 Remove the alternator with reference to Chapter 12. Also remove the mounting bracket (photo).

14 Unscrew the nuts and withdraw the thermostat housing from the studs on the front left-hand side of the cylinder head. Remove the gasket (photos).

15 Remove the exhaust manifold from the cylinder head with reference to Chapter 3.

8.3A Removing the automatic transmission driveplate

8.3B Removing the flange plate from the flywheel

8.4A Remove the flywheel ...

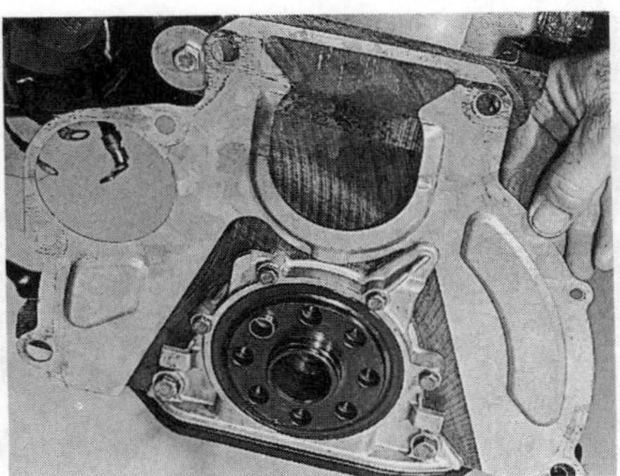
8.4B ... and rear engine plate

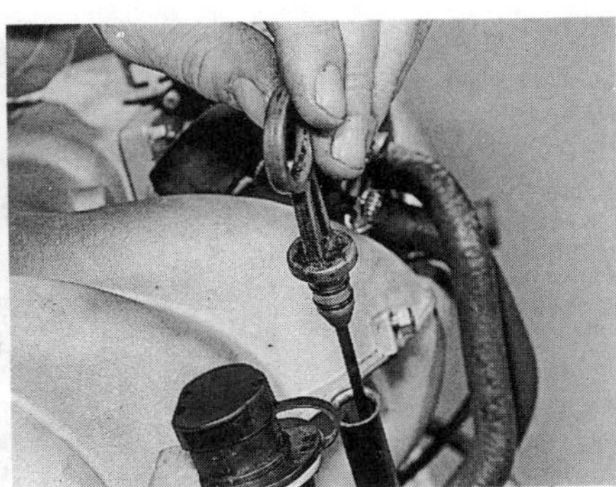
8.6 Engine oil level dipstick removal

8.7A Unscrew the bolts ...

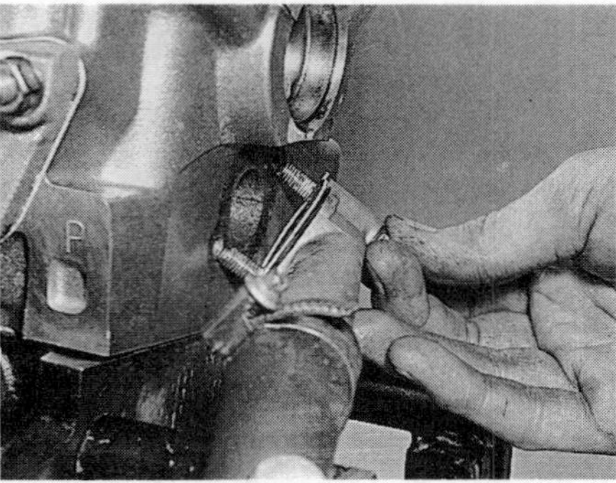

8.7B ... and remove the rear outlet from the cylinder head

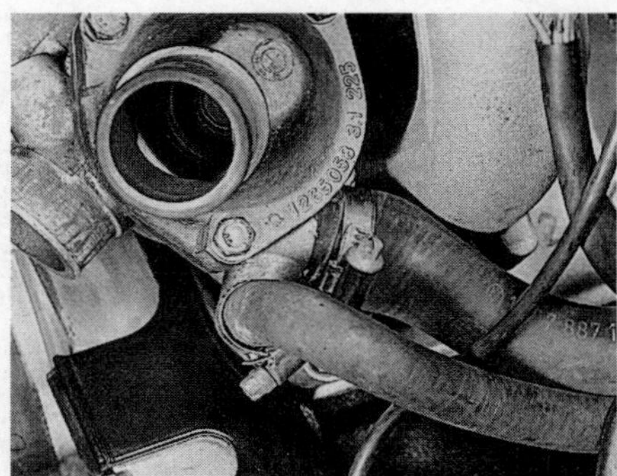

8.8A Disconnect the hoses from the thermostat housing

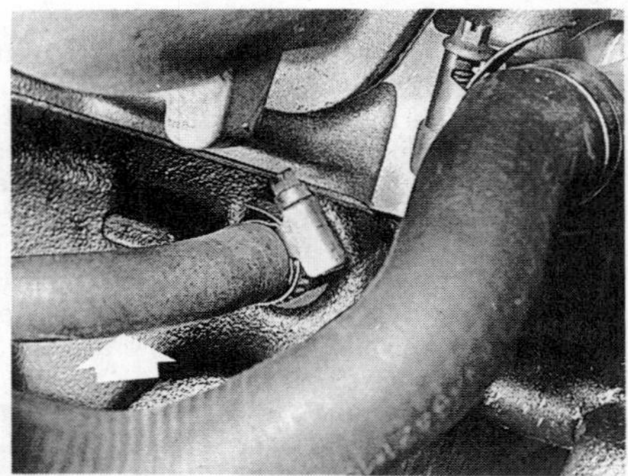

8.8B Coolant hose (arrowed) for the throttle housing located on the left-hand side of the cylinder block

8.9 HT lead conduit located on the valve cover

16 Remove the rubber cover from the side of the timing covers (photos).
17 Unscrew the centre nut securing the upper and lower timing covers, noting that the alternator adjustment link is also connected to the same stud (photo).
18 Unscrew the two upper and one lower bolt securing the upper timing cover to the cylinder head and remove the cover (photos).
19 Turn the engine with a socket on the crankshaft pulley bolt until number 1 piston is at TDC on compression. If necessary, the distributor rotor may be temporarily refitted in order to determine the correct position.
20 Align the timing marks on the camshaft sprocket and cylinder head, and also on the crankshaft pulley and timing cover (photos).
21 Unclip and remove the TDC sensor from the lower timing cover.
22 Unscrew the lower bolt and remove the lower timing cover from the front of the cylinder block.
23 Unscrew the bolts securing the crankshaft pulley and vibration damper to the hub, then remove them (photos). The vibration damper is located on the hub with a dowel.
24 Remove the front engine lifting eye bracket from the dowels on the cylinder head (photo).
25 Loosen the timing cover stud and the bolt securing the tensioner to the cylinder head (photos). Push in the tensioner roller and tighten the upper bolt to hold the tensioner away from the belt.
26 If the timing belt is to be re-used, mark it so that it can be refitted in the same running direction as removed.
27 Slide the timing belt off the tensioner roller, then remove it from the crankshaft sprocket, intermediate shaft and camshaft sprocket (photo).
28 Unscrew the nuts securing the valve cover to the cylinder head noting the location of the wiring harness clips (photo).
29 Disconnect the crankshaft ventilation hose then remove the valve cover. Remove the gasket from the studs (photos).
30 Prise the rubber plugs from the front and rear of the cylinder head noting that their flanges are located on the inside of the casting (photo).
31 Hold the camshaft sprocket stationary then unscrew the sprocket

8.10A Disconnect the wire from the oil pressure switch ...

8.10B ... and from the plastic tie on the front of the block

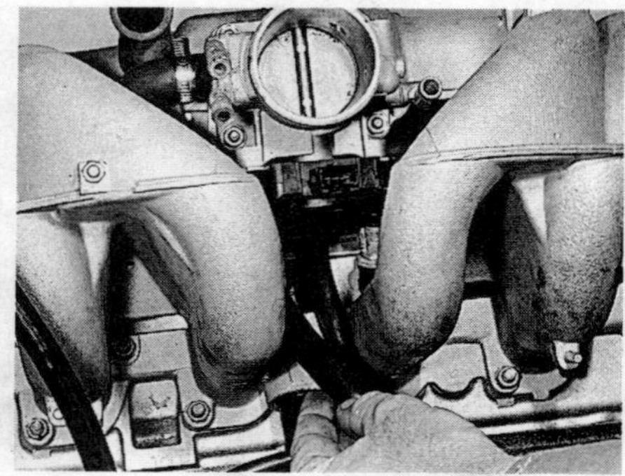

8.11 Withdrawing the engine wiring harness through the inlet manifold centre branches

8.13 Alternator mounting bracket

8.14A Unscrew the nuts ...

8.14B ... and withdraw the thermostat housing from the cylinder head

8.16A Unclip the rubber cover (arrowed) ...

8.16B ... then remove it (arrowed) from the side of the timing covers

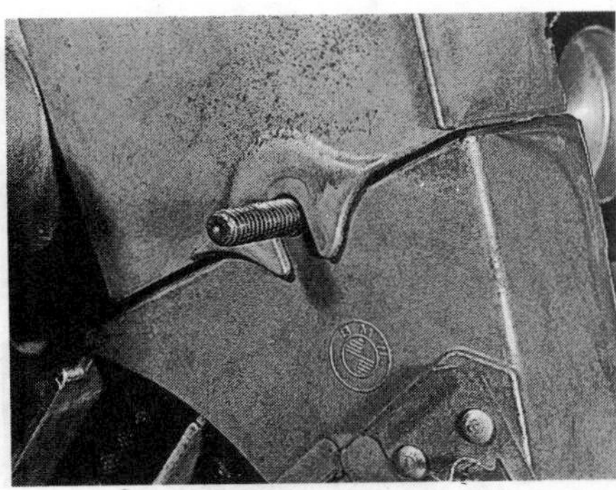

8.17 Timing cover centre stud

8.18A Upper timing cover mounting bolt (arrowed)

8.18B Upper and lower timing covers

8.20A Timing marks on the camshaft sprocket and cylinder head

8.20B Timing marks on the crankshaft pulley

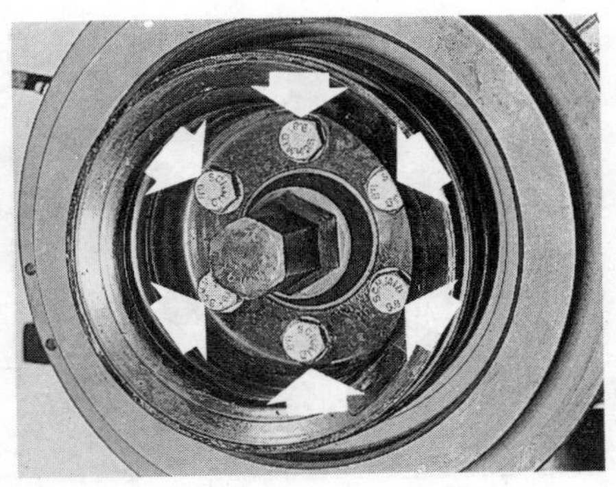

8.23A Unscrew the bolts (arrowed) ...

8.23B ... and remove the crankshaft pulley ...

8.23C ... and vibration damper

8.24 Front engine lifting eye bracket (arrowed)

8.25A Loosening the timing cover stud ...

8.25B ... and upper tensioner bolt

8.27 Removing the timing belt

8.28 Valve cover nut and wiring harness clip

8.29A Disconnect the crankcase ventilation hose (arrowed) ...

8.29B ... remove the valve cover ...

8.29C ... and remove the gasket

8.30 Removing the rubber plugs from the cylinder head

8.32 Removing the adaptor plate and camshaft sprocket

8.33 Using a small pair of grips to hold the tensioner spring and pin

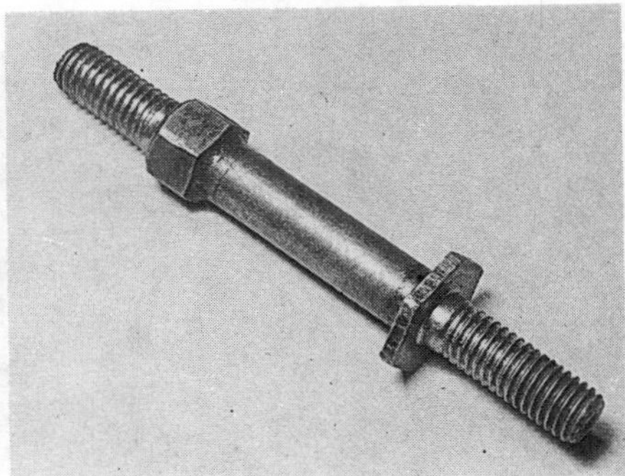
8.34 Timing cover stud fitted to the bottom of the tensioner

8.37 Lifting the cylinder head from the cylinder block

8.38 Removing the cylinder head gasket

8.39 Removing the intermediate shaft sprocket

centre bolt using a Torx key. Several methods may be used to hold the sprocket stationary – the method shown in photograph 11.44 uses an old timing belt bolted to a long length of metal bar, but grips may be used with an old timing belt in a similar way.

32 With the bolt removed, remove the adaptor plate followed by the camshaft sprocket (photo). If necessary mark the outer face of the sprocket to ensure correct refitting but note that it will only locate in one position due to the dowel.

33 The timing belt tensioner spring must now be restrained. BMW technicians use a special tool which holds the spring and pin in position on the tensioner by gripping the inner end of the pin. The tensioner pin is therefore held away from the water pump. A small pair of grips can be used to hold the pin (photo).

34 Unscrew the stud and bolt and remove the tensioner. Note that the narrow hexagon flange is fitted to the outside of the stud (photo).

35 Unbolt the water pump from the front of the cylinder block and remove the gasket.

36 Unscrew the cylinder head bolts evenly in the reverse order to that shown in Fig. 1.7. Remove the bolts and washers.

37 Lift the cylinder head from the location dowel on the block and place it on the bench (photo).

38 Remove the gasket from the cylinder block (photo).

39 Hold the intermediate shaft sprocket stationary then unscrew the centre bolt and withdraw the sprocket from the shaft (photo). Note the location dowel. Use a length of metal bar with long bolts positioned so that they can be inserted in the holes in the intermediate shaft sprocket to hold the sprocket stationary. Alternatively, use the method given in paragraph 31.

40 Unbolt the power steering pump bracket from the front left-hand side of the block (photos).

41 Turn the engine upside down on the bench. As oil and water will run out, place some rags on the bench first.

42 Unscrew the sump bolts and lift the sump from the crankcase. Remove the gasket (photos).

43 If necessary, remove the oil level dipstick tube from the block using grips, but mark it for position first to ensure correct refitting.

8.40A Unscrew the power steering pump bracket front bolt (arrowed) ...

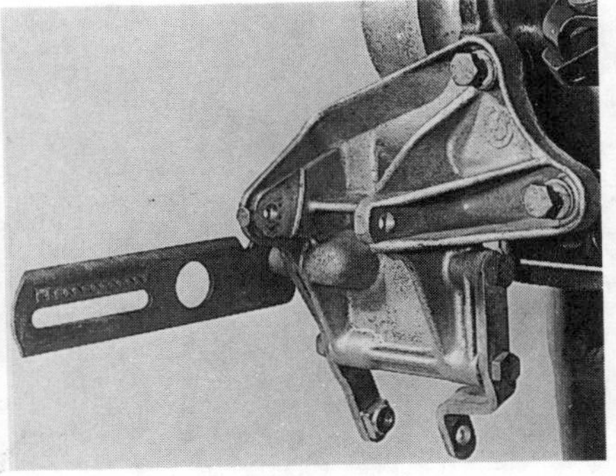
8.40B ... and rear bolts, and remove the bracket

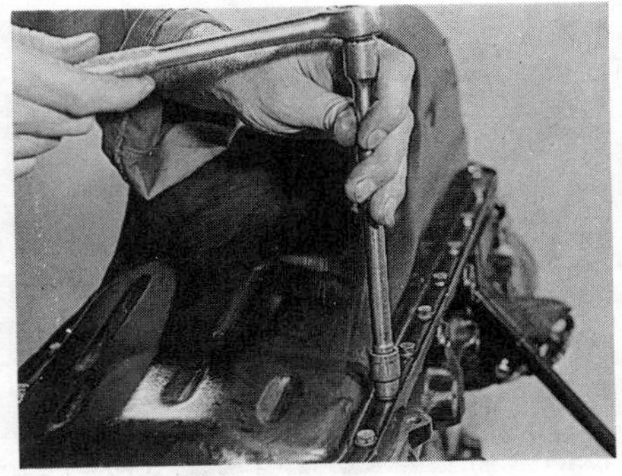
8.42A Unscrew the bolts ...

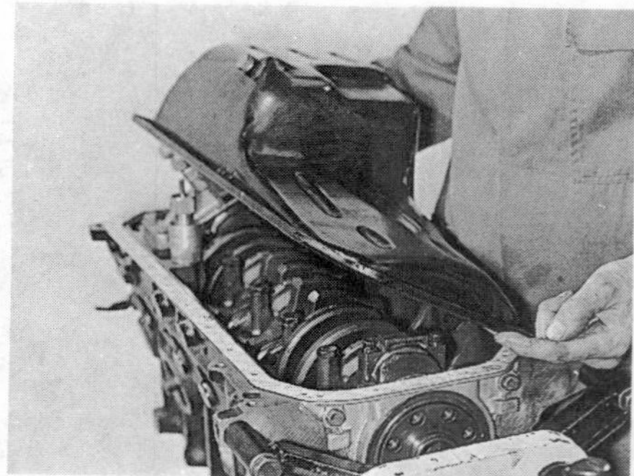
8.42B ... and remove the sump ...

8.42C ... and gasket

8.44 Oil pressure relief valve located on the bottom of the block

8.45 Oil pressure switch

8.46A Unscrew the bolts (arrowed) ...

8.46B ... and remove the crankshaft rear oil seal housing

8.47A Removing the oil pump ...

8.47B ... and oil pump driveshaft

8.48 Front crankshaft pulley bolt

8.49A Slide the pulley hub/sprocket from the nose of the crankshaft ...

8.49B ... and extract the Woodruff key (arrowed)

8.50A Front oil seal housing upper bolts (arrowed) ...

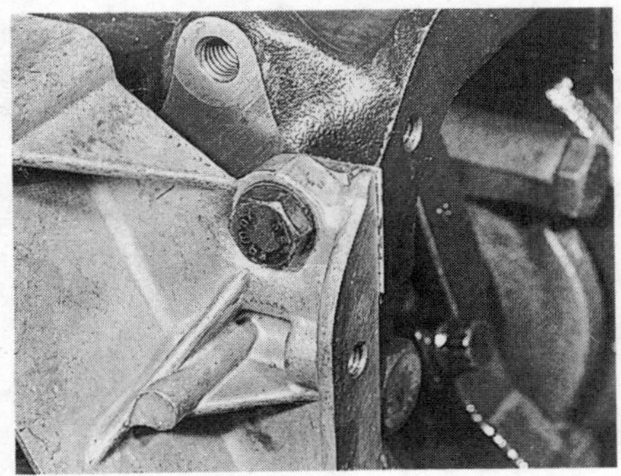
8.50B ... and lower bolts

8.50C Removing the front oil seal housing

8.52A Remove the bearing ...

8.52B ... and extract the oil pump drive gear

8.53A Using an impact driver to loosen the intermediate shaft guide plate screws

8.53B Intermediate shaft guide plate removal

8.54A Intermediate shaft removal

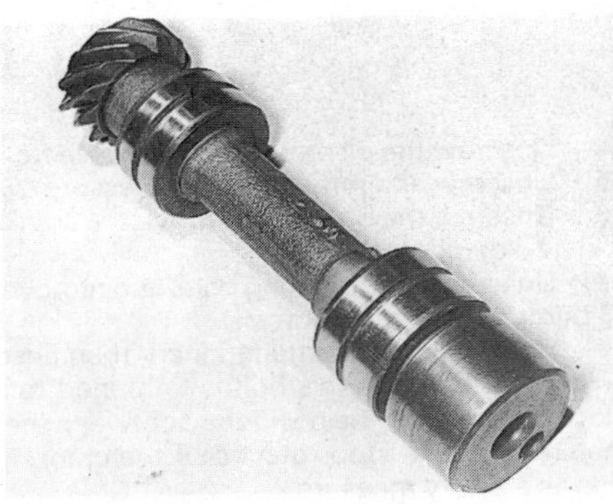
8.54B Intermediate shaft

8.55 Connecting rod and cap marked with a centre punch

8.56 Removing a big-end cap

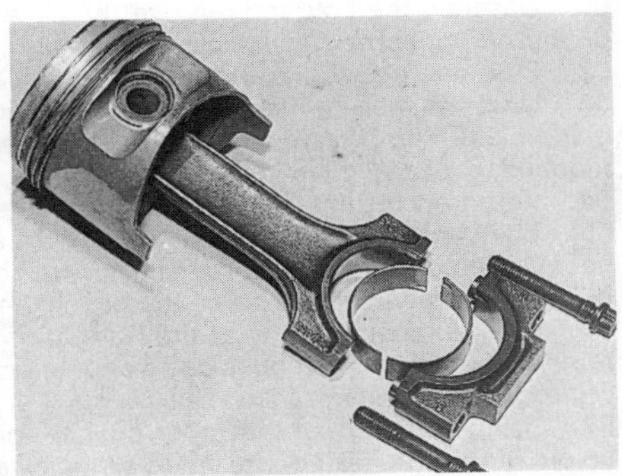
8.57 Piston and connecting rod components

8.59A Checking the crankshaft endfloat with a dial gauge ...

8.59B ... and a feeler blade

8.60A Main bearing cap numbering (arrowed)

8.60B Removing a main bearing cap

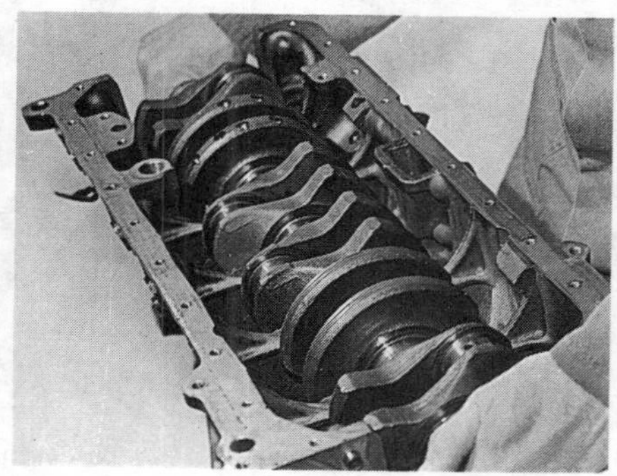
8.62 Lifting the crankshaft from the crankcase

44 Unscrew the oil pressure relief valve from the block (photo).
45 Unscrew and remove the oil pressure switch (photo).
46 Unscrew the bolts and remove the crankshaft rear oil seal housing and gasket (photos).
47 Unscrew the mounting bolts and remove the oil pump. Pull out the oil pump driveshaft (photos).
48 Hold the crankshaft stationary then unscrew the front crankshaft pulley bolt (photo). This bolt is tightened to a very high torque and a block of wood may be positioned between the front crankshaft web and the crankcase to stop rotation of the crankshaft. Lie the engine on its side as a safety measure.
49 Slide the pulley hub/sprocket from the nose of the crankshaft. Extract the Woodruff key (photos).
50 Unscrew the bolts and remove the front oil seal housing. Remove the gasket (photos).
51 Unscrew the bolt and remove the clamp securing the oil pump driveshaft upper bearing in the cylinder block.
52 Prise out the bearing and extract the drive gear (photos).
53 Unscrew the slot-head screws and extract the intermediate shaft guide plate. The screws are very tight and an impact driver may be required to release them (photos).
54 Withdraw the intermediate shaft from the cylinder block (photos).
55 The connecting rods and their caps are engraved for match, but not numbered for sequence, so mark and number them from the timing belt end of the engine using a centre punch (photo).
56 With number 1 piston at the bottom of its stroke, unscrew and remove the big-end cap bolts using a multi-spline socket. Remove the cap together with its bearing shell (photo).
57 Using the handle of a hammer, push the piston and connecting rod up out of the bore taking care not to allow the connecting rod to scrape the bore surface. Make sure that the upper bearing shell is not left behind on the crankshaft. Temporarily refit the cap and shell to the bottom of the connecting rod and place the assembly to one side (photo).
58 Repeat the procedure given in paragraphs 56 and 57 for the remaining piston assemblies.
59 Check the endfloat of the crankshaft using either a dial gauge on the front or rear of the crankshaft, or a feeler blade between number 6 main bearing side flange and the crankshaft web (photos). This will determine whether new main bearings are required, in particular whether the number 6 bearings which include the side flanges, are worn.
60 The main bearing caps are numbered one to seven from the timing belt end of the engine. Note which way round the caps are fitted. Starting with number one cap, unscrew the bolts and lift the cap from the crankcase. If it is tight tap it lightly with a hammer to release it. Keep the main bearing shell together with the cap to ensure correct reassembly (photos).
61 Repeat the procedure given in paragraph 60 to remove the remaining caps.
62 Lift the crankshaft from the crankcase (photo).
63 Remove the lower main bearing shells from the crankcase, keeping them identified for position.

9 Engine components – examination and renovation

Cylinder block and crankcase

1 Examine the casting carefully for cracks, especially around the bolt holes and between cylinders.
2 The cylinder bores must be checked for taper, ovality (out-of-round), scoring and scratching. Start by examining the top of the cylinder bores. If they are at all worn, a ridge will be felt on the thrust side. This ridge marks the limit of piston ring travel. The owner will have a good indication of bore wear prior to dismantling by the quantity of oil consumed and the emission of blue smoke from the exhaust, especially when the engine is cold.

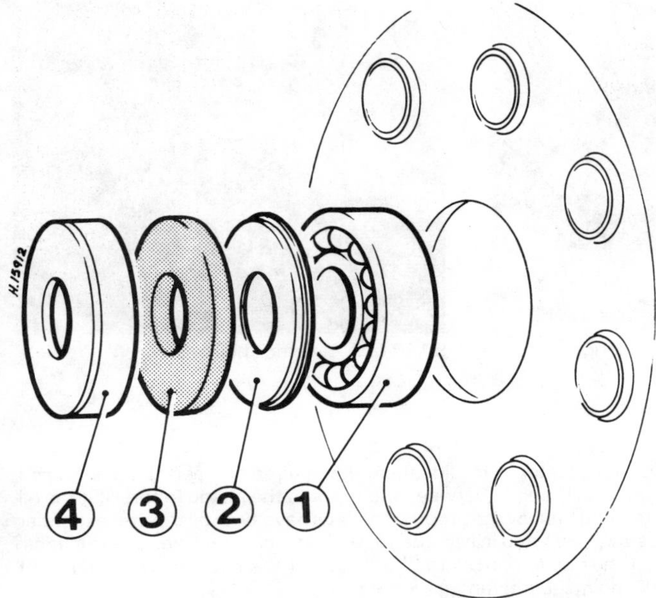

Fig. 1.2 Clutch spigot bearing components located in the rear of the crankshaft (Sec 9)

1 Bearing
2 Cover
3 Felt ring
4 Spacer

3 An internal micrometer or dial gauge can be used to check bore wear and taper against the Specifications, but this is a pointless operation if the engine is obviously in need of reboring due to excessive consumption.
4 Your engine reconditioner will be able to rebore the block for you and supply the correct oversize pistons to give the specified running clearance.
5 If the engine has reached the limit for reboring then cylinder liners can be fitted, but here again this is a job for your engine reconditioner.
6 To rectify minor bore wear it is possible to fit proprietary oil control rings, as described later in this Section. A good way to test the condition of the engine is to have it at normal operating temperature with the spark plugs removed. Disconnect the HT lead from the centre of the ignition coil and connect it to earth with a bridging wire. Screw a compression tester (available from most motor accessory stores) into the first plug hole. Hold the accelerator fully depressed and crank the engine on the starter motor for several revolutions. Record the reading. Zero the tester and check the remaining cylinders in the same way. All six compression figures should be approximately equal and within the tolerance given in the Specifications. If they are low, suspect piston ring or cylinder bore wear. If only one reading is down, suspect a valve not seating.
7 Check the core plugs in the cylinder block for signs of leakage (photo). To renew a core plug, first drill a hole in the centre and screw in a large self-tapping screw. A pair of grips or a suitable slide hammer and adaptor can then be attached to the screw and the core plug pulled out.
8 Clean the core plug seating and apply a little sealant, then locate the new core plug squarely in the hole and use a metal tube to tap it into position.

Crankshaft and bearings

9 Examine the surfaces of the crankpins and journals for signs of scoring or scratching and check for ovality or taper using a micrometer. If the crankpin or journals are not within the dimensional tolerances given in the Specifications then the crankshaft will have to be reground.
10 Wear in a crankshaft can be detected while the engine is running. Big-end bearing and crankpin wear is indicated by distinct metallic knocking, particularly noticeable when the engine is pulling from low engine speeds. Low oil pressure will also occur.
11 Main bearing and journal wear is indicated by engine rumble increasing in severity as the engine speed increases. Low oil pressure will again be an associated condition.

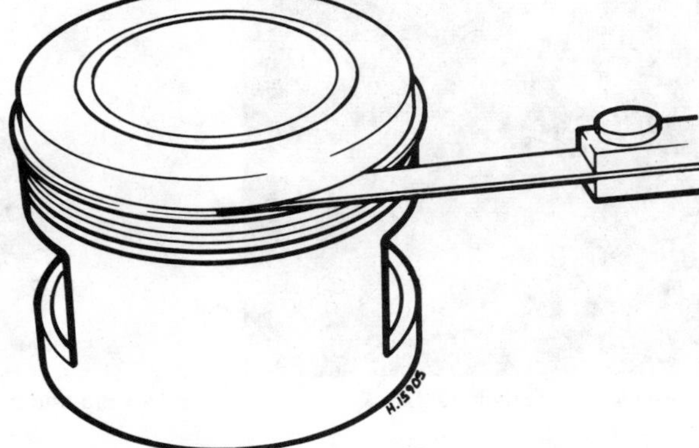

Fig. 1.3 Checking the piston ring-to-groove clearance (Sec 9)

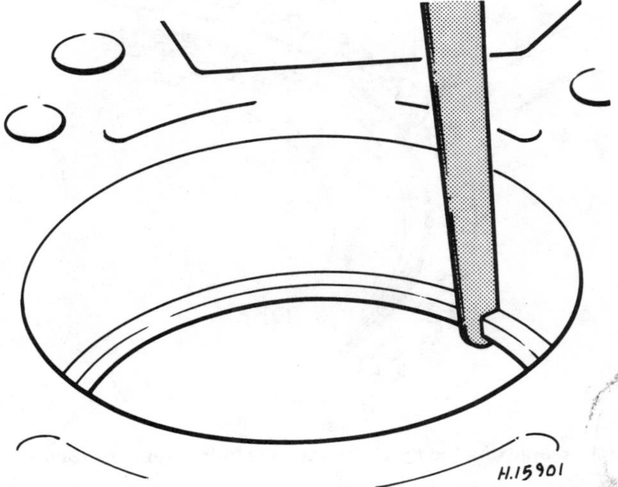

Fig. 1.4 Checking the piston ring end gap (Sec 9)

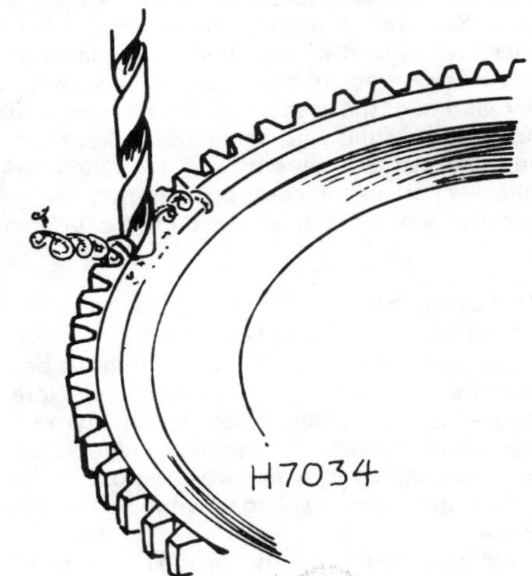

Fig. 1.5 Drilling the flywheel ring gear prior to removal (Sec 9)

12 Due to the fact that the crankshaft has a special surface treatment, grinding and the supply of matching shells should only be carried out by BMW. The service is carried out through their dealers.
13 Inspect the connecting rod big-end and main bearing shells for signs of general wear, scoring, pitting and scratching. The bearings should be matt grey in colour. If a copper colour is evident, then the bearings are badly worn and the surface material has worn away to expose the underlay. Renew the bearing shells as a complete set.
14 At time of major overhaul it is worthwhile renewing the bearing

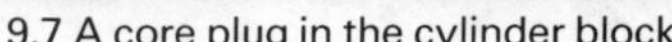
9.7 A core plug in the cylinder block

9.14A Big-end bearing shell markings

9.14B Main bearing shell markings

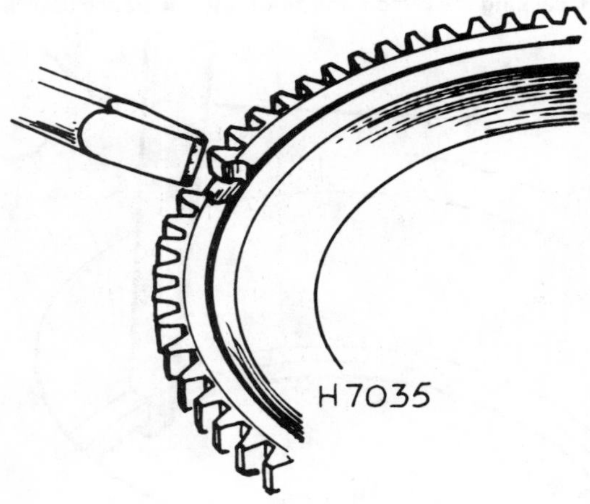

Fig. 1.6 Splitting the flywheel ring gear before removal (Sec 9)

shells as a matter of routine even if they appear to be in reasonably good condition. Bearing shells can be identified by the marking on the back of the shell (photos). Standard sized shells are usually marked STD or 0.00. Undersized shells are marked with the undersize such as 0.25 mm.

15 Finally, on manual transmission models, check the clutch spigot bearing in the rear end of the crankshaft. If it is worn it will have to be renewed. Extract the bearing with a suitable puller. Note the order of removal of the components as shown in Fig. 1.2. When the new bearing has been fitted, pack it with 1 gram of multi-purpose grease. When fitting the cover, make sure that it has the domed side facing out.

Pistons/connecting rods

16 To remove a piston from a connecting rod, extract the circlips and push out the gudgeon pin (photo). If it is too tight to be removed by finger pressure, warm the piston in hot water first. Note which way round the piston is fitted in relation to the connecting rod.

17 New pistons are supplied with matching gudgeon pins. The piston sets should be of the same make and weight group. If the engine has been rebored then new oversize pistons with rings and gudgeon pins will be supplied.

18 If the purpose of removing the pistons was to fit new rings, proceed in the following way.

19 Expand the rings with the fingers and remove them from the piston in an upward direction.

20 Clean the piston ring grooves of carbon deposits. A piece of broken piston ring is useful for this. Make sure that the groove oil return holes are clear.

21 The top compression ring of new ring sets should be stepped to avoid the ring contacting the wear ridge at the top of the bore. Most proprietary piston ring sets are supplied stepped.

22 Check each ring in its piston groove to see that it has the specified clearance.

23 Push each ring down the cylinder bore and check the end gap. This should be within the specified tolerance. The safest way to fit the new rings to the piston is to slide them down three old feeler blades, placed at equidistant points between the ring and the piston (photo). Fit the oil control ring first. Some proprietary rings have two rails and an expander and should be fitted in accordance with the manufacturer's instructions.

24 When all the rings are fitted, stagger the end gaps at equidistant (120°) points to prevent gas blow-by.

25 When fitting new piston rings for use in the worn cylinder bores, the hard glaze in the bores should be removed using a glaze busting tool or by rubbing with fine glasspaper. Try and obtain a cross-hatched appearance. This roughening of the bores will help the new rings to bed in.

26 Check the alignment of the connecting rods visually. If you suspect distortion, have them checked by your dealer or engine reconditioner on the special jig which he will have.

27 Refit the pistons to their relevant connecting rods, oil the gudgeon pins and press them into position. If necessary, heat the pistons in hot water first. If the original gudgeon pins are being re-used they should be refitted the same way round as when removed.

Flywheel

28 On manual transmission models, check the clutch mating surface of the flywheel. If it is deeply scored (due to failure to renew a worn disc) then it may be possible to have its surface ground, provided the thickness of the flywheel is not reduced below the specified minimum. If lots of tiny cracks are visible on the surface of the flywheel then this will be due to overheating caused by slipping of the clutch or by riding the clutch pedal.

29 The pre-engaged starter motor fitted does not cause excessive wear to the ring gear, but if the ring gear is worn it can be renewed separately from the flywheel.

30 To remove the ring gear, drill a hole between the roots of two teeth, taking care not to damage the flywheel, and then split the ring with a sharp cold chisel.

31 The new ring gear must be heated to between 200°C and 230°C so if you do not have the facilities for obtaining these temperatures, leave the job to your dealer or engine reconditioner. If you have access to a thermocolor pencil or accurate oven, heat the ring to the correct temperature then tap it onto the flywheel with the chamfered teeth facing the engine side.

Timing belt and tensioner

32 Examine the belt for cracking or tooth wear. If any of these conditions is evident or if the belt has been in service for more than 40 000 miles (60 000 km) it is recommended that it is renewed.

33 The tensioner should not be noisy or rough when spun, and the spring should show no signs of weakness. Where these conditions are not met, renew the tensioner complete.

Intermediate shaft

34 Inspect the condition of the shaft journals. If they are worn or scored, renew the shaft.

35 If the gear teeth on the end of the shaft are worn or chipped, renew the shaft.

36 If there is excessive endfloat in the shaft, renewing the retainer plate may eliminate the problem.

37 If the bearings in the crankcase are excessively worn, a BMW

9.16 Gudgeon pin circlip in the piston (arrowed)

9.23 Using an old feeler blade to fit the piston rings

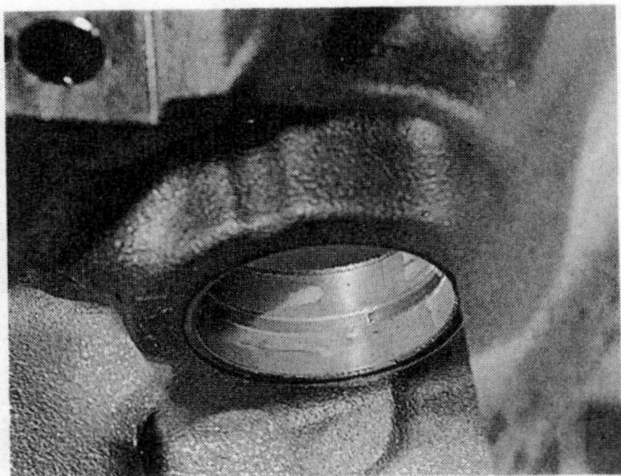
9.37 Intermediate shaft bearing in the crankcase

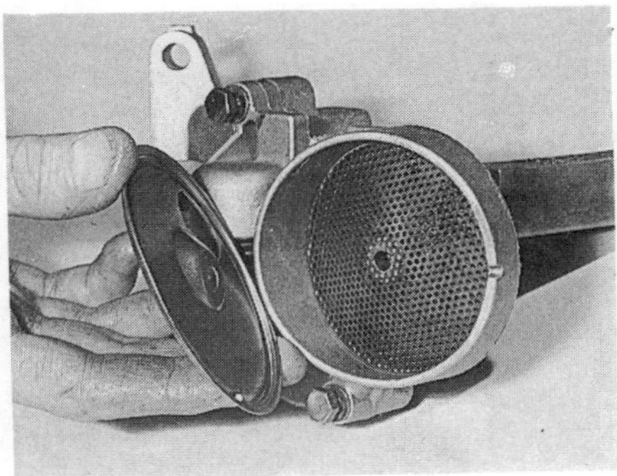
9.38 Removing the oil pump baffle plate

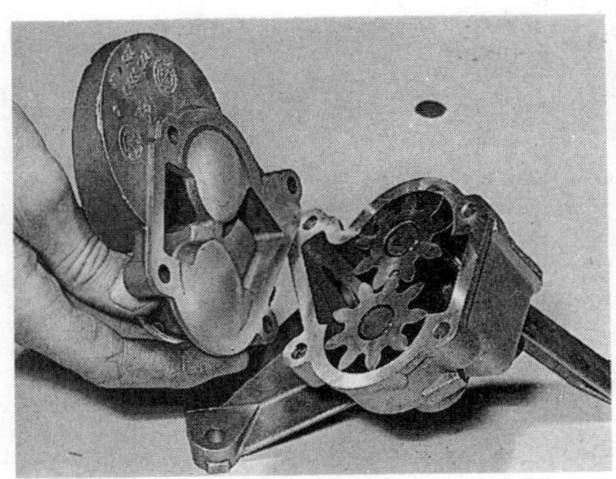
9.39 Removing the oil pump cover

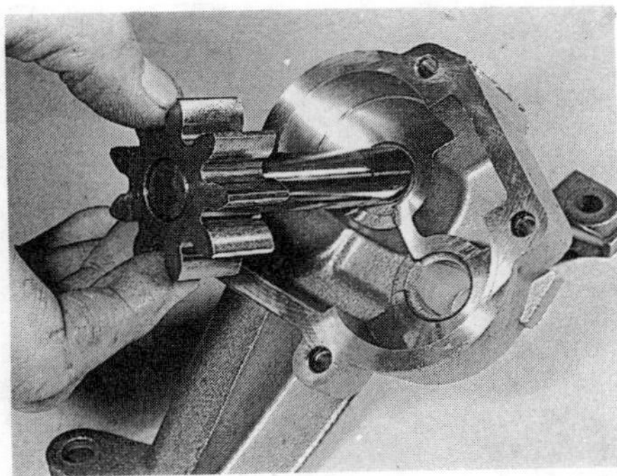
9.40 Removing the oil pump gears

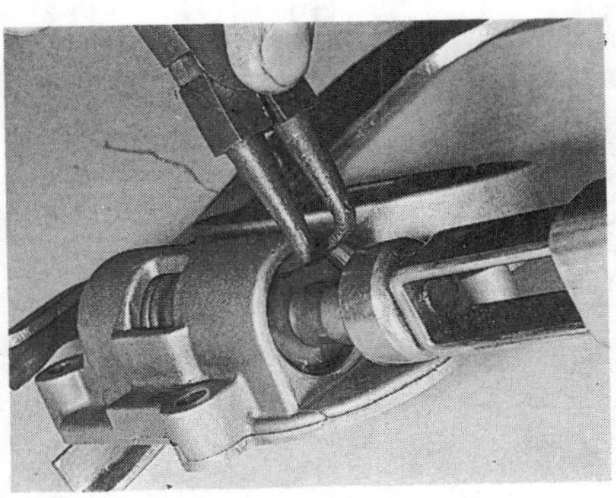
9.41A Extract the circlip ...

9.41B ... and remove the oil pressure relief valve spring and valve

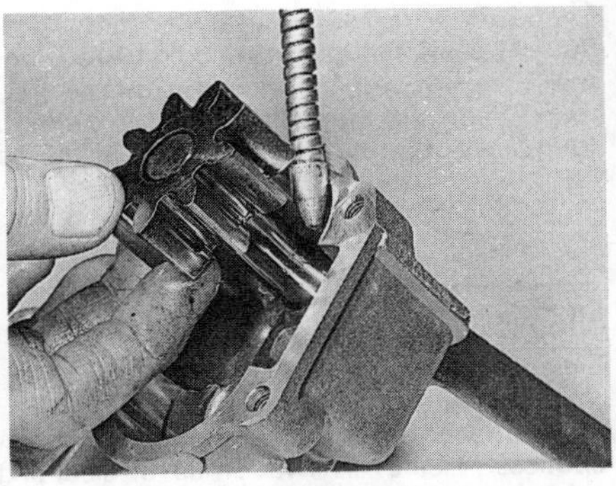
9.43A Inserting the oil pump drive gear ...

dealer should be consulted. BMW state that these bearings cannot be renewed (photo).

Oil pump and relief valve

38 Unscrew the bolt securing the baffle plate to the oil pump and remove the baffle plate (photo). The bolt also holds the cover on the main housing.
39 Unscrew the remaining bolts and remove the cover (photo).
40 Mark the gears in relation to each other then remove them from the housing (photo).
41 To remove the oil pressure relief valve, use a valve spring compressor to compress the spring then extract the circlip and washer and withdraw the spring and valve (photos).
42 Thoroughly clean all the components and examine them for wear and damage.
43 Lightly oil the gear shafts and insert them in the housing in their original positions and with the previously made marks aligned (photos).
44 Using feeler gauges check the following clearances (photos):

- (a) *Gear teeth to body*
- (b) *Gear backlash*
- (c) *Gear endfloat, using a straight-edge and feeler blade across the top of the body*

45 If any of the clearances are outside the specified tolerances, either renew the components or preferably obtain a new oil pump.
46 Measure the length of the oil pressure relief valve spring (photo). If it is less than the specified amount, obtain a new one.
47 Check the sealing surface of the valve and if there is any sign of wear or damage, renew the complete pump.
48 Refit the valve by compressing the spring, then refit the washer and circlip.
49 Lubricate the gears with oil then refit the cover and baffle plate, insert the bolts and tighten them to the specified torque (photo). Note that the baffle plate has a location 'pip' which must engage with the cut-out in the housing.

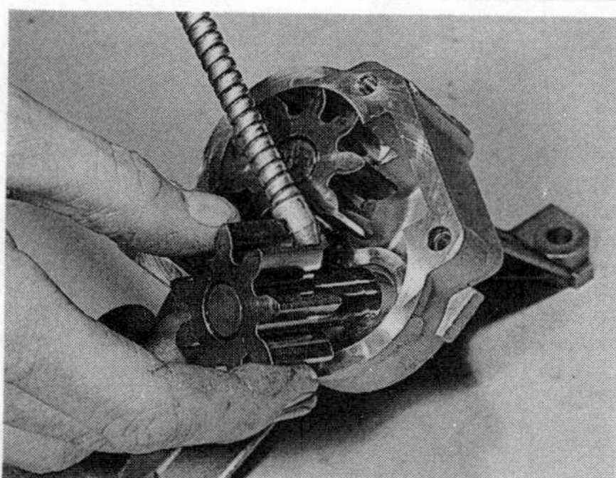
9.43B ... and driven gear

9.44A Using a feeler blade to check the oil pump clearance for gear teeth to body ...

9.44B ... gear backlash ...

9.44C ... and gear endfloat

9.46 Checking the length of the oil pressure relief valve spring

9.49 Reassembled oil pump

Oil seals and gaskets

50 All seals and gaskets should be renewed as a matter of course at major engine overhaul. Make sure that each seal is fitted the correct way round – some of the seals have an arrow moulded onto their outer face to indicate the rotational direction of the component on which they bear.

10 Engine reassembly – general

To ensure maximum life with minimum trouble from a rebuilt engine, not only must all parts be correctly assembled, but they must be spotlessly clean. All oilways must be clear of debris. Oil all bearings and other working surfaces thoroughly with clean engine oil during assembly. Renew any nuts, bolts or studs with damaged threads.

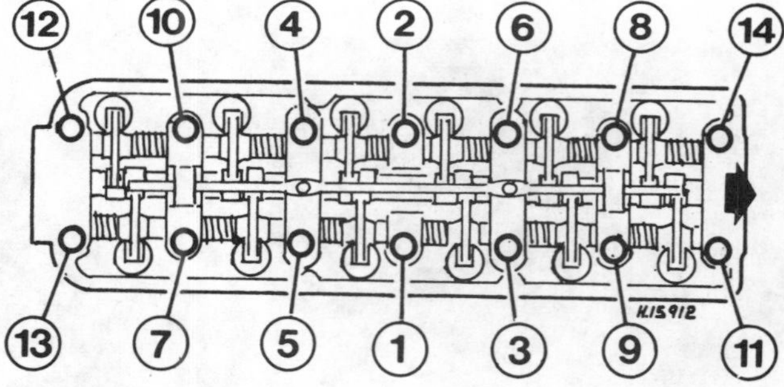

Fig. 1.7 Cylinder head bolt tightening sequence (Sec 11)

11 Engine – complete reassembly

1 Clean the crankcase recesses and locate the main bearing shells so that the oil holes are correctly aligned (photos). The shell which incorporates the thrust flanges is located in number 6 position, counting from the timing belt end of the engine. Make sure that the tabs are located in the cut-outs in the crankcase.
2 Oil the shells (photo) and lower the crankshaft into position.
3 Wipe the main bearing recesses in the main bearing caps and fit the shells making sure that the tabs engage the cut-outs (photo).
4 Refit the main bearing caps in their correct order and facing the same way round as noted when removing them. Insert the bolts and tighten them evenly to the specified torque (photo). Refit number 6 main bearing first, and, with the bolts slightly loose, tap the front and rear of the crankshaft with a mallet in order to align the top and bottom shells, then tighten the bolts.
5 Check that the crankshaft turns freely.

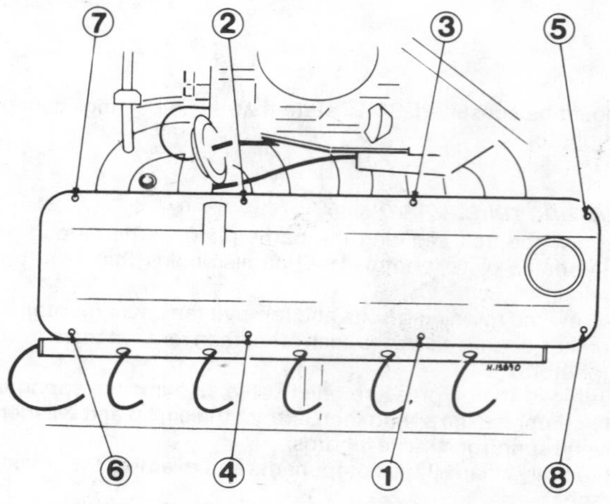

Fig. 1.8 Valve cover nut tightening sequence (Sec 11)

11.1A Inserting a plain main bearing shell

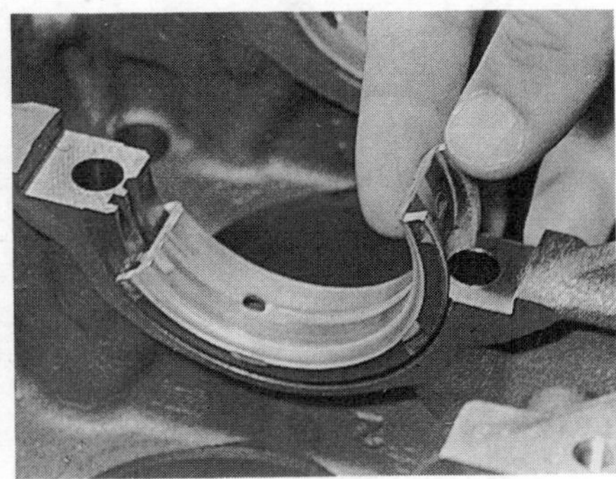
11.1B Inserting number 6 main bearing shell

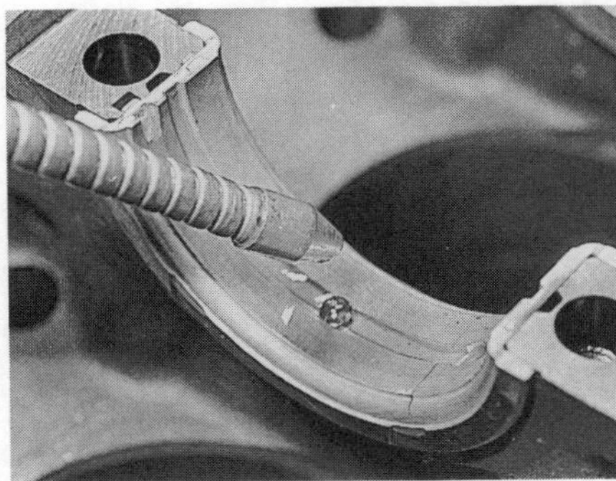
11.2 Oiling the main bearing shells

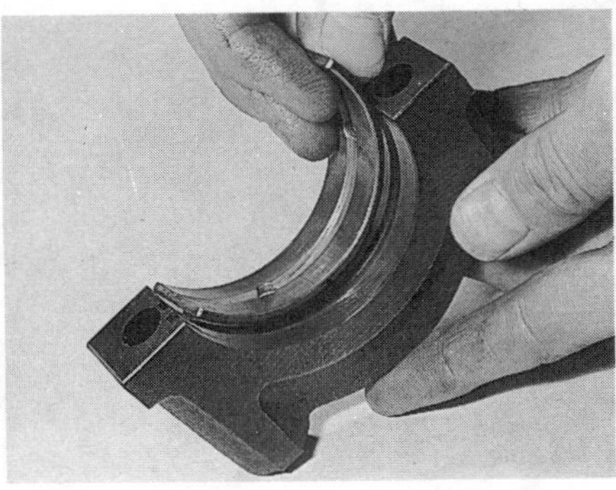
11.3 Inserting a main bearing shell in the cap

11.4 Tightening the main bearing cap bolts

11.9 Oiling the cylinder bore

11.10 Inserting a piston in its bore, showing the ring compressor fitted over the rings

11.11 The arrow on the piston crown must face the front of the engine

11.12 Driving the piston into its bore with the handle of a hammer

6 Check the crankshaft endfloat using either a dial gauge on the front or rear of the crankshaft, or a feeler blade between number 6 main bearing side flange and the crankshaft web. It should be as given in the Specifications.

7 Turn the crankshaft so that number 1 crankpin is at the bottom of its stroke.

8 Position the number 1 piston ring gaps so that they are at 120° intervals.

9 Oil the piston and rings liberally and fit a ring compressor. Also oil the bore (photo).

10 Fit the upper big-end bearing shell into the connecting rod recess and then insert the rod into number 1 bore so that the compressor stands squarely on the top face of the cylinder block (photo). Do not allow the connecting rod to scratch the bore.

11 Check that the piston directional arrow is towards the timing belt end of the engine (photo).

12 Place the wooden handle of a hammer on the centre of the piston crown and drive the pinion downwards (photo). The piston and rings will enter the bore and the compressor will be released.

13 Oil the crankpin then draw the connecting rod down and guide it onto the crankpin.

14 Fit the lower big-end bearing shell in number 1 big-end cap making sure that the tab engages the cut-out in the cap. Oil the shell (photos).

15 Fit the cap then insert the bolts and tighten them evenly to the specified torque. Now angle-tighten the bolts as specified (photos).

16 Oil the intermediate shaft bearings in the cylinder block, then insert the shaft and refit the guide plate (photo). Insert and tighten the slot-head screws.

17 Insert the oil pump drive gear through the aperture in the side of the cylinder block making sure that the hollow end of the gear enters first (photos).

18 Fit a new O-ring to the bearing cap then press the cap into the aperture (photos). Fit the clamp and tighten the bolt to secure.

19 Using a screwdriver or cold chisel, drive the old oil seals from the front oil seal housing. Clean the seatings then press new seals squarely into position with a block of wood or suitable metal tube. The new seals

11.14A Fit the big-end bearing shell to the cap ...

11.14B ... and oil it

11.15A Torque tightening the big-end bearing cap bolts

11.15B Angle tightening the big-end bearing cap bolts

11.16 Oiling the intermediate shaft bearings

should be positioned between 1 and 2 mm deeper than the original seals which would have been flush with the outer surface of the housing. Use vernier calipers to measure the depth of the seals. Oil the inner lips of the seals (photos).

20 Clean the mating surfaces then refit the front oil seal housing together with a new gasket and tighten the bolts to the specified torque. Make sure that the oil seals are centralised before tightening the bolts.

21 Insert the Woodruff key in the slot in the nose of the crankshaft and tap it firmly into position (photo).

22 Slide the pulley hub/sprocket onto the crankshaft, engaging it with the key.

23 Screw in the pulley bolt. With the engine on its side, insert a block of wood between the front crankshaft web and the crankcase, then tighten the bolt to the specified torque (photo). Remove the block of wood.

24 Position the engine upside down on the bench.

25 Insert the oil pump driveshaft into the drive gear on the end of the intermediate shaft.

26 Refit the oil pump, insert the bolts and tighten them to the specified torque (photo).

27 Drive out the oil seal from the rear oil seal housing. Clean the seating then squarely press in a new seal with a block of wood or metal tube (photo). The new seal should be positioned between 1 and 2 mm deeper than the original seal which would have been flush with the outer surface of the housing. Use vernier calipers to measure the depth of the seal. Oil the inner lips of the oil seal.

28 Clean the mating surfaces and refit the rear oil seal housing together with a new gasket. Insert and tighten the bolts to the specified torque.

29 Refit and tighten the oil pressure switch.

30 Refit and tighten the oil pressure relief valve in the bottom of the block.

31 Apply a little sealant to the end of the oil dipstick tube, then drive it into the cylinder block with the previously made marks aligned (photo).

32 Clean the mating surfaces of the sump and crankcase. Apply a suitable brush-on type of sealant to the bottom surfaces of the front and rear oil seal housings.

33 Locate a new gasket on the crankcase and fit the sump. Insert and

11.17A Oil pump drive gear blocked shaft end ...

11.17B ... and hollow shaft end

11.18A Fitting a new O-ring to the bearing cap

11.18B Roller bearing (arrowed) in the bearing cap

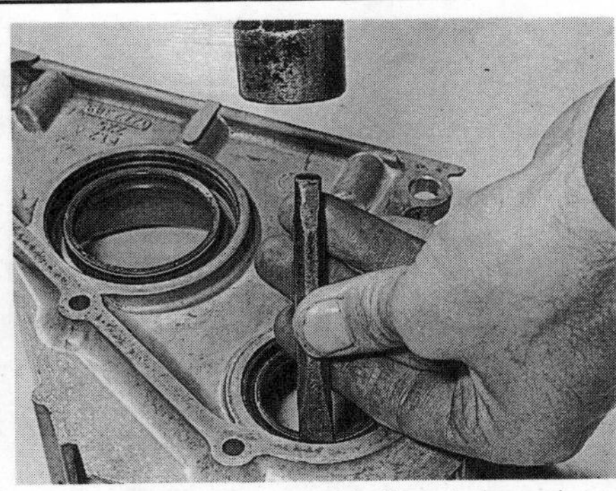
11.19A Driving out the old oil seals from the front oil seal housing

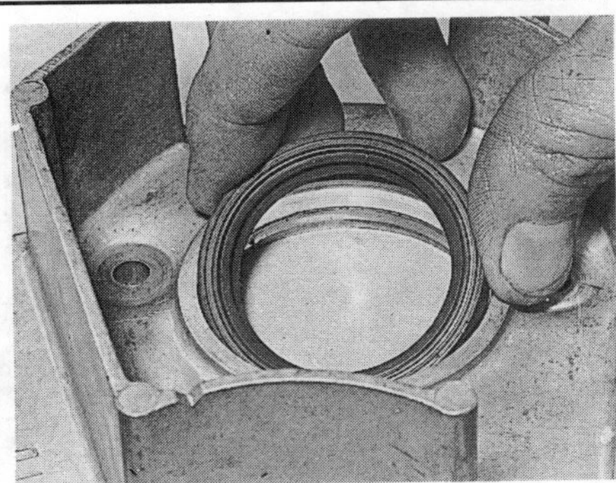
11.19B Fitting a new oil seal

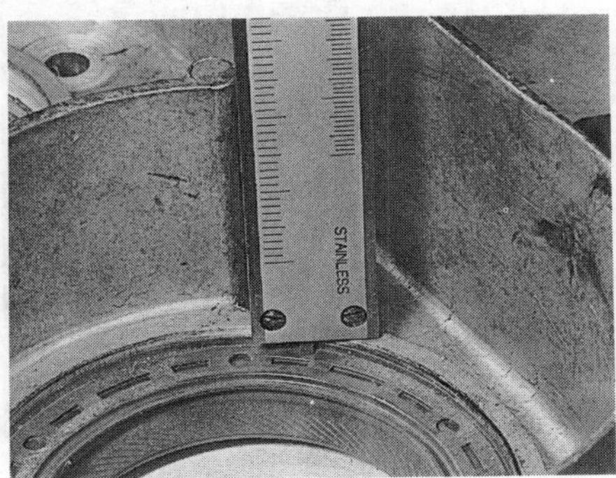

11.19C Checking the position of the oil seal with vernier calipers

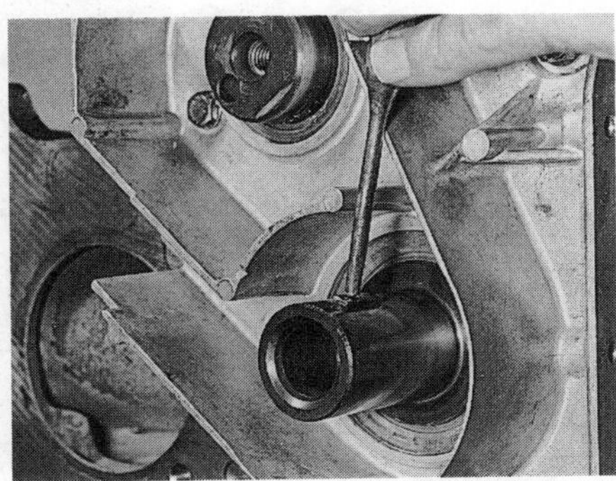
11.21 Tapping the Woodruff key into the slot in the nose of the crankshaft

11.23 Tightening the crankshaft pulley bolt

11.26 Tightening the oil pump bolts

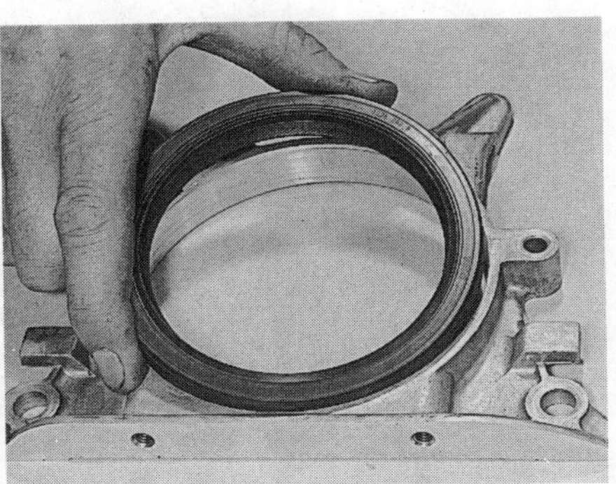
11.27 Fitting a new oil seal to the rear oil seal housing

11.31 Driving the oil dipstick tube into the cylinder block

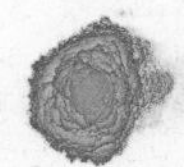

tighten the sump bolts evenly to the specified torque.
34 Position the engine upright on the bench and support with blocks of wood.
35 Fit the power steering pump bracket to the front left-hand side of the block, insert the bolts and tighten them to the specified torque.
36 Fit the timing sprocket to the intermediate shaft and insert the bolt.
37 Hold the sprocket stationary and tighten the bolt to the specified torque (photo).
38 Clean the cylinder head bolts and lubricate the threads and heads with a light coating of oil.
39 Locate a new gasket in position on the block, making sure that all oil and water holes are correctly aligned. Make sure that the location dowel is fitted correctly (photos).
40 Lower the cylinder head onto the gasket, then insert the bolts together with washers and screw in the bolts finger-tight.
41 Tighten the bolts in the sequence shown in Fig. 1.7 through the first three stages given in the Specifications (photo).
42 Refit the water pump together with a new gasket and tighten the bolts to the specified torque.
43 Refit the timing belt tensioner together with the spring but only tighten the mounting bolts finger-tight at this stage (photo). Note that the narrow hexagon flange of the stud is located on the outside.
44 Refit the camshaft sprocket and adaptor plate. Insert the bolt and tighten it to the specified torque while holding the sprocket stationary (photo).
45 Reconnect and tension the timing belt with reference to Section 13.
46 Check and adjust the valve clearances as described in Section 12.
47 Fit new rubber plugs to the front and rear of the cylinder head with their flanges located on the inside of the casting.

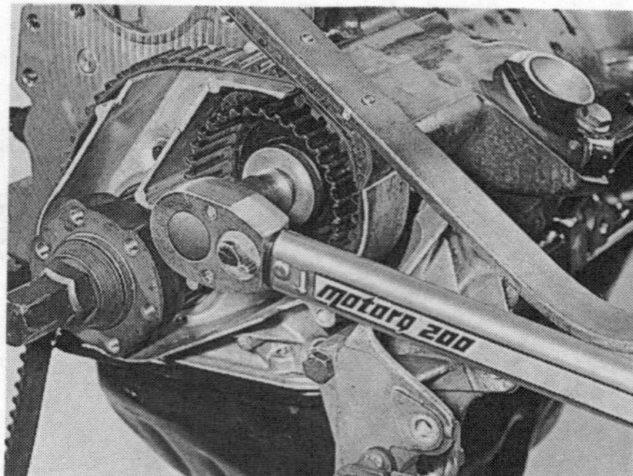

11.37 Tightening the intermediate shaft sprocket bolt

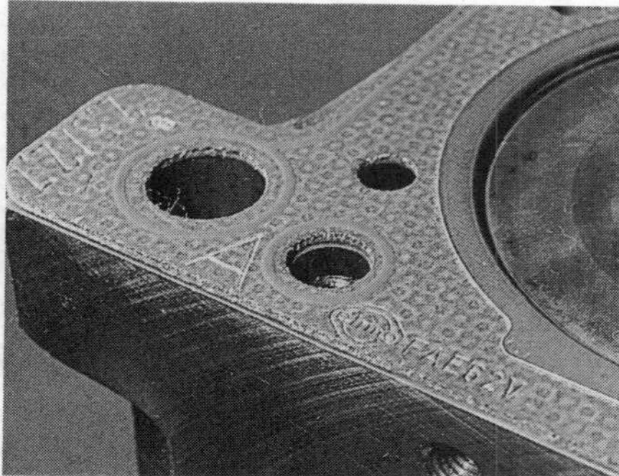
11.39A Make sure that all the holes are correctly aligned when locating the new gasket on the cylinder block

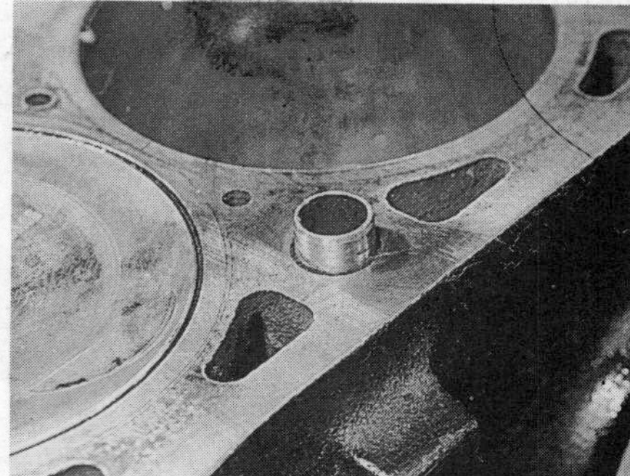
11.39B Cylinder head location dowel in the block

11.41 Tightening the cylinder head bolts

11.43 Timing belt tensioner with spring held by a pair of grips, prior to refitting to the engine

11.44 Tightening the camshaft sprocket bolt

11.65 Location dowel in the rear flange of the crankshaft (arrowed)

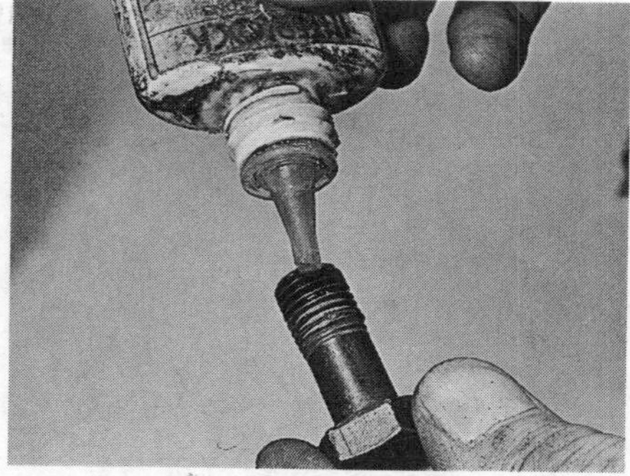
11.67A Applying thread-locking fluid to the flywheel mounting bolts

11.67B Tightening the flywheel bolts (automatic transmission driveplate also shown)

48 Refit the valve cover together with a new gasket. Locate the wiring harness clips and HT lead conduit on their studs, then refit and tighten the nuts in the order shown in Fig. 1.8.
49 Refit the front engine lifting eye bracket to the dowels on the cylinder head.
50 Refit the vibration damper and pulley to the hub on the front of the crankshaft. Tighten the bolts to the specified torque.
51 Refit the lower timing cover and tighten the lower bolt.
52 Refit the TDC sensor to the lower timing cover.
53 Refit the upper timing cover and tighten the bolts. Note that the alternator adjustment link is located on the front centre stud.
54 Refit the rubber cover to the side of the timing covers.
55 Refit the exhaust manifold with reference to Chapter 3.
56 Refit the thermostat housing together with a new gasket to the front left-hand side of the cylinder head. Tighten the nuts.
57 Refit the alternator bracket and alternator with reference to Chapter 12.
58 Refit the inlet manifold with reference to Chapter 3.
59 Reconnect the wiring harness to the engine.
60 Reconnect the single wire to the oil pressure switch and secure it to the plastic tie on the front of the block.
61 Refit the rotor arm, dust cover, spark plugs, distributor cap and HT leads with reference to Chapter 4.
62 Refit the hoses to the thermostat housing on the front of the head and to the rear left-hand side of the cylinder block.
63 Refit the rear coolant outlet together with a new gasket. Reconnect the hoses to the rear left-hand side of the cylinder head and block.
64 Refit the engine oil level dipstick.
65 Wipe clean the flywheel and crankshaft rear flange and make sure that the location dowel is secure in the flange (photo).
66 Fit the rear engine plate on its dowels.
67 Fit the flywheel to the rear of the crankshaft and refit the flange plate together with the driveplate, where applicable. The bolts should be renewed as a matter of course. Apply thread-locking fluid to the threads of the bolts then insert them and tighten to the specified torque while holding the flywheel stationary (photos).

11.68 Topping-up the engine oil

68 Refill the engine with the correct grade and quantity of oil (photo).
69 After the engine has been refitted, it should be run for 25 minutes, then the cylinder head bolts should be angle-tightened with reference to the Specifications and the valve clearances checked and adjusted if necessary.

12 Valve clearances – adjustment

1 The valve clearances should be checked with the engine cold. First remove the spark plugs (Chapter 4).
2 Unscrew the nuts securing the valve cover to the cylinder head noting the location of the wiring harness clips and the HT lead conduit (photo).
3 Unbolt the support bracket from the valve cover and inlet manifold then remove the valve cover. Due to the location of the brake linkage across the front of the bulkhead, it may be necessary to lever the engine forwards slightly in order to remove the valve cover from the studs.
4 Using a socket on the crankshaft pulley bolt, turn the engine until number 1 piston is at TDC on its compression stroke. Place a finger over number 1 spark plug hole while the engine is being turned in order to determine when the piston is moving up the bore. With number 1 piston at TDC, the valves will be rocking on number 6 cylinder (exhaust valve closing and inlet valve opening).
5 Adjust the valves in the following sequence, counting from the front (timing belt end) of the engine.

Valves to adjust	Valves rocking
Cylinder number 1	*Cylinder number 6*
Cylinder number 5	*Cylinder number 2*
Cylinder number 3	*Cylinder number 4*
Cylinder number 6	*Cylinder number 1*
Cylinder number 2	*Cylinder number 5*
Cylinder number 4	*Cylinder number 3*

6 The valve clearances on both inlet and exhaust valves are the same (see Specifications).
7 Check the valve clearances with a feeler blade of the specified thickness. If adjustment is required, release the locknut on the rocker arm and move the eccentric cam by inserting a cranked rod (2.5 mm diameter) in the hole provided. The clearance is correct when the feeler blade is a firm sliding fit. Tighten the locknut after making the adjustment (photo).
8 On completion refit the valve cover, using a new gasket if required and tighten the nuts to the specified torque. Also refit the support bracket.

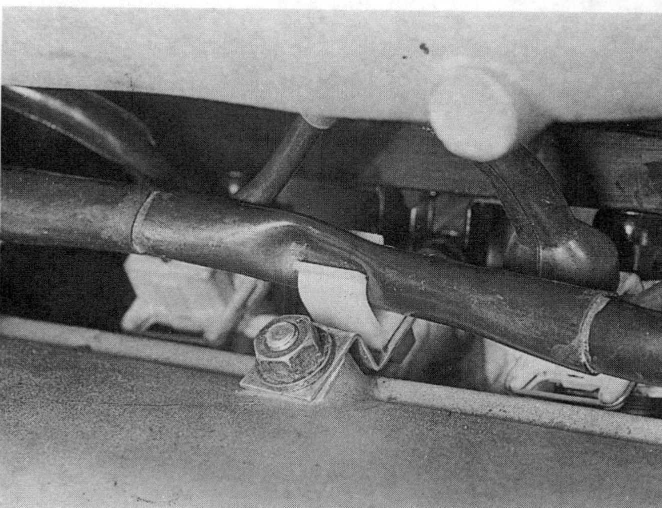
12.2 Wiring harness clip location on the valve cover mounting nut

13 Timing belt – removal and refitting

1 Disconnect the battery negative lead.
2 Remove the radiator with reference to Chapter 2, but disconnect the top and bottom hoses from the thermostat housing. Also remove the viscous fan.
3 Remove the distributor cap, rotor, adaptor and dust cover with reference to Chapter 4.
4 Unscrew the two upper timing cover mounting bolts.
5 Remove the rubber cover from the side of the timing covers.
6 Unscrew the centre nut and remove the upper timing cover. Also unbolt and remove the alternator adjusting link.
7 Temporarily refit the adaptor to the end of the camshaft.
8 Using a socket on the front pulley bolt, turn the engine until number 1 piston is at TDC compression. The timing marks must also be aligned on the camshaft sprocket and cylinder head, and on the crankshaft pulley and lower timing cover.
9 Remove the driveshafts for the alternator, power steering pump, and where applicable the air conditioning compressor, with reference to the relevant Chapter.
10 Unbolt the pulley and vibration damper from the pulley hub.
11 The crankshaft must now be held stationary while the hub bolt is unscrewed. To do this, BMW technicians use a special lever tool bolted

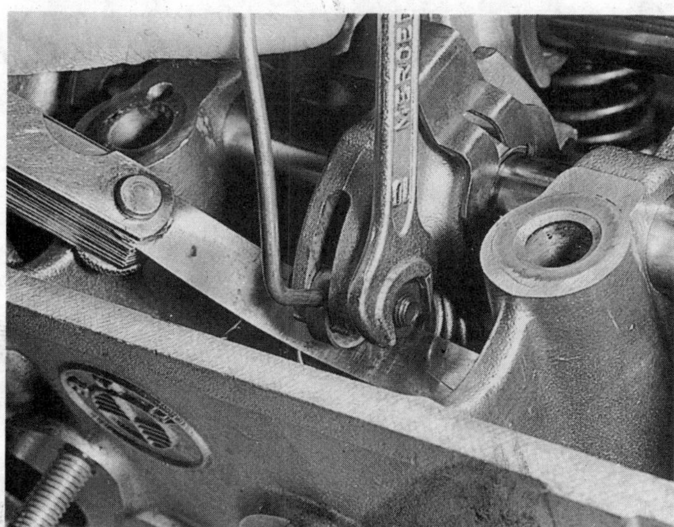
12.7 Adjusting the valve clearances

to the pulley in place of the vibration damper. If this arrangement cannot be used, remove the starter motor and insert a wide-bladed screwdriver in the starter ring gear teeth. In fact, the timing belt can be removed without removing the pulley hub/sprocket, but it may be damaged as it is inserted past the hub flange so it is better to remove the hub first.

12 Unscrew the hub bolt and remove the pulley hub/sprocket. If it is tight, use a puller to remove it.

13 Unclip and remove the TDC sensor from the lower timing cover.

14 Unscrew the lower bolt and remove the lower timing cover.

15 Loosen the stud and bolt on the timing belt tensioner, push the tensioner plate inwards at the top, then tighten the upper bolt to retain the tensioner in its retracted position.

16 Mark the timing belt to indicate its running direction if it is to be re-used.

17 Remove the timing belt from the camshaft, intermediate shaft, and crankshaft sprockets.

18 **Do not** turn the crankshaft while the belt is removed.

19 To refit the belt, first check that the timing marks are still correctly aligned (photos). Temporarily refit the crankshaft pulley hub to confirm that the timing mark is still aligned. Engage the timing belt with the crankshaft sprocket, intermediate shaft sprocket and the camshaft sprocket. Locate the belt over the tensioner roller. Check that the timing marks are still aligned.

20 Loosen the upper tensioner bolt and allow the spring to tension the belt. Check again that the timing marks are still aligned then tighten the tensioner bolts.

21 Refit the lower timing cover and clip the TDC sensor into position.

22 Refit the crankshaft pulley hub and tighten the bolt to the specified torque while holding the crankshaft stationary.

23 Refit the vibration damper and pulley and tighten the bolts.

24 Turn the engine in its normal direction one or two revolutions, then, without turning it backwards, loosen the tensioner bolts again and allow the belt to be tensioned. Tighten the bolts.

25 Refit the drivebelts for the alternator, power steering pump, and where applicable the air conditioning compressor, and tension them with reference to the relevant Chapter.

26 Refit the upper timing cover and alternator link, and tighten the centre nut.

27 Refit the rubber cover to the side of the timing covers.

28 Insert and tighten the two upper timing cover bolts.

29 Refit the dust cover, adaptor, rotor, and distributor cap with reference to Chapter 4.

30 Refit the viscous fan and radiator with reference to Chapter 2, and reconnect the top and bottom hoses to the thermostat housing.

31 Reconnect the battery negative lead.

14 Camshaft oil seal - renewal

1 Drain the cooling system as described in Chapter 2.

2 Disconnect the battery negative lead.

3 Disconnect the coolant hoses from the thermostat housing on the front of the head.

4 Remove the HT leads, distributor cap, rotor arm and dust cover with reference to Chapter 4.

5 Remove the rubber cover from the side of the timing covers.

6 Unscrew the centre nut securing the upper and lower timing covers, noting that the alternator adjustment link is also connected to the same stud.

7 Unscrew the two upper and one lower bolt securing the upper timing cover to the cylinder head and remove the cover.

8 Turn the engine with a socket on the crankshaft pulley bolt until number 1 piston is at TDC on compression. If necessary the distributor rotor may be temporarily refitted in order to determine the correct position.

9 Align the timing marks on the camshaft sprocket and cylinder head, and also on the crankshaft pulley and timing cover.

10 Remove the front engine lifting eye bracket from the dowels on the cylinder head.

11 Loosen the timing cover stud and the bolt securing the tensioner to the cylinder head. Push in the tensioner roller and tighten the upper bolt to hold the tensioner away from the belt.

12 Slide the timing belt off the tensioner roller then remove it from the camshaft sprocket.

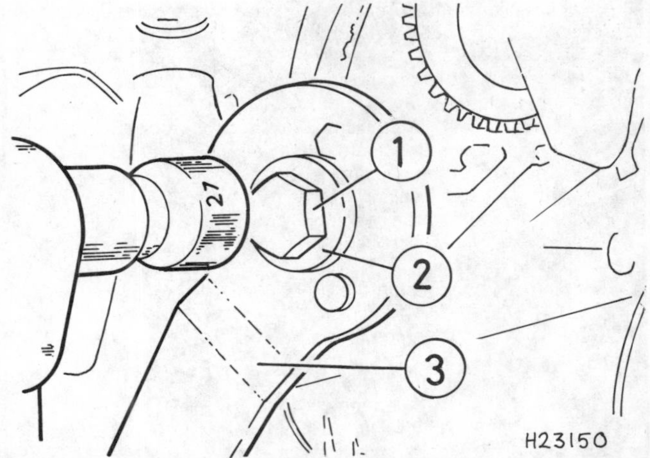

Fig. 1.9 Unscrewing the crankshaft pulley bolt (Sec 13)

1 *Bolt*
2 *Washer*
3 *Holding tool*

13.19A Timing marks on the camshaft sprocket and cylinder head (arrowed)

13.19B Timing marks on the crankshaft pulley hub and lower timing cover

13 Hold the camshaft sprocket stationary then unscrew the sprocket centre bolt using a Torx key. Remove the adaptor plate followed by the camshaft sprocket.
14 Unscrew the bolts and remove the oil seal housing from the front of the cylinder head.
15 Drive the oil seal from the camshaft front oil seal housing and clean the seating. Press a new seal into the housing. Also renew the O-ring on the inner shoulder of the housing.
16 Refit the oil seal housing to the front of the cylinder head. Insert and tighten the bolts to the specified torque.
17 Refit the camshaft sprocket and adaptor plate and tighten the bolt to the specified torque.
18 Reconnect and tension the timing belt with reference to Section 13.
19 Locate the front engine lifting eye bracket on the dowels on the cylinder head.
20 Refit the upper timing cover and tighten the bolts.
21 Refit and tighten the timing cover centre nut then refit the rubber cover.
22 Refit the HT leads, distributor cap, rotor arm and dust cover with reference to Chapter 4.
23 Reconnect the coolant hoses and battery negative lead.
24 Fill the cooling system with reference to Chapter 2.

15 Cylinder head – removal and refitting

1 Apply the handbrake then jack up the front of the car and support on axle stands.
2 Drain the cooling system as described in Chapter 2.
3 Disconnect the exhaust front pipes with reference to Chapter 3 and remove the gaskets.
4 Disconnect the battery negative lead.
5 Disconnect the accelerator cable, kick-down cable (automatic transmission models), and cruise control cable (where fitted).
6 Remove the air cleaner and mixture regulator/fuel distributor (K-Jetronic) or the air cleaner and airflow sensor (L-Jetronic and Motronic) with reference to Chapter 3.
7 Remove the inlet and exhaust manifolds with reference to Chapter 3.
8 Disconnect the wiring plugs from the injectors and from the temperature sensors.
9 Disconnect the HT lead and LT leads from the ignition coil.
10 Remove the wiring harness from the engine and tie it to one side.
11 Loosen the clips and disconnect the coolant hoses from the rear left-hand side of the cylinder head. The rear outlet may be unbolted if necessary. Also disconnect the hoses from the thermostat housing on the front of the head.
12 Remove the HT leads, spark plugs, distributor cap, rotor arm and dust cover with reference to Chapter 4. Unscrew the valve cover nuts and remove the HT lead conduit.
13 Unscrew the nuts and withdraw the thermostat housing from the studs on the front left-hand side of the cylinder head. Remove the gasket.
14 Remove the rubber cover from the side of the timing covers.
15 Unscrew the centre nut securing the upper and lower timing covers, noting that the alternator adjustment link is also connected to the same stud.
16 Unscrew the two upper and one lower bolt securing the upper timing cover to the cylinder head and remove the cover.
17 Turn the engine with a socket on the crankshaft pulley bolt until number 1 piston is at TDC on compression. If necessary the distributor rotor may be temporarily refitted in order to determine the correct position.
18 Align the timing marks on the camshaft sprocket and cylinder head, and also on the crankshaft pulley and timing cover.
19 Remove the front engine lifting eye bracket from the dowels on the cylinder head.
20 Loosen the timing cover stud and the bolt securing the tensioner to the cylinder head. Push in the tensioner roller and tighten the upper bolt to hold the tensioner away from the belt.
21 Slide the timing belt off the tensioner roller then remove it from the camshaft sprocket.
22 Unscrew the nuts securing the valve cover to the cylinder head noting the location of the wiring harness clips. Remove the valve cover and gasket. Due to the location of the brake linkage across the front of the bulkhead, it may be necessary to lever the engine forwards slightly in order to remove the valve cover from the studs.
23 Prise the rubber plugs from the front and rear of the cylinder head, noting that their flanges are located on the inside of the casting.
24 Unscrew the cylinder head bolts evenly in the reverse order to that shown in Fig. 1.7. Remove the bolts and washers.
25 Lift the cylinder head from the location dowel on the block and place it on the bench.
26 Remove the gasket from the cylinder block.
27 If the cylinder head is to be dismantled and reconditioned, refer to Section 16, otherwise remove all carbon and dirt from the head and block, and also remove the carbon from the piston crowns. Prevent carbon from dropping down between the pistons and bores by first pressing some grease around the tops of the pistons. After removing the carbon, the grease (which will now have collected some carbon) can be wiped out.
28 Mop out any dirt or oil from the bolt holes in the cylinder block. Any oil left in these holes could cause the block to crack as the bolts are screwed in.
29 Clean the cylinder head bolts and lubricate the threads and heads with a light coating of oil.
30 Locate a new gasket in position on the block making sure that all oil and water holes are correctly aligned. Make sure that the location dowel is fitted correctly.
31 Lower the cylinder head onto the gasket, then insert the bolts and washers and screw in the bolts finger-tight.
32 Tighten the bolts in the sequence shown in Fig. 1.7 through the first three stages given in the Specifications.
33 Reconnect and tension the timing belt with reference to Section 13.
34 Check and adjust the valve clearances as described in Section 12.
35 Refit the remaining components using a reversal of the removal procedure.
36 After the engine has been run to operating temperature, tighten the cylinder head bolts through the angle specified for Stage 5 (photo). No further tightening of the cylinder head bolts is required.

15.36 Angle-tightening the cylinder head bolts

16 Cylinder head – dismantling, decarbonising and reassembling

1 Unscrew the union nuts and remove the rocker arm oil supply pipe (photo).
2 Release the cam adjuster nuts and set all the valve clearances to maximum. Although it is not essential to loosen all the adjusters, this makes removal of the rocker shafts easier.
3 Hold the camshaft sprocket stationary then unscrew the sprocket centre bolt using a Torx key. Remove the adaptor plate followed by the

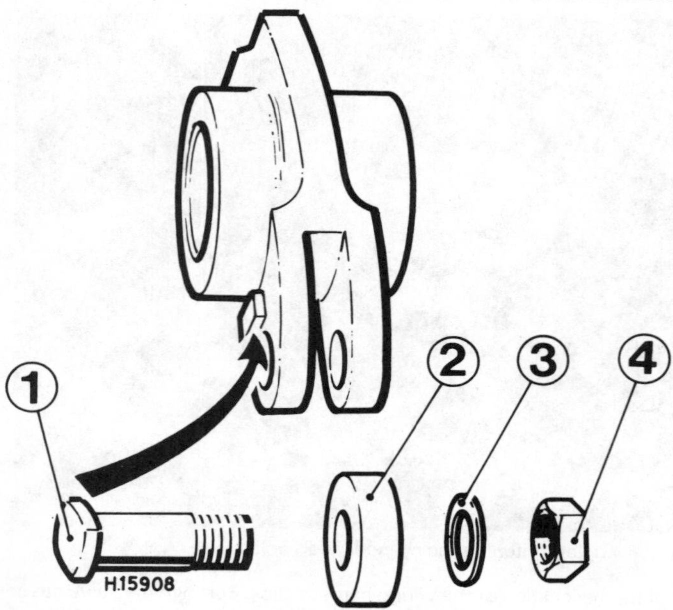

Fig. 1.10 Rocker arm components (Sec 16)

1 *Setscrew (note flat on head)*
2 *Eccentric*
3 *Washer*
4 *Nut*

camshaft sprocket. To turn the camshaft, the adaptor plate may be temporarily refitted.

4 Remove the retaining plate from the end of the rocker shafts and then extract the spring clips noting which way round they are fitted (photos).

5 Identify the fitted position of the rocker shafts, then turn the camshaft so that number 6 valves are rocking.

6 Push the number 6 exhaust rocker to one side of the valve then turn the camshaft slightly clockwise and check that all of the remaining exhaust rockers are free of the valves (photo).

7 Using a metal drift, drive the exhaust rocker shaft out of the cylinder head from rear to front (photo). To ensure correct reassembly, refit the rocker to the shaft in their original positions.

8 Turn the camshaft slightly anti-clockwise. Push the number 6 inlet rocker to one side of the valve and check that all of the remaining inlet rockers are free of the valves.

9 Using the metal drift, drive the inlet rocker shaft out of the cylinder head from rear to front (photo). Refit the rockers to the shaft in their original positions.

10 Remove the adaptor plate, then unscrew the bolts and remove the oil seal housing from the front of the cylinder head (photos).

11 Carefully withdraw the camshaft from the cylinder head (photos).

12 To remove the valves, compress the first valve spring with a compressor and extract the collets (photo). If the spring refuses to compress, tap the end of the compressor with a hammer rather than apply additional pressure on the compressor.

13 Release the compressor and take off the spring retainer, valve spring, and spring seat (photos).

14 Remove the valve from the combustion chamber (photo).

15 Prise the valve stem seal from the valve guide.

16 Keep all of the components in numbered sequence so that they can be refitted in their original positions. A small box with divisions is useful for this purpose (photos).

17 Remove the other valves in the same manner.

18 Examine the head of the valves for pitting and burning, paying particular attention to the heads of the exhaust valves. The valve seats should be examined at the same time. If the pitting on the valve and seat is only slight, the marks can be removed by grinding the seats and valves together with coarse, and then fine, grinding paste. Where bad

16.1 Removing the rocker arm oil supply pipe (arrowed)

16.4A Rocker shaft retaining plate removal

16.4B Removing the rocker shaft spring clips

16.6 Number 6 exhaust rocker pushed to one side

16.7 Removing the exhaust rocker shaft (arrowed)

16.9 Removing the inlet rocker shaft (arrowed)

16.10A Unscrew the bolts ...

16.10B ... and remove the oil seal housing from the front of the cylinder head

16.11A Withdrawing the camshaft from the cylinder head

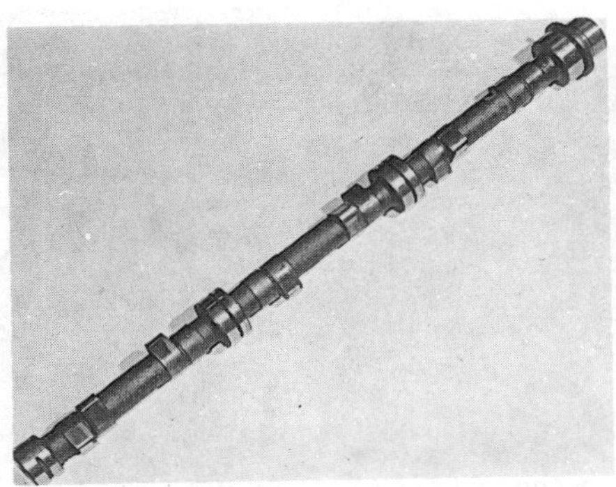
16.11B The camshaft

16.12 Using a compressor to compress the valve spring and remove the collets

pitting has occurred, it will be necessary to renew the valve and have the valve seat re-cut.

19 Scrape all carbon from the valve stems and heads.

20 Scrape away all carbon from the cylinder head using a blunt scraper and wire brush. Take care not to damage the alloy surfaces. Thoroughly clean the ports and valve guides.

21 Check the valve guides for wear by inserting their respective valves and attempting to rock the valve. There should be only a minimum of movement, otherwise the guides will need to be renewed by a garage or engine reconditioner.

22 Valve grinding is carried out as follows. Smear a small quantity of coarse carborundum paste around the contact surface of the valve or seat, and insert the valve into its guide. Apply a suction grinder tool to the valve head, and grind in the valve by semi-rotary motion. This is produced by rolling the valve grinding tool between the palms of the hands. When grinding action is felt to be at an end, extract the valve, turn it and repeat the operation as many times as is necessary to produce a uniform matt grey surface over the whole seating area of the valve head and valve seat. Repeat the process using fine grinding paste.

23 Carefully clean away every trace of grinding paste, taking care not to leave any in the ports or valve guides.

24 Check the valve springs for weakening by comparing their height with a new spring. If any spring appears to be weak, renew all of the springs as a set.

25 Using a straight-edge and feeler blade, check the gasket face of the cylinder head for distortion. The head may be surface ground by an engine reconditioner provided that its height is not reduced to less than 125.1 ± 0.1 mm. Note that a 0.3 mm thicker gasket should be used with a cylinder head which has been reground.

26 Examine the camshaft journals and bearing surfaces for excessive wear. Also check the cam lobes for wear especially on their peaks. The bearings are machined directly in the head and therefore if they are worn excessively a new head must be obtained. If only the camshaft itself is worn, obtain a new one. Note that it is colour-coded according to the model. For 520i models manufactured before March 1983, the camshaft is coded in white for LE-Jetronic models and plain for K-Jetronic models. From March 1983 it is coded in yellow. On 525e models the camshaft has a 236° identification on its front end and has only four bearings.

27 Examine the rocker arms for loose, scored or worn pads. Where evident, renew the arm(s).

28 The rocker shafts and arms should show no signs of scoring or wear. If they do, renew them.

29 The valve oil seals and camshaft front oil seal should be renewed as a matter of course.

30 Flush through the rocker arm oil supply pipe and make sure that the oil jet holes are clear of any obstruction. Check the flared ends of the pipe for fractures (photos).

31 Commence reassembly by oiling the stem of the first valve and inserting it into its guide from the combustion chamber side.

32 Wrap a piece of adhesive tape around the end of the valve stem so that the collet grooves are covered. Oil the new oil seal then slide it over the valve and press it onto the valve guide (photo). Strong plastic tubing may be used to do this. Remove the tape.

33 Refit the spring seat, followed by the valve spring and spring retainer.

34 Compress the valve spring until the split collets can be inserted onto the grooves in the valve stem. A little grease may be used to stick the collets to the valves.

35 Gently release the compressor, checking that the collets are not displaced, then remove the compressor.

36 Refit the remaining valves in their original positions in the same manner.

37 Oil the camshaft bearings and carefully insert the camshaft into the cylinder head.

38 Drive the oil seal from the camshaft front oil seal housing and clean the seating. Press a new seal into the housing. Also renew the O-ring on the inner shoulder of the housing (photos).

39 Refit the oil seal housing to the front of the cylinder head. Insert and tighten the bolts to the specified torque.

40 Refit the rocker arms and shafts in the reverse order to their removal, making sure that the large lubrication holes in the shafts point

16.13A Removing the valve spring retainer ...

16.13B ... valve spring ...

16.13C ... and spring seat

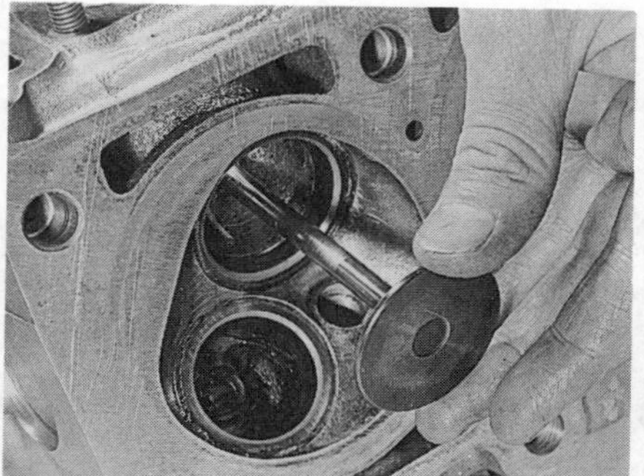
16.14 Removing an inlet valve

16.16A Valve spring components and valve stem oil seal

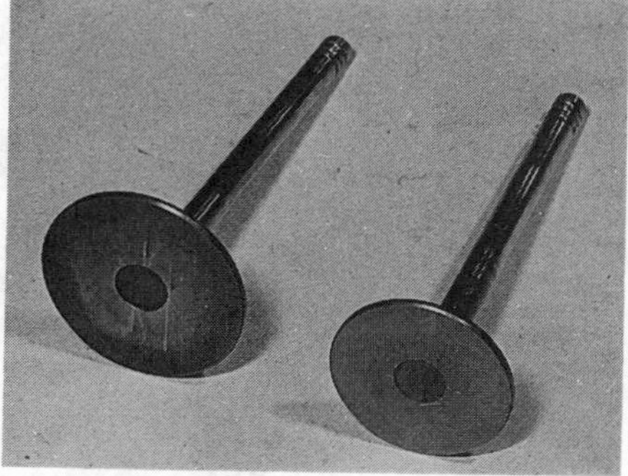
16.16B Inlet valve (left) and exhaust valve (right)

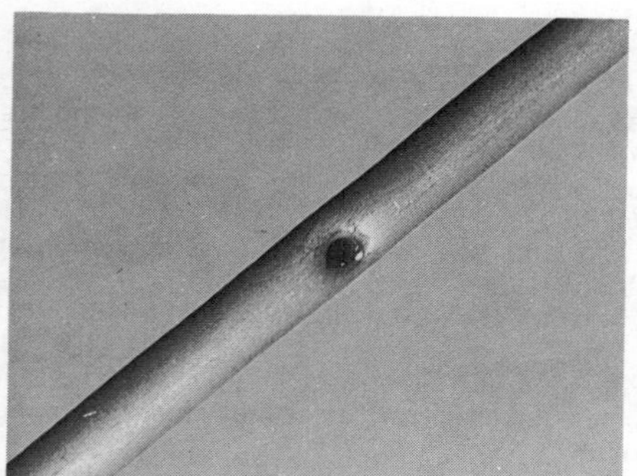
16.30A Check that the oil jet holes in the rocker arm oil supply pipe are clear

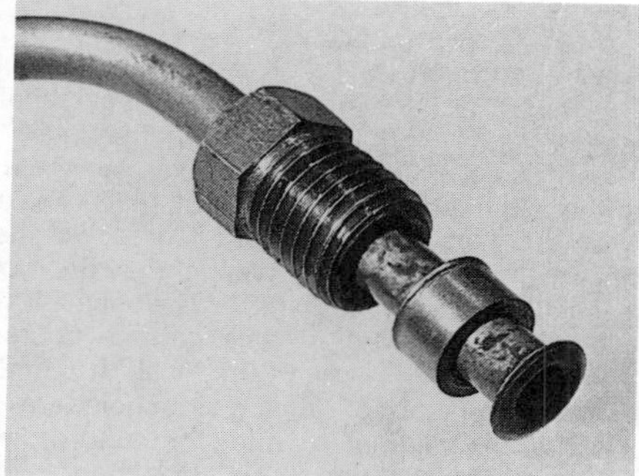
16.30B Flared end and union nut on the rocker arm oil supply pipe

16.32 Fitting a new valve stem oil seal to a valve guide

16.38A New oil seal fitted to the camshaft front oil seal housing

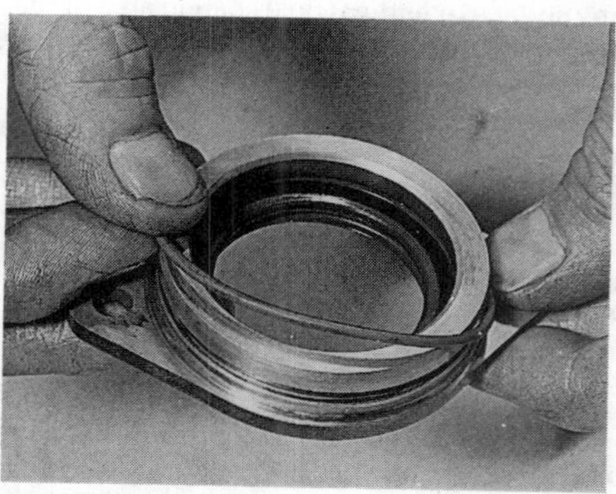
16.38B Fitting a new O-ring to the camshaft front oil seal housing

towards the valve guides and the small holes face inwards. Refit the spring clips so that the straight edges locate in the grooves in the rocker shafts.

41 Locate the sprocket on the front of the camshaft, fit the adaptor plate, then insert the centre bolt. Tighten the bolt to the specified torque while holding the sprocket stationary.

42 Refit the rocker arm oil supply pipe and tighten the union nuts.

17 Camshaft and tappets - removal and refitting

The removal and refitting of the camshaft and tappets is covered in the dismantling and reassembly of the cylinder head described in Section 16. It is not possible to remove the camshaft without first removing the cylinder head.

18 Intermediate shaft - removal and refitting

1 Remove the front end cover as described in Section 21.

2 Unscrew the slot-head screws and extract the intermediate shaft guide plate. The screws are very tight and an impact driver may be required to release them.

3 Withdraw the intermediate shaft from the cylinder block.

4 To refit the shaft oil the intermediate shaft bearings in the cylinder block, then insert the shaft carefully so that it engages the oil pump drive gear, then refit the guide plate. Insert and tighten the slot-head screws.

5 Refit the front end cover with reference to Section 21.

19 Sump and oil pump - removal and refitting

1 Jack up the front of the car and support on axle stands. Alternatively, position the car over an inspection pit.

2 Unbolt and remove the splash guard.

3 Unscrew the drain plug and drain the oil into a suitable container taking suitable precautions against scalding, as the oil may be hot. Clean the plug and renew the washer if necessary, then refit and tighten it to the specified torque.

4 Unbolt and remove the cover from the front of the transmission. On automatic transmission models the cover housing must also be unbolted from the cylinder block.

5 Unscrew the bolts securing the sump to the crankcase, and lower the sump onto the crossmember. If it is tight, carefully lever the sump from the crankcase using a screwdriver.

6 Reach in over the sump and unbolt the oil pump from the crankcase. Lower the pump into the sump. The oil pump driveshaft may drop down at this stage.

7 Withdraw the sump from over the crossmember and lower it to the floor. Remove the gasket.

8 Clean the mating surfaces of the sump and crankcase. Apply a suitable brush-on type of sealant to the bottom surfaces of the front and rear oil seal housings.

9 Clean the mating surfaces of the oil pump and crankcase.

10 Lower the oil pump into the sump.

11 Refit the oil pump driveshaft into the drive gear on the end of the intermediate shaft.

12 Locate a new gasket on the sump, then offer the sump into position over the crossmember.

13 Refit the oil pump making sure that the driveshaft engages correctly. Tighten the bolts to the specified torque.

14 Lift the sump onto the crankcase, insert the bolts and tighten them evenly to the specified torque.

15 Refit the cover to the front of the transmission and tighten the bolts.

16 Refit the splash guard.

17 Lower the car to the ground.

18 Fill the engine with the correct grade and quantity of oil.

20 Oil pump drive gear bearings - renewal

1 Remove the oil pump with reference to Section 19.

2 Unbolt and remove the clamp securing the drive gear upper bearing, then prise out the bearing.

3 Extract the drive gear.

4 Using a suitable drift, drive out the lower bearing from bottom to top (photo).

5 Lubricate the new bearing with grease and drive it into position against its stop.

6 Insert the gear with the hollow end facing downwards.

7 Fit a new O-ring to the new upper bearing, then press it into position.

8 Refit the clamp and tighten the bolt.

9 Refit the oil pump with reference to Section 19.

21 Front end cover oil seals - renewal

1 Remove the timing belt and crankshaft front hub/sprocket as described in Section 13.

2 Hold the intermediate shaft sprocket stationary then unscrew the centre bolt and withdraw the sprocket from the shaft. Note the location dowel. To hold the sprocket stationary, use a length of metal bar with long bolts positioned so that they can be inserted in the holes in the intermediate shaft sprocket.

3 Unscrew the bolts securing the housing to the front of the cylinder block and to the sump, and remove the front oil seal housing. Remove the gasket. Take care not to damage the sump gasket. If it is damaged, the sump will have to be removed and the gasket renewed.

4 Using a screwdriver or cold chisel, drive the old oil seals from the front oil seal housing. Clean the seatings then press new seals squarely into position with a block of wood or suitable metal tube. The new seals should be positioned between 1 and 2 mm deeper than the original seals which would have been flush with the outer surface of the housing. Use vernier calipers to measure the depth of the seals. Oil the inner lips of the oil seals.

5 Apply a brush-on type sealant to the front upper area of the sump gasket.

6 Clean the mating surfaces then refit the front oil seal housing together with a new gasket and tighten the bolts to the specified torque. Make sure that the oil seals are centralised before tightening the bolts.

7 Refit the intermediate shaft sprocket and tighten the bolt to the specified torque.

8 Refit the timing belt and crankshaft front hub/sprocket with reference to Section 13.

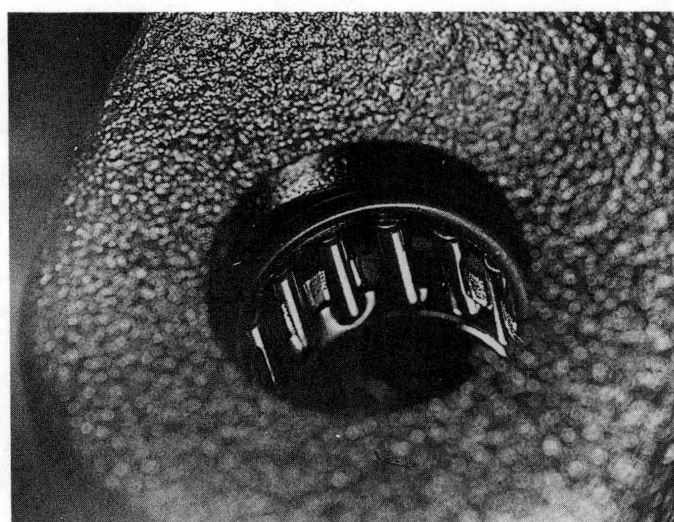

20.4 Oil pump drive gear lower bearing in the crankcase

22 Pistons/connecting rods – removal and refitting

1 Although it is possible to remove the pistons/connecting rods with the engine *in situ*, it is recommended that the engine be removed and placed on the bench. It will then be easier to remove the pistons and there will be less likelihood of dirt and grime entering the engine.
2 Refer to Sections 8 and 10 for the procedures involved.

23 Flywheel/driveplate – removal and refitting

1 Remove the transmission with reference to Chapter 6.
2 On manual transmission models remove the clutch with reference to Chapter 5.
3 Hold the crankshaft stationary either with a wide-bladed screwdriver engaged in the starter ring gear teeth or with a socket on the front pulley bolt.
4 Unscrew the bolts and remove the flange plate, and where applicable the driveplate, then lift the flywheel from the crankshaft.
5 Refit the flywheel and flange plate, and where applicable the driveplate. Apply thread-locking fluid to the threads of the bolts, then insert them and tighten to the specified torque.
6 Refit the clutch on manual transmission models.
7 Refit the transmission with reference to Chapter 6.

24 Crankshaft rear oil seal – renewal

1 Remove the transmission with reference to Chapter 6.
2 On manual transmission models remove the clutch with reference to Chapter 5.
3 Hold the crankshaft stationary either with a wide-bladed screwdriver engaged in the starter ring gear teeth or with a socket on the front pulley bolt.
4 Unscrew the bolts and remove the flange plate, and where applicable the driveplate, then lift the flywheel from the crankshaft.
5 Unscrew the bolts securing the rear oil seal housing to the cylinder block and sump then remove the housing and gasket. Take care not to damage the sump gasket. If it is damaged, the sump will have to be removed and the gasket renewed.
6 Drive out the oil seal, then clean the seating. Squarely press in a new seal with a block of wood or metal tube. The new seal should be positioned between 1 and 2 mm deeper than the original seal which would have been flush with the outer surface of the housing. Use vernier calipers to measure the depth of the seal. Oil the inner lips of the oil seal.
7 Clean the mating surfaces and refit the rear oil seal housing together with a new gasket. Apply sealant to the lower corners of the housing where it contacts the sump gasket. Insert and tighten the bolts to the specified torque.
8 Refit the flywheel and flange plate, and where applicable the driveplate. Apply thread-locking fluid to the threads of the bolts, then insert them and tighten to the specified torque.
9 Refit the clutch on manual transmission models.
10 Refit the transmission with reference to Chapter 6.

25 Engine mountings – removal and refitting

1 Apply the handbrake then jack up the front of the car and support on axle stands. Remove the engine splash guard.
2 Attach a hoist to the engine and take its weight. Lifting eyes are located on the front of the cylinder head and on the left-hand rear side of the cylinder block.
3 If the left-hand side mounting is to be removed, first remove the air cleaner and ducting as described in Chapter 3. On models with K-Jetronic fuel injection, remove the mixture regulator/fuel distributor. On models with L-Jetronic or Motronic fuel injection, remove the airflow sensor.
4 Unscrew the engine mounting lower nuts from the underbody, then unbolt the mounting from the cylinder block and remove it. For better access to the right-hand mounting remove the oil filter, and also note that the engine earth strap is attached to this mounting.
5 Refitting is a reversal of removal, but before tightening the bolts, rock the engine by hand to ensure correct alignment. Tighten the nuts and bolts to the specified torque.

26 Fault diagnosis – engine

Symptom	Reason(s)
Engine fails to start	Discharged battery Loose battery connection Loose or broken ignition leads Moisture on spark plugs, distributor cap, or HT leads Cracked distributor cap or rotor Empty fuel tank! Faulty fuel pump Faulty starter motor Low cylinder compression
Engine idles erratically	Inlet manifold or air duct air leak Leaking cylinder head gasket Worn camshaft lobes Loose crankcase ventilation hose or leaking ventilation tube O-ring Idle mixture incorrect Uneven cylinder compressions
Engine misfires	Spark plugs gap incorrect Faulty ignition component Burnt out valve Leaking cylinder head gasket Cracked distributor cap or rotor Idle mixture incorrect Uneven cylinder compressions

Symptom	Reason(s)
Engine stalls	Idle adjustments incorrect Inlet manifold or air duct air leak Ignition timing incorrect
Excessive oil consumption	Worn pistons and cylinder bores Valve guides and valve stem oil seals worn Oil leaking from crankshaft oil seals, valve cover gasket etc
Engine backfires	Idling adjustments incorrect Ignition timing incorrect Inlet manifold or air duct air leak Sticking valve
Engine lacks power	Incorrect ignition timing Incorrect spark plug gap Low cylinder compression Excessive carbon build-up in engine Air filter choked

Chapter 2 Cooling system

Contents

Specifications

System type	Pressurized radiator and expansion tank, belt-driven water pump, thermostat, viscous-coupled cooling fan, transmission fluid cooler incorporated in radiator side tank on automatic transmission models	
Thermostat		
Opening commences	80° C	
Pressure cap		
Opens at	1.0 ± 0.1 bar	
Vacuum valve opens until	0.9 bar	
Viscous-coupled cooling fan		
Standard type:		
De-activating speed:	**9-blade fan**	**8-blade fan**
Cold	2300 to 2700 rpm	2900 to 3700 rpm
Hot	2000 to 2400 rpm	2600 to 3400 rpm
Maximum rotor axial play	1.4 mm	
Rotor radial play	0.5 mm	
Temperature and speed controlled type:		
Switch-on temperature	82° ± 4°C	
Switch-off temperature	≧ 60°C	
Fan speed at engine speed of 3500 rpm (coupling switched on)	2400 ± 100 rpm	
Maximum rotor axial play	0.4 mm	
Rotor radial play	0.5 mm	
Water pump		
Clearance between body and impeller	0.8 to 1.2 mm	
Distance from drive flange to end of shaft	3.0 to 3.5 mm	
Coolant		
System capacity:		
520i models	10.5 litres (9.2 pints)	
525e models	11.0 litres (9.7 pints)	
Antifreeze:		
Type	Ethylene glycol based antifreeze with corrosion inhibitor (Duckhams Universal Antifreeze and Summer Coolant)	
Concentration	40% antifreeze/60% soft water	

Torque wrench settings

	Nm	lbf ft
Coolant drain plug in cylinder block	50 to 56	36 to 40
Water pump:		
M8 bolts	20 to 24	15 to 17
M6 bolts	9 ± 1	6 to 7
Viscous coupled cooling fan to drive flange	40 to 50	29 to 36
Fan to fan clutch	9 ± 1	6.5 ± 0.5
Water pump pulley	9 ± 1	6.5 ± 0.5
Temperature gauge sender unit	18 ± 1	13 ± 0.5
Thermostat housing	9 ± 1	6.5 ± 0.5
Coolant bleeder screw	6 to 10	4.5 to 7.0
Radiator	9 to 10	6.5 to 7.0
Radiator drain plug	2	1.5
Expansion tank	8 to 9	6 to 6.5

1 General description

The cooling system is of pressurized type with a front-mounted radiator, belt-driven water pump, thermostat and an expansion tank (photo). A belt-driven viscous-coupled fan is fitted which may be of either standard type or of temperature and speed controlled type. On automatic transmission models a transmission fluid cooler is incorporated in the radiator side tank.

The system functions as follows. Cold water from the water pump is forced around the cylinder block and head, then via by-pass hoses through the throttle housing and back to the inlet side of the water pump. Additional circulation occurs through the car heater matrix. When the engine reaches the predetermined temperature, the thermostat commences to open and the coolant then circulates through the radiator to provide extra cooling.

The viscous-coupled cooling fan operates via a film of oil which effectively limits the maximum speed of the fan, thereby reducing noise and providing a saving in energy. On some models its operation is controlled by a temperature switch which prevents the fan operating when the engine is cold.

1.0 The expansion tank

2 Routine maintenance

Warning: *DO NOT attempt to remove the pressure cap/filler cap when the engine is hot, as there is a very great risk of scalding.*

Carry out the following at the intervals given in *Routine maintenance* at the front of this manual.

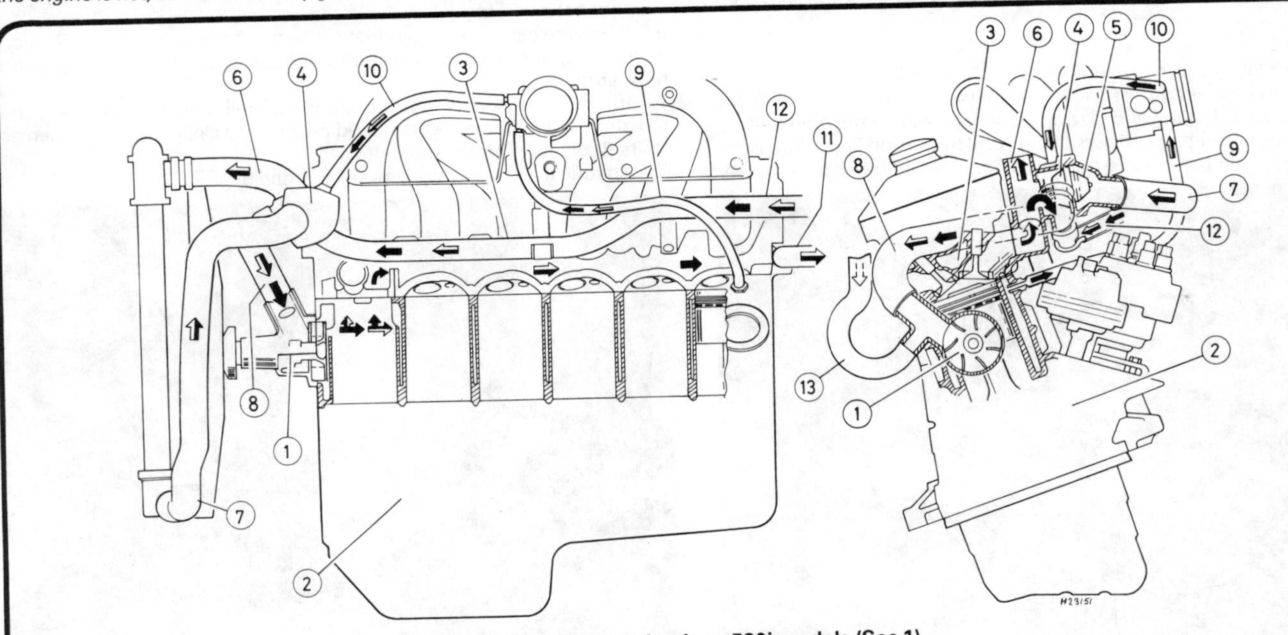

Fig. 2.1 Coolant circuit on 520i models (Sec 1)

1 *Water pump*
2 *Crankcase*
3 *Cylinder head*
4 *Thermostat housing*
5 *By-pass circuit*
6 *Radiator inlet*
7 *Radiator outlet*
8 *To water pump*
9 *Throttle housing feed*
10 *Throttle housing return*
11 *To heater*
12 *From heater*
13 *To expansion tank*

2.7 Checking the drivebelt tension midway between the pulleys

Check coolant level and concentration

1 With the engine cold the coolant level should be up to the maximum mark on the expansion tank. The tank is translucent and the level may be checked without removing the cap. If the engine is warm the level may be slightly higher.
2 If necessary, top up the level using the correct antifreeze mixture. If the engine is warm, place a cloth over the expansion tank filler cap, then unscrew the cap slowly to allow all the pressure to escape before completely removing the cap.
3 If necessary check the antifreeze concentration at this stage using a special hydrometer for this purpose. The hydrometer may be obtained from a motor accessory shop.
4 Refit the cap after topping-up the level.

Check cooling system hoses

5 Examine the cooling system hoses for deterioration and damage and renew them as required. Check that the hose clips are correctly tightened.

Check the water pump/alternator drivebelt

6 Check the full length of the water pump/alternator drivebelt for signs of cracking, fraying and glazing. If evident, renew the drivebelt.
7 Check the drivebelt tension using firm thumb or finger pressure midway between the pulleys (photo). There should be approximately 10 to 15 mm (0.4 to 0.6 in) deflection. If adjustment is necessary, carry out the procedure given in Section 13.

Change coolant

8 Renew the coolant at the specified intervals with reference to Sections 3, 4 and 5.

3 Cooling system – draining

1 It is preferable to drain the cooling system when the engine is cold. If this is not possible, place a cloth over the expansion tank filler cap, then unscrew the cap slowly, and allow all pressure to escape before completely removing it.
2 With the expansion cap removed, position the heater temperature control lever to maximum heat.
3 Position a suitable container beneath the radiator then unscrew the drain plug and drain the coolant into it (photo).
4 Unscrew the drain plug located on the side of the cylinder block and drain the coolant into another container (photo).
5 Dispose of the old coolant or keep it in a covered container if it is to be re-used.

4 Cooling system – flushing

1 Whenever the cooling system is drained it should be flushed through with clean water in order to clear away any accumulations of rust, scale or sediment. If the coolant has not been regularly changed, there may be a severe accumulation of sediment, and reverse flushing may then be necessary to clear the system.
2 Drain the cooling system as described in Section 3.
3 Disconnect the top and bottom hoses from the radiator, then insert a garden hose in the top of the radiator, and allow the water to circulate through the matrix and out of the bottom of the radiator until it runs clear.
4 Insert the hose in the expansion tank, and allow water to run through the supply hose.
5 Insert the hose in the top hose, and allow water to run through the cylinder head and block.
6 In severe cases of contamination, remove the radiator (see Section 9), invert it, and flush with water until clear water runs out of the top hose stub.
7 If, after a reasonable period the water still does not run clear, the radiator can be flushed with a good proprietary cleaning agent, such as Holts Radflush or Holts Speedflush.
8 To refill the cooling system, see Section 5.

3.3 Radiator drain plug (arrowed)

3.4 Cylinder block drain plug

5.3 Air bleed screw (arrowed) located on the thermostat housing

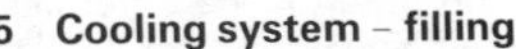

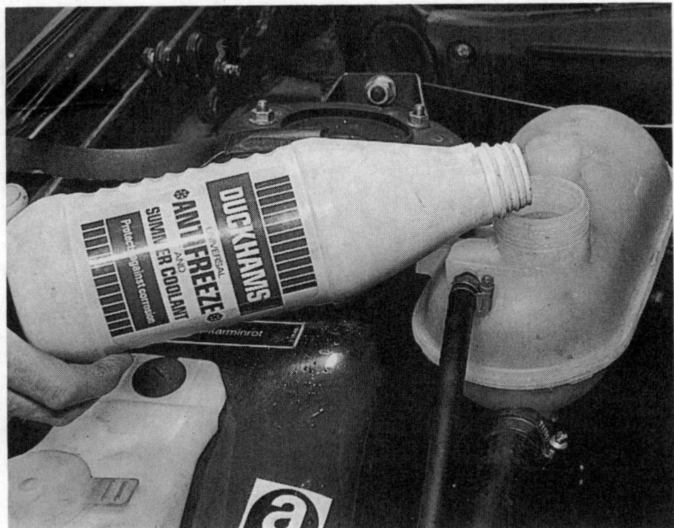

5.4 Adding antifreeze to the cooling system

5 Cooling system – filling

1 Reconnect all hoses and tighten the retaining clips. Also tighten the drain plugs on the radiator and cylinder block.

2 Position the heater temperature control lever to maximum heat.

3 Loosen the air bleed screw located on the thermostat housing (photo).

4 Pour coolant mixture slowly into the expansion tank (photo) until it starts to run from the bleed screw, then tighten the bleed screw.

5 Continue to pour the mixture into the expansion tank to the maximum level mark then refit and tighten the filler cap.

6 Run the engine at a fast idle until normal operating temperature is reached, then stop the engine and allow it to cool for approximately ten minutes.

7 Position the heater temperature control lever to maximum heat.

8 Place a cloth over the expansion tank filler cap, then unscrew the cap slowly, and allow all pressure to escape before completely removing it.

9 With the engine running at a fast idle, loosen the bleed screw on the thermostat housing and wait until the escaping coolant is free of air bubbles, then retighten the screw.

10 Top up the expansion tank to slightly above the maximum level mark and refit the filler cap.

6 Antifreeze mixture

1 The cooling system is filled at the factory with a mixture which contains a long-life antifreeze and corrosion inhibitor. The antifreeze mixture prevents freezing but also raises the boiling point of the coolant, thus delaying the tendency of the coolant to boil. The corrosion inhibitor reduces corrosion and the formation of scale. For these reasons the cooling system should be filled with antifreeze all the year round.

2 The concentration of the antifreeze should be maintained at the same level throughout the year. When topping-up the cooling system, always use the same mixture of water and antifreeze which the system contains. Topping-up using water only will gradually reduce the antifreeze concentration and lower the level of protection against both freezing and boiling.

3 The antifreeze mixture should be changed at the recommended periods in order to maintain its qualities and ensure the efficiency of the cooling system.

7 Viscous cooling fan – removal, checking and refitting

1 On models fitted with air conditioning unbolt the fan cowl from the rear of the radiator.

2 Unscrew the nut (left-hand thread) securing the fan unit to the water pump drive flange. BMW technicians use a special tool which engages the drivebelt pulley mounting bolts to hold the flange stationary, but if this tool or a similar home made tool is not available, the pulley can be held still by removing the drivebelt and gripping the pulley with an old drivebelt using a pair of grips. Remove the fan unit (photos).

3 Examine the viscous coupling for signs of damage and leakage of oil. Check that the fan moves freely without sticking. If necessary unbolt the fan from the unit.

4 Refitting is a reversal of removal, but tighten the nut to the specified torque. If removed, tension the drivebelt as described in Section 13.

8 Temperature gauge sender unit – removal and refitting

1 The temperature gauge sender unit is located on the thermostat housing on the front left-hand side of the cylinder head. It has just one wire attached to it, whereas the other temperature transmitters on the same housing have two wires each.

2 Drain the cooling system as described in Section 3.

3 Disconnect the wiring then unscrew and remove the sender unit.

4 Clean the thermostat housing then refit the sender unit together with a new gasket, and tighten it to the specified torque. Reconnect the wiring.

5 Fill the cooling system as described in Section 5.

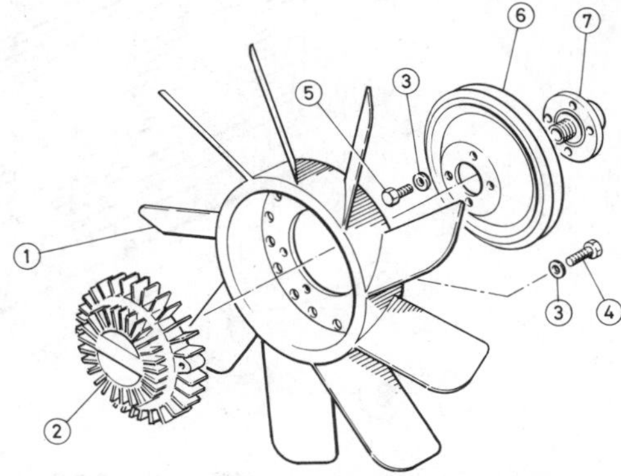

Fig. 2.2 Viscous coupled cooling fan components (Sec 7)

1 Fan blade (9-blade type shown)
2 Viscous coupling
3 Wave washer
4 Bolt
5 Bolt
6 Pulley
7 Drive flange

7.2A Using a cranked spanner to unscrew the viscous cooling fan nut (**left-hand** thread)

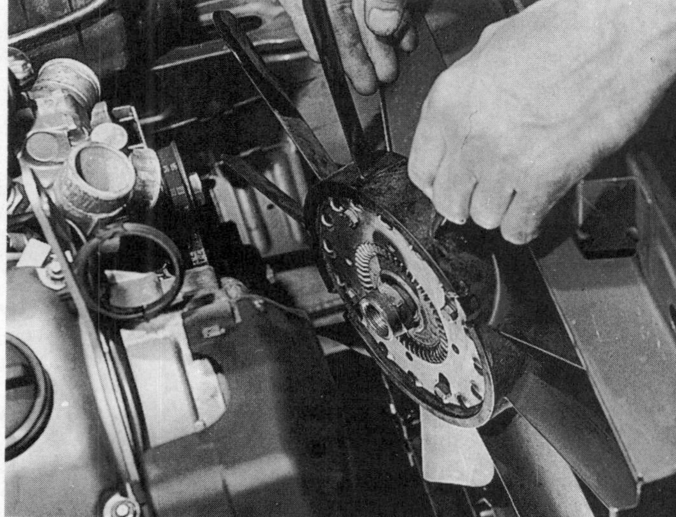

7.2B Removing the viscous cooling fan

9 Radiator – removal, inspection, cleaning and refitting

1 Drain the cooling system as described in Section 3.

2 Loosen the clips and disconnect the coolant hoses from the radiator, including the expansion tank hose (photos).

3 On automatic transmission models, position a suitable container beneath the radiator, then unscrew the union nuts for the automatic transmission fluid cooler, disconnect the lines and allow the fluid to drain (photos).

4 On models fitted with air conditioning, unbolt the fan cowl from the rear of the radiator and disconnect the wiring from the temperature switches. Also remove the radiator grilles as described in Chapter 11, then unbolt the condenser from the front of the radiator (refer to Chapter 11 if necessary).

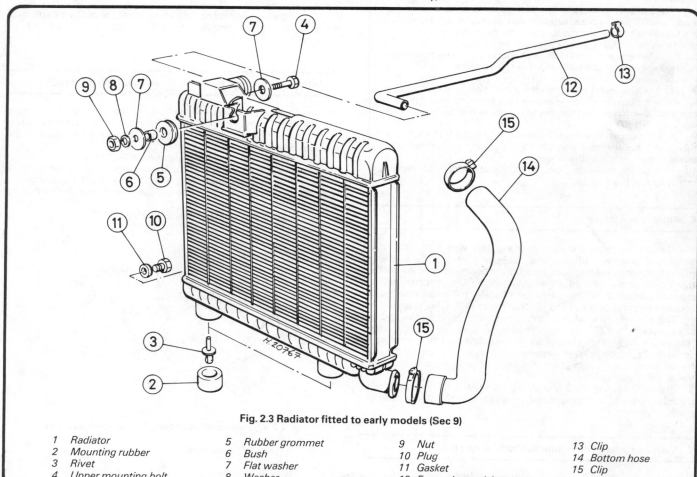

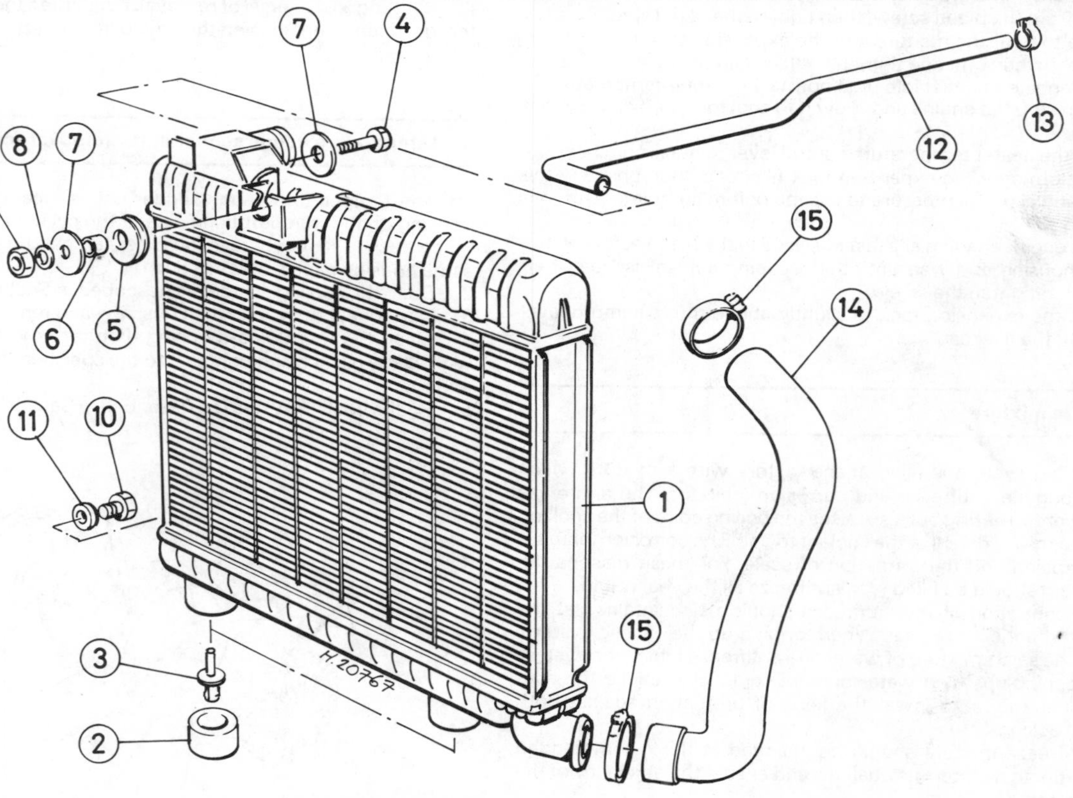

Fig. 2.3 Radiator fitted to early models (Sec 9)

1 Radiator
2 Mounting rubber
3 Rivet
4 Upper mounting bolt
5 Rubber grommet
6 Bush
7 Flat washer
8 Washer
9 Nut
10 Plug
11 Gasket
12 Expansion tank hose
13 Clip
14 Bottom hose
15 Clip

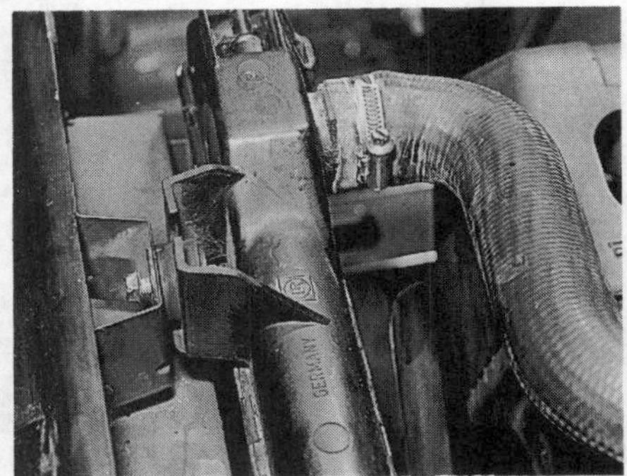

9.2A Top hose connection to the radiator – also showing a radiator top mounting

9.2B Disconnecting the expansion tank hose from the radiator

9.3A Automatic transmission fluid cooler line connection to the right-hand ...

9.3B ... and left-hand side of the radiator (arrowed)

9.6 Removing the radiator

9.9 View of the radiator mounting rubbers and automatic transmission fluid cooler lines with the radiator removed

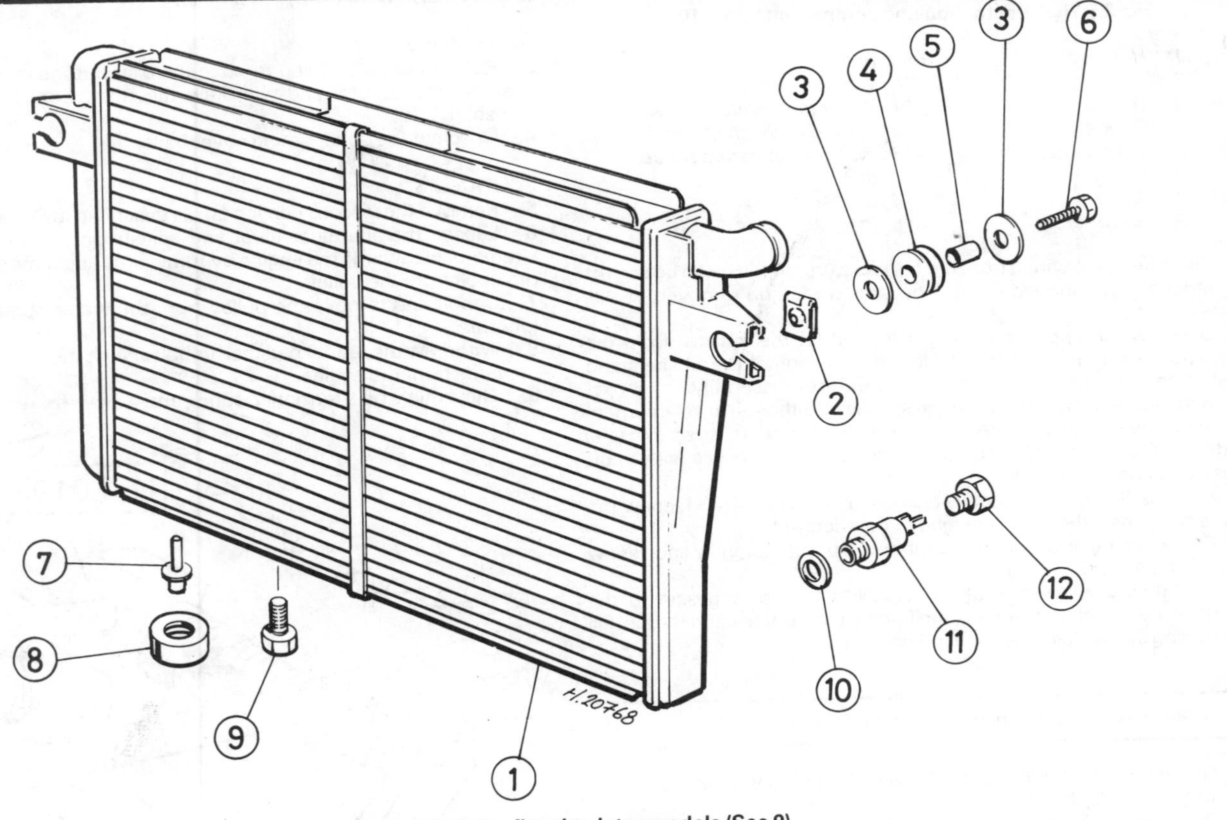

H.20768

Fig. 2.4 Radiator fitted to later models (Sec 9)

1 Radiator
2 Body nut
3 Flat washer
4 Rubber grommet
5 Bush
6 Mounting bolt
7 Rivet
8 Rubber mounting
9 Plug
10 Gasket
11 Temperature switch
12 Plug

10.3A Unscrew the bolts ...

10.3B ... remove the cover ...

10.3C ... and withdraw the thermostat

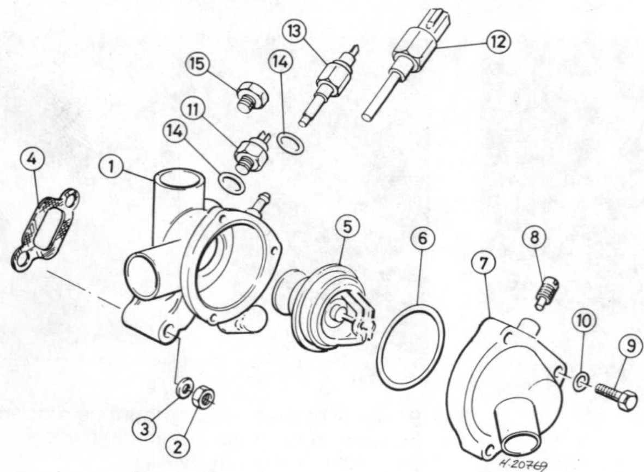

Fig. 2.5 Thermostat housing components (Sec 10)

1	*Housing*	*9*	*Bolt*
2	*Nut*	*10*	*Washer*
3	*Washer*	*11*	*Water temperature sensor*
4	*Gasket*	*12*	*Temperature time switch*
5	*Thermostat*	*13*	*Water temperature sender unit*
6	*O-ring*	*14*	*Gasket*
7	*Cover*	*15*	*Plug*
8	*Bleed screw*		

5 Disconnect the wiring from the temperature switch in the bottom of the radiator left-hand side tank. The switch may be removed at this stage if necessary.
6 Unscrew the upper mounting bolts and lift the radiator from the lower mounting rubbers (photo). Note the position of the washers and bushes on the upper mountings to ensure correct assembly.
7 Radiator repair is best left to the specialist, although in an emergency, minor leaks can be cured using a radiator sealant such as Holts Radweld. Clean the radiator matrix of flies and small leaves with a soft brush or by hosing with water.
8 Reverse-flush the radiator as described in Section 4, and renew the hoses and clips if they are damaged or deteriorated.
9 Check the radiator mounting rubbers for deterioration and renew them as necessary (photo).
10 Refitting is a reversal of removal, but fit a new gasket to the temperature switch if removed and tighten it to the specified torque. Fill the cooling system as described in Section 5.

10 Thermostat – removal, testing and refitting

1 The thermostat is located in a housing bolted to the front left-hand side of the cylinder head.
2 Drain the cooling system as described in Section 3.
3 Unbolt the thermostat housing cover and withdraw the thermostat (photos). Remove the O-ring seal. There is no need to disconnect the hoses from the housing cover.
4 If the thermostat is suspected of being faulty, suspend it in a pan of water and gradually heat the water. The thermostat valve should begin to open at the specified temperature. If not, it is faulty and should be renewed.
5 Check the condition of the hoses and clips and renew them if necessary.
6 Refitting is a reversal of removal, but make sure that the bar on the thermostat faces outwards, renew the O-ring seal, and refill the cooling system as described in Section 5.

11 Water pump – removal and refitting

All models

1 Drain the cooling system as described in Section 3.

520i models

2 Unbolt the wiring harness from the front engine lifting eye, then unbolt the eye from the cylinder head.

525e models

3 Refer to Chapter 4 and remove the distributor cap and rotor, then unscrew the adaptor and withdraw the cover from the front of the camshaft.
4 Unscrew the upper timing cover bolts.

All models

5 Remove the viscous cooling fan as described in Section 7.
6 Loosen the alternator pivot and adjustment nuts and swivel the alternator in towards the engine by turning the adjustment bolt. Slip the drivebelt from the pulley.
7 Unbolt and remove the pulley from the water pump drive flange (photo).
8 Withdraw the rubber pad then unbolt and lift the upper timing cover upwards from the engine.
9 The timing belt tensioner spring must now be restrained. BMW

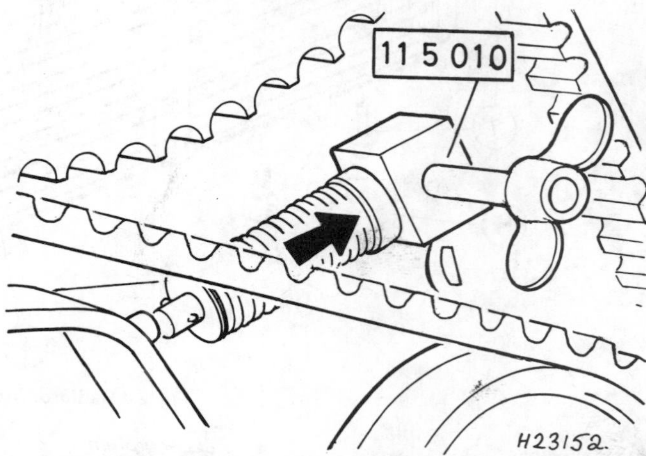

Fig. 2.6 Special BMW tool for holding the timing belt tensioner spring away from the water pump (Sec 11)

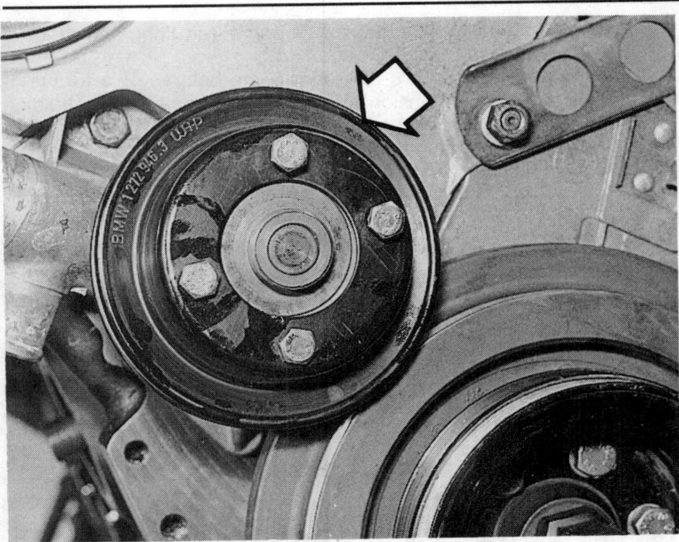

11.7 Water pump pulley (arrowed)

technicians use a special tool (see Fig. 2.6) which holds the spring and pin in position on the tensioner by gripping the inner end of the pin. The tensioner pin is therefore held away from the water pump. A small pair of grips may be used to hold the pin.

10 Loosen the clips and disconnect the hoses from the water pump.

11 Unbolt the water pump from the cylinder block and remove the gasket (photo). Clean away the old gasket.

12 Examine the hoses for deterioration and renew them as necessary.

13 Refitting is a reversal of removal, but fit a new gasket and tighten all bolts to the specified torque. Make sure that the tensioner pin is correctly located in the water pump.

11.11 Removing the water pump from the cylinder block

14 Tension the drivebelt as described in Section 13. Refill the cooling system with reference to Section 5.

12 Water pump – overhaul

1 If a pump is well worn, noisy and leaking from around the bearing/shaft, it is recommended that a new pump is obtained. However, for

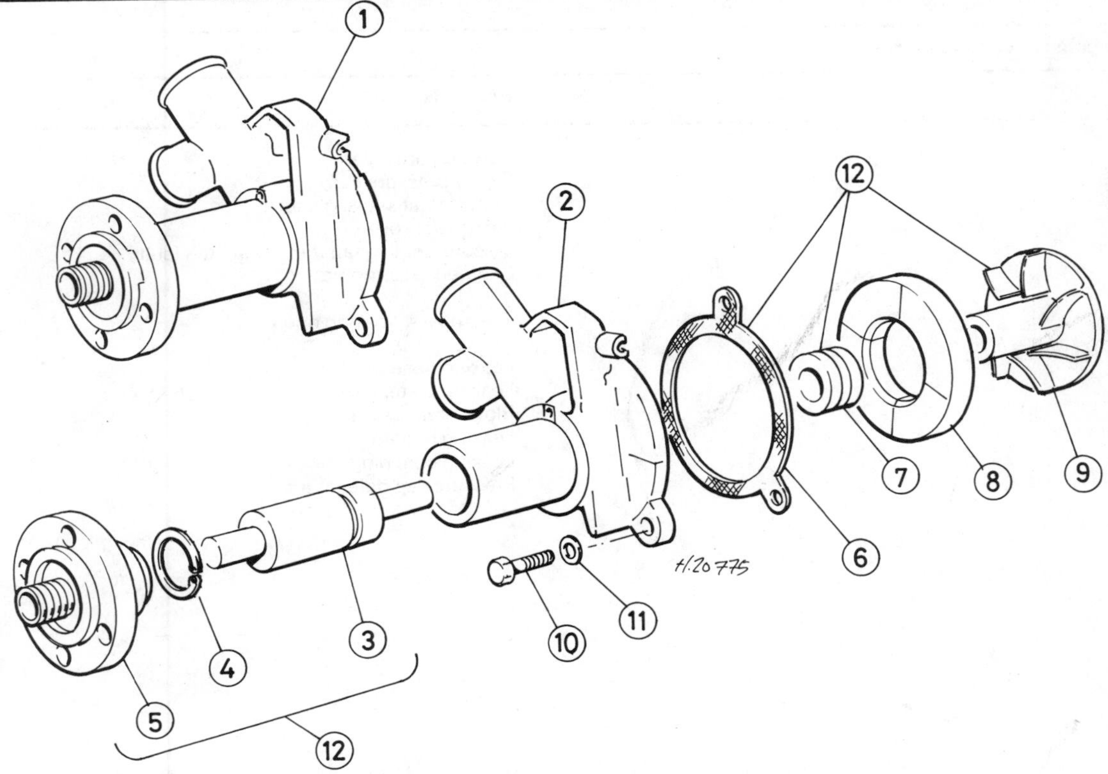

H.20775

Fig. 2.7 Exploded view of the water pump (Sec 12)

1 Water pump assembly
2 Water pump body
3 Bearing
4 Circlip
5 Drive flange
6 Gasket
7 Slip ring seal
8 Ring cover
9 Impeller
10 Bolt
11 Washer
12 Repair kit

those preferring to overhaul the original pump, proceed in the following way.
2 Use an extractor to pull off the drive flange.
3 Extract the circlip then press the shaft/bearing out of the pump body and impeller.
4 Press out the seal from the body.
5 Obtain a repair kit which will contain a new shaft/bearing and seal. Check that the impeller is still serviceable.
6 Clean all the components and examine them for wear and damage. Renew them as necessary.
7 Press the new seal into the body.
8 Support the body then press the shaft/bearing into the body with its longer end towards the impeller end.
9 Refit the circlip into the groove in the end of the body.
10 Support the front end of the shaft on the bench then press on the impeller, but only far enough to provide a gap between 0.4 and 0.8 mm between the blades of the impeller and the pump body.
11 Support the shaft on the impeller end using a metal dowel rod in a vice, then press on the drive flange so that the end of the shaft projects by between 4.1 and 4.4 mm. Do not support the pump on the impeller otherwise the previous clearance will be reduced.
12 Check that the shaft impeller and drive flange rotate freely.

13 Water pump/alternator drivebelt – removal, refitting and adjustment

1 Loosen the alternator pivot and adjustment nuts and swivel the alternator in towards the engine by turning the adjustment bolt (photo). Slip the drivebelt from the water pump, alternator and crankshaft pulleys. On the B27 engine it may be necessary to turn the engine in order to pull the drivebelt up over the pulley, as there is insufficient adjustment to allow the alternator to fully release the drivebelt.
2 Fit the new drivebelt to the pulleys and pull out the alternator by hand to hold the drivebelt in place.
3 Make sure that the alternator pivot bolt is not tight, and that the alternator moves freely.
4 Using a torque wrench on the tensioning bolt, apply a torque of 7 Nm (5 lbf ft). This will tension the drivebelt correctly. While holding the torque wrench, tighten the nut on the inner end of the adjustment bolt to retain the alternator in the correct position.
5 Tighten the pivot bolt nut to the specified torque.

13.1 Alternator adjustment bolt – locking nut is on the inner end of the bolt (arrowed)

14 Fault diagnosis – cooling system

Symptom	Reason(s)
Overheating	Low coolant level Faulty pressure cap Thermostat sticking shut Drivebelt broken Viscous cooling fan thermo-switch faulty Clogged radiator matrix
Slow warm up	Thermostat sticking open
Coolant loss	Leaking hose Leaking water pump or cooling system joint Blown cylinder head gasket Leaking radiator Leaking core plug Pressure cap defective

Chapter 3 Fuel and exhaust systems

Contents

Specifications

General

Type and application:

520i models	Bosch K, L or LE-Jetronic fuel injection system
525e models	Bosch Motronic (DME-controlled L-Jetronic) fuel injection system
Fuel octane rating	95 RON (for suitability for unleaded fuel, consult a BMW dealer)
Fuel tank capacity	70 litres (15.4 gal)

Air cleaner element

Type:

Pre-1986 models	Champion U504
1986-on models	Champion U527

K-Jetronic

Injector spray angle	35°
Injector operating pressure	4.5 to 5.2 bar
Maximum leak rate	1 drop per minute at test pressure of 2.5 bar
Temperature time switch switching point	35 ± 5°C
Temperature time switch period	8 ± 3 seconds
Temperature time switch resistance:	
Coolant temperature below 30°C:	
Terminal G to earth	25 to 40 ohms
Terminal W to earth	Zero ohms
Terminal G to W	25 to 40 ohms
Coolant temperature above 40°C:	
Terminal G to earth	50 to 80 ohms
Terminal W to earth	100 to 300 ohms
Terminal G to W	50 to 80 ohms
Warm-up regulator maximum activating time	6.5 minutes
Warm-up regulator final pressure with warm engine:	
With vacuum	3.55 to 3.95 bar
Without vacuum	2.5 to 2.9 bar
Throttle bypass valve gap at 20 ± 1°C	5.3 to 5.7 mm
Cold start valve spray angle	Approximately 80°
Cold start valve winding resistance at 20°C	3 to 5 ohms
Fuel pump pressure (with vacuum hose disconnected from pressure regulator)	2.3 to 2.7 bar
Idle speed	800 to 900 rpm
CO content	1.5% maximum

L-Jetronic

Air-flow meter resistance	95 to 335 ohms
Coolant temperature sensor resistance	250 to 410 ohms
Air temperature and airflow meter resistance	90 to 330 ohms
Throttle switch resistance:	
Idle	2.0 ohms
Part-load	800 ohms
Full-load	2.0 ohms
Fuel pump pressure (vacuum hose disconnected from pressure regulator)	2.3 to 2.7 bar
Idle speed (vacuum hose attached to pressure regulator):	
Up to September 1982	800 to 900 rpm
September 1982 on	750 to 850 rpm
CO content	0.5 to 1.5%
Injector resistance	2 to 3 ohms
Cold start valve winding resistance at 20°C	3 to 5 ohms

DME-Motronic

Idle speed regulation:	
Normal	680 to 720 rpm
With air conditioner on	800 to 900 rpm
During warm-up	900 to 1000 rpm
Coolant temperature sensor resistance:	
−10°C	7 to 11.6 ohms
+20°C	2.1 to 2.9 ohms
+80°C	0.2 to 0.4 ohms
Injector resistance	15 to 17.5 ohms
Idle speed:	
Up to 1985	660 to 740 rpm
1986 on (control unit 0 261 200 074	680 to 760 rpm
CO content:	
Control unit 0 261 200 007	0.2 to 1.2%
All other models	0.5 to 1.5%
HC content (control unit 0 261 200 007 only)	300 ppm

Fuel pump

Minimum delivery rate	2.0 litres
Operating pressure:	
K-Jetronic	4.5 to 5.0 bar
L-Jetronic	2.5 to 3.0 bar

Fuel tank sender unit

Resistance with fuel tank	2.5 to 3.9 ohms
Resistance with empty tank	69.4 to 74.0 ohms

Torque wrench settings

	Nm	lbf ft
Inlet manifold	30 to 33	22 to 24
Exhaust manifold	22 to 25	16 to 18
Injector union (K-Jetronic)	25	18
Fuel line bolt (K-Jetronic):		
M8	7.5 to 9.5	5.5 to 6.5
M12	20 to 25	14.5 to 18.0
Fuel line to pressure regulator (L-Jetronic)	25 to 30	18 to 22
Return hose to pressure regulator (L-Jetronic)	26 to 28	19 to 20
Temperature time switch	20 to 25	15 to 18
Coolant temperature sensor	12 to 14	9 to 10
Temperature switch	25 to 30	18 to 22
Warm-up regulator	22 to 24	16 to 17
Fuel tank drain plug	21 to 25	15 to 18
Fuel pump mounting	6 to 7	4.5 to 5

1 General description

Warning: *Many of the procedures in this Chapter require the removal of fuel lines and connections which may result in some fuel spillage. Before carrying out any operation on the fuel system refer to the precautions given in Safety First! at the beginning of this Manual and follow them implicitly. Petrol is a highly dangerous and volatile liquid and the precautions necessary when handling it cannot be overstressed.*

A Bosch fuel injection system is fitted being of K, L or LE-Jetronic type for 520i models and of Motronic type for 525e models.

The basic K-Jetronic system consists of a mechanical airflow sensor to monitor the volume of air entering the engine, a fuel distributor integral with the airflow sensor, a cold start valve and throttle bypass valve for cold starting, and a warm-up regulator to lean out the mixture gradually during the warm-up period. A temperature time switch energises the cold start valve during initial cold starting only when the starter is operating, the length of period depending on the engine temperature. The injectors, which are located in the inlet manifold, point towards the inlet valves and operate continuously, the amount of fuel delivered being dependent upon the position of the airflow sensor arm.

The L-Jetronic system consists of an electronic airflow sensor, various sensors to monitor the engine condition, an electronic control

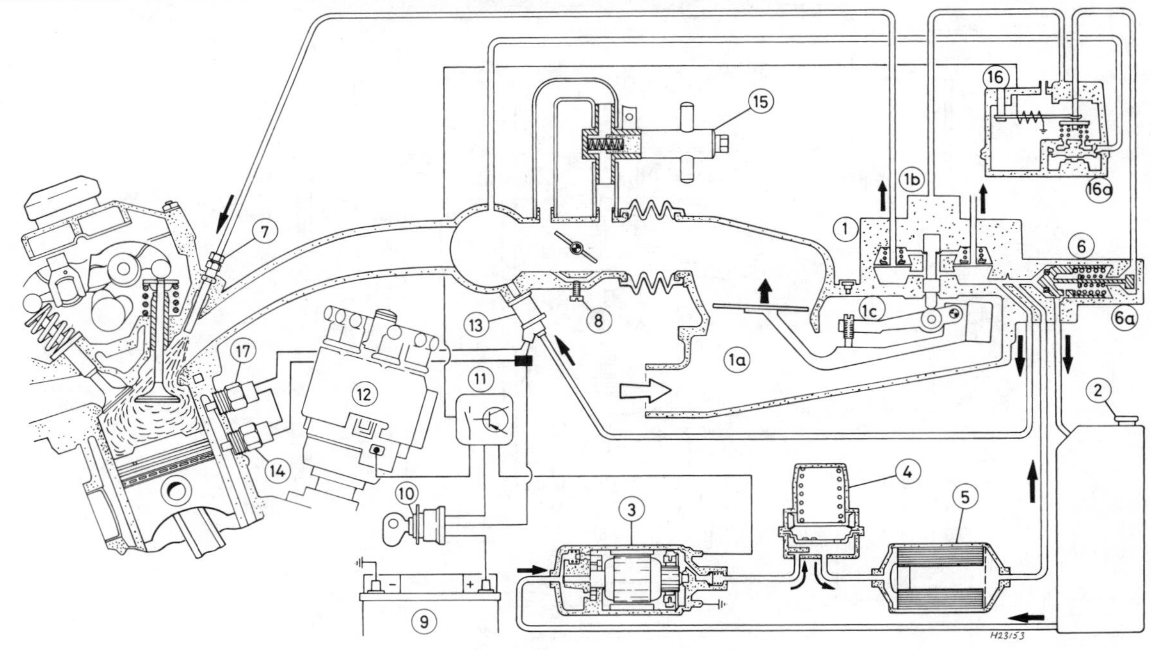

Fig. 3.1 K-Jetronic fuel injection system (Sec 1)

1 Fuel metering unit
1a Airflow sensor
1b Fuel distributor
1c Idle mixture control screw
2 Fuel tank
3 Electric fuel pump
4 Fuel accumulator
5 Fuel filter
6 Fuel pressure regulator
6a Valve
7 Fuel injector
8 Idle speed control screw
9 Battery
10 Ignition switch
11 Control relay
12 Distributor
13 Cold start valve
14 Temperature time switch
15 Throttle bypass valve
16 Warm-up regulator
16a Full load diaphragm
17 Temperature switch

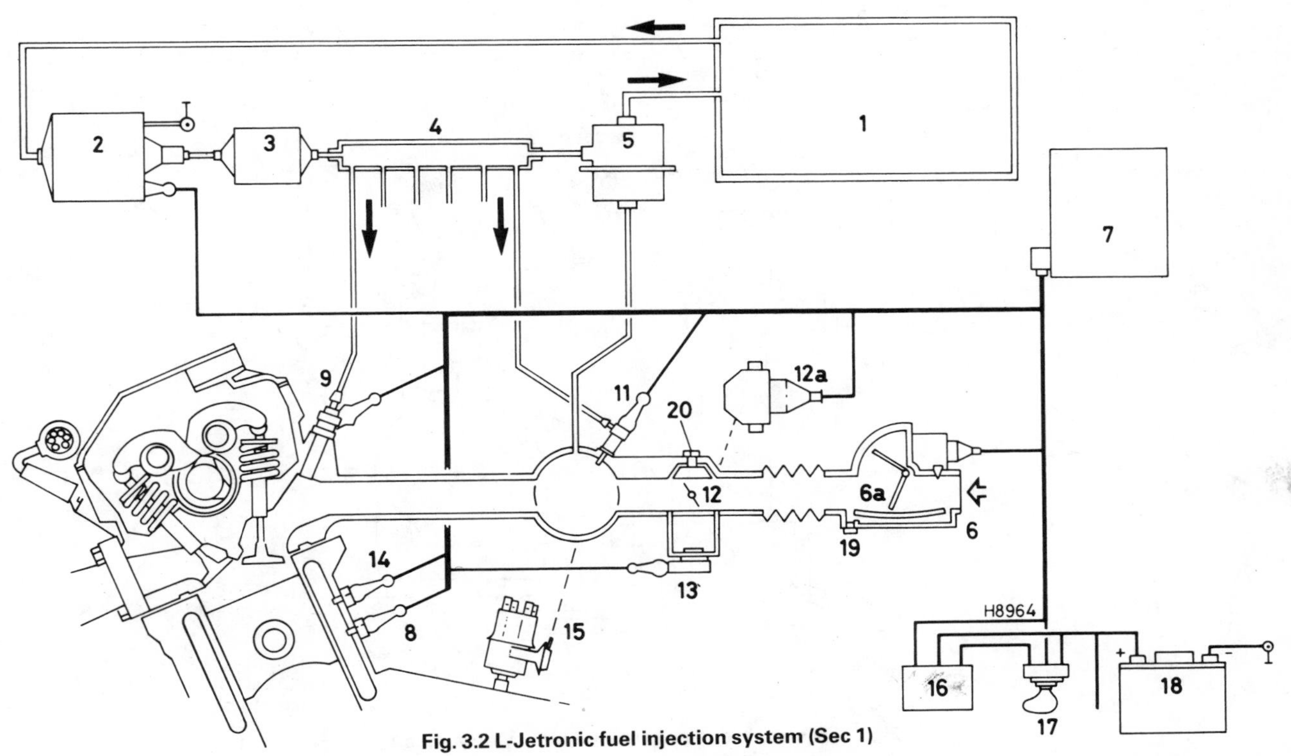

Fig. 3.2 L-Jetronic fuel injection system (Sec 1)

1 Fuel tank
2 Fuel pump
3 Fuel filter
4 Injection tube
5 Pressure regulator
6 Airflow sensor
6a Sensor plate
7 Control unit
8 Coolant temperature sensor
9 Injector
10 Intake pipe
11 Cold start valve
12 Throttle butterfly
12a Throttle switch
13 Throttle bypass valve (coolant heated)
14 Temperature time switch
15 Distributor
16 Fuel pump relay
17 Ignition switch
18 Battery
19 Mixture control screw
20 Idle speed control screw

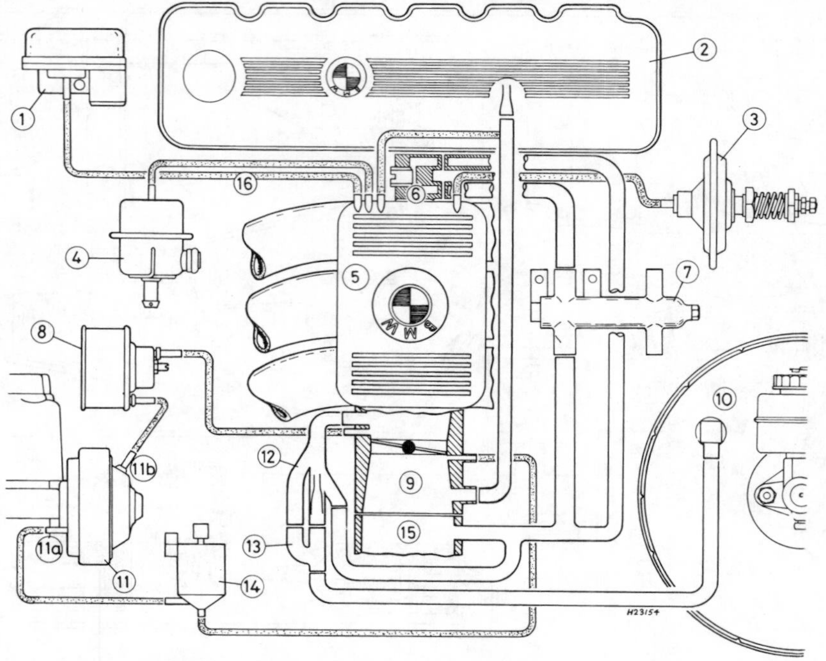

Fig. 3.3 Hose routing on the L-Jetronic fuel injection system (Sec 1)

1 *Partial throttle switch*
2 *Valve cover*
3 *Idle speed control valve*
4 *Fuel pressure regulator*
5 *Inlet manifold*
6 *Bypass air housing*
7 *Throttle bypass valve*
8 *2/3 way valve*
9 *Throttle housing*
10 *Brake servo*
11 *Distributor vacuum capsule*
11a *Ignition advance connection*
11b *Ignition retard connection*
12 *Bypass connection*
13 *Double check valve*
14 *Switch valve (not fitted to UK models)*
15 *Air intake cowl*
16 *Temperature sensor for electronic heater*

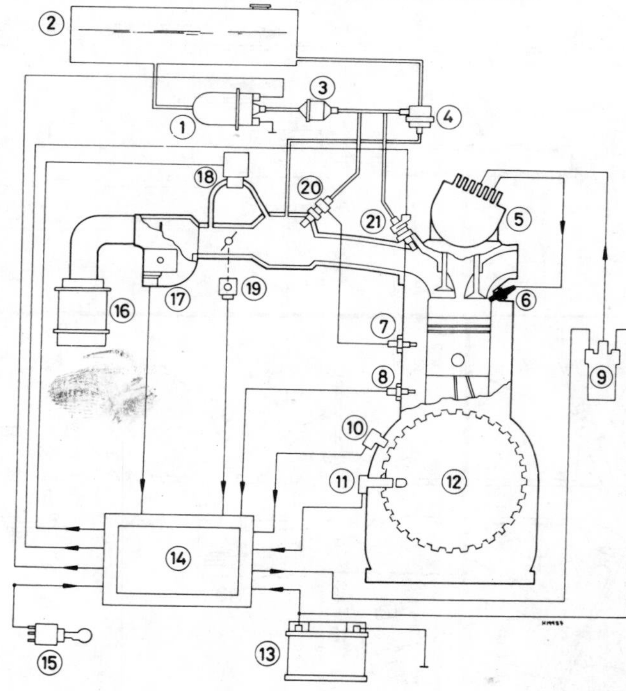

Fig. 3.4 Motronic engine management system (Sec 1)

1 *Electric fuel pump*
2 *Fuel tank*
3 *Fuel filter*
4 *Fuel pressure regulator*
5 *Ignition distributor*
6 *Spark plugs*
7 *Coolant temperature sensor*
8 *Coolant temperature sensor*
9 *Ignition coil*
10 *Speed sensor*
11 *Reference sensor (timing)*
12 *Flywheel/driveplate ring gear*
13 *Battery*
14 *Control unit*
15 *Ignition lock*
16 *Air cleaner*
17 *Airflow sensor*
18 *Idle speed control*
19 *Throttle butterfly switch*
20 *Cold start valve*
21 *Fuel injectors*

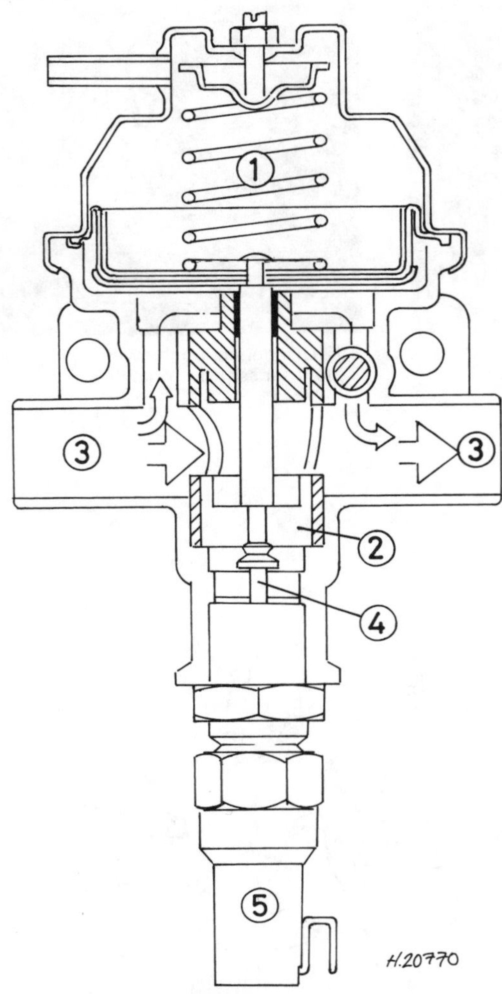

Fig. 3.5 Idle speed adjuster (Sec 1)

1 *Spring*
2 *Valve*
3 *Bypass port*
4 *Piston*
5 *Temperature operating motor*

unit to process the signals from the sensors, and electronic injectors which operate simultaneously and for a period dependent upon the engine condition. The fuel pressure to the injectors is controlled by a regulator which is vacuum- sensitive so that the pressure varies with the vacuum present in the inlet manifold. This ensures that the amount of fuel injected can be controlled by varying the time that the injectors are opened. A cold start valve is provided for initial enrichment during operation of the starter motor, and thereafter enrichment is controlled by the length of time the injectors are opened during the warm-up period. The LE-Jetronic system (fitted to 520i models from 1984) functions in the same way as the L-Jetronic system but has additional sensors. The Motronic system is a full engine management system which controls both the fuel and ignition timing requirements of the engine through a single electronic control unit (ECU). The injection system is still L-Jetronic. The volume of fuel injected and the ignition timing are constantly varied according to engine speed and load, to provide the optimum fuel economy consistent with performance. An automatic idle speed adjuster is fitted. On early models it is operated by vacuum but on later models it is controlled by the electronic control unit. Some models may be fitted with a cruise control unit as an optional extra. The control unit is located beneath the facia.

2 Routine maintenance

Carry out the following at the intervals given in *Routine maintenance* at the front of this manual.

Lubricate accelerator linkages

1 Apply a little engine oil to the accelerator linkages and levers on the throttle housing and bulkhead. Where applicable also lubricate the cruise control linkages.

Renew the air cleaner element

2 Refer to Section 3.

Check the fuel lines, tank and hoses

3 Raise the car on a ramp or axle stands and examine the fuel lines, fuel tank and all fuel hoses for deterioration, security and damage.

Renew the fuel filter

4 Refer to Section 7

Check the exhaust system

5 Raise the car on a ramp or axle stands, then start the engine to allow it to idle. Check the full length of the exhaust system for leakage and general condition. Also check the rubber mountings.

Check the idle speed and CO

6 Refer to Section 13.

3 Air cleaner – removal and refitting

Air cleaner element

1 Unscrew the nuts and remove the washers from the air cleaner mountings near the fusebox on the left-hand side of the engine compartment (photo).
2 Prise open the spring clips securing the air cleaner lower section to the upper section (photo).
3 Lift the upper section slightly then remove the air cleaner element from the lower section (photo).
4 Wipe clean the inner surfaces of the upper and lower sections taking care not to damage the airflow sensor in the upper section.

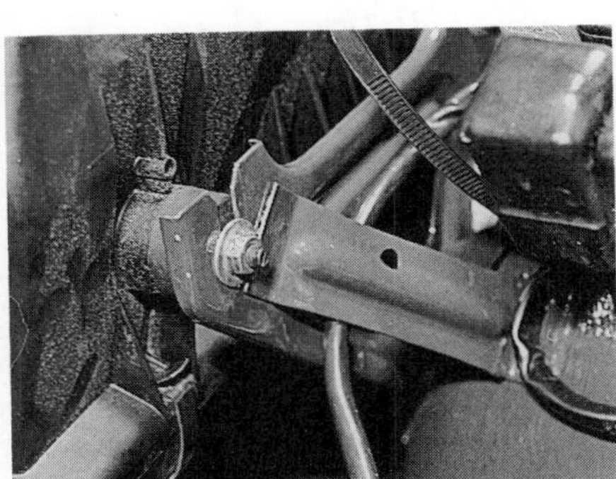

3.1 Air cleaner mounting (Motronic)

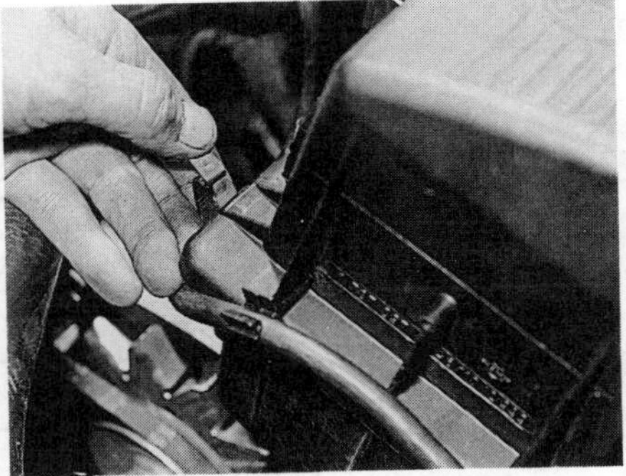

3.2 Unclipping the air cleaner lower section (Motronic)

3.3 Removing the air cleaner element (Motronic)

3.9 Releasing the inlet duct from the front of the air cleaner (Motronic)

3.10 Wiring cable (arrowed) attached to the air cleaner (Motronic)

3.12 Disconnecting the wiring plug from the airflow sensor (Motronic)

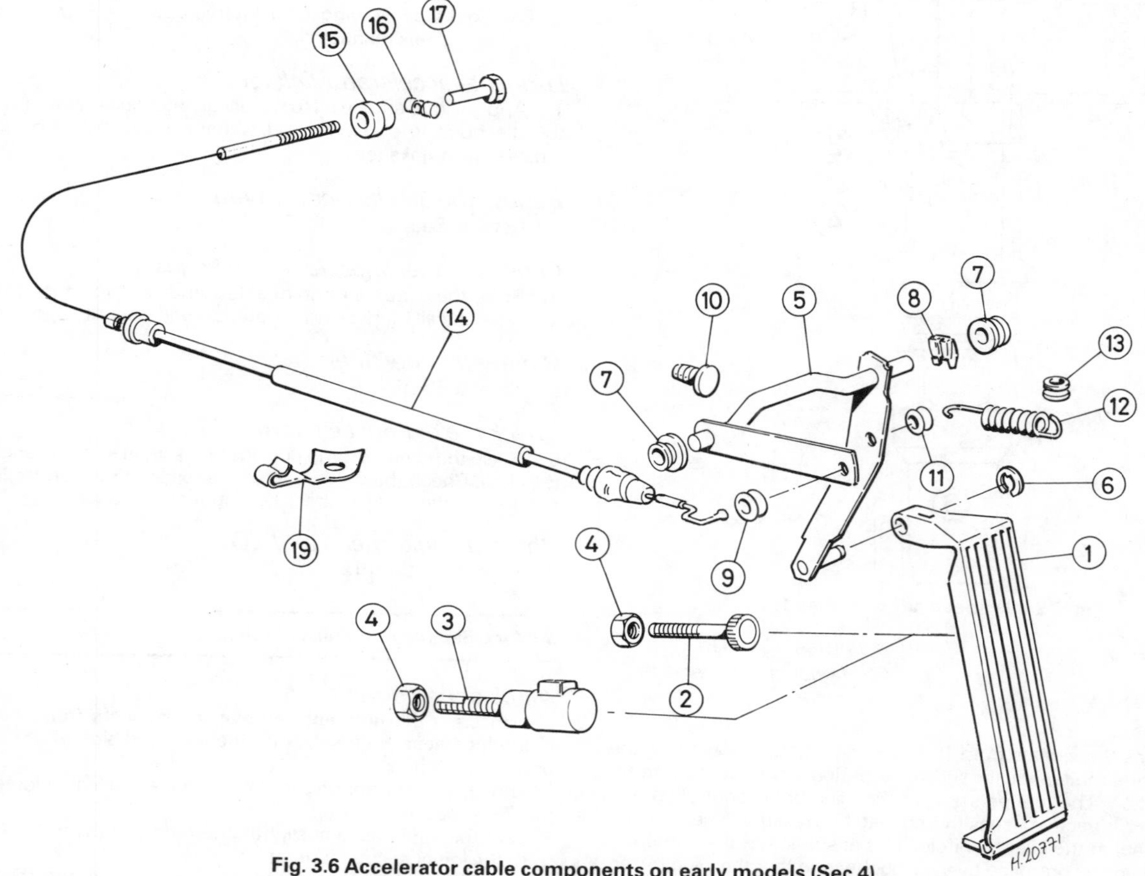

Fig. 3.6 Accelerator cable components on early models (Sec 4)

1 Pedal
2 Adjusting stop
3 Stopper
4 Nut
5 Lever
6 Circlip
7 Bush
8 Circlip
9 Grommet
10 Stop
11 Grommet
12 Spring
13 Grommet
14 Cable
15 Grommet
16 Pin
17 Adjusting nut

5 Fit the new element, making sure that it is seated correctly, then connect the two sections together and snap on the spring clips.
6 Refit the upper section in the mounting brackets, then fit the washers and tighten the nuts.

Air cleaner assembly

7 Remove the element as described previously.
8 On models with L-Jetronic remove the airflow sensor as described in Section 15.
9 Release the inlet duct from the front of the air cleaner (photo).
10 Unclip the cable from the inner section (photo).
11 Where applicable, loosen the clip and disconnect the air duct leading from the air inlet sensor to the throttle housing.
12 Where applicable disconnect the wiring plug from the air inlet sensor (photo).
13 Lift the air cleaner assembly from the engine compartment. Unbolt the airflow sensor with reference to Section 15.
14 Refitting is a reversal of removal.

4 Accelerator cable – removal, refitting and adjustment

Early models

1 Release the inner cable end fitting from the lever on the throttle housing.

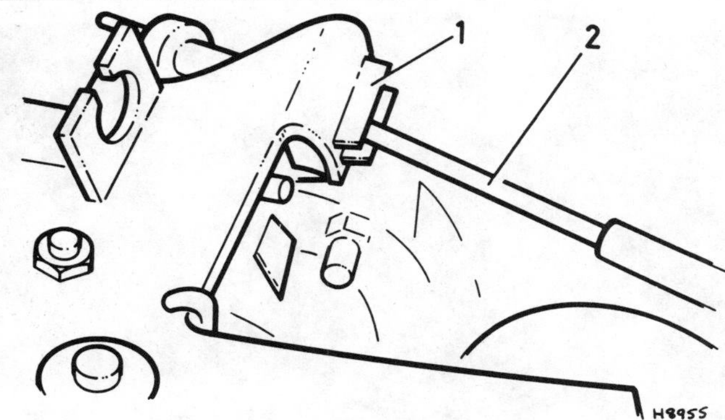

Fig. 3.7 Accelerator cable clamp (1) and cable (2) – L-Jetronic (Sec 4)

2 Loosen the adjustment ferrule nuts and disconnect the outer cable from the bracket on the inlet manifold.
3 Working inside the car, remove the lower facia panel with reference to Chapter 11.
4 Unhook the inner cable from the accelerator pedal, then remove the inner cable fitting from the lever assembly. Recover the grommets.
5 Release the outer cable grommet from the bulkhead. On some models it may be necessary to first compress the plastic locking claws.
6 Release the cable from the clips and withdraw it from inside the engine compartment.

Later models

7 Working in the engine compartment, open the throttle lever then pull the inner cable plastic block from the bracket on the throttle housing.
8 Release the outer cable from the bracket on the inlet manifold.
9 Release the inner cable end fitting from the accelerator pedal upper lever located on the right-hand side of the bulkhead (photo). Remove the grommet.
10 Disconnect the outer cable and grommet from the bracket on the bulkhead.
11 Release the cable from the clips and withdraw it from inside the engine compartment.

All models

12 Refitting is a reversal of removal, but adjust the cable as follows. Make sure that the accelerator pedal is on its stop, and that the automatic choke is not operating (ie the fast idle stop is not in contact with the cam).
13 Unscrew the adjusting nut(s) until there is just free play on the inner cable.
14 Have an assistant fully depress the accelerator pedal, then adjust the accelerator pedal stop inside the car until there is 0.5 mm clearance between the throttle lever on the throttle housing and its full open stop. Note that approximately $1\frac{1}{2}$ turns on the adjusting bolt is equivalent to this clearance. Lock the bolt after making the adjustment.
15 On automatic transmission models refer to Chapter 6 for adjustment of the kickdown cable.
16 On models fitted with cruise control, adjust the inner cable on the throttle lever so that there is a gap of 1 to 2 mm between the knurled nut and the adaptor on the bracket.

5 Accelerator pedal – removal and refitting

1 Remove the lower facia panel with reference to Chapter 11.
2 Unhook the return spring.
3 Extract the circlip and disconnect the pedal.
4 Press off the right-hand bush, move the pedal to the right, then disconnect the cable or rod as applicable (photo).

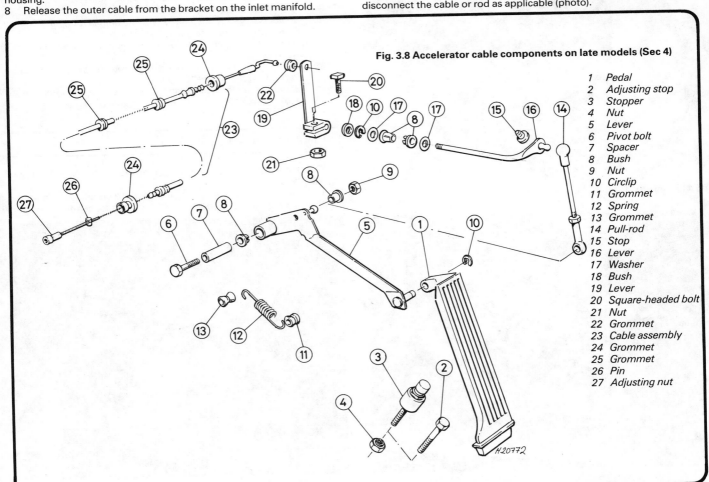

Fig. 3.8 Accelerator cable components on late models (Sec 4)

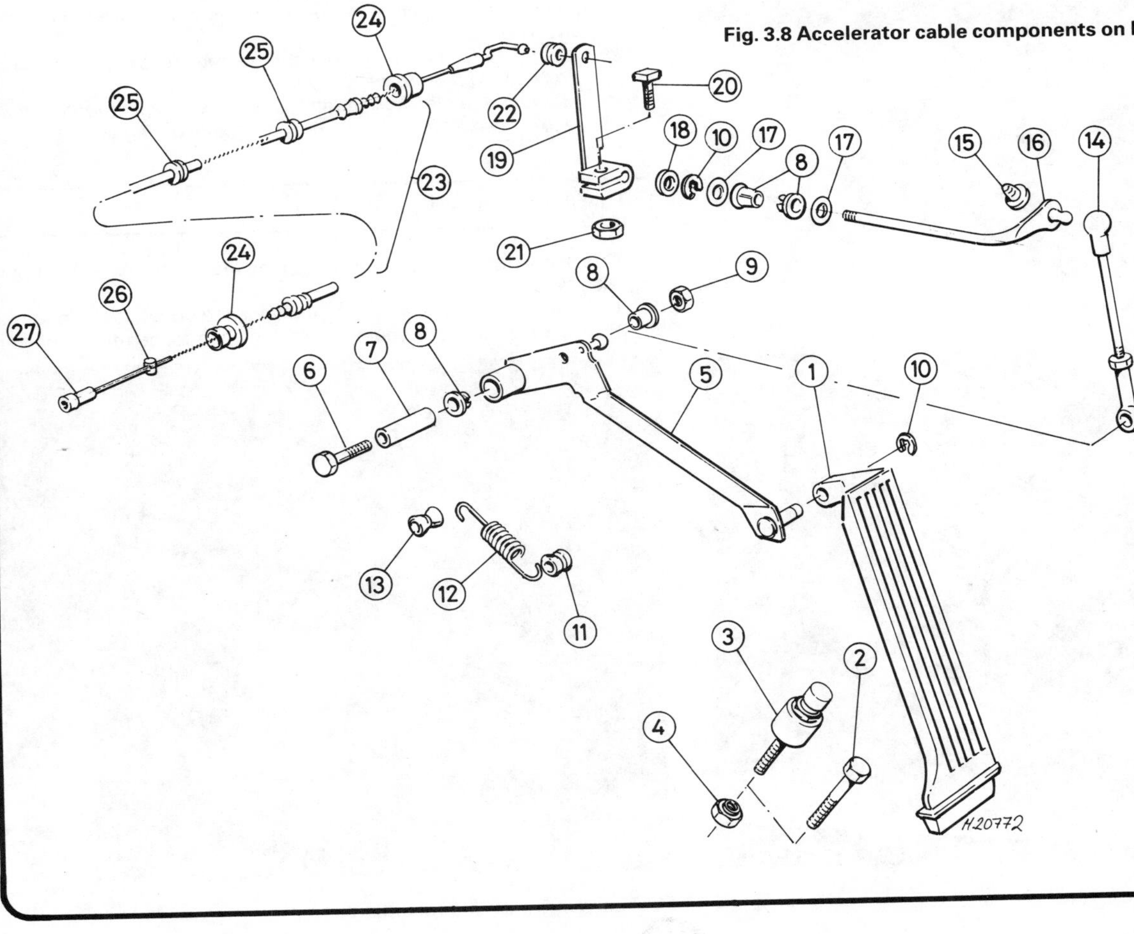

1 *Pedal*
2 *Adjusting stop*
3 *Stopper*
4 *Nut*
5 *Lever*
6 *Pivot bolt*
7 *Spacer*
8 *Bush*
9 *Nut*
10 *Circlip*
11 *Grommet*
12 *Spring*
13 *Grommet*
14 *Pull-rod*
15 *Stop*
16 *Lever*
17 *Washer*
18 *Bush*
19 *Lever*
20 *Square-headed bolt*
21 *Nut*
22 *Grommet*
23 *Cable assembly*
24 *Grommet*
25 *Grommet*
26 *Pin*
27 *Adjusting nut*

H.20772

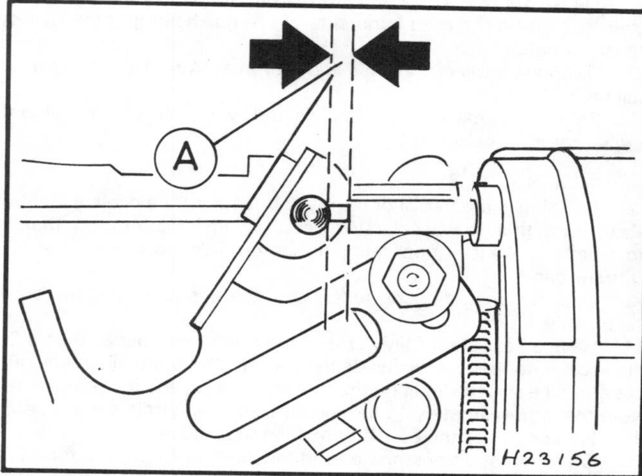

Fig. 3.9 Cruise control cable adjustment (Sec 4)

A = 1 to 2 mm

4.9 Accelerator cable attachment to the pedal upper lever

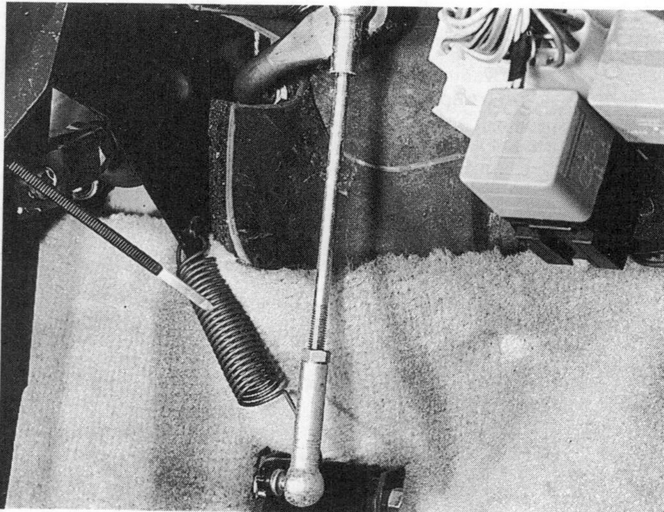

5.4 Linkage rod from the accelerator pedal to the upper lever

5 Remove the pedal assembly.
6 Refitting is a reversal of removal, but grease the bearing surfaces and adjust the cable as described in Section 4.

6 Fuel injection system – precautions

The fuel injection system is normally trouble-free. Avoid damage to the electrical components by observing the following precautions.

(a) Do not disconnect the battery with the engine running
(b) Do not use a boost charger as a starting aid
(c) Do not disconnect or reconnect wiring plugs with the ignition switched on
(d) Before performing a cylinder compression test, unplug the control relay to disable the fuel pump
(e) Remove the electronic control unit if the ambient temperature will exceed 80°C as for example in a paint drying oven.

7 Fuel filter – renewal

1 Chock the front wheels then jack up the rear of the car and support on axle stands.
2 Using a hose clamp, clamp the filter inlet and outlet hoses (photo).
3 Position a container beneath the filter, then loosen the clips and

7.2 Fuel filter outlet hose (arrowed)

7.4 Fuel pump and filter mounting clamp

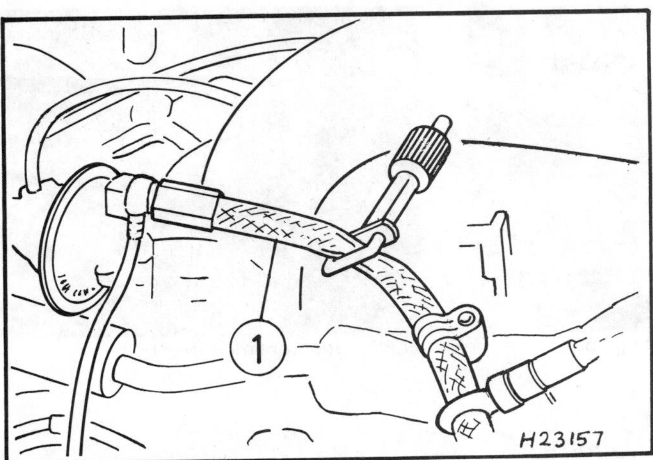

Fig. 3.10 Clamp hose (1) when checking the fuel pressure (Sec 8)

disconnect the hoses. Some fuel will escape, so take suitable precautions.
4 Unscrew the clamp nut and pull the filter from the mounting bracket (photo).
5 Fit the new filter using a reversal of the removal procedure, but make sure that the arrow faces the direction of flow.

8 Fuel pump delivery rate and pressure – checking

Note: *To carry out the following tests it will be necessary to obtain a suitable pressure gauge and adaptors.*

K-Jetronic

1 Disconnect the centre fuel line from the top of the fuel distributor (ie the line from the warm-up regulator).
2 Connect the pressure gauge and adaptors to the line and re-connect to the fuel distributor.
3 Clamp the hose shown in Fig. 3.10.
4 Pull the pump relay from its socket on the side of the fusebox, then use a bridging wire to connect terminal 87 in the socket with battery positive. The pump will now run.
5 Check that the delivery pressure is as given in the Specifications.
6 Re-connect the relay and fuel line.

L-Jetronic

7 Disconnect the feed line from the delivery tube located on the inlet manifold, and hold it over a measuring glass.
8 Pull the pump relay from its socket on the side of the fusebox, then use a bridging wire to connect terminal 87b in the socket with battery positive. Run the pump for the specified time and check that it delivers the correct amount of fuel.
9 To check the fuel pressure, disconnect an injector feed line from the delivery tube and fit a pressure gauge and further line in place of the removed line. Clamp the line to the delivery tube.
10 Connect the bridging wire as described in paragraph 8 and check that the pressure is as given in the Specifications.
11 Re-connect the relay and fuel lines.

9 Fuel pump – removal and refitting

1 Chock the front wheels then jack up the rear of the car and support on axle stands.
2 The fuel pump is located on the right-hand side underbody.
3 Push back the caps where fitted unscrew the nuts, and disconnect the wires from the pump. If necessary identify the wires for position before removing them.
4 Using hose clamps, clamp the fuel pump inlet and fuel filter outlet hoses.
5 On K-Jetronic models, loosen the clips then disconnect the inlet hose from the pump and the fuel hose from the pipe. Remove the guard, then unscrew the union nuts and disconnect the fuel line. Unbolt the strap and withdraw the fuel filter together with its holder.
6 On L-Jetronic and Motronic models, loosen the two clips and disconnect the hoses from the pump and filter. Unscrew the bracket nuts and bolt and withdraw the fuel pump together with the filter from the underbody. Unbolt the clamp. Disconnect the hose and remove the rubber ring from the filter. Disconnect the hose from the pump and remove the mounting rubber.
7 Refitting is a reversal of removal, but where the filter has been removed make sure that it is refitted the correct way round so that the flow marks point in the correct direction.

10 Fuel gauge sender unit – removal and refitting

1 Working inside the boot, remove the carpet then unscrew the screws and remove the cover from over the fuel gauge sender unit (photo).
2 Disconnect the hoses and wiring plug (photo).
3 Using two crossed screwdrivers, turn the fuel gauge sender unit

10.1 Removing the fuel gauge sender unit cover

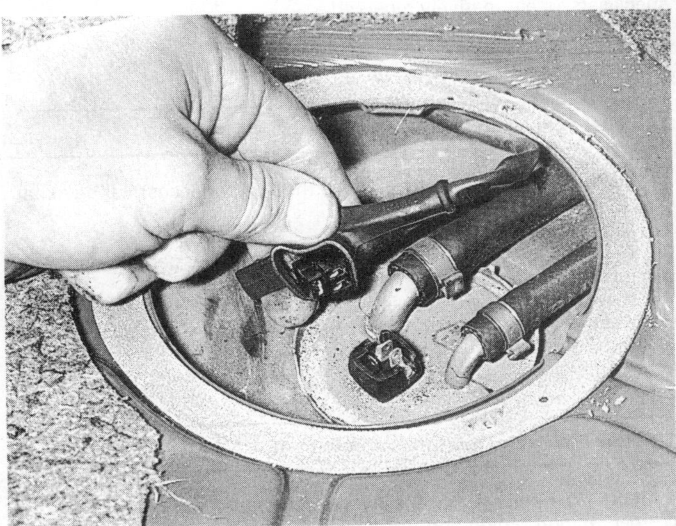

10.2 Disconnecting the fuel gauge sender unit wiring plug

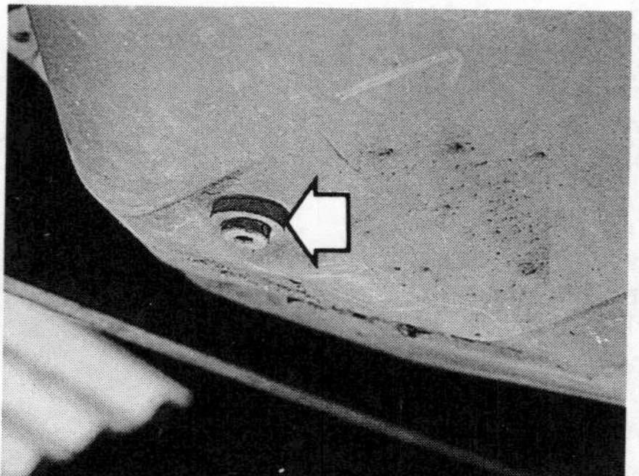
11.2 Fuel tank drain plug (arrowed)

11.8A Fuel tank side mounting bolt (arrowed) ...

11.8B ... and front mounting bolt

anti-clockwise then withdraw it from the tank. Recover the cord seal.
4 If the old unit is to be refitted, clean the filter screen in the bottom of the tube.
5 Refitting is a reversal of removal, but fit a new cord seal smeared with a little petroleum jelly – the seal will expand in contact with the fuel, thus ensuring a perfect joint. If a new seal is being fitted, remove the temporary spring clip before fitting it.

11 Fuel tank – removal, repair and refitting

1 Chock the front wheels then jack up the rear of the car and support on axle stands.
2 Remove the filler cap. Drain the fuel tank by syphoning or by unscrewing the plug where fitted (photo).
3 Remove the rubber cover from the filler neck and disconnect the vent hoses.
4 Working inside the boot, remove the carpet then unscrew the screws and remove the cover from over the fuel gauge sender unit.
5 Disconnect the hoses and wiring plug.
6 Unhook the exhaust system rear mountings then lower the exhaust and support it on an axle stand.
7 Support the weight of the tank on a trolley jack.
8 Unscrew the mounting bolts (photo), remove the retaining strap and lower the tank to the floor.
9 If the tank is to be renewed, remove the fuel gauge sender unit and fit it to the new unit with reference to Section 10. The rubber packing should be fitted to the top of the new tank using suitable adhesive.
10 If the tank is contaminated with sediment or water, remove the gauge sender unit as described in Section 10 and swill the tank out with clean fuel. If the tank is damaged or leaks, it should be repaired by specialists, or alternatively renewed.
11 Refitting is a reversal of removal.

12 Fuel expansion tank – removal and refitting

1 Working inside the boot, remove the trim for access to the expansion tank.
2 Disconnect the hoses.
3 Unscrew the mounting bolt, withdraw the expansion tank, and disconnect the hose.
4 If necessary clean or repair the tank with reference to Section 11.
5 Refitting is a reversal of removal but make sure that the tab is located in the mounting bracket.

13 Idle speed and mixture – adjustment

Note: *The engine should be at normal operating temperature, with correct ignition timing and valve clearances. The air filter should be in good condition and all electrical components should be switched off.*

K-Jetronic

1 Start the engine and allow it to idle.
2 Connect a tachometer to the engine.
3 Check that the idle speed is as given in Specifications. If not, remove the tamperproof cap from the throttle housing and turn the idle adjustment screw until the speed is correct (Fig. 3.11).
4 Connect an exhaust gas analyzer to the engine. BMW technicians use a special tester with two probes connected into the front and rear exhaust manifolds. There are two plugs on the manifolds for this purpose.
5 Run the engine at idle speed and check that the CO reading is as specified in the Specifications.

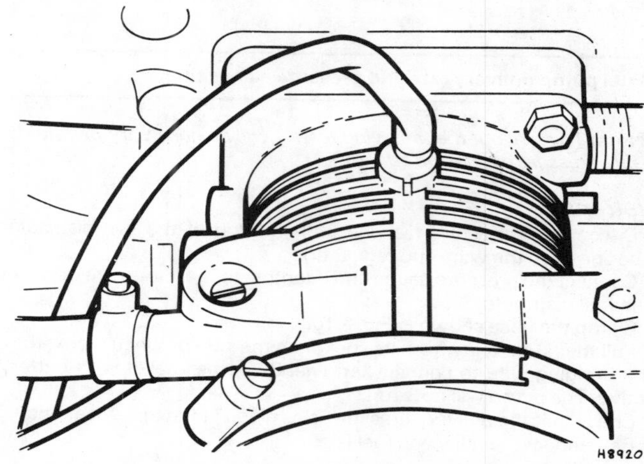

Fig. 3.11 Idle speed screw (1) – K-Jetronic (Sec 13)

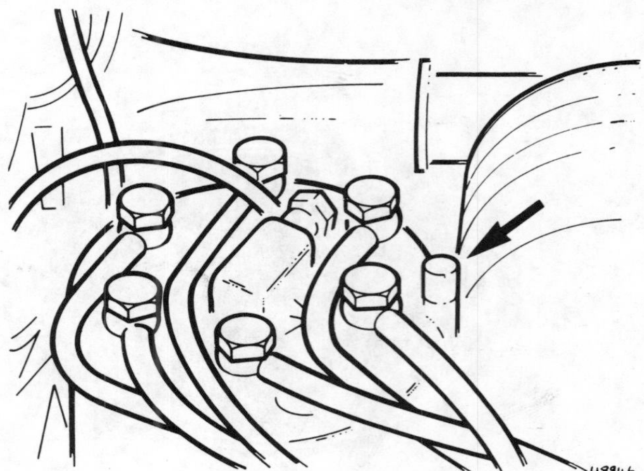

Fig. 3.12 Tamperproof cap (arrowed) – K-Jetronic (Sec 13)

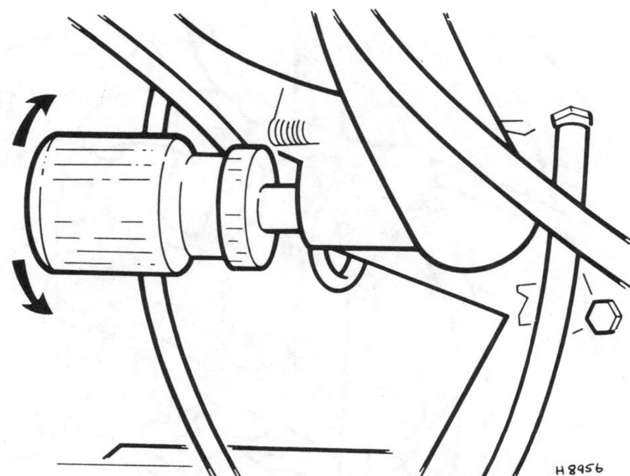

Fig. 3.13 Idle speed screw adjustment – L-Jetronic (Sec 13)

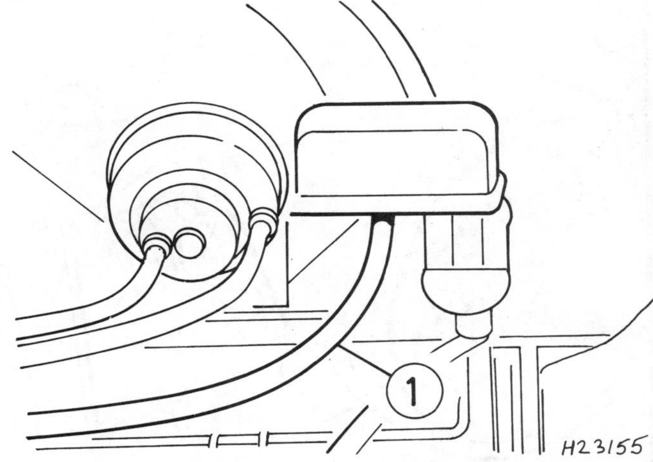

Fig. 3.14 Pull off vacuum hose (1) and check that the CO level rises (Sec 13)

13.13 Adjusting the idle mixture (Motronic)

6 If adjustment is necessary, remove the tamperproof cap (Fig. 3.12) from the fuel distributor and use the special wrench (tool number 13 0 010) to turn the mixture adjustment screw. Turn the wrench clockwise to richen the mixture and anti-clockwise to weaken it. After making an adjustment, remove the wrench and briefly accelerate the engine before checking the setting again.
7 Refit the plugs and disconnect the exhaust gas analyzer.

L-Jetronic

8 The procedure is similar to that described in paragraphs 1 to 7, except that the mixture control screw is located on the airflow sensor and the special tool (number 13 1 060) must be used to make any adjustments.
9 Before disconnecting the exhaust gas analyzer, pull off and plug the vacuum hose shown in Fig. 3.14 and check that the CO level rises by approximately 2.5%.

Motronic

10 On models fitted with an electronic rotary idle adjuster, it is not possible to adjust the idle speed manually as the rotary idle adjuster is controlled by the electronic control unit. If the idle speed is not within the specified range with the engine at normal operating temperature, check for a leak in the air inlet system and also check the operation of the idle rotary adjuster.
11 On models fitted with the vacuum-operated type of idle adjuster, run the engine to normal operating temperature then check the idle speed with a tachometer. If adjustment is required, turn the screw located on the adjuster body as necessary. To check the fast idle speed, disconnect and plug the vacuum hose. If adjustment is required, loosen the locknut and turn the temperature operating motor on the opposite end of the adjuster.
12 Connect an exhaust gas analyzer to the engine. Run the engine at idle speed and check that the CO reading is as specified in the Specifications.
13 If adjustment is required, prise out the tamperproof plug from the airflow sensor and use an Allen key to set the CO content (photo). Fit a new tamperproof plug on completion.

14 Fuel injection components – adjustments and checks

Basic throttle setting (K and L-Jetronic and Motronic)

1 Remove the air intake duct and disconnect the accelerator cable.
2 Referring to Fig. 3.15, release the nut (1) and screw (2) until the stop (3) is just free (photo).
3 Tighten the screw through a further half-turn and tighten the locknut.
4 Adjust the accelerator cable as described in Section 4.
5 If the throttle housing is removed, the above setting may be made using a feeler blade. First loosen the screw, then slide a 0.05 mm feeler blade between the throttle and the housing in the area of the bore for the vacuum advance ignition control. Tighten the screw until the throttle just starts to lift off the feeler blade, then tighten the locknut. Make sure that the vacuum advance holes in the bore are not completely covered by the throttle after making the adjustment.

Throttle bypass valve (K-Jetronic)

6 Pull the plug from the warm-up regulator (Fig. 3.16).
7 Disconnect both hoses from the bypass valve.
8 If the engine is cold, the air valve should be half open. Switch on the ignition and operate the starter. Check that current is present at the pin of the plug which is connected to the green/yellow wire.
9 Reconnect the plug and the two hoses, and the plug to the regulator. With the engine running, the air valve should close after five minutes. To check it, disconnect the hose on the inlet duct and blow air through. There should be no flow.

Mixture regulator/fuel distributor (K-Jetronic)

10 Detach the air inlet duct from the regulator and throttle housing (Fig. 3.17).
11 Pull the fuel pump relay (and diode relay where applicable) from the socket by the fusebox and connect a bridging wire between terminal 87 and battery positive (Fig. 3.18).
12 With the pump running, raise the baffle plate slowly using the hand or a magnet. Uniform resistance should be felt over the entire distance.
13 Lower the plate slowly then pull it up again immediately. Resistance should be felt immediately without any free play.
14 The baffle plate should be flush with the start of the tapered

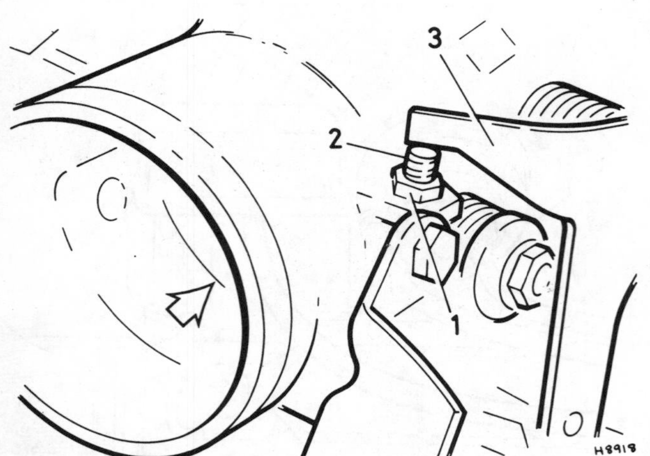

Fig. 3.15 Basic throttle butterfly setting – K-Jetronic (Sec 14)

1 Locknut
2 Screw
3 Stop
Throttle butterfly arrowed

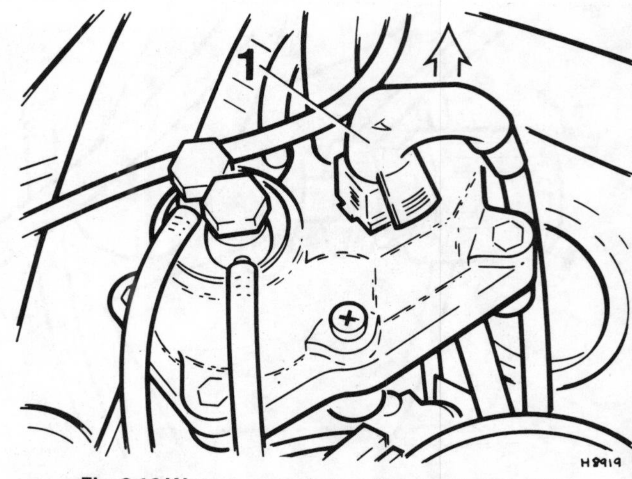

Fig. 3.16 Warm-up regulator – K-Jetronic (Sec 14)

Pull off the plug (1) in the direction arrowed

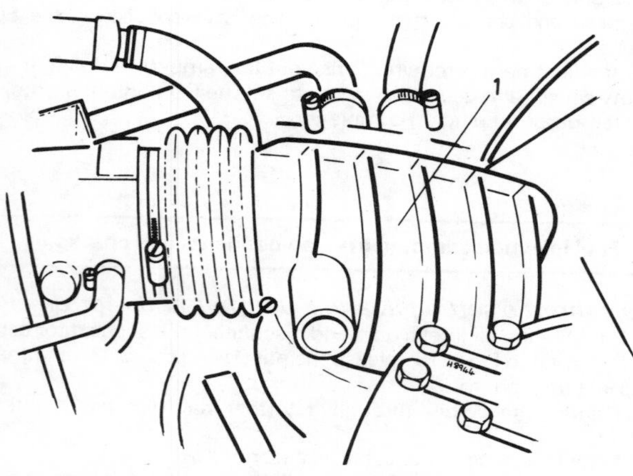

Fig. 3.17 Air intake duct (1) – K-Jetronic (Sec 14)

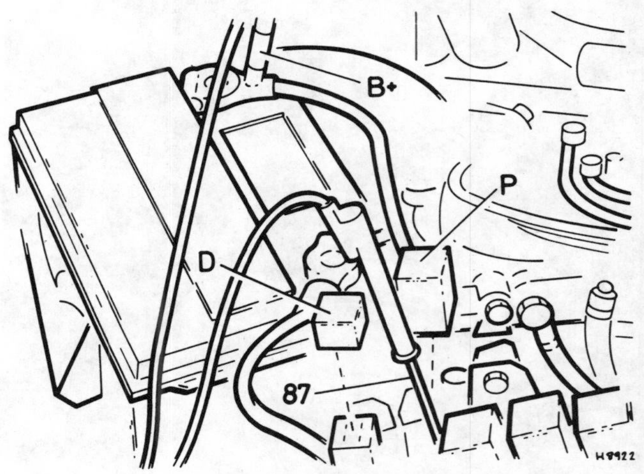

Fig. 3.18 Running the fuel pump (Sec 14)

B + Battery positive terminal
D Diode delay
P Pump relay
87 Probe to contact

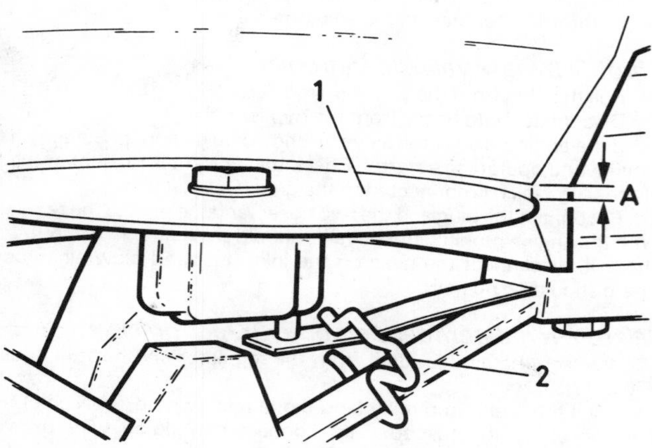

Fig. 3.19 Baffle plate (1) and shaped spring (2) – K-Jetronic (Sec 14)

A Maximum baffle plate depth

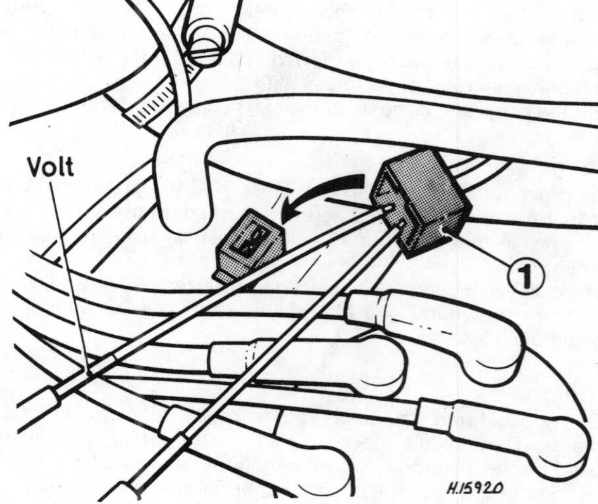

Fig. 3.20 Voltmeter connection to warm-up regulator plug (1) – K-Jetronic (Sec 14)

14.2 Throttle valve stop adjusting screw with tamperproof cap (arrowed)

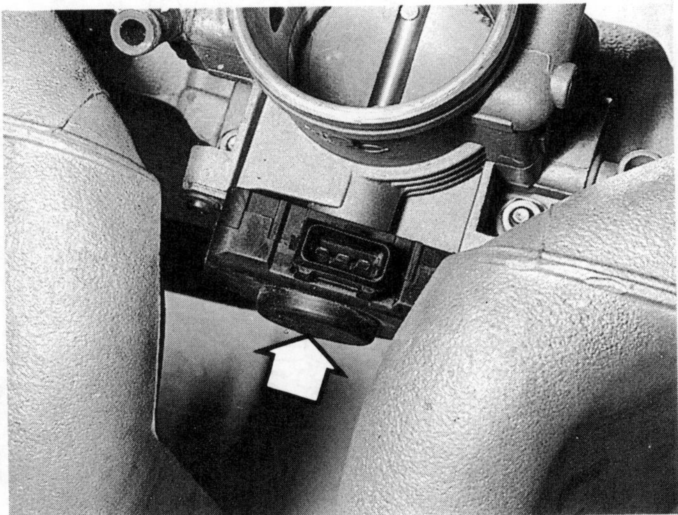

14.25 Throttle valve switch (arrowed)

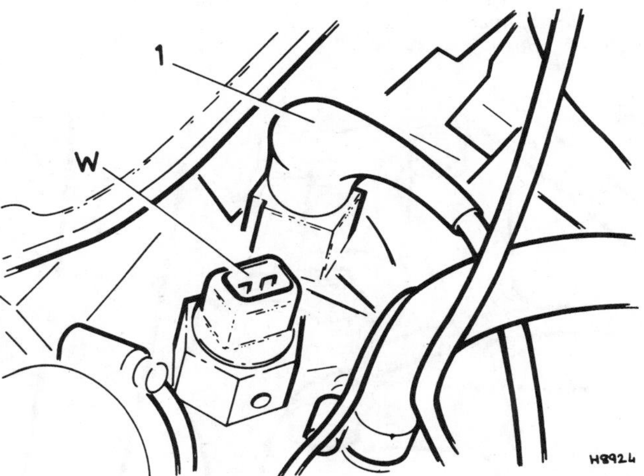

Fig. 3.21 Temperature time switch (Sec 14)

1 Plug *W Switch terminal*

section of the air venturi or at most 0.5 mm below. If necessary, remove the unit from the intermediate housing and bend the shaped spring (Fig. 3.19). If the baffle plate is too high the engine will run on, and if it is too low poor starting will result. The gap between the baffle plate and the venturi must also be uniform right around the plate. If necessary, loosen the screw and reposition the plate, then tighten the screw.

Cold start valve (K-Jetronic)

15 Remove the valve with the fuel line attached, and hold it over a measuring glass.

16 Connect bridging leads between the valve terminals, battery positive and earth.

17 Pull the fuel pump relay from the socket by the fusebox and connect a bridging wire between terminal 87 and battery positive. Check that the spray is even and that the injection rate is as given in Specifications.

18 Pull off the wires and dry the valve. No fuel must drip for a period of one minute.

19 The resistance of the internal windings may be checked if necessary by connecting an ohmmeter across the two terminals.

Warm-up regulator (K-Jetronic)

20 Pull the plug from the warm-up regulator, connect an ohmmeter to the heater windings, and check for an open circuit.

21 Connect a voltmeter to the regulator as shown in Fig. 3.20, then start the engine (which should be cold). Battery voltage should be present.

Temperature time switch (K and L-Jetronic)

22 This switch controls the opening of the cold start valve in relation to the coolant temperature.

23 Disconnect the plug and connect a testlamp between the battery positive and terminal W (Fig. 3.21). The switch should be on at coolant temperatures below 35°C and permanently off at higher temperatures.

24 To check the switch heater windings, disconnect the testlamp and use an ohmmeter to check the resistances between the terminals and earth as given in the Specifications.

Throttle switch (L-Jetronic and Motronic)

25 Disconnect the wiring plug from the throttle valve switch (photo).

26 Connect an ohmmeter between the centre terminal (18) and the outer terminal (2). With the throttle closed the reading should be zero ohms.

27 Connect the ohmmeter between the centre terminal (18) and the outer terminal (3). With the throttle fully open the reading should be zero ohms. If necessary loosen the screws and adjust the switch as required, then tighten the screws.

Fuel injectors

28 The fuel injectors may be checked in a similar manner to that described for the cold start valve in paragraphs 15 to 19, but it must be emphasized that adequate fire precautions be taken as there will be a very real danger of fire when fuel is being sprayed from the injectors. It will also be necessary to connect an extension line to the fuel delivery tube so that the tube and injectors can be held over a suitable container away from the engine during the test. If the correct extension cannot be obtained it is recommended that checking the fuel injectors is limited to testing their winding resistances with an ohmmeter.

15 Fuel injection components – removal and refitting

K-Jetronic

Mixture regulator/fuel distributor

1 Remove the air intake duct.

2 Unscrew the unions and disconnect the fuel lines from the fuel distributor (Fig. 3.22).

3 Unscrew the bolts and lift off the mixture regulator together with the fuel distributor.

4 Unscrew the three slotted screws and remove the fuel distributor.

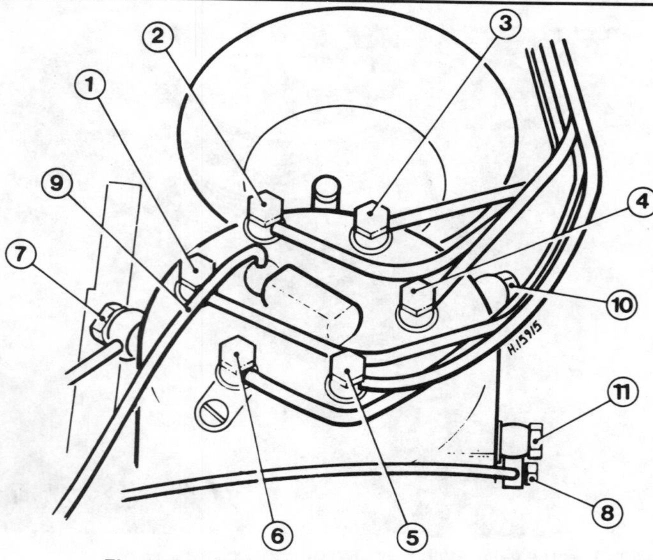

Fig. 3.22 Fuel distributor – K-Jetronic (Sec 15)

1 *Injector connection*
2 *Injector connection*
3 *Injector connection*
4 *Injector connection*
5 *Injector connection*
6 *Injector connection*
7 *Cold start valve connection*
8 *Warm-up regulator connection*
9 *Warm-up regulator connection*
10 *Fuel filter connection*
11 *Return hose connection*

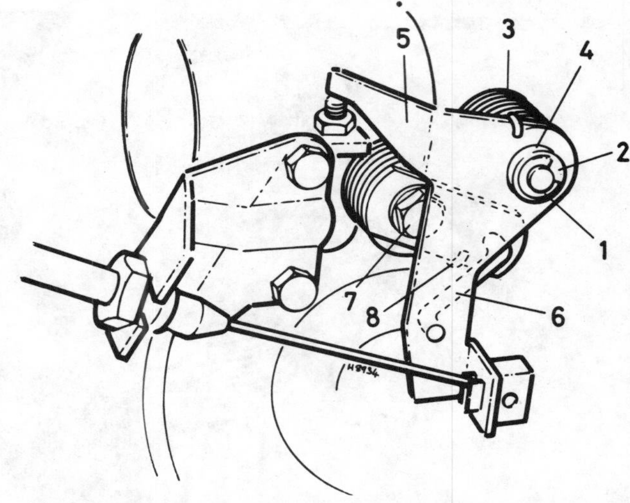

Fig. 3.23 Throttle butterfly connections – K-Jetronic (Sec 15)

1 *E-clip*
2 *Wave washer*
3 *Spring*
4 *Bush*
5 *Lever*
6 *Linkage*
7 *Nut*
8 *Spring*

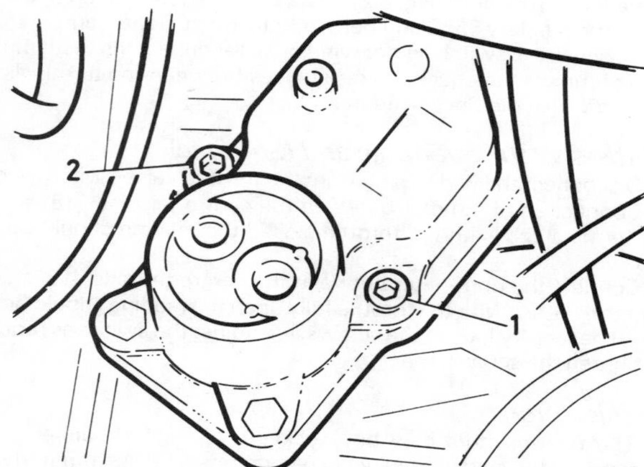

Fig. 3.24 Warm-up regulator fixing bolts (1 and 2) – K-Jetronic (Sec 15)

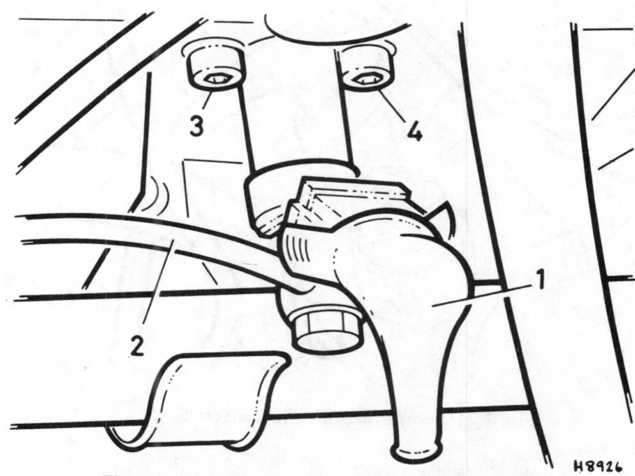

Fig. 3.25 Cold start valve – K-Jetronic (Sec 15)

1 *Plug*
2 *Fuel line*
3 *Retaining bolt*
4 *Retaining bolt*

5 Refitting is a reversal of removal, but use a new O-ring, gasket and new sealing washers. Adjust the idle speed and mixture on completion as described in Section 13.

Fuel injectors

6 Disconnect the valve cover breather hose and unscrew the injector pipe union nuts.

7 Pull out the injectors using a screwdriver to lever them out if necessary. Remove the rubber insulating sleeves.

8 Refitting is a reversal of removal, but smear a little petroleum jelly on the insulating sleeves before refitting the injectors.

Throttle butterfly return springs

9 Disconnect the accelerator cable.

10 Referring to Fig. 3.23, remove the circlip (1), wave washer (2) and unhook the spring end (3).

11 Remove the lever (5) and the bush (4).

12 Unscrew the nut and remove the linkage and springs.

13 Remove the lock washer, lever, sleeve and spring.

14 Reassembly is a reversal of dismantling, but adjust the throttle butterfly on completion as described in Section 14.

Warm-up regulator

15 Remove the fuel distributor cap, identify and disconnect the feed and return lines, and remove the vacuum hose and plug from the regulator.

16 Unscrew the bolts (1 and 2 in Fig. 3.24) and remove the warm-up regulator.

17 Refitting is a reversal of removal.

Cold start valve

18 Disconnect the wiring plug and fuel line from the cold start valve (Fig. 3.25).

19 Unscrew the socket-headed bolts and pull out the cold start valve. Remove the O-ring seal.

20 Refitting is a reversal of removal, but renew the O-ring seal (Fig. 3.26).

Throttle housing

21 Remove the intake duct and then pull off the white and black vacuum hoses.

22 Disconnect and plug the coolant hoses (engine cold).

23 Disconnect the accelerator cable with reference to Section 4.

24 Unscrew the mounting nuts and remove the throttle housing together with its gasket (photo).

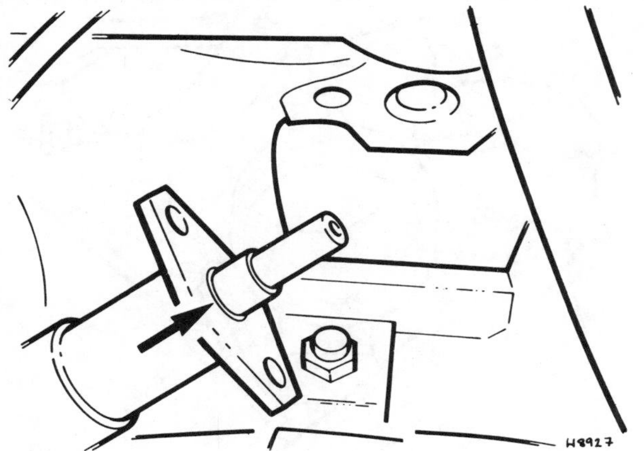

Fig. 3.26 Removing the cold start valve – K-Jetronic (Secs 14 and 15)

O-ring arrowed

Fig. 3.27 Throttle housing – K-Jetronic (Sec 15)

1 *Vacuum hose*
2 *Vacuum hose*
3 *Coolant hose*
4 *Coolant hose*

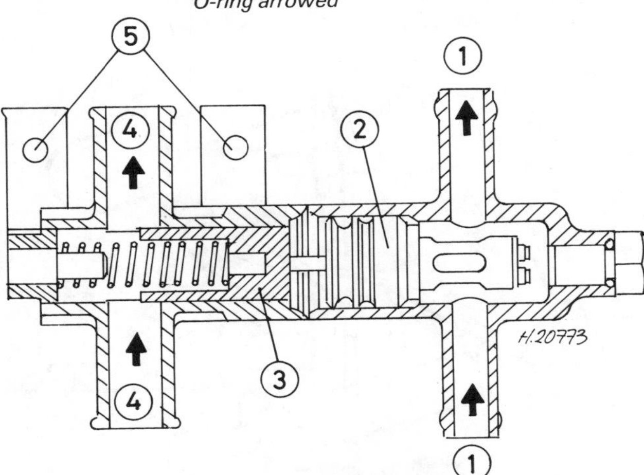

Fig. 3.28 Sectional view of the throttle bypass valve (Sec 15)

1 *Coolant connections*
2 *Expansion element*
3 *Piston*
4 *Auxiliary air connections*
5 *Mounting bars*

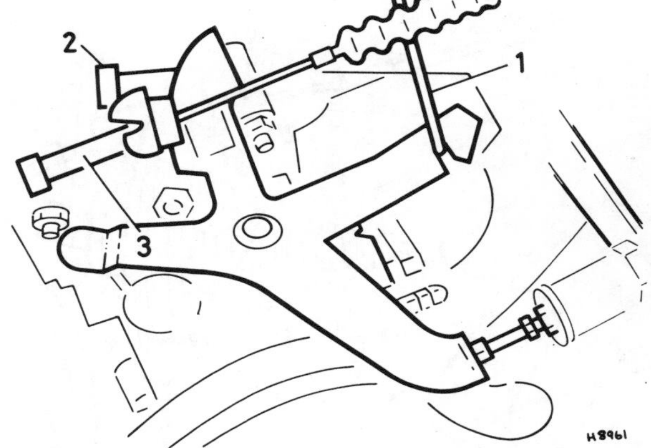

Fig. 3.29 Throttle housing cables – L-Jetronic (Sec 15)

1 *Automatic transmission*
2 *Accelerator*
3 *Cruise control*

25 Refitting is a reversal of removal, but fit a new gasket and adjust the accelerator cable as described in Section 4. Bleed the cooling system on completion as described in Chapter 2.

Throttle bypass valve

26 Disconnect the coolant hoses, engine cold (Fig. 3.28).
27 Disconnect the air hoses from the unit.
28 Disconnect the mounting rubbers and remove the valve.
29 Refitting is a reversal of removal but bleed the cooling system with reference to Chapter 2.

L-Jetronic

Fuel pressure regulator

30 Position a suitable container beneath the regulator, then disconnect the fuel hose and vacuum hose (photo).
31 Unscrew the bolts and pull the regulator from the fuel delivery tube (photo). Remove the O-ring seal.
32 Refitting is a reversal of removal, but renew the O-ring seal. If a new regulator is being fitted, make sure that its code is correct for the engine.

15.24 Throttle housing

15.30 Fuel hose connection to the pressure regulator

15.31 Fuel pressure regulator (arrowed)

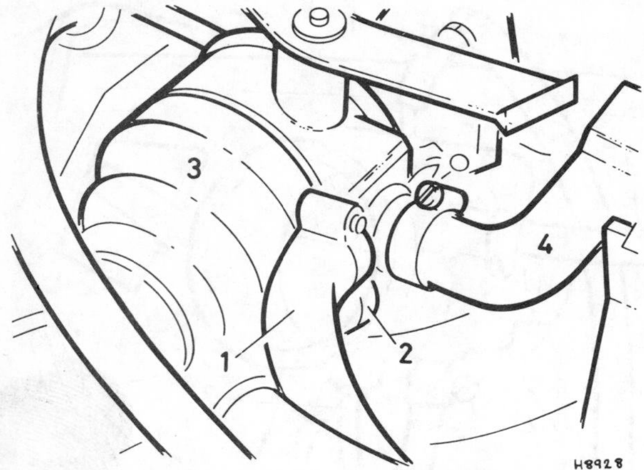

Fig. 3.30 Throttle housing hoses – L-Jetronic (Sec 15)

1 Coolant
2 Coolant
3 Air
4 Air

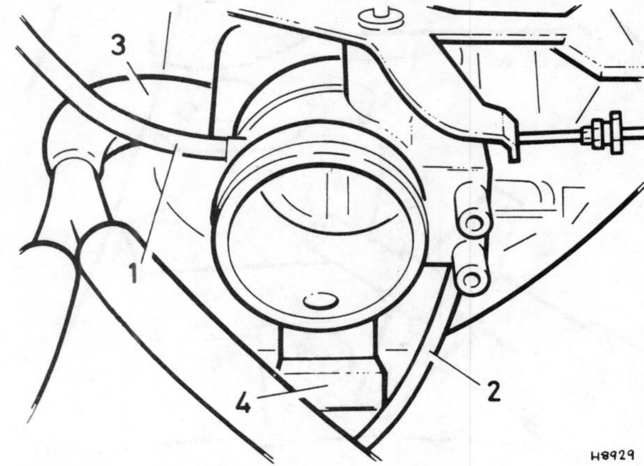

Fig. 3.31 Throttle housing connections – L-Jetronic (Sec 15)

1 Vacuum hose
2 Vacuum hose
3 Air hose
4 Plug

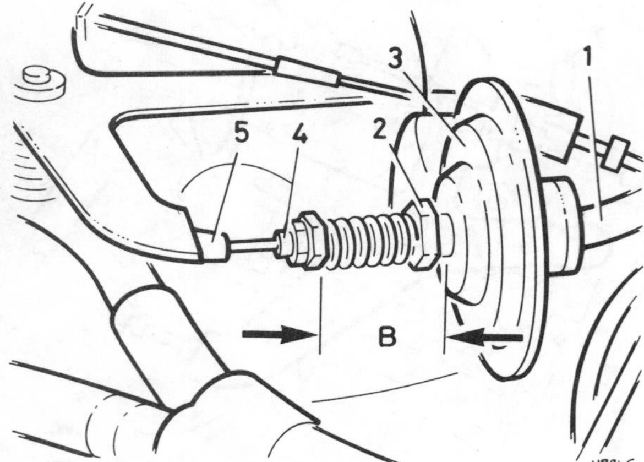

Fig. 3.32 Throttle vacuum control – L-Jetronic (Sec 15)

B Setting dimension
1 Hose
2 Nut
3 Vacuum control
4 Screw
5 Screw

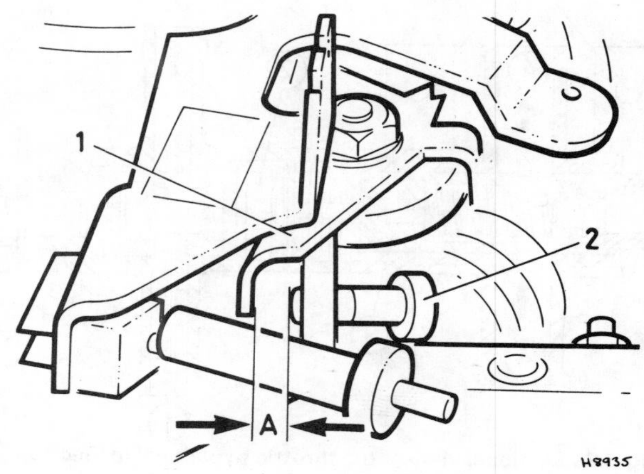

Fig. 3.33 Throttle vacuum control – L-Jetronic (Sec 15)

A Setting dimension
1 Control lever
2 Stop screw

Throttle housing

33 Referring to Fig. 3.29, disconnect the cables (1, 2 or 3) as applicable.

34 Referring to Fig. 3.30, disconnect and plug the coolant hoses, with the engine cold (photos).

35 Disconnect the vacuum and air hoses.

36 Referring to Fig. 3.31, disconnect the vacuum hoses (1 and 2), the air hose (3) and pull off the multi-pin plug (4) (photos).

37 Unscrew the mounting nuts and remove the throttle housing. Do not remove the throttle switch unless a new housing is being fitted otherwise it will have to be adjusted.

38 Refitting is a reversal of removal but use a new gasket and bleed the cooling system as described in Chapter 2. Finally adjust the cables.

Throttle vacuum control

39 Referring to Fig. 3.32, pull of the hose (1), release the nut (2) and remove the vacuum control (3).

40 When refitting, adjust dimension (B) to 33 ± 0.3 mm using screw (4).

41 Referring to Fig. 3.33, adjust the dimension (A) to 2.8 ± 0.2 mm

Control unit

42 Open the glovebox and pull the pins from the retaining straps. Remove the cover.

43 With the ignition switched off, depress the retainer and pull out the multi-pin plug. Note which way round the plug is fitted for correct refitting.

44 Unbolt and remove the control unit (photo).

45 Refitting is a reversal of removal, but make sure that the multi-pin plug is fitted correctly and finally adjust the idle speed and mixture with reference to Section 13.

Airflow sensor

46 Release the clamp and disconnect the duct from the airflow sensor to the throttle housing.

47 Remove the air cleaner as described in Section 3.

48 Disconnect the multi-pin plug, unscrew the fixing nuts and withdraw the airflow sensor from the mounting bracket or air cleaner as applicable (photo). Remove the gasket/seal (Fig. 3.34) and also remove the rubber mountings where applicable.

49 Refitting is a reversal of removal. Renew the seal and mountings if necessary. Finally adjust the engine idle speed and mixture as described in Section 13.

Temperature time switch

50 The temperature time switch is located on the thermostat housing (photo). Pull off the plug (Fig. 3.35) and unscrew and remove the switch.

51 Refit the switch using a new sealing washer.

Coolant temperature sensor

52 Pull off the plug (Fig. 3.36) and unscrew the sensor. Refit using a new sealing washer.

Cold start valve

53 Referring to Fig. 3.37, pull of the plug (1) and disconnect the fuel line (2).

54 Unscrew the mounting bolts (3 and 4) and withdraw the valve.

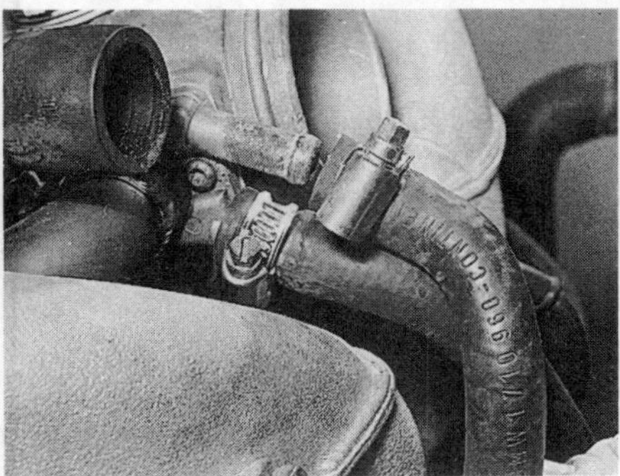
15.34A Disconnecting the upper coolant hose ...

15.34B ... and lower coolant hose from the throttle housing

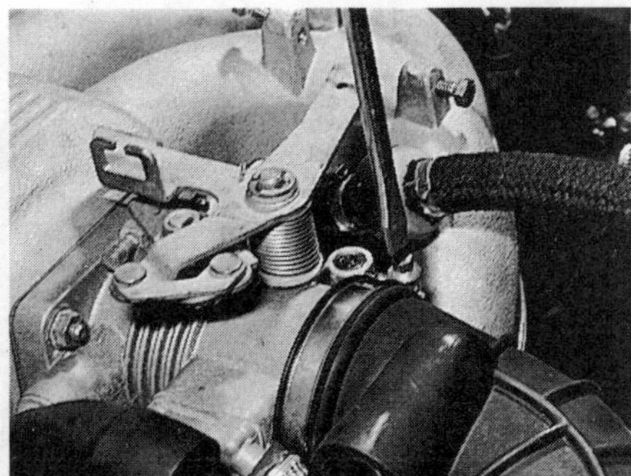
15.36A Disconnecting the air duct ...

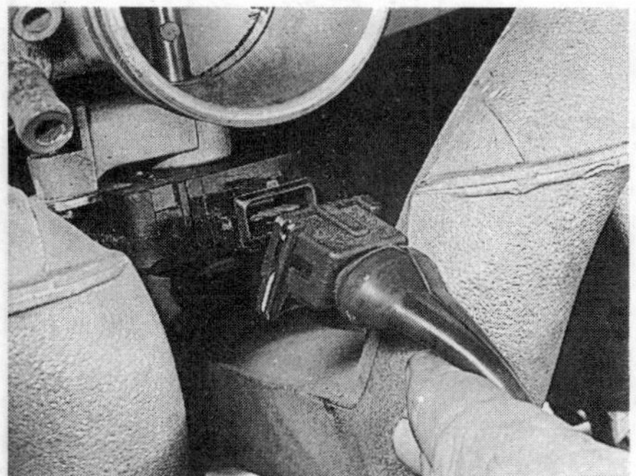
15.36B ... and throttle switch plug

15.44 Control unit located behind the glovebox

15.48 Airflow sensor to air cleaner mounting nuts (Motronic)

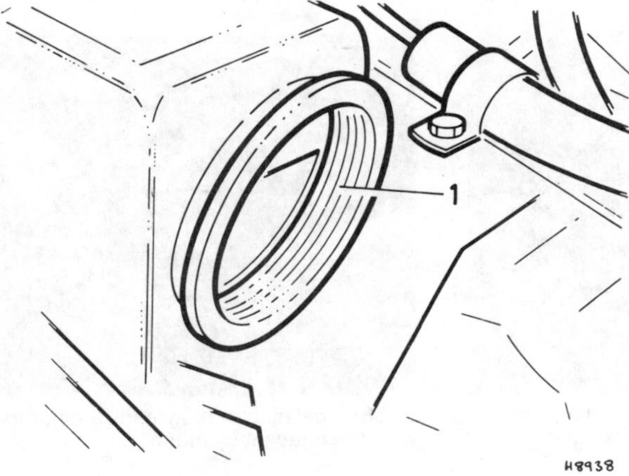

Fig. 3.34 Airflow sensor seal (1) – L-Jetronic (Sec 15)

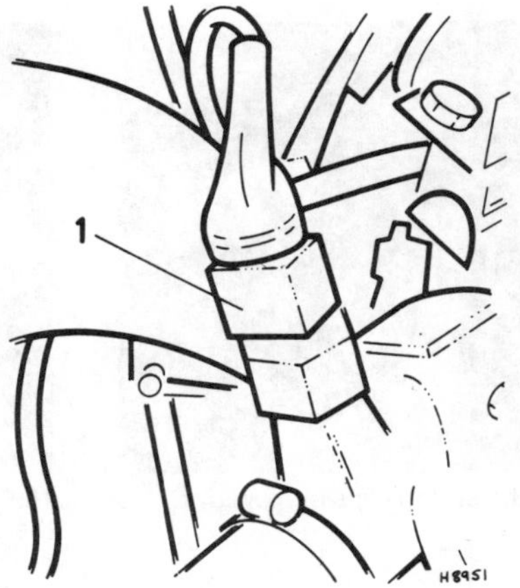

Fig. 3.35 Temperature time switch – L-Jetronic (Sec 15)

1 Plug

55 Fit a new seal when refitting.

Fuel injectors

56 Unscrew the four fuel delivery tube bolts, then push the tube upwards until the fuel injectors have cleared the guide in the inlet manifold. Disconnect the pressure regulator fuel and vacuum hoses and withdraw the assembly from the inlet manifold (photos). If necessary for additional working room, remove the inlet manifold support bracket from the valve cover and manifold.

57 Pull off the plug (Fig. 3.38) and extract the spring clips. Pull the injectors from the delivery tube. Remove the O-ring seals and the plastic washers (photo).

58 When refitting the injectors it is easier to fit them into the inlet manifold first, then press the delivery tube onto them, press on the spring clips and connect the plugs. Note that the plug leads are numbered with the relevant cylinder. Use new O-ring seals and washers. Tighten the mounting bolts to the specified torque (photos).

Throttle shaft return springs

59 Disconnect the accelerator cable, and the automatic transmission and cruise control cables if applicable.

60 Remove the circlip (1), washer (2) and disconnect the linkage (3) on the lever (4) (photo).

61 Raise the lever and turn it to relieve the spring tension. Remove the lever.

62 Remove the spring.

63 Referring to Fig. 3.39, disconnect the spring (1) and unscrew the nut (2).

15.50 Temperature time switch (arrowed)

15.56A Fuel delivery tube mounting bolt (arrowed)

15.56B Vacuum hose connection to the pressure regulator

15.57 An injector

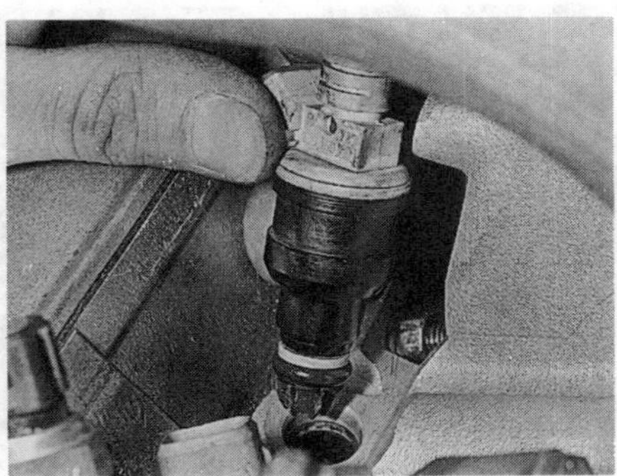
15.58A Insert the injectors ...

15.58B ... press on the delivery tube ...

15.58C ... refit the spring clips (arrowed) ...

15.58D ... reconnect the plugs, and tighten the delivery tube mounting bolts

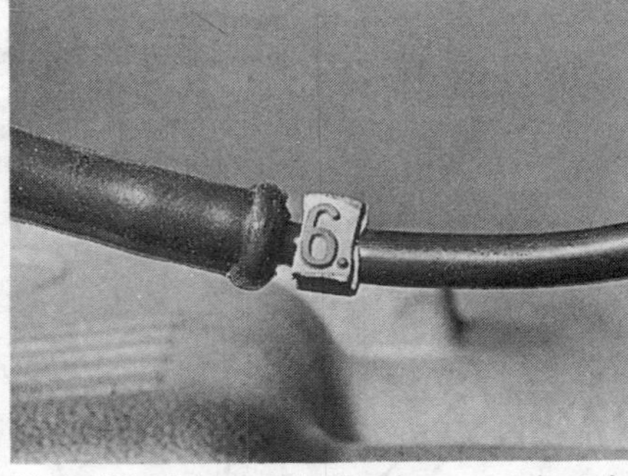

15.58E The injector plug leads are numbered with the relevant cylinder

64 Referring to Fig. 3.40, remove the washer (1) and lever (2).

65 Referring to Fig. 3.41, remove the sleeve (1) and spring (2). Also remove the wave washer.

66 Reassemble in the reverse order to dismantling and adjust in the following way. Pull off the tamperproof lock (1) and loosen the screw (2) until the lever (3) no longer rests on the screw (Fig. 3.42). Place a finger on the lever and tighten the screw until the lever just begins to move. Turn the screw a quarter-turn more and fit the tamperproof lock.

67 Adjust the kick-down cruise control and accelerator cables, as applicable, after reference to the appropriate Chapter.

Throttle bypass valve

68 Disconnect the air inlet duct from the throttle housing.

69 Disconnect and plug the coolant hoses, with the engine cold.

70 Disconnect the two air hoses.

71 Unscrew the mounting nuts and remove the bypass valve from its bracket.

72 Refitting is a reversal of removal, but first check that the dimension shown in Fig. 3.43 is as given in the Specifications.

Motronic

Idle control valve

73 Disconnect the air hoses (photo).

74 Pull off the vacuum hose from the vacuum controlled unit fitted up to September 1985.

75 Disconnect the wiring plug (photo).

76 Unbolt and remove the idle control valve, then disconnect it from the bracket (photo).

77 Refitting is a reversal of removal, but on models up to September 1985 adjust the engine idle speed as described in Section 13.

Fuel pressure regulator

78 Refer to paragraphs 30 to 32 inclusive.

Throttle housing

79 Refer to paragraphs 33 to 38 inclusive.

Throttle shaft return springs

80 Refer to paragraphs 59 to 67 inclusive.

Control unit

81 Refer to paragraphs 42 to 45, noting that on some models it may be necessary to unbolt an access plate.

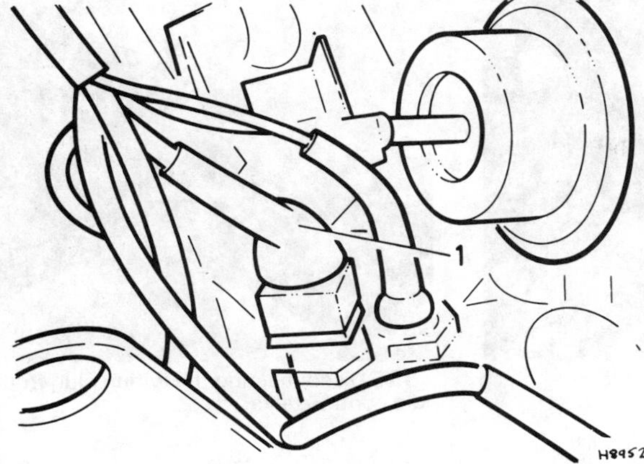

Fig. 3.36 Coolant temperature sensor – L-Jetronic (Sec 15)

1 Plug

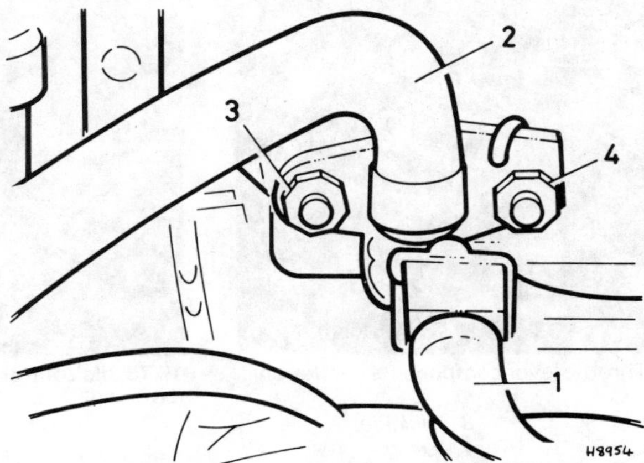

Fig. 3.37 Cold start valve – L-Jetronic (Sec 15)

1 Plug
2 Fuel line
3 Mounting bolt
4 Mounting bolt

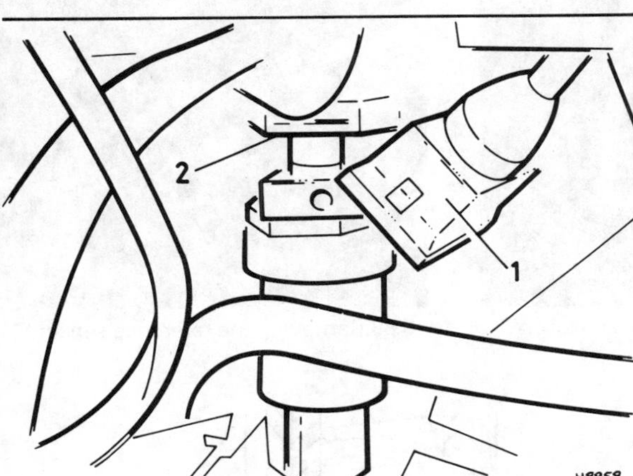

Fig. 3.38 Fuel injector plug (1) and circlip (2) – L-Jetronic (Sec 15)

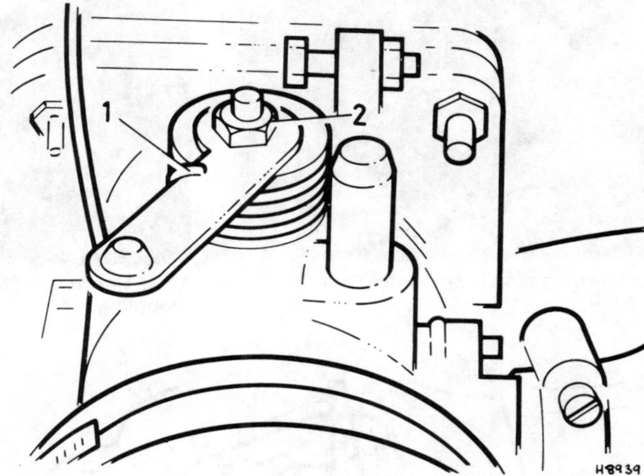

Fig. 3.39 Throttle shaft return spring (1) and nut (2) – L-Jetronic (Sec 15)

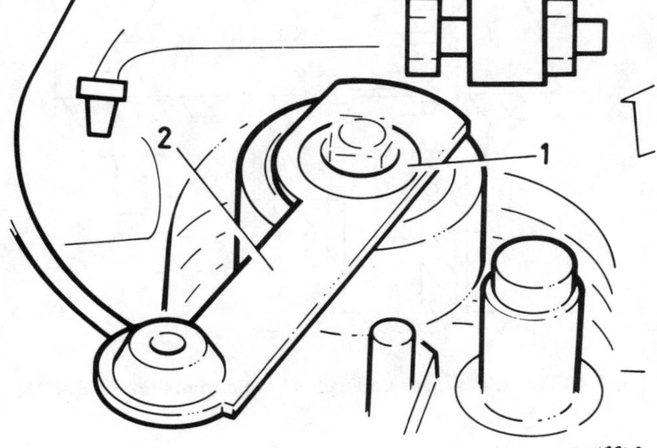

Fig. 3.40 Throttle shaft washer (1) and lever (2) – L-Jetronic (Sec 15)

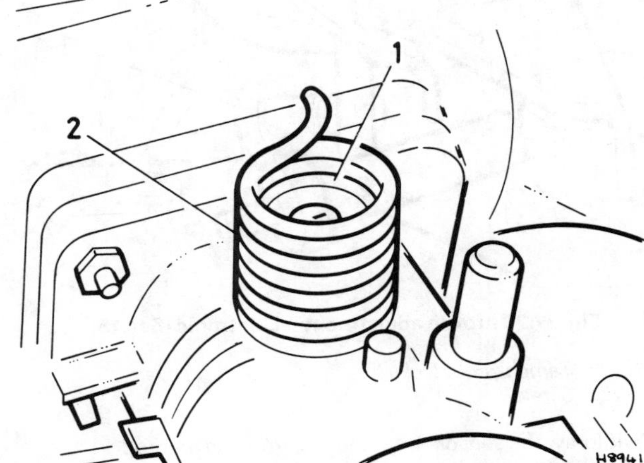

Fig. 3.41 Throttle shaft sleeve (1) and spring (2) – L-Jetronic (Sec 15)

Airflow sensor

82 Refer to paragraphs 46 to 49 inclusive.

Coolant temperature sensor

83 Refer to paragraph 52.

Fuel injectors

84 Refer to paragraphs 56 to 58 inclusive.

Reference and speed sensors

85 Apply the handbrake then jack up the front of the car and support on axle stands.

86 Disconnect the sensor wiring plugs located in the bracket on the left-hand side of the cylinder block.

87 Working beneath the car, note the location of each sensor then unscrew the mounting bolts using an Allen key (photo). The reference sensor with the grey cable tie attached to its lead is located in the bottom hole and the plug on the upper end of the lead is coloured grey.

15.60 Throttle lever components – L-Jetronic

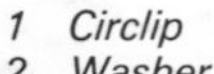

1 Circlip
2 Washer
3 Linkage
4 Lever

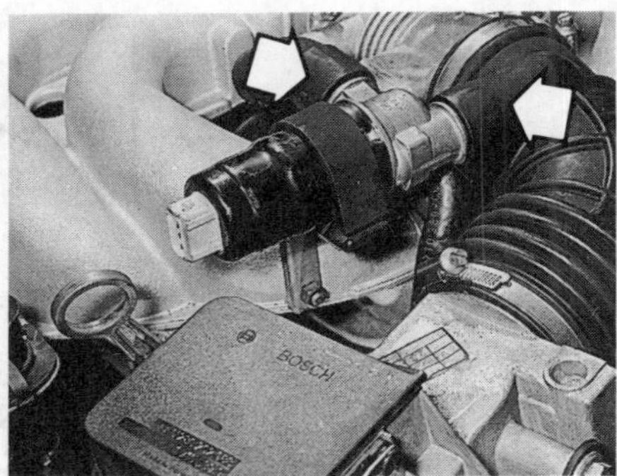

15.73 Idle control valve and air hoses (arrowed)

15.75 Disconnecting the wiring plug from the idle control valve

15.76 Idle control valve mounting nut (arrowed)

15.87 Unscrewing the reference sensor mounting bolt

15.88 Removing the reference sensor

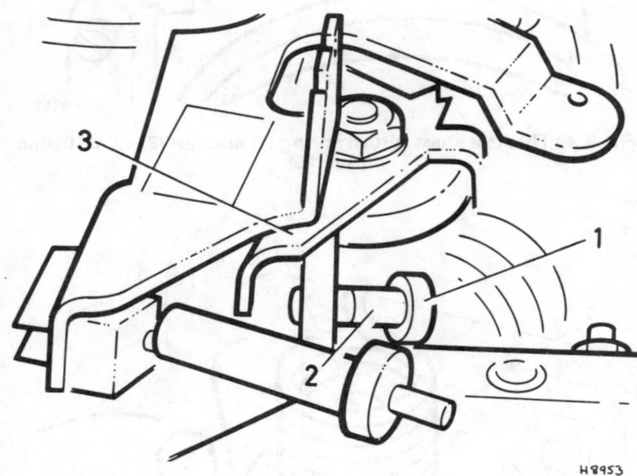

Fig. 3.42 Throttle adjustment – L-Jetronic (Sec 15)

1 *Tamperproof lock*
2 *Screw*
3 *Lever*

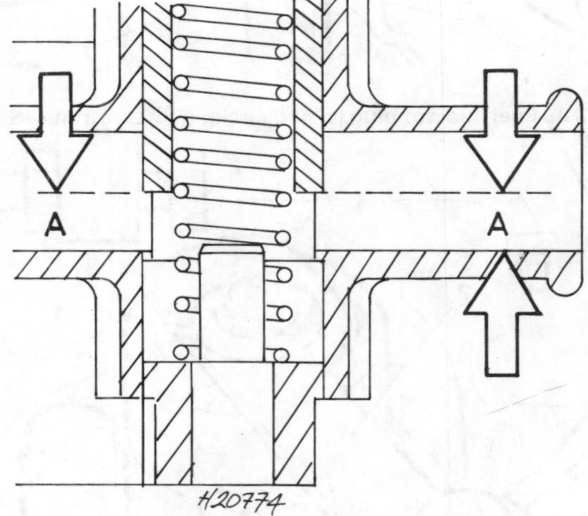

Fig. 3.43 Throttle bypass valve checking dimension (A) (Sec 15)

88 Withdraw the sensors from the transmission (photo).
89 Where applicable, transfer the protective sleeve and clips to the new sensor.
90 Refitting is a reversal of removal, but lightly grease the seal.

16 Inlet manifold – removal and refitting

1 Disconnect the battery negative lead.
2 Remove the throttle housing with reference to Section 15, but if there is no necessity to separate the two items, it may remain in position.
3 Remove the accelerator cable, kickdown and cruise control cables (where applicable) and bracket(s) from the inlet manifold with reference to Section 4 and Chapter 6. If necessary the kickdown cable (where applicable) and accelerator cable may be left attached to the bracket(s) (photos).
4 Remove the cold start valve or idle speed valve with reference to Section 15.
5 Remove the fuel injectors with reference to Section 15.
6 Disconnect the brake servo vacuum hose from the inlet manifold (photo).

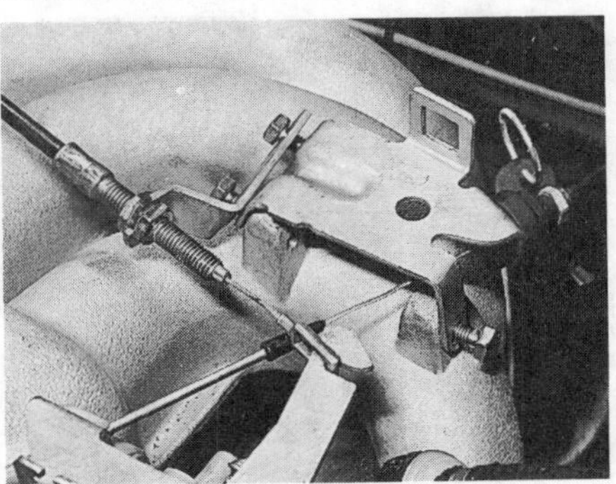
16.3A Removing the kickdown cable bracket from the inlet manifold

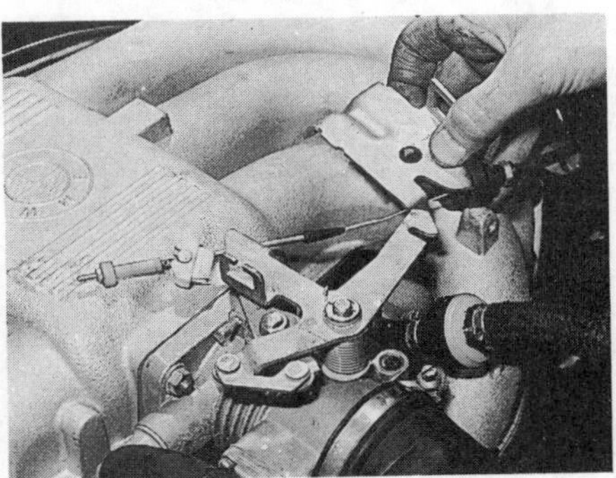
16.3B Removing the accelerator cable bracket from the inlet manifold

16.6 Disconnecting the brake servo vacuum hose from the inlet manifold

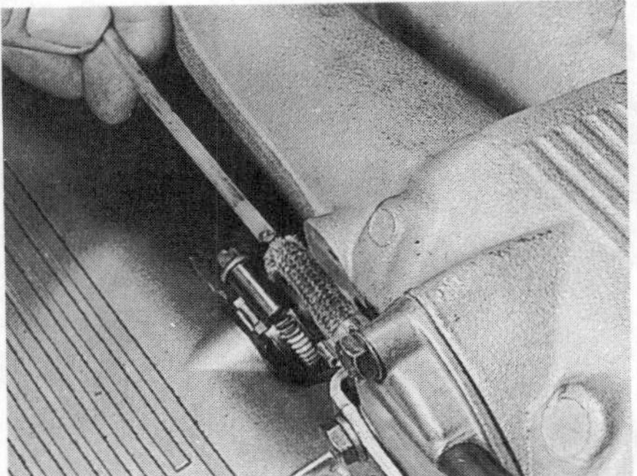
16.7 Disconnecting the vacuum take-off hoses

16.8A Diagnostic socket and bracket

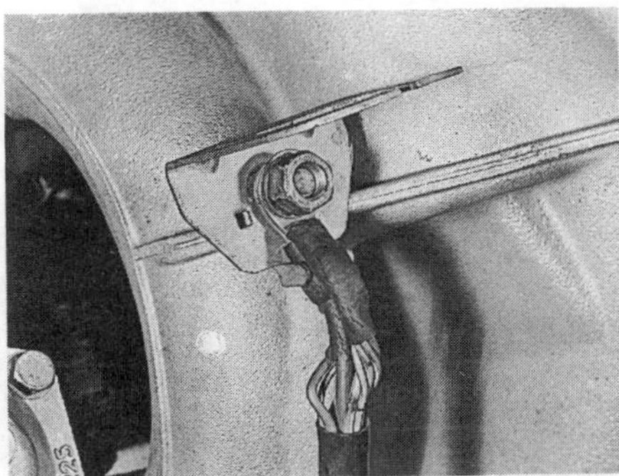
16.8B Removing the diagnostic socket bracket and earth cable

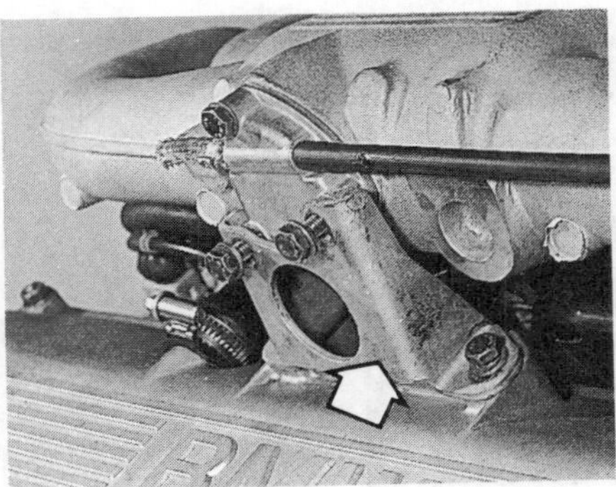
16.9 Removing the inlet manifold support bracket (arrowed)

16.10A Pull the crankcase ventilation tube from the inlet manifold ...

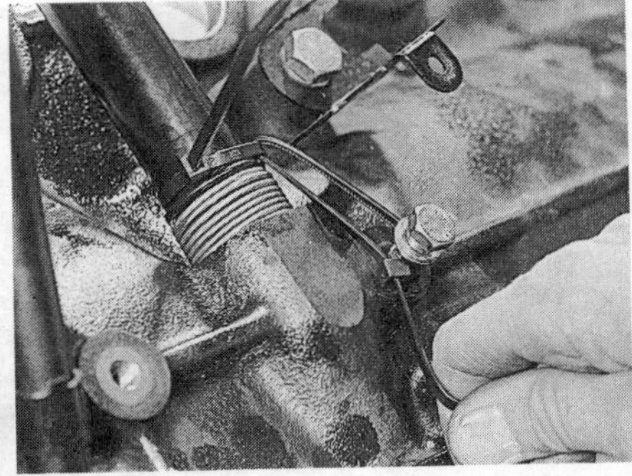
16.10B ... and hold it down with a plastic cable tie

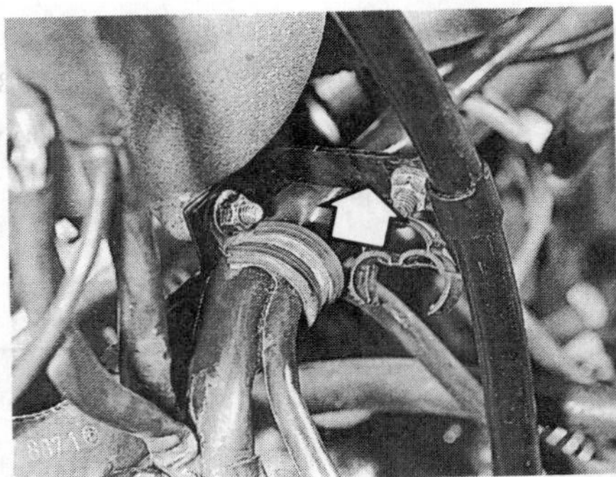
16.11A Bracket holding the wiring harness and engine oil dipstick tube to the front of the inlet manifold (arrowed)

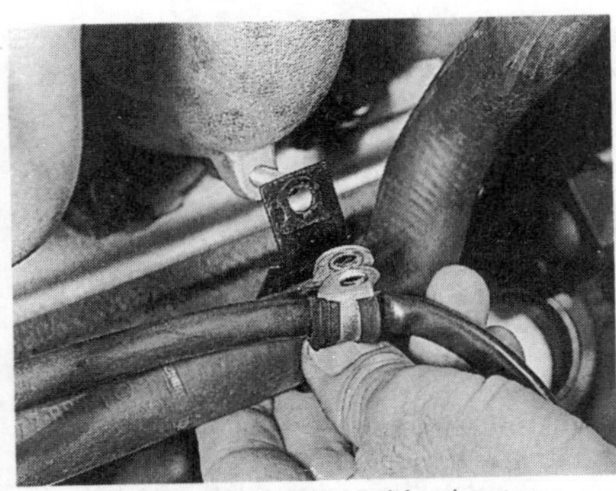
16.11B Disconnecting the wiring harness from the rear of the inlet manifold

16.12A Unscrew the mounting nuts ...

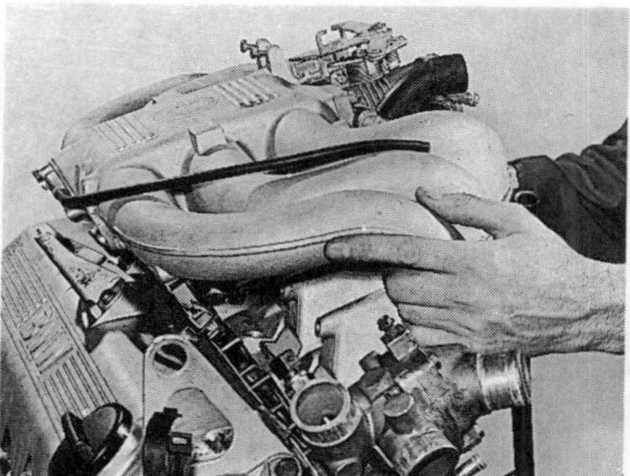
16.12B ... remove the inlet manifold ...

16.12C ... disconnect the crankcase ventilation hose ...

16.12D ... and remove the gaskets

16.13A Removing the crankcase ventilation tube and spring from the cylinder block

16.13B Vacuum take-off flange on the inlet manifold

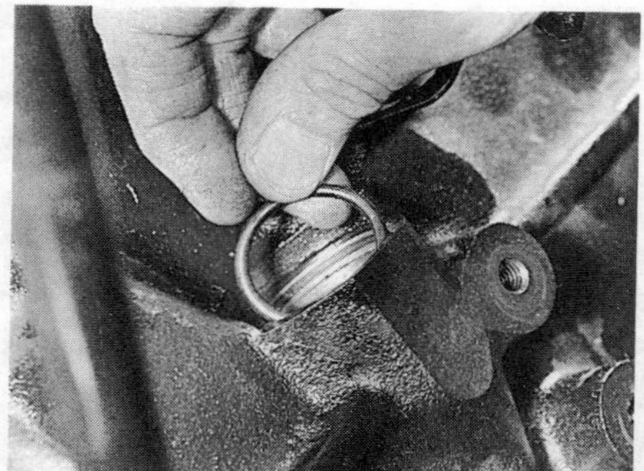
16.14A Locating a new ventilation tube O-ring in the cylinder block

16.14B Crankcase ventilation tube correctly located in the inlet manifold with a new O-ring

7 Disconnect the vacuum take-off hoses (photo).

8 Detach the diagnostic socket from the bracket on the inlet manifold, then unscrew the nut and disconnect the earth cable, and remove the bracket (photos).

9 Unbolt the bracket supporting the inlet manifold on the valve cover (photo).

10 Before removing the inlet manifold, pull the crankcase ventilation tube down from the underside of the manifold against the spring tension and hold it down using a plastic cable tie (photos).

11 Unscrew the nuts securing the wiring harness to the studs on the manifold. The engine oil level dipstick tube bracket may also be unbolted from the tube (photos).

12 Unscrew the mounting nuts and withdraw the inlet manifold from the cylinder head. At the same time disconnect the crankcase ventilation hose from the valve cover. Remove the gasket(s) (photos). It may be necessary to tilt the manifold in order to clear the thermostat housing cover on the B27 engine, or alternatively the cover may be removed.

13 If necessary, remove the crankcase ventilation tube and spring from the cylinder block and clean out any accumulated sediment. The vacuum take-off flange may also be unbolted from the manifold and the gasket renewed (photos).

14 Refitting is a reversal of removal, but fit new gaskets and also a new O-ring to the top and bottom of the ventilation tube (photos). On completion adjust the idle speed and mixture.

17 Exhaust manifold – removal and refitting

1 Apply the handbrake then jack up the front of the car and support on axle stands.

2 On early models unbolt the hot air shrouds from the top of the exhaust manifolds.

3 Unscrew the nuts securing the downpipes to the manifold. Lower the downpipes and support on axle stands. Remove the gasket(s) (photo).

17.3 Bottom flange of the exhaust manifold

17.4A Unscrew the mounting nuts ...

17.4B ... and remove the exhaust manifold

17.5 Removing the exhaust manifold gaskets and heat shield

4 Unscrew the nuts securing the manifold to the cylinder head, then withdraw the manifold from the studs (photos).
5 Remove the gasket(s) and where fitted the heat shield (photo).
6 If necessary on early models the two exhaust manifold halves may be disconnected by unscrewing the stud nuts. Separate the two halves and remove the collar and ring.
7 Clean the contact surfaces of the manifold and cylinder head.
8 Refitting is a reversal of removal, but fit new gaskets and tighten the nuts to the specified torque. On early models with two halves do not tighten the intermediate stud nuts until the main mounting nuts have been fully tightened.

18 Exhaust system – removal and refitting

1 Jack up the front and rear of the car and support on axle stands, or position the car over an inspection pit.
2 Unscrew the nuts securing the downpipes to the exhaust manifold, lower the downpipes and remove the gasket (photo).
3 Unscrew the two bolts securing the exhaust front support bracket to the transmission. Also unscrew the clamp bolt and detach the bracket from the exhaust system (photos).
4 Unscrew the two nuts and remove the clamp ring from the rear silencer (photo). Alteratively, just loosen one and remove the other so that the ring can be swivelled to one side.
5 Unhook the rubber suspension rings and lower the exhaust system to the ground (photos).
6 Separate the front and rear sections by unscrewing the flange nuts and removing the sealing rings (photos).

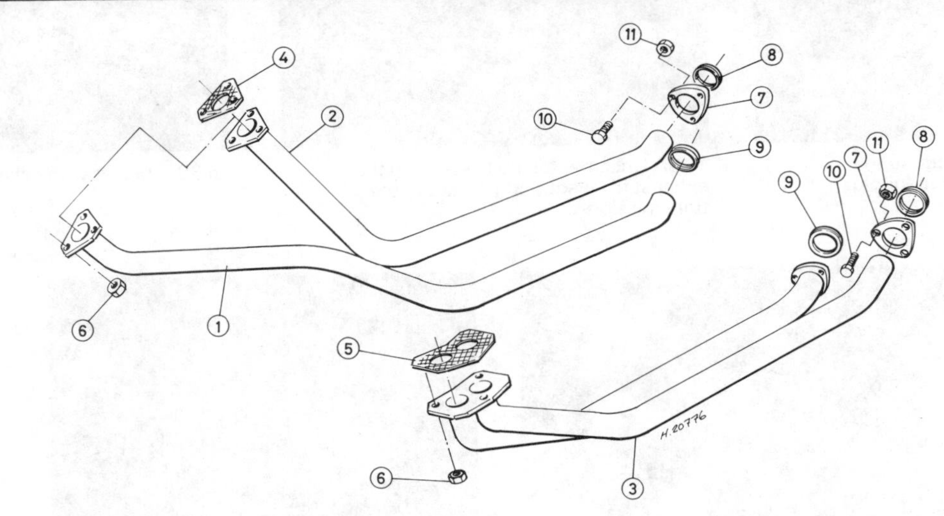

Fig. 3.44 Exhaust system downpipes (Sec 18)

1 *Early lower downpipe for 520i*
2 *Early upper downpipe for 520i*
3 *Later downpipe assembly for 520i and 525e*
4 *Early gasket*
5 *Later gasket*
6 *Nut*
7 *Flange*
8 *Sealing ring*
9 *Sealing ring*
10 *Bolt*
11 *Nut*

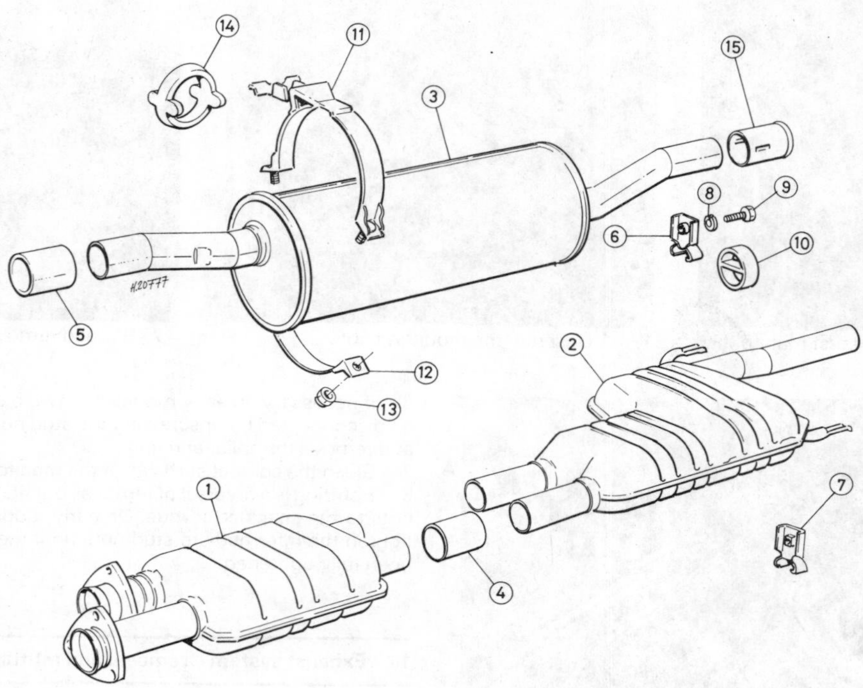

Fig. 3.45 Exhaust silencer components (Sec 18)

1 *Front silencer*
2 *Intermediate silencer*
3 *Rear silencer*
4 *Sleeve*
5 *Sleeve*
6 *Bracket*
7 *Bracket*
8 *Flat washer*
9 *Bolt*
10 *Suspension rubber ring*
11 *Upper clamp ring*
12 *Lower clamp ring*
13 *Nut*
14 *Suspension rubber ring*
15 *Chrome extension*

18.2 Unscrew the nuts securing the downpipes to the exhaust manifold

18.3A Unscrew the bolts securing the exhaust front support bracket to the transmission ...

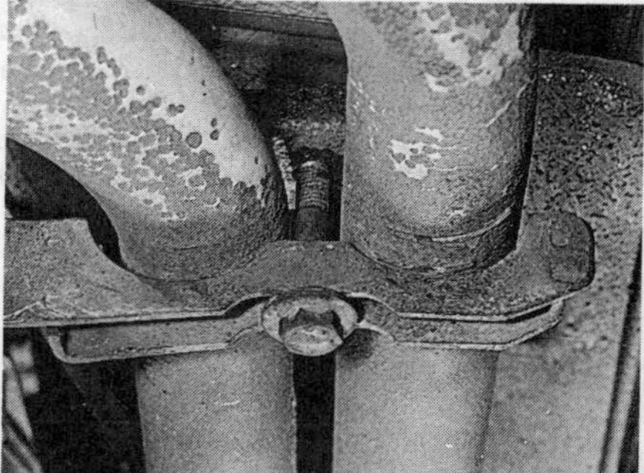
18.3B ... unscrew the clamp bolt ...

18.3C ... and detach the bracket

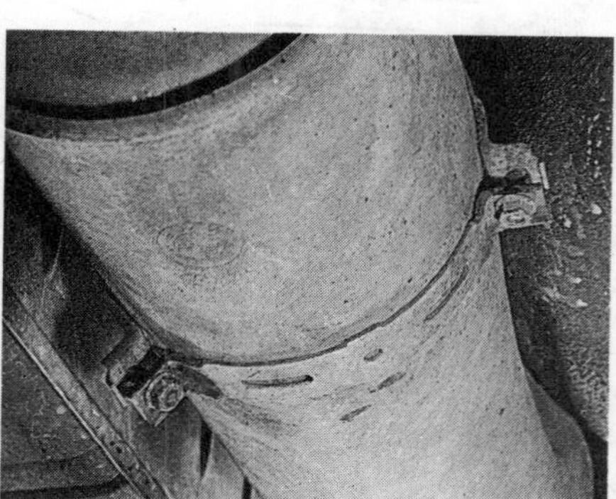
18.4 Rear silencer clamp ring

18.5A Front view of the rubber suspension rings (arrowed) supporting the front silencer

18.5B Close-up of a front silencer rubber suspension ring

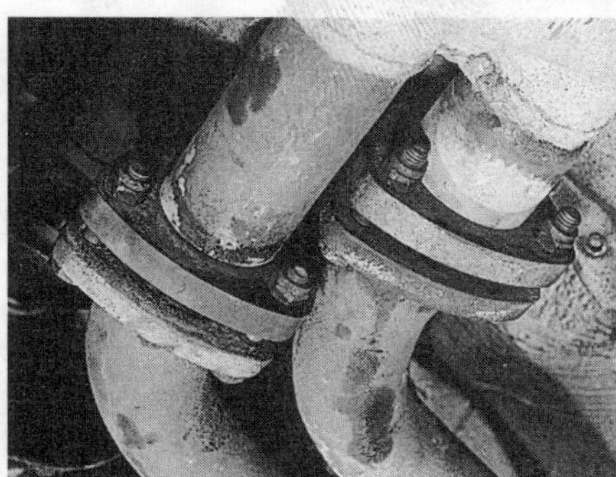
18.6A Flanges connecting the front and rear sections of the exhaust system

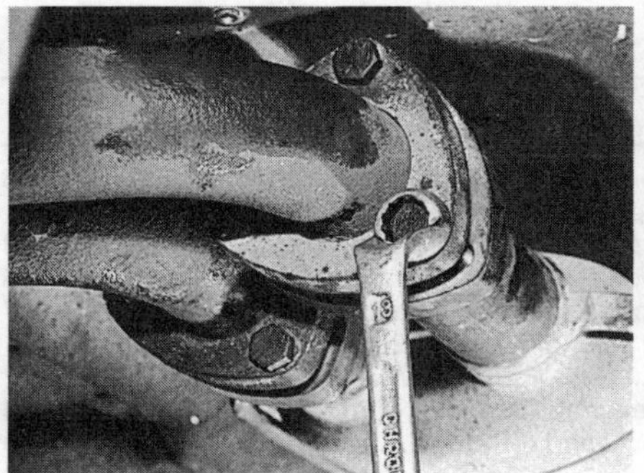
18.6B Unscrew the bolts ...

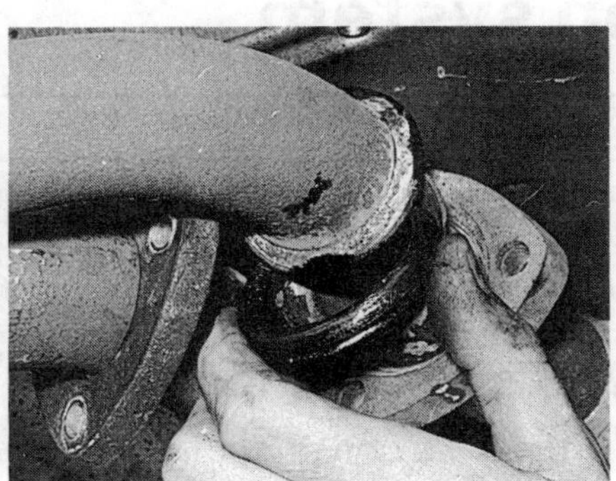
18.6C ... separate the two sections, and remove the sealing rings

18.7 Heatshield mounting bolts above the rear silencer

7 The front and rear sections may be removed separately if necessary, with the exhaust system still in the car, by disconnecting the flanges. The front and rear silencers may be renewed separately if necessary, though this requires the relevant section to be cut and sleeves fitted. If necessary the heat shield above the rear silencer may be removed by unbolting it from the underbody (photo).

8 Holts Flexiwrap and Holts Gun Gum exhaust repair systems can be used for effective repairs to exhaust pipes and silencer boxes, including ends and bends. Holts Flexiwrap is an MOT approved permanent exhaust repair.

9 Refitting is a reversal of removal, but renew the suspension rings as required and fit a new gasket and sealing ring. Apply a little copper paste to the studs on the manifold and fit new self-locking nuts.

19 Fault diagnosis – fuel and exhaust systems

Symptom	Reason(s)
Excessive fuel consumption	Mixture setting incorrect (where applicable) Air cleaner element blocked Fuel leak Fuel metering unit faulty Warm-up regulator faulty (K and L-Jetronic) Inlet manifold air leak
Insufficient fuel supply or weak mixture	Fuel pump faulty Mixture setting incorrect (where applicable) Fuel filter blocked Fuel leak Faulty cold start valve (K-Jetronic)

Chapter 4 Ignition system

Contents

Specifications

General

System type:

520i models	Electronic, with breakerless distributor driven by intermediate shaft
525e models	Computerized and incorporated in Motronic Engine Management System
Firing order	1 - 5 - 3 - 6 - 2 - 4 (No 1 at front of engine)

Distributor

Type

520i models	Breakerless, driven by intermediate shaft
525e models	Rotor located on front of the camshaft, distributor cap located on front of the timing cover
Direction of rotor arm rotation	Clockwise
Clearance between stator and reluctor (520i models)	0.3 to 0.7 mm (0.012 to 0.028 in)
Rotor resistance	1.0 k ohms
Pulse sensor coil resistance (520i models)	990 to 1210 ohms

Ignition coil

	520i	525e
Primary resistance	0.82 ohm	0.5 ohm
Secondary resistance	8250 ohms	6000 ohms

Ignition HT leads

Spark plug connector resistance	5.0 k ohm

Reference transmitter (525e models)

Resistance at 25°C	70 to 90 ohms

Ignition timing

Engine at normal operating temperature, vacuum disconnected

520i models:	
Up to 1985	22° BTDC at 2000 ± 50 rpm
1986 on	23° BTDC at 5000 ± 50 rpm
525e models:	
Up to 1985	6° to 12° BTDC at 700 ± 50 rpm
1986 on	6° to 12° BTDC at 720 ± 40 rpm

Spark plugs

Type (520i models):	
All models to 1987	Champion N9YCC or N9YC
All models from 1988	Champion N9YCC or N9YCX
Type (525e models)	Champion N9YCC or N9YC
Electrode gap:	
N9YC and N9YCX	0.7 mm (0.028 in)
N9YCC	0.8 mm (0.032 in)
Spark plug firing voltage	6 to 14 kV
Firing voltage difference between cylinders (maximum permissible)	3 kV

Torque wrench settings

	Nm	lbf ft
Distributor:		
520i models	20 to 22	14 to 16
525e models	2.7 ± 0.1	2.0 ± 0.1
Spark plugs	26 ± 2	19 ± 1.5
Speed and reference transmitters	7 ± 1	5 ± 0.5

1 General description and precautions

Warning: *The voltages produced by the electronic ignition system are considerably higher than those produced by conventional systems. Extreme care must be taken when working on the system with the ignition switched on. Persons with surgically-implanted cardiac pacemaker devices should keep well clear of the ignition circuits, components and test equipment*

The ignition system is of electronic breakerless type on 520i models and is computerized and incorporated in the Motronic Engine Management System on 525e models. The Motronic system is also referred to as the Digital Motor Electronics (DME) system and incorporates a grid control which is pre-programmed to apply the correct ignition timing for different engine operating conditions.

To achieve optimum performance from an engine, and to meet stringent exhaust emission requirements, it is essential that the fuel/air mixture in the combustion chamber is ignited at exactly the right time relative to the engine speed and load. The ignition system provides the spark necessary to ignite the mixture, and automatically varies the instant at which ignition occurs according to the engine requirements.

The ignition system consists of a primary low tension (LT) circuit and a secondary high tension (HT) circuit. When the ignition is switched on, current is fed to the coil primary windings and a magnetic field is established. At the required point of ignition, the primary circuit is interrupted electronically. The magnetic field collapses and a secondary high tension voltage is induced in the secondary windings. This HT voltage is fed via the distributor rotor arm to the relevant spark plug. After delivering the spark the primary circuit is re-energized and the cycle is repeated.

The ignition timing is controlled by the distributor centrifugal weights and vacuum capsule on 520i models, and by a computerized control unit on 525e models.

On 520i models, from March 1983 the vacuum capsule has been moved to the opposite side of the distributor, and retard is now ported from the larger diaphragm. The vacuum take-off point has also been moved from the inlet manifold to the throttle housing. Note that there is no retard action on automatic transmission models.

To prevent damage to the electronic control unit and coil, the following precautions should be observed. Do not start the engine if the distributor cap is removed or if the wire has been disconnected from the coil terminal 4. Do not disconnect the battery leads while the engine is running. Do not fit any ignition coil other than the correct one for the model. Do not connect a capacitor or test lamp to the ignition coil terminal 1. Do not connect the ignition coil terminal 1 to earth or battery positive, as may be instructed in some burglar alarm kits – in this case the starter terminal 50 could be used as an alternative. Before checking the engine compression, disconnect the control unit plug.

The ignition coil and HT leads are insulated to withstand up to 30 000 volts.

2 Routine maintenance

Carry out the following at the intervals given in *Routine maintenance* at the front of this manual.

Renew the spark plugs

1 Refer to Section 14.

Check and adjust ignition timing (520i models only)

2 Refer to Section 6.

3 Distributor (520i models) – removal and refitting

1 With the ignition switched off, disconnect the wiring plug and earth wire from the distributor. Also remove the guard cover where fitted.
2 Remove the distributor cap by pushing and twisting the fasteners, then remove the rotor and dust cap.
3 Identify the vacuum advance and retard hoses for location, then

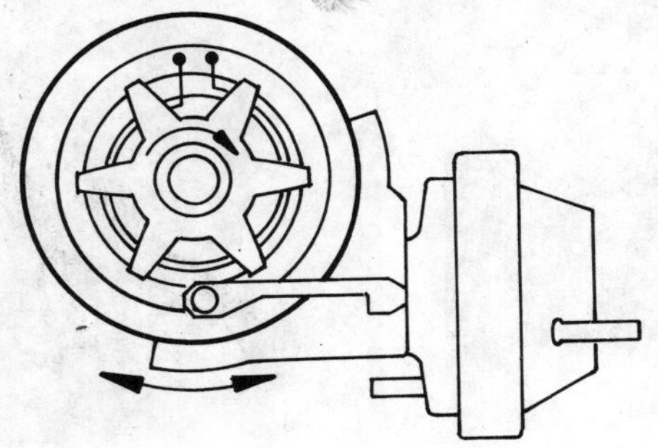

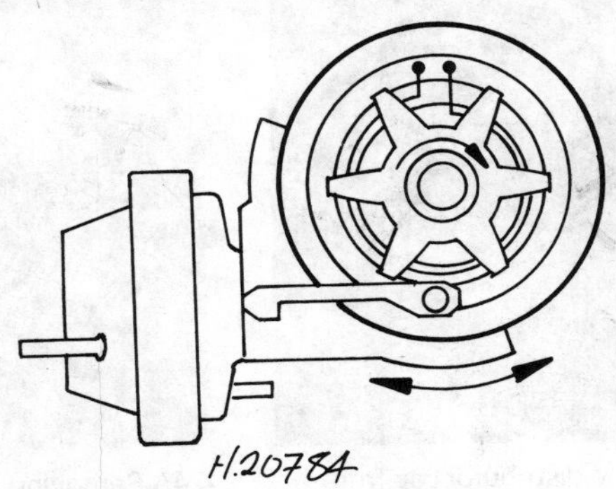

Fig. 4.1 Vacuum capsule positions for the distributor on 520i models (Sec 1)
Left – up to March 1983 Right – March 1983 on

disconnect them from the vacuum capsule. The black hose is for advance, and the white, or black and white, hose for retard. Note that on the 520i model fitted with automatic transmission, no vacuum hose is fitted for retard.

4 Refit the distributor rotor then turn the engine clockwise with a socket on the crankshaft pulley bolt until the mark on the rotor is aligned with the mark on the rim of the distributor. The TDC mark on the vibration damper should also be aligned with the mark on the lower timing cover. Remove the socket from the crankshaft pulley bolt.

5 Mark the distributor body in relation to the cylinder block to ensure correct refitting.

6 Unscrew the clamp plate bolt and remove the clamp plate.

7 Withdraw the distributor from the cylinder block.

8 Wipe clean the distributor body and location hole in the cylinder block. Check the rubber O-ring on the distributor and if necessary renew it.

9 Before refitting the distributor, check that No 1 piston is still at TDC and that the timing marks are correctly aligned.

10 Hold the distributor over its hole so that it is in its original relative position to the cylinder block. Turn the rotor so that it is aligned with the mark on the rim, then turn it an additional 20.0 mm clockwise from the mark.

11 Insert the distributor directly into its hole. As the gears mesh, the rotor will turn anti-clockwise until it is aligned with the mark on the rim. Make sure that the marks on the body and cylinder block remain in alignment.

12 Refit the clamp plate and tighten the bolt.

13 Reconnect the vacuum advance and retard hoses to the vacuum capsule.

14 Remove the rotor, refit the dust cap, then refit the rotor and distributor cap.

15 Reconnect the wiring plug and earth wire.

16 Check and adjust the ignition timing as described in Section 6.

4.1 Unclipping the plastic cap from the distributor on the 525e engine

4 Distributor cap and rotor (525e models) – removal, checking and refitting

1 Unclip and slide the plastic cap from the distributor on the front of the camshaft (photo).

4.2A Cylinder numbers moulded on the distributor cap (arrowed) on the 525e engine

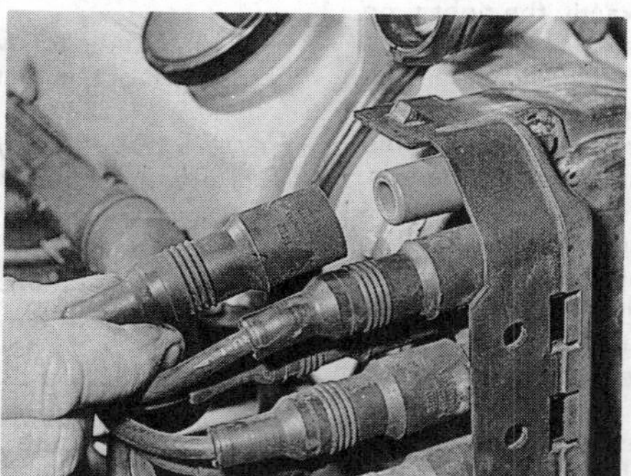

4.2B Disconnecting the HT leads from the distributor cap

4.3A Distributor cap mounting bolts (arrowed)

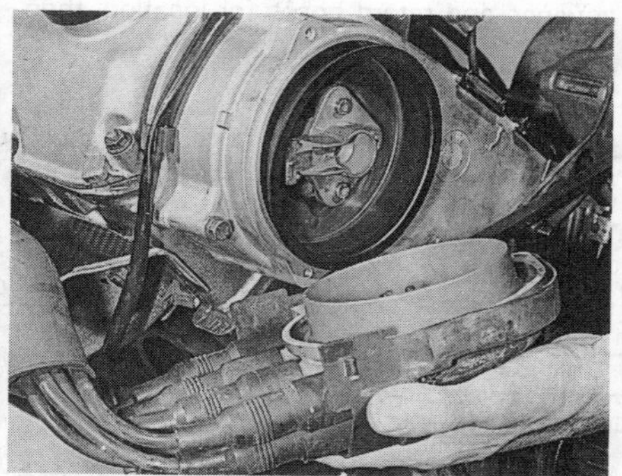

4.3B Withdrawing the distributor cap from the front of the timing cover

4.4A Removing the distributor rotor ...

4.4B ... and plastic cover

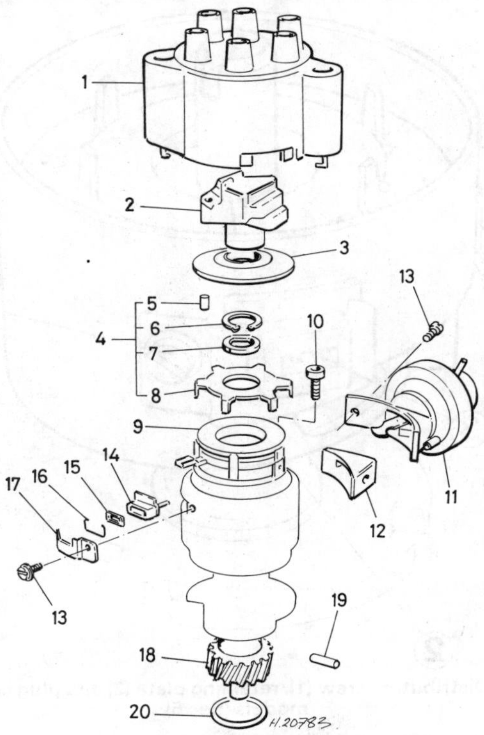

Fig. 4.2 Exploded view of the distributor for 520i models (Sec 5)

1	*Distributor cap*	11	*Vacuum capsule*
2	*Rotor*	12	*Bracket*
3	*Dust cap*	13	*Screw*
4	*Reluctor repair kit*	14	*Bush*
5	*Dowel pin*	15	*Gasket*
6	*Circlip*	16	*Clip*
7	*Diaphragm spring*	17	*Bracket*
8	*Reluctor*	18	*Gear*
9	*Pulse transmitter*	19	*Dowel pin*
10	*Screw*	20	*O-ring*

2 Identify the HT leads for position then disconnect them from the distributor cap. The cap has moulded numbers corresponding to the relevant cylinder next to each HT lead and each lead is marked along its length with its cylinder number (photos).
3 Unscrew the bolts and withdraw the distributor cap from the front of the timing cover (photos). If necessary remove the bolts and separate the protection cover from the distributor cap.
4 Using an Allen key, unscrew the three bolts and withdraw the rotor from the end of the crankshaft. Also remove the plastic cover (photos).
5 Check and clean the cap and rotor with reference to Section 5.
6 Refitting is a reversal of removal, but make sure that the HT leads are located in their correct positions on the cap.

5 Distributor (520i models) – checking and overhaul

Pulse transmitter – checking

1 The distributor pulse transmitter may be checked as follows while still fitted to the engine. First disconnect the wiring plug and connect a voltmeter across the two terminals. Crank the engine on the starter motor (approximately 300 rpm) and check that the pulse transmitter produces a voltage of between 1.5 and 2.0 volts. If no voltage is registered, the transmitter is faulty and should be renewed with reference to the following paragraphs after removing the distributor from the engine.

Pulse transmitter – removal and refitting

2 Remove the screws securing the advance/retard capsule to the distributor body, press down on the connecting rod to disconnect it, then withdraw the capsule.
3 Using circlip pliers, extract the circlip from the centre shaft, followed by the diaphragm spring (Fig. 4.3).
4 Using two screwdrivers on opposite sides, prise off the pulse sensor gear (reluctor). Recover the location pin (Fig. 4.4).
5 Remove the thrustwasher (Fig. 4.5).
6 Using a 3 mm Allen key, unscrew the three mounting screws through the carrier plate.
7 Extract the circlip from the centre shaft.
8 Unbolt the wiring connector holder and pull out the plug (Fig. 4.6).

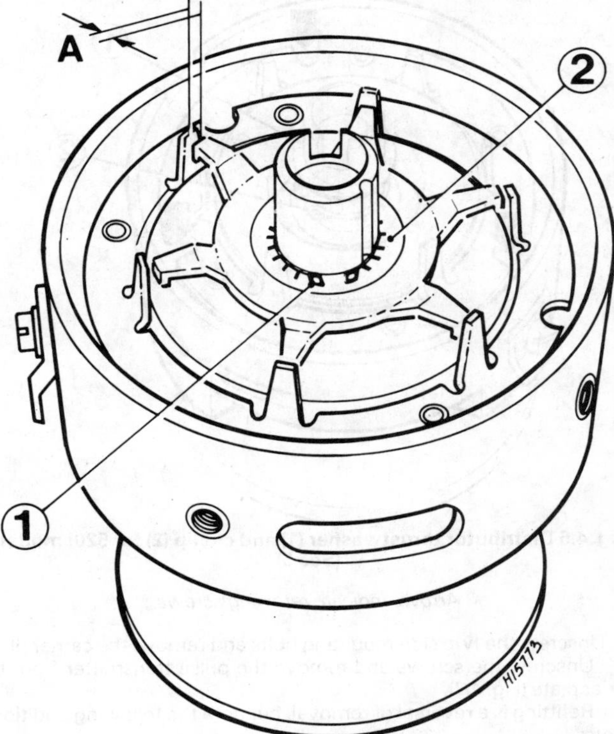

Fig. 4.3 Distributor circlip (1) and washer (2) for 520i models (Sec 5)

A = air gap

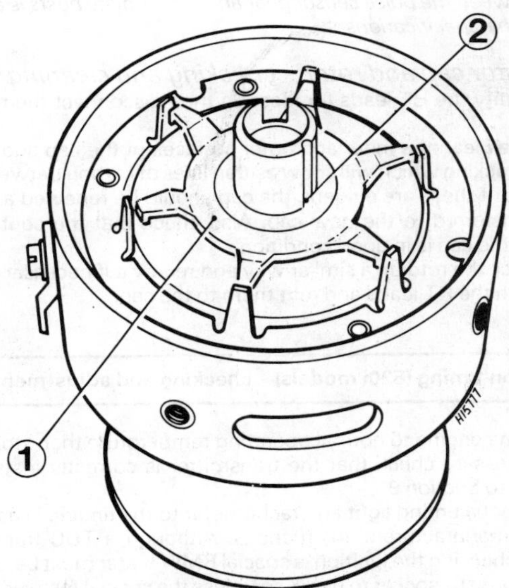

Fig. 4.4 Distributor reluctor (1) and location pin (2) for 520i models (Sec 5)

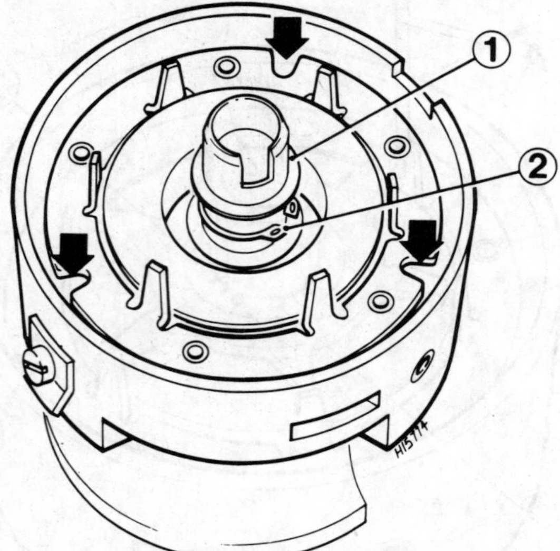

Fig. 4.5 Distributor thrustwasher (1) and circlip (2) for 520i models (Sec 5)

Arrows indicate retaining screws

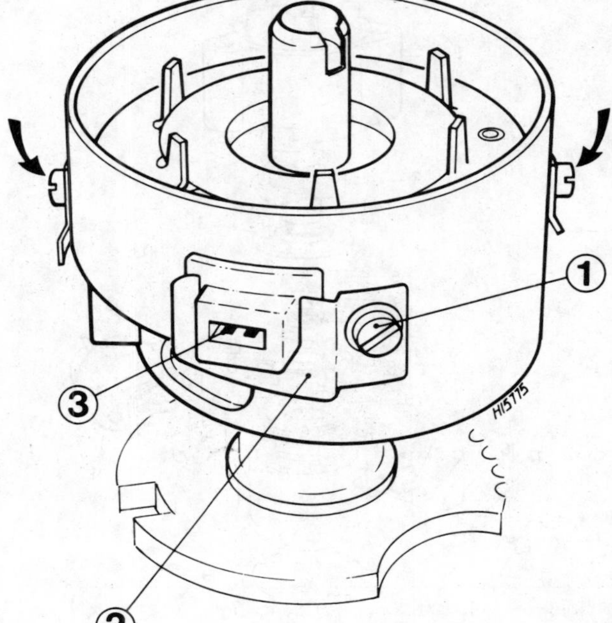

Fig. 4.6 Distributor screw (1), retaining plate (2) and plug (3) for 520i models (Sec 5)

Arrows indicate stator screws

9 Unscrew the two side mounting bolts and remove the carrier plate.
10 Unscrew the screws and remove the pulse transmitter from the carrier plate (Fig. 4.7).
11 Refitting is a reversal of removal, but note the following additional points:

(a) *When fitting the pulse transmitter to the carrier plate, align the terminals with the plug opening*
(b) *Using non-magnetic feeler blades, check that the air gap between the pulse sensor gear and carrier plate posts is as given in the Specifications*

Distributor cap and rotor – checking and cleaning

12 Identify the HT leads for location then disconnect them from the cap.
13 Wipe clean the inner and outer surfaces of the cap and check for signs of tracking which will show as thin lines of carbon between the HT segments. If these are evident, the cap should be renewed and the HT leads transferred to the new cap. Also check that the contact in the centre of the cap is in good condition.
14 Check the rotor in a similar way and renew it if necessary.
15 Clean the HT leads and refit them to the cap.

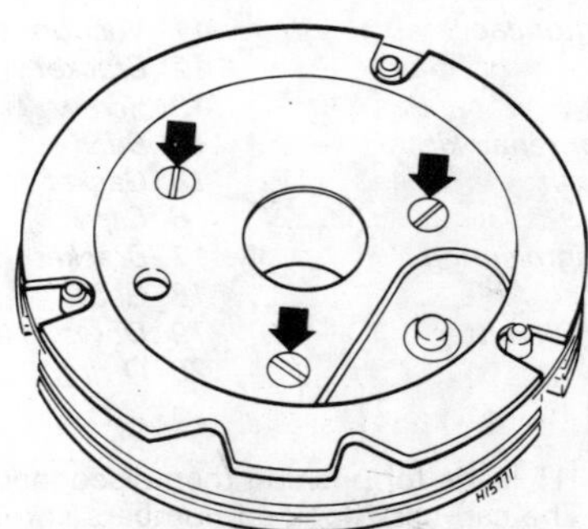

Fig. 4.7 Distributor pulse transmitter fixing screws for 520i models (Sec 5)

6 Ignition timing (520i models) – checking and adjustment

1 Run the engine to normal operating temperature then stop it.
2 If necessary check that the transmitter is correctly installed with reference to Section 9.
3 Connect a timing light and tachometer to the engine in accordance with the manufacturers' instructions. Although a TDC transmitter is fitted for checking the ignition, a special BMW tester must be connected to the diagnostic socket to use it, so unless the special tester is available, a conventional timing light should be used. The ignition timing mark should be on the crankshaft vibration damper, but if it is not, the TDC mark will be. If the timing light is of the adjustable delay type, then the ignition timing may be determined by zeroing the adjustment then turning the adjustment until the TDC marks are aligned and then reading off the amount of advance from the timing light. If a standard timing light is being used, make a mark on the vibration damper in accordance with the specified advance using the following formula:

$$\frac{2nr \times advance}{360}$$

where n = 3.142
r = radius of vibration damper
advance = specified advance BTDC in degrees

4 Disconnect and plug both vacuum hoses from the distributor advance and retard capsule and identify them for location. Note that from March 1983 the capsule is located on the opposite side of the distributor and therefore the advance and retard hoses are in opposite positions.
5 Start the engine and run it at the specified speed.
6 Point the timing light towards the ignition timing marks on the vibration damper. Both marks should appear stationary and in alignment. If they are not, loosen the distributor clamp bolt and turn the distributor body anti-clockwise to advance the ignition or clockwise to retard the ignition. Tighten the bolt after making the adjustment, then recheck the setting and stop the engine.
7 Reconnect the vacuum hoses and disconnect the timing light and tachometer.

7 Ignition timing (525e models) – checking and adjustment

On 525e models, the ignition timing is controlled by the Motronic Engine Management System and is not therefore adjustable. However, it may be checked using a timing light in the same manner as described in Section 6.

8.2A Rubber boot pulled from the top of the ignition coil

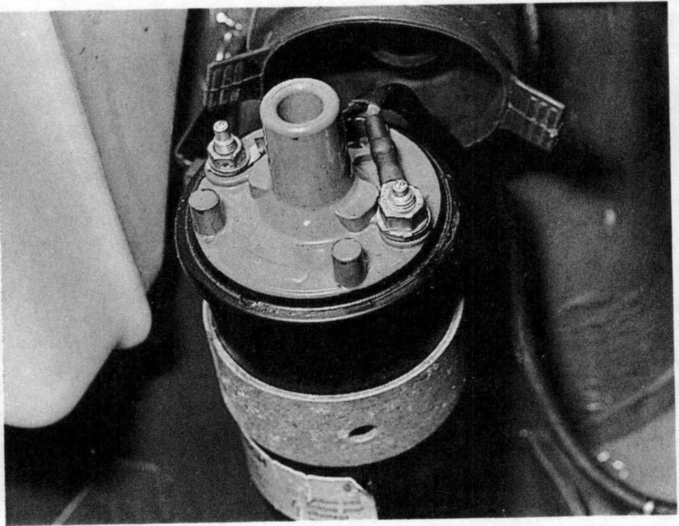

8.2B Ignition coil with HT lead disconnected

8 Ignition coil – description and testing

1 The ignition coil is located on the left-hand side of the engine compartment in front of the fusebox on 520i models, and on the right-hand side of the engine compartment next to the washer reservoir on 525e models.
2 Pull off the rubber boot, disconnect the LT and HT leads from the coil, then check if the internal compound has leaked out (photos).
3 Connect an ohmmeter to terminals 15 and 1 on the coil and check if the primary resistance is as given in the Specifications.
4 Connect the ohmmeter to terminals 15 and 4 on the coil and check if the secondary resistance is as given in the Specifications.
5 Renew the coil if the resistances are incorrect or if it is leaking.
6 Reconnect the wiring after making the test.

9 TDC transmitter – removal and refitting

1 Carefully press the TDC diagnostic socket from the bracket on the top of the engine.
2 Release the TDC transmitter from the wire clips on the wiring harness.
3 Unclip the transmitter from the clip on the front of the engine timing cover.
4 Refitting is a reversal of removal, but check that the transmitter is correctly seated.

10 Ignition amplifier module (520i models) – removal and refitting

1 The ignition amplifier module is located on the bulkhead.
2 Remove the cap then release the wire clip and disconnect the plug.
3 Unscrew the bolts or nuts and remove the unit from the bulkhead.
4 Refitting is a reversal of removal, but check and if necessary adjust the ignition timing as described in Section 6.

11 Ignition vacuum control solenoid valve (520i models) – checking

1 The solenoid valve is energized when the inlet manifold temperature is in excess of 17°C. When the valve is open the vacuum to the distributor is vented to atmosphere.
2 Run the engine to normal operating temperature and check that vacuum can be felt on the valve upper outlet to atmosphere, proving that the solenoid valve is open. Disconnect the lower outlet and check that there is no vacuum.
3 Disconnect the wiring plug and check that the vacuum stops from the upper outlet but is present at the lower outlet to the distributor.
4 On completion reconnect the vacuum hose.

12 Coasting shut-off valve (520i models) – checking and adjustment

1 This valve dampens the vacuum shut-off point. A vacuum pump is necessary for this check. Refer to Fig. 4.8 and connect the vacuum pump to the outlet P1.
2 Slowly increase the vacuum. The valve should switch to outlet P2 at a vacuum of approximately 670 mbar.
3 Decrease the vacuum and check that the valve switches back to outlet P1 at approximately 615 mbar.
4 If necessary the valve may be adjusted by turning the screw in the centre of the valve.
5 Disconnect the vacuum pump and reconnect the hoses in their original positions.

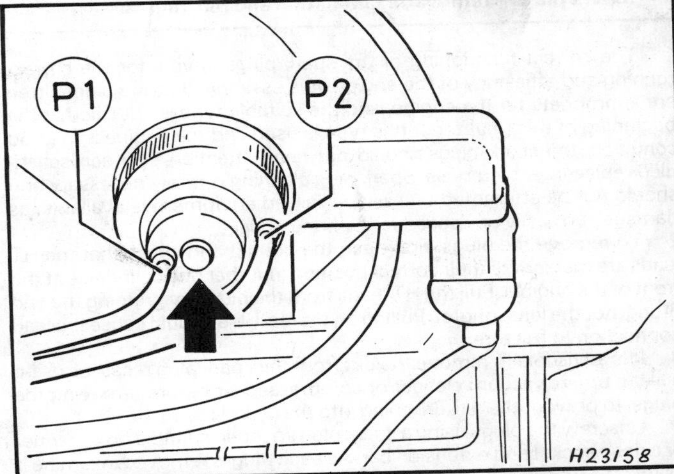

Fig. 4.8 Testing the coasting shut-off valve (Sec 12)

P1 Vacuum pump connection
P2 Switched vacuum connection
Arrow indicates adjusting screw

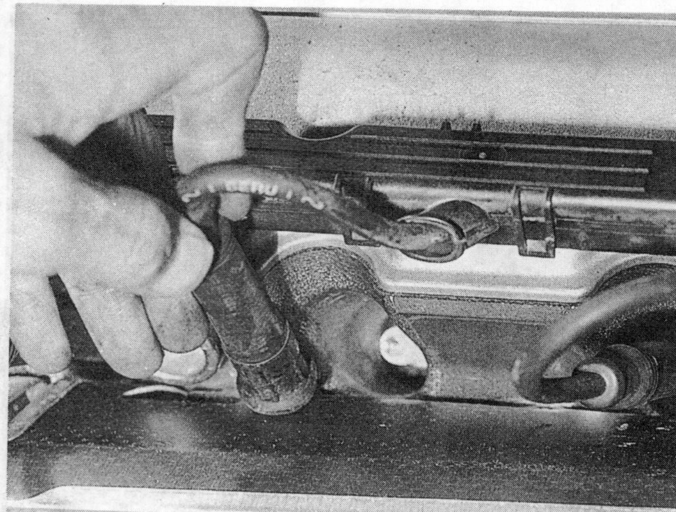

14.2 Disconnecting an HT lead from the sparking plug

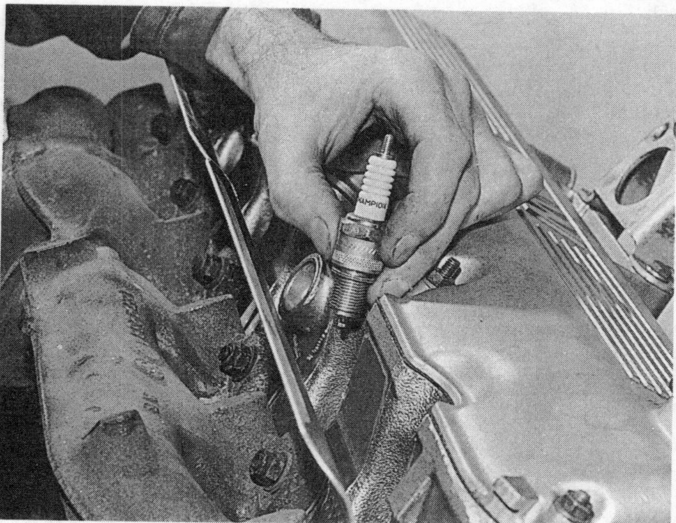

14.4 Removing a spark plug

13 Ignition reference and speed transmitters (525e models) – checking, removal and refitting

1 The ignition reference and speed transmitters are located together on the front of the transmission. In order to carry out a comprehensive test on the transmitters, a multimeter test scope is required. This is not likely to be available to the home mechanic so it is recommended that if a comprehensive test is required the transmitters be tested by a BMW garage using the special BMW test unit. However, it is possible to check the resistance of the transmitters using an ohmmeter and compare the result with the information given in the Specifications.
2 To remove either one of the units, first locate the supply wire plug on the bracket and disconnect the appropriate plug. If both units are being removed, note the location of each one to ensure correct refitting.
3 Unscrew and remove the wire harness retaining clamp.
4 Using an Allen key, unscrew the transmitter mounting bolt and withdraw the unit from the transmission casing.
5 Refitting is a reversal of removal, but make sure that the transmitters are located in their correct positions. The reference transmitter is marked with a grey ring and its plug is also grey.

14 Spark plugs – removal, examination and refitting

1 The correct functioning of the spark plugs is vital for the correct running and efficiency of the engine. It is essential that the plugs fitted are appropriate for the engine, and the suitable type is specified at the beginning of this Chapter. If this type is used and the engine is in good condition, the spark plugs should not need attention between scheduled replacement intervals. Spark plug cleaning is rarely necessary and should not be attempted unless specialized equipment is available, as damage can easily be caused to the firing ends.
2 To remove the plugs, first open the bonnet and check that the HT leads are marked for their correct position (number one cylinder is at the front of the engine). Pull the HT leads from the plugs by gripping the end fitting, not the lead (photo). Pulling on the lead itself could cause the lead connection to fracture.
3 It is advisable to remove the dirt from the spark plug recesses using a clean brush, vacuum cleaner or compressed air before removing the plugs, to prevent the dirt dropping into the cylinders.
4 Unscrew the plugs using a spark plug spanner, suitable box spanner or a deep socket and extension bar. As each plug is removed, examine it as follows (photo).
5 Examination of the spark plugs will give a good indication of the condition of the engine. If the insulator nose of the spark plug is clean and white, with no deposits, this is indicative of a weak mixture or too hot a plug (a hot plug transfers heat away from the electrode slowly, a cold plug transfers heat away quickly).
6 If the tip and insulator hose are covered with hard black-looking deposits, then this is indicative that the mixture is too rich. Should the plug be black and oily, then it is likely that the engine is fairly worn, as well as the mixture being too rich.
7 If the insulator nose is covered with light tan to greyish brown deposits, then the mixture is correct and it is likely that the engine is in good condition.
8 The spark plug gap is of considerable importance as, if it is too large or too small, the size of the spark and its efficiency will be seriously impaired. For the best results the spark plug gap should be set in accordance with the Specifications at the beginning of this Chapter.
9 To set it, measure the gap with a feeler gauge, and then bend open, or close, the outer plug electrode until the correct gap is achieved. The centre electrode should never be bent, as this may crack the insulation and cause plug failure, if nothing worse.
10 Special spark plug electrode gap adjusting tools are available from most motor accessory shops.
11 Before fitting the spark plugs check that the threaded connector sleeves are removed (not required with the special HT lead connectors) and that the plug exterior surfaces and threads are clean.
12 Screw in the spark plugs by hand where possible, then tighten them to the specified torque. Take extra care to enter the plug threads correctly, as the cylinder head is of aluminium.
13 Reconnect the HT leads in their correct order.

15 HT leads – general

1 The HT leads require no routine attention other than being kept clean and wiped over regularly. When attending to the spark plugs, it is a good idea to remove each plug lead in turn from the distributor cap. Water can find its way into the joints giving rise to a white corrosive deposit which must be carefully removed from the end of each cable and the terminal sockets in the distributor cap.
2 The HT leads fitted as original equipment have connectors which are of the resistor type and may be checked using an ohmmeter. The resistance of each connector should be as shown in the Specifications. Renew all the HT leads and connectors if the resistance is excessive.

16 Fault diagnosis – ignition system

Since the ignition primary circuit is controlled electronically, it is relatively trouble-free compared to other systems. Any faults occurring in the primary circuit are most likely to be caused by broken or disconnected leads or bad contact caused by corrosion. The ignition

Are your plugs trying to tell you something?

Normal.
Grey-brown deposits, lightly coated core nose. Plugs ideally suited to engine, and engine in good condition.

Heavy Deposits.
A build up of crusty deposits, light-grey sandy colour in appearance.
Fault: Often caused by worn valve guides, excessive use of upper cylinder lubricant, or idling for long periods.

Lead Glazing.
Plug insulator firing tip appears yellow or green/yellow and shiny in appearance.
Fault: Often caused by incorrect carburation, excessive idling followed by sharp acceleration. Also check ignition timing.

Carbon fouling.
Dry, black, sooty deposits.
Fault: over-rich fuel mixture.
Check: carburettor mixture settings, float level, choke operation, air filter.

Oil fouling.
Wet, oily deposits. Fault: worn bores/piston rings or valve guides; sometimes occurs (temporarily) during running-in period.

Overheating.
Electrodes have glazed appearance, core nose very white – few deposits. Fault: plug overheating. Check: plug value, ignition timing, fuel octane rating (too low) and fuel mixture (too weak).

Electrode damage.
Electrodes burned away; core nose has burned, glazed appearance. Fault: pre-ignition. Check: for correct heat range and as for 'overheating'.

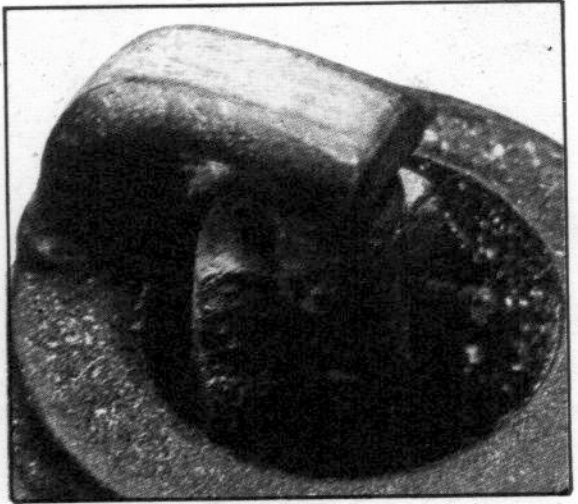

Split core nose.
(May appear initially as a crack). Fault: detonation or wrong gap-setting technique. Check: ignition timing, cooling system, fuel mixture (too weak).

WHY DOUBLE COPPER IS BETTER FOR YOUR ENGINE.

Champion Double Copper plugs are the first in the world to have copper core in both centre and earth electrode. This innovative design means that they run cooler by up to 100°C – giving greater efficiency and longer life. These double copper cores transfer heat away from the tip of the plug faster and more efficiently. Therefore, Double Copper runs at cooler temperatures than conventional plugs giving improved acceleration response and high speed performance with no fear of pre-ignition.

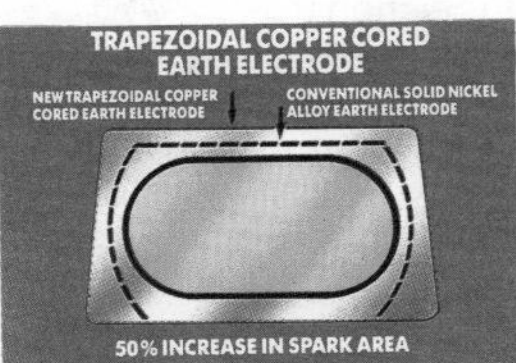

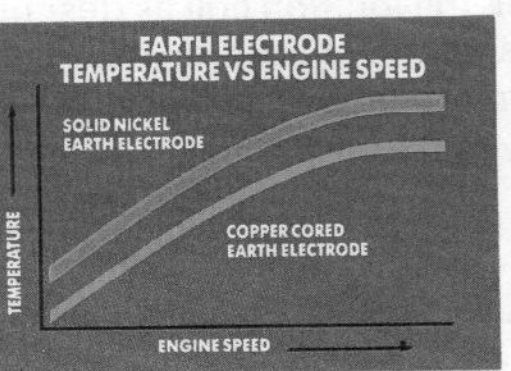

Champion Double Copper plugs also feature a unique trapezoidal earth electrode giving a 50% increase in spark area. This, together with the double copper cores, offers greatly reduced electrode wear, so the spark stays stronger for longer.

 **FASTER COLD STARTING**

 **FOR UNLEADED OR LEADED FUEL**

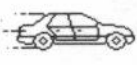 **ELECTRODES UP TO 100°C COOLER**

 **BETTER ACCELERATION RESPONSE**

 **LOWER EMISSIONS**

 **50% BIGGER SPARK AREA**

THE LONGER LIFE PLUG

Plug Tips/Hot and Cold.

Spark plugs must operate within well-defined temperature limits to avoid cold fouling at one extreme and overheating at the other.

Champion and the car manufacturers work out the best plugs for an engine to give optimum performance under all conditions, from freezing cold starts to sustained high speed motorway cruising.

Plugs are often referred to as hot or cold. With Champion, the higher the number on its body, the hotter the plug, and the lower the number the cooler the plug. For the correct plug for your car refer to the specifications at the beginning of this chapter.

Plug Cleaning

Modern plug design and materials mean that Champion no longer recommends periodic plug cleaning. Certainly don't clean your plugs with a wire brush as this can cause metal conductive paths across the nose of the insulator so impairing its performance and resulting in loss of acceleration and reduced m.p.g.

However, if plugs are removed, always carefully clean the area where the plug seats in the cylinder head as grit and dirt can sometimes cause gas leakage.

Also wipe any traces of oil or grease from plug leads as this may lead to arcing.

coil, distributor cap and HT leads should be checked as described in the appropriate Sections of this Chapter.

On the breakerless transistorized ignition system, check the pulse transmitter as described in Section 5. The power supply to the amplifier module may be checked by disconnecting the multi-plug and connecting a voltmeter across terminals 4 and 2.

The high tension circuit on all models is of conventional type, and the associated faults are covered in the following paragraphs. There are two main symptoms indicating ignition faults. Either the engine will not start or fire, or the engine is difficulty to start and misfires.

Engine fails to start

1 If the starter motor fails to turn the engine, check the battery and starter motor with reference to Chapter 12.

2 Disconnect an HT lead from any spark plug and hold the end of the cable approximately 5 mm away from the cylinder head using *well-insulated pliers.* While an assistant spins the engine on the starter motor check that a regular blue spark occurs. If necessary, re-gap or renew the spark plugs as described in Section 14.

3 If no spark occurs, disconnect the main feed HT lead from the distributor cap and check for a spark as in paragraph 2. If sparks now occur, check the distributor cap, rotor arm, and HT leads as described in Sections 4, 5 and 15.

4 If no sparks occur, check the continuity of the main feed HT lead using an ohmmeter and renew as necessary. Should the lead be serviceable, check that all wiring and multi-plugs are secure in the low tension circuit.

5 Check the ignition coil as described in Section 8.

6 If the above checks reveal no faults but there is still no spark, the control unit must be suspect. Consult a BMW dealer for further testing, or test by substitution.

Engine misfires

7 If the engine misfires regularly, run it at a fast idling speed. Pull off each of the plug HT leads in turn and listen to the note of the engine. *Hold the plug leads with a well-insulated pair of pliers as protection against a shock from the HT supply.*

8 No difference in engine running will be noticed when the lead from the defective circuit is removed. Removing the lead from one of the good cylinders will accentuate the misfire.

9 Remove the plug lead from the end of the defective plug and hold it about 5 mm away from the cylinder head. Restart the engine. If the sparking is fairly strong and regular, the fault must lie in the spark plug.

10 The plug may be loose, the insulation may be cracked, or the points may have burnt away giving too wide a gap for the spark to jump. Worse still, one of the points may have broken off. Either renew the plug, or reset the gap and then test it.

11 If there is no spark at the end of the plug lead, or if it is weak and intermittent, check the HT lead from the distributor to the plug. If the insulation is cracked or perished, or if its resistance is incorrect, renew the lead. Check the connection at the distributor cap.

12 If there is still no spark, examine the distributor cap carefully for tracking. This can be recognized by a very thin black line running between two or more electrodes, or between an electrode and some other part of the distributor. These lines are paths which now conduct electricity across the cap thus letting it run to earth. The only answer is a new distributor cap.

13 If the engine fails to start due to either damp HT leads or distributor cap, a moisture dispersant, such as Holts Wet Start, can be very effective. To prevent the problem recurring, Holts Damp Start can be used to provide a sealing coat, so excluding any further moisture from the ignition system. In extreme difficulty, Holts Cold Start will help to start a car when only a very poor spark occurs.

Chapter 5 Clutch

Contents

Specifications

Type

Single dry plate, diaphragm spring with hydraulic actuation

Clutch disc

Diameter	228.0 mm
Maximum thickness deviation	0.15 mm
Maximum lateral run-out	0.5 mm
Minimum lining thickness	7.5 mm

Clutch cover

Diaphragm finger tip height maximum deviation	0.6 mm

Release bearing

Total length:	
B20 engine	51.6 to 52.4 mm
B27 engine:	
Fichtel & Sachs	48.6 to 49.4 mm
SKF	50.5 to 52.5 mm
Bearing length:	
B20 engine	29.75 to 30.25 mm
B27 engine	24.75 to 25.25 mm

Clutch pedal

Height	250 to 261 mm

Hydraulic fluid

Type/specification	Hydraulic fluid to SAE J1703 or DOT 4 (Duckhams Universal Brake and Clutch Fluid)

Torque wrench settings

	Nm	lbf ft
Clutch cover to flywheel:		
8.8 bolt	22 to 24	16 to 17
10.9 bolt	30 to 35	22 to 25
Hydraulic pipe coupling bolt	13 to 16	9.5 to 11.5
Clutch master cylinder to bulkhead	22 to 24	16 to 17
Master cylinder stop bolt	21	15
Clutch master cylinder to bracket	9	6.5
Slave cylinder	24	17

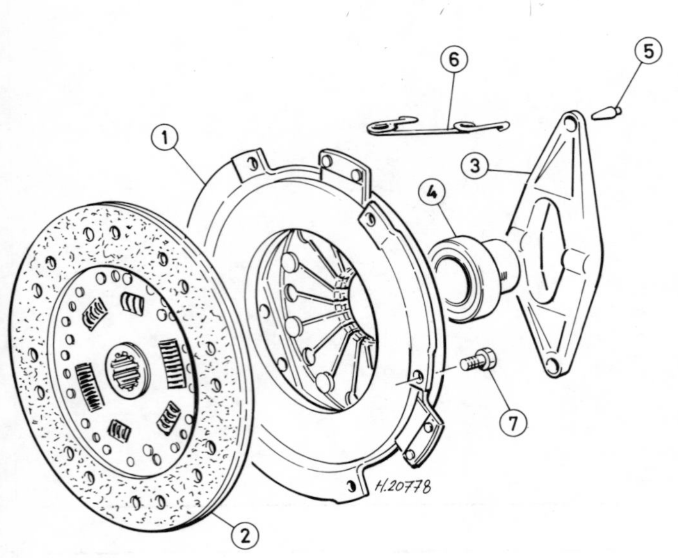

Fig. 5.1 Clutch cover, disc and release bearing components (Sec 1)

1 Clutch cover
2 Friction disc
3 Release lever
4 Release bearing
5 Ball stud
6 Lever retaining spring
7 Bolt

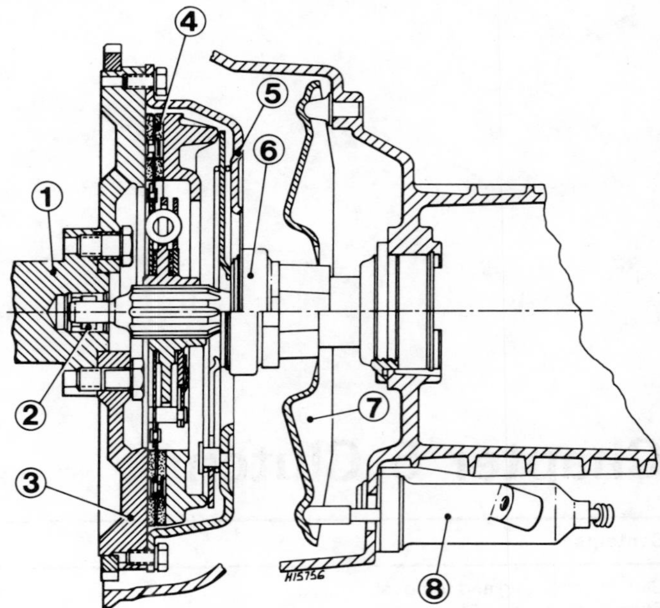

Fig. 5.2 Sectional view of the clutch mechanism (Sec 1)

1 Crankshaft
2 Needle-roller bearing
3 Flywheel
4 Friction disc
5 Cover assembly
6 Release bearing
7 Release lever
8 Slave cylinder

1 General description

The clutch is of single dry plate and diaphragm spring type with hydraulic operation. It is only fitted to the 520i model.

The clutch cover is bolted to the rear face of the flywheel. The friction disc is located between the flywheel and the pressure plate and slides on splines on the gearbox input shaft. When the clutch is engaged, the diaphragm spring forces the pressure plate onto the friction disc which in turn is forced against the flywheel. Drive is then transmitted from the flywheel through the friction plate to the gearbox input shaft. On disengaging the clutch, the pressure plate is lifted from the friction disc, and drive to the gearbox is then disconnected.

The clutch is operated by a foot pedal suspended under the facia which pushes a rod onto the clutch master cylinder piston. Through hydraulic action the slave cylinder is operated and the release lever is moved. The release bearing is then forced against the fingers of the diaphragm spring in the clutch cover. The spring is sandwiched between two rings which act as fulcrums. As the centre of the spring is moved in, the periphery moves out to lift the pressure plate and disengage the clutch. The reverse takes place when the pedal is released.

As the friction disc wears, the fingers of the diaphragm spring will return to a higher position when the clutch is released, but this will automatically be compensated for by the hydraulic fluid being forced back through the master cylinder, so it is not necessary to adjust the clutch.

2 Routine maintenance

Carry out the following at the intervals given in *Routine maintenance* at the front of this manual.

Check hydraulic fluid level

1 The hydraulic fluid for the clutch is supplied from the brake fluid reservoir. Check that the level of fluid in the reservoir is on or near the maximum mark. If necessary, top it up using the specified hydraulic fluid, but if frequent topping-up is required, check the complete brake and clutch hydraulic circuits for leakage, and rectify.

Check clutch disc wear

2 Check the wear of the clutch disc linings as described in Section 7 paragraphs 1 and 2. If worn excessively the disc must be renewed.

3 Clutch pedal – removal and refitting

1 Remove the lower facia panel from beneath the steering wheel as described in Chapter 11.

2 Disconnect the clutch pedal return spring from the pedal and bracket.

3 Unscrew the nut and pull out the eccentric pivot bolt securing the clutch pedal to the master cylinder. To ensure that the bolt is refitted in the same position, mark it before removal.

4 Note how the pedal components are fitted to the pivot bolt then unscrew the nut and pull out the bolt sufficiently to remove the clutch pedal.

5 If necessary, the pedal bearing bushes may be renewed by pressing out the spacer sleeves followed by the bushes. Press in the new bushes then apply a little grease to the sleeves and press them in also.

6 Refitting is a reversal of removal, but adjust the pedal height as follows. With the pedal fully released, measure the distance from the bulkhead to the bottom edge of the rubber pad on the pedal (Fig. 5.3). If not as given in the Specifications, adjust it by turning the eccentric pivot bolt as necessary. Tighten the nut after making the adjustment.

4 Clutch master cylinder – removal, overhaul and refitting

1 Working in the engine compartment, unscrew the filler cap and

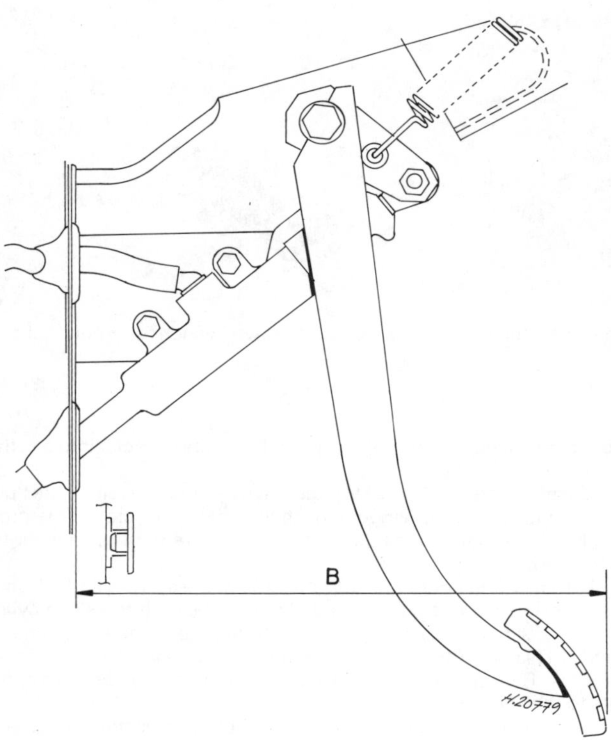

Fig. 5.3 Clutch pedal height adjustment diagram (Sec 3)

B = 250 to 261 mm

remove the level float from the brake and clutch fluid reservoir, then syphon off the fluid until the level is below the clutch outlet.

2 Apply the handbrake then jack up the front of the car and support on axle stands.

3 Unscrew the union nut and disconnect the slave cylinder hydraulic line from the clutch master cylinder. Operate the clutch pedal several times and drain the fluid into a suitable container.

4 Remove the lower facia panel from under the steering wheel as described in Chapter 11.

5 Unscrew the nut and pull out the eccentric pivot bolt securing the clutch pedal to the master cylinder. To ensure that the bolt is refitted in the same position, mark it before removal.

6 Pull the fluid supply line from the top of the master cylinder.

7 Unscrew the two bolts and withdraw the master cylinder from the pedal bracket and through the rubber grommet (where fitted) in the bulkhead.

8 Pull off the dust excluder, extract the circlip and withdraw the piston assembly. Also prise out the inlet plug.

9 Examine the surfaces of the piston and cylinder bore. If they are corroded or scored, renew the complete cylinder. If the bore is in good condition, discard the piston assembly and obtain a repair kit which will consist of a new piston assembly, a circlip, a new dust excluder, and a new inlet plug. Clean all parts in hydraulic fluid or methylated spirit. Dip the piston in clean hydraulic fluid and insert it into the cylinder, followed by the other components.

10 Refitting is a reversal of removal, but make sure that with the clutch pedal fully depressed to the floor, the locknut on the pushrod is located in the cut-out in the side of the pedal. If necessary loosen the locknut and reposition it, then retighten it. If this precaution is not taken there is a danger of the pushrod breaking as a result of contacting the side of the pedal. Tighten all nuts and bolts to the specified torque, adjust the pedal height as described in Section 3, and bleed the hydraulic system as described in Section 6.

5 Clutch slave cylinder – removal, overhaul and refitting

1 Working in the engine compartment, unscrew the filler cap and

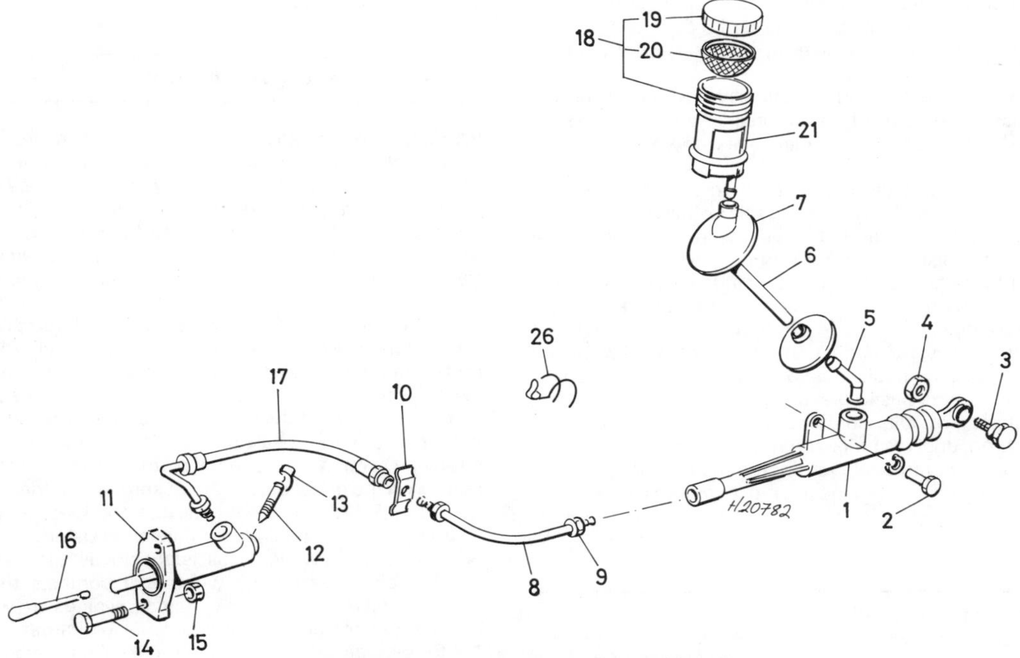

Fig. 5.4 Clutch hydraulic components (Sec 4)

1 Clutch master cylinder
2 Bolt
3 Eccentric bolt
4 Self-locking nut
5 Connector
6 Hose
7 Rubber grommet
8 Hydraulic pipe
9 Union nut
10 Clip
11 Slave cylinder
12 Bleed screw
13 Dust cap
14 Bolt
15 Self-locking nut
16 Push rod
17 Hose
18 Fluid reservoir assembly
19 Filler cap
20 Filter
21 Fluid reservoir

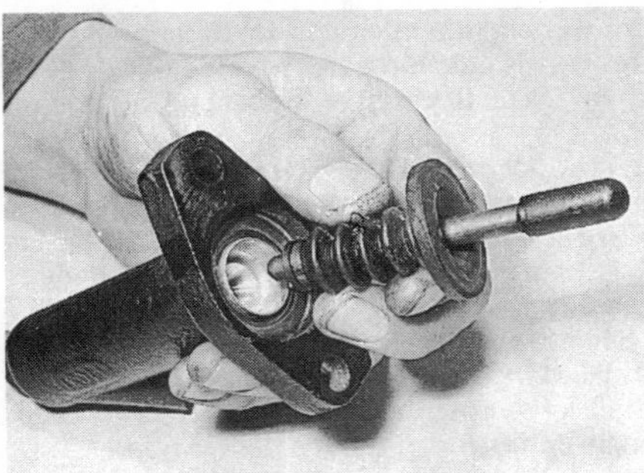

5.5A Removing the slave cylinder pushrod ...

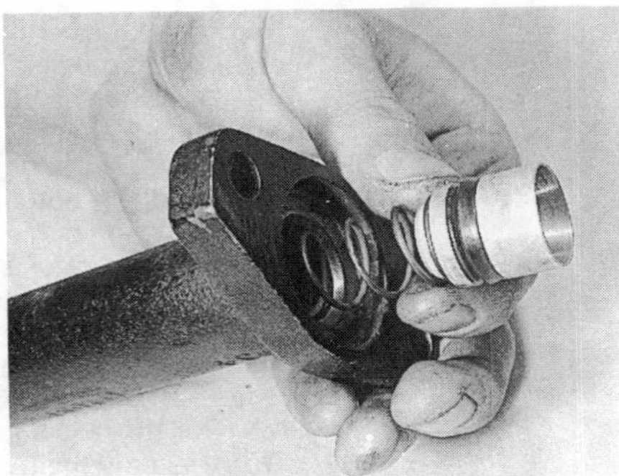

5.5B ... followed by the piston and return spring

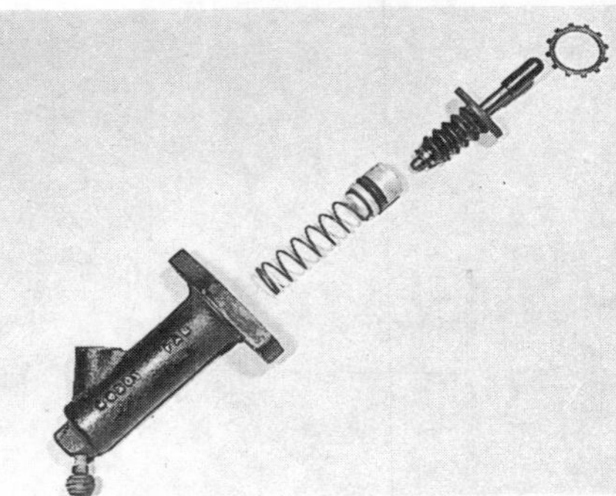

5.5C Clutch slave cylinder components

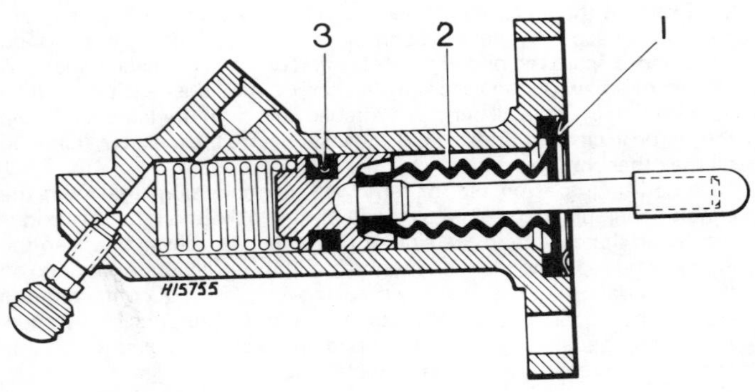

Fig. 5.5 Sectional view of the clutch slave cylinder (Sec 5)

1 *Truarc ring*
2 *Dust excluder*
3 *Seal*

remove the level float from the brake and clutch fluid reservoir, then syphon off the fluid until the level is below the clutch outlet.

2 Apply the handbrake then jack up the front of the car and support on axle stands.

3 Unscrew the two nuts and withdraw the slave cylinder from the transmission. Release the pipe run from its bracket where necessary. Note that the bleed screw on the cylinder faces downwards when installed.

4 Unscrew the union nut and disconnect the hydraulic line from the clutch slave cylinder. Drain the fluid into a suitable container.

5 Prise out the retaining ring and remove the pushrod and dust excluder, followed by the piston and return spring (photos).

6 Examine the surfaces of the piston and cylinder bore. If they are corroded or scored, renew the complete slave cylinder. If the components are in good condition, discard the piston assembly and obtain a repair kit which will consist of a dust excluder and a new piston assembly. Clean all parts in hydraulic fluid or methylated spirit. Apply a little molybdenum disulphide based grease to the tips of the pushrod. Dip the piston in clean hydraulic fluid and insert it into the cylinder followed by the pushrod, dust excluder and retaining ring.

7 Refitting is a reversal of removal, but tighten the mounting nuts to the specified torque and finally bleed the hydraulic system as described in Section 6.

6 Clutch hydraulic system – bleeding

1 The procedure is similar to that described in Chapter 9 for the braking system but only using the pressure bleeding kit method. First apply the handbrake then jack up the front of the car and support on axle stands.

2 Unscrew the filler cap and remove the level float from the brake and clutch fluid reservoir.

3 Top up the fluid level.

4 Connect the pressure bleeding kit to the reservoir. Also connect a tube to the bleed screw on the slave cylinder and direct it into a suitable container.

5 Unscrew the bleed screw on the slave cylinder and allow the fluid to escape until it is free of air bubbles then tighten the screw. Operate the clutch pedal several times during this procedure to purge any air from the system.

6 Unscrew the mounting nuts and remove the slave cylinder from the transmission. **Do not** depress the clutch pedal with the slave cylinder detached. Slowly press the pushrod fully into the cylinder then release it slowly. This will force any remaining trapped air back into the fluid reservoir. Refit the slave cylinder to the transmission and tighten the nuts to the specified torque.

7 Disconnect the pressure bleeding kit from the reservoir and remove the tube from the slave cylinder.

8 A similar method may be used when bleeding the system without a pressure bleeding kit, but since the bleed screw is located on the bottom of the slave cylinder, several attempts may be necessary to purge all air from the system.

9 Top up the fluid level in the reservoir then refit the float and tighten the filler cap.

10 Lower the car to the ground.

7 Clutch – checking and removal

Warning: *Dust created by clutch wear and deposited on the clutch components may contain asbestos, which is a health hazard. DO NOT blow it out with compressed air or inhale any of it. DO NOT use petrol or petroleum-based solvents to clean off the dust. Brake system cleaner or methylated spirit should be used to flush the dust into a suitable receptacle. After the clutch components are wiped clean with rags, dispose of the contaminated rags and cleaner in a sealed, marked container*

1 BMW technicians use a special tool to determine the extent of wear on the clutch disc linings. The tool is shown in Fig. 5.6 and consists of a metal plate which is inserted into a slot in the slave cylinder housing. With the clutch pedal released, the inner end of the plate normally bears on the metal part of the slave cylinder pushrod, but when the linings are worn excessively it bears on the raised tip on the end of the pushrod. A cut-away section on the metal plate is used to determine if the plate is resting on the metal part of the pushrod or on the raised tip.

2 If the BMW tool is not available, the wear may be determined by inserting a plain metal plate while an assistant holds the clutch pedal depressed. Then while the assistant slowly releases the pedal the plate can be felt to determine whether it contacts the raised tip of the pushrod. If it does, then the clutch disc linings are worn excessively.

3 Remove the gearbox as described in Chapter 6.

4 Before removing the clutch, check the height of the diaphragm spring fingers using a straight-edge and vernier calipers. If they deviate by more than that given in the Specifications, the cover assembly will need to be renewed as well as the disc. If the car has covered a high mileage it is wise to renew the cover as a matter of course,.

5 Unscrew the clutch cover bolts a turn at a time in diagonally opposite sequence until the diaphragm spring pressure is relieved.

6 Remove the bolts and lift the cover and disc from the flywheel (photo).

7.6 Removing the clutch cover and disc

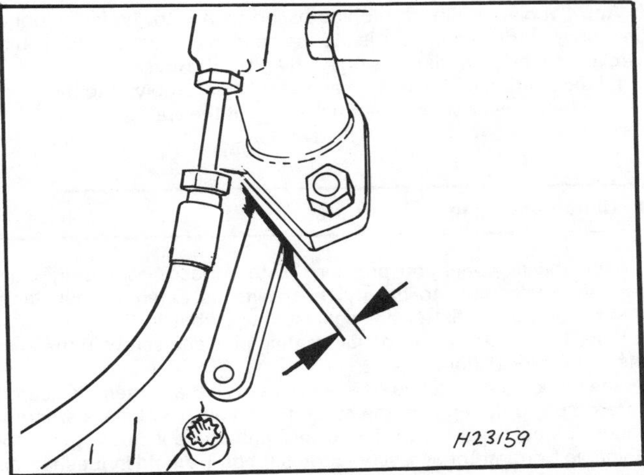

Fig. 5.6 Using the special BMW tool for checking the wear of the clutch linings (Sec 7)

If indicated gap is present, clutch linings are worn excessively

8 Clutch – inspection

1 Examine the surfaces of the pressure plate and flywheel for scoring. If this is only light the parts may be re-used, but if scoring is excessive renew both the cover assembly and the flywheel.
2 If the pressure plate has any blue discoloured areas, the clutch has been overheated at some time and renewal is necessary.
3 Examine the clutch cover for loose components and for distortion of the diaphragm spring.
4 Renew the friction disc if the linings are worn down to, or near the rivets. If the linings appear oil stained, the cause of the oil leak must be found and rectified. This is most likely to be a failed gearbox input shaft oil seal or crankshaft rear oil seal. Check the friction disc hub and centre splines for wear.
5 Spin the release bearing in the clutch housing and check it for roughness. If any excessive movement or roughness is evident, renew the release bearing as described in Section 9.

9 Release bearing and arm – removal and refitting

1 With the gearbox removed, release the spring holding the end of the release lever to the pivot ball.
2 Slide the release lever together with the bearing from the input shaft then separate the bearing from the lever.
3 If the bearing is noisy when spun with the fingers, or has been in use for a high mileage, it should be renewed.
4 Where necessary remove the bearing from the carrier and press the new one on so that it is positioned as shown in Fig. 5.8.

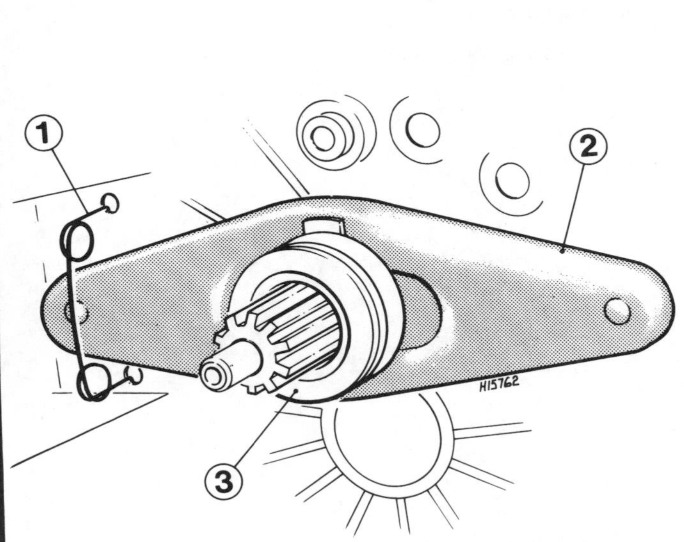

Fig. 5.7 Clutch release bearing and arm (Sec 9)

1 Spring   *2 Release lever*   *3 Release bearing*

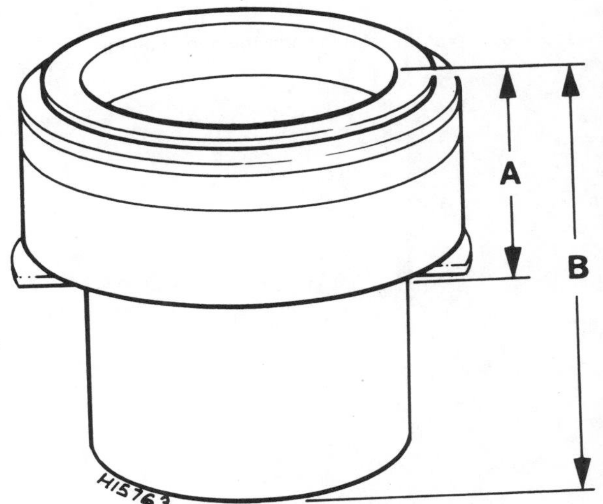

Fig. 5.8 Release bearing setting on carrier (Sec 9)

A = Bearing length (see Specifications)
B = Total length (see Specifications)

5 Apply molybdenum disulphide-based grease to the inner lubrication groove in the bearing carrier, to the bearing contact surfaces on the lever, and to the pivot dimples on each end of the lever.
6 Fit the bearing to the lever, then slide the assembly onto the guide.
7 Locate the lever on the pivot ball and refit the spring.

10 Clutch – refitting

1 With the flywheel and pressure plate surfaces absolutely clean, offer the driven plate to the flywheel with its extended hub facing outwards (ie with its flatter side against the flywheel).
2 Locate the clutch cover on its locating pins and screw in the cover bolts evenly finger-tight.
3 The friction disc must now be centralized so that, when the gearbox is offered up to the engine, the input shaft splines will pass smoothly through the hub of the disc. To do this, either use a clutch guide tool obtainable from motor accessory stores (photo), an old input shaft or a rod bound with tape to match the diameter of the friction disc hub hole.
4 Slide the tool into the friction disc hub until its end engages in the pilot bearing in the rear end of the crankshaft. This will have the effect of centralizing the friction disc. Tighten the cover bolts evenly and in diagonal sequence to the specified torque, then remove the tool.
5 Apply a trace of grease to the input shaft splines then refit the gearbox with reference to Chapter 6.

10.3 Centralizing the clutch friction disc

11 Fault diagnosis – clutch

Symptom	Reason(s)
Judder when taking up drive	Friction disc linings worn or contaminated with oil Worn splines on friction disc or gearbox input shaft Engine/gearbox mountings loose or deteriorated
Clutch drag (failure to disengage)	Friction disc sticking on input shaft splines Crankshaft spigot bearing seizing Clutch pedal adjustment incorrect
Clutch slip (engine speed increases without increase in road speed)	Friction disc linings worn or contaminated with oil Weak or broken diaphragm spring
Noise when depressing clutch pedal (engine stopped)	Worn diaphragm spring Pedal shaft dry
Noise when depressing clutch pedal (engine running)	Dry or worn release bearing

Chapter 6 Manual gearbox and automatic transmission

Contents

Specifications

Part A: Manual gearbox

Type ... 4 or 5 forward speeds with synchromesh, and reverse (with synchromesh on 5-speed transmission)

Ratios	**240**	**242**	**245**	**ZF**
1st	3.72:1	3.76:1	3.76:1	3.72:1
2nd	2.02:1	2.04:1	2.32:1	2.04:1
3rd	1.32:1	1.32:1	1.61:1	1.34:1
4th	1.00:1	1.00:1	1.22:1	1.00:1
5th	0.81:1		0.81:1	0.82:1
Reverse	3.45:1	4.10:1	3.68:1	3.54:1

Gearbox overhaul data

Output shaft endplay	0 to 0.9 mm
Input shaft endplay:	
Except ZF	0 to 0.9 mm
ZF	1.1 to 1.3 mm
Layshaft endplay (none on ZF):	
Except 240	0.1 to 0.2 mm
240	0.13 to 0.23 mm

Lubrication

Lubricant type/specification	Gear oil, viscosity SAE 80 to API GL4, or single-grade mineral-based engine oil, viscosity SAE 20, 30 or 40, to API SG (Duckhams Hypoid 80)
Capacity:	
240	1.05 litres (1.8 pints)
242	1.0 litres (1.7 pints)
245	1.5 litres (2.6 pints)
ZF	1.15 litres (2.0 pints)

Torque wrench settings	**Nm**	**lbf ft**
Gearbox to engine:		
M8 hex	22 to 27	16 to 20
M10 hex	47 to 51	34 to 37
M12 hex	66 to 82	48 to 59

Torque wrench settings (continued)	Nm	lbf ft
M8 Torx	20 to 24	14 to 17
M10 Torx	38 to 47	27 to 34
M12 Torx	64 to 80	46 to 58
Front cover	22 to 24	16 to 17
Oil filler and drain plugs	40 to 60	29 to 43
Guide tube:		
M8x22	18	13
M8x30	25	18
M6	10	7
Output flange	100	72
Rear crossmember to underbody	22 to 24	16 to 17

Part B: Automatic transmission

Type	3 or 4 forward speeds and reverse

Application

520i models	ZF-3HP-22 3-speed, or ZF-4HP-22 4-speed
525e models	ZF-4HP-22 4-speed

Ratios	ZF-3HP-22	ZF-4HP-22
1st	2.478:1	2.48:1 (2.73:1 from 9.85)
2nd	1.470:1	1.48:1 (1.56:1 from 9.85)
3rd	1.000:1	1.000:1
4th		0.73:1
Reverse	2.090:1	2.090:1

Lubrication

Fluid type	Dexron II type ATF (Duckhams D-Matic)
Fluid capacity (fluid change):	
ZF-3HP-22	2.0 litres (3.5 pints)
ZF-4HP-22	3.0 litres (5.3 pints)
Refill from dry:	
ZF-3HP-22	5.7 to 6.1 litres (10.0 to 10.7 pints)
ZF-4HP-22	6.4 to 7.5 litres (11.3 to 13.2 pints)

Torque converter

Stall speed:	
ZF-3HP-22	2250 to 2350 rpm
ZF-4HP-22:	
520i	1990 to 2240 rpm
525e	1890 to 2050 rpm

Torque wrench settings	Nm	lbf ft
Torque converter-to-engine:		
M8	24	17
M10	45	32
M12	78 to 86	57 to 62
M8 Torx	21	15
M12 Torx	63	46
Reinforcement plate	22 to 24	16 to 17
Cover	8 to 9	6 to 6.5
Oil pan:		
ZF-3HP-22	8 to 9	6 to 6.5
ZF-4HP-22	6 to 7	4.5 to 5
Oil drain plug	15 to 17	11 to 12

PART A: MANUAL GEARBOX

1 General description

One of four different gearboxes may be fitted, depending upon model and year of production.

Both the four and five-speed gearboxes have synchromesh on all forward speeds. The five-speed units have synchromesh on reverse as well.

Gear change is by means of a floor-mounted remote control rod and lever.

2 Routine maintenance

Carry out the following at the intervals given in *Routine maintenance* at the front of this manual.

Check the oil level

1 Jack up the front and rear of the car and support on axle stands so that it is level.

2 Using an Allen key, unscrew the oil level/filler plug from the side of the gearbox.

3 Check that the level is up to the bottom of the plug hole. If not, top up with the correct grade of oil until it starts to run out of the plug hole.

4 Refit and tighten the plug.
5 Lower the car to the ground.

Change the oil

6 The gearbox should be at normal operating temperature.
7 Jack up the front and rear of the car and support on axle stands so that it is level.
8 Position a suitable container beneath the gearbox.
9 Unscrew and remove both the filler/level and drain plugs and allow the oil to drain. The oil will be hot, so take suitable precautions against scalding.
10 Clean the drain plug and renew the sealing washer if necessary, then refit and tighten it.
11 Using a flexible oil container with an extension tube, inject the correct grade and quantity of oil into the gearbox. The level should be up to the bottom of the filler/level plug hole, as described in paragraph 3.
12 Refit and tighten the plug.
13 Lower the car to the ground.

3 Gearbox – removal and refitting

1 Jack up the front and rear of the car and support on axle stands. Alternatively, position the car over an inspection pit.
2 Disconnect the battery negative lead.
3 Remove the front exhaust pipes and support bracket with reference to Chapter 3.
4 Refer to Chapter 7 and detach the propeller shaft centre bearing, then disconnect the shaft from the rear of the gearbox by bending down the centre bearing. Tie the shaft to one side. Alternatively, completely remove the propeller shaft from the car.
5 Disconnect the selector rod from the gearbox selector shaft by extracting the circlip, removing the washer and pulling out the rod.
6 Disconnect the wiring from the reversing light switch on the rear of the gearbox.
7 Where applicable, unscrew the two socket-headed gearchange lever mounting bracket bolts using an Allen key. These are very tight due to thread-locking fluid having been applied to their threads.
8 Remove the clutch slave cylinder with reference to Chapter 5 but leaving the hydraulic line still connected. Tie the cylinder to one side, taking care not to strain the hydraulic line.
9 Unbolt the lower front cover from the gearbox.
10 Unbolt the starter motor and move it forward. Leave the wiring connected but support the starter motor to prevent straining the wires.
11 Support the weight of the gearbox with a trolley jack.
12 Mark the position of the gearbox rear mounting crossmember on the underbody, then unscrew the mounting nuts. Also unbolt the crossmember from the gearbox. Note the location of any shims.
13 Position a thin piece of wood between the front crossmember and the engine sump, then lower the gearbox until the sump is resting on the piece of wood. The trolley jack must still support the weight of the gearbox.
14 Unscrew and remove all the gearbox-to-engine mounting bolts using an Allen key and extension socket where necessary.
15 Refitting is a reversal of removal but apply a little grease to the end of the input shaft so that it will enter the spigot bearing easily. Tighten all the gearbox-to-engine bolts to the specified torque before raising the gearbox otherwise there is not enough room to reach the upper bolts. Where applicable, renew the two socket-headed gearchange lever mounting bracket bolts and apply thread-locking fluid to them before inserting and tightening them to the specified torque. Refer to Chapters 3 and 7 as necessary. Check the oil level as described in Section 2.

4 Gearbox overhaul – general notes and precautions

1 If a gearbox is well worn and has been in service for a high mileage, consideration should be given to obtaining a new or exchange unit. This may well be more economical than the purchase of a large number of internal components.
2 Where perhaps only a synchromesh unit or bearing is worn then obviously overhaul will be a viable proposition.
3 Before overhauling a gearbox, clean away external dirt using a water soluble solvent, a steam cleaner or paraffin and a stiff brush.
4 A bearing puller, a two-legged extractor or a press will be needed for some operations, including dismantling of the mainshaft.
5 Certain adjustment shims will be required if new components are fitted and it may be possible to obtain a selection of various thicknesses in advance of overhaul on a sale or return basis.
6 Renew all circlips, roll pins, oil seals and gaskets as a matter of course.

5 Gearbox (Getrag 242, 4-speed) – overhaul

Dismantling into major assemblies

1 Unscrew the drain plug and drain the oil.
2 Unscrew the nut and remove the mounting rubber.
3 From within the main casing bellhousing, detach the spring and remove the clutch release arm with the release bearing. Refer to Chapter 5 if necessary.
4 Unbolt and remove the guide sleeve (Fig. 6.1). Retain the shims.
5 Extract the bearing circlip and remove the thrustwasher.
6 The front bearing must now be removed, either by using a proper bearing puller or, if the bearing is to be renewed, by inserting two hooked rods between the balls and attaching them to a slide hammer.
7 Use a pair of pincers to pull out the cap (3) and then remove the spring (2) and selector shaft plunger (1) (Fig. 6.2) noting which way round it is fitted.
8 Unscrew and remove the lockbolt (1) (Fig. 6.3).
9 Unscrew and remove the bolts which hold the rear casing section to the main casing. Drive out the two location dowels.
10 Separate the main casing from the rear casing, retaining any shims which are located on the input shaft or layshaft.
11 Unscrew the plug (1) then remove the spring (2) and lockpin (3) (Fig. 6.4).

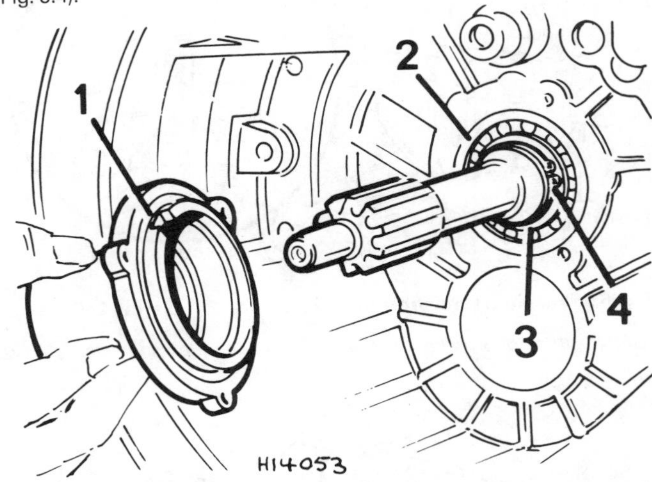

Fig. 6.1 Clutch guide sleeve (1), shim(s) (2), thrustwasher (3) and bearing circlip (4) – Getrag 242 (Sec 5)

Fig. 6.2 Selector shaft plunger (1), spring (2) and cap (3) – Getrag 242 (Sec 5)

Fig. 6.3 Lockbolt (1) – Getrag 242 (Sec 5)

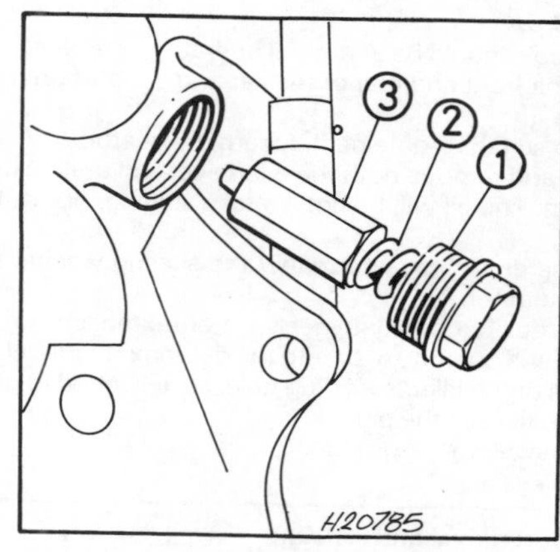

Fig. 6.4 Plug (1), spring (2) and lockpin (3) – Getrag 242 (Sec 5)

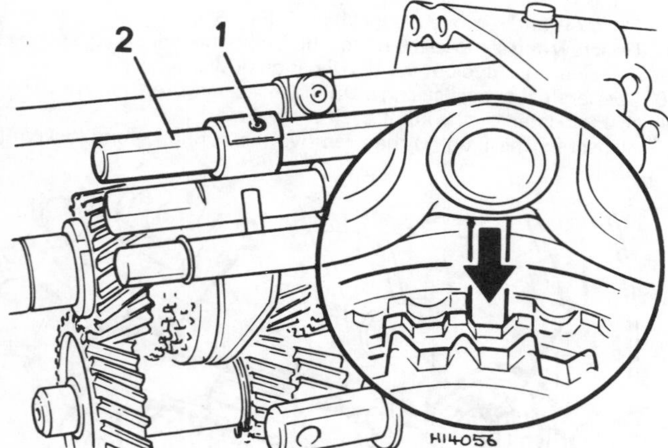

Fig. 6.5 Roll pin (1) and 3rd/4th selector fork (2) – Getrag 242 (Sec 5)

Inset: Position the synchro so that the pin has enough space for removal

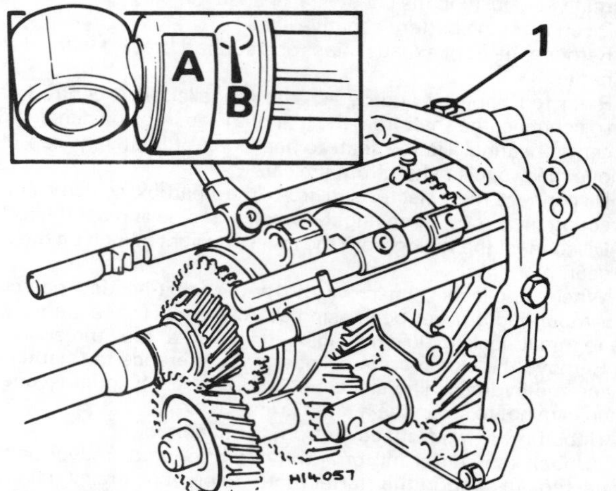

Fig. 6.6 Selector rod locking screw (1) – Getrag 242 (Sec 5)

A Sleeve *B Pin*

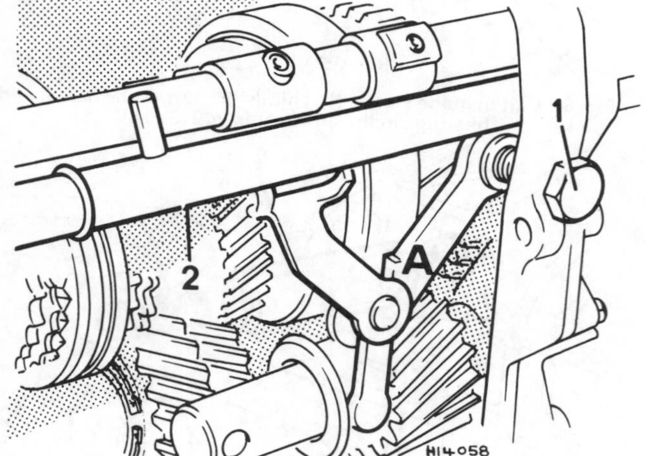

Fig. 6.7 Reverse gear selector lever (A), securing bolt (1) and reverse selector shaft (2) – Getrag 242 (Sec 5)

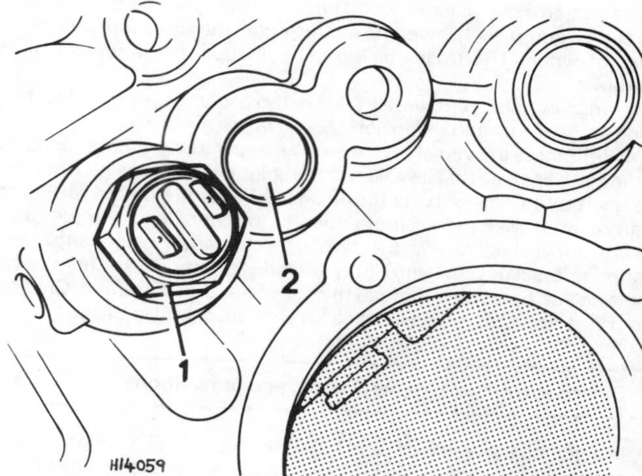

Fig. 6.8 Reverse lamp switch (1) and plug (2) – Getrag 242 (Sec 5)

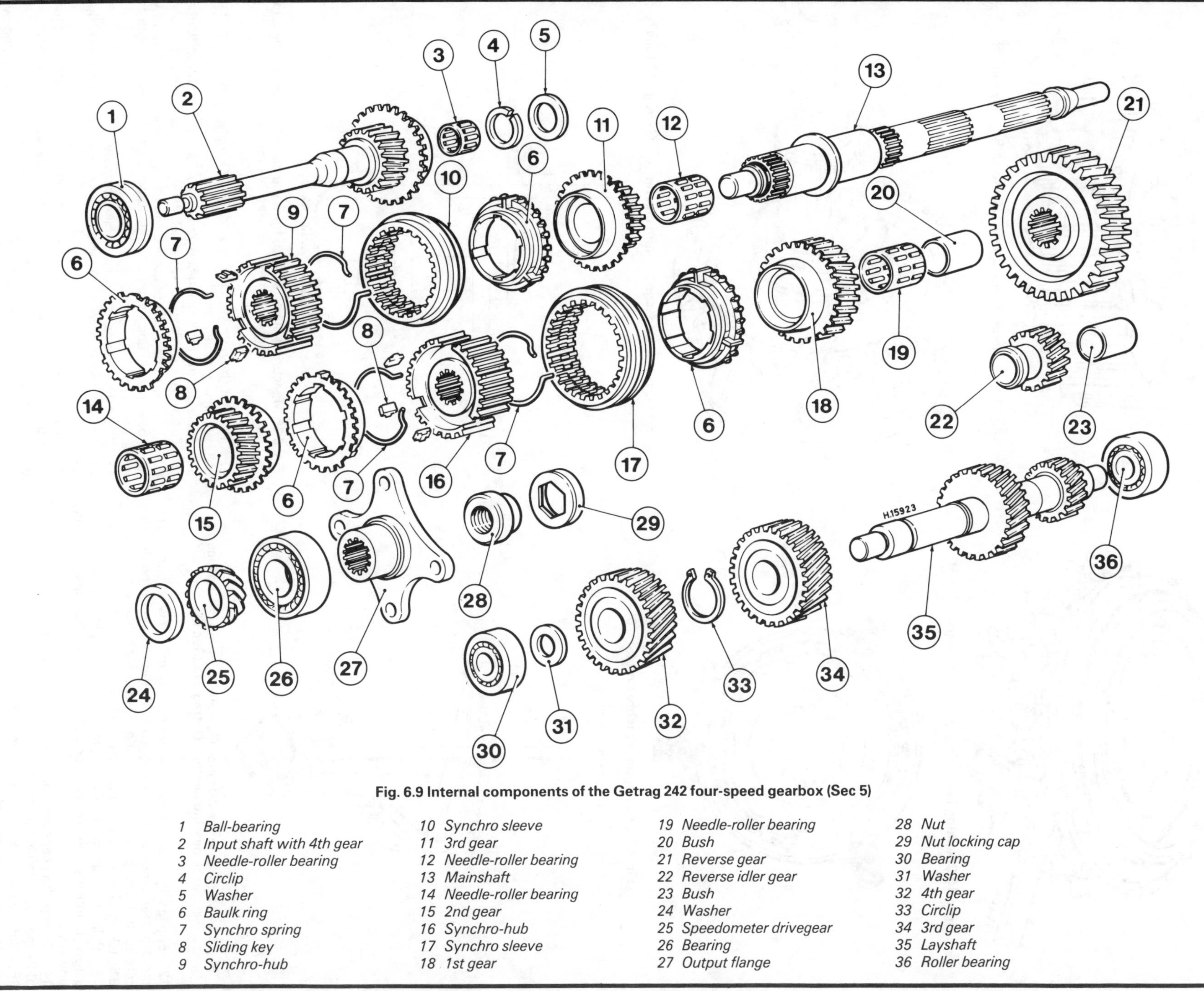

Fig. 6.9 Internal components of the Getrag 242 four-speed gearbox (Sec 5)

1 *Ball-bearing*
2 *Input shaft with 4th gear*
3 *Needle-roller bearing*
4 *Circlip*
5 *Washer*
6 *Baulk ring*
7 *Synchro spring*
8 *Sliding key*
9 *Synchro-hub*
10 *Synchro sleeve*
11 *3rd gear*
12 *Needle-roller bearing*
13 *Mainshaft*
14 *Needle-roller bearing*
15 *2nd gear*
16 *Synchro-hub*
17 *Synchro sleeve*
18 *1st gear*
19 *Needle-roller bearing*
20 *Bush*
21 *Reverse gear*
22 *Reverse idler gear*
23 *Bush*
24 *Washer*
25 *Speedometer drivegear*
26 *Bearing*
27 *Output flange*
28 *Nut*
29 *Nut locking cap*
30 *Bearing*
31 *Washer*
32 *4th gear*
33 *Circlip*
34 *3rd gear*
35 *Layshaft*
36 *Roller bearing*

Fig. 6.10 Checking baulk ring-to-gear cone gap (Sec 5)

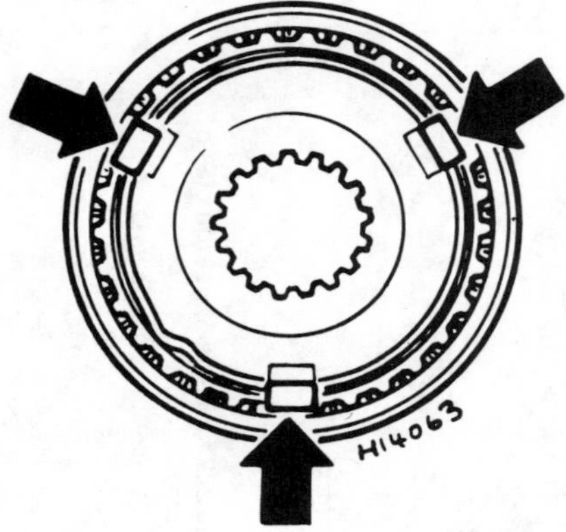

Fig. 6.12 Assemble synchro unit (Sec 5)

Sliding keys arrowed

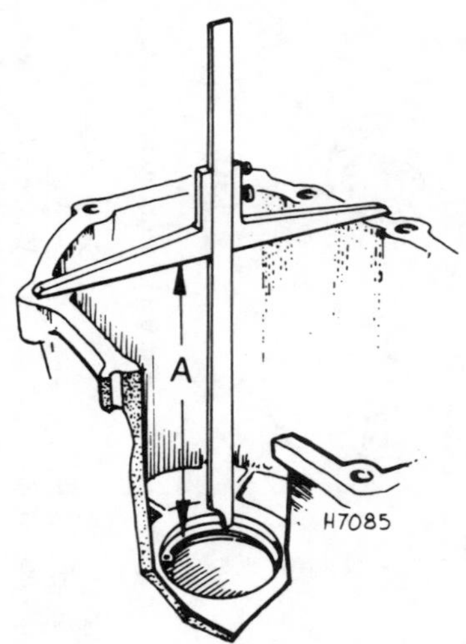

Fig. 6.14 Measuring the distance (A) from the main casing face to the bearing circlip – Getrag 242 (Sec 5)

Fig. 6.11 Synchro-hub with spring and sliding key (Sec 5)

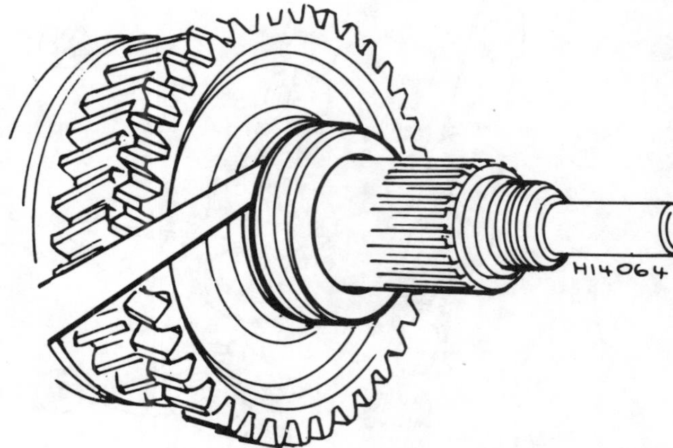

Fig. 6.13 Checking spacer-to-shim clearance – Getrag 242 (Sec 5)

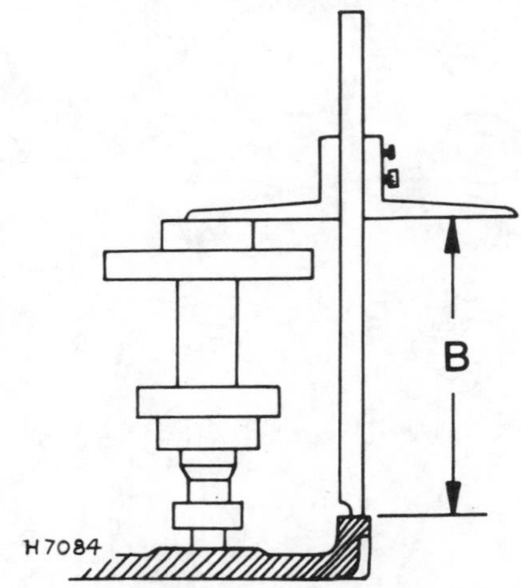

Fig. 6.15 Measuring dimension (B) from the casing gasket to the end of the layshaft – Getrag 242 (Sec 5)

12 Engage 3rd gear and turn the input shaft until the wide opening in the 3rd gear synchro dogs is aligned with the roll pin in the 3rd/4th selector fork. Drive out the roll pin and withdraw the selector shaft (Fig. 6.5), taking care not to lose the detent balls from the casing.
13 Pull off the sleeve (A) (Fig. 6.6) and tap out the pin (B). Slacken the screw (1) until the selector shaft can be turned to set the finger pointing upwards.
14 Engage 4th gear then pull the selector shaft out towards the front of the gearbox. Retain the rollers.
15 Remove the 3rd/4th selector fork.
16 Unscrew the bolt (1) (Fig. 6.7) until the reverse gear selector lever (A) can be removed.
17 Pull out the reverse selector shaft (2), taking care not to lose the balls which will be displaced.
18 Prise out the nut locking cup and then unscrew the output flange nut. To do this use a deep socket which will have to be ground to reduce the thickness of its walls, as there is very little clearance. Alternatively use a box spanner and hold the flange stationary by bolting a length of metal bar to it.
19 Pull off the flange, using a puller if necessary.
20 Unbolt and remove the rear cover then take out and retain the shims.
21 Remove the mainshaft rear bearing with a bearing puller or, if the bearing is to be renewed, by inserting two hooked rods between the balls and attaching them to a slide hammer.
22 Drive out the roll pin from the 1st/2nd selector shaft then withdraw the shaft taking care not to lose the detent balls from the casing.
23 Withdraw the input and output shafts followed by the layshaft.

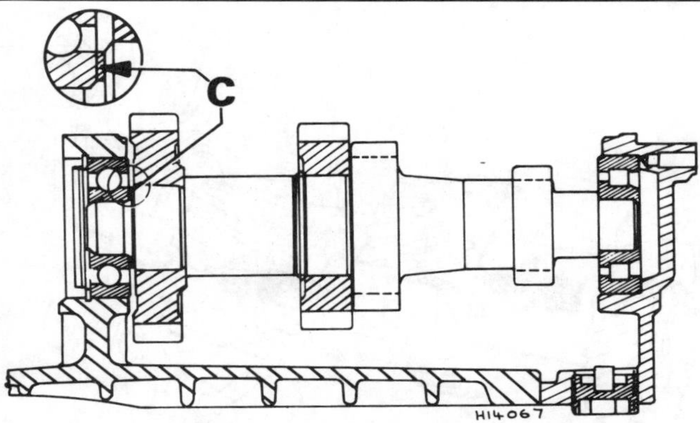

Fig. 6.16 Location of layshaft shim(s) (C) – Getrag 242 (Sec 5)

24 Unscrew the reverse lamp switch (1) and prise out the plug (2) (Fig. 6.8).
25 If any gears or synchromesh units are worn, then dismantle the shafts in the following way.

Mainshaft – dismantling

26 Remove the circlip (4), thrustwasher (5), 4th baulk ring, 3rd/4th synchro and the 3rd baulk ring (6) (Fig. 6.9).
27 Remove the 3rd gear (11) and the needle-roller bearing (12).
28 Support the 2nd gear and press the shaft out of the remaining components, or alternatively draw them from the shaft with a suitable puller. Keep all the components identified for position. Note that the needle-roller bearings have slots at 90° or 120° intervals in order to guarantee uniform support.

Gears, synchromesh units and selector forks – inspection

29 Renew any gears which have chipped teeth.
30 Although a worn synchromesh unit will already be known as a result of noisy gear changing, check for wear in all synchro units in the following way.
31 Fit the baulk ring to the gear cone and check the gap (Fig. 6.10) adjacent to the stop blocks with a feeler gauge. If the gap is less than 1.0 mm renew the baulk ring.
32 If the synchro teeth are worn, renew the component concerned.
33 When reassembling the unit engage the hooked ends of the springs in the same groove, but make sure that they run in opposite directions in relation to each other. The springs must engage in the grooves in the sliding keys (Figs. 6.11 and 6.12).
34 Examine the selector forks for wear and loose sliding pads. It is unlikely that the grooves in the synchro sleeves will be found to be worn.

Mainshaft – reassembly

35 To the front end of the shaft, fit the needle-roller bearing, 3rd gear, the baulk ring and the 3rd/4th synchro unit. Fit the synchro so the chamfer on the synchro sleeve is towards 4th gear.
36 Fit the thrustwasher and circlip.
37 To the opposite end of the shaft, fit 2nd gear with the needle-roller bearing.
38 Fit the 2nd baulk ring.
39 Fit the 1st/2nd synchro unit and the 1st baulk ring.
40 Fit the 1st gear and the needle-roller bearing with the spacer bush.
41 Fit the reverse gear to the splines on the end of the mainshaft.
42 Locate the shim then press on the spacer and check that the clearance between the gear and shim is between zero and 0.09 mm (Fig. 6.13). Note that the spacer must be pressed against the collar on the shaft. If the clearance is incorrect select a different shim.

Layshaft

43 The bearings may be drawn off for renewal. The rear taper roller bearing outer track can be removed from the rear casing by heating the casing to approximately 80°C.
44 3rd and 4th gears can be pressed from the shaft, but 3rd gear has a retaining circlip.
45 When fitting the gears, heat to between 120° and 150°C and note that the raised shoulders on both gears must be towards 2nd gear.
46 The rear layshaft bearing outer track must be located in the rear casing with its larger diameter and rollers facing the main casing. If new bearings are fitted, then the following calculation must be made to determine the thickness of the shim to fit to the layshaft next to the ball bearing. Measure the distance (A) (Fig. 6.14) from the face of the main casing to the bearing circlip. Press the new ball bearing onto the front of the layshaft without a shim and also press the rear taper bearing inner track onto the rear of the layshaft. Locate the layshaft in the rear casing. Place a new joint gasket in position on the rear casing, then measure

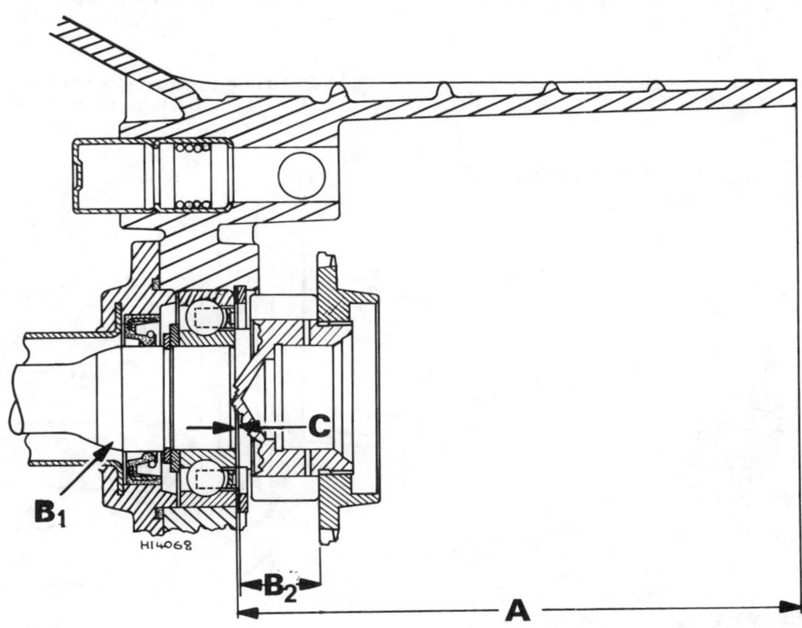

Fig. 6.17 Measuring diagram for the input shaft shim – Getrag 242 (Sec 5)

A Casing face to bearing track *B1 Engraved marks on shaft* *B2 Dimension indicated by B1*

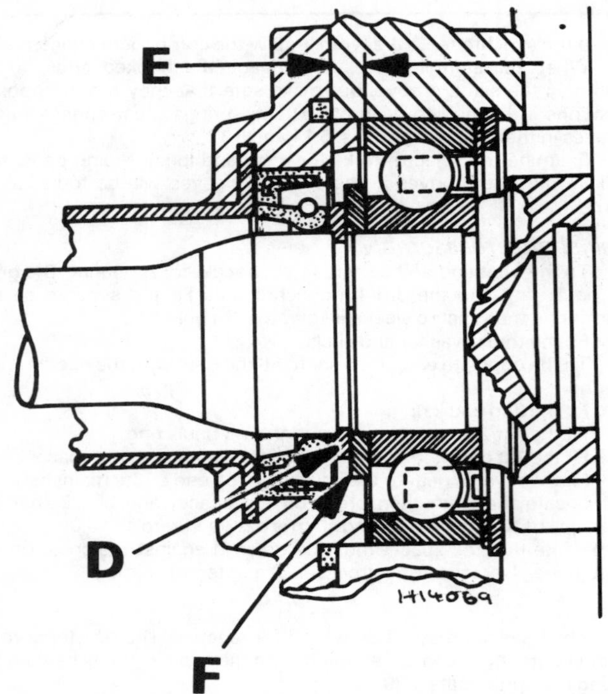

Fig. 6.18 Measuring diagram for the input shaft spacer washer – Getrag 242 (Sec 5)

D Thickness of input shaft circlip *E Circlip-to-bearing clearance* *F Spacer washer*

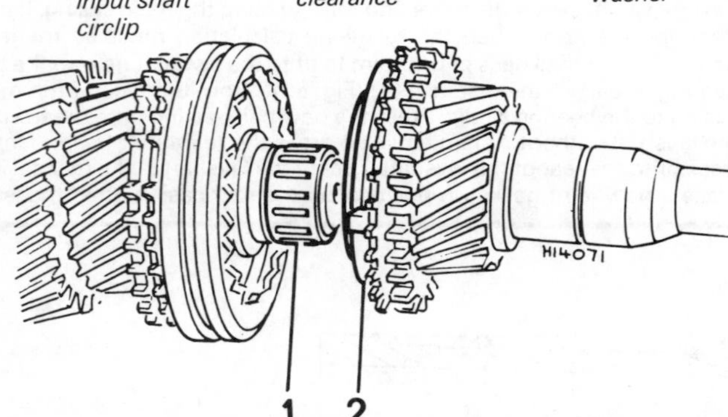

Fig. 6.20 Input shaft needle roller bearing (1) and baulk ring (2) – Getrag 242 (Sec 5)

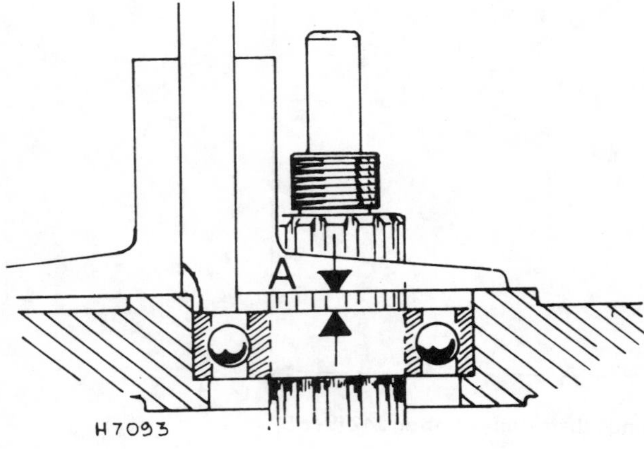

Fig. 6.22 Measuring dimension (A) – casing surface to bearing (Sec 5)

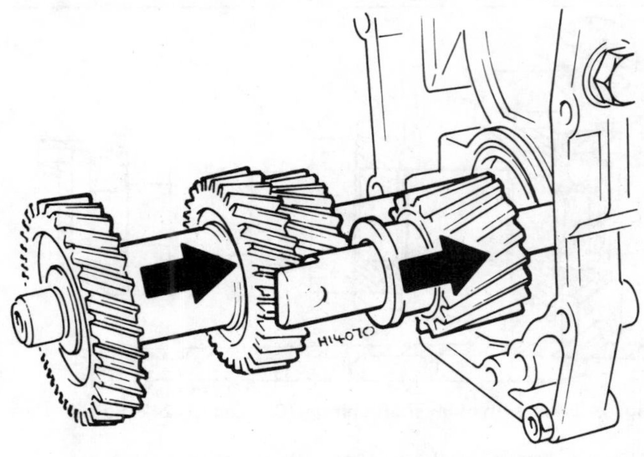

Fig. 6.19 Mesh the reverse idler gear and layshaft together and insert them into the rear casing – Getrag 242 (Sec 5)

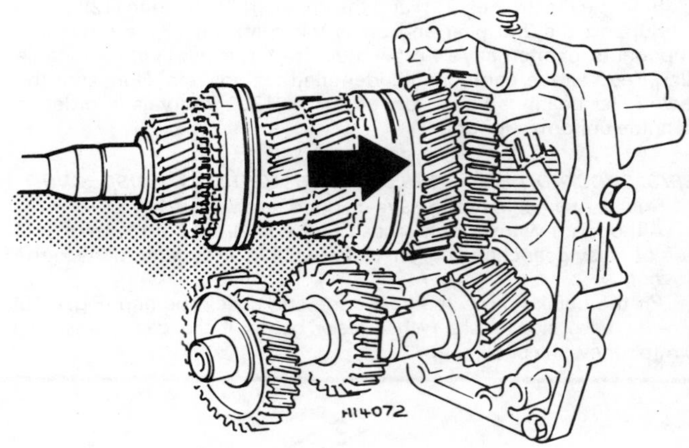

Fig. 6.21 Fitting the mainshaft/input shaft assembly to the rear casing – Getrag 242 (Sec 5)

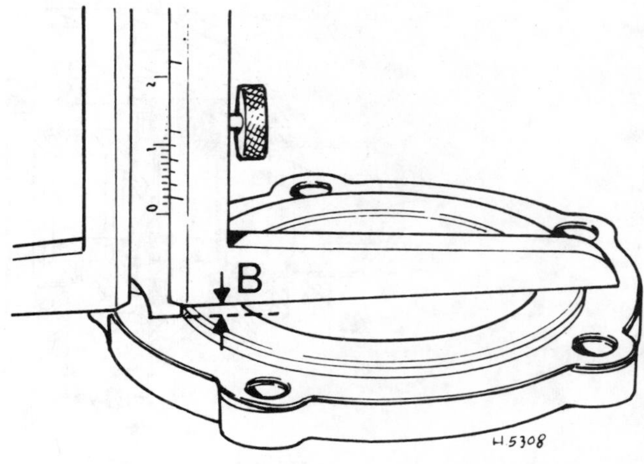

Fig. 6.23 Measuring the rear cover shoulder height (B) (Sec 5)

A new gasket is in position

Fig. 6.24 Fitting the reverse selector shaft (arrowed) – Getrag 242 (Sec 5)

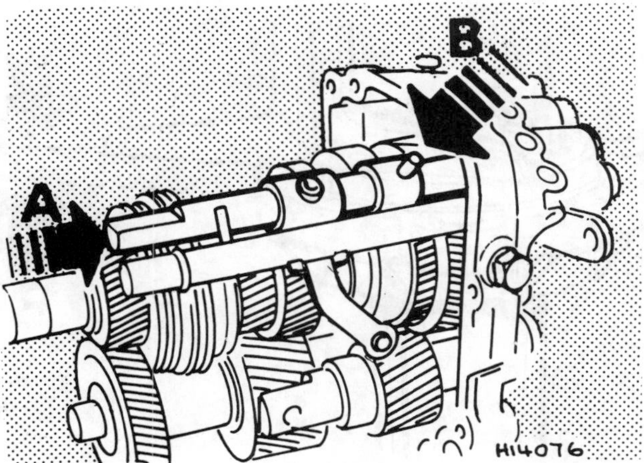

Fig. 6.25 Fitting 1st/2nd selector shaft – Getrag 242 (Sec 5)

A Push the shaft into position
B Fit the roll pin to secure the selector fork to the shaft

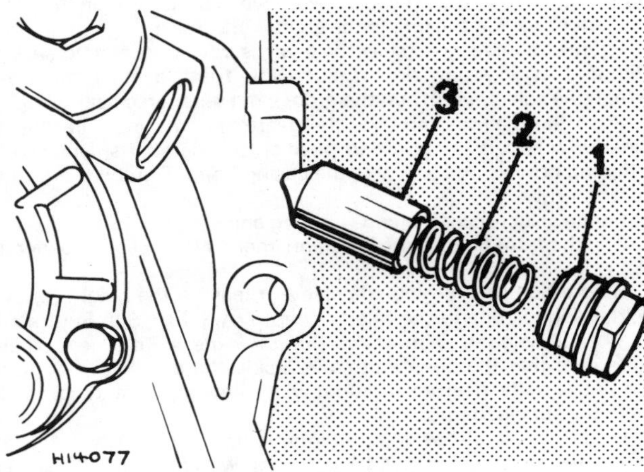

Fig. 6.26 Fit the selector plunger (3), the spring (2) and plug (1) – Getrag 242 (Sec 5)

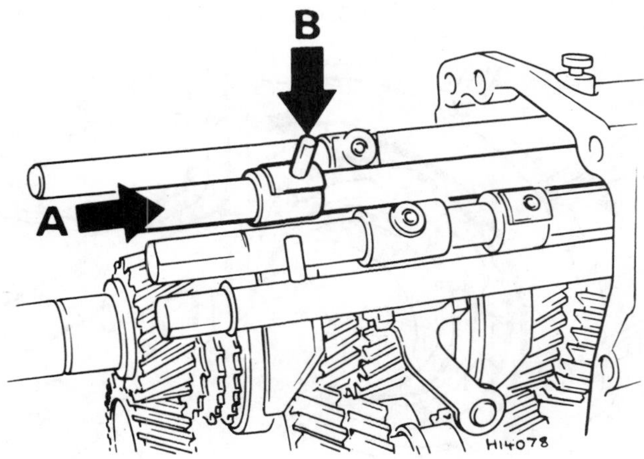

Fig. 6.27 Fitting the 3rd/4th selector shaft – Getrag 242 (Sec 5)

A Push the shaft into position
B Fit the roll pin to secure the selector fork to the shaft

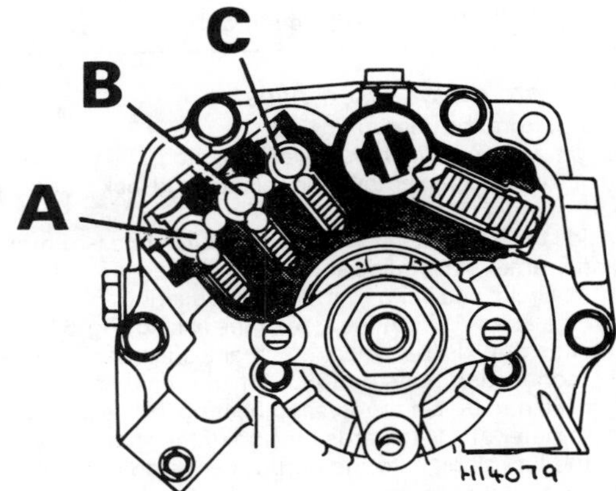

Fig. 6.28 Fitted positions of the detents – Getrag 242 (Sec 5)

A Reverse selector
B 1st/2nd selector
C 3rd/4th selector

from the surface of the gasket to the further edge of the front ball bearing outer track (B) (Fig. 6.15). Subtract (B) from (A) then deduct from this 0.1 to 0.2 mm, the latter being the required axial play. The resulting dimension is the thickness of the shim required (C) (Fig. 6.16) to fit on the front of the layshaft before fitting the ball-bearing.

Input (clutch) shaft

47 Only the needle-roller bearing and ball-bearing can be renewed. If the gear teeth are chipped or worn, renew the shaft complete. If a new ball- bearing is to be fitted, locate a 1.0 mm thick shim in the main casing and fit the new bearing.

48 Measure (A) (Fig. 6.17) from the end of the main casing to the face of the bearing outer track. Note the dimension (B) engraved on the input (clutch) shaft. Refer to the following table and read off the thickness of the shim (C) which will be required.

A (mm)	B (engraved mark)	B (mm)	C (mm)
159.9	*3 or 4 lines*	*24.0*	*0.5*
159.9	*1 or 2 lines*	*23.9*	*0.6*
159.8	*3 or 4 lines*	*24.0*	*0.4*
159.8	*1 or 2 lines*	*23.9*	*0.5*
159.7	*3 or 4 lines*	*24.0*	*0.3*
159.7	*1 or 2 lines*	*23.9*	*0.4*
159.6	*3 or 4 lines*	*24.0*	*0.2*
159.6	*1 or 2 lines*	*23.9*	*0.3*

49 Remove the input shaft bearing from the main casing, fit the shim then refit the bearing.

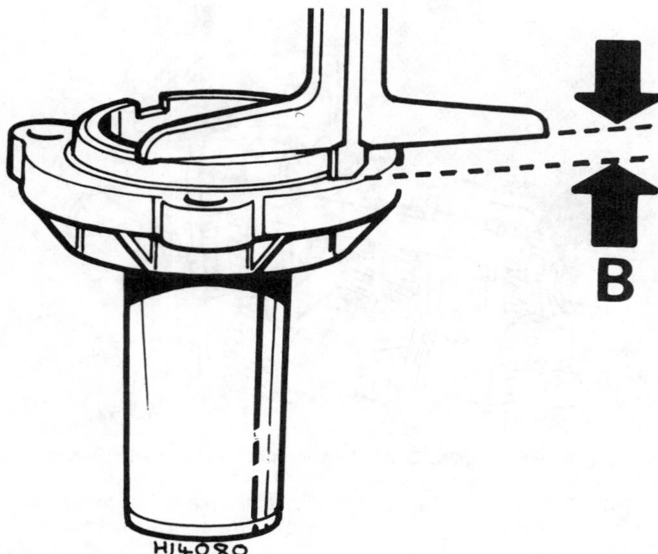

Fig. 6.29 Measuring the guide sleeve shoulder (B) – Getrag 242 (Sec 5)

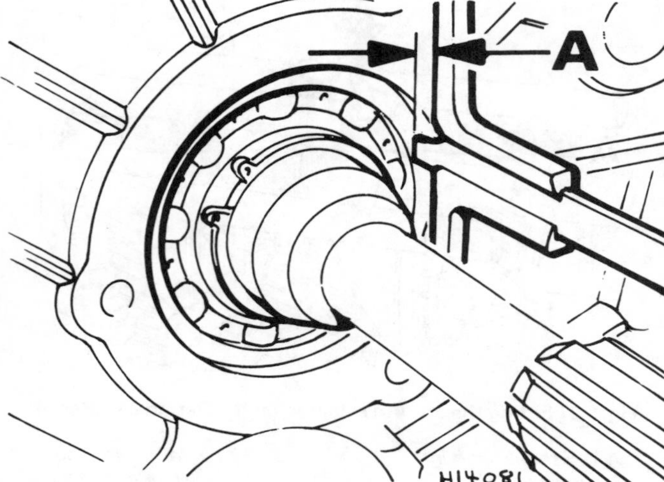

Fig. 6.30 Measuring the depth of the bearing (A) – Getrag 242 (Sec 5)

50 Now measure the thickness (D) of the input shaft bearing circlip (Fig. 6.18). Measure (E) to determine the circlip-to-bearing dimension. Subtract (D) from (E) and select a spacer washer (F) of this thickness. Fit the spacer washer and circlip to the input shaft.

Reassembly of gearbox

51 Mesh the reverse idler gear with the layshaft and fit both units into the rear casing (Fig. 6.19).
52 Connect the input (clutch) shaft to the mainshaft, making sure that the needle-roller bearing is in the recess in the end of the input shaft and the baulk ring correctly located (Fig. 6.20).
53 Fit the shafts to the rear casing (Fig. 6.21).
54 Locate the bearing on the rear end of the mainshaft and then tap it down the shaft and into the casing.
55 Using a depth gauge, measure the recess (A) (Fig. 6.22) of the rear bearing from the casing surface.
56 Now measure the height (B) (Fig. 6.23) of the end cover shoulder without a gasket but subtract 0.2 mm from the dimension to allow for the compressed gasket. Subtract (B) from (A) to determine the thickness of the shim to fit next to the rear bearing. Fit the shim.
57 Fit a new oil seal to the rear cover then fit the cover to the rear casing together with a new gasket and tighten the bolts to the specified torque.
58 Fit the output flange, and screw on the nut. Hold the flange against rotation and tighten the nut to the specified torque. Fit a new nut locking cup and stake it into the cut-out provided.
59 Insert the locking ball into the hole in the rear casing and then fit the reverse selector shaft (Fig. 6.24). If there is any difficulty in inserting the shaft, hold the ball depressed with a dummy shaft which will then be displaced by the real shaft as it is pushed into position.
60 Drive out the roll pin and separate the 1st/2nd selector fork from its shaft. Locate the 1st/2nd selector fork in the synchro sleeve groove.
61 Insert the locking and detent balls into the hole in the rear casing and push the 1st/2nd selector shaft into position (Fig. 6.25). Hold the balls depressed with a dummy shaft, if necessary. Reconnect the fork to the shaft by driving in the roll pin.
62 Locate 3rd/4th selector fork in its synchro sleeve groove. Move the sleeve to 4th gear position.
63 Push the selector shaft into the rear casing and turn it so that the selector finger points downwards.
64 Insert and tighten the locking screw, then engage neutral.
65 Check that the bush in the rear casing is positioned so that the plunger hole is aligned correctly. Fit the selector plunger, spring and plug (Fig. 6.26) having applied thread-locking fluid to the plug threads.
66 Insert the interlock and detent balls into the rear casing and push 3rd/4th selector shaft into position (Figs. 6.27 and 6.28), again using the dummy shaft if required. The shaft will have passed through the hole in the selector fork. Pin the fork to the shaft with a roll pin.
67 Fit the reverse gear selector lever, screw in the reverse lamp switch and tap in a new detent plug. Note that clearance must exist between the selector arm and the groove of the reverse gear wheel.
68 Push the main casing over the geartrains, making sure that the original or selected shims are in position on the shafts. Drive in the positioning dowels and screw in the casing bolts. Tighten them to the specified torque.
69 Fit the selector shaft plunger, spring and cap.
70 Tap the front bearing into position, then fit the spacer washer and circlip.
71 Before bolting on the guide sleeve, measure the height (B) of its shoulder (Fig. 6.29) and the bearing depth (A) (Fig. 6.30). Subtract (B) from (A) and select a shim of the same thickness. Fit a new oil seal, making sure that the open end faces inside the gearbox, then fit the guide sleeve to the gearbox together with a new gasket and tighten the bolts to the specified torque.
72 Fit the clutch release components, as described in Chapter 5, and screw in the drain plug. Fill the transmission with the correct grade and quantity of oil after it is fitted in the car.

6 Gearbox (Getrag 240, 5-speed) – overhaul

Dismantling into major assemblies

1 Drain the oil from the gearbox.
2 Unscrew and remove the reverse lamp switch.
3 Using a pair of pincers, remove the selector rod lock plunger cap (1), spring (2) and plunger (3) (Fig. 6.32).
4 From inside the bellhousing, remove the clutch release components and unbolt and remove the guide sleeve and spacer.
5 Extract the circlip and shim from the front bearing.
6 Unscrew the bolts (1) from the side of the casing (Fig. 6.33).
7 Tap out the dowels between the main and rear casings, then unscrew the connecting bolts and pull off the main casing. Note the position of the 60 mm bolt. If the layshaft bearing is displaced, note that the smaller diameter of it is towards the end of the shaft.
8 Release the lockplate, hold the output flange against rotation and unscrew the output flange nut. Draw off the flange using a puller, if necessary.
9 Unscrew the bolts (1 and 3) and remove the holder (2) (Fig. 6.34).
10 Remove the reverse idler shaft with the gear and needle-roller bearing.
11 Drive out the roll pin (1), pull out the selector rail (3) and take off the operating lever (2) (Fig. 6.35).
12 Move the synchro sleeve to engage 4th gear. Drive the roll pin (1) out far enough to be able to withdraw the selector rod (Fig. 6.36). Watch for the selector rod rollers. The oil seal will also be pulled out.
13 Unbolt the detent plate (Fig. 6.37) and extract the three detent springs.

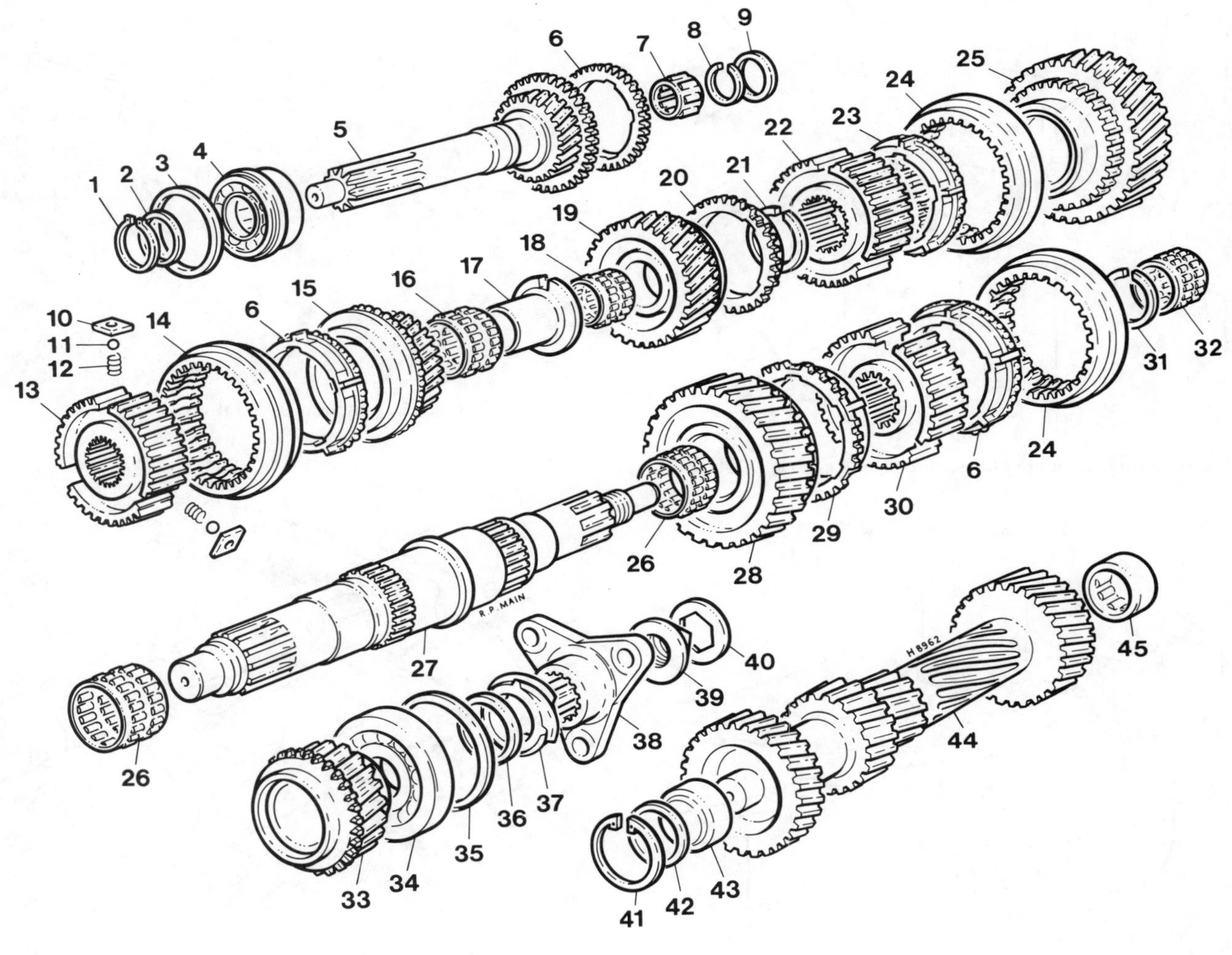

Fig. 6.31 Internal components of the Getrag 240 5-speed gearbox (Sec 6)

1 *Circlip*
2 *Spacer*
3 *Spacer*
4 *Bearing*
5 *Input shaft with 4th gear*
6 *Baulk ring*
7 *Needle-roller bearing*
8 *Circlip*
9 *Spacer*
10 *Sliding key*
11 *Ball*
12 *Spring*
13 *3rd/4th synchro-hub*
14 *3rd/4th synchro sleeve*
15 *3rd gear*
16 *Needle-roller bearing*
17 *Bearing sleeve*
18 *Needle-roller bearing*
19 *2nd gear*
20 *Baulk ring*
21 *Circlip*
22 *1st/2nd synchro-hub*
23 *Baulk ring*
24 *1st/2nd synchro sleeve*
25 *1st gear*
26 *Needle-roller bearing*
27 *Mainshaft*
28 *Reverse gear*
29 *Baulk ring*
30 *Reverse/5th synchro-hub*
31 *Circlip*
32 *Needle-roller bearing*
33 *5th gear*
34 *Bearing*
35 *Spacer*
36 *Spacer*
37 *Spacer*
38 *Output flange*
39 *Nut*
40 *Nut locking cup*
41 *Circlip*
42 *Spacer*
43 *Bearing*
44 *Layshaft*
45 *Bearing*

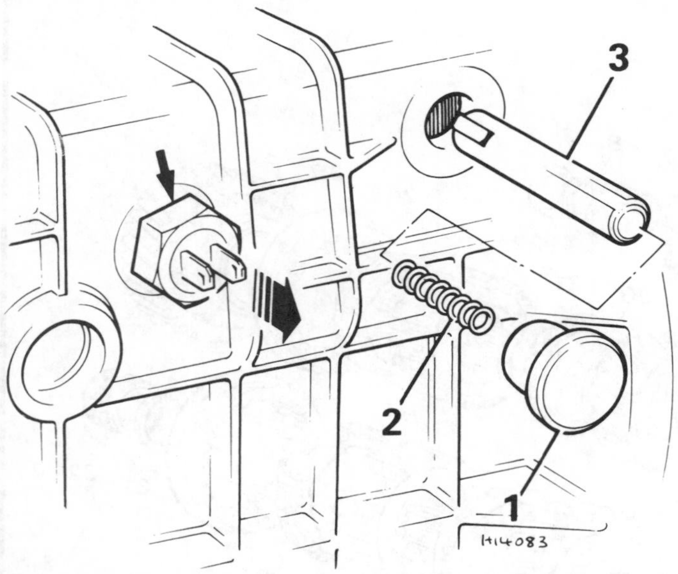

Fig. 6.32 Selector rod plunger (3), spring (2) and cap (1) – Getrag 240 (Sec 6)

Reverse switch arrowed

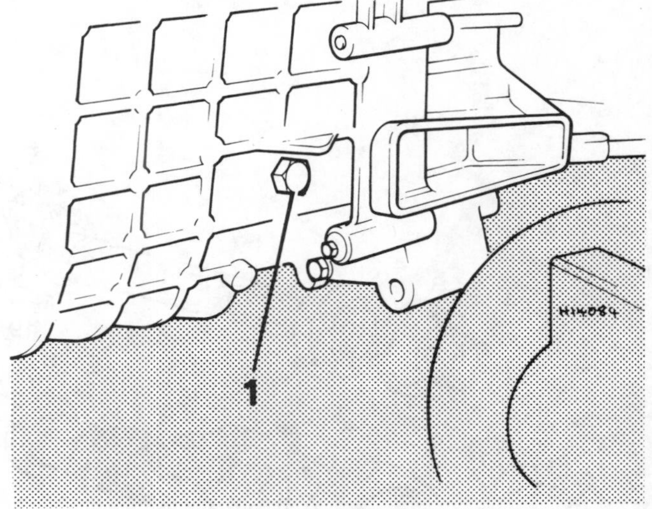

Fig. 6.33 Lockbolt (1) – Getrag 240 (Sec 6)

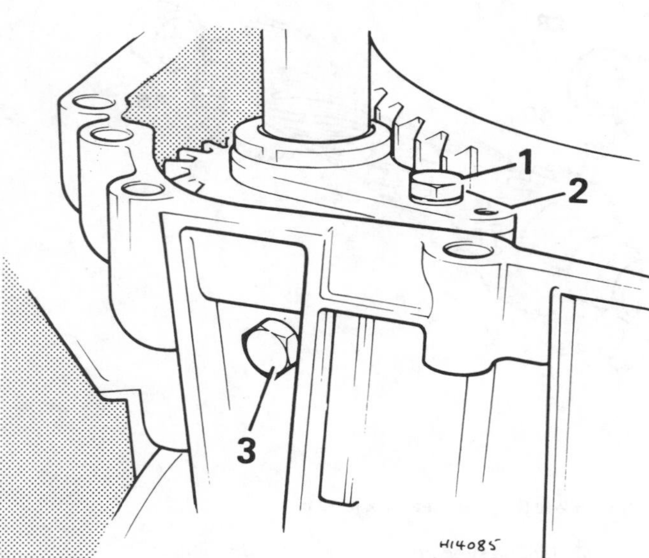

Fig. 6.34 Holder (2) and holder bolts (1 and 3) – Getrag 240 (Sec 6)

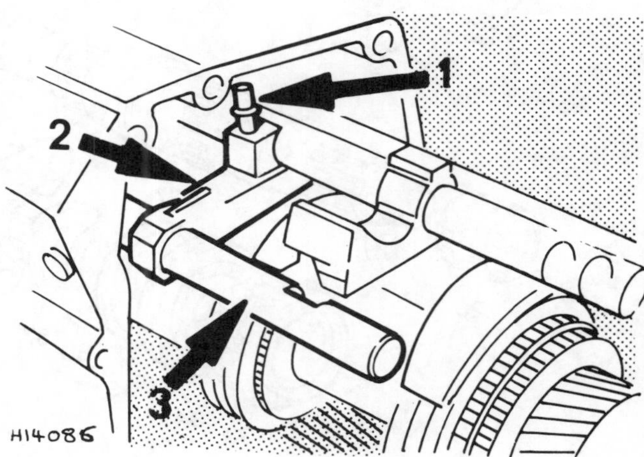

Fig. 6.35 Selector operating lever roll pin (1), operating lever (2) and selector rail (3) – Getrag 240 (Sec 6)

14 Prise out the selector shaft end plug.

15 Drive out the roll pin from the 3rd/4th selector fork (Fig. 6.38) and draw the shaft out towards the front of the gearbox, noting the interlock pin.

16 Select 2nd gear and reverse gears together by pushing their respective selector rods towards the front of the gearbox.

17 Press or tap the input shaft, output shaft and layshaft simultaneously together with the selector shafts out of the rear casing. Retrieve all the detent balls and springs.

Mainshaft – dismantling

18 Pull the input (clutch) shaft from the mainshaft, take off the baulk ring (nickel-plated) and extract the needle-roller bearing.

19 A puller or press may be needed to remove some assemblies from the shaft. Remove the 5th gear (1), the baulk ring (2) (brass), and the needle-roller bearing (3) (Fig. 6.39) from the rear end of the mainshaft.

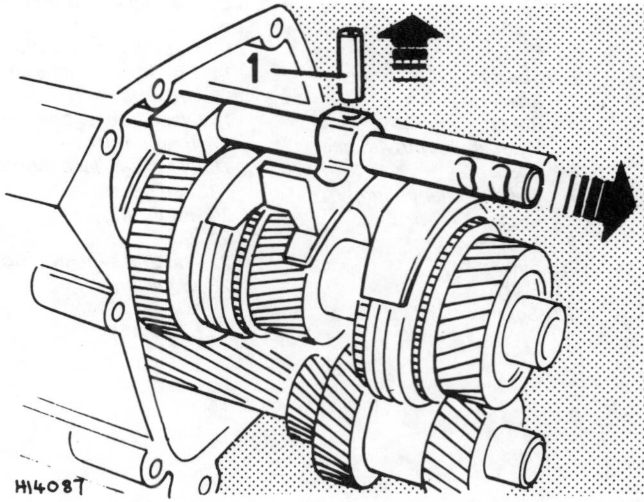

Fig. 6.36 Remove the roll pin (1) and withdraw the selector rod – Getrag 240 (Sec 6)

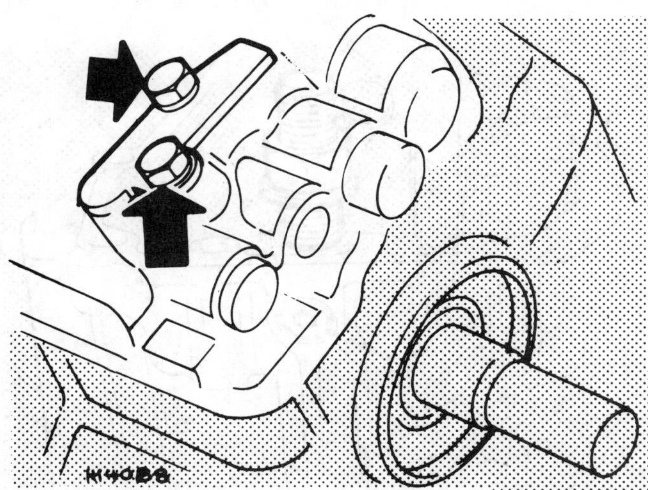

Fig. 6.37 Detent end plate securing bolts (arrowed) – Getrag 240 (Sec 6)

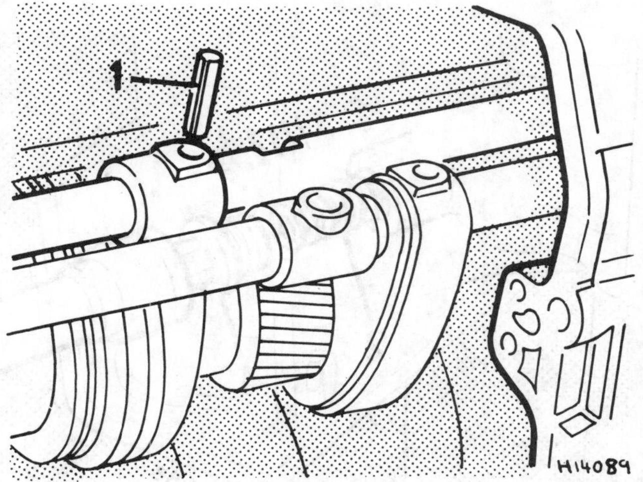

Fig. 6.38 3rd/4th selector fork roll pin (1) – Getrag 240 (Sec 6)

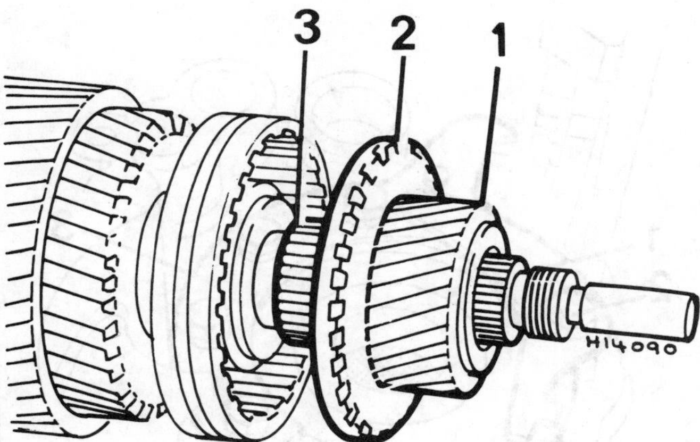

Fig. 6.39 Remove 5th gear (1), the baulk ring (2), and needle-roller bearing (3) from the mainshaft – Getrag 240 (Sec 6)

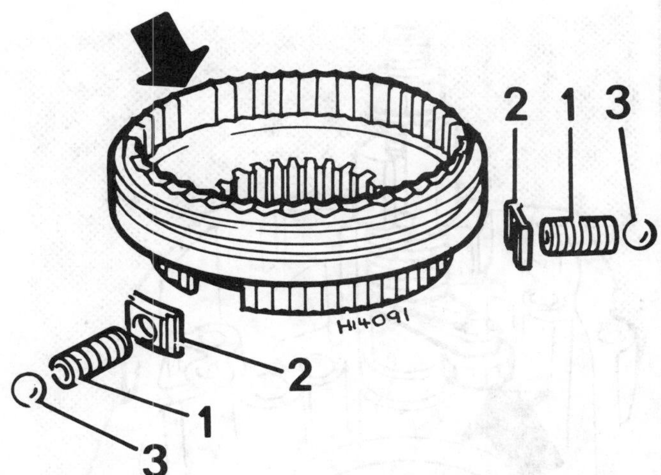

Fig. 6.40 Synchro components – Getrag 240 (Sec 6)

1 Spring
2 Sliding key
3 Ball

The flat teeth of the sleeve (arrowed) must align with the sliding keys

20 Extract the circlip and remove the spacer from the front end of the shaft.
21 Remove the 3rd gear and the needle-roller bearing with the 3rd/4th synchro unit.
22 Remove the bearing sleeve and 2nd gear. Take off the baulk ring (nickel-plated) and the needle-roller bearing.
23 Extract the circlip and remove 1st gear, the needle-roller bearing and the 1st/2nd synchro unit.
24 Extract the circlip and remove the reverse gear together with the 5th/reverse synchro unit and needle-roller bearing.

Gears, synchromesh units and selector forks – inspection

25 Renew any gears which have chipped teeth.
26 Although a worn synchromesh unit will already be known as a result of noisy gear changing, check for wear in all synchro units in the following way.
27 Fit the baulk ring to the gear cone and check the gap between the dog faces on the baulk ring and gear adjacent to the stop blocks with a feeler gauge. If the gap is less than 0.8 mm renew the baulk ring. Chipped or worn teeth in the synchro components will mean the purchase of new parts.
28 Mark the synchro sleeve in relation to its hub, then wrap the unit in cloth and push out the hub. The springs, balls and sliding keys will be ejected.
29 When reassembling, note the following points. Align the flat teeth on the sleeve with the sliding keys (Fig. 6.40). On the 3rd/4th unit, the groove in the sleeve must be adjacent to the narrow projection on the

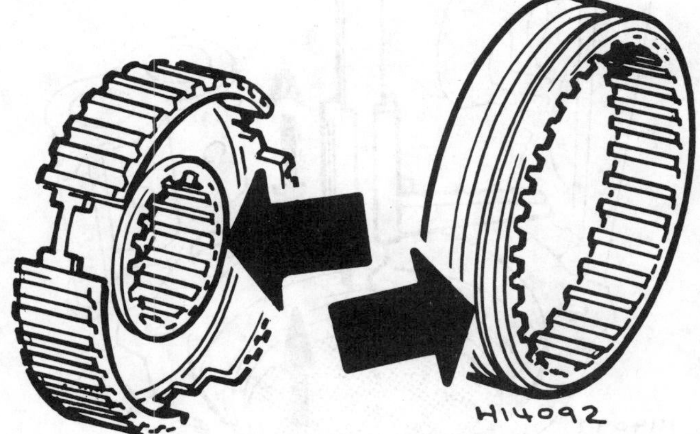

Fig. 6.41 3rd/4th synchro-hub and sleeve alignment – Getrag 240 (Sec 6)

The groove on the sleeve must be adjacent to the smaller hub projection

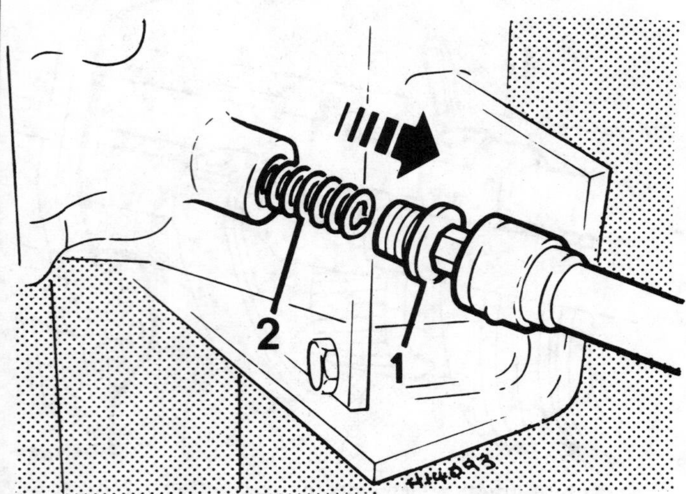

Fig. 6.42 Bolt (1) and spring (2) in the rear casing – Getrag 240 (Sec 6)

Fig. 6.43 Socket-headed bolt (1) in the rear casing – Getrag 240 (Sec 6)

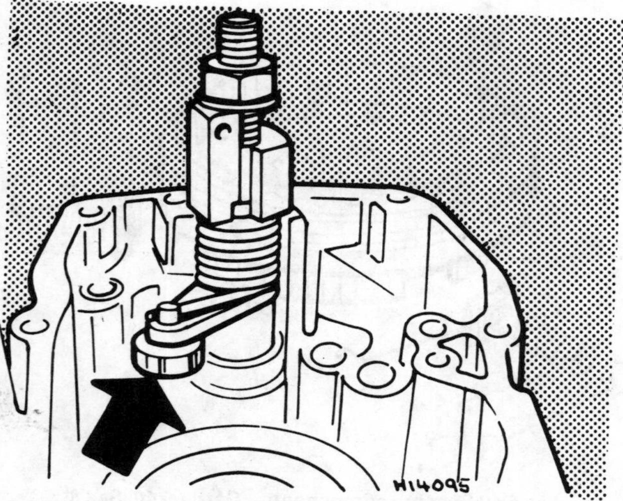

Fig. 6.44 Selector arm – Getrag 240 (Sec 6)

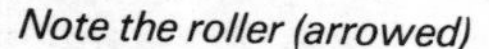

Note the roller (arrowed)

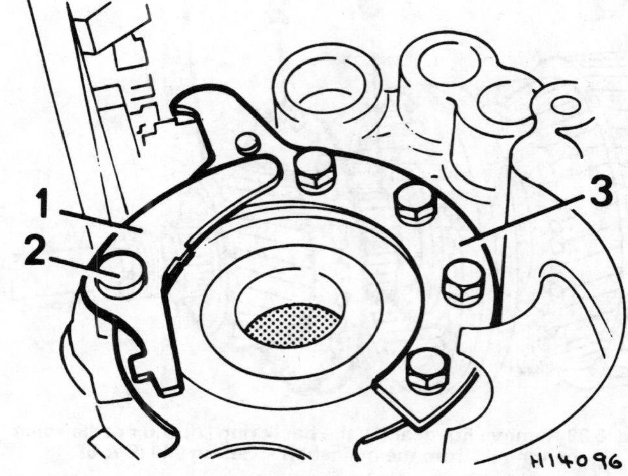

Fig. 6.45 Unbolt and remove the locking lever (1), the spacer (2) and the bearing holder (3) – Getrag 240 (Sec 6)

Fig. 6.46 Measuring the bearing recess depth (A) – Getrag 240 (Sec 6)

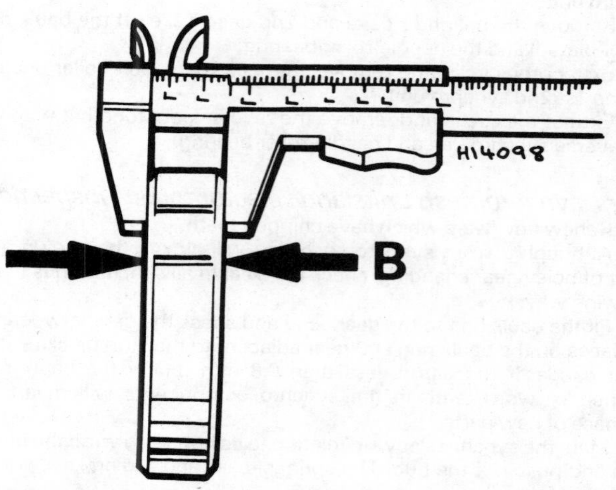

Fig. 6.47 Measuring the width of the new bearing (B) – Getrag 240 (Sec 6)

Fig. 6.48 1st/2nd and 5th/reverse selector shafts and forks located in their mainshaft synchro sleeve grooves – Getrag 240 (Sec 6)

hub (Fig. 6.41). Make sure that the stepped side of the sliding key is towards the synchro sleeve.

30 Examine the selector forks for wear and loose sliding pads. It is unlikely that the grooves in the synchro sleeves will be found to be worn.

Input shaft and mainshaft bearings – renewal

31 Wear in the shaft bearings should be rectified by renewing the bearings in the following way.

32 To remove the input shaft bearing from the main casing, extract the circlip and shim and press or draw the bearing from its seat.

33 To remove the mainshaft bearing from the rear casing, unscrew the bolt (1) (Fig. 6.42) and remove the spring (2).

34 Remove the socket-headed bolt and the selector arm (Figs. 6.43 and 6.44). The BMW tool shown in Fig. 6.44 would assist the removal of the arm.

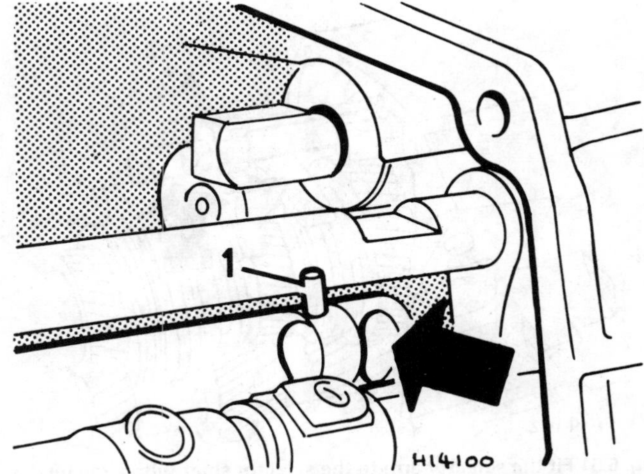

Fig. 6.49 3rd/4th selector shaft interlock pin (1) Getrag 240 (Sec 6)

Arrow indicates detent groove

35 Unscrew and remove the bolt, locking lever (1), spacer (2) and the bearing holder (3) (Fig. 6.45).

36 Extract the oil seal, bearing and shim.

37 To select the shim for use with the new bearing, measure the dimension (A) (Fig. 6.46), then the width of the new bearing (B) (Fig. 6.47). Subtract (B) from (A) for the thickness of the shim to fit.

38 When fitting the bearing, heat the casing in boiling water, place the selected shim in the bearing seat and press in the bearing so that its sealed face enters first.

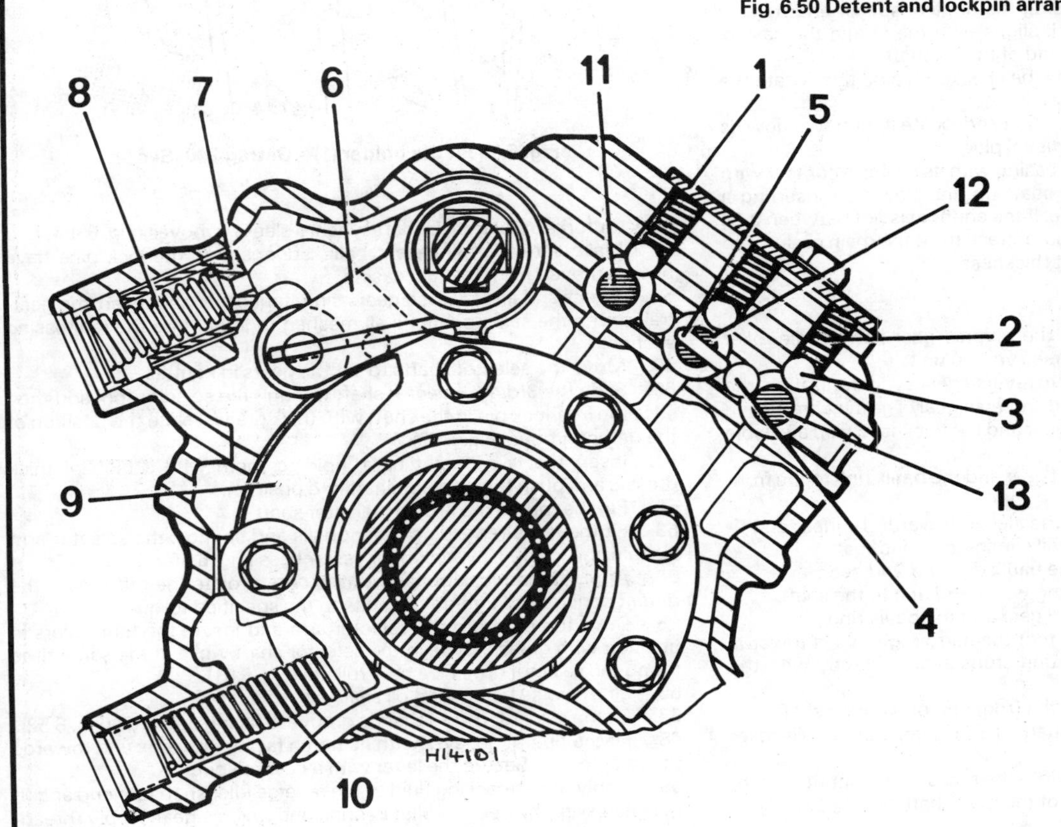

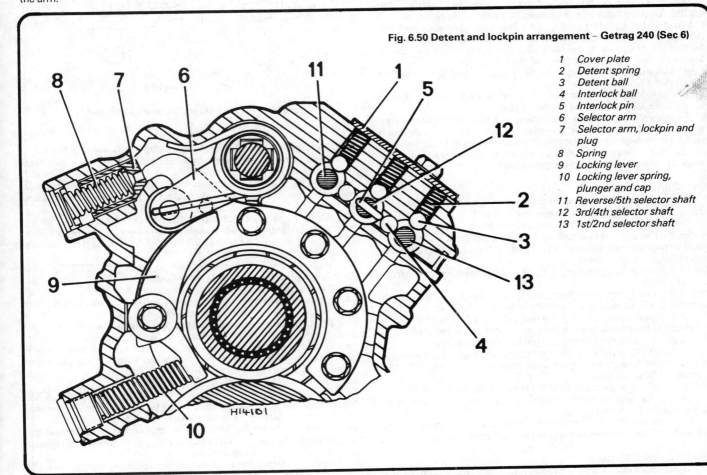

Fig. 6.50 Detent and lockpin arrangement – Getrag 240 (Sec 6)

1 Cover plate
2 Detent spring
3 Detent ball
4 Interlock ball
5 Interlock pin
6 Selector arm
7 Selector arm, lockpin and plug
8 Spring
9 Locking lever
10 Locking lever spring, plunger and cap
11 Reverse/5th selector shaft
12 3rd/4th selector shaft
13 1st/2nd selector shaft

Fig. 6.51 Fit the selector arm to the selector shaft with a roll pin (1) – Getrag 240 (Sec 6)

The grooves in the shaft (arrowed) must face outwards

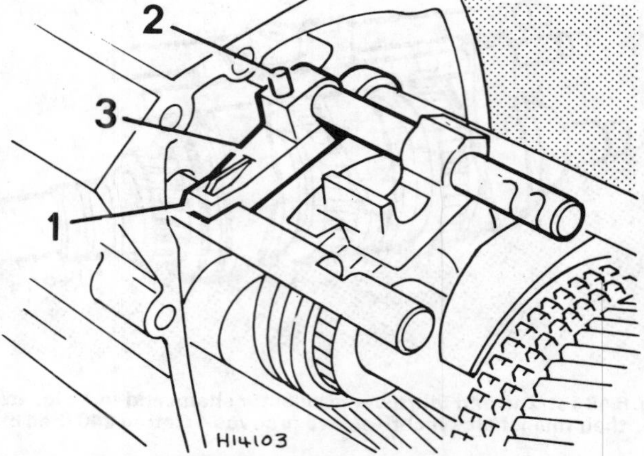

Fig. 6.52 Fitting the selector rail – Getrag 240 (Sec 6)

1 Groove
2 Roll pin
3 Operating lever

Fig. 6.53 Fit the holder (1) – Getrag 240 (Sec 6)

39 Refit the bearing holder and selector arm and tighten all bolts to the specified torque. Make sure that the selector arm roller is located over the locking lever. The socket-headed bolt, and bolt (1) in paragraph 33 should be installed with thread-locking fluid.

Layshaft bearings – renewal

40 The gears cannot be removed from the layshaft, but to renew the layshaft bearing in the rear casing, use a suitable puller to extract the outer track from the casing, then draw the inner race from the end of the layshaft. Fit the new bearing by reversing the removal operations, but align the slot in the track with the casing lock bead in the rear casing.
41 To renew the layshaft bearing in the main casing, remove the outer track and press in the new one, using the original spacer and making sure that the oil groove in the track aligns with the one in the casing. Remove the bearing race from the end of the layshaft.
42 The layshaft endfloat must now be checked. To do this, locate the layshaft in the rear casing bearing track.
43 Lower the main casing into position and locate it with two dowels and two bolts. Unscrew the oil filler/level plug.
44 Locate a dial gauge on the rear casing with its probe in contact with a tooth of the layshaft. Move the shaft up and down by inserting a screwdriver through the oil filler hole. If the endfloat is not between 0.13 and 0.23 mm, remove the bearing outer track from the main casing and change the shim for one of different thickness.

Mainshaft – reassembly

45 To the mainshaft rear end fit the reverse gear and needle-roller bearing, the baulk ring and 5th/reverse synchro unit.
46 On gearboxes which do not have reverse gear synchronization, the circlip in the sleeve must face towards reverse gear. The synchro sleeve should be pushed towards reverse gear and the thickest circlip available fitted to eliminate all endfloat.
47 Fit the needle-roller bearing, 1st gear and the baulk ring to the front end of the shaft.
48 Fit the 1st/2nd synchro. Push the sleeve towards 1st gear and fit the thickest circlip available which will eliminate all endfloat.
49 Fit the needle-roller bearing, the baulk ring and 2nd gear.
50 Heat the bearing sleeve in boiling water and fit it to the shaft.
51 Fit the needle-roller bearing, 3rd gear and the baulk ring.
52 Fit the 3rd/4th synchro unit so that the narrow groove is towards 4th gear. Make sure that the baulk ring stops align correctly with the openings in the synchro sleeve.
53 Fit the spacer and the circlip to the front end of the mainshaft.
54 To the rear end of the mainshaft fit 5th gear, the needle-roller bearing and the baulk ring.
55 Insert the needle-roller bearing into the recess in the input (clutch) shaft and connect it to the front end of the mainshaft.

Gearbox – reassembly

56 Locate the 1st/2nd and 5th/reverse selector shafts with all the selector forks in their mainshaft synchro sleeve grooves (Fig. 6.48).
57 Make sure that all detent balls, springs and interlock pins have been removed from the rear casing.
58 Select 2nd and reverse gears simultaneously and insert the geartrains with the selector shafts all meshed together into the rear casing section.
59 Move the selector shafts to set the gears in neutral.
60 Slide the 3rd/4th selector shaft through the selector fork and then stick the interlock pin in the shaft with thick grease. Note the position of the detent groove (Fig. 6.49).
61 Insert the two detent balls, holding them with a blob of thick grease, and push the selector shaft into position.
62 Pin the fork to the 3rd/4th selector shaft.
63 Fit the three remaining detent balls and springs. the selector arm lockpin and locking lever plunger assemblies (Fig. 6.50).
64 Apply thread-locking fluid to the detent plate then fit it over the detent springs and tighten the bolts to the specified torque.
65 Drive the pin from the selector arm and locate the four rollers in position with grease. Slide in the selector shaft while at the same time fitting the selector arm. Fit a new roll pin (Fig. 6.51).
66 Fit a new selector shaft oil seal.
67 Fit the selector rod so that its groove is facing upwards (Fig. 6.52).
68 Fit the operating lever with its notch facing upwards and towards the selector rail. Secure the lever with a new roll pin.
69 Apply thread-locking fluid to the reverse idler shaft rear end and fit the shaft with the needle-roller bearing and reverse gear. Apply thread-locking fluid to the lock bolt and screw it into position.
70 Fit the holder (1) (Fig. 6.53), align, then insert and tighten the bolts.
71 Fit the output flange. Apply thread-locking fluid and tighten the nut

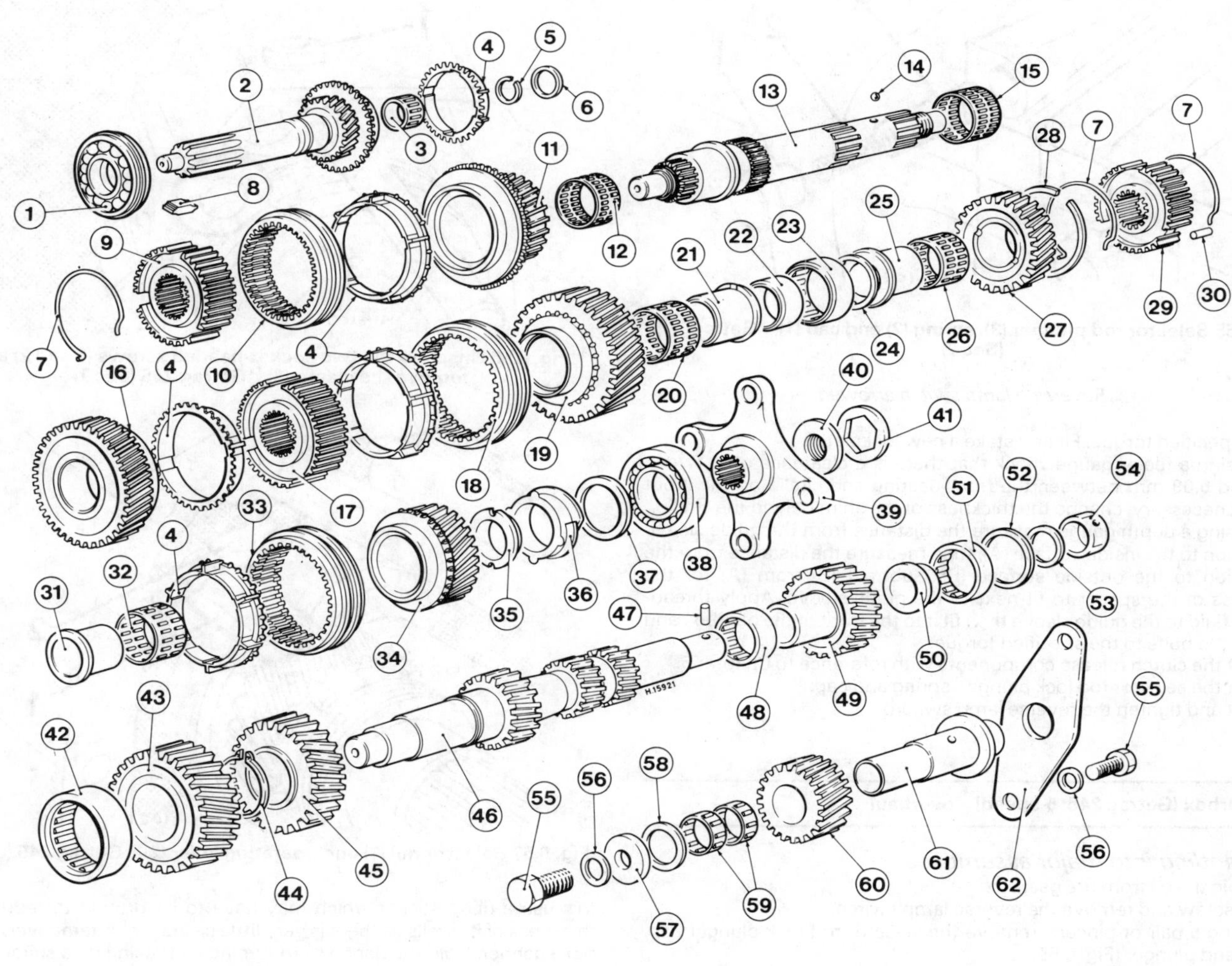

Fig. 6.54 Internal components of the Getrag 245 5-speed overdrive gearbox (Sec 7)

1 *Ball bearing*
2 *Input shaft*
3 *Needle-roller bearing*
4 *Baulk ring*
5 *Circlip*
6 *Washer*
7 *Synchro spring*
8 *Sliding key*
9 *3rd/4th synchro-hub*
10 *3rd/4th synchro sleeve*
11 *3rd gear*
12 *Needle-roller bearing*
13 *Mainshaft*
14 *Lockball*
15 *Needle-roller bearing*
16 *2nd gear*
17 *1st/2nd synchro-hub*
18 *1st/2nd synchro sleeve*
19 *1st gear*
20 *Needle-roller bearing*
21 *Bearing bush*
22 *Bearing inner track*
23 *Roller bearing*
24 *Shim (X)*
25 *Bearing bush*
26 *Needle-roller bearing*
27 *Reverse gear*
28 *Circlip*
29 *Reverse/5th synchro-hub*
30 *Sliding key*
31 *Bearing bush*
32 *Needle-roller bearing*
33 *Reverse/5th synchro sleeve*
34 *5th gear*
35 *Washer*
36 *Spacer*
37 *Washer*
38 *Ball-bearing*
39 *Output flange*
40 *Nut*
41 *Nut locking cup*
42 *Roller bearing*
43 *4th gear*
44 *Circlip*
45 *3rd gear*
46 *Layshaft*
47 *Pin*
48 *Roller bearing*
49 *5th gear*
50 *Bearing inner track*
51 *Roller bearing*
52 *Washer*
53 *Washer*
54 *Collar*
55 *Reverse idler shaft bolt*
56 *Lockwasher*
57 *Washer*
58 *Thrustwasher*
59 *Needle-roller bearing*
60 *Reverse idler gear*
61 *Reverse idler shaft*
62 *Reverse idler shaft holder*

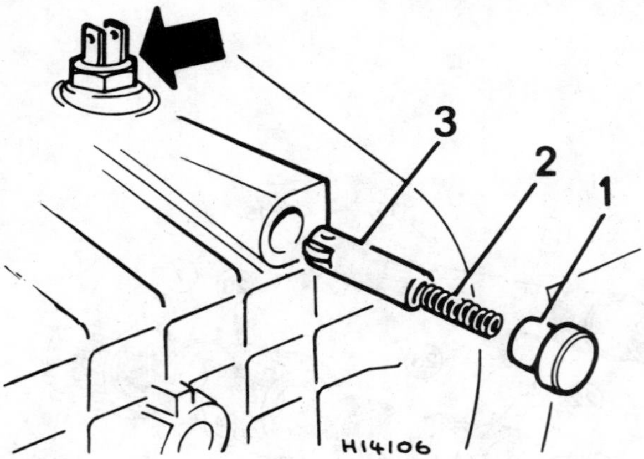

Fig. 6.55 Selector rod plunger (3), spring (2) and cap (1) – Getrag 245 (Sec 7)

Reversing lamp switch arrowed

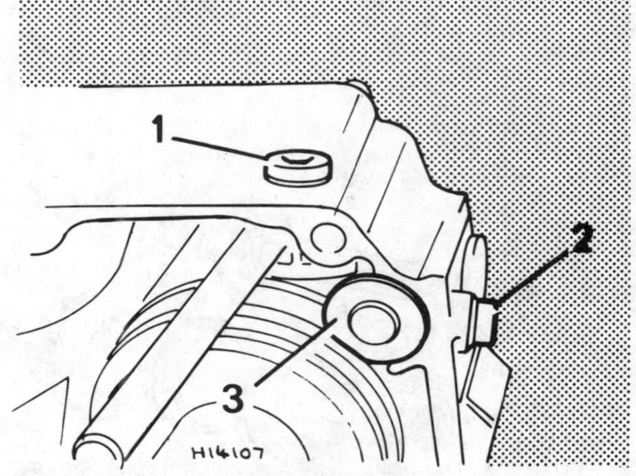

Fig. 6.56 Unscrew the two socket-headed screws (1 and 2) and remove the clamp (3) – Getrag 245 (Sec 7)

to the specified torque. Fit and stake a new lockplate.

72 Using a feeler gauge check that there is a clearance of between zero and 0.09 mm between the front bearing and circlip on the input shaft. If necessary, change the thickness of the shim behind the circlip.

73 Using a depth gauge measure the distance from the guide sleeve protrusion to the inside surface (A), then measure the distance from the protrusion to the outside surface (B). Subtract (B) from (A) for the thickness of the spacer to fit next to the guide sleeve. Apply thread-locking fluid to the guide sleeve then fit it to the front of the gearbox and tighten the bolts to the specified torque.

74 Fit the clutch release components with reference to Chapter 5.

75 Fit the selector rod lock plunger, spring and cap.

76 Fit and tighten the reverse lamp switch.

7 Gearbox (Getrag 245, 5-speed) – overhaul

Dismantling into major assemblies

1 Drain the oil from the gearbox.

2 Unscrew and remove the reverse lamp switch.

3 Using a pair of pincers, remove the selector rod lock plunger cap, spring and plunger (Fig. 6.55).

4 From inside the bellhousing, remove the clutch release components and unbolt and remove the guide sleeve and spacer.

5 Extract the circlip and shim from the front bearing.

6 Tap out the dowels between the main and rear casings.

7 Unscrew and remove the casing connecting bolts including the socket-headed bolt.

8 Withdraw the main casing from the intermediate casing. Take care to catch the shaft bearings which may be displaced.

9 Prise out the locking cup then unscrew the output flange nut. To do this use a deep socket which may have to be ground to reduce the thickness of its walls as there is very little clearance. Alternatively, use a box spanner. Hold the flange from turning by making up a suitable tool (photo). Pull off the flange using a suitable puller, if necessary.

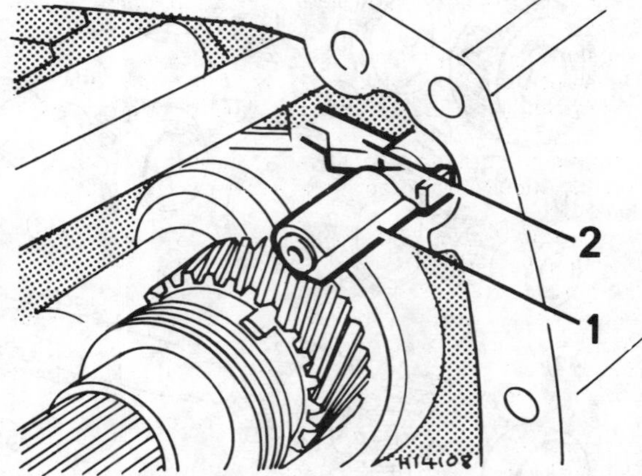

Fig. 6.57 Selector rail (1) and operating lever (2) – Getrag 245 (Sec 7)

10 Unbolt and remove the rear cover and gasket together with any shims.

11 Drive out the dowels from the rear cover and unscrew the single bolt from the top of the rear casing.

12 Engage 2nd gear then pull off the rear casing taking care not to drop the rollers on the selector shaft or the layshaft bearing.

13 Drive the ball-bearing out of the rear cover and remove the sealing cover. Also unscrew and remove the oil drain plug.

7.9 Tool for holding output flange

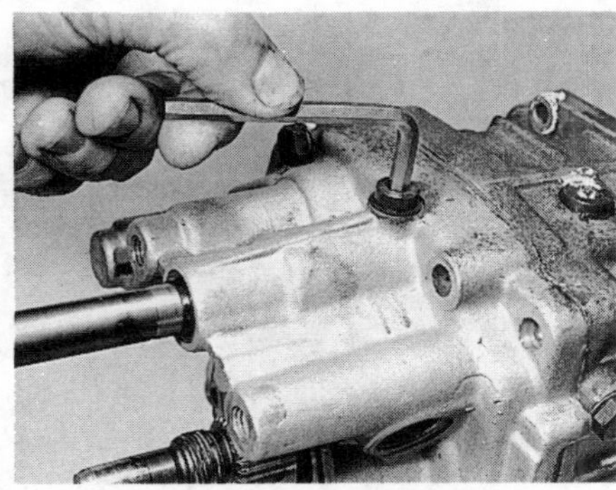

7.15 Operating lever socket screw

7.36 Drawing 3rd gear and synchro unit from the mainshaft

14 Unscrew the two socket-headed screws (1 and 2) and remove the clamp (3) (Fig. 6.56).
15 Withdraw the selector rail (1) towards the rear of the gearbox and remove the operating lever (2) held by a socket-headed screw (photo and Fig. 6.57).
16 Drive out the roll pin from the dog (Fig. 6.58). Pull the selector rod towards the rear of the gearbox, take off the selector arm.
17 Where applicable, pull the spacer from the end of the mainshaft.
18 Drive out the pin from the end of the layshaft and remove the spacer sleeve and shims.
19 Draw off the layshaft 5th gear with bearing race.
20 Remove the 5th gear, 5th baulk ring and the needle-roller bearing from the mainshaft.
21 Push the 5th/reverse selector shaft towards the rear of the gearbox and then drive the roll pin from the selector fork. During this operation, the synchro sleeve will probably separate from its hub and release the sliding keys.
22 Slide the fork, with the synchro from the 5th/reverse selector shaft, but avoid removing the shaft unless absolutely essential. If it must be done, watch for ejection of the spring-loaded balls and note that the shaft detent grooves are towards the bottom of the gearbox. To completely remove the shaft the selector groove must face upwards.
23 Drive the roll pins from the 1st/2nd selector fork and selector dog then remove the selector shaft and dog, taking care not to lose the detent balls.
24 Engage 3rd gear by moving the synchro sleeve.
25 Drive out the roll pin which holds the fork to the 3rd/4th selector shaft. Align the roll pin so that it passes out into the gap in the synchro teeth.
26 Remove the 3rd/4th selector shaft taking care not to lose the detent balls. Should the detent balls jam use a length of thin wire to dislodge them.
27 Remove the 1st/2nd and 3rd/4th selector forks from their respective synchro units.
28 Unscrew the two socket-headed screws (Fig. 6.59) and remove the reverse gear holder. Unscrew the reverse gear idler shaft fixing bolt and remove the washer (Fig. 6.60).
29 Screw a bolt into the reverse idler shaft and tap out the reverse gear and shaft. Note the position of the flat on the washer.
30 From the mainshaft pull off the reverse gear and remove the flanged bush and needle-roller bearing.
31 Pull the bearing bush from the mainshaft and remove the shim.
32 Remove the layshaft and mainshaft from the intermediate casing while meshed together.
33 From the rear end of the mainshaft, take off the shim. Separate the input (clutch) shaft from the mainshaft and remove the baulk ring and needle-roller bearing.

Mainshaft – dismantling

34 A press or puller will be required to remove some gears and synchro units from the shaft.
35 Extract the circlip from the front end of the shaft and take off the spacer washer.
36 Remove the 3rd/4th synchro unit, the 3rd baulk ring and the 3rd gear together using a puller (photo).
37 Remove the split needle-roller bearing.
38 Pull off the following parts together in one operation from the rear of the mainshaft – 1st gear and needle-roller bearing, 1st/2nd synchro unit and baulk rings, bearing track and the spacer, 2nd gear and needle-roller bearing.

Fig. 6.58 1st/2nd selector shaft roll pins (1 and 2) – Getrag 245 (Sec 7)

3 *Dog*

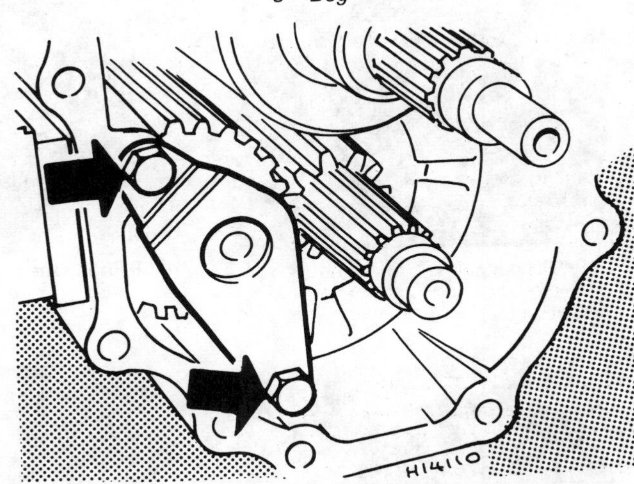

Fig. 6.59 Reverse gear holder retaining screws (arrowed) – Getrag 245 (Sec 7)

Gears, synchromesh units and selector forks – inspection

39 Refer to Section 5 paragraphs 29 to 34 inclusive.

Layshaft – inspection

40 The 3rd, 4th and 5th gears can be removed from the layshaft if the

7.41 Layshaft roller bearing

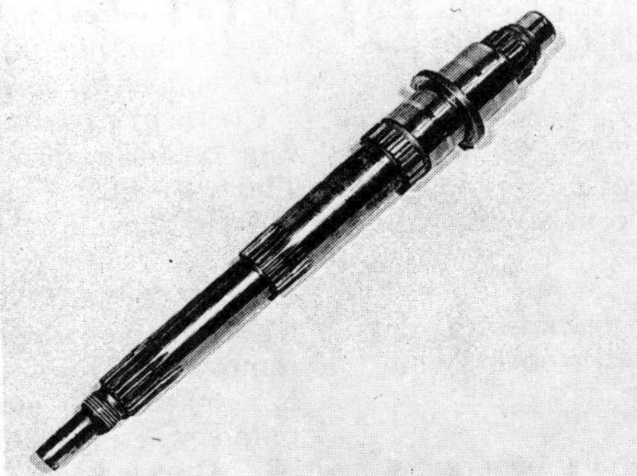

7.42A Mainshaft stripped

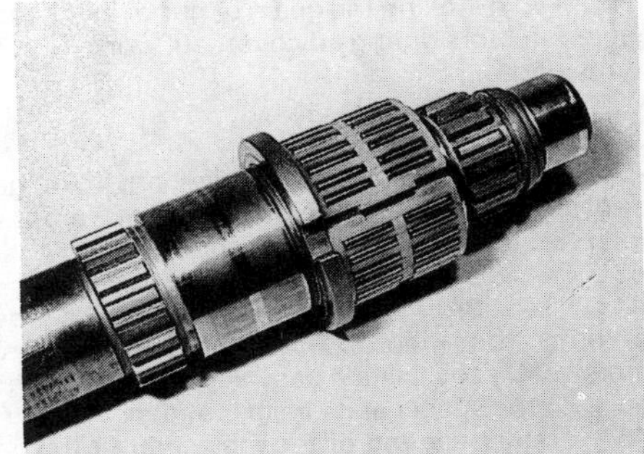

7.42B 3rd gear needle-roller bearing

7.42C Fitting 3rd gear to the mainshaft

7.43 Fitting the baulk ring to 3rd gear

7.44 Fitting 3rd/4th synchro (arrow indicates groove)

7.45A Spacer

7.45B Fitting the circlip

7.46A 2nd gear needle-roller bearing

7.46B Fitting 2nd gear

7.47A Baulk ring

7.47B 1st/2nd synchro

teeth show signs of wear or damage.

41 Avoid striking the gears or gripping the teeth in a vice without soft jaw protectors during any overhaul work. The roller bearings are of split type (photo).

Mainshaft – reassembly

42 To the front end of the mainshaft, fit 3rd gear needle-roller bearing and the gear (photos). Note that slots are provided at 90° or 120° intervals to provide uniform support.

43 Fit the 3rd baulk ring (photo).

44 Fit the 3rd/4th synchro unit so that its groove is towards the front of the gearbox (photo). The synchro unit can be warmed in boiling water if necessary to facilitate easy engagement with the splines.

45 Fit the spacer and circlip (photos).

46 To the rear end of the mainshaft fit the needle-roller bearing and 1st gear (photos).

47 Fit the 1st baulk ring followed by the 1st/2nd synchro unit (photos).

48 Fit the 2nd baulk ring (photo).

49 Fit the needle-roller bearing and 2nd gear, followed by the flanged bush and the roller bearing inner track (photos).

50 If new reverse/5th components have been fitted, then the thickness of the shim (X) must be calculated in the following way. Measure the distance (A) between the shaft collar and the bearing inner track (Fig. 6.61). Dismantle the reverse/5th synchro unit and then push the reverse gear bush into the synchro-hub and measure the distance (B) from the hub to the bush (Fig. 6.62). Subtract (B) from (A) for the thickness of the shim to fit next to the rear bearing when reassembling the gearbox.

Gearbox – reassembly

51 If new bearings are being fitted, then the outer tracks should be removed and refitted after heating the casing in boiling water.

52 Insert a 2.0 mm thick shim under the mainshaft bearing track before pressing the track into the casing.

53 The clearance between the layshaft bearing and its circlip in the casing must be adjusted by means of shims to give an endplay to the layshaft of between 0.1 and 0.2 mm (Fig. 6.63). The layshaft endcover must be fitted using thread-locking fluid.

54 Commence reassembly by inserting the needle-roller bearing into

7.48 2nd baulk ring

7.49A 1st gear, needle-roller bearing and flanged bush

7.49B Fitting roller bearing inner track

7.54A Fitting baulk ring to 3rd/4th synchro

7.54B Connecting the input shaft to the mainshaft

7.55 Fitting the geartrains to the intermediate casing

7.56A Shim (X) on the mainshaft

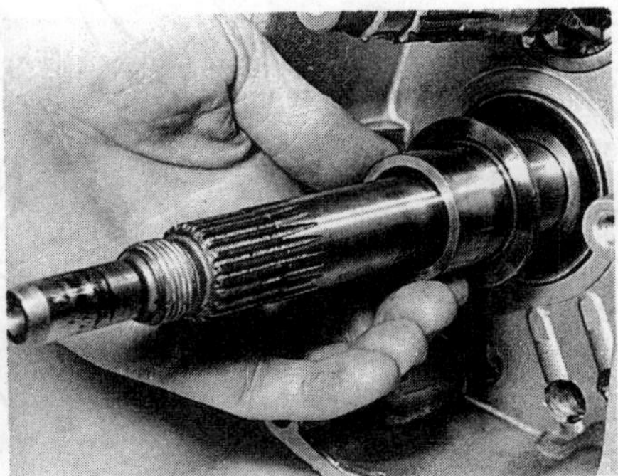
7.56B Flanged bush on the mainshaft

7.56C Needle-roller bearing on the mainshaft

the recess in the end of the input (clutch) shaft. Fit the 4th baulk ring to the 3rd/4th speed synchro sleeve and then connect the input shaft to the front end of the mainshaft (photos).

55 Mesh the mainshaft and layshaft together and fit them into the intermediate casing (photo).

56 To the rear of the mainshaft fit the selected shim (X), the flanged bush and the reverse gear needle-roller bearing (photos). Heat the flanged bush in boiling water before fitting it.

57 Fit reverse gear to the mainshaft (photo).

58 Assemble the reverse idler gear, shaft and bearing (photo).

59 Fit the shaft with the reverse idler gear and bearing. Screw in the retaining bolt, noting the position of the cut-away edge of the thrust-washer (photos).

60 Fit the reverse gear holder (photo). Apply thread-locking fluid to the threads of the socket-headed retaining screws.

61 Engage the 1st/2nd and 3rd/4th selector forks in their synchro sleeve grooves (photo). Make sure that the angled corners of the forks are towards each other.

62 Insert the 1st/2nd selector shaft detent ball and spring into its hole in the intermediate casing (photo). Keep the detent ball depressed and pass the selector shaft through the dog and fork and into the casing.

63 Pin the fork and dog to the selector shaft (photo).

64 Insert the 3rd/4th selector shaft detent ball and spring (photo). Keep the detent ball depressed and pass the selector shaft through its fork and into the intermediate casing. Note that the cut-out on the selector shaft must face the 5th gear selector shaft position.

65 Pin the fork to the selector shaft.

66 Push the reverse/5th selector fork onto its shaft.

67 Locate the fork in the groove of the reverse/5th synchro sleeve and fit the shaft, fork and synchro as an assembly (photo), but only just enter

Fig. 6.60 Reverse gear idler shaft bolt (1) and washer (2) – Getrag 245 (Sec 7)

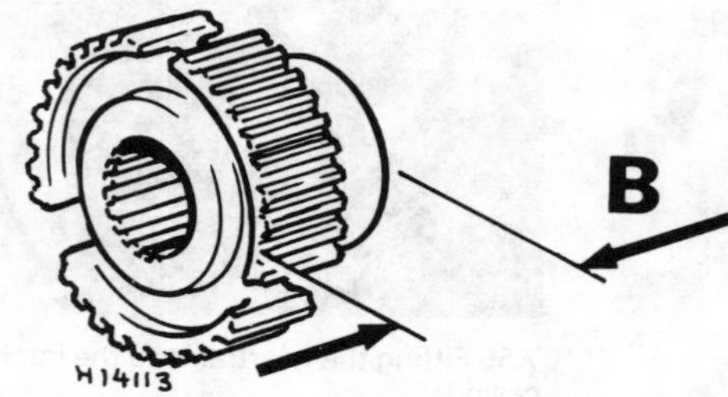

Fig. 6.62 Measure the distance (B) from the hub to the bush – Getrag 245 (Sec 7)

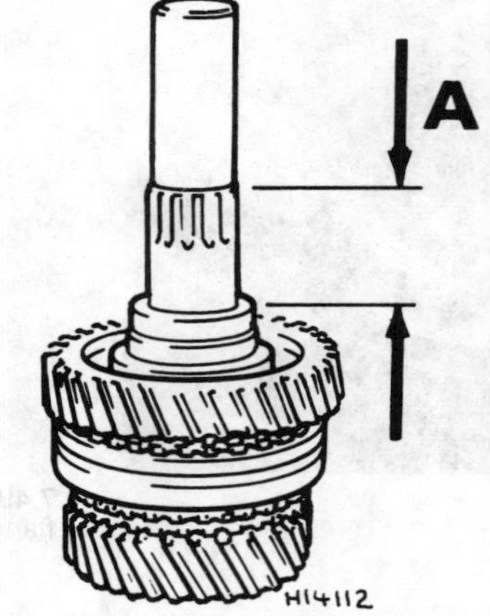

Fig. 6.61 Measure the distance (A) between the shaft collar and the bearing inner track – Getrag 245 (Sec 7)

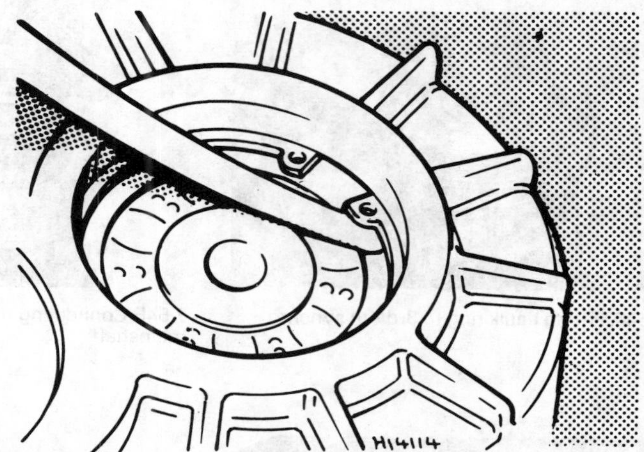

Fig. 6.63 Checking the layshaft bearing-to-circlip clearance – Getrag 245 (Sec 7)

the shaft into the intermediate casing. The boss on the fork must be towards the front of the gearbox.

68 Drop the remaining interlock ball into position, follow with the reverse/5th detent ball and spring. Hold the ball depressed and push the selector shaft into position. The shaft detent grooves must be towards the bottom of the gearbox. On no account push the shaft so far that the square cut-outs in it align with the detent ball, otherwise the ball will jam.

69 Pin the reverse/5th fork to the selector shaft (photo).

70 To the mainshaft, fit the flanged bush up against the synchro-hub so that the pins engage in the flange notches (photo). Make the fitting easier by warming the bush in boiling water.

71 Fit the split needle-roller bearing, baulk ring and 5th gear to the mainshaft (photos).

72 To the layshaft, fit the 5th gear and the bearing inner track so that its flange is towards the gear (photo). If necessary heat the gear before fitting it.

73 Pin the collar with the spacer, shim and washer to the end of the layshaft (photos). The chamfer on the collar should be towards the end of the shaft. Eliminate any play by using a shim of different thickness if necessary.

74 To the end of the mainshaft fit the notched spacer with its chamfer to the end of the shaft (photo).

75 Where applicable fit the spacer to the end of the mainshaft. Heat it in boiling water first if necessary.

76 Fit the layshaft rear roller race (photo).

77 Push the selector rod with a new oil seal into the intermediate casing. Make sure that the notches in the rod are away from the selector shafts and make sure that it passes through the dog as it is pushed into position. Pin the dog to the rod (photo).

78 Fit the selector rail and operating lever (photos). Screw in the lever socket-headed screw having applied thread-locking fluid to the screw threads.

79 Fit the clamp and screw (photos). The clamp chamfer should face the selector fork, and the screw should be fitted with thread-locking fluid.

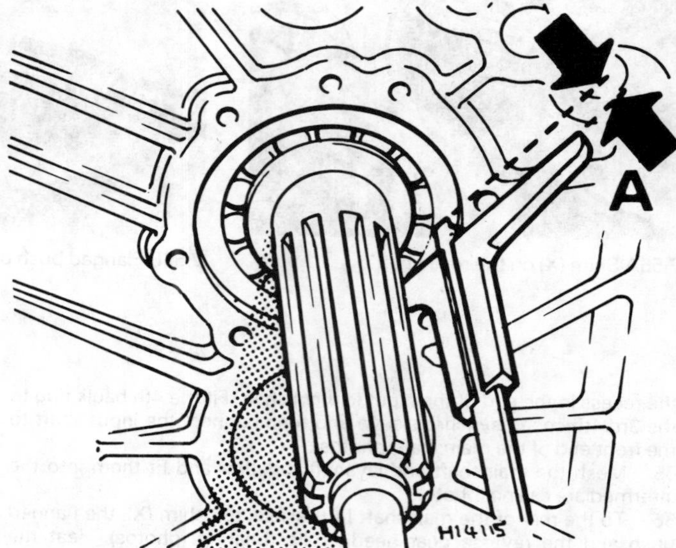

Fig. 6.64 Measuring the distance (A), the depth of the bearing below the surface of the casing – Getrag 245 (Sec 7)

80 Stick the small rollers to the selector rod (photo).

81 Locate the spring-loaded selector arm on the selector rod (photo).

82 Stick the interlock plunger, using thick grease into its hole in the casing (photo). Make sure that it is not displaced as the casing is fitted.

7.57 Reverse gear

7.58 Reverse gear, shaft and bearing

7.59A Reverse gear thrustwasher

83 Smear the casing mating flanges with gasket cement. Engage 2nd gear by pushing the 1st/2nd synchro sleeve towards the front of the gearbox.
84 Join the rear casing to the intermediate casing (photo). If the casings will not close together, drive out the 1st/2nd selector fork and dog roll pins to allow the fork and dog to 'float' as the casings are joined. Refit the roll pins on completion.
85 Tap the dowels into position and screw in the casing bolt (photos). Select neutral.
86 Insert the two selector arm plungers into the hole in the rear casing (photo). It is essential that the projection on the lower plunger is aligned with the gearbox centre line, and the projections where the two plungers join are opposite each other. Insert the spring and screw in the threaded plug.
87 Fit the selector rod lock plunger, spring and cap (photos).
88 Apply sealant to the threads of the reverse lamp switch and screw it into position (photo).
89 Apply thread-locking fluid to the new detent ball plugs and drive them into position (photo).
90 Drive the rear bearing into position.
91 Fit the spacer to the rear bearing (photo). If new components have been fitted, determine the shim thickness as described in Section 5 paragraphs 55 and 56.
92 Fit the rear cover together with a new oil seal and gasket (photo). Fill the seal lips with grease.
93 Fit the output flange, screw on the nut (thread-locking fluid on its threads) and tighten to the specified torque (photos).
94 Locate a new nut locking cup and stake it into the cut-out provided (photo).
95 Fit the roller bearing races to the front ends of the mainshaft and layshaft (photos).
96 Apply sealant to the main casing flanges and push it into position on the intermediate casing (photo). Should it not mate completely, this will probably be due to one of the shaft front split type bearings having expanded. Remove the bearing and place it in the casing instead of on the shaft.
97 Tap in the dowels and screw in the casing connecting bolts.
98 Fit the front bearing to the input shaft, heating the inner race first if

7.59B Reverse shaft retaining bolt

7.60 Reverse gear holder

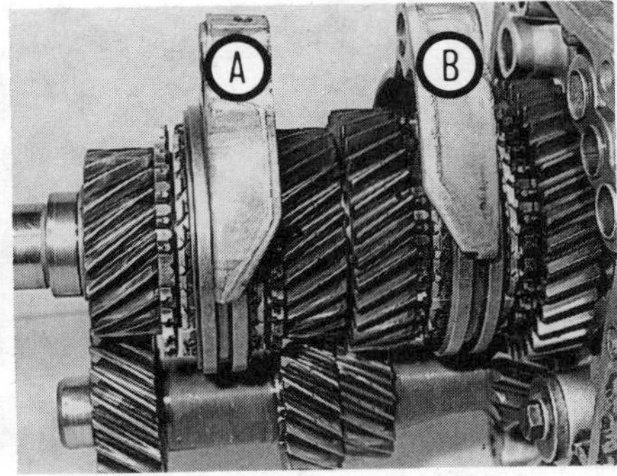

7.61 Selector forks

A 3rd/4th *B 1st/2nd*

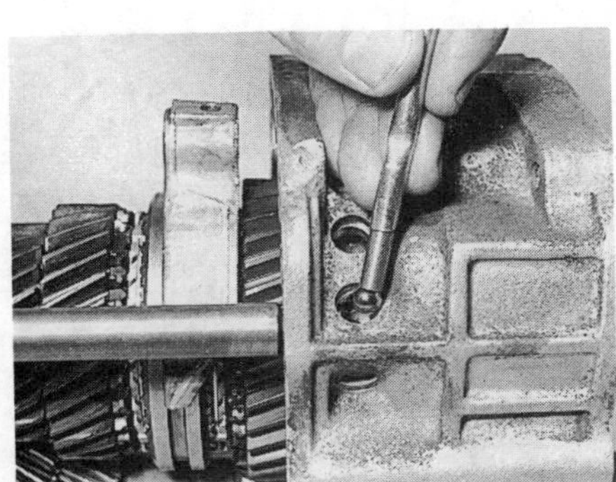
7.62 1st/2nd detent ball

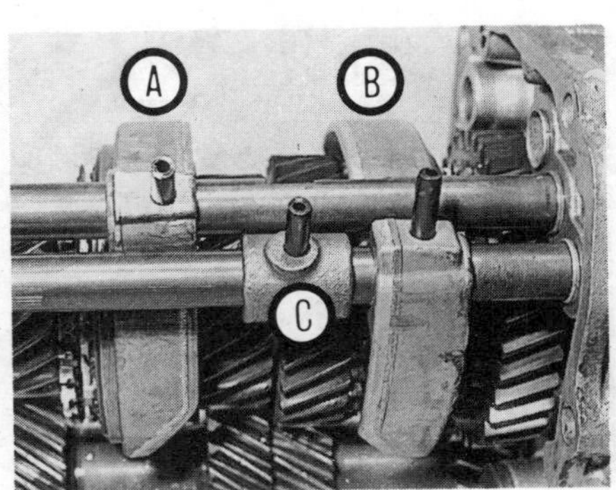

7.63 Selector fork pins

A 3rd/4th *B 1st/2nd* *C Dog*

7.64 3rd/4th detent ball

7.67 5th/reverse synchro, fork and shaft

7.69 5th/reverse fork pin

7.70 Flanged bush on the mainshaft

7.71A Split needle-roller bearing

7.71B 5th gear on the mainshaft

7.72 5th gear on the layshaft

7.73A Spacer on the layshaft

7.73B Shim on the layshaft

7.73C Washer on the layshaft

7.73D Collar on the layshaft

7.73E Pinning the collar to the layshaft

7.74 Notched spacer on the mainshaft

7.76 Layshaft roller race

7.77 Selector rod dog and pin

7.78A Fitting the selector rail

7.78B Selector rail operating lever and screw

7.79A Selector rail clamp

7.79B Selector rail clamp screw

7.80 Selector rod rollers

7.81 Spring-loaded selector arm

7.82 Interlock plunger

7.84 Joining the rear and intermediate casings

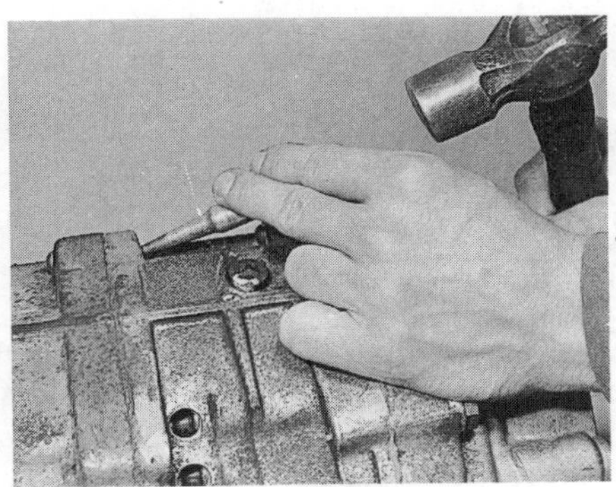
7.85A Driving home a dowel pin

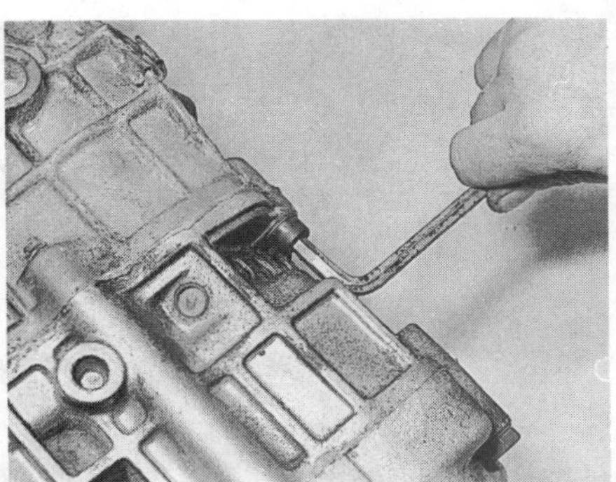
7.85B Tightening a casing bolt

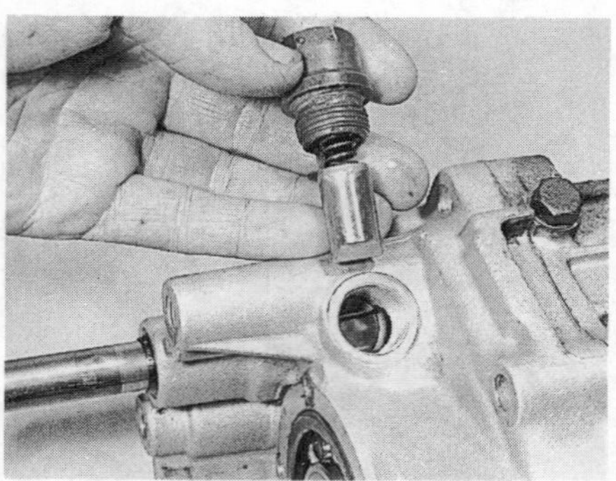
7.86 Fitting the selector arm plunger, spring and plug

7.87A Selector rod plunger

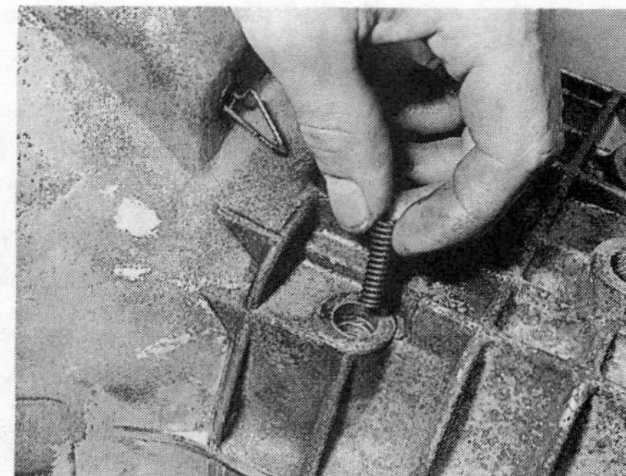
7.87B Selector rod plunger spring

7.87C Selector rod plunger cap

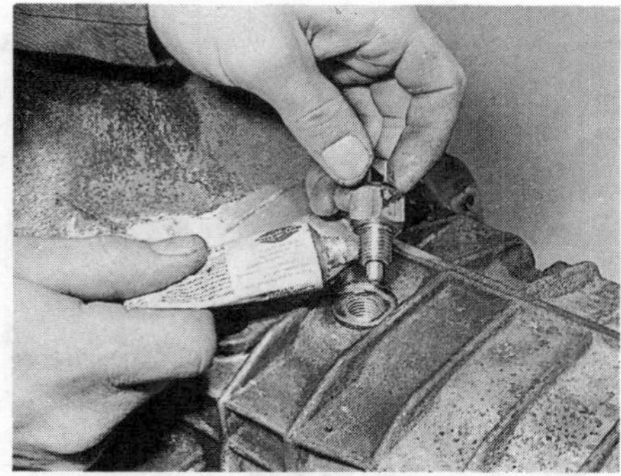
7.88 Applying sealant to the reverse lamp switch

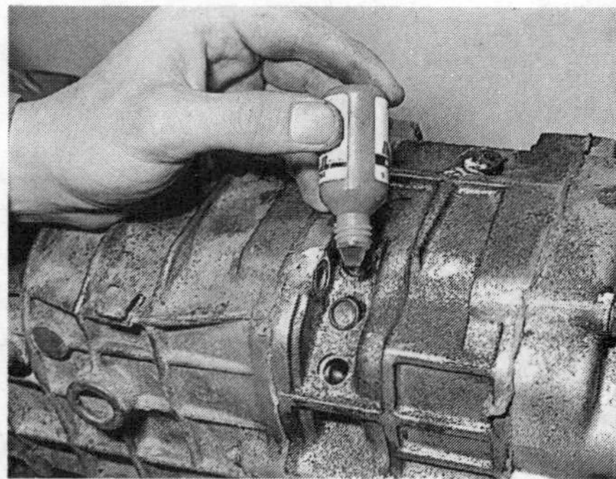
7.89 Applying thread-locking fluid to the detent ball plug

7.91 Rear bearing spacer

7.92 Tightening a rear cover bolt

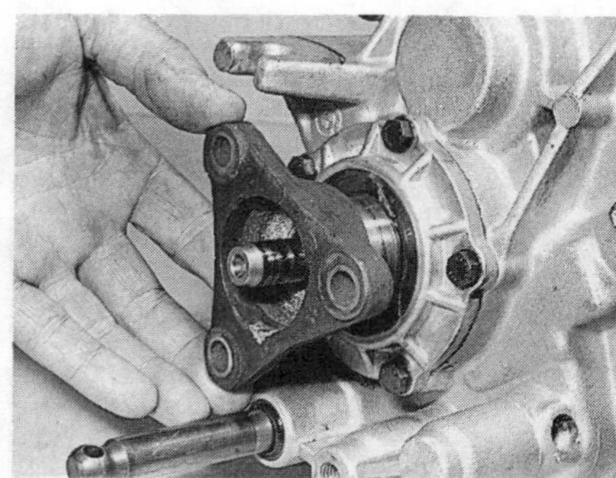
7.93A Fitting the output flange

7.93B Flange nut

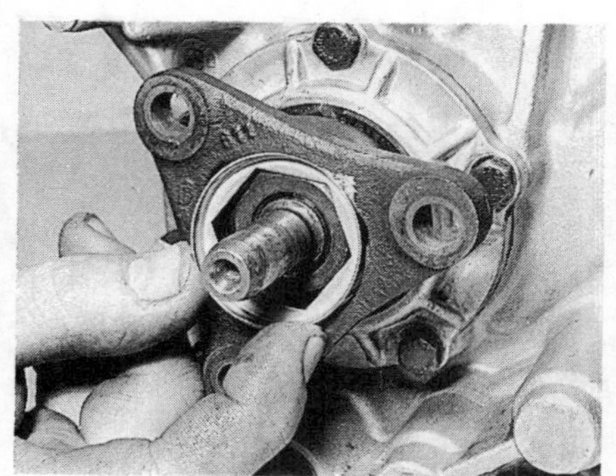
7.94 Output flange nut locking cup

7.95A Layshaft front bearing

7.95B Mainshaft front bearing

7.96 Joining main and intermediate casings

7.98A Input shaft bearing

7.98B Spacer

7.98C Circlip

7.98D Input shaft bearing circlip fitted

necessary. Fit the spacer, shim and circlip (photos).

99 If new components have been fitted, carry out the following shim selection procedure. Using a depth gauge, measure the distance (A) of the bearing below the surface of the casing (Fig. 6.64). Measure the dimensions (B) and (C) on the guide sleeve (Figs. 6.65 and 6.66). Subtract (A) from (B) then subtract (C) from the result. This will give the thickness of the shim to be used.

100 Fit the guide sleeve fitted with a new oil seal. Apply gasket cement to the sleeve flange and bolt it into position so that the oil drain channel is at the bottom.

101 Fit the clutch release components as described in Chapter 5.

102 Refill the gearbox with the correct grade and quantity of oil after it has been fitted to the car.

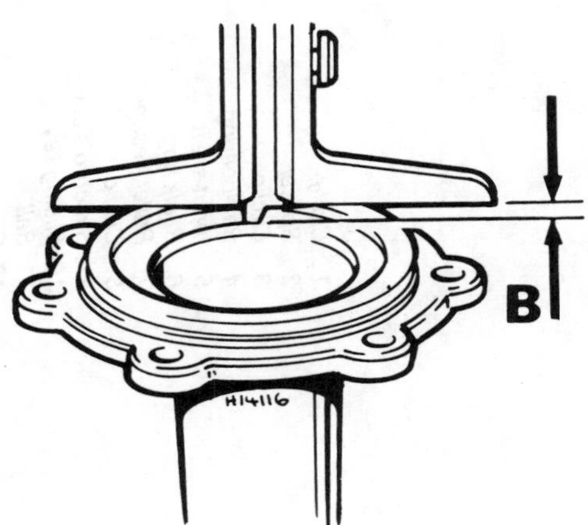

Fig. 6.65 Measuring the distance (B), the depth of the recess in the clutch sleeve – Getrag 245 (Sec 7)

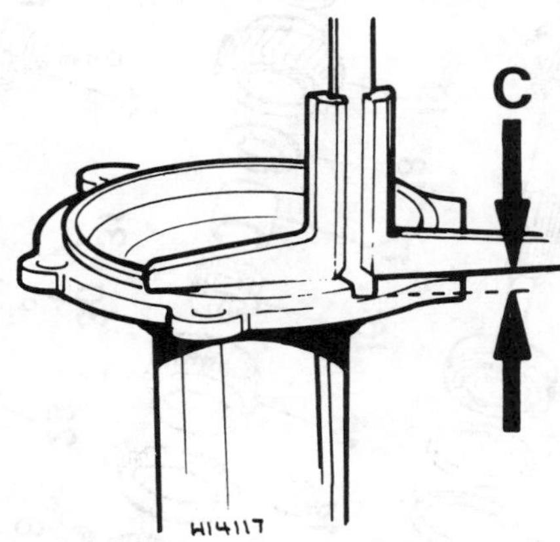

Fig. 6.66 Measuring the distance (C), the depth of the clutch sleeve shoulder – Getrag 245 (Sec 7)

8 Gearbox (ZF S 5-16, 5-speed) – overhaul

Dismantling into major assemblies

1 Drain the oil from the gearbox.

2 From inside the bellhousing, remove the clutch release components and unbolt and remove the guide sleeve and spacer.

3 Extract the bearing circlip.

4 Unscrew the reverse lamp switch.

5 Tap out the dowels and unscrew and remove the bolts which hold the rear casing to the main casing.

6 Pull the main casing from the rear casing. Remove the gasket.

7 Remove the magnet from the rear casing and wipe it clean.

8 Remove the plug (1) (Fig. 6.68).

9 Drive out the ball-bearing towards the front of the gearbox.

10 Remove the output flange as described in Section 5, paragraphs 18 and 19.

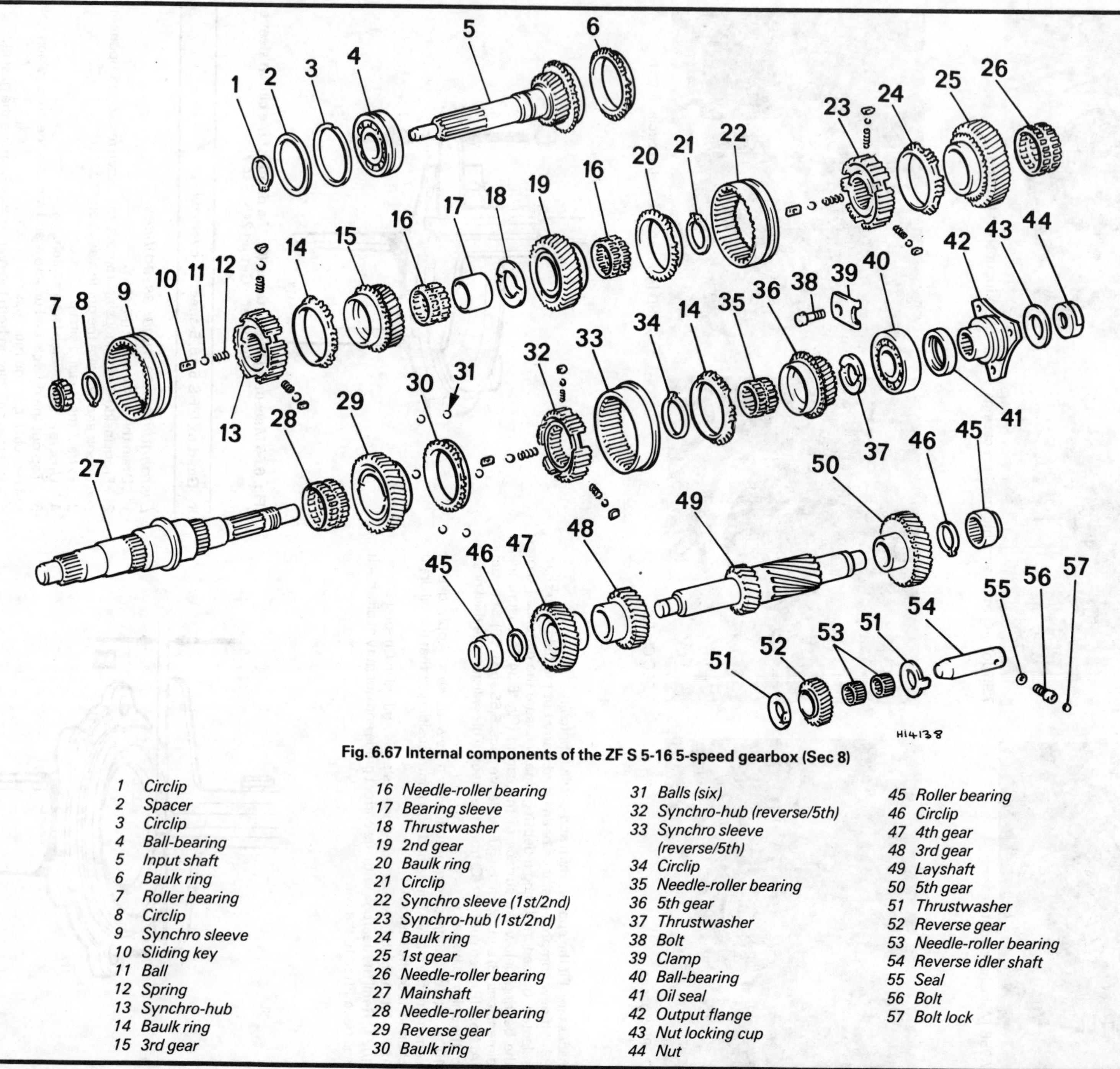

Fig. 6.67 Internal components of the ZF S 5-16 5-speed gearbox (Sec 8)

1 *Circlip*
2 *Spacer*
3 *Circlip*
4 *Ball-bearing*
5 *Input shaft*
6 *Baulk ring*
7 *Roller bearing*
8 *Circlip*
9 *Synchro sleeve*
10 *Sliding key*
11 *Ball*
12 *Spring*
13 *Synchro-hub*
14 *Baulk ring*
15 *3rd gear*
16 *Needle-roller bearing*
17 *Bearing sleeve*
18 *Thrustwasher*
19 *2nd gear*
20 *Baulk ring*
21 *Circlip*
22 *Synchro sleeve (1st/2nd)*
23 *Synchro-hub (1st/2nd)*
24 *Baulk ring*
25 *1st gear*
26 *Needle-roller bearing*
27 *Mainshaft*
28 *Needle-roller bearing*
29 *Reverse gear*
30 *Baulk ring*
31 *Balls (six)*
32 *Synchro-hub (reverse/5th)*
33 *Synchro sleeve (reverse/5th)*
34 *Circlip*
35 *Needle-roller bearing*
36 *5th gear*
37 *Thrustwasher*
38 *Bolt*
39 *Clamp*
40 *Ball-bearing*
41 *Oil seal*
42 *Output flange*
43 *Nut locking cup*
44 *Nut*
45 *Roller bearing*
46 *Circlip*
47 *4th gear*
48 *3rd gear*
49 *Layshaft*
50 *5th gear*
51 *Thrustwasher*
52 *Reverse gear*
53 *Needle-roller bearing*
54 *Reverse idler shaft*
55 *Seal*
56 *Bolt*
57 *Bolt lock*

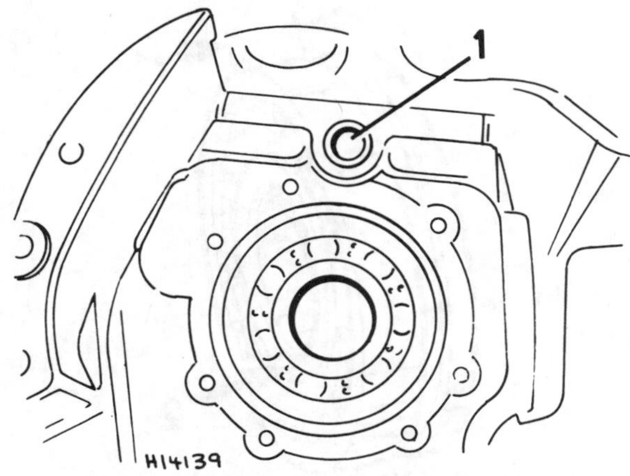

Fig. 6.68 Casing plug (1) – ZF S 5-16 (Sec 8)

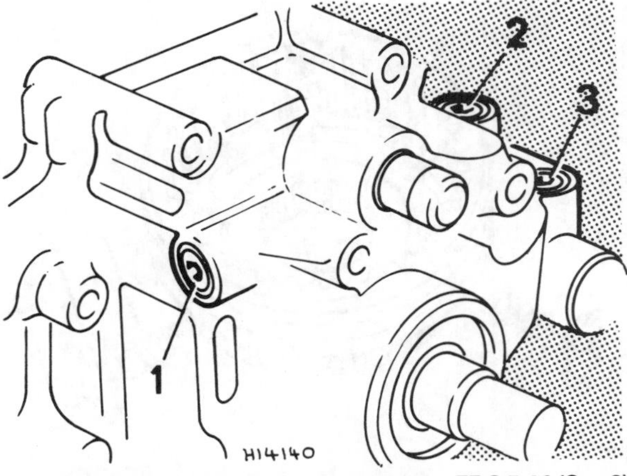

Fig. 6.69 Detent spring caps (1, 2 and 3) – ZF S 5-16 (Sec 8)

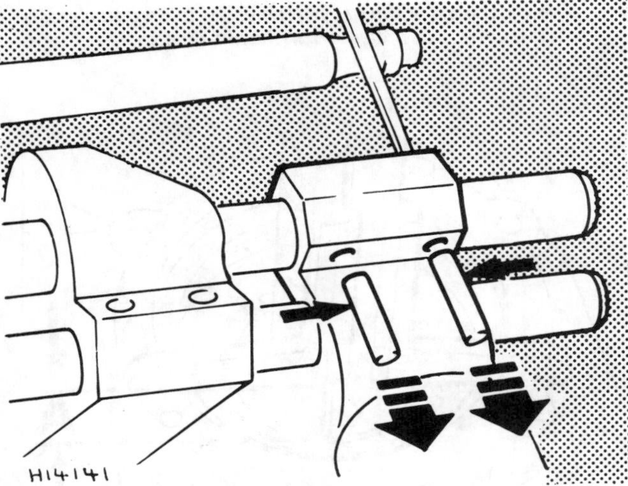

Fig. 6.70 Removing the 3rd/4th selector fork roll pins (arrowed) – ZF S 5-16 (Sec 8)

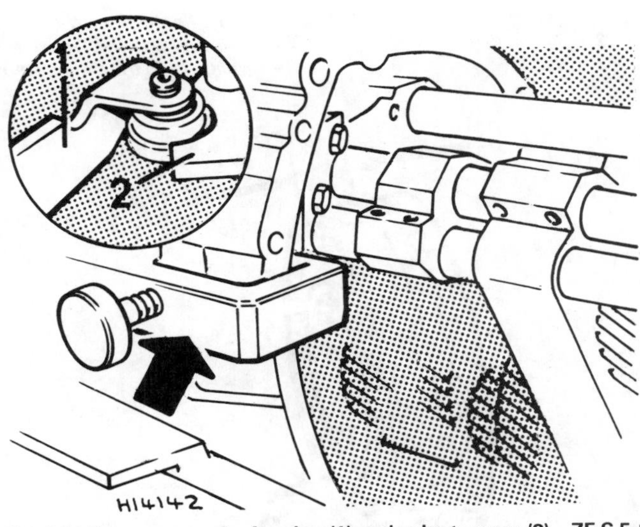

Fig. 6.71 Reverse gear leaf spring (1) and selector arm (2) – ZF S 5-16 (Sec 8)

Note use of small clamp (arrowed)

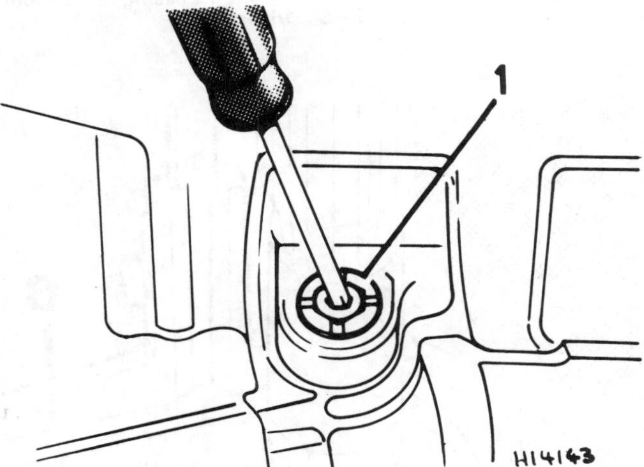

Fig. 6.72 Removing the socket-headed bolt (1) – ZF S 5-16 (Sec 8)

11 Remove the detent spring caps from the end cover (Fig. 6.69). Extract the detent springs.

12 Pull out the three detent plungers using circlip pliers. The plungers can only be completely removed after removing the stem locks.

13 Drive out the roll pins from the fork on the 3rd/4th selector shaft (Fig. 6.70).

14 Using a small clamp, push back the reverse gear leaf spring (1) until the selector (2) is accessible (Fig. 6.71).

15 Swing the selector arm out of the groove in the selector shaft.

16 Pull out the 3rd/4th selector shaft and then unscrew the bolt (1) (Fig. 6.72).

17 Remove the reverse gear shaft, reverse gear, the needle-roller bearing and the thrustwasher.

18 Remove the operating lever bolt.

19 Select reverse gear by moving the synchro sleeve forward.

20 Press the gear trains out of the rear casing.

Mainshaft – dismantling

21 Separate the input (clutch) shaft from the mainshaft. Take off the 4th baulk ring and the needle-roller bearing from the recess in the end of the input shaft.

22 Extract the mainshaft front synchro circlip.

23 Support 3rd gear and press the mainshaft out of the gear and 3rd/4th synchro unit. Remove the needle-roller bearing.

24 Press the shaft out of the bearing sleeve, thrustwasher and the 2nd gear. Take off the needle-roller bearing and the 2nd baulk ring.

25 Extract the circlip and press the shaft from 1st gear. Remove the needle- roller bearing.

26 Press the output shaft from 5th gear. Remove the 5th baulk ring and needle-roller bearing.

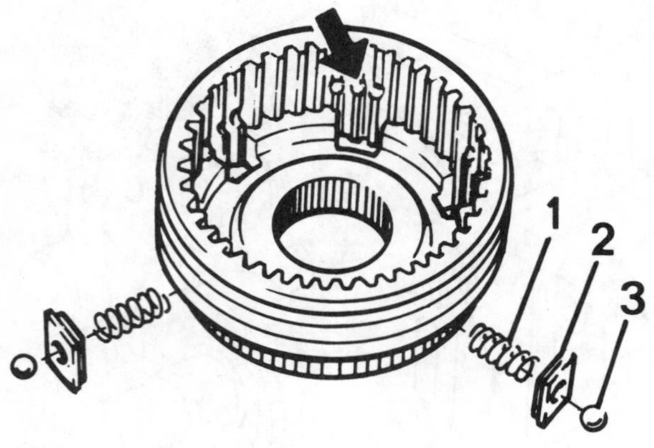

Fig. 6.73 Synchro components – ZF S 5-16 (Sec 8)

1 *Spring*
2 *Sliding key*
3 *Ball*

The flat teeth on the sleeve (arrowed) must align with the sliding keys

Fig. 6.74 1st/2nd synchro – ZF S 5-16 (Sec 8)

The wider band of the sleeve (1) must be towards the greater projection on the hub (2)

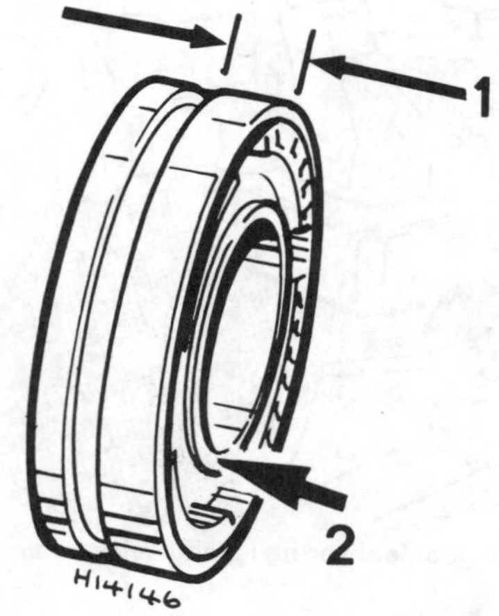

Fig. 6.75 5th/reverse synchro – ZF S 5-16 (Sec 8)

The wider band of the sleeve (1) must be towards the lesser projection on the hub (2)

Fig. 6.76 Measuring the distance (A) from the casing to the input shaft – ZF S 5-16 (Sec 8)

27 Extract the circlip and press the output shaft from reverse gear and the 5th/reverse synchro unit. Remove the 5th baulk ring and the six balls.

Gears, synchromesh units and selector forks – inspection

28 Refer to Section 6, paragraphs 25 to 30 but note that the stepped side of the sliding keys is towards the synchro-hub. On the 1st/2nd synchro unit the wider band of the sleeve is towards the greater projection on the hub. On the 5th/reverse synchro unit the wider band of the sleeve is towards the less projecting side of the hub (Figs. 6.73, 6.74 and 6.75).

Input shaft and mainshaft bearings – renewal

29 The bearings should be removed from, and refitted to, the casing sections after having heated the casing in boiling water. Always fill the lips of new oil seals with grease.
30 The input (clutch) shaft endfloat must be checked and adjusted in the following way, with the main casing in position. Using a depth gauge, measure the distance (A) between the surface of the casing and the input shaft (Fig. 6.76).
31 Measure the distance (B) from the surface of the casing to the bearing circlip (Fig. 6.77).

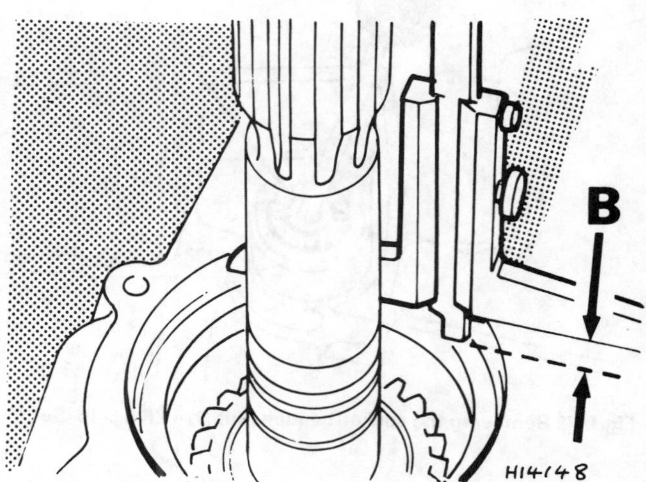

Fig. 6.77 Measuring the distance (B) from the casing to the circlip – ZF S 5-16 (Sec 8)

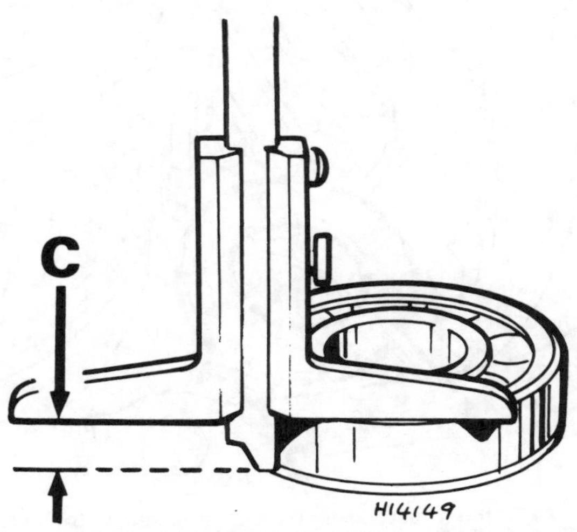

Fig. 6.78 Measuring the distance (C) from the bearing outer track to the circlip – ZF S 5-16 (Sec 8)

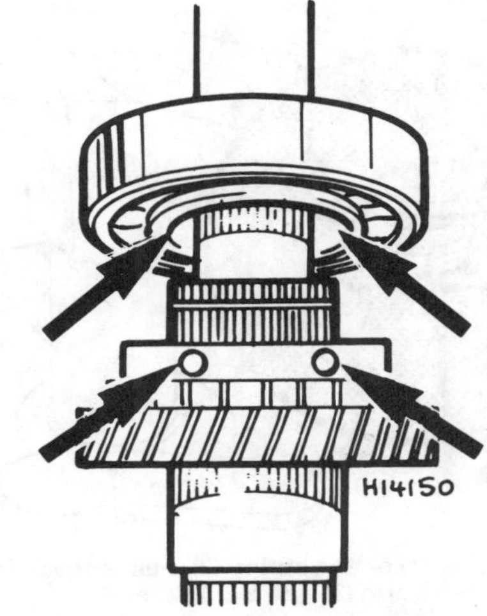

Fig. 6.79 Assembling the mainshaft – ZF S 5-16 (Sec 8)

Arrows show location of two of the six reverse gear synchro balls

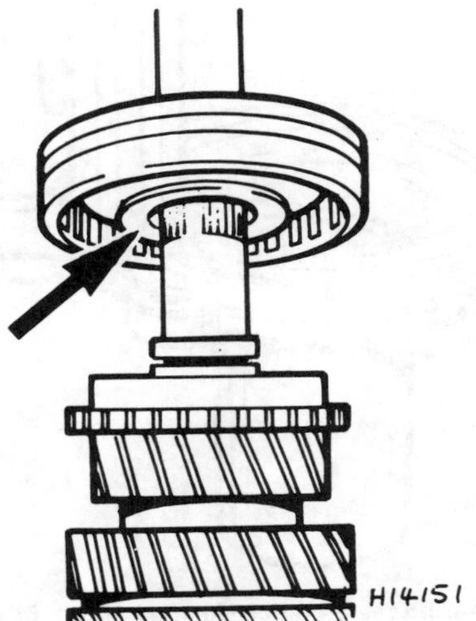

Fig. 6.80 Fitting the 3rd/4th synchro – ZF S 5-16 (Sec 8)

The greater projection on the hub (arrowed) must face 3rd gear

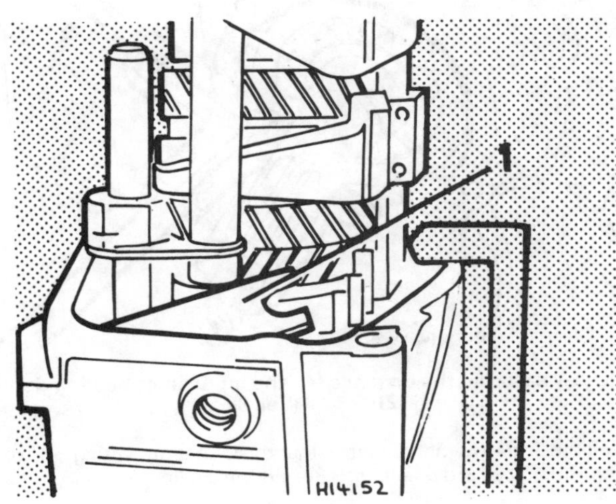

Fig. 6.81 Fitting the operating lever (1) – ZF S 5-16 (Sec 8)

32 Measure the distance (C) from the bearing outer track to the circlip (Fig. 6.78).

33 Subtract (B) from (A) then subtract (C) from the result to give the required endfloat of between 1.3 and 1.5 mm. Select a suitable circlip to provide this.

Mainshaft – reassembly

34 Fit the needle-roller bearing, reverse gear and the reverse baulk ring with six balls held in position with grease.

35 Fit the 5th/reverse synchro unit so that the narrow hub projection is towards the reverse gear.

36 Move the 5th/reverse synchro sleeve in the direction of reverse gear and fit a circlip which is thick enough to eliminate all endfloat in the synchro-hub.

37 Fit the 5th baulk ring, needle-roller bearing and the 5th gear.

38 Heat the thrustwasher in boiling water and fit it to the shaft.

39 Fit the needle-roller bearing, 1st gear and the 1st baulk ring.

40 Fit the 1st/2nd synchro unit with the narrow projecting side of the hub towards 1st gear. Make sure that the baulk ring engages correctly.

41 Move the synchro sleeve in the direction of 1st gear and fit a circlip which is thick enough to eliminate all endfloat in the synchro-hub.

42 Fit the 2nd baulk ring, needle-roller bearing and the 2nd gear.

43 Heat the thrustwasher and the bearing sleeve in boiling water and fit to the shaft.

44 Fit the needle-roller bearing, 3rd gear and the 3rd baulk ring.

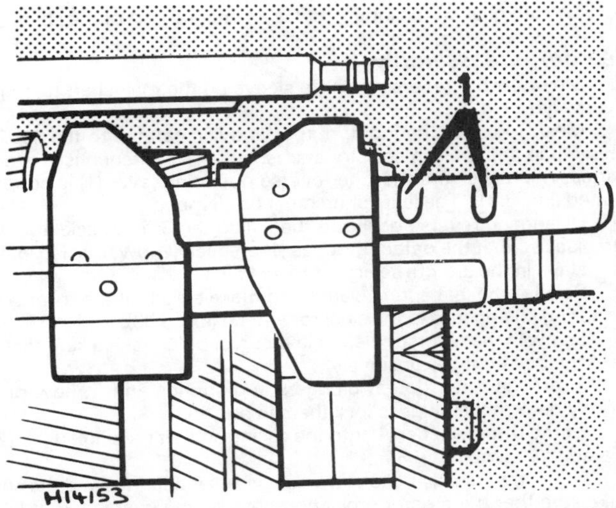

Fig. 6.82 3rd/4th selector shaft detent grooves (1) – ZF S 5-16 (Sec 8)

Fig. 6.83 The roller (1) on the spring (2) must engage in the selector arm (3) – ZF S 5-16 (Sec 8)

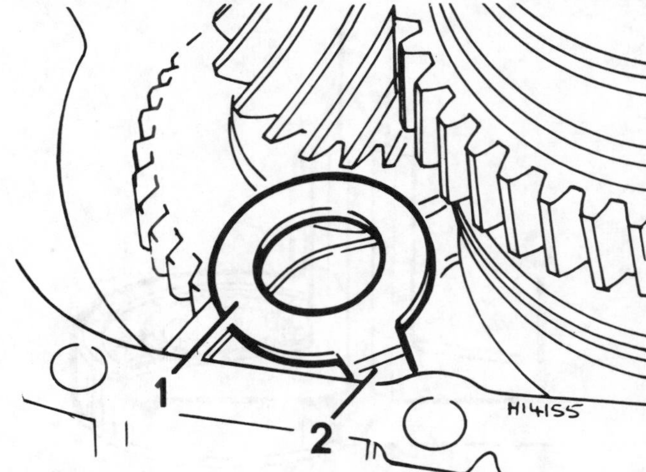

Fig. 6.84 Fit the thrustwasher (1) into the casing with the angled tab (2) positioned thus – ZF S 5-16 (Sec 8)

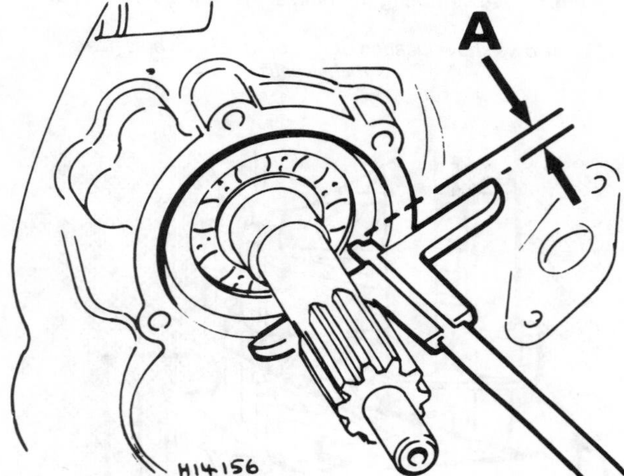

Fig. 6.85 Measuring the distance (A), the input shaft bearing depth – ZF S 5-16 (Sec 8)

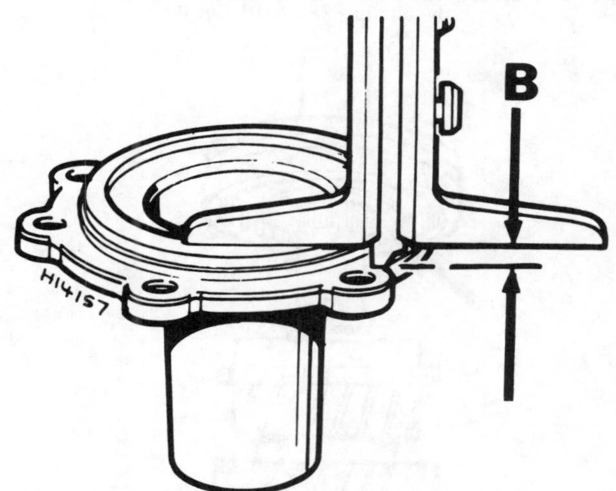

Fig. 6.86 Measuring the distance (B), the height of the clutch guide sleeve shoulder – ZF S 5-16 (Sec 8)

New gasket in position

45 Fit the 3rd/4th synchro unit so that the longer projecting side of the synchro-hub faces 3rd gear (Fig. 6.80). Fit the circlip.

Layshaft and input (clutch) shaft gears

46 The gears on the shafts are fitted during production and removal should not be attempted. Leave the removal and fitting of new gears to your dealer.

47 The 5th gear on the input shaft is an integral part of the shaft.

Gearbox – reassembly

48 Move the 5th/reverse synchro sleeve on the mainshaft to engage reverse gear.

49 Mesh together the input, output and layshafts with the 1st/2nd, 5th/reverse and 3rd/4th selector shafts. Install simultaneously into the rear casing. Make sure that the reverse operating lever (1) is correctly located (Fig. 6.81). The leaf spring must be clamped.

50 Disengage reverse gear and then slide the 3rd/4th selector shaft into place so that the detent grooves (1) are facing upwards (Fig. 6.82).

51 Drive in the 3rd/4th selector fork roll pins.

52 Release the leaf spring clamp and make sure that the roller (1) on the spring (2) engages in the selector arm (3) (Fig. 6.83).

53 Screw in the reverse selector lever pivot bolt, making sure that the tip of the bolt engages positively.

54 Insert the three detent plungers and springs and fit new plugs. Slightly deform the plugs to lock them in position.

55 Fit the thrustwasher (1) into the casing so that the angled tab (2) is located as shown (Fig. 6.84).

56 Fit the reverse idler gear, two needle-roller bearings and the shaft. Make sure that the greater projecting boss on the gear is towards the casing.

57 Fit the lockbolt with a new seal, and the cover.

58 Fit the output flange and nut, having applied thread-locking fluid to the threads. Fit and stake the nut lockplate.

59 Fit the magnet and a new end plug.

60 If not already fitted, install the main casing bearing.

61 Fit the main casing to the rear casing together with a new gasket. Tap in the dowels and screw in the bolts to the specified torque.

62 Warm the front end of the main casing then fit the input shaft bearing. Fit the spacer, shim and circlip.

63 Fit the reverse lamp switch.

64 Measure the input shaft bearing recess (A) (Fig. 6.85).

65 Measure the distance (B) – the shoulder height of the clutch guide sleeve with the gasket in position (Fig. 6.86). Subtract (B) from (A) for the thickness of the shim and fit it against the bearing.

66 Fit the clutch guide sleeve together with a new oil seal and flange gasket.

67 Refill the gearbox with the correct grade and quantity of oil after it has been fitted to the car.

9 Gearchange mechanism – general

Gear lever – removal and refitting

1 Apply the handbrake then jack up the front of the car and support on axle stands.

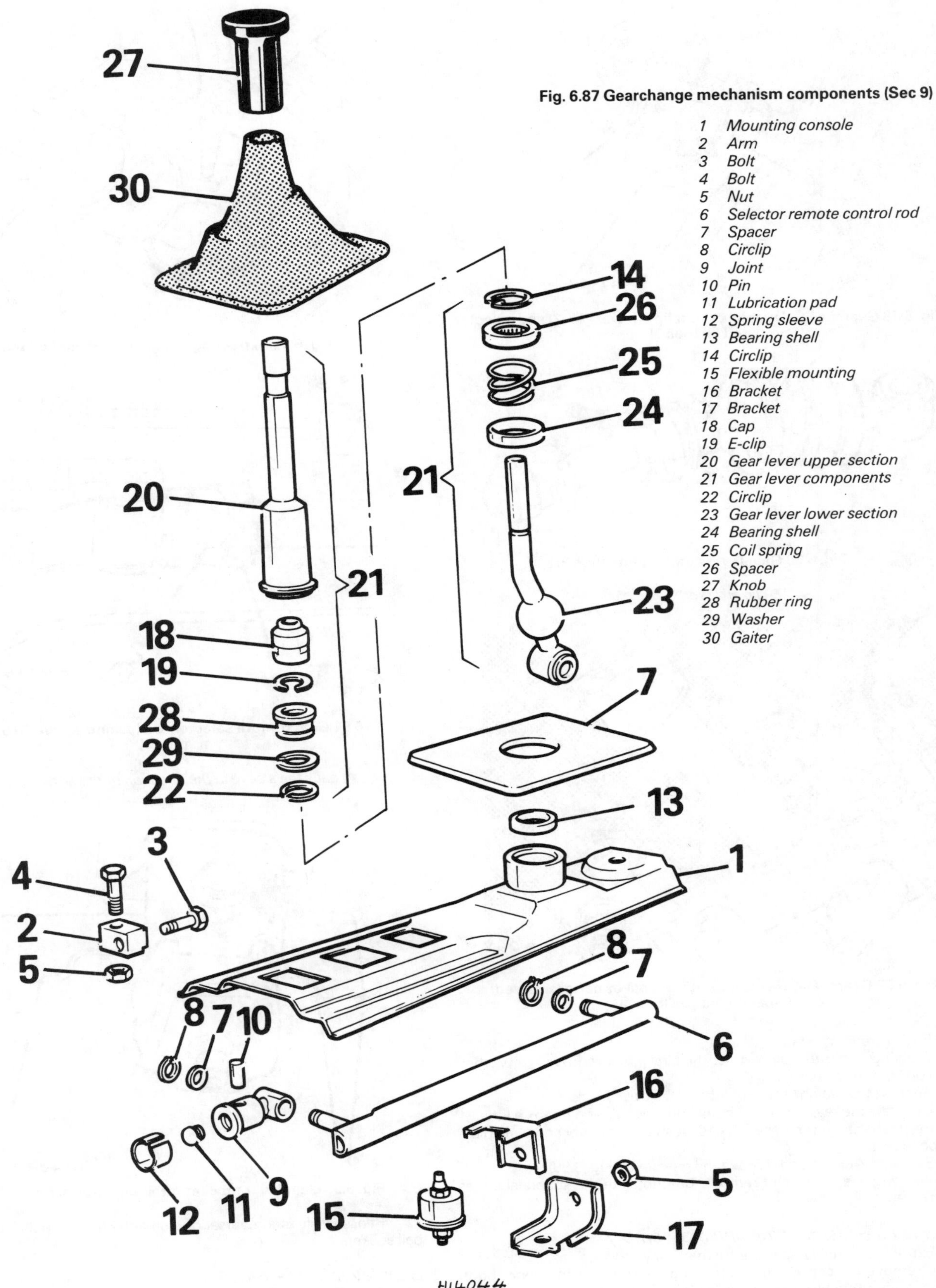

Fig. 6.87 Gearchange mechanism components (Sec 9)

1 *Mounting console*
2 *Arm*
3 *Bolt*
4 *Bolt*
5 *Nut*
6 *Selector remote control rod*
7 *Spacer*
8 *Circlip*
9 *Joint*
10 *Pin*
11 *Lubrication pad*
12 *Spring sleeve*
13 *Bearing shell*
14 *Circlip*
15 *Flexible mounting*
16 *Bracket*
17 *Bracket*
18 *Cap*
19 *E-clip*
20 *Gear lever upper section*
21 *Gear lever components*
22 *Circlip*
23 *Gear lever lower section*
24 *Bearing shell*
25 *Coil spring*
26 *Spacer*
27 *Knob*
28 *Rubber ring*
29 *Washer*
30 *Gaiter*

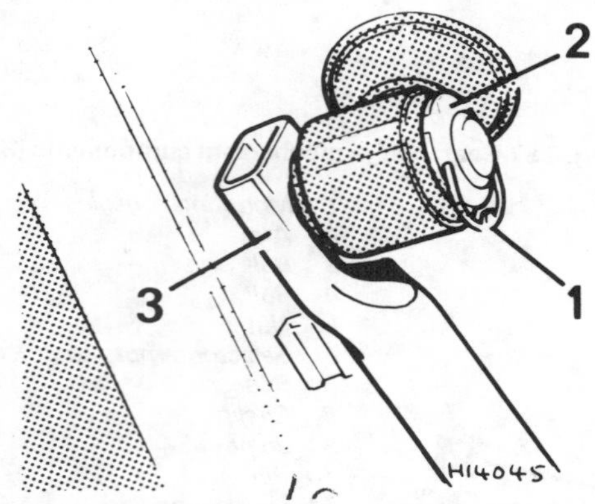

Fig. 6.88 Gearchange lever lower circlip (1), washer (2) and selector rod (3) (Sec 9)

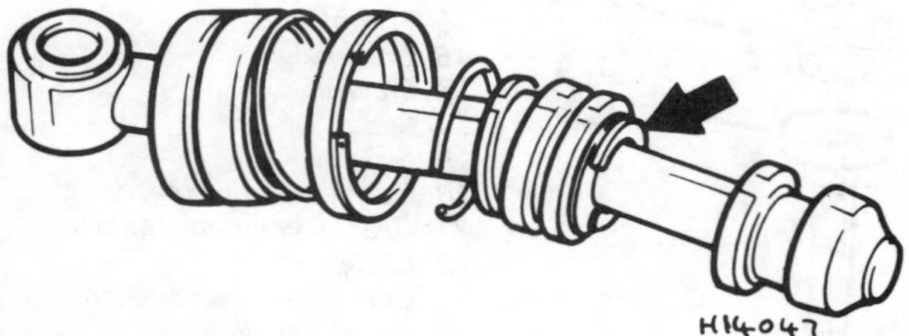

Fig. 6.90 Gear lever components (Sec 9)

E-clip arrowed

Fig. 6.92 Gearchange lever mounting bracket bolts (arrowed) – 4-speed gearbox (Sec 9)

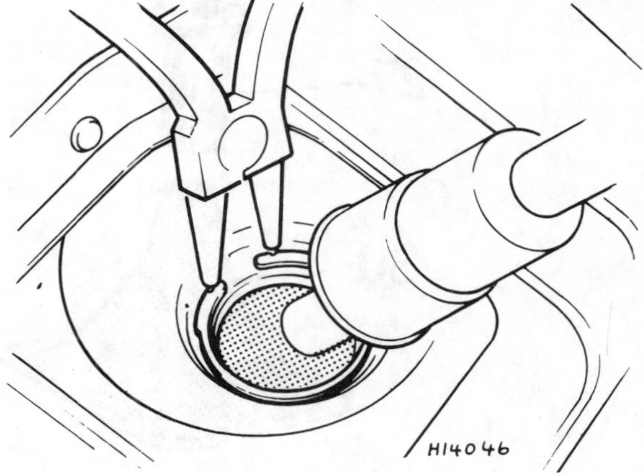

Fig. 6.89 Extracting the gear lever circlip (Sec 9)

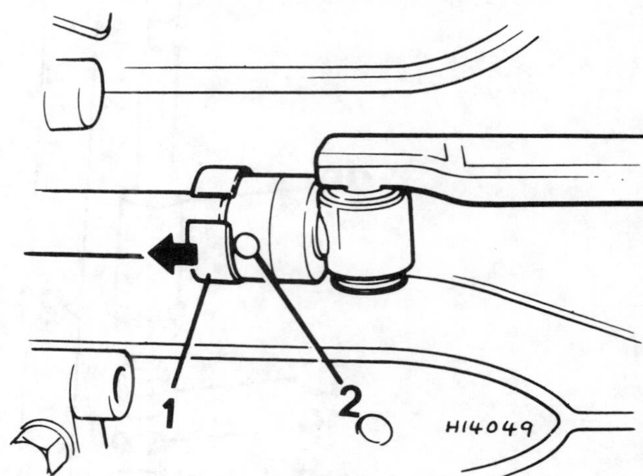

Fig. 6.91 Gear remote selector rod locking sleeve (1) and pin (2) (Sec 9)

Push back the sleeve in the direction of the arrow to remove the pin

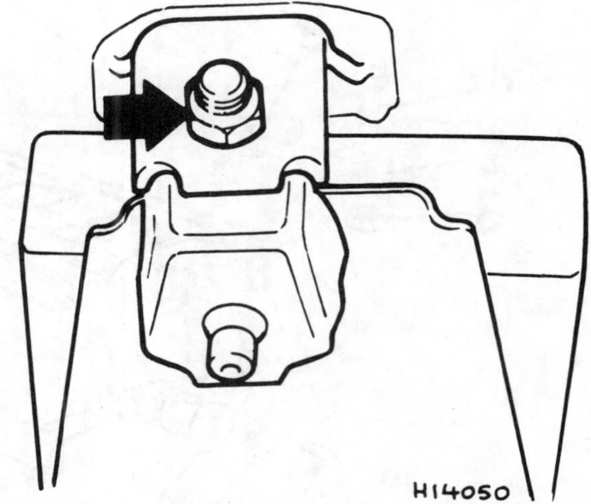

Fig. 6.93 Gear lever bracket retaining nut – arrowed (Sec 9)

2 Engage reverse gear.

3 Working under the car, extract the circlip and remove the washer, then pull out the selector rod (Fig. 6.88).

4 Support the weight of the gearbox on a trolley jack.

5 Unscrew the rear mounting bolts, then lower the gearbox a little.

6 Inside the car remove the felt pad, push up the cover and pull up the rubber cover.

7 Extract the circlip and remove the gear lever (Fig. 6.89).

8 Refitting is a reversal of removal but lubricate the spherical plates with grease.

Gear lever – dismantling and reassembly

9 Extract the circlip and separate the gear lever sections.

10 Remove the cap, circlip. rubber ring, washer, circlip, rubber boot, circlip, spring retainer, spring, upper spherical plate and lower ribbed spherical plate (Fig. 6.90).

11 Clean, check and renew the components as necessary.

12 Reassembly is a reversal of dismantling, but apply grease to the ball sockets.

Gear lever boot – renewal

13 Pull off the gear lever knob.

14 Disconnect the boot from the centre console aperture, then pull it up off the lever.

15 Fit the new boot using a reversal of the removal procedure.

Gear lever selector rod joint bushes – renewal

16 Apply the handbrake then jack up the front of the car and support on axle stands.
17 Disconnect the propeller shaft from the transmission with reference to Chapter 7.
18 Engage reverse gear and remove the circlip and washer from the base of the gear lever under the car. Disconnect the selector rod.
19 Refer to Fig. 6.91 and push back the locking sleeve (1), then move the selector rod into 3rd gear, drive out the pin, and disconnect the selector rod from the gearbox selector shaft.
20 Renew the bushes as necessary.
21 Reassembly is a reversal of dismantling, but lubricate the joint with grease.

Gearchange lever mounting bracket – removal and refitting

22 Remove the gear lever as previously described.
23 Disconnect the wires from the plug and the reversing lamp switch.
24 Unscrew the two front socket-headed mounting bolts (Fig. 6.92).
25 Unscrew the rear mounting nut and remove the bracket (Fig. 6.93).
26 Refitting is a reversal of removal, but renew the front mounting bolts and tighten them to the specified torque.

10 Fault diagnosis – manual gearbox

Symptom	Reason(s)
Ineffective synchromesh	Worn synchro baulk rings
Jumps out of gear	Detent spring weak or broken Worn selector forks or dogs Worn synchro unit or gears
Noisy operation	Worn bearings or gears
Difficult engagement of gears	Worn selector components Worn synchro unit Worn gear engagement dogs Clutch fault Seized needle-roller bearing in end of crankshaft

PART B: AUTOMATIC TRANSMISSION

11 General description

A four-speed automatic transmission is standard on 525e models, while on 520i models either a three or four-speed transmission may be fitted as an option depending on the year of manufacture. The four-speed transmission incorporates a torque converter 4th gear lock-up function which provides a direct drive for improved economy.

From September 1985 an electronic four-speed automatic transmission may be fitted as an option on 525e models, but at the time of writing no information was available for specific maintenance work on this transmission. The transmission is coded EH (electronic-hydraulic) and incorporates a control knob on the centre console next to the selector lever with three positions. It is possible to select 'E' for economy, 'S' for sports, and '3.2.1' for direct. A main electronic control unit controls the transmission according to the mode selected, and a further control unit is fitted for downshift protection. The road speed is monitored by a pulse wheel and speed sensor, and the ECU determines the shift points for optimum performance and fuel economy. The EH transmission is very similar to the standard four-speed transmission except for the fitting of control solenoids to the hydraulic control valve assembly.

12 Routine maintenance

Carry out the following at the intervals given in *Routine maintenance* at the front of this manual.

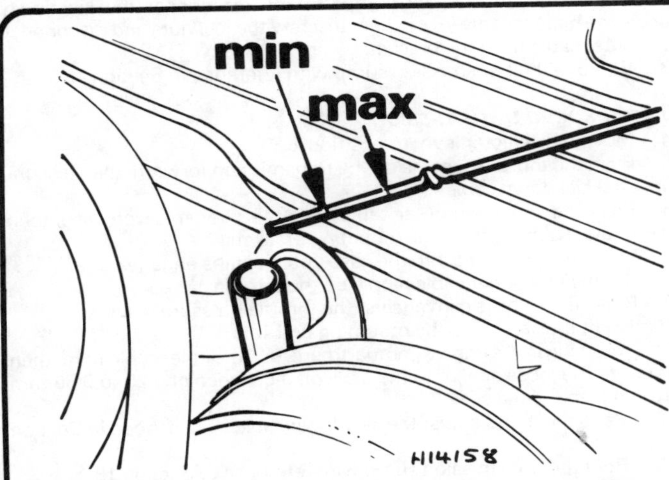

Fig. 6.94 Dipstick markings – automatic transmission (Sec 12)

Min to max = 0.3 litre (0.5 pint) approx

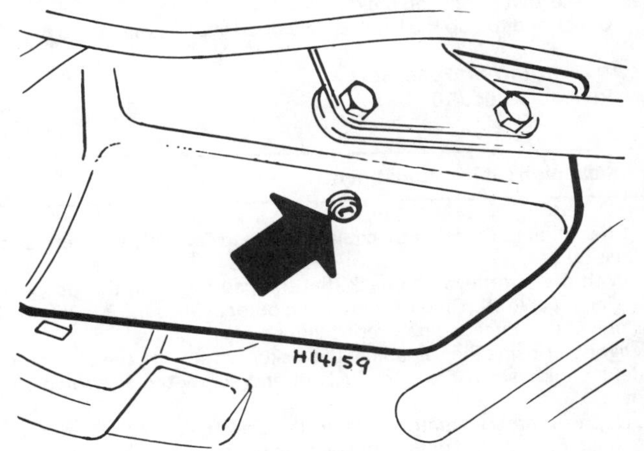

Fig. 6.95 Sump pan drain plug (arrowed) – automatic transmission (Sec 12)

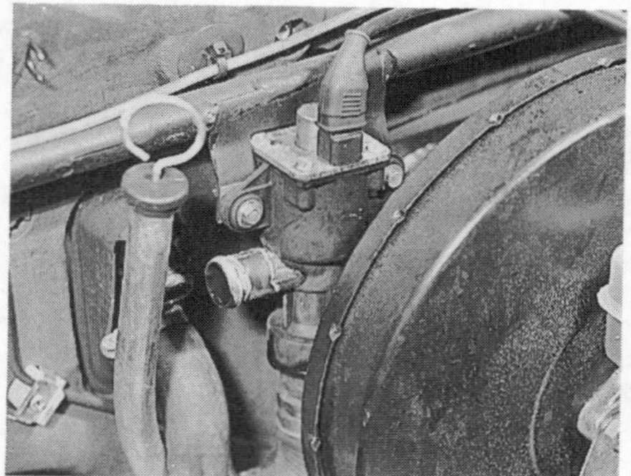
12.3 Automatic transmission fluid level dipstick

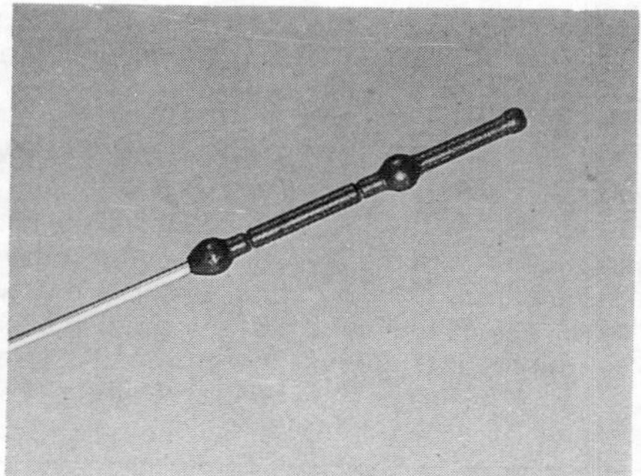
12.4 Minimum and maximum level marks on the automatic transmission fluid level dipstick

12.5 Topping up the automatic transmission fluid level

Check the fluid level

1 Position the car on level ground with the transmission at normal operating temperature.

2 Select 'P' then start the engine and allow it to idle.

3 Withdraw the fluid level dipstick (photo) and wipe clean with a non-fluffy rag.

4 With the engine still idling, re-insert the dipstick and withdraw again. The level should be between the two notch marks (photo and Fig. 6.94).

5 If the level is low, top it up by pouring fresh fluid of the correct type into the dipstick tube, using a funnel if necessary (photo). The space between the two notches represents approximately 0.3 litre (0.5 pint). Do not overfill the transmission otherwise the transmission may overheat.

6 Refit the dipstick and switch off the engine.

Change the fluid

7 The transmission should be at normal temperature, and the car should be on level ground.

8 Apply the handbrake then jack up the front of the car and support on axle stands.

9 Position a container beneath the transmission. Unscrew the transmission drain plug (Fig. 6.95) and allow the fluid to drain into the container. Since the fluid will be very hot, take suitable precautions to prevent scalding.

10 If the fluid smells burnt and is black, this indicates damage to the internal clutches and professional advice should be sought. If regular servicing has been neglected it may be necessary to clean the filter screen as described in Section 18.

11 Clean the drain plug and renew the sealing washer if necessary, then refit and tighten it to the specified torque.

12 Lower the car to the ground.

13 Pour fresh fluid of the correct type into the dipstick tube until it reaches the lower notch on the dipstick.

14 Check and top up the level as described in paragraphs 1 to 6.

Clean the fluid filter screen

15 Refer to Section 18.

13 Kickdown cable – adjustment

1 Check that the accelerator cable is adjusted correctly with reference to Chapter 3.

2 With the throttle shut, check that the gap between the kickdown cable inner cable stop and the end of the outer cable is 0.5 ± 0.25 mm. If not, adjust the outer cable by repositioning the locknuts.

3 Working inside the car, adjust the kickdown stop on the accelerator pedal as follows. Unscrew the locknut and screw the kickdown stop right in.

4 Depress the accelerator pedal to the transmission pressure point, then unscrew the stop until it touches the pedal.

5 Depress the accelerator to the kickdown position and check that the gap between the kickdown cable stop and the end of the outer cable seal is now at least 44 mm.

6 Lower the car to the ground.

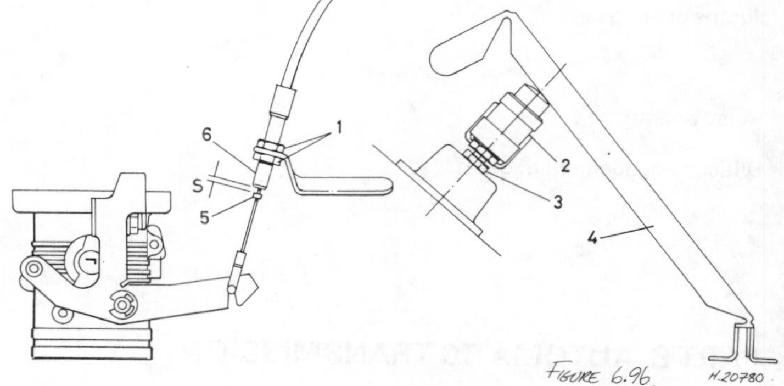

Fig. 6.96 Kickdown cable adjustment – automatic transmission (Sec 13)

1 Adjustment nuts
2 Kickdown stop
3 Locknut
4 Accelerator pedal
5 Stop
6 Sleeve
S = 0.050 ± 0.25 mm

14 Kickdown cable – renewal

1 Apply the handbrake then jack up the front of the car and support on axle stands.

2 Working in the engine compartment, disconnect the kickdown cable from the throttle lever, then unscrew the locknuts and disconnect the outer cable from the bracket.

3 Remove the transmission sump with reference to Section 18.

Three-speed transmission

4 Move the selector lever to position 'N'.

5 Push the throttle cam inside the transmission forward, then disconnect the kickdown cable.

6 Push the kickdown outer cable out of the transmission case, then withdraw the cable from the mounting brackets.

7 Push the new cable into the case until the tabs engage.

8 Connect the inner cable nipple on the throttle cam.

9 Press the throttle cam against the throttle pressure valve.

10 Refit the cable into the mounting brackets.

11 Working in the engine compartment, pull the inner cable tight, then squeeze the loose seal onto the cable at a distance of 0.25 to 0.50 mm from the end of the seal.

12 Reconnect and adjust the kickdown cable as described in Section 13.

13 Refit the transmission sump with reference to Section 18.

Four-speed transmission

14 Remove the filter screen with reference to Section 18.

15 Using a Torx key, unbolt and remove the valve body. Make sure

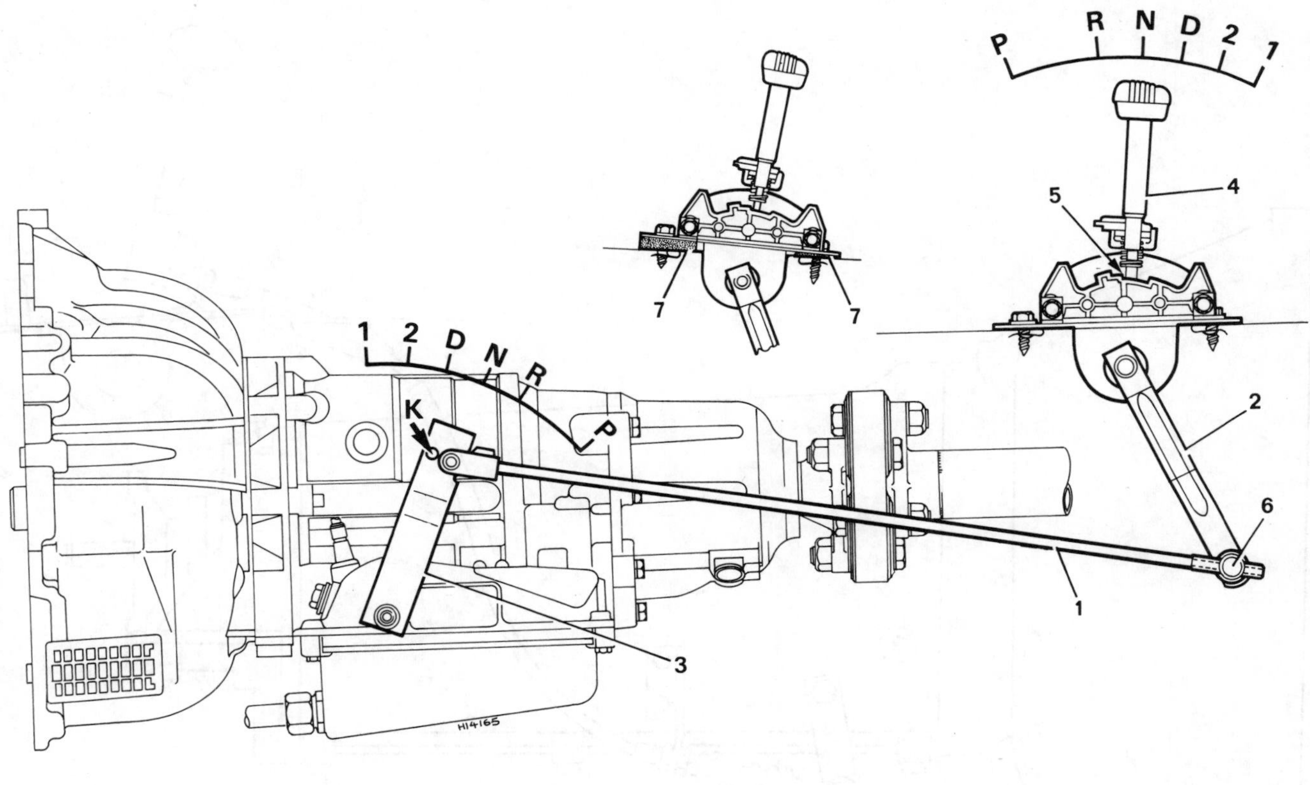

Fig. 6.97 Selector lever linkage – three-speed transmission (Sec 15)

1 Selector rod
2 Selector lever lower section
3 Transmission lever
4 Selector lever
5 Stop
6 Pin
7 Blocks
K Hole for use with air conditioned cars

that only the bolts with the 12 mm heads are unscrewed.

16 Disconnect the cable from the cam, then press the outer cable out of the transmission case. Withdraw the cable from the mounting brackets.

17 Push the new cable into the case until the tabs engage.

18 Preload the cam spring by turning the cam one turn anti-clockwise, then reconnect the nipple on the inner cable to the cam.

19 Refit the valve body and tighten the bolts.

20 Press the throttle cam against the throttle pressure valve.

21 Refit the cable into the mounting brackets.

22 Working in the engine compartment, pull the inner cable tight, then squeeze the loose seal onto the cable at a distance of 0.25 to 0.50 mm from the end of the seal.

23 Reconnect and adjust the kickdown cable as described in Section 13.

24 Refit the transmission sump with reference to Section 18.

15 Selector lever linkage – adjustment

Three-speed transmission

1 Apply the handbrake then jack up the front of the car and support on axle stands.

2 Make sure that the shift control console is secure before carrying out the adjustment.

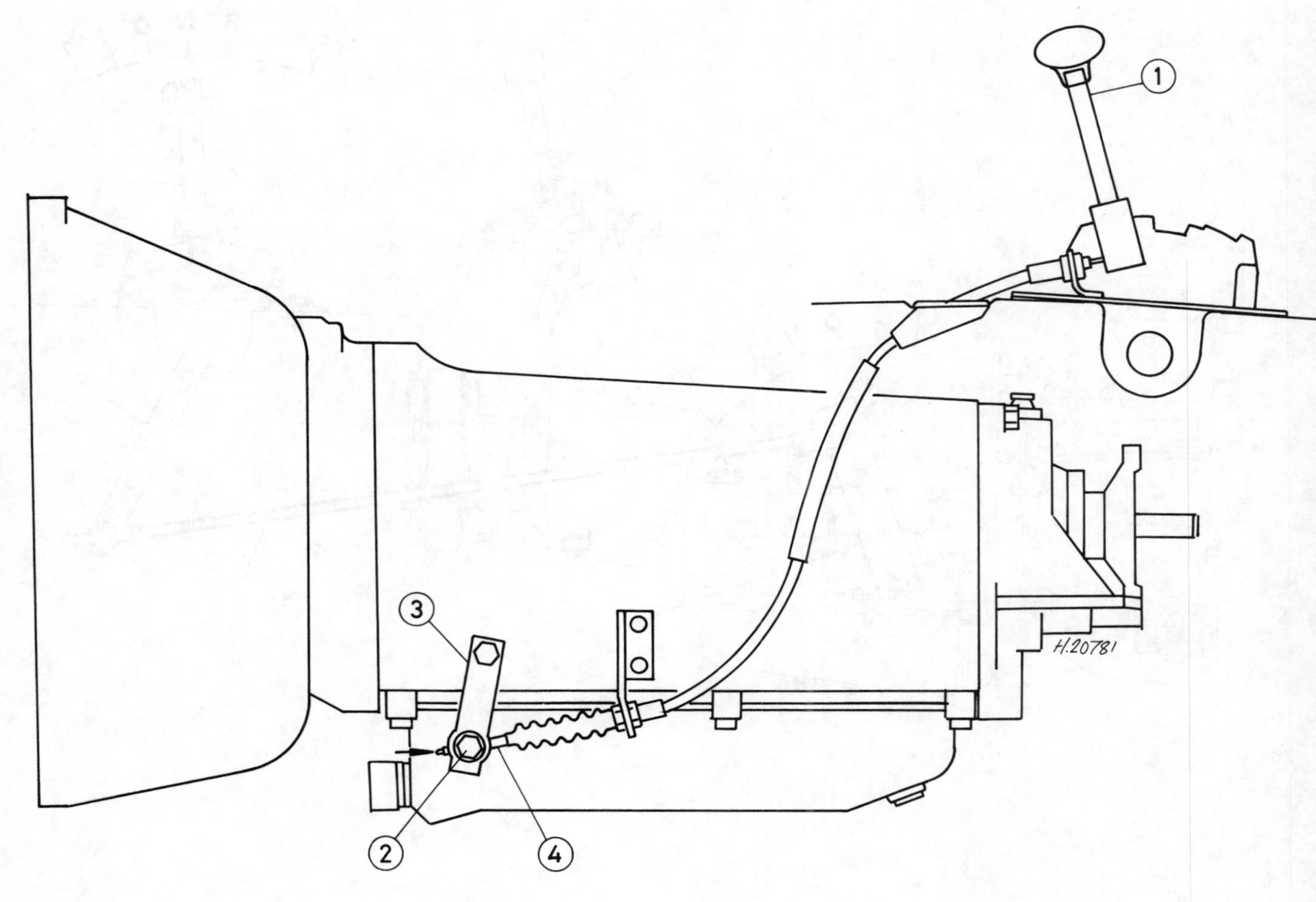

Fig. 6.98 Selector lever linkage – four-speed transmission (Sec 15)

1 Selector lever *2 Nut* *3 Transmission lever* *4 Cable end*

3 Working under the car, disconnect the selector rod from the base of the selector lever (Fig. 6.97).
4 Move the selector arm on the side of the transmission until it clicks in the 'N' detent. This position can be determined by counting three clicks from the fully forward position.
5 Push the hand control lever against its stop on the selector gate so that it engages 'N'.
6 Adjust the length of the selector rod until the trunnion pivot pin will just slide through the hole in the lever. Now reduce the length of the selector rod by screwing in the trunnion by between one and two turns. Connect the rod to the lever.
7 Lower the car to the ground.

Four-speed transmission

8 Apply the handbrake then jack up the car and support on axle stands.
9 Move the hand control lever to position 'P'.
10 Working under the car, loosen the nut securing the selector cable to the transmission lever.
11 Push the transmission lever forward to the 'P' position.
12 Move the selector cable slightly to the rear in order to tension it, then tighten the securing nut.
13 Lower the car to the ground.

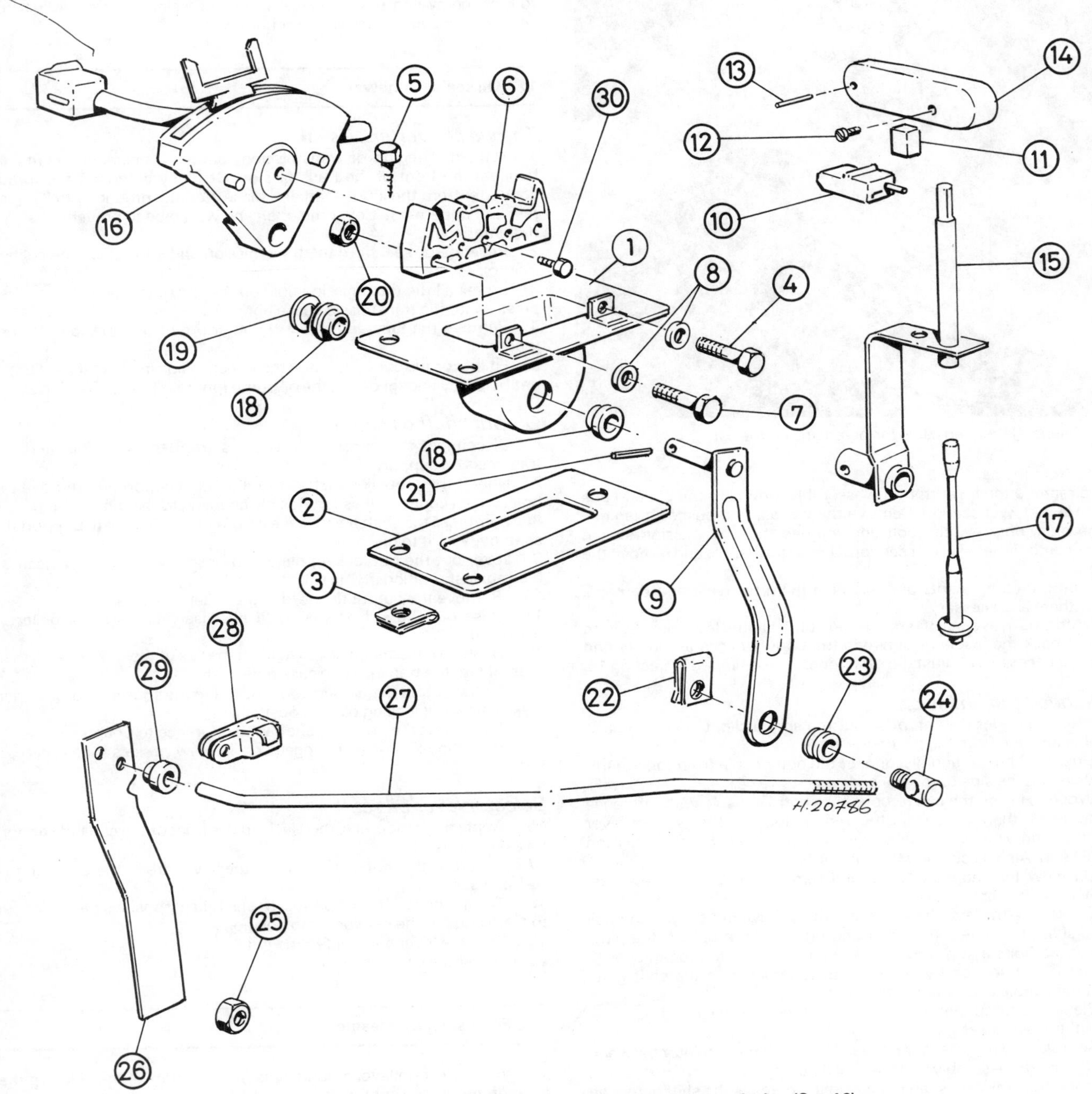

Fig. 6.99 Selector lever components – three-speed transmission (Sec 16)

1 *Bearing shell*
2 *Sealing plate*
3 *Spring nut*
4 *Bolt*
5 *Screw*
6 *Shift gate*
7 *Bolt*
8 *Washer*
9 *Selector lever lower section*
10 *Push button*
11 *Spring element*
12 *Stud*
13 *Dowel pin*
14 *Handle*
15 *Selector lever*
16 *Transmission switch*
17 *Pull rod*
18 *Bearing sleeve*
19 *Shim*
20 *Nut*
21 *Key*
22 *Retainer*
23 *Joint sleeve*
24 *Shaft*
25 *Nut*
26 *Selector lever bracket*
27 *Selector rod*
28 *Spring clip*
29 *Sleeve*
30 *Screw*

16 Selector lever – removal and refitting

1 Disconnect the battery negative lead.
2 Apply the handbrake then jack up the front of the car and support on axle stands.

Three-speed transmission

3 Working under the car, prise out the spring clip, then disconnect the selector rod from the transmission lever.
4 Remove the centre console with reference to Chapter 11.
5 Disconnect the wiring plug from the selector lever assembly.
6 Unscrew the mounting bolts and remove the selector lever as-

16.12 Selector lever and cable (arrowed) inside the car

sembly from the car.

7 To remove the lever from the assembly, drive out the pin and pull out the lever lower section. Remove the washer and bushes, then pull off the plug, unscrew the bolt and remove the transmission switch together with the lever upper section. Unbolt the handle and remove the pullrod.

8 Clean the components and examine them for wear and damage. Renew them as necessary.

9 Refitting is a reversal of removal, but lubricate the lever bushes with grease. Check the insulator between the body and the assembly and renew it if necessary. Adjust the selector rod as described in Section 15.

Four-speed transmission

10 Working under the car, prise out the spring clip, then disconnect the cable end eye from the pin on the lever.

11 Unscrew the nut and disconnect the outer cable from the mounting bracket on the side of the transmission.

12 Working inside the car, remove the centre console with reference to Chapter 11, then disconnect the wiring plugs for the selector lever assembly, and where applicable the wiring for the EH transmission control knob. Also disconnect the cable (photo).

13 Unscrew the mounting bolts and remove the selector lever assembly from the car.

14 To remove the lever from the assembly, drive out the pin and pull out the shaft. Remove the washer and bushes, then pull off the plug, unscrew the bolts and remove the transmission switch together with the lever upper section by tilting it out together with the shift gate. Unbolt the handle and remove the pullrod.

15 Clean the components and examine them for wear and damage. Renew them as necessary.

16 Refitting is a reversal of removal, but check the insulator between the body and the assembly and renew it if necessary. Make sure that the pins on the transmission shaft engage in the bores of the shift gate. The fork of the switch must engage above the selector lever. Adjust the selector cable as described in Section 15.

17 Oil seals – renewal

Torque converter oil seal

1 With the engine or transmission removed, position a container beneath the front of the transmission. Carefully withdraw the torque converter from the input shaft and place it on the ground with its open rear end uppermost. Cover the open end with tape to prevent dust and dirt entering it.

2 Prise the oil seal from the transmission and wipe clean the seating (photo).

3 Smear a little transmission fluid on the lips of the new oil seal, then press it into the transmission case until flush.

4 Remove the tape and clean the outer rim of the torque converter (photo).

5 Fit the torque converter over the transmission input shaft and turn it until it is fully engaged with the oil pump (photo). Refer to Section 20 (b).

Output shaft oil seal

6 Disconnect the exhaust downpipes from the manifold and the transmission support.

7 Unbolt the propeller shaft centre bearing support and remove the bolts which connect the shaft flexible coupling to the output flange.

8 Compress the shaft and release it from the output shaft. Support the shaft by tying it to one side.

9 Lever out the nut locking plate and unscrew the nut. This can be held against rotation if 'P' is selected.

10 Remove the output flange, using a puller if necessary.

11 Prise out the old oil seal, or if necessary use a small puller to remove it.

12 Smear a little transmission fluid on the lips of the new oil seal, then press it into the transmission case until flush.

13 Fit the output flange, screw on the nut to the specified torque, then stake a new nut locking plate in position.

14 Reconnect the propeller shaft with reference to Chapter 7.

15 Refit the exhaust pipes together with new gaskets where necessary.

Selector lever oil seal

16 Apply the handbrake, then jack up the front of the car and support on axle stands.

17 Unscrew the nut and remove the lever from the side of the transmission.

18 Tap in one side of the oil seal to eject the opposite side. Lever out the seal and tap the new one into position.

19 Refit the lever and tighten the nut.

20 Lower the car to the ground.

18 Filter screen – cleaning

1 With the car on level ground, apply the handbrake then jack up the front of the car and support on axle stands.

17.2 Torque converter oil seal (arrowed)

17.4 Torque converter rim (arrowed) which engages the oil pump

17.5 Automatic transmission and input shaft before fitting the torque converter

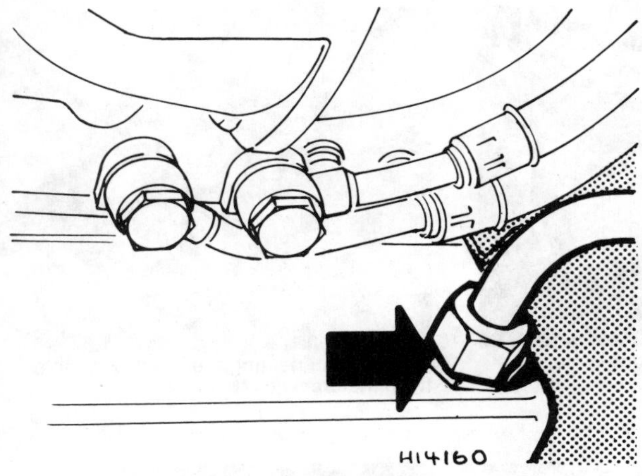

Fig. 6.100 Fluid level/dipstick guide tube bolt (arrowed) – automatic transmission (Sec 18)

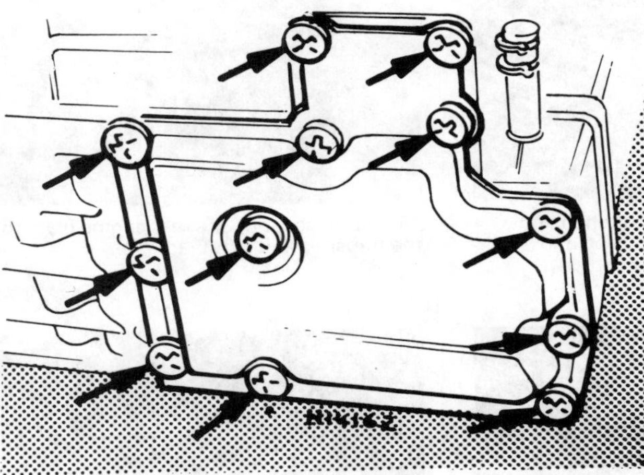

Fig. 6.101 Filter screen fixing screws (arrowed) – three-speed automatic transmission (Sec 18)

2 Unscrew the drain plug and drain the transmission fluid into a suitable container. If the car has just been used, the fluid will be very hot, so take suitable precautions against scalding.
3 If the fluid smells burnt and is black, this indicates damage to the internal clutches and professional advice should be sought.
4 Unscrew the union nut and disconnect the oil filler tube from the transmission sump (Fig. 6.100).
5 Unscrew the bolts and lower the sump from the transmission.
6 Using a Torx key, unbolt and remove the filter screen (Fig. 6.101).
7 Clean the screen in fuel or a suitable cleaning fluid and examine it for damage. If the screen is beginning to gum up with a brown residue, it should be renewed. On the four-speed transmission renew the O-ring on the upper face of the screen. At the same time it is also worth flushing out and cleaning the oil cooler in the bottom of the radiator in order to clear away any dirt or residue.
8 Refit the screen and tighten the bolts to the specified torque.
9 Clean the sump and magnets of any accumulated residue. Place the magnets back in the sump.
10 Refit the sump together with a new gasket and tighten the bolts to the specified torque. Make sure that the small bracket on each bolt is positioned with its shorter leg on the sump (Fig. 6.102).
11 Reconnect the oil filler tube and tighten the union nut.
12 Renew the copper washer then refit and tighten the drain plug.
13 Lower the car to the ground.
14 Fill the transmission with the correct type and quantity of fresh fluid with reference to Section 12.

19 Transmission – removal and refitting

1 Apply the handbrake then jack up the front of the car and support on axle stands, or alternatively position the car on a ramp or over an inspection pit.
2 Unscrew the drain plug (photo) and drain the transmission fluid. Also disconnect the battery negative lead.
3 Disconnect the kickdown cable from the throttle lever by first opening the lever, then loosen the locknuts and release the cable from the bracket (photos).
4 Disconnect the exhaust downpipes from the manifold and release the pipe support from the transmission.
5 Refer to Chapter 7, then detach the propeller shaft from the transmission and also detach the centre bearing. Tie the propeller shaft to one side.
6 Disconnect the selector rod or cable from the lever on the transmission or alternatively from the bottom of the selector lever (photo). On the EH transmission also disconnect the wiring for the hydraulic valve assembly control solenoids.
7 Unbolt and remove the cover plate/housing from the lower face of the torque converter housing and from the bottom of the cylinder block as applicable. Also unscrew the single bolt securing the engine rear plate to the transmission (photos).
8 Disconnect the fluid filler pipe from the sump pan and the fluid cooler pipes from the transmission (photos).
9 Unscrew and remove the bolts which connect the torque converter to the driveplate. Turn the crankshaft while doing this to bring each bolt into view (photo).
10 Support the rear end of the transmission and unbolt the mounting crossmember from the underbody (photo).
11 Place a piece of wood over the front anti-roll bar. Use a plastic tie to keep it in position (photo).
12 Lower the transmission and engine until they are just resting on the front crossmember and anti-roll bar.
13 Unscrew and remove the transmission-to-engine bolts. A long extension will be required to reach the upper bolts (photos).
14 Prise out the plastic grille from the bottom of the transmission (photo).
15 Withdraw the transmission from the engine, and at the same time insert a lever through the grille opening and prise the torque converter from the driveplate towards the rear so that it is kept in full engagement with the transmission oil pump. Do not allow the torque converter to move forwards otherwise fluid will be lost.
16 Lower the transmission to the ground.
17 Retain the torque converter in the transmission with a length of flat bar bolted to the torque converter housing flange (Fig. 6.103).
18 While the transmission is removed, examine the driveplate. Any cracks or distortion will indicate the need for a new one. Always fit new bolts when refitting the driveplate and apply thread-locking fluid to their threads.

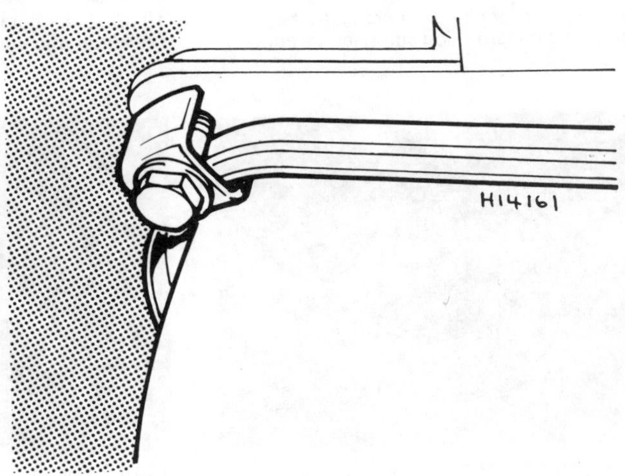

Fig. 6.102 Sump pan fixing clamps – automatic transmission (Sec 19)

19.2 Automatic transmission drain plug

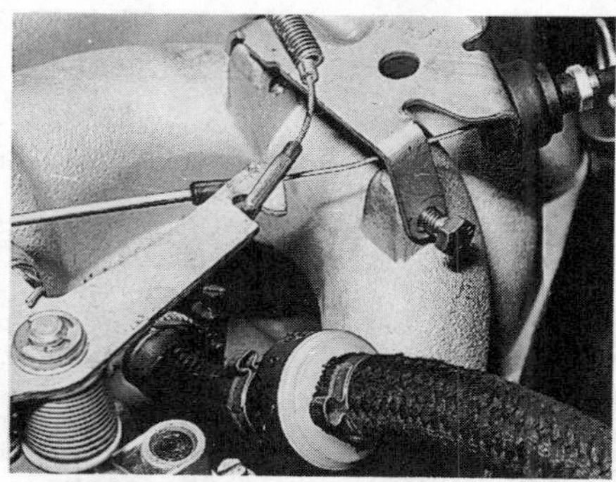
19.3A Disconnecting the kickdown cable from the throttle lever

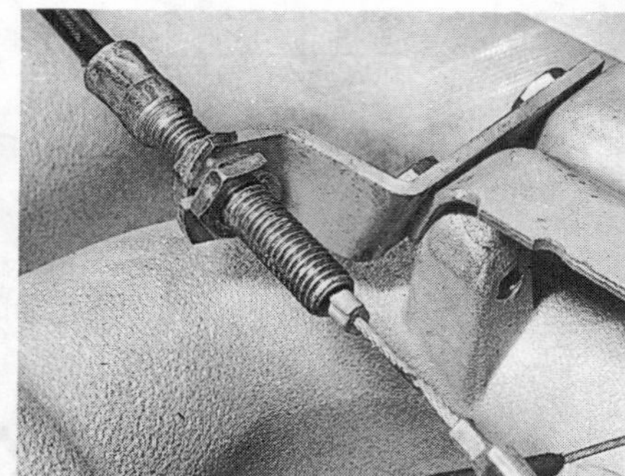
19.3B Disconnecting the kickdown cable from the bracket

19.6 Selector cable on the side of the automatic transmission

19.7A Removing the cover plate/housing from the torque converter housing and cylinder block

19.7B Bolt securing the rear engine plate to the transmission (arrowed)

19.8A Fluid filler pipe connection to the automatic transmission sump (arrowed)

19.8B Lower fluid cooler pipe connection to the automatic transmission

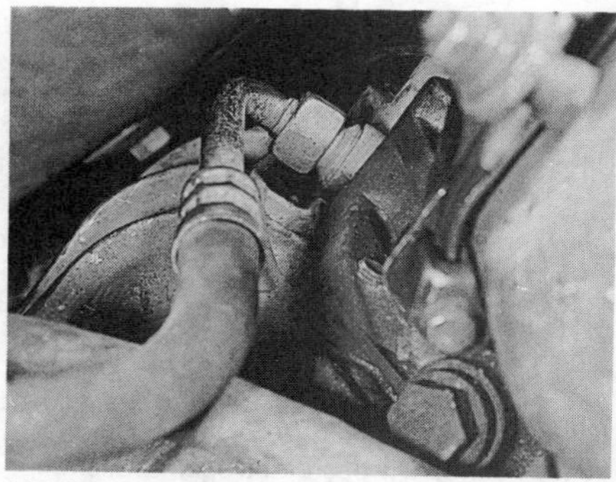
19.8C Upper fluid cooler pipe connection to the automatic transmission

19.9 Unscrewing the torque converter-to-driveplate bolts

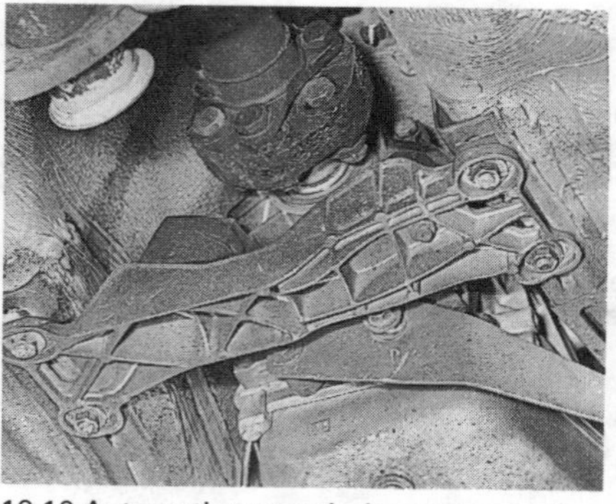
19.10 Automatic transmission rear mounting crossmember

19.11 Piece of wood positioned to protect the front anti-roll bar

19 If the transmission is being exchanged, transfer the following components before parting with the old unit:

- *(a) Selector rod, if applicable – attach it to the transmission lever with the special spring clip fitted from top to bottom*
- *(b) Rear crossmember and exhaust bracket*
- *(c) Cover plate*

20 Refitting is a reversal of removal, but note the following:

- *(a) Blow through the fluid cooler pipes and flush twice with new fluid before re-connecting*
- *(b) Check that the torque converter is fully engaged with the oil pump by measuring the distance from the flange face to the dogs on the torque converter (photo). This should be approximately 30.5 mm. Turn the torque converter if necessary so that it is fully engaged*
- *(c) Apply thread-locking fluid to the threads of the driveplate-to-torque converter bolts before refitting them*
- *(d) Adjust the kickdown cable and selector lever as described in Sections 13 and 15*
- *(e) Preload the propeller shaft centre bearing as described in Chapter 7*
- *(f) Tighten all bolts to the specified torque. Make sure that the rear mounting crossmember is positioned within the elongated bolt slots without pressure either forward or rearwards (photo)*
- *(g) Fill the transmission with the specified type and quantity of fresh fluid*

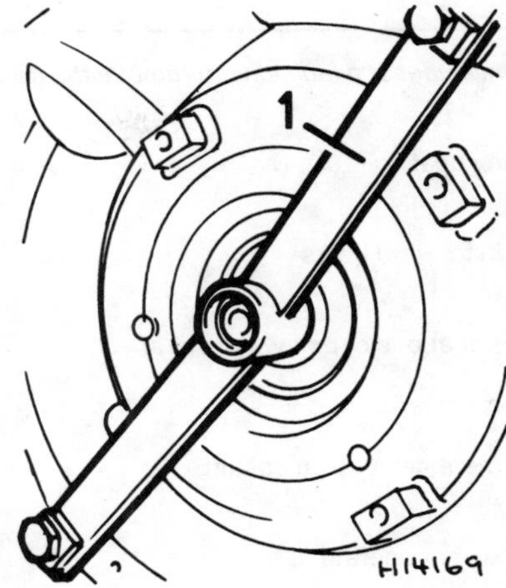

Fig. 6.103 Torque converter retaining strap (1) – automatic transmission (Sec 19)

19.13A Using an extension bar to unscrew the upper mounting bolts

19.13B Transmission-to-engine bolt (arrowed)

19.14 Removing the plastic grille from the bottom of the transmission

19.20A Checking that the torque converter is fully engaged with the oil pump

19.20B Automatic transmission rear mounting, showing the elongated bolt slot

Fault diagnosis overleaf

20 Fault diagnosis – automatic transmission

Symptom	Reason(s)
Caution: *In the event of a fault, do not remove the transmission from the car before having a full test and diagnosis procedure carried out by a BMW dealer*	
No drive in any gear	Fluid level too low Faulty control unit or solenoid on EH transmission only
Erratic drive in forward gears	Fluid level too low Filter screen dirty
Gear changes at above or below normal speed	Dirty fluid
Gear engagement jerky	Idle speed too high
Gear engagement delayed on upshift	Fluid level too low Kickdown cable adjustment incorrect
Kickdown does not operate	Kickdown cable adjustment incorrect
Fluid dirty or discoloured	Brake bands and clutches wearing
Parking lock not effective	Selector lever out of adjustment Parking lock defective

Chapter 7 Propeller shaft and driveshafts

Contents

Specifications

Propeller shaft

Type	Two-section, tubular with rubber flexible joint at front, two universal joints and a rubber mounted centre bearing
Front coupling type	Jurid rubber disc

Driveshafts

Type	Solid, with two constant velocity joints
Grease capacity per joint:	
520i	80 grams
525e	120 grams

Torque wrench settings

	Nm	lbf ft
Front flexible joint	72	52
Propeller shaft to final drive	72	52
Centre mounting to underbody	22	16
Threaded sleeve	20	14.5
Driveshaft to final drive and hub	58 to 63	42 to 45

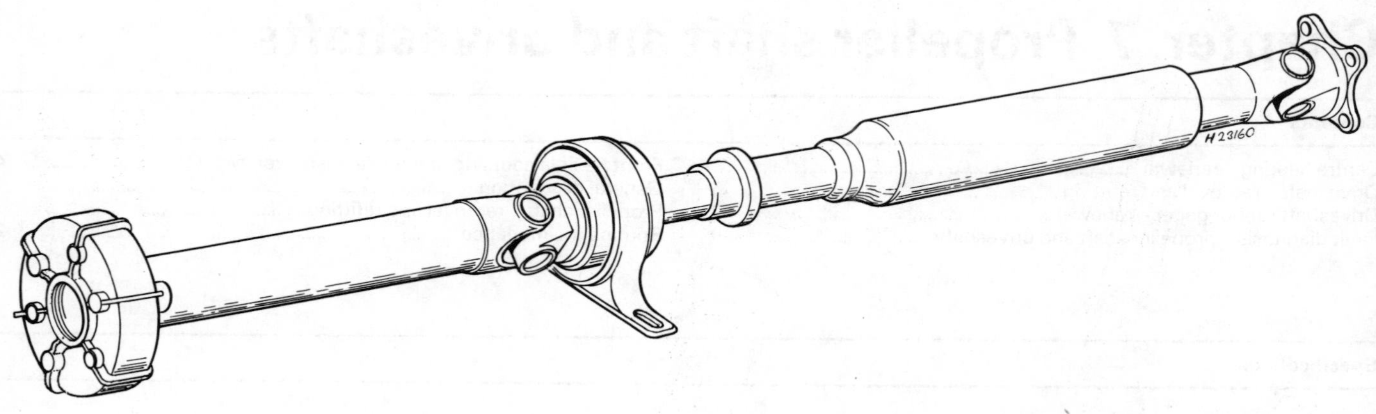

Fig. 7.1 Two section propeller shaft (Sec 1)

1 General description

The propeller shaft is of two-piece tubular type having a rubber flexible coupling at the front of the transmission output flange. Conventional universal joints are fitted at the centre and rear of the propeller shaft, but it is not possible to renew them separate from the main shaft. The rear section is splined to allow for movement of the final drive unit.

The driveshafts incorporate double constant velocity joints.

2 Routine maintenance

Carry out the following at the intervals given in *Routine maintenance* at the front of this manual.

Check driveshaft rubber gaiters

1 Chock the front wheels, then jack up the rear of the car and support on axle stands.

2 With the handbrake released, examine the driveshaft rubber gaiters for signs of splits and deterioration. Turn the wheels during the check so that all areas of the gaiters are visible.

3 Propeller shaft – removal and refitting

1 Jack up the front and rear of the car and support on axle stands.

2 Remove the exhaust system as described in Chapter 3.

3 Where fitted, unbolt and remove the heatshield from the underbody (photo).

4 Unscrew and remove the three bolts securing the front propeller shaft flexible coupling to the gearbox or automatic transmission output flange. Note that the nuts are fitted at the flange end (photo).

5 Release the handbrake, then unscrew the nuts and remove the special bolts securing the rear of the propeller shaft to the final drive flange (photo). Note which way round the bolts are fitted. Support the propeller shaft on an axle stand if necessary.

6 Support the centre of the propeller shaft, then unscrew the centre mounting nuts.

7 Lower the centre of the propeller shaft so that it is released from the pin on the transmission output shaft, then withdraw it from under the car.

8 The propeller shaft is a balanced assembly and therefore it is preferable to renew it complete if it is excessively worn or damaged. It is not possible to renew the universal joints as they are swaged into the shafts. If necessary, dismantle the propeller shaft and renew the components described in Sections 4 and 5. It is recommended that all self-locking nuts are renewed as a matter of course.

9 Commence refitting by locating the front coupling onto the transmission output shaft, then locate the rear of the propeller shaft onto the final drive flange and lift the centre bearing into position, supporting it with an axle stand. Loosely fit one of the rear bolts to hold it in position on the flange.

10 Locate the centre mounting on the special bolts and screw on the nuts loosely.

11 Fit all of the front and rear coupling bolts in their previously noted positions, then tighten them to the specified torque. When tightening the front bolts, only turn the nuts or bolts in contact with the output flange in order not to distort the coupling itself.

12 Preload the centre mounting in a forward direction by 2.0 to 4.0 mm for pre-1985 models, and 4.0 to 6.0 mm for 1985-on models, then tighten the nuts fully. Note that the propeller shaft must be in a central position on the underbody. This can be verified by measuring from identical points on each side of the car. Also the centre bearing must be at a right-angle to the propeller shaft.

13 If new components have been fitted, loosen the threaded sleeve and then retighten it to the specified torque. BMW technicians use a special tool to do this, but it may be possible to use a conventional tool such as a pair of grips instead. It is also worth checking that the centre mounting is correctly aligned in relation to the front and rear sections. The BMW tool for this check firstly checks the attitude of the engine

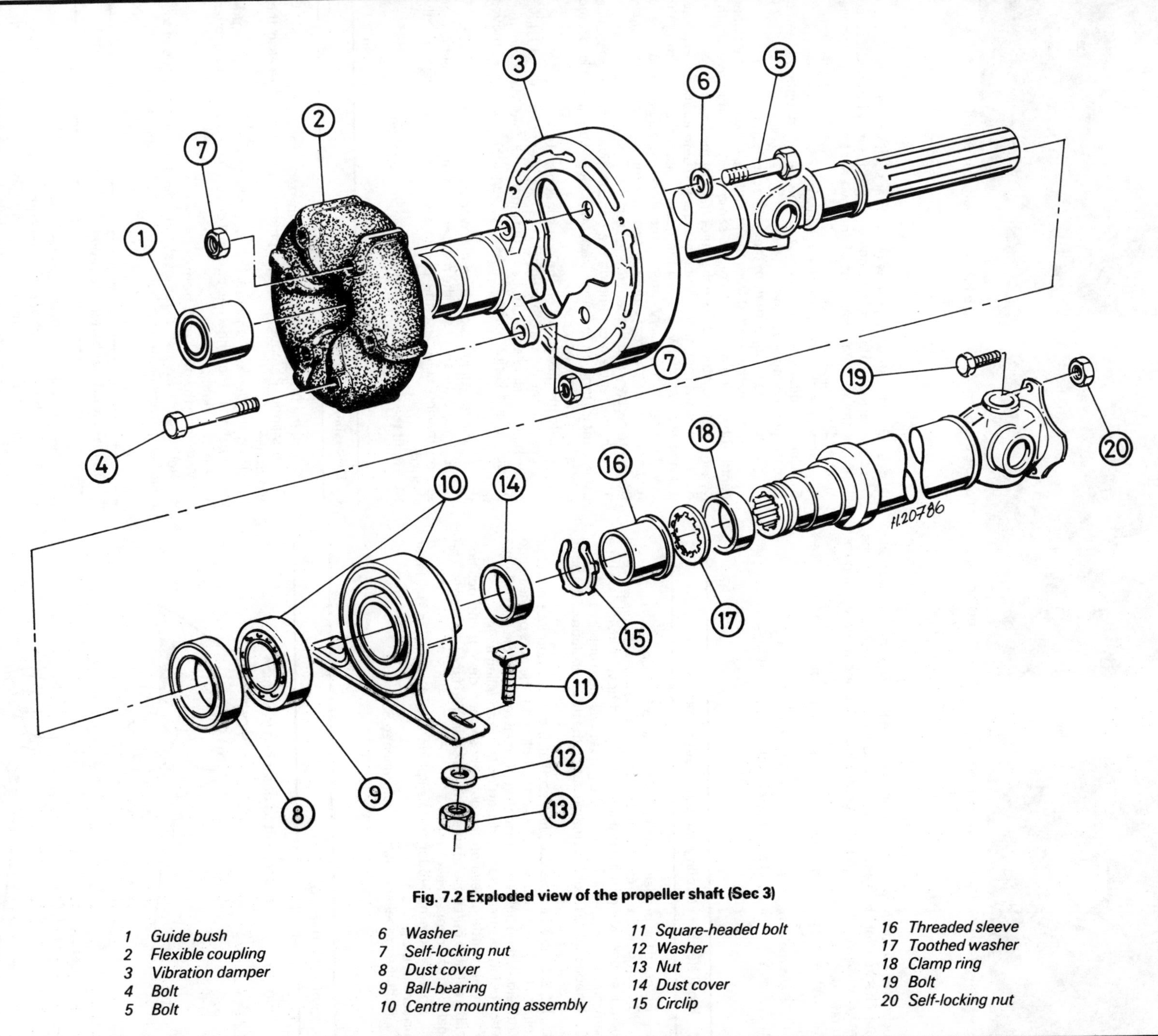

Fig. 7.2 Exploded view of the propeller shaft (Sec 3)

1 *Guide bush*
2 *Flexible coupling*
3 *Vibration damper*
4 *Bolt*
5 *Bolt*
6 *Washer*
7 *Self-locking nut*
8 *Dust cover*
9 *Ball-bearing*
10 *Centre mounting assembly*
11 *Square-headed bolt*
12 *Washer*
13 *Nut*
14 *Dust cover*
15 *Circlip*
16 *Threaded sleeve*
17 *Toothed washer*
18 *Clamp ring*
19 *Bolt*
20 *Self-locking nut*

3.3 Heatshield mounting screw (arrowed)

3.4 Propeller shaft front flexible coupling (arrowed)

3.5 Propeller shaft rear coupling

using the oil sump flange as a reference, then the front and rear sections are checked for the same attitude. If adjustment is necessary, shims may be positioned between the centre mounting and the underbody as required.
14 Where necessary, refit the heatshield to the underbody and tighten the bolts.
15 Refit the exhaust system with reference to Chapter 3.
16 Apply the handbrake and lower the car to the ground.

4 Front flexible coupling and guide bush – renewal

1 Remove the propeller shaft as described in Section 3.
2 To remove the guide bush, fill the centre cavity with grease then locate a close fitting metal rod in the bush and drive it inwards with a hammer. The hydraulic action of the grease will force out the bush.
3 Unbolt the old flexible coupling noting the fitted position of the bolts (Fig. 7.3).
4 Fit the new flexible coupling so that the arrows on its perimeter point to the flange bolt holes. Insert the bolts with the nuts on the flange extensions, then tighten them to the specified torque. Hold the bolts still when doing this to avoid any distortion in the coupling itself.
5 Smear a little grease on the guide bush then drive it into position with a suitable drift making sure that the sealing lip faces outwards. The final protrusion must be 4.5 mm.
6 Apply a little molybdenum disulphide based grease to the inner surfaces of the guide bush.
7 Refit the propeller shaft with reference to Section 3.

5 Centre bearing – renewal

1 Remove the propeller shaft as described in Section 3.

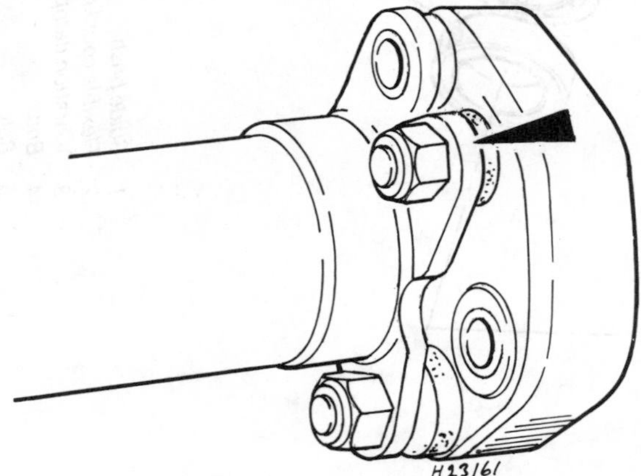

Fig. 7.3 Arrows on the front flexible coupling (Sec 4)

2 Unscrew the threaded screw on the rear section. BMW technicians use a special tool to do this, but a pair of large grips may be used instead.
3 Mark the relative alignment of the two sections of the propeller shaft and then separate them.
4 Extract the circlip and remove the dust guard.
5 Using a suitable extractor, draw off the centre mounting together with the grooved ball-bearing.
6 Remove the dust guard from the rear section stub.
7 To separate the bearing from the mounting, position the mounting centre tube over a metal tube of the same diameter and drive out the bearing using another tube on the outer track of the bearing.
8 Examine the mounting rubber for wear and deterioration and renew it if necessary. Otherwise clean the bearing seating before fitting the new bearing. If necessary remove the threaded sleeve, washer and rubber ring from the rear stub and examine them for damage. Renew them if necessary and fit them to the stub.
9 With the centre mounting on the bench, drive in the new bearing using a metal tube on the outer track only. Make sure that it is located centrally in the mounting.
10 Locate the dust guard on the rear section stub.
11 Position the centre mounting on the propeller shaft stub and drive on the bearing using a metal tube on the inner track only. Make sure that the dust guard is flush with the bearing and that the bearing moves freely.
12 Fit the remaining dust guard followed by the circlip.
13 Lubricate the splines of the rear section stub, then slide on the rear section making sure that the previously made marks are correctly aligned.
14 Refit the propeller shaft with reference to Section 3.

6 Driveshaft – removal and refitting

1 Chock the front wheels then jack up the rear of the car and support on axle stands. Remove the appropriate roadwheel and release the handbrake.
2 Using an Allen key, unscrew the socket-headed bolts which secure the driveshaft to the wheel hub and final drive flanges (photos). Recover the reinforcement plates.
3 Withdraw the driveshaft from under the car.
4 Refitting is a reversal of removal, but clean the contact faces of the drive flanges and tighten the bolts to the specified torque.

7 Driveshaft rubber gaiter – renewal

1 Remove the driveshaft as described in Section 6.
2 Prise out the sealing cover from the outboard end.
3 Extract the circlip and release the gaiter clip.
4 Release the gaiter from the constant velocity joint, then rest the joint on a vice and press out the driveshaft. Make sure that the inner hub of the joint is resting on the vice otherwise the joint may be damaged.
5 Remove the rubber gaiter from the driveshaft.
6 Wipe clean the driveshaft then fit the new gaiter.
7 Thoroughly clean the splines on the driveshaft and joint, then apply

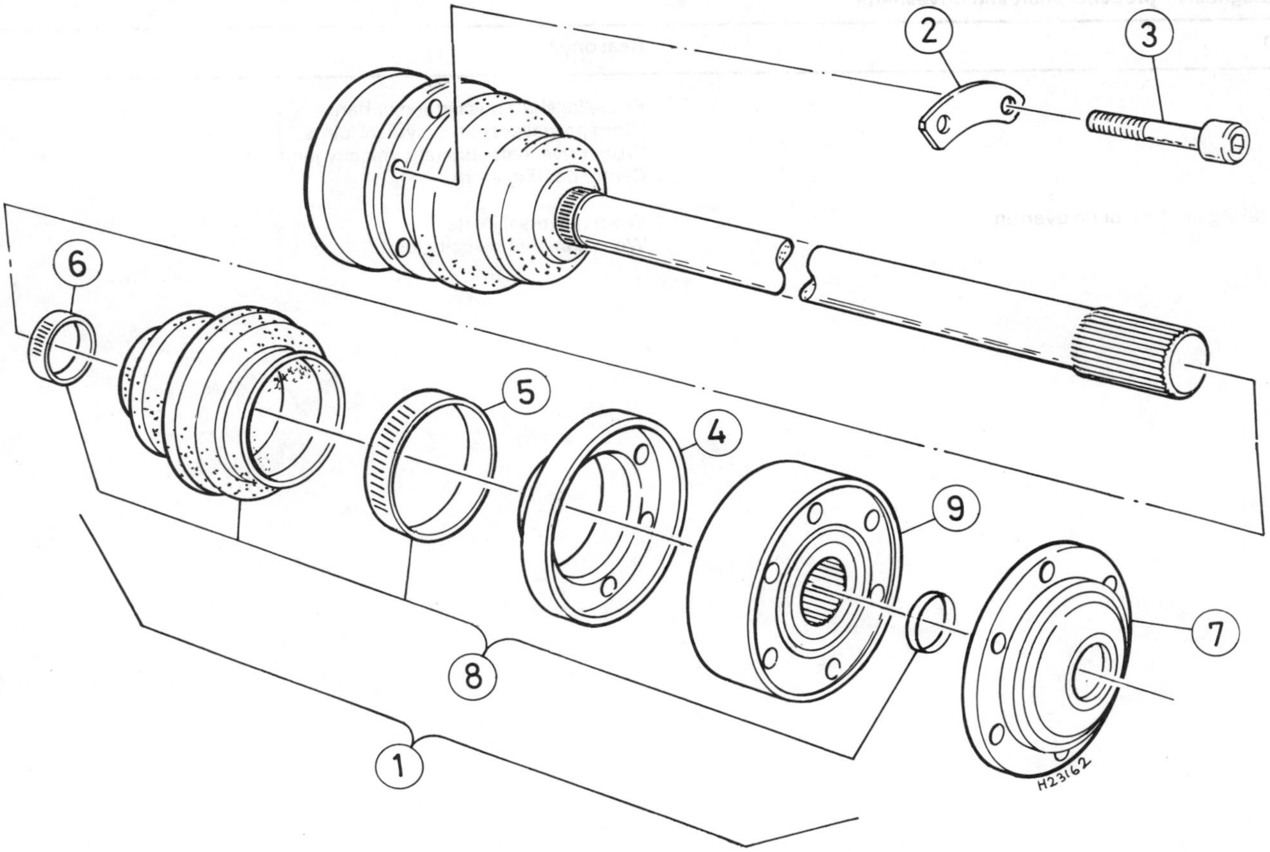

Fig. 7.4 Exploded view of the driveshaft (Sec 6)

1 *Driveshaft*
2 *Reinforcement plate*
3 *Socket-headed bolt*
4 *Cover*
5 *Clip*
6 *Clip*
7 *Sealing cover*
8 *Repair kit (rubber boot)*
9 *Repair kit (constant velocity joint)*

6.2A Driveshaft-to-wheel hub mounting bolts

6.2B Driveshaft-to-final drive mounting bolts

a little thread-locking fluid to them. Do not allow the fluid to enter the joint itself.

8 Refit the constant velocity joint with the inner collar facing inwards. Drive the joint onto the driveshaft using a metal tube on the inner hub.

9 Refit the circlip into its groove.

10 Scoop out any remaining grease from the joint, then pack it with the new grease supplied with the new gaiter. Some of the grease may be packed into the gaiter.

11 Clean the contact surfaces of the gaiter and joint and apply a suitable adhesive. Locate the gaiter on the joint then refit and tighten the clip.

12 Apply a suitable sealant to the sealing cover then locate it on the outboard end of the driveshaft.

13 Refit the driveshaft with reference to Section 6.

8 Fault diagnosis – propeller shaft and driveshafts

Symptom	Reason(s)
Vibration	Propeller shaft misaligned or bent Worn propeller shaft universal joints Worn driveshaft constant velocity joints Centre bearing worn
'Clonk' on taking up drive or on overrun	Worn universal joints Worn constant velocity joints

Chapter 8 Final drive and differential

Contents

Specifications

Type	Hypoid bevel pinion with open driveshafts, optional limited slip differential
Ratios	
520i:	
Manual gearbox:	
To 1985	3.91:1
From 1986	4.10:1
Automatic transmission:	
To 1985	3.73:1
From 1986	3.91:1
525e (automatic transmission only)	3.07:1
Lubrication	
Lubricant type/specification	BMW-approved hypoid gear oil, viscosity SAE 90 (Duckhams D12001–only available to the motor trade; refer to BMW dealer)
Lubricant capacity (drain and refill):	
520i:	
To 1985	1.5 litres (2.6 pints)
1986 on	1.7 litres (3.0 pints)
525e	1.7 litres (3.0 pints)

Torque wrench settings	**Nm**	**lbf ft**
Final drive unit to rear axle carrier	110 to 123	81 to 91
Final drive unit to rubber mounting	80 to 87	59 to 64
Oil filler and drain plugs	50 to 60	37 to 44
Electronic speedometer sensor	9 to 10	6 to 7
Flange to drive pinion (minimum)	150	111
Rubber mounting to underbody	43 to 48	32 to 35

1 General description

The final drive unit is of hypoid bevel gear type mounted on the rear axle carrier at its front end and on a rubber mounting on the underbody at its rear. Drive to the unit is from a two-section propeller shaft, and drive from the differential side gears is transmitted through two open driveshafts to the rear wheels.

A limited slip differential is available as an option, and may be identified by the letter S cast in the final drive casing. Compared with the standard differential this has several advantages, including the prevention of wheel slip on wet or rough surfaces.

Due to the need for special tools and gauges, it is recommended that only the operations described in this Chapter are carried out by the home mechanic. Where a complete overhaul is necessary the unit should be taken to a BMW dealer, or alternatively a new or reconditioned unit fitted.

2 Routine maintenance

Carry out the following at the intervals given in *Routine maintenance* at the front of this manual.

2.2 Final drive unit filler plug (A) and drain plug (B) (arrowed)

Check final drive unit oil level

1 Position the car over an inspection pit or alternatively jack up the front and rear of the car and support on axle stands so that it is level.
2 Using a hexagon key, unscrew the filler plug from the final drive rear cover (photo).
3 Using a short length of wire, check that the oil level is up to the bottom of the filler hole. If not, top up with the specified grade of oil as necessary.
4 Clean the plug and washer and check them for condition. Renew as necessary.
5 Refit and tighten the plug to the specified torque.
6 Lower the car to the ground.

Change final drive unit oil

7 Proceed as described in paragraphs 1 and 2.
8 Position a container beneath the unit, then unscrew the drain plug and drain the oil. On completion, clean the drain plug and washer to examine them for condition. Renew as necessary.
9 With the oil drained, refit and tighten the drain plug to the specified torque.
10 Fill the unit with the specified quantity and grade of oil, finally checking the level as described in paragraph 3.
11 Proceed as described in paragraphs 4 to 6 inclusive.

3 Drive flange oil seal – renewal

1 Chock the front wheels then jack up the rear of the car and support on axle stands.
2 Remove the appropriate roadwheel and release the handbrake.
3 Using an Allen key, unscrew the socket-headed bolts which secure the driveshaft to the final drive flange. Recover the reinforcement plates. Support the driveshafts on an axle stand.
4 Using two levers, prise out the drive flange against the resistance of its internally-expanding circlip. Take care not to damage the final drive casing.
5 Prise out the old oil seal and dust cover.
6 Clean the oil seal seating, then dip the new seal in gear oil and drive it squarely into position using a piece of tubing.
7 Check the internally-expanding circlip for damage and stretching, and renew it if necessary.
8 Locate the circlip in the groove inside the differential housing making sure that both ends of the circlip are fully engaged.
9 Refit the drive flange, pushing it in by hand and turning it slightly so

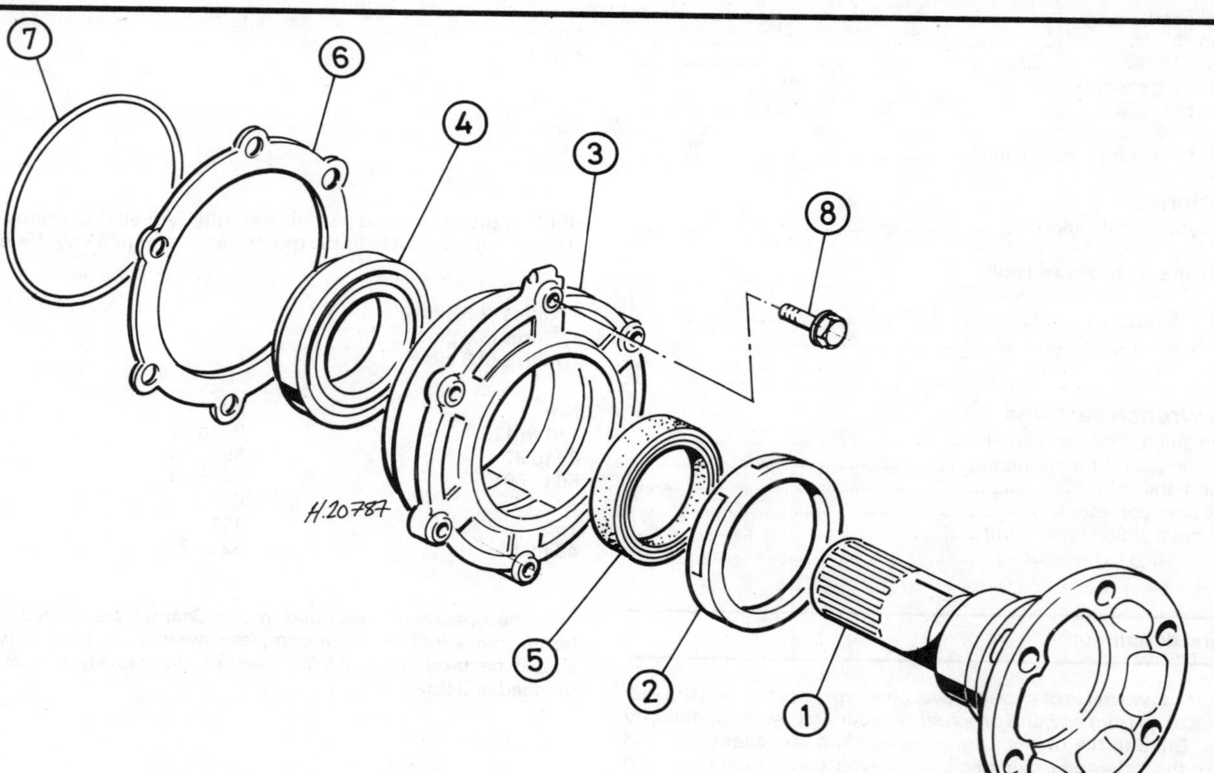

H.20787

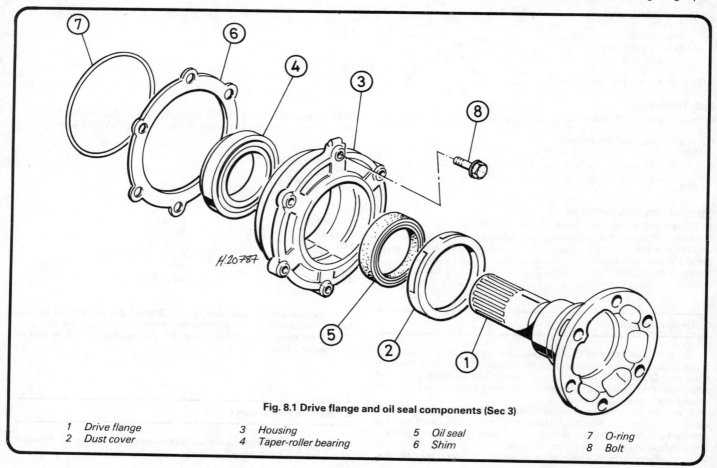

Fig. 8.1 Drive flange and oil seal components (Sec 3)

1 Drive flange
2 Dust cover
3 Housing
4 Taper-roller bearing
5 Oil seal
6 Shim
7 O-ring
8 Bolt

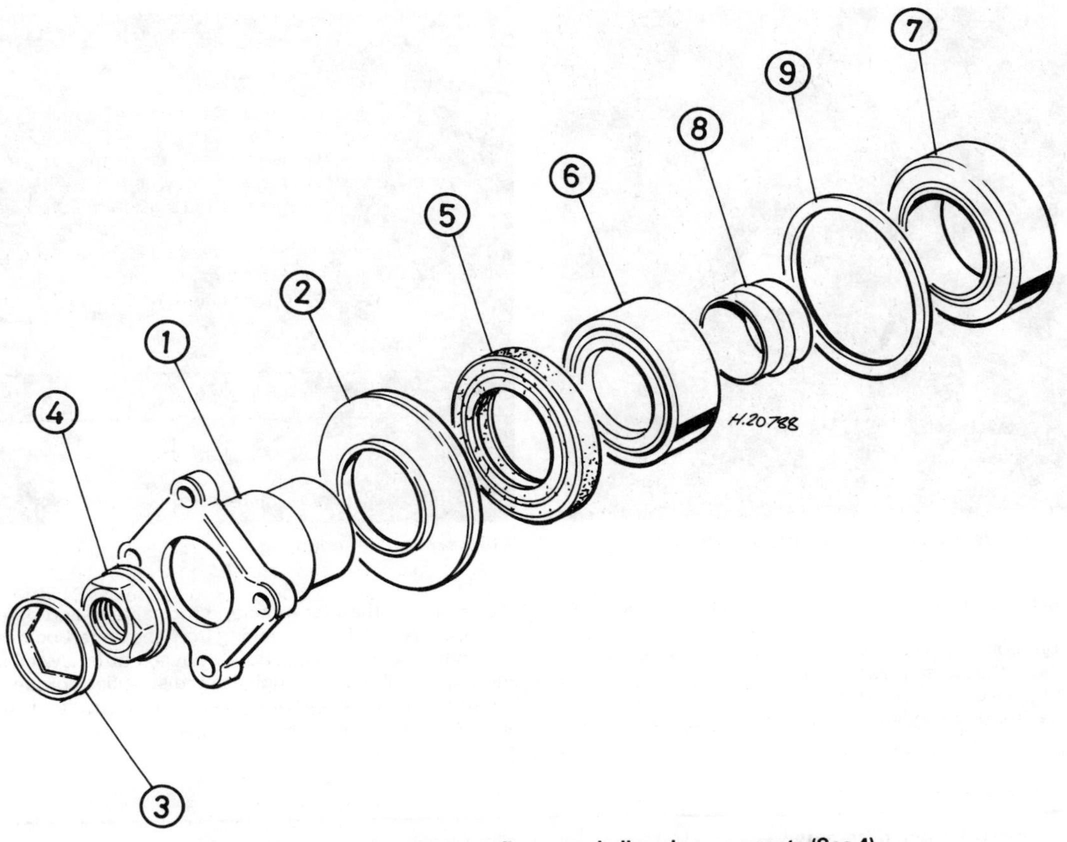

Fig. 8.2 Final drive unit pinion flange and oil seal components (Sec 4)

1 *Drive flange*
2 *Dust cover*
3 *Lockplate*
4 *Nut*
5 *Oil seal*
6 *Taper-roller bearing (outer)*
7 *Taper-roller bearing (inner)*
8 *Collapsible spacer*
9 *Shim*

that the circlip slides over the splines and is heard to snap into its location groove.

10 Clean the contact faces of the drive flanges, then refit the driveshaft, insert the bolts together with their reinforcement plates, and tighten them to the specified torque.

11 Refit the roadwheel, apply the handbrake then lower the car to the ground.

4 Pinion oil seal – renewal

1 Remove the final drive unit as described in Section 5.

2 Accurately mark the pinion, nut and flange in relation to each other. This is necessary in order to preserve the bearing preload of the pinion bearings when reassembling.

3 Hold the pinion flange stationary using a length of metal bolted to it, then unscrew and remove the nut and lockplate. Initially the lockplate will resist movement as it is staked into the flange, but once it is free the nut may be unscrewed normally.

4 Withdraw the flange from the pinion. If it is tight, use a puller or alternatively use two bolts as a puller by inserting them through opposite bolt holes in the flange with nuts on the inner side. By tightening the bolts onto pads of metal on the final drive casing the flange will be forced off. Take care not to damage the casing.

5 Remove the dust cover then prise out the oil seal with a screwdriver or suitable extractor.

6 Clean the seal seating in the casing. Also clean the flange and dust cover. Check that the nut is still serviceable and renew it if necessary.

7 Dip the new oil seal in gear oil and drive it squarely into the casing until it is flush.

8 Tap the dust cover onto the front of the casing.

9 Slide the flange onto the pinion so that the previously made marks are in alignment.

10 Screw on the nut, then hold the flange stationary and tighten the nut until the previously made marks are in alignment. **Do not** over-tighten the nut otherwise the internal collapsible spacer will be over-compressed thus making the bearing preload incorrect. If this happens the complete final drive must be dismantled and the collapsible spacer renewed, and this work is best carried out by a suitably equipped BMW dealer or an engineering works.

11 Fit the lockplate on the nut and stake it into the flange to secure.

12 Refit the final drive unit with reference to Section 5.

5 Final drive unit – removal and refitting

1 Chock the front wheels then jack up the rear of the car and support on axle stands.

2 Remove the exhaust system as described in Chapter 3.

3 Where fitted, unbolt and remove the heatshield from the under-body.

4 Release the handbrake, then unscrew the nuts and remove the special bolts securing the rear of the propeller shaft to the final drive flange. Note which way round the bolts are fitted. Support the propeller shaft on an axle stand if necessary.

5 Using an Allen key, unscrew the socket-headed bolts which secure the driveshafts to the final drive flanges. Recover the reinforcement plates. Support the driveshafts on axle stands or tie them to one side.

6 Position a container beneath the final drive unit, then unscrew the drain plug using a hexagon key and drain the oil from the unit. Refit and tighten the plug to the specified torque on completion.

7 Support the final drive unit on a trolley jack.

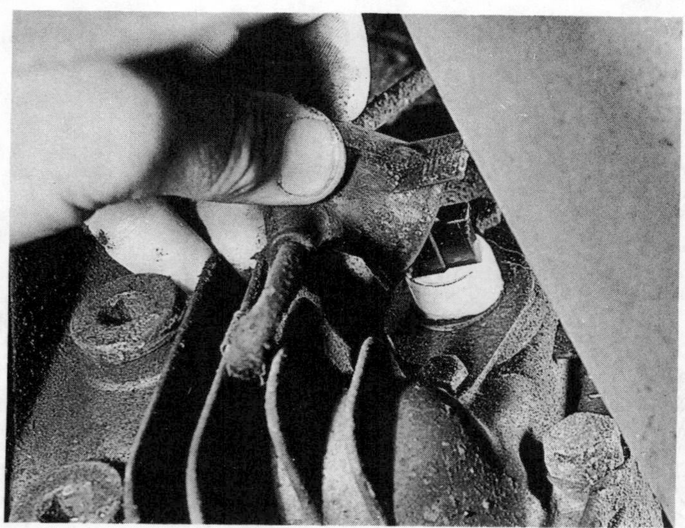
5.10 Disconnecting the wire from the speed pulse sensor

5.11 Rear flexible mounting

8 Unscrew the top bolts which hold the final drive unit to the rear axle carrier.
9 Unscrew the front bolts from both sides.
10 Pull the leads from the speed pulse sensor (photo).
11 Unscrew and remove the bolt from the rear flexible mounting (photo) and lower the final drive unit to the floor. Withdraw the unit from under the car.

12 Examine the rear mounting for damage and deterioration, and if necessary renew it by unbolting from the underbody.
13 Refitting is a reversal of removal, but renew all self-locking nuts and tighten all nuts and bolts to the specified torque. With the car on level ground, fill the final drive unit with the specified grade and quantity of oil (refer to Section 2 if necessary).

6 Fault diagnosis – final drive and differential

Symptom	Reason(s)
Knock when moving off or changing gear	Excessive backlash Excessive play in propeller shaft splines
Noise – general	Excessive wear
Oil leaks	Worn oil seals Breather clogged Incorrect oil grade

Chapter 9 Braking system

Contents

Specifications

System type	Front discs with single piston floating calipers, rear drums or discs, hydraulic system split diagonally and vacuum-assisted, mechanical handbrake to rear wheels, anti-lock braking system (ABS) optional

Front brakes

Minimum pad lining thickness	2.0 mm (0.079 in)
Brake disc wear limit:	
Non-ventilated	10.0 mm
Ventilated	20.0 mm
Brake disc regrinding limit:	
Non-ventilated	10.4 mm
Ventilated	20.4 mm
Brake disc maximum run-out:	
Removed	0.05 mm
Installed	0.2 mm

Rear drum brakes

Maximum shoe lining thickness	2.0 mm (0.079 in)
Drum machining limit	251 mm
Drum maximum radial run-out	0.05 mm

Rear disc brakes

Minimum pad lining thickness	2.0 mm (0.079 in)
Brake disc wear limit	8.0 mm
Brake disc regrinding limit	8.4 mm
Brake disc maximum run-out:	
Removed	0.05 mm
Installed	0.2 mm

ABS system

Clearance between sensor and transmitter	0.25 to 0.67 mm

Brake pedal

Pedal height	231 + 10 mm

Brake fluid type/specification

Hydraulic brake fluid to SAE J 1703 or DOT 4 (Duckhams Universal Brake and Clutch Fluid)

Torque wrench settings

	Nm	lbf ft
Bleed screw	4 to 6	3 to 4
Brake caliper to steering knuckle	110 to 123	80 to 89
Caliper guide bolt	30 to 35	22 to 25
Wheel cylinder	9 to 10	6.5 to 7.0
Rear brake backplate	60 to 67	44 to 49
Brake caliper to trailing arm	60 to 67	44 to 49
Rigid brake line union nut	10 to 15	7 to 10
Flexible brake hose union	13 to 16	9.5 to 11.5
Master cylinder	26 to 32	19 to 23
Pedal pushrod locknut	27	20

1 General description

The braking system is of four wheel dual-circuit, hydraulic type with discs at the front and drums or discs at the rear. The front calipers are of single piston floating type. The hydraulic system is split diagonally in the interests of safety so that in the event of failure of one circuit, the remaining circuit still functions.

A vacuum servo unit is fitted to all models to provide assistance to the driver when applying the brake.

The master cylinder and servo unit are located on the left-hand side of the engine compartment, and a rod linkage is provided from the brake pedal on the right-hand side.

The handbrake is operated mechanically on the rear wheels. On rear drum models, the same rear shoes are used for both the main footbrake and the handbrake, however on rear disc models separate brake shoes are fitted which operate inside a drum integral with the disc.

An anti-lock braking system (ABS) is optional on certain models.

Warning: *Dust created by the braking system may contain asbestos, which is a health hazard. Never blow it out with compressed air and don't inhale any of it. An approved filtering mask should be worn when working on the brakes. DO NOT use petroleum based solvents to clean brake parts. Use brake cleaner or methylated spirit only.*

2 Routine maintenance

Carry out the following at the intervals given in *Routine maintenance* at the front of this manual.

Check brake fluid level

1 Check that the level of fluid in the reservoir on the master cylinder is on or near the maximum mark. If necessary top it up using the specified hydraulic fluid (photo), however if frequent topping-up is required, check the complete hydraulic circuit for leakage, and rectify.

Check brake linings

2 Check the front and (where fitted) the rear brake pad linings for wear with reference to Sections 3 and 8, and renew them as complete sets if necessary.

3 At the same time check the brake discs for wear.

4 Also lightly grease the roadwheel centering spigots before refitting the wheels.

Check brake hydraulic circuit

5 Jack up the front and rear of the car and support on axle stands.

6 Examine all the brake lines and components for leakage and damage. On rear drum models, remove the drums and check the wheel cylinders for leakage around the dust covers.

Check handbrake adjustment

7 Check and adjust the handbrake as described in Section 12.

Change the brake fluid

8 Syphon all the fluid from the reservoir.

9 Refer to Section 17 and pump the brake pedal until all fluid is forced from each bleed screw.

10 Fill the reservoir with new fluid and bleed the hydraulic system with reference to Section 17.

Check the handbrake linings

11 Refer to Section 11.

3 Front brake pads – inspection and renewal

1 Apply the handbrake then jack up the front of the car and support on axle stands. Remove the roadwheels.

2 Looking through the small hole in each caliper, check that the thickness of the pads is not less than that given in Specifications. If any one pad is less than the specified amount, renew the complete front set of pads together.

3 Prise the plastic caps from the upper and lower guide bolts (photo).

4 If working on the left-hand side, disconnect the pad wear warning lamp wire.

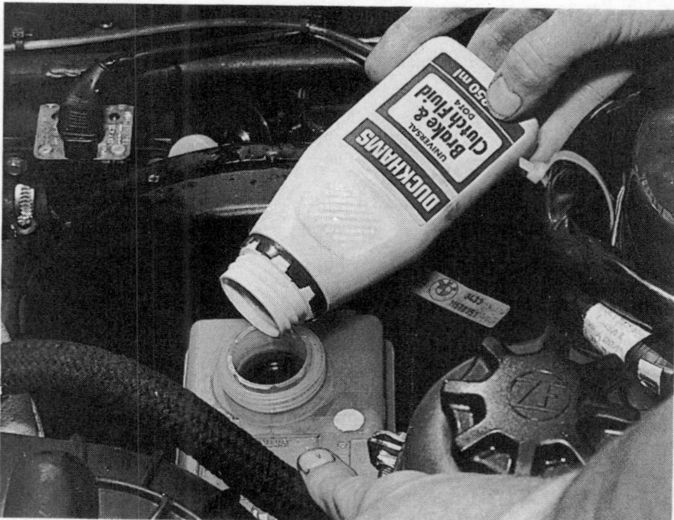

2.1 Topping-up the brake fluid level

3.3 Removing the plastic caps from the front brake caliper

3.5 Prising out the front brake caliper retaining spring clip

3.6 Unscrewing the front brake caliper guide bolts

3.7 Removing the front brake caliper

3.8A Removing the front brake inner pad ...

3.8B ... and outer pad

5 Using a screwdriver, prise out the spring clip securing the caliper to the bracket (photo).
6 Using an Allen key, unscrew the two guide bolts and remove them (photo).
7 Remove the caliper and support on an axle stand without straining the flexible hose (photo).
8 Remove the inner brake pad which is retained in the caliper piston with an internally expanding spring, following by the outer brake pad from the bracket (photos).
9 Brush out all dust from the caliper, but **do not** inhale it as *it is injurious to health.*
10 The caliper piston must now be depressed in order to accommodate the new thicker pads. It should be possible to do this with the fingers, but if the piston is tight use a lever, taking care not to damage the piston or caliper.
11 Fit the inner brake pad with its spring located in the piston, then locate the outer brake pads on the bracket.
12 Locate the caliper over the outer brake pad and disc.
13 Clean the guide bolts but do not apply any grease or lubricant. Insert them through the caliper and screw them into the bracket. Tighten them to the specified torque using an Allen key. Refit the plastic caps.
14 Insert the spring clip in the caliper holes and locate the extension legs on the bracket.
15 If working on the left-hand side, reconnect the pad wear warning lamp wire.
16 Repeat the procedure on the remaining front brake.
17 Apply the footbrake hard several times in order to set the pads in their normal position.
18 Refit the roadwheels and lower the car to the ground.
19 Check the hydraulic fluid level in the reservoir as described in Section 2, and top up if necessary.
20 Avoid harsh braking if possible during the initial bedding-in period as the friction linings adapt to the irregularities of the discs.

4 Front brake caliper – removal, overhaul and refitting

1 Apply the handbrake then jack up the front of the car and support on axle stands. Remove the appropriate roadwheel.
2 Fit a brake hose clamp to the flexible hose leading to the caliper. Alternatively, draw off the fluid from the fluid reservoir on the master cylinder in order to reduce the loss of fluid when the cylinder is removed.
3 Loosen the flexible hose connection at the caliper.
4 Remove the brake pads as described in Section 3.
5 Unscrew the caliper from the flexible hose.
6 Unscrew the bolts securing the caliper bracket to the strut and remove the bracket (photo).
7 Clean away all external dirt from the caliper.
8 Position a piece of wood in the caliper as a cushion for the piston when it is removed. Prise the piston dust cover from the groove in the caliper.
9 Force out the piston using *low* air pressure from a foot or hand pump in the fluid inlet.
10 Using a non-metallic instrument, prise out the piston seal from the caliper. Also remove the dust cover from the piston.
11 Clean all the components with methylated spirit and allow to dry.
12 Examine the components for excessive wear and corrosion. In particular check the piston and cylinder bore surfaces for scoring. If the components are in good condition, obtain a new set of rubber seals, otherwise renew the caliper complete.
13 Commence reassembly by dipping the piston seal in fresh hydraulic fluid then locating it in its groove inside the caliper bore. Smear a little fluid on the bore surface.
14 Fit the dust cover in the piston groove.
15 Press the piston into the caliper bore, turning it slightly to ensure that it passes through the seal easily.
16 Locate the dust cover in the groove in the caliper.

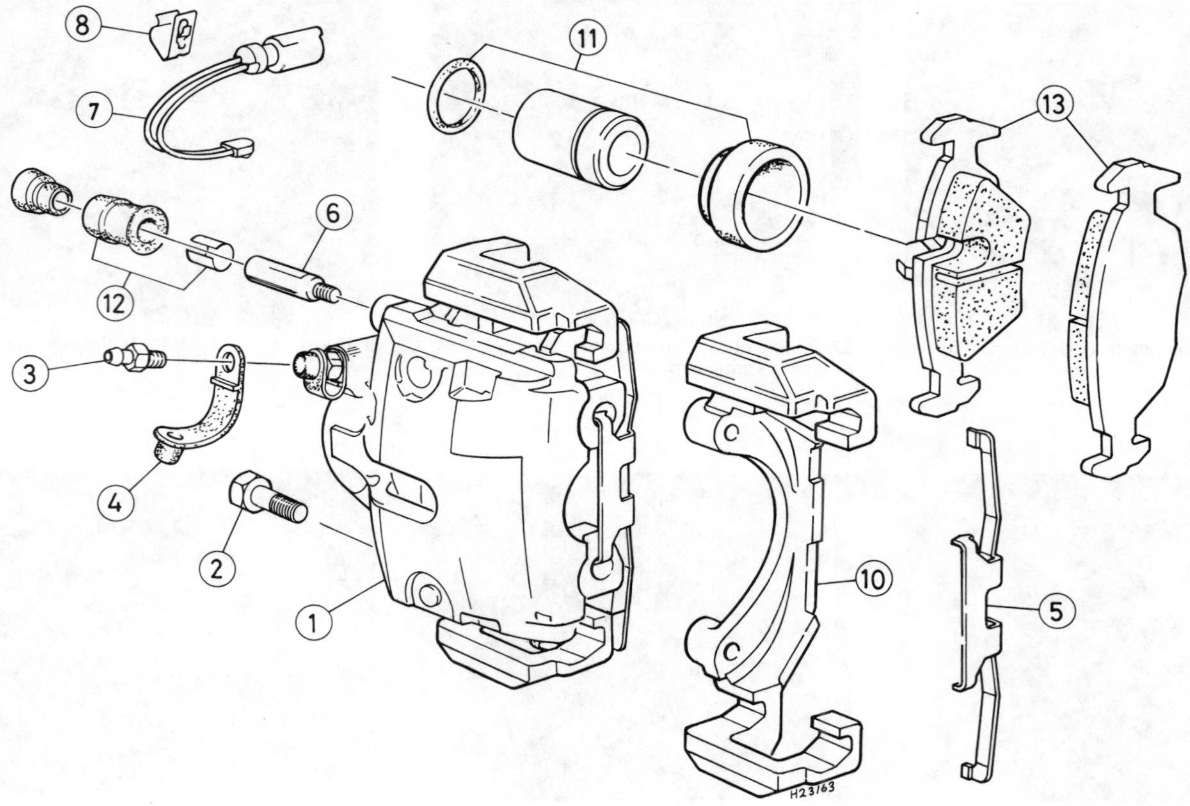

Fig. 9.1 Exploded view of the front brake caliper (Sec 4)

1 Caliper housing
2 Caliper bracket bolt
3 Bleed screw
4 Dust cap
5 Spring clip
6 Guide bolt
7 Pad wear warning lamp wire
8 Cable clamp
9 Plastic pad
10 Bracket
11 Piston, seal and dust cover
12 Guide bush
13 Brake pads

4.6 Front brake caliper bracket mounting bolts (arrowed)

17 Refit the caliper bracket to the strut and tighten the bolts to the specified torque.
18 Screw the caliper onto the flexible hose and tighten moderately.
19 Refit the brake pads as described in Section 3.
20 Fully tighten the flexible hose connection at the caliper, but make sure that the hose is not twisted.
21 Top up the brake fluid in the reservoir and bleed the system as described in Section 17.
22 Refit the roadwheel and lower the car to the ground.

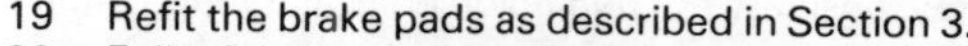

5 Front brake disc – checking, removal and refitting

1 Apply the handbrake, jack up the front of the car and support on axle stands. Remove the appropriate roadwheel.
2 Unscrew and remove the caliper bracket mounting bolts, then disconnect the pad wear wire (where applicable) and withdraw the complete caliper from the disc. Support it to one side without straining the flexible hose.
3 Secure the disc using wheelbolts and washers.
4 Measure the thickness of the disc at eight equidistant points around the disc, using a micrometer. Compare the maximum run-out with that given in Specifications. A dial gauge may be used instead but in this case the wear of the wheel bearings must be taken into account.
5 Check the disc for scoring, deep grooving and cracking. Light scoring is normal, but if it is excessive or if the run-out is outside the specified amount the disc must be renewed or reground by a specialist. Note that in order to maintain equal braking on both sides of the car, both front discs should be renewed or reground at the same time.
6 To remove the disc, unscrew the socket-headed screw using an Allen key and withdraw the disc from the hub (photo).

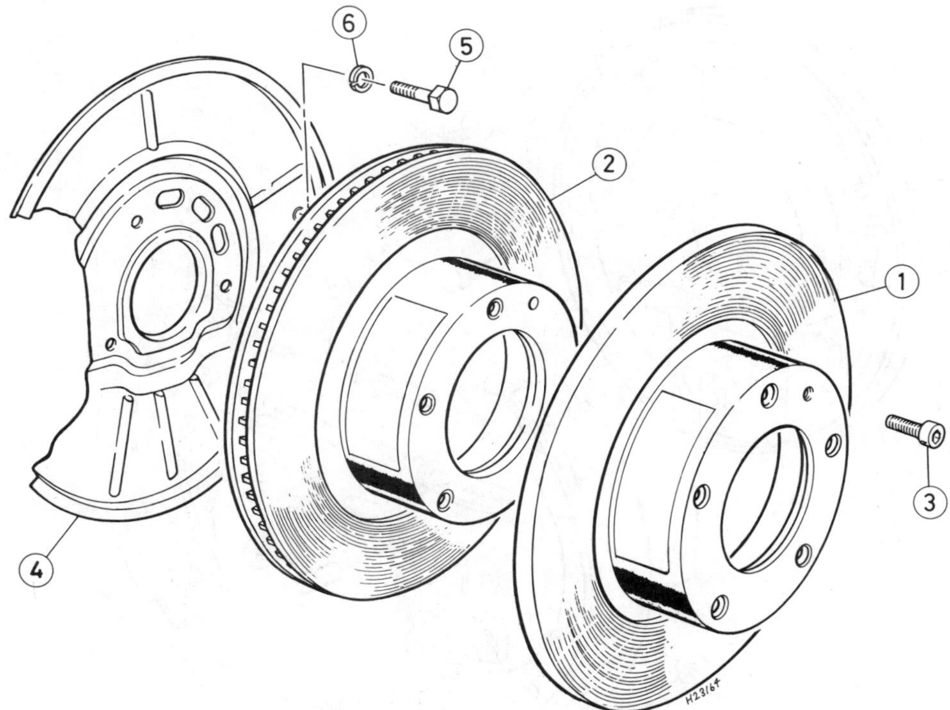

Fig. 9.2 Front brake discs (Sec 5)

1 *Non-ventilated disc*
2 *Ventilated disc*
3 *Socket-headed screw*
4 *Shield*
5 *Bolt*
6 *Washer*

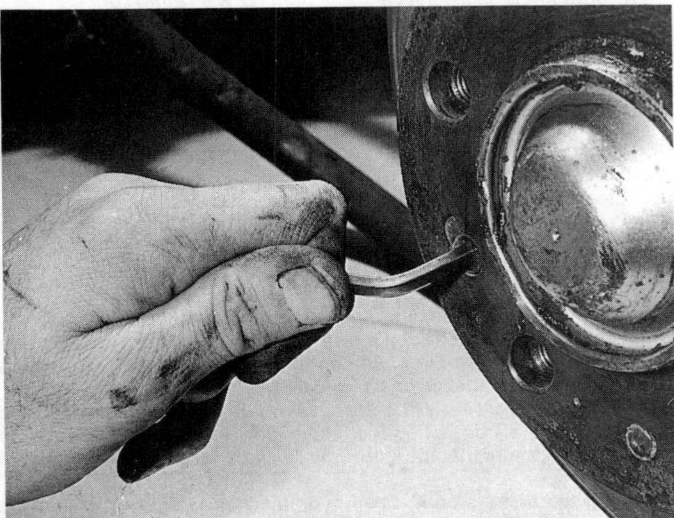

5.6 Unscrewing the front brake disc retaining screw

7 Refitting is a reversal of removal, but clean the disc-to-hub surfaces and tighten all bolts to the specified torque. With the car on the ground depress the footbrake pedal fully several times to set the pads in their normal position.

6 Rear brake shoes (520i models to 1987) – inspection and renewal

1 Chock the front wheels then jack up the rear of the car and support on axle stands. Alternatively, position the car on ramps or over an inspection pit.

2 Prise the inspection plugs from the backplates and check the thickness of the linings on the brake shoes. If they are still serviceable, refit the plugs and lower the car to the ground. If they are worn down to or near the minimum thickness given in Specifications, a more thorough investigation is necessary.

3 Remove the rear roadwheels.

4 Working on one side, unscrew the bolt and withdraw the brake drum using a wooden or hide mallet if necessary. If the brake drum binds on the shoes and will not come off, disconnect the handbrake cables and use a drift to drive the small pin visible through the inspection hole into the brake shoe until the handbrake lever on the shoe moves back to allow the shoes to retract.

5 Brush away all dust from the shoes taking care not to inhale it as it is injurious to health. Check both shoes for wear of the linings, and if any one shoe is worn below the specified minimum amount renew all the rear brake shoes as a complete set. Note the position of the return springs if the shoes are to be removed. At the same time check the brake drum for wear. Light scoring is normal but if it is excessive the drum should be renewed.

6 To remove the shoes first depress the steady springs with a screwdriver and slide them from the pins. Remove the pins from the backplate.

7 Unhook the lower shoe return spring and detach the bottom of the shoes from the anchor post.

8 Overlap the bottom ends of the shoes then release the top of the shoes from the wheel cylinder.

9 Unhook the handbrake cable from the operating lever on the rear (trailing) shoe and withdraw the two shoes together from the backplate.

10 Unhook the upper return spring and the spring from the automatic adjuster, and separate the shoes.

11 Drive out the pin and remove the automatic adjuster lever from the leading shoe. Note how it is fitted.

12 Examine the automatic adjuster for wear. Turn the adjuster nut so that the adjuster is at its minimum length.

13 If the small pin described in paragraph 4 has been driven in to remove the brake drum, drive it back through the brake shoe in order to provide a stop for the handbrake lever.

14 Fit the automatic adjuster lever to the new leading shoe.

15 Fit the upper ends of the shoes to the automatic adjuster, then refit

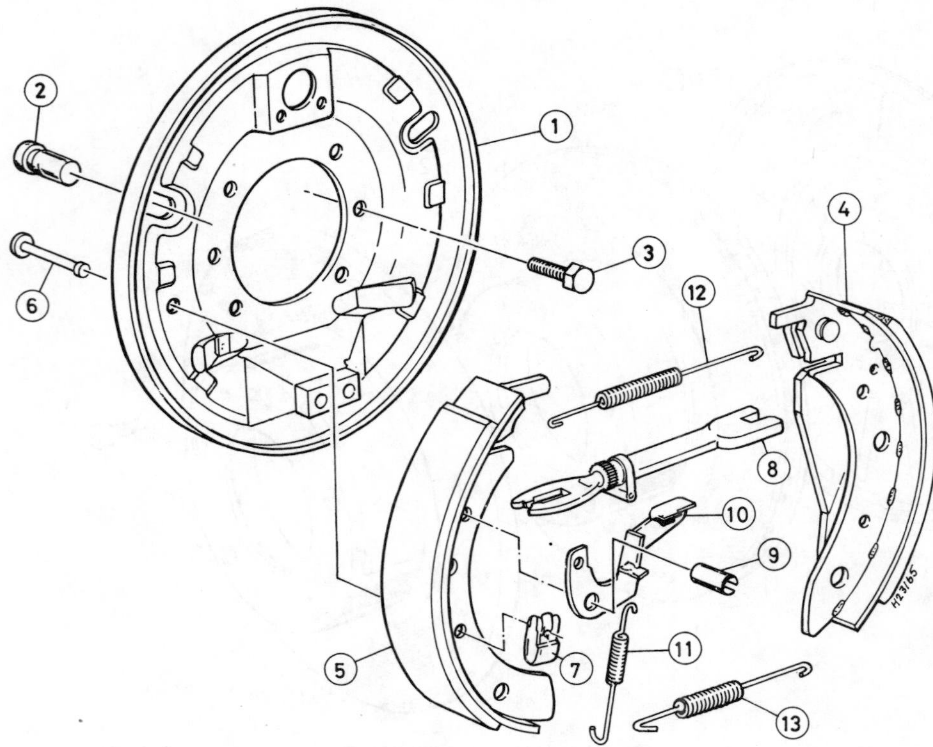

Fig. 9.3 Rear brake shoe components (Sec 6)

1 *Backplate*
2 *Inspection plug*
3 *Bolt*
4 *Trailing brake shoe*
5 *Leading brake shoe*
6 *Steady spring pin*
7 *Steady spring*
8 *Automatic adjuster*
9 *Pivot roll pin*
10 *Automatic adjuster lever*
11 *Automatic adjuster return spring*
12 *Upper return spring*
13 *Lower return spring*

the upper return spring and the spring for the automatic adjuster. Make sure that the adjuster lever engages with the nut.

16 Locate the shoes on the backplate and reconnect the handbrake cable to the lever on the rear (trailing) shoe.

17 With the upper ends of the shoes located on the wheel cylinder, locate the lower ends to the anchor post and refit the lower return spring.

18 Insert the pins from the rear of the backplate and refit the steady springs so that their closed ends are downwards.

19 Refit the brake drum and securing bolt. If removed, refit the inspection plugs.

20 Repeat the procedure given in paragraphs 4 to 19 on the remaining side.

21 Refit the roadwheels.

22 Apply the footbrake hard several times until the rear adjusters do not click any more.

23 Adjust the handbrake as described in Section 12.

24 Lower the car to the ground.

7 Rear wheel cylinder (520i models to 1987) – removal, overhaul and refitting

1 Remove the brake shoes from the appropriate side as described in Section 6.

2 Fit a brake hose clamp to the flexible rear hose located by the appropriate semi-trailing arm. Alternatively, draw off the fluid from the reservoir on the master cylinder to reduce the loss of fluid in the subsequent procedure.

3 Unscrew the union nut securing the rigid brake line to the wheel cylinder, pull out the line sufficiently to clear the cylinder and plug it. Also unscrew and remove the bleed screw.

4 Unscrew the two mounting bolts and withdraw the wheel cylinder from the backplate.

5 Clean the exterior surfaces of the wheel cylinder.

6 Prise off the two dust covers and press out the pistons and return spring.

7 Note how the rubber seals are fitted to the pistons then prise them out of their grooves with a screwdriver.

8 Clean all the components in methylated spirit and allow to dry.

9 Examine the surfaces of the pistons and cylinder bore for corrosion and scoring. If they are in good condition, obtain a repair kit of seals which will also include pistons if from a BMW source.

10 Discard the old seals. Dip the new seals in fresh hydraulic fluid and fit them to the pistons using the fingers only to manipulate them into position. Make sure that the lips of the seals are facing the inner ends of the pistons.

11 Dip the first piston in clean hydraulic fluid and insert it into the cylinder bore, taking care not to damage the seal.

12 Smear a little brake grease on the interior surface of the dust cover then fit it to the cylinder so that it engages the groove.

13 Insert the return spring. Dip the second piston in clean hydraulic fluid and insert it into the cylinder bore, again taking care not to damage the seal.

14 Smear a little brake grease on the final dust cover and fit it to the groove in the cylinder.

15 Clean the backplate and wheel cylinder mounting faces then locate the wheel cylinder on the backplate and insert the bolts. Tighten them to the specified torque.

16 Screw in the bleed screw and tighten by hand.

17 Refit the rigid brake line and tighten the union nut.

18 Remove the brake hose clamp if fitted. Top up the hydraulic fluid reservoir with fresh fluid.

19 Refit the brake shoes with reference to Section 6.

20 Bleed the hydraulic system as described in Section 17.

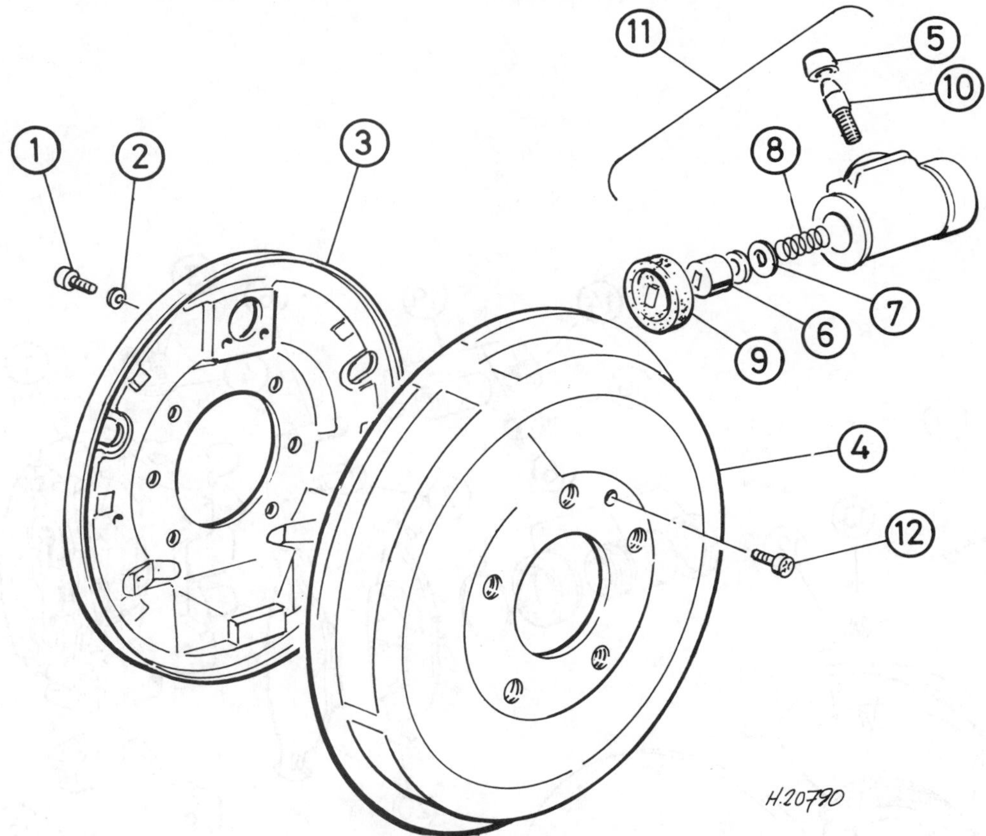

Fig. 9.4 Rear brake drum and wheel cylinder (Sec 7)

1 *Bolt*
2 *Washer*
3 *Backplate*
4 *Brake drum*
5 *Dust seal*
6 *Piston*
7 *Seal*
8 *Spring*
9 *Dust cover*
10 *Bleed screw*
11 *Wheel cylinder*
12 *Drum retaining screw*

8 Rear brake pads (all 525e models, and 520i models from 1988) – inspection and renewal

1 Chock the front wheels then jack up the rear of the car and support on axle stands. Remove the roadwheels.

2 Looking through the small hole in each caliper, check that the thickness of the pads is not less than that given in Specifications. If any one pad is less than the specified amount, renew the complete rear set of pads together.

3 Prise the plastic pads from the upper and lower guide bolts (photo).

4 If working on the right-hand side, disconnect the pad wear warning lamp wire (photo).

5 Using a screwdriver, prise out the spring clip securing the caliper to the bracket (photo).

6 Using an Allen key, unscrew the two guide bolts and remove them (photo).

7 Remove the caliper and support on an axle stand without straining the flexible hose (photo).

8 Remove the outer brake pads from the bracket followed by the inner brake pad which is retained in the caliper piston with an internally expanding spring (photo).

9 Brush out all dust from the caliper, but **do not** *inhale it as it is injurious to health.*

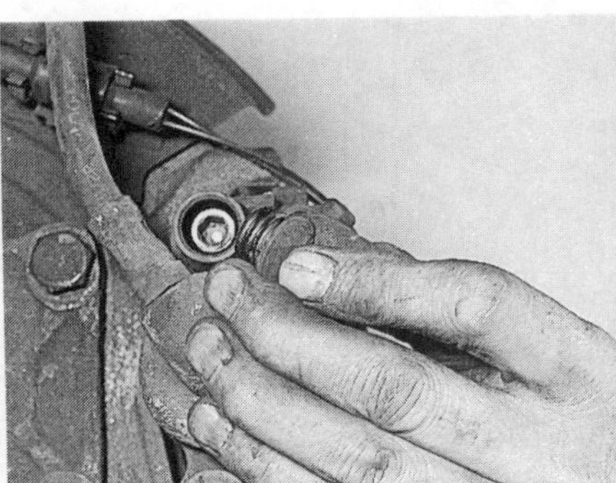

8.3 Removing the rear brake caliper guide bolt plastic pads

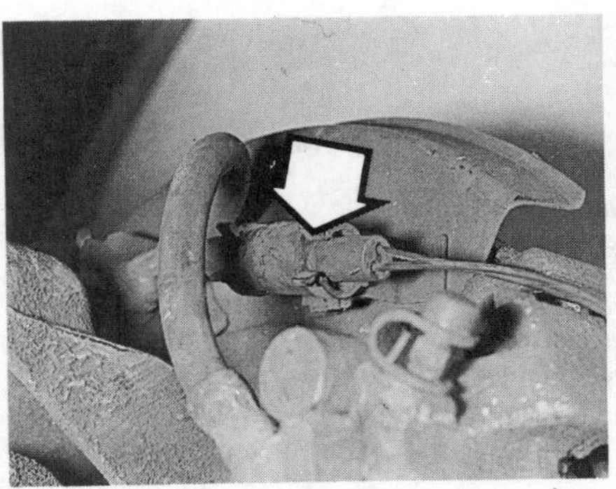

8.4 Rear brake pad wear warning lamp wire connector (arrowed)

8.5 Rear brake caliper retaining spring clip (arrowed)

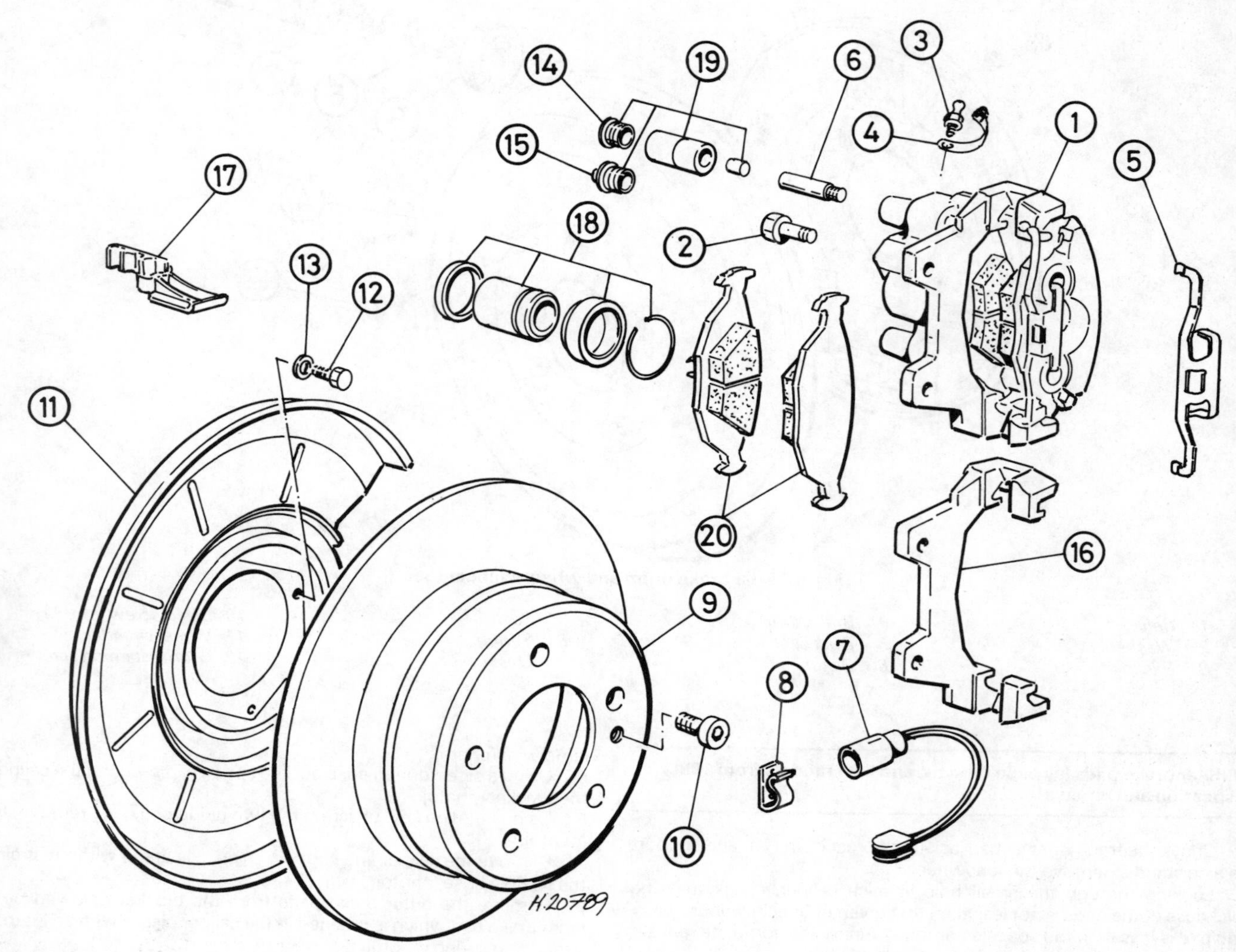

Fig. 9.5 Rear disc brake components (Sec 8)

1 *Caliper*
2 *Bracket mounting bolt*
3 *Bleed screw*
4 *Dust cap*
5 *Spring clip*
6 *Guide bolt*
7 *Brake pad wear warning lamp wire*
8 *Cable clamp*
9 *Brake disc*
10 *Socket-headed screw*
11 *Shield*
12 *Bolt*
13 *Washer*
14 *Plastic pad*
15 *Plastic pad*
16 *Caliper bracket*
17 *Cable clamp*
18 *Piston repair kit*
19 *Guide bush repair kit*
20 *Brake pads*

8.6 Unscrewing the rear brake caliper guide bolts

8.7 Removing the rear brake caliper

8.8 Removing the inner brake pad from the rear brake caliper

10 The caliper piston must now be depressed in order to accommodate the new thicker pads. It should be possible to do this with the fingers, but if the piston is tight use a lever, taking care not to damage the piston or caliper.
11 Fit the inner brake pad with its spring located in the piston, then locate the outer brake pad on the bracket.
12 Locate the caliper over the outer brake pad and disc.
13 Clean the guide bolts but do not apply any grease or lubricant. Insert them through the caliper and screw them into the bracket. Tighten them to the specified torque using an Allen key. Refit the plastic pads.
14 Insert the spring clip in the caliper holes and locate the extension legs on the bracket.
15 If working on the right-hand side, reconnect the pad wear warning lamp wire.
16 Repeat the procedure on the remaining rear brake.
17 Apply the footbrake hard several times in order to set the pads in their normal position.
18 Refit the roadwheels and lower the car to the ground.
19 Check the hydraulic fluid level in the reservoir as described in Section 2, and top up if necessary.
20 Avoid harsh braking if possible during the initial bedding-in period as the friction linings adapt to the irregularities of the discs.

9 Rear brake caliper (all 525e models, and 520i models from 1988) – removal, overhaul and refitting

1 Chock the front wheels then jack up the rear of the car and support on axle stands. Remove the appropriate roadwheel.
2 Fit a brake hose clamp to the flexible hose leading to the caliper. Alternatively, draw off the fluid from the fluid reservoir on the master cylinder in order to reduce the loss of fluid when the cylinder is removed.
3 Loosen the flexible hose connection at the caliper.
4 Remove the brake pads as described in Section 8.
5 Unscrew the caliper from the flexible hose.
6 Unscrew the bolts securing the caliper bracket to the semi-trailing arm and remove the bracket (photos).
7 Clean away all external dirt from the caliper.
8 Position a piece of wood in the caliper as a cushion for the piston when it is removed. Prise the piston dust cover from the groove in the caliper.
9 Force out the piston using *low* air pressure from a foot or hand pump in the fluid inlet.
10 Using a non-metallic instrument, prise out the piston seal from the caliper. Also remove the dust cover from the piston.
11 Clean all the components with methylated spirit and allow to dry.
12 Examine the components for excessive wear and corrosion. In particular check the piston and cylinder bore surfaces for scoring. If the components are in good condition, obtain a new set of rubber seals, otherwise renew the caliper complete.
13 Commence reassembly by dipping the piston seal in fresh hydraulic fluid then locating it in its groove inside the caliper bore. Smear a little fluid on the bore surface.
14 Fit the dust cover in the piston groove.
15 Press the piston into the caliper bore, turning it slightly to ensure that it passes through the seal easily.
16 Locate the dust cover in the groove in the caliper.
17 Refit the caliper bracket to the semi-trailing arm and tighten the bolts to the specified torque.
18 Screw the caliper onto the flexible hose and tighten moderately.
19 Refit the brake pads as described in Section 8.

9.6A Unscrew the bolts ...

9.6B ... and remove the rear brake caliper mounting bracket

20 Fully tighten the flexible hose connection at the caliper, but make sure that the hose is not twisted.
21 Top up the brake fluid in the reservoir and bleed the system as described in Section 17.
22 Refit the roadwheel and lower the car to the ground.

10 Rear brake disc (all 525e models, and 520i models from 1988) – checking, removal and refitting

1 Chock the front wheels then jack up the rear of the car and support on axle stands. Remove the appropriate roadwheel.
2 Unscrew and remove the caliper bracket mounting bolts, then disconnect the pad wear wire (where applicable) and withdraw the complete caliper from the disc. Support it to one side without straining the flexible hose.
3 Secure the disc using wheelbolts and washers.
4 Measure the thickness of the disc at eight equidistant points around the disc, using a micrometer. Compare the maximum run-out with that given in Specifications. A dial gauge may be used instead but in this case the wear of the wheel bearings must be taken into account.
5 Check the disc for scoring, deep grooving and cracking. Light scoring is normal, but if it is excessive or if the run-out is outside the specified amount the disc must be renewed or reground by a specialist. Note that in order to maintain equal braking on both sides of the car, both rear discs should be renewed or reground at the same time.
6 To remove the disc, unscrew the socket-headed screw using an Allen key and withdraw the disc from the hub (photo).
7 Refitting is a reversal of removal, but clean the disc-to-hub surfaces and tighten all bolts to the specified torque. With the car on the ground depress the footbrake pedal fully several times to set the pads in their normal position. Adjust the handbrake as described in Section 12. If new brake discs have been fitted, the handbrake shoes must be bedded in as follows, then re-adjusted. Drive the car at 30 mph and then, where it is safe to do so, stop it using the handbrake only. Do this five times then allow the brakes to cool off for several minutes. Repeat the procedure for five more stops.

11 Handbrake shoes (all 525e models, and 520i models from 1988) – inspection and renewal

1 Remove both rear brake discs as described in Section 10.

10.6 Removing the rear brake disc

2 Brush all dust from the shoes and inside the drums – **do not** *inhale it as it is injurious to health.*
3 Check all shoes for wear of the linings, and if any one shoe is worn below the specified minimum amount renew all the shoes as a complete set.
4 Working on one side, note the position of the return springs, then unhook and remove the upper return spring (photo).
5 Using a small screwdriver, depress the steady spring pins and turn them through 90° to disconnect them from the backplate (photo). Remove the pins and springs from the shoes.
6 Disconnect the shoes from the expander and adjuster and unhook the lower return spring (photo).
7 To remove the expander unit, pull it from the housing and press out the pivot pin which is attached to the cable.
8 Repeat the procedure given in paragraphs 4 to 7 on the remaining side.
9 Clean the backplates and expander units and check for wear and damage.
10 Apply a little molybdenum disulphide based grease to the sliding surfaces of the expander units.
11 Working on one side, attach the expander unit to the cable and

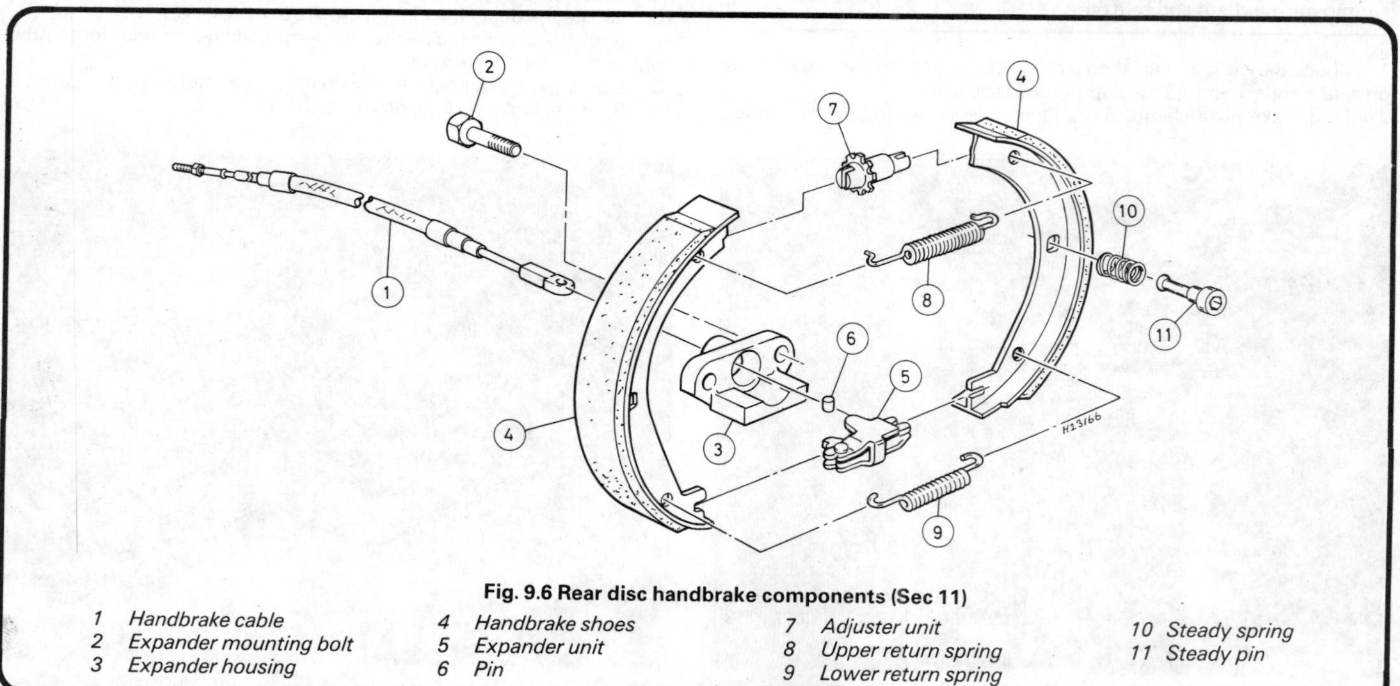

Fig. 9.6 Rear disc handbrake components (Sec 11)

1 Handbrake cable
2 Expander mounting bolt
3 Expander housing
4 Handbrake shoes
5 Expander unit
6 Pin
7 Adjuster unit
8 Upper return spring
9 Lower return spring
10 Steady spring
11 Steady pin

11.4 Rear handbrake shoe expander and return spring

11.5 Rear handbrake shoe steady spring (arrowed)

11.6 Rear handbrake shoe adjuster and lower return spring

press in the pivot pin. Locate the unit against the housing to prevent the pivot pin from dropping out.

12 Hook the front return spring to the lower ends of the brake shoes, then locate the shoes on the expander unit.

13 Refit the steady springs and pins, turning the pins through 90° to lock them onto the backplate.

14 Hook the rear return spring to the brake shoes.

15 Repeat the procedure given in paragraphs 11 to 14 on the remaining side.

16 Refit both rear brake discs with reference to Section 10.

12 Handbrake – adjustment

Rear drum brakes

1 Chock the front wheels then jack up the rear of the car and support on axle stands. Release the handbrake lever.

2 Working inside the car prise the rubber boot from the base of the handbrake lever in order to expose the cable adjusting nuts.

3 Back off the adjusting nuts then apply the footbrake pedal hard several times to set the shoes in their normal position.

4 Apply the handbrake lever to the third notch.

5 Tighten the cable adjusting nuts equally until it is just possible to turn each rear wheel uniformly but without them being locked.

6 Release the handbrake lever and check that the rear wheels can now be turned freely. With the ignition switched on, the warning light should not be lit – if it is, check the warning light switch by the handbrake lever.

7 Prise the inspection plugs from the rear backplates and check that with the lever released, the levers on the rear brake shoes are just clear of the pins but not more than 1 mm away from them.

8 Refit the plugs and lower the car to the ground.

Rear disc brakes

9 Before adjusting the handbrake it is recommended that the surfaces of the drums be cleaned by driving the car with the handbrake applied until resistance is felt plus a further notch. Do not drive the car for more than 400 m (1300 ft).

10 Chock the front wheels then jack up the rear of the car and support on axle stands. Fully release the handbrake lever.

11 Working inside the car, lift off the cover plate over the handbrake lever in order to expose the cable adjusting nuts.

12 Back off the adjusting nuts.

13 Unscrew and remove one wheel bolt from each rear roadwheel.

14 Working on one side, turn the wheel so that the wheel bolt hole is positioned 45° to the rear from its centre-bottom position. Using a screwdriver, rotate the adjuster until the wheel is locked, then back off the adjuster 4 to 6 threads (photo). Rotating the adjuster clockwise (viewed from above) expands the shoes and rotating it anti-clockwise contracts the shoes. Check that the wheel turns freely after making the adjustment.

12.14 Adjusting the rear handbrake shoes

15 Adjust the handbrake on the remaining side in the same manner.

16 Apply the handbrake lever 5 notches.

17 Working inside the car, adjust the cable adjusting nuts until both rear wheels can just be turned uniformly without being locked.

18 Fully release the handbrake lever and check that the rear wheels can be turned freely. If not, the handbrake cables may be partially seized.

19 Refit the handbrake lever cover plate, then lower the car to the ground.

13 Handbrake lever – removal and refitting

1 Remove the centre console. On rear drum models prise the rubber boot from the base of the handbrake lever. On rear disc models lift off the cover from the handbrake lever (photo).

2 Unscrew the nuts from the ends of the cables (photo).

3 Unscrew the nut and press the pivot bolt through the handbrake lever assembly. Withdraw the assembly from the car.

4 If necessary the locking element, pawl and push rod may be removed from the main lever but note how it is fitted to ensure correct reassembly.

5 The handbrake lever warning switch may be removed if necessary

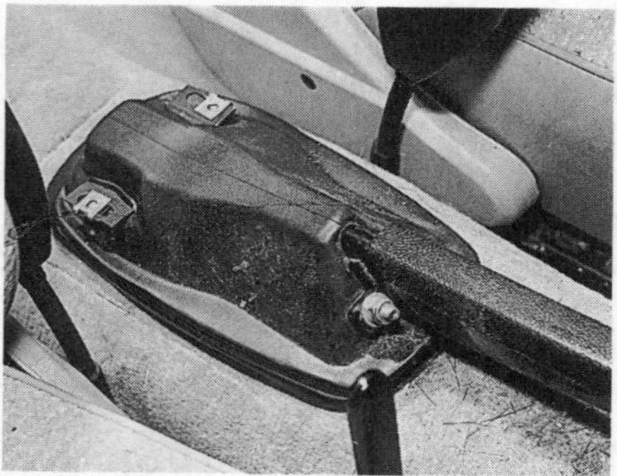
13.1 Handbrake lever and cover

13.2 Handbrake cable adjusting nut (arrowed)

13.5 Handbrake lever warning switch (arrowed)

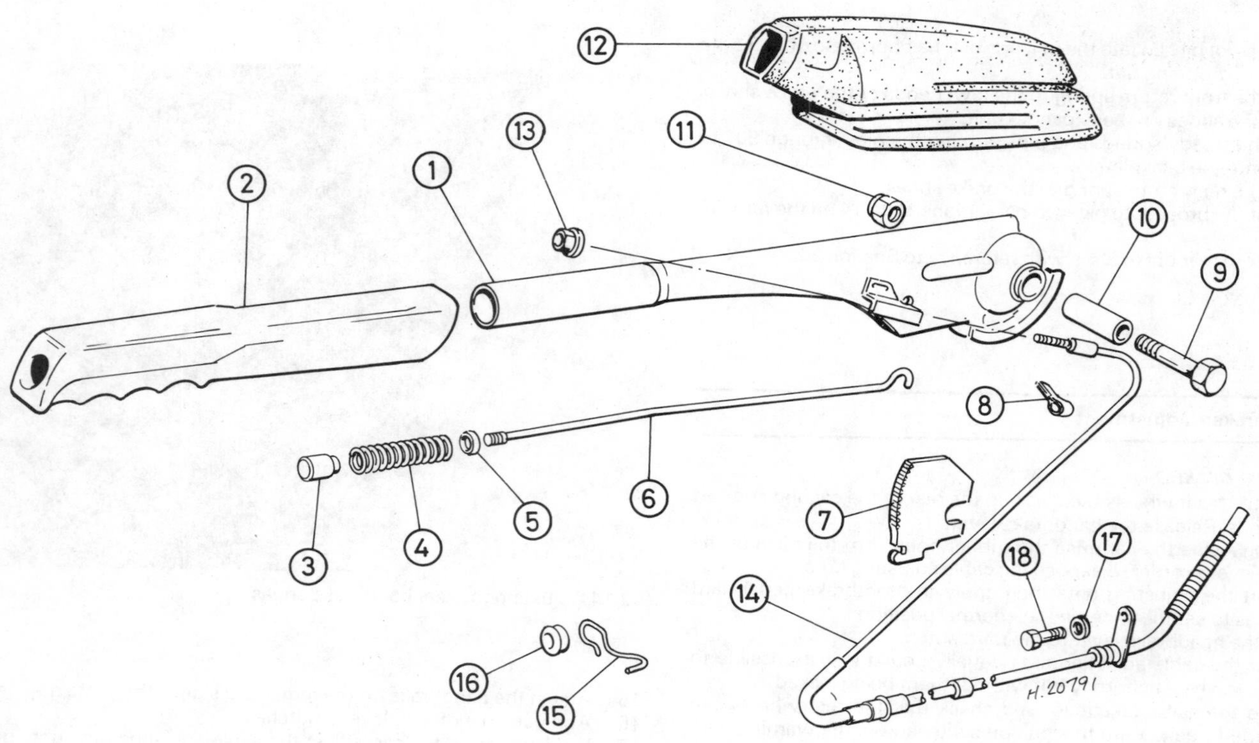

Fig. 9.7 Handbrake lever components (Sec 13)

1 *Handbrake lever*
2 *Hand grip*
3 *Push button*
4 *Spring*
5 *Rubber washer*
6 *Pushrod*
7 *Ratchet plate*
8 *Guide*
9 *Pivot bolt*
10 *Bush*
11 *Self-locking nut*
12 *Rubber boot*
13 *Cable nut*
14 *Handbrake cable*
15 *Hook*
16 *Grommet*
17 *Wave washer*
18 *Bolt*

by unscrewing the bolt from under the car and disconnecting the wiring (photo).

6 Reassembly and refitting is a reversal of removal, but tighten the pivot bolt to the specified torque, and adjust the handbrake as described in Section 12.

14 Handbrake cable – removal and refitting

1 Remove the appropriate rear brake shoes as described in Sections 6 or 11 as applicable.

2 Working inside the car, on rear drum models prise the rubber boot from the base of the handbrake lever, and on rear disc models lift off the cover plate over the handbrake lever.

3 On rear drum models unscrew the nut from the end of the appropriate handbrake cable.

4 On rear disc models remove the handbrake lever completely as described in Section 13.

5 Unclip the handbrake cable from the semi-trailing arm.

6 Remove the handbrake cable from the backplate and withdraw from under the car.

7 Refitting is a reversal of removal but adjust the handbrake cable as described in Section 12.

15.6 Brake master cylinder

15 Master cylinder – removal, overhaul and refitting

1 Unscrew the filler cap from the fluid reservoir and draw off the fluid using a syringe.
2 Place some cloth rags beneath the master cylinder to soak up any spilled fluid.
3 Disconnect the clutch master cylinder supply hose from the fluid reservoir.
4 Unscrew the union nuts and disconnect the rigid hydraulic lines from the master cylinder. If necessary identify them for position.
5 Pull the reservoir from the top of the master cylinder. Prise out the rubber grommets if necessary.
6 Unscrew the mounting nuts and withdraw the master cylinder from the vacuum servo unit (photo). Remove the rubber O-ring.
7 Apply light finger pressure to the end of the piston, then unscrew the stop bolt.
8 Extract the circlip from the mouth of the cylinder and pull out the primary piston. Keep all of the components in their correct order of removal to ensure correct reassembly.
9 Remove the secondary piston by tapping the cylinder on the bench.
10 Examine the surfaces of the cylinder bore and pistons for corrosion and scoring. If this is excessive renew the master cylinder complete, but if the bore and pistons are in good condition obtain a repair kit which will obtain all the necessary seals.
11 From the primary piston remove the stop washer, seal, intermediate ring, seal, and bearing noting their fitted position.
12 Unscrew the bolt from the inner end of the piston and withdraw the spring retainer, spring, support ring, seal, and shim.
13 From the secondary piston remove the spring, support ring, seal and shim. Prise the intermediate seals from the front of the piston.
14 Clean all of the components with methylated spirit.
15 During the reassembly procedure dip the piston components in fresh hydraulic fluid.
16 Fit the intermediate seals to the front of the secondary piston using the fingers only to manipulate them into position. Make sure that the seal lips face away from each other. These seals are colour-coded to identify them from the other seals.
17 To the secondary piston fit the shim, seal (lip facing the rear of the piston), support ring, and spring. Make sure that the support ring is correctly located.
18 To the inner end of the primary piston fit the shim, seal, support ring, spring, and spring retainer. Make sure that the support ring is correctly located.
19 To the outer end of the primary piston fit the bearing, seal, intermediate ring, seal, and stop washer. The lips of both seals must face the inner end of the piston. Coat the space between the two seals, the intermediate ring, and the piston skirt with silicone grease.
20 Dip the secondary piston assembly in fresh hydraulic fluid and insert it into the cylinder. Take care not to distort the seal lips.
21 Dip the primary piston assembly in fresh hydraulic fluid and insert it into the cylinder again taking care not to distort the seal lips. Depress the piston and refit the circlip into the groove in the mouth of the cylinder.
22 Fit a new copper washer to the stop bolt, then apply light finger pressure to the end of the piston and tighten the stop bolt into the cylinder body.
23 Clean the mating faces then locate the master cylinder on the vacuum servo unit together with a new O-ring and tighten the mounting nuts to the specified torque. Note that insufficient sealing of the O-ring will affect the vacuum within the servo unit.
24 Fit new rubber grommets to the top of the master cylinder and smear a little brake fluid on the inner diameters. Press the reservoir fully into the grommets.
25 Reconnect the rigid hydraulic lines and tighten the union nuts.
26 Reconnect the clutch master cylinder supply hose to the reservoir.
27 Top up the reservoir with fresh fluid and bleed the hydraulic system as described in Section 17.

16 Flexible hoses and rigid pipelines – renewal

1 Before removing any brake line or hose it will be necessary to draw off the hydraulic fluid from the reservoir on the master cylinder to reduce the loss of fluid.
2 To remove a flexible hose first unscrew the rigid pipeline union from it, holding the hose end fitting against rotation with another open-ended

16.2A Front brake flexible hose to rigid line connection

16.2B Rear brake flexible hose

spanner. A special brake union split-ring spanner is to be preferred to release the unions as they can be very tight (photos).

3 The hose end fittings are secured to the brackets by a spring plate located beneath the union.

4 To remove a rigid brake line, unscrew the end unions then release the line from the body clips by unscrewing the bolts and removing the retaining plates.

5 New rigid pipes are available from BMW dealers or can be made to pattern by most garages.

6 When fitting new brake lines or hoses, do not over-tighten the unions as the flared ends may be distorted and cause leakage. If possible use a torque wrench to tighten them.

7 On completion it will be necessary to bleed the complete hydraulic system as described in Section 17.

17 Hydraulic system – bleeding

1 If any of the hydraulic components in the braking system have been removed or disconnected, or if the fluid level in the reservoir has been allowed to fall appreciably, air will have been introduced into the system. The following paragraphs describe the procedure for removing the air.

2 The two diagonal hydraulic circuits are entirely separate, therefore on non-ABS models, unless the master cylinder has been removed or the brake fluid is being changed, it will only be necessary to bleed the circuit which has been disturbed. On ABS models the complete system must always be bled.

3 There are a variety of do-it-yourself brake bleeding kits available from motor accessory shops, and it is recommended that one of these kits is used wherever possible as they greatly simplify the bleeding operation. A pressure bleeding kit is particularly recommended for models fitted with ABS, although this is not essential. Follow the kit manufacturer's instructions in conjunction with the following procedure.

4 During the bleeding operation do not allow the brake fluid level in the reservoir to drop below the minimum mark, and only use new fluid for topping- up. Never re-use fluid bled from the system.

5 Before starting, check that all rigid pipes and flexible hoses are in good condition and that all hydraulic unions are tight. Take great care not to allow hydraulic fluid to come into contact with the vehicle paintwork, otherwise the finish will be seriously damaged. Wash off any spilt fluid immediately with cold water.

6 If a brake bleeding kit is not being used, gather together a clean jar, a suitable length of plastic or rubber tubing which is a tight fit over the bleed screws and a new tin of brake fluid.

7 Clean the area around the bleed screw on the right-hand rear brake and remove the dust cap (photo). Connect one end of the tubing to the bleed screw and immerse the other end in the jar containing sufficient brake fluid to keep the end of the rubber tube submerged.

8 Open the bleed screw half a turn, then have an assistant first depress the brake pedal to the floor, and then slowly release it. Tighten the bleed screw at the end of each downstroke to prevent the expelled air and fluid from being drawn back into the system. Continue this procedure until clean brake fluid, free from air bubbles, can be seen flowing into the jar, and then finally tighten the bleed screw. On models fitted with ABS it will be necessary to operate the brake pedal at least twelve times. Note that if a pressure bleeding kit is being used on models fitted with ABS, the brake pedal must still be fully operated at least twelve times.

9 Remove the tube and refit the dust cap.

10 On non-ABS models, the diagonally opposite brake may be bled next followed by the rear left and front right brakes. On ABS models, however, the rear left brake should be bled next followed by the front right and front left brakes.

11 When bleeding is complete, top up the fluid level in the reservoir and refit the cap.

18 Vacuum servo unit – testing, removal and refitting

1 To test the vacuum servo unit, first depress the footbrake pedal approximately ten times in order to dissipate the vacuum. With the pedal depressed, start the engine and check that the pedal is felt to move towards the floor, indicating that the unit is functioning correctly. If the pedal remains stationary, the check valve, vacuum hoses, and the

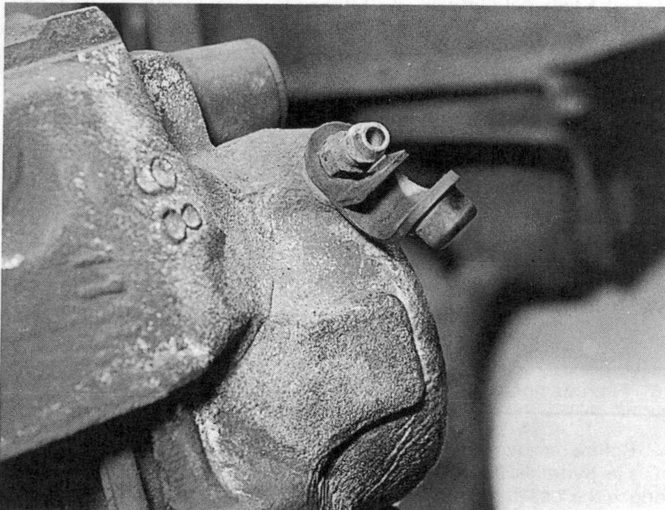
17.7 Brake hydraulic system bleed screw and dust cap

18.5 Brake linkage pullrod (A) and servo unit pushrod (B)

18.6 Brake servo unit mounting nuts (arrowed)

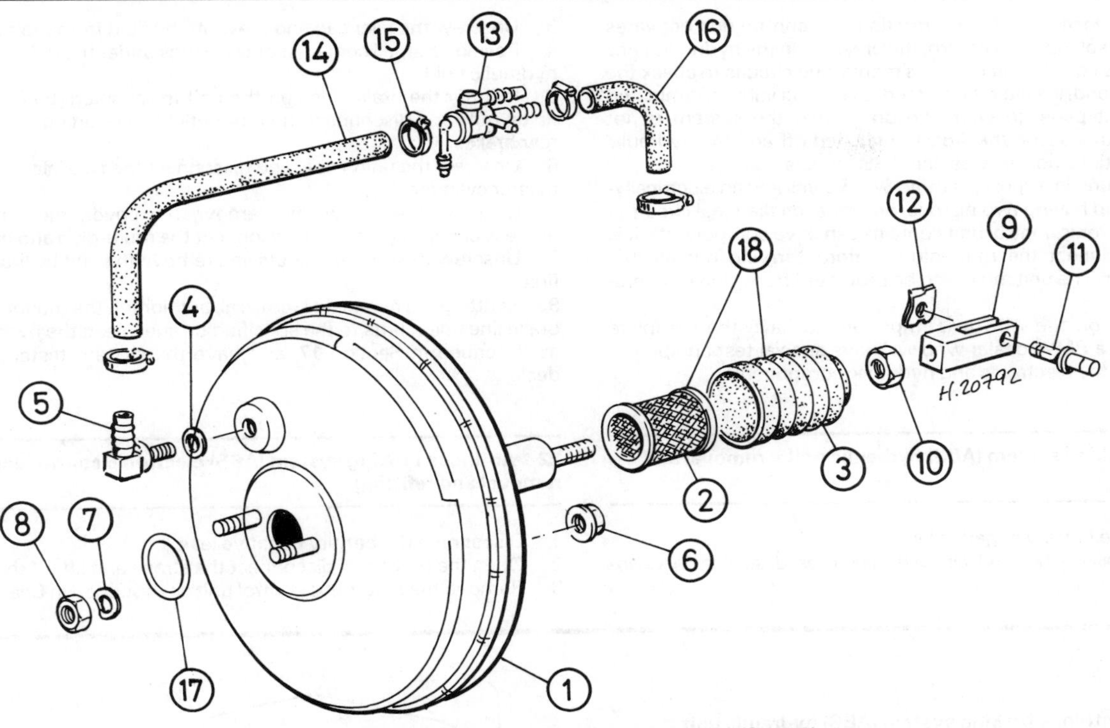

Fig. 9.8 Vacuum servo unit components (Sec 18)

1 Servo unit housing
2 Air filter
3 Rubber boot
4 Gasket
5 Connector
6 Mounting nut
7 Washer
8 Nut
9 Clevis
10 Locknut
11 Clevis pin
12 Spring clip
13 Non-return valve
14 Hose
15 Clamp
16 Hose
17 O-ring
18 Air filter repair kit

master cylinder-to-servo unit O-ring should be checked.

2 To remove the unit first remove the master cylinder as described in Section 15.

3 Disconnect the vacuum hose from the check valve.

4 Remove the glovebox from inside the car.

5 Working inside the car, remove the clevis pin securing the servo unit pushrod to the pedal linkage (photo).

6 Unscrew the mounting nuts and withdraw the servo unit from the bulkhead in the engine compartment (photo).

7 If necessary the filter may be cleaned. First unscrew the locknut and clevis, then remove the rubber boot, holder, damper and finally the filter. Clean the damper and filter, then reassemble in reverse order. The slots of the damper and filter should be offset to each other by 180°.

8 To remove the check valve, loosen the clamp where fitted and pull the valve from the rubber grommet. Refitting is a reversal of removal, but make sure that the arrow or the black side of the valve faces the inlet manifold.

9 Refitting of the servo unit is a reversal of removal. Refer to Section 15 for details of refitting the master cylinder.

19 Stoplamp switch – removal, refitting and adjustment

1 Remove the lower facia trim from beneath the steering wheel.

2 Disconnect the wiring from the switch (photo).

3 Unscrew the lower locknut and withdraw the switch from the bracket.

4 Refitting is a reversal of removal, but adjust the switch as follows. With the brake pedal fully released, check that the distance between the threaded end of the switch and the pedal is between 5 and 6 mm. If necessary loosen the locknuts and reposition the switch as required, then retighten the locknuts.

20 Anti-lock braking system (ABS) – description and precautions

The ABS system prevents the wheels locking when braking hard, and by so doing ensures that the car remains in full control for steering. By maintaining optimum friction between the tyres and road, the car can be stopped in the minimum distance.

The system consists of an electronic control unit, hydraulic unit, and speed sensors on the wheels.

The electronic control unit incorporates a computer which collates signals from the wheel sensors and compares this with the actual speed

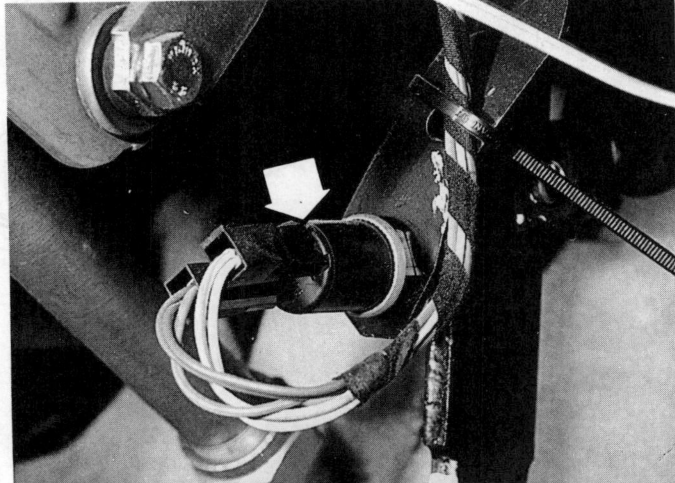

19.2 Stoplamp switch (arrowed)

of the car. After processing the information, the control unit activates the hydraulic unit solenoids to control the pressure in the hydraulic lines to the wheels. The control unit contains monitoring circuits to check the system functions and, if a fault is detected, a warning light is illuminated on the instrument panel to warn the driver that the system is not working. Should this occur, the ABS is switched off and the hydraulic system then functions normally as non-ABS models.

The hydraulic unit incorporates three-way valves and an electrically-driven return pump having two pistons, one for each diagonal circuit.

Since the electronic control unit contains sensitive components, it is essential to disconnect the multi-plugs before carrying out electric welding on the car. The unit must also be protected from high temperatures.

After working on the ABS it is important to have the complete system tested by a BMW dealer who will have special test equipment for checking both the electronic and hydraulic components.

21 Anti-lock braking system (ABS) hydraulic unit – removal and refitting

1 Disconnect the battery negative lead.

2 Remove the air cleaner and air flow sensor as described in Chapter 3.

3 Unscrew the filler cap and draw off the fluid from the reservoir.

4 Position a small container or cloth rags under the unit to collect spilt hydraulic fluid.

5 Identify the brake lines on the unit for position, then unscrew the union nuts and disconnect the four outlet lines leading to the front and rear brakes.

6 Unscrew the union nuts and disconnect the two inlet lines from the master cylinder.

7 Unscrew the screw and remove the cover, then unscrew the harness clamp screws, and disconnect the multi-plug and earth wire.

8 Unscrew the mounting nuts and remove the unit by lifting the front first.

9 Refitting is a reversal of removal, but tighten the mounting nuts and brake line union nuts to the specified torque, bleed the hydraulic circuit as described in Section 17, and have the system tested by a BMW dealer.

22 Anti-lock braking system (ABS) electronic control unit – removal and refitting

1 Disconnect the battery negative lead.

2 Open the glovebox, disconnect the straps and lift off the cover.

3 Remove the L-Jetronic control unit as described in Chapter 3.

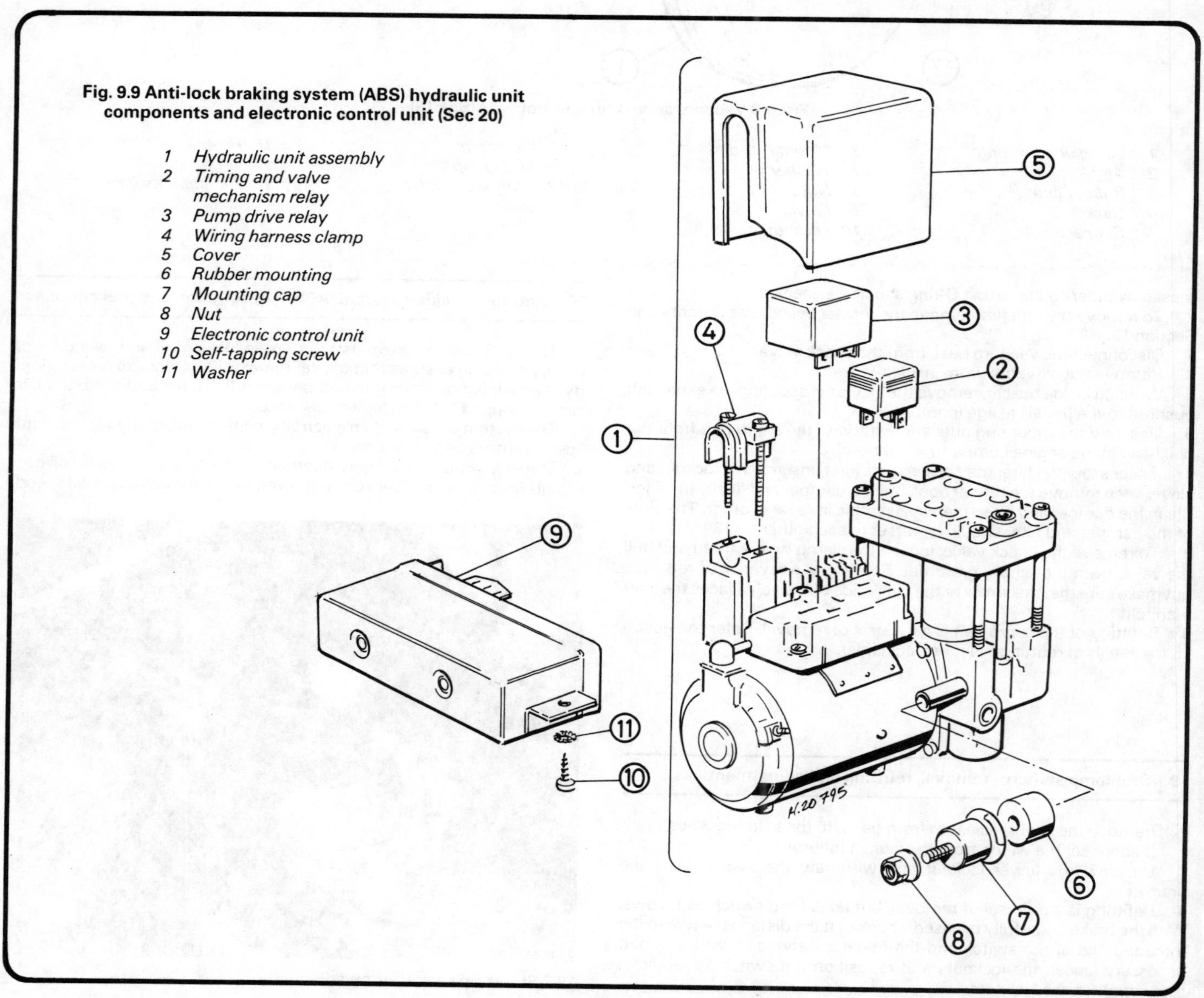

Fig. 9.9 Anti-lock braking system (ABS) hydraulic unit components and electronic control unit (Sec 20)

1 Hydraulic unit assembly
2 Timing and valve mechanism relay
3 Pump drive relay
4 Wiring harness clamp
5 Cover
6 Rubber mounting
7 Mounting cap
8 Nut
9 Electronic control unit
10 Self-tapping screw
11 Washer

4 Working on the anti-lock braking system electronic control unit, release the clamp then pull out the multi-plug on the right-hand side and disconnect it on the left-hand side.
5 Unbolt the unit from the body.
6 Refitting is a reversal of removal but on completion have the complete ABS system tested by a BMW dealer.

23 Anti-lock braking system (ABS) front speed sensor – removal and refitting

1 Switch off the ignition.
2 Apply the handbrake then jack up the front of the car and support on axle stands.
3 Using an Allen key, unscrew the sensor mounting screw, lift out the wire and remove the sensor. If necessary, disconnect the plug in the engine compartment and pull the wires down.
4 Check the condition of the seal and renew it if necessary.
5 Clean the sensor, then apply some molybdenum based grease to the sensor and housing.
6 Refit the sensor by reversing the removal procedure and noting that it is fitted without a spacer. When reconnecting the wire, make sure that it is not strained. On completion have the complete ABS system checked by a BMW dealer.

24 Anti-lock braking system (ABS) rear speed sensor – removal and refitting

1 Switch off the ignition.
2 Chock the front wheels, then jack up the rear of the car and support on axle stands.
3 Remove the rear brake caliper as described in Chapter 9.
4 Using an Allen key, unscrew the sensor mounting screw, lift out the wire and remove the sensor. If necessary separate the plug, unclip the wires and remove them from the rubber grommet.
5 Check the condition of the seal and renew it if necessary.
6 Clean the sensor then apply some molybdenum based grease to the sensor and housing.
7 Refit the sensor by reversing the removal procedure. On completion have the complete ABS system checked by a BMW dealer.

25 Anti-lock braking system (ABS) pulse wheel – removal and refitting

1 The front pulse wheels are integral with the front wheel hubs (see Chapter 10).
2 The rear pulse wheels are integral with the driveshafts (see Chapter 7).

26 Anti-lock braking system (ABS) hydraulic unit relay – renewal

1 Unscrew the screw and remove the cover from the hydraulic unit.
2 Pull out the motor relay (larger) or valve relay.
3 Press the new relay direct into the hydraulic unit.
4 Refit the cover and tighten the screw.

27 Brake pedal – removal and refitting

1 Remove the lower facia panel from beneath the steering wheel as described in Chapter 11.

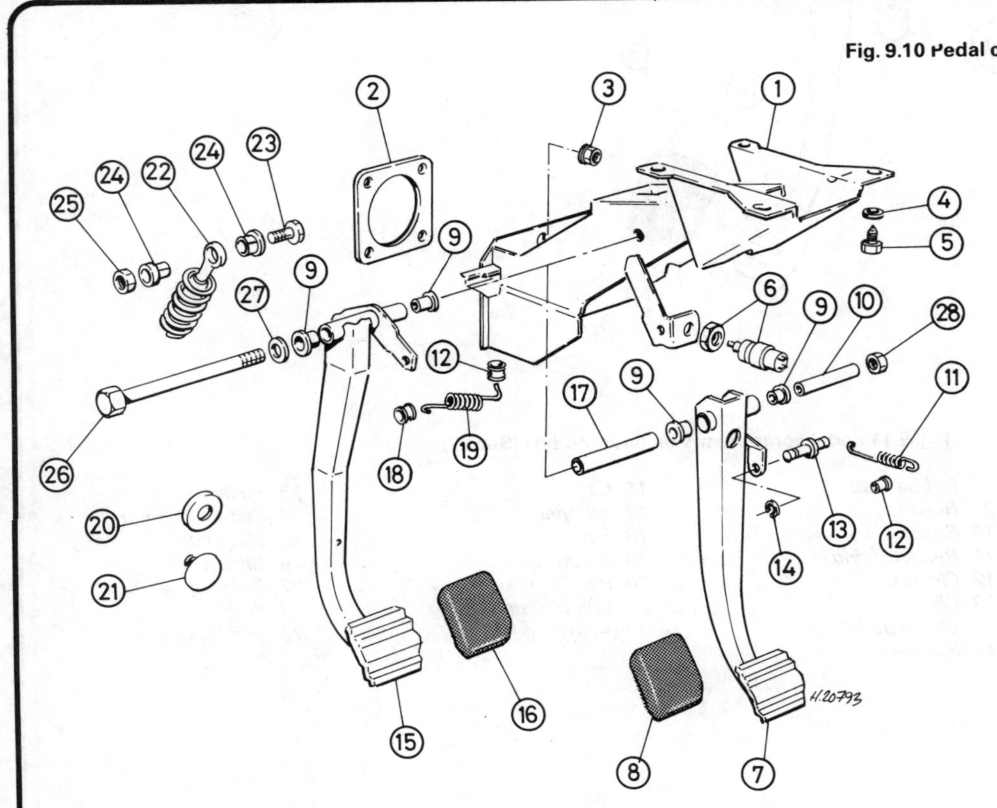

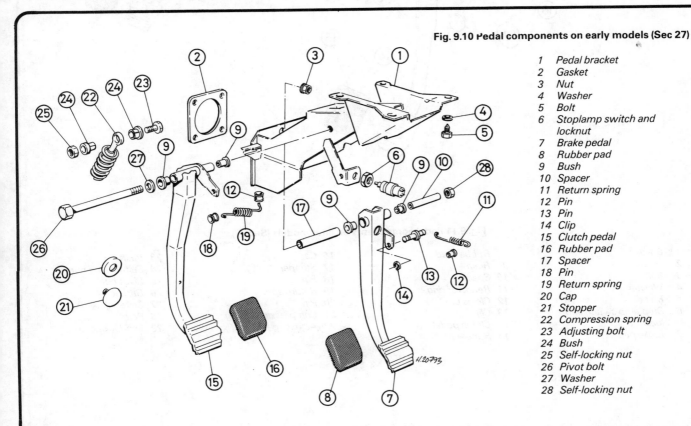

Fig. 9.10 Pedal components on early models (Sec 27)

1 Pedal bracket
2 Gasket
3 Nut
4 Washer
5 Bolt
6 Stoplamp switch and locknut
7 Brake pedal
8 Rubber pad
9 Bush
10 Spacer
11 Return spring
12 Pin
13 Pin
14 Clip
15 Clutch pedal
16 Rubber pad
17 Spacer
18 Pin
19 Return spring
20 Cap
21 Stopper
22 Compression spring
23 Adjusting bolt
24 Bush
25 Self-locking nut
26 Pivot bolt
27 Washer
28 Self-locking nut

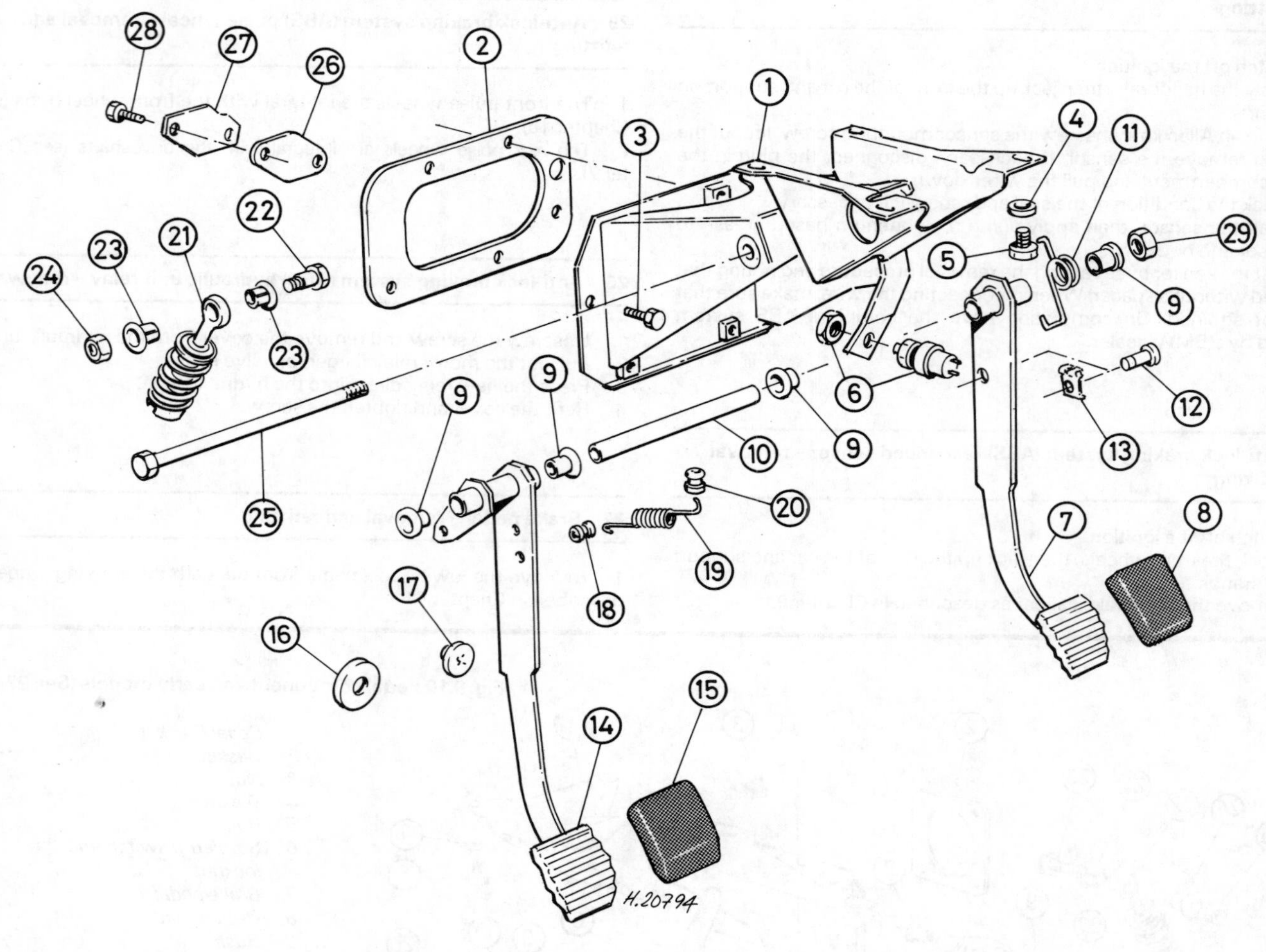

Fig. 9.11 Pedal components on later models (Sec 27)

1 Bracket
2 Gasket
3 Bolt
4 Washer
5 Bolt
6 Stoplamp switch and locknut
7 Brake pedal
8 Rubber pad
9 Bush
10 Spacer
11 Return spring
12 Clevis pin
13 Clip
14 Clutch pedal
15 Rubber pad
16 Cap
17 Stopper
18 Pin
19 Return spring
20 Pin
21 Compression spring
22 Adjusting bolt
23 Bush
24 Self-locking nut
25 Pivot bolt
26 Gasket
27 Cover plate
28 Bolt
29 Self-locking nut

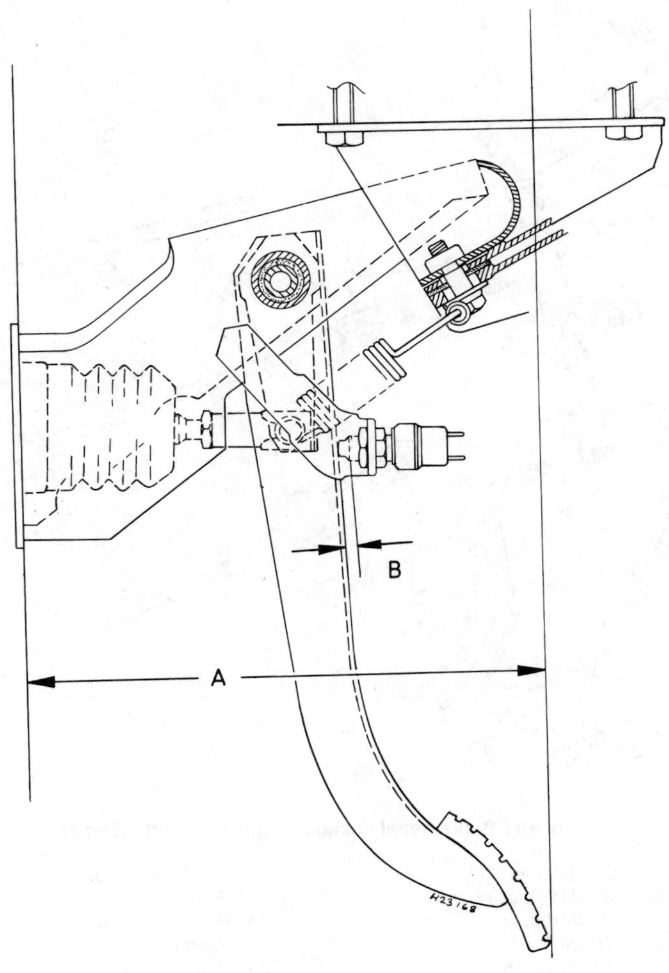

Fig. 9.12 Brake pedal height and stoplamp switch adjustment (Sec 27)

A = 231 + 10 mm *B = 5 to 6 mm*

2 On 520i manual transmission models, disconnect the clutch pedal return spring where necessary.
3 On all models disconnect the brake pedal return spring.
4 Extract the special spring clip from the end of the clevis pin securing the linkage pushrod to the pedal, extract the pin and disconnect the pushrod.
5 On 520i manual transmission models, unscrew the nut from the eccentric pivot bolt securing the clutch pedal to the clutch master cylinder, and extract the bolt. To ensure that the bolt is refitted in the same position, mark it before removal otherwise it will have to be adjusted with reference to Chapter 5.
6 Note how the pedal components are fitted to the pivot bolt then unscrew the nut and pull out the bolt sufficient to remove the brake pedal.
7 If necessary the pedal bearing bushes may be renewed by pressing out the spacer sleeves followed by the bushes. Press in the new bushes then apply a little grease to the sleeves and press them in also.
8 Refitting is a reversal of removal, but check the pedal height from the bulkhead (Fig 9.12) and compare with that given in Specifications. If necessary adjust it by loosening the nuts on the linkage pushrod, repositioning them as necessary, then tightening them. Tighten all nuts and bolts to the specified torque. Check and if necessary adjust the stoplamp switch as described in Section 19.

28 Brake pedal linkage – removal and refitting

1 The brake pedal linkage is located on the front face of the bulkhead in the engine compartment (photos). Access to the interconnecting linkages is gained by removing the lower facia panels and glovebox. Refer to Chapter 11 for details of this procedure.
2 The linkage components are shown in Figs. 9.13 and 9.14.
3 When reassembling and refitting the linkage make sure that all nuts and bolts are tightened to the specified torque and that all clevis pins are secure. Lightly grease the bearing surfaces of bushes before assembling them and finally adjust the pedal height with reference to Section 27.

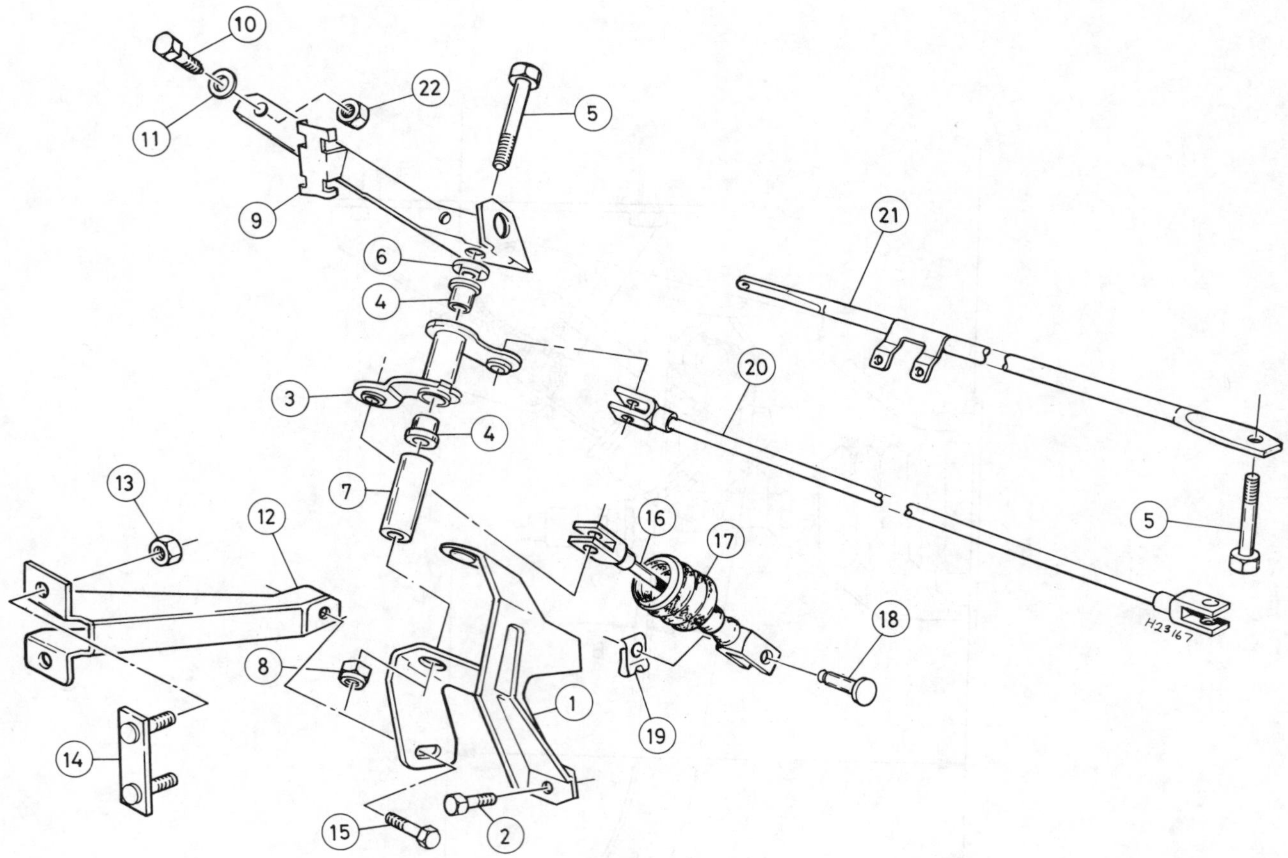

Fig. 9.13 Brake pedal linkage – right-hand side (Sec 28)

1 Bracket
2 Bolt
3 Lever
4 Bush
5 Bolt
6 Washer
7 Spacer
8 Self-locking nut
9 Support
10 Bolt
11 Washer
12 Support
13 Self-locking nut
14 Plate
15 Bolt
16 Pushrod
17 Rubber boot
18 Clevis pin
19 Clip
20 Pullrod
21 Brace
22 Self-locking nut

28.1A Brake pedal linkage on the right-hand side of the bulkhead (arrowed)

28.1B Brake pedal linkage on the left-hand side of the bulkhead

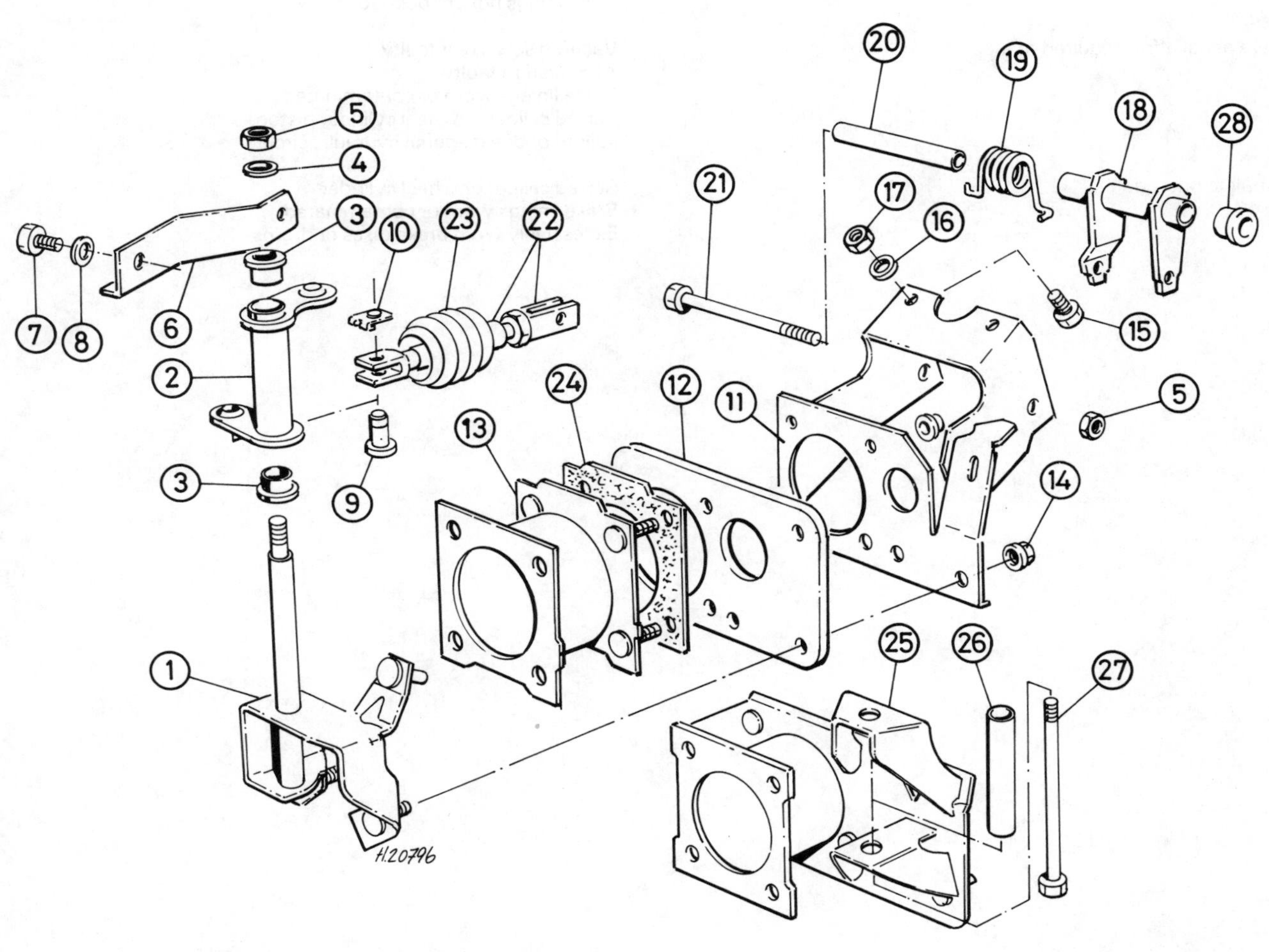

Fig. 9.14 Brake pedal linkage – left-hand side (Sec 28)

1 *Bracket*
2 *Lever*
3 *Bush*
4 *Washer*
5 *Self-locking nut*
6 *Support*
7 *Bolt*
8 *Washer*
9 *Clevis pin*
10 *Clip*
11 *Bracket*
12 *Gasket*
13 *Support*
14 *Nut*
15 *Bolt*
16 *Washer*
17 *Self-locking nut*
18 *Lever*
19 *Return spring*
20 *Spacer*
21 *Pivot bolt*
22 *Pushrod*
23 *Rubber boot*
24 *Gasket*
25 *Bracket*
26 *Spacer*
27 *Bolt*
28 *Bush*

29 Fault diagnosis – braking system

Symptom	Reason(s)
Excessive pedal travel	Air in hydraulic system Faulty master cylinder Loss of brake fluid Rear brake self-adjusters faulty (520i only)
Brake pedal feels spongy	Air in hydraulic system Faulty master cylinder New linings not yet bedded-in
Excessive pedal effort required to stop	Vacuum servo unit faulty ABS system faulty Brake linings worn or contaminated Seized caliper or wheel cylinder piston Failure of one diagonal hydraulic circuit
Brakes pull to one side	Seized caliper or wheel cylinder Brake linings worn or contaminated Excessively worn brake discs or drums

Chapter 10 Suspension and steering

Contents

Specifications

Front suspension

Type	Independent MacPherson struts with double track control arms and two front suspension lower balljoints on each side, anti-roll bar

Rear suspension

Type	Independent, with semi-trailing arms and struts incorporating coil springs and shock absorbers, anti-roll bar
Rear wheel toe setting	2.0 ± 0.8 mm or 0° 18′ ± 7′ toe-in
Rear wheel camber angle	–1° 45′ ± 30′ (negative)

Steering

Type	Recirculating-ball and nut steering gear, power-assisted, safety steering column
Turns lock-to-lock	3.5
Camber angle	–20′ ± 30′ (negative)
Maximum camber variation between sides	30′
Castor angle:	
At ± 10° wheel lock	8° ± 30′
At ± 20° wheel lock	8° 20′ ± 30′
Steering axle inclination:	
At ± 10° wheel lock	11° 57′ ± 30′
At ± 20° wheel lock	12° ± 30′
Toe setting	2.0 ± 0.6 mm toe-in
Toe difference angle at 20° lock of inside wheel	–1° 50′ ± 30′
Maximum difference in tolerance between left and right sides	30′
Power steering fluid:	
Type/specification	Dexron II type ATF (Duckhams D-Matic)
Capacity	1.2 litres (2.1 pints)
Power steering drivebelt deflection	approx 10 mm (0.4 in)

Roadwheels

Type	Aluminium
Size	5½J x 14H2

Tyres

Size:		
To 1985 models	175 HR14	
From 1986 models	195/70 HR14	
Pressures (cold) – bar (lbf/in²):	**Front**	**Rear**
Up to 4 persons	2.2 (32)	2.2 (32)
5 persons and luggage	2.2 (32)	2.6 (38)

Torque wrench settings	**Nm**	**lbf ft**
Front suspension		
Front axle carrier to body:		
M10	42	30
M12	77	56
Control arm to carrier	77.5	57
Control arm to strut	65	47
Strut upper mounting	22	16
Hub nut	290	210
Strut shock absorber piston	75	54
Shock absorber threaded ring	130	94
Anti-roll bar mounting	22	16
Anti-roll bar link	33	24
Rear suspension		
Semi-trailing arm to rear axle carrier	67 to 75	49 to 54
Rear strut upper mounting	22 to 24	16 to 17
Rear strut to semi-trailing arm	125 to 143	90 to 103
Hub nut:		
Yellow code (chromatized)	400 to 470	295 to 347
Waxed white code:		
520i	175 to 195	129 to 144
525e	234 to 260	173 to 192
Steering		
Steering gear:		
M10	42	30.5
M12	80 ± 8	57 ± 5
Tie-rod end nut	36.5 ± 3.5	26.5 ± 2.5
Tie-rod end clamp bolt	14	10
Drop arm to steering gear	140 (min)	102 (min)
Steering idler to carrier:		
M10	42	30
M12	85	63
Roadwheels		
Wheel bolt	100 ± 10	72 ± 7

1 General description

The front suspension (Fig. 10.1) comprises independent MacPherson struts with double track control arms on each strut, and two lower suspension balljoints on each side. An anti-roll bar is fitted with link arms attached to the struts. Shock absorbers are incorporated within the struts, and the shock absorber pistons are coated with teflon film for improved response.

The rear suspension (Fig. 10.2) comprises semi-trailing arms with struts incorporating coil springs and shock absorbers, and an anti-roll bar.

The steering is of recirculating-ball type and is power-assisted. A safety steering column is fitted which collapses in the event of a major front end crash.

2 Routine maintenance

Carry out the following at the intervals given in *Routine maintenance* at the front of this manual.

Check power steering pump drivebelt

1 Examine the full length of the power steering pump drivebelt for signs of deterioration and cracking.

2 Check the tension of the drivebelt. BMW technicians use a special tool for this, which will not be generally available to the home mechanic, so the following method should be used.

3 Press on the drivebelt at the mid-point of its longest run, and check that the deflection is approximately 10 mm (0.4 in) under moderate finger pressure. If adjustment is necessary, raise the front of the car and support on axle stands then remove the splash guard and loosen the pump adjustment and pivot bolts. Turn the adjustment gear until the required tension is obtained then tighten the bolt to lock the gear. Alternatively tighten the gear to between 8 and 8.5 Nm (6.0 lbf ft) and lock it in this position. Also tighten the pivot bolts (photos).

4 Refit the splash guard and lower the car to the ground.

Check power steering fluid level

5 With the engine stopped, unscrew the reservoir filler cap and wipe dry the dipstick.

6 Insert the dipstick by resting the filler cap on the reservoir filler neck, then remove it and check that the level is between the two marks (photo).

7 If necessary top up to the maximum level with the specified grade of fluid.

8 Run the engine for a short period then recheck the level again with the engine still running and top up if necessary.

9 Switch off the engine. The level may rise up to 5 mm (0.2 in) above the maximum mark, but this is in order.

10 Refit the filler cap.

11 If regular topping-up is required, the associated hoses and hydraulic lines should be inspected for leakage.

Check steering

12 With the front of the car raised and supported on axle stands, examine the steering gear and linkages for excessive wear. If possible have an assistant turn the steering wheel from side to side while checking the balljoints and linkages. Also check the balljoint dust covers.

Check suspension

13 With the front of the car raised and supported on axle stands, examine the suspension balljoints and linkages for excessive wear. In particular check the front suspension lower balljoints for wear.

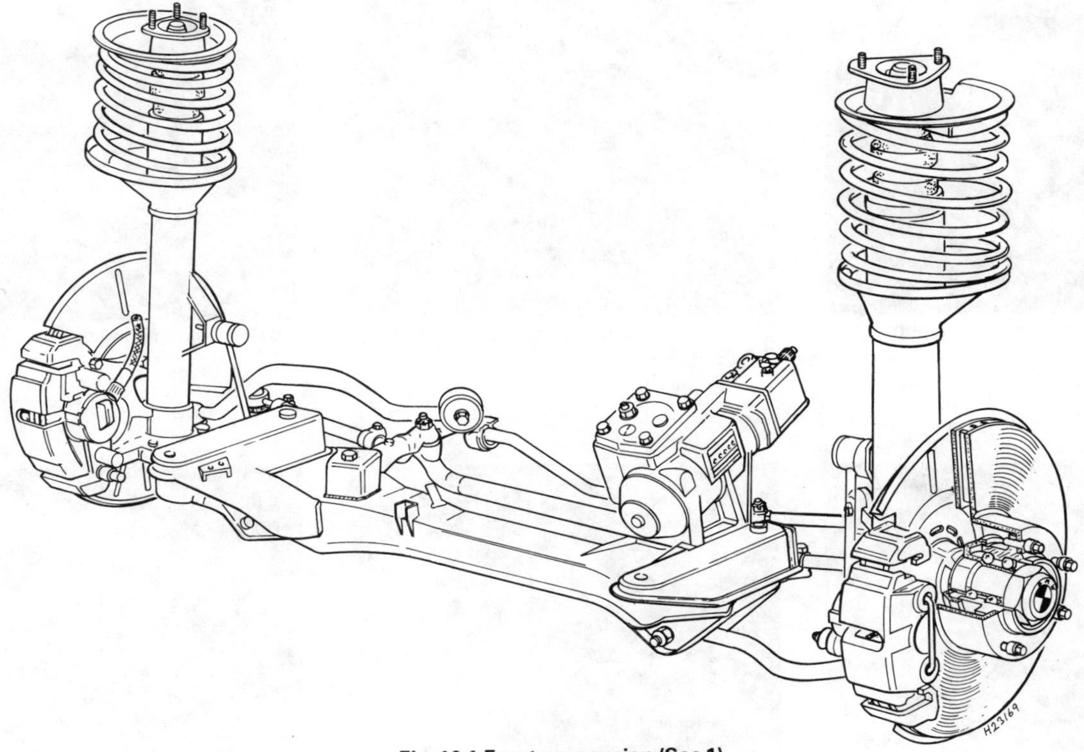

Fig. 10.1 Front suspension (Sec 1)

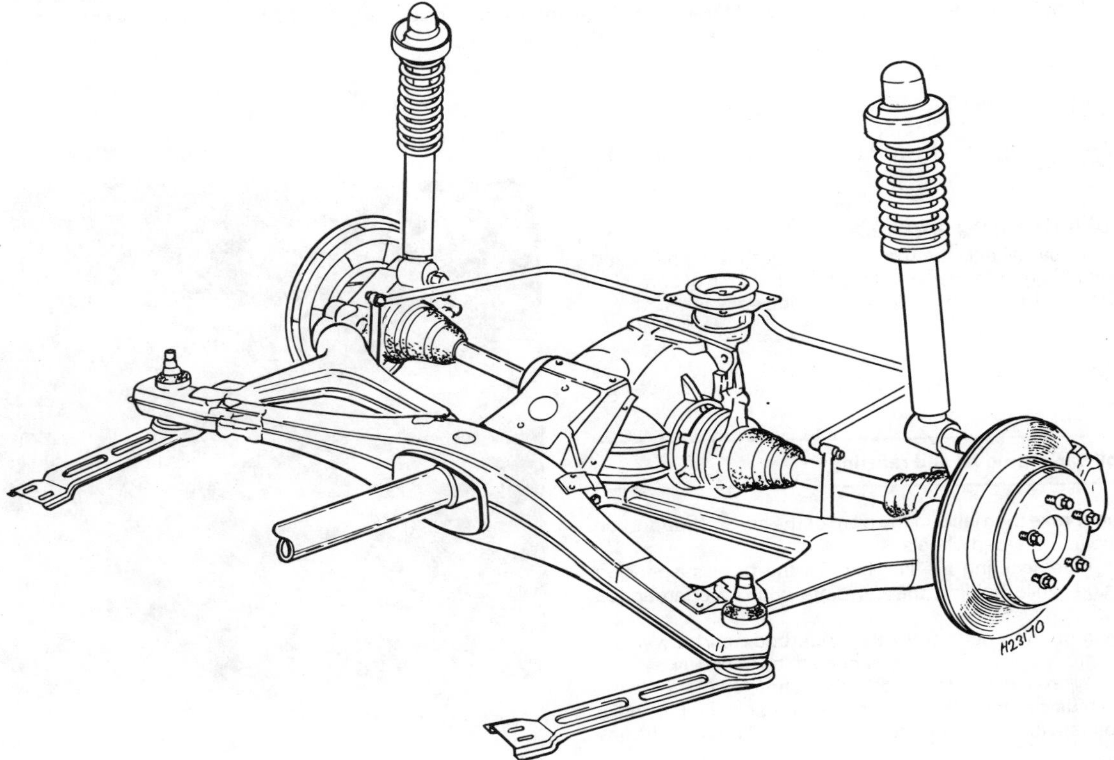

Fig. 10.2 Rear suspension (Sec 1)

Check tyres and pressures

14 Examine the tyres for wear and condition with reference also to Section 23. If any part of the tyre thread is worn down below the legal limit, renew the tyre. Where there are signs of uneven wear, check the front wheel alignment as described in Section 22.

Check front wheel bearing play

15 Raise the front of the car and support on axle stands.

16 Working on each side in turn, grip the top and bottom of the tyre and attempt to rock the wheel. If excessive movement is evident, the wheel bearing is probably worn, however to prove this conclusively

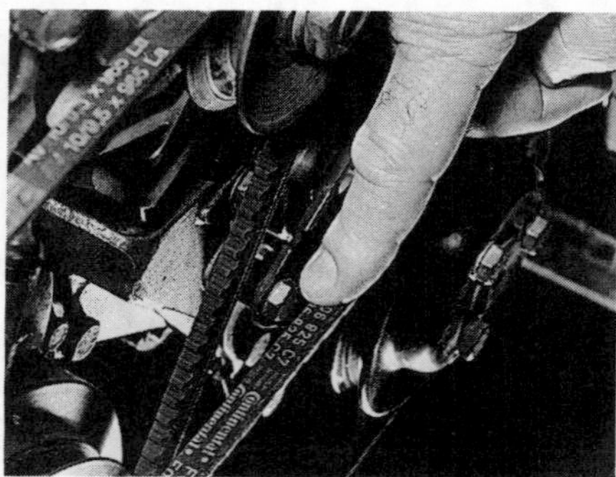
2.3A Checking the power steering pump drivebelt tension

2.3B Adjusting the power steering pump drivebelt tension

2.6 Checking the power steering reservoir fluid level

3.2A Front anti-roll bar link upper mounting nut

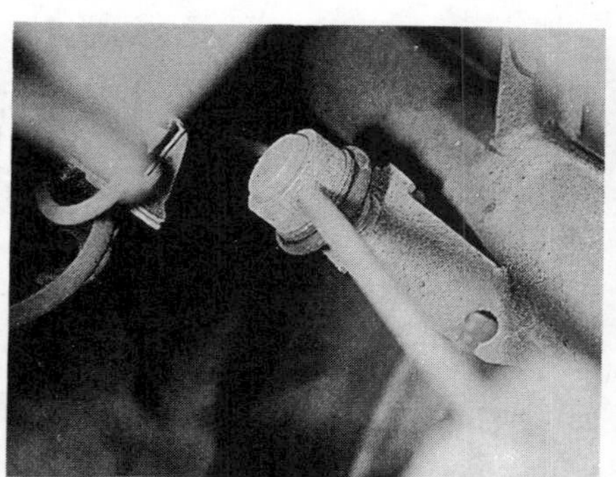
3.2B View of the front anti-roll bar link upper mounting on the front strut

3.3 Front anti-roll bar mounting bolt and clamp

have an assistant rock the wheel while observing the hub from the inside.

Grease roadwheel centres and hubs

17 Whenever the roadwheels are removed, check that the hubs and roadwheel centres are greased to prevent the accumulation of corrosion through the interaction of the aluminium wheels and steel hubs.

3 Front anti-roll bar – removal and refitting

1 Apply the handbrake then jack up the front of the car and support on axle stands. Remove both roadwheels.
2 Unscrew the nuts securing the link bars to the front suspension struts on each side while holding the balljoints with an open-ended spanner (photos).
3 Unscrew the mounting bolts from the underbody and lower the anti-roll bar to the ground. The clamps may need to be prised away with a screwdriver if they are stuck to the underbody (photo).
4 Unscrew the nuts securing the link bars to the anti-roll bar while holding the balljoints with an open-ended spanner, and remove the link bars (photo).
5 Prise off the mounting rubbers.
6 Examine the anti-roll bar, links and mounting rubbers for damage and deterioration and renew them if necessary. Check that the bonded rubbers in the links are not perished.
7 Refitting is a reversal of removal, but make sure that the slotted ends of the mounting rubbers face the rear of the car, and delay fully tightening the nuts to the specified torques until the weight of the car is on the front suspension.

3.4 Link to anti-roll bar nut

4 Track control arm – removal, overhaul and refitting

1 Apply the handbrake, then jack up the front of the car and support on axle stands. Remove the appropriate front roadwheel.
2 Unscrew the bolts securing the steering arm bracket to the bottom of the front suspension strut, and lower it (photo).

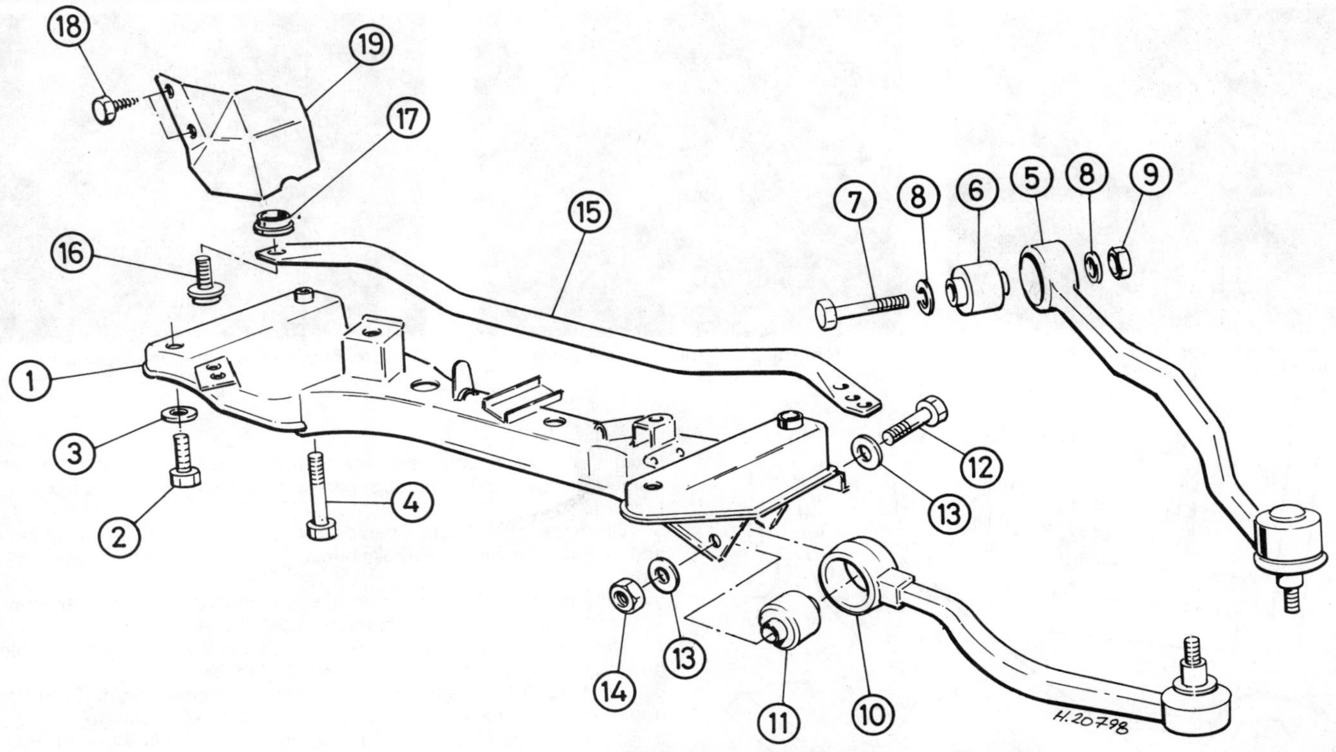

Fig. 10.3 Track control arm and crossmember components (Sec 4)

1 Crossmember
2 Mounting bolt
3 Washer
4 Bolt
5 Rear track control arm
6 Bush
7 Pivot bolt
8 Washer
9 Self-locking nut
10 Front control arm
11 Bush
12 Pivot bolt
13 Washer
14 Nut
15 Brace
16 Bolt
17 Nut
18 Screw
19 Heat resistant plate

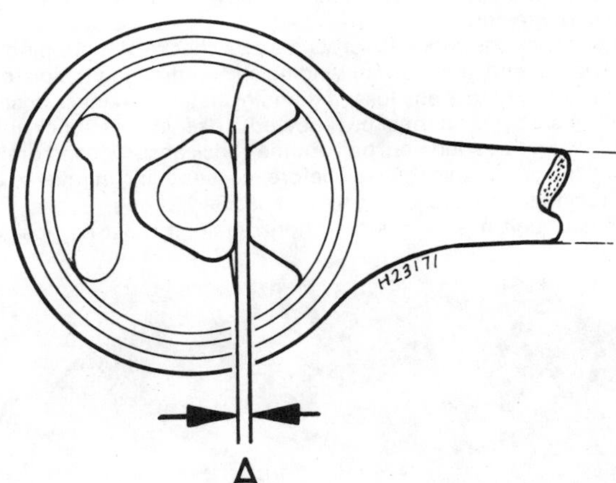

Fig. 10.4 Track control arm bush measuring dimension (Sec 4)

A = 0.8 to 1.8 mm

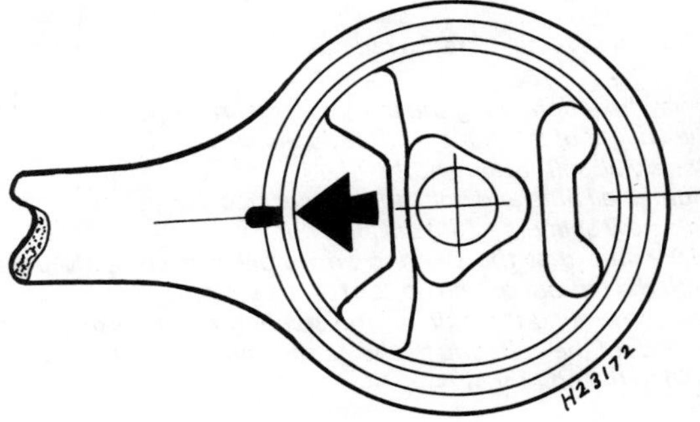

Fig. 10.5 Correct location of the track control arm bush (Sec 4)

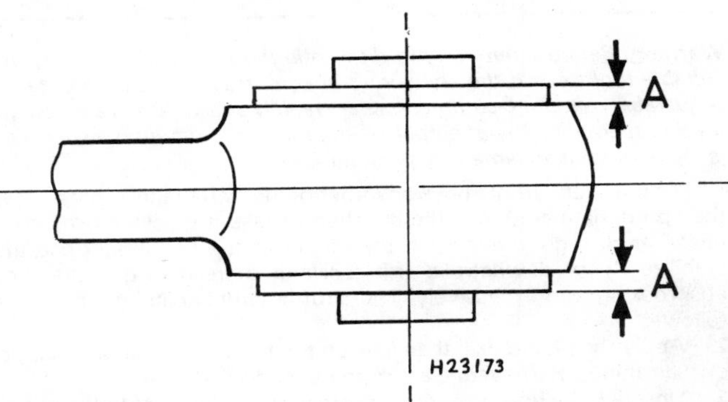

Fig. 10.6 Track control arm bush must be fitted centrally so that dimensions A are equal (Sec 4)

3 Extract the split pin and unscrew the balljoint nut, then separate the balljoint from the bracket using a balljoint removal tool.

4 Unscrew and remove the inner pivot bolt from the crossmember or underbody bracket as applicable, noting that a washer is fitted on each side (photos).

5 To check the pivot bush, refer to Fig. 10.4 and use a feeler blade to measure the dimension given. If it is not within the specified tolerance, renew the bush by pressing it out with a bench press or by using a long bolt, nut and washer. When pressing in the new bush make sure that it is located as shown in Figs. 10.5 and 10.6.

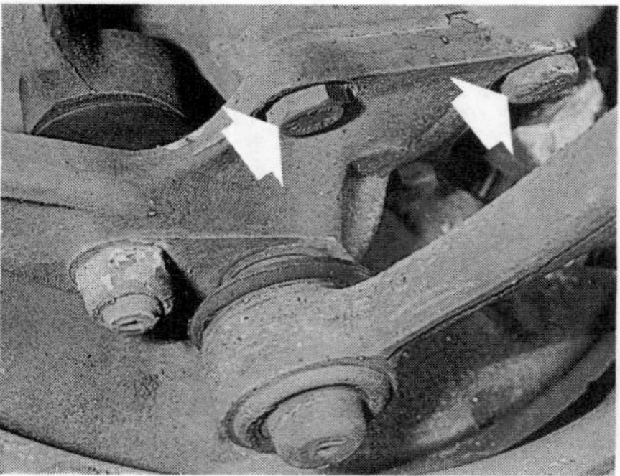
4.2 Steering arm bracket-to-front suspension strut bolts (arrowed)

4.4A Front track control arm inner pivot (arrowed)

4.4B Rear track control arm inner pivot (arrowed)

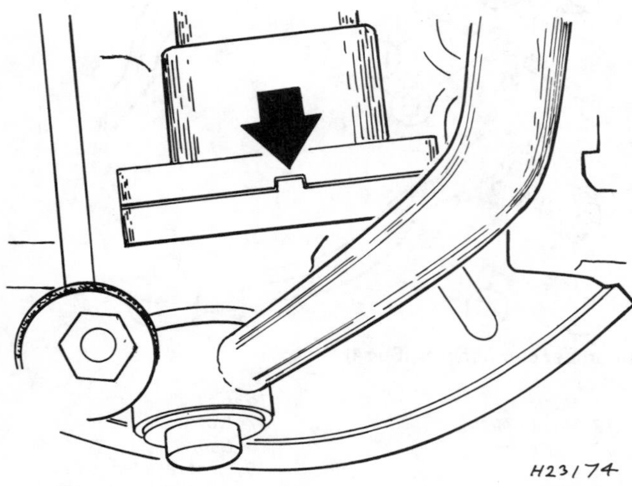

Fig. 10.7 Steering arm bracket location cut-out (Sec 4)

6 Refitting is a reversal of removal, but note the following additional points:

- (a) *Delay fully tightening the track control arm inner pivot bolt until the weight of the car is on the suspension*
- (b) *Renew all self-locking nuts*
- (c) *Tighten all nuts and bolts to the specified torque*
- (d) *Fit a new split pin to the balljoint nut*
- (e) *Make sure that the steering arm bracket is correctly engaged with the cut-out on the bottom of the strut*
- (f) *Before refitting the bolts to the steering arm bracket, clean the threads of the bolts and the holes and apply a little thread-locking fluid to the bolt threads*

5 Front suspension strut – checking, removal, overhaul and refitting

Warning: *Before attempting to dismantle the front suspension strut, a suitable tool to hold the coil spring in compression must be obtained. Adjustable coil spring compressors are readily available and are essential for this operation. Any attempt to dismantle the strut without such a tool is likely to result in damage or personal injury.*

1 To check the front shock absorber before removing it, press down the appropriate corner of the car then release it quickly. If the shock absorber is in good condition the corner of the car should rise then stabilize on the downstroke. If it oscillates more than this, the shock absorber is worn excessively. The strut assembly can be removed as follows.

2 Apply the handbrake, then jack up the front of the car and support on axle stands. Remove the appropriate roadwheel.

3 Unscrew the bolts securing the steering arm bracket to the bottom of the front suspension strut, and withdraw the bracket.

4 If necessary extract the split pins and unscrew the castle nuts securing the track control arm and tie-rod end balljoints to the bracket. Using a balljoint removal tool, separate the track control arms from the bracket.

5 Disconnect the disc pad wear sensor plug and the earth connection and then slip the wires and brake hose out of the clips on the suspension strut.

6 Unbolt the brake caliper from the strut and tie it up out of the way. There is no need to disconnect the hydraulic hose.

7 Unscrew the nuts securing the anti-roll bar links to the strut while holding the balljoint with an open-ended spanner.

8 Working in the engine compartment, unscrew the nuts from the upper mounting and lower the strut from under the car (photo).

9 If the strut is to be stored for some time it should be kept in an upright position, otherwise the shock absorber may be noisy when refitted.

10 To dismantle the strut first compress the coil spring using a coil spring compressor. Do not attempt to use any other method to compress the coil.

11 Remove the cap and unscrew the self-locking nut while counter-holding the piston rod. Remove the washer.

12 Lift off the upper mounting from the piston rod, and recover the washer.

13 Remove the upper spring retainer followed by the coil spring and lower spring retainer.

14 If necessary the shock absorber may be checked by gripping it in a vice at its lower end, then fully extending and contracting the piston rod several times. If there is any loss of damping action, jerkiness or seizure the shock absorber/strut must be renewed. To renew the shock absorber, unscrew the threaded ring, pull out the shock absorber and drain out the oil. Fill the unit with engine oil before reassembling in reverse order and tightening the threaded ring to the specified torque.

15 If a new unit has been stored horizontally it must be positioned

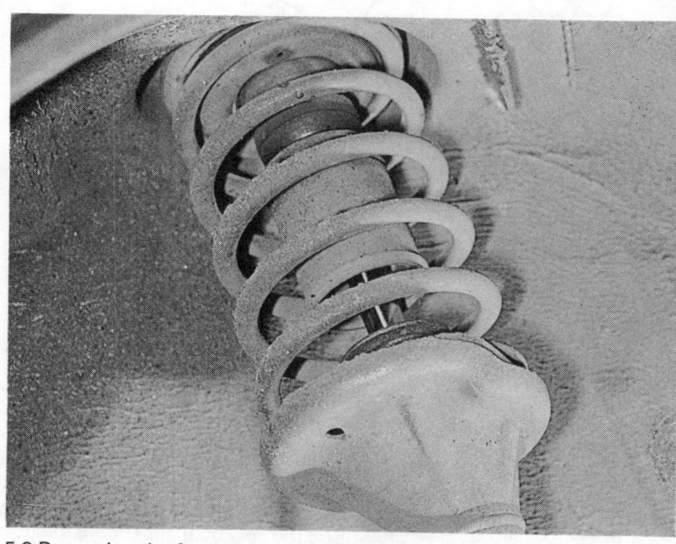
5.8 Removing the front suspension strut from under the car

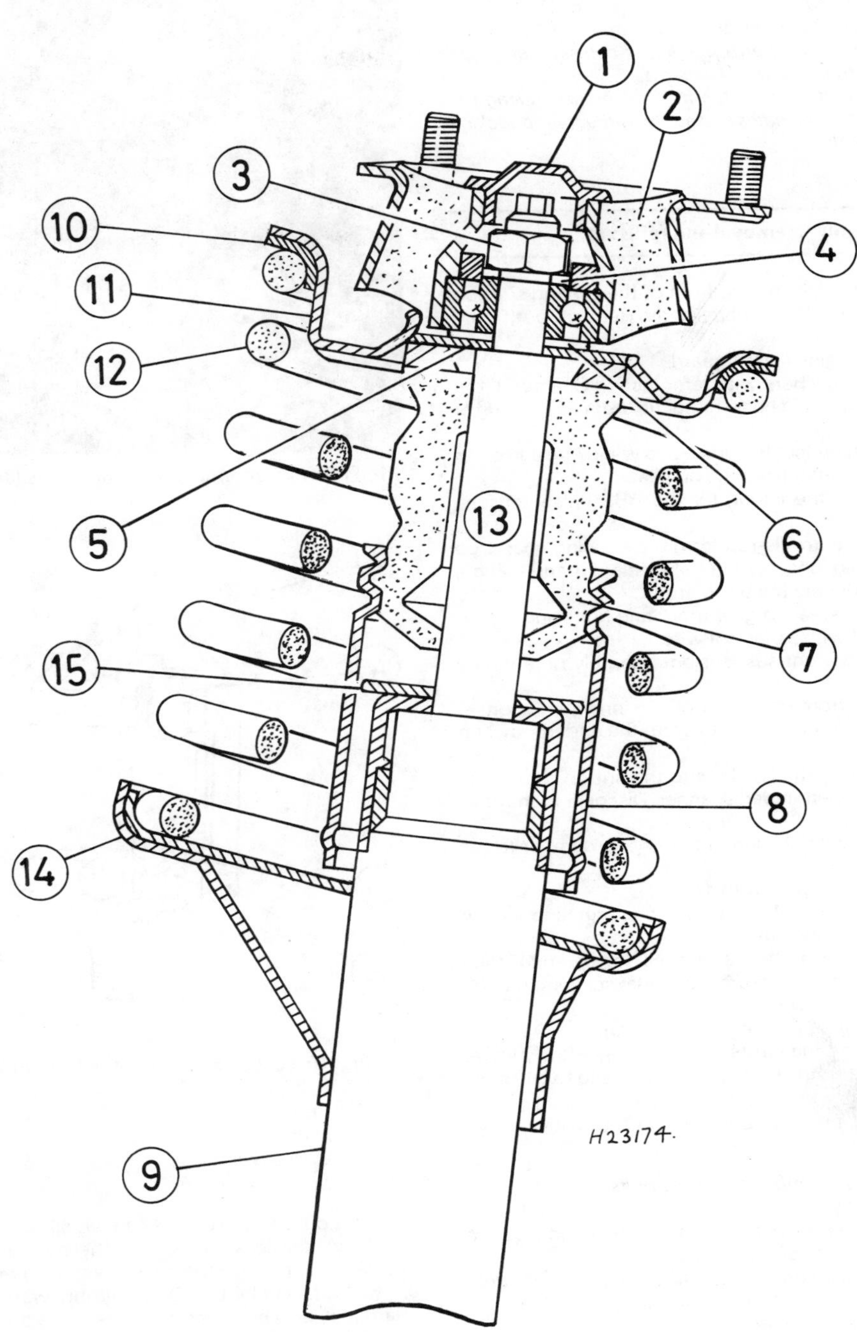

Fig. 10.8 Cross-section view of the front suspension strut (Sec 5)

1 Cap
2 Mounting
3 Self-locking nut
4 Washer
5 Insulator
6 Washer
7 Rubber damper
8 Protective tube
9 Strut
10 Upper spring rubber
11 Spring retainer
12 Coil spring
13 Shock absorber piston rod
14 Lower spring rubber
15 Screw-on ring

vertically, fully extended, for 24 hours before fitting to the car.

16 Examine the spring pads, top mounting and mounting rubbers for condition and renew them if necessary. If possible compare the free length of the coil spring with a new one and renew it if necessary.

17 Reassembly is a reversal of dismantling, but make sure that the spring retainers are correctly located – the upper retainer rubber has a thickness of 9 mm on coil springs with a red colour code. Renew the self-locking nut and tighten to the specified torque.

18 Refitting is a reversal of removal but note the following additional points:

(a) *Renew all self-locking nuts*
(b) *Tighten all nuts and bolts to the specified torque*
(c) *Make sure that the steering arm bracket is correctly engaged with the cut-out on the bottom of the strut*
(d) *Before refitting the bolts to the steering arm bracket, clean the threads of the bolts and the holes and apply a little thread-locking fluid to the bolt threads*

6 Front suspension assembly – removal and refitting

1 Apply the handbrake, then jack up the front of the car and support on axle stands positioned beneath the underbody. Remove both front roadwheels.
2 Unbolt and remove the engine splash guard.
3 Remove both front brake calipers with reference to Chapter 9, but do not disconnect the hydraulic fluid hose. Either tie them to one side or support them on axle stands.
4 On the left-hand side, disconnect the brake pad wear wire and earth wire. Also pull the rubber grommet from the bracket.
5 On both sides disconnect the wiring for the ABS pulse sensors, where fitted.
6 Disconnect the steering centre tie-rod from the steering gear drop arm by extracting the split pin, unscrewing the castle nut and using a balljoint removal tool to disconnect the balljoint.
7 Unscrew and remove the steering gear mounting bolts and tie the steering gear to the bulkhead with a piece of wire.
8 Support the weight of the front suspension assembly on a trolley jack.
9 Unscrew and remove the front track control arm inner pivot bolts.
10 Unscrew the anti-roll bar mounting bolts from the underbody and prise away the clamps.
11 Unscrew the nuts securing the link bars to the anti-roll bar while holding the balljoints with an open-ended spanner. Disconnect the links and withdraw the anti-roll bar.
12 Unscrew and remove the bolt securing the engine damper to the crossmember.
13 Support the weight of the engine with a hoist.
14 Unscrew the lower nuts from the engine mountings and loosen only the upper right-hand mounting nut.
15 Support the front suspension struts at their lower ends, then working in the engine compartment, unscrew the nuts securing the top mountings to the body lower sections.
16 Unscrew the crossmember mounting bolts (photo).
17 With assistants supporting the struts on both sides, slowly lower the assembly to the ground. The struts must not be allowed to fall to the ground otherwise the balljoints would be damaged.
18 Refitting is a reversal of removal, but observe the following additional points:

(a) *Fit washers to the crossmember mounting bolts*
(b) *Renew all self-locking nuts*
(c) *Make sure that the location pegs on the engine mountings are correctly engaged in the bracket cut-outs*
(d) *Delay tightening the track control arm and anti-roll bar bolts until the weight of the car is on the front suspension*
(e) *Fit new split pins to the tie-rod end nuts*
(f) *Tighten all nuts and bolts to the specified torque wrench settings*
(g) *On completion have the front axle and steering alignment checked.*

7 Front hub bearings – renewal

1 Apply the handbrake then jack up the front of the car and support on axle stands. Remove the roadwheel.
2 Remove the brake caliper and bracket with reference to Chapter 9, but do not disconnect the hydraulic hose. Tie the caliper to one side or support it on axle stands.
3 Unscrew the socket-headed screw and withdraw the brake disc from the hub.

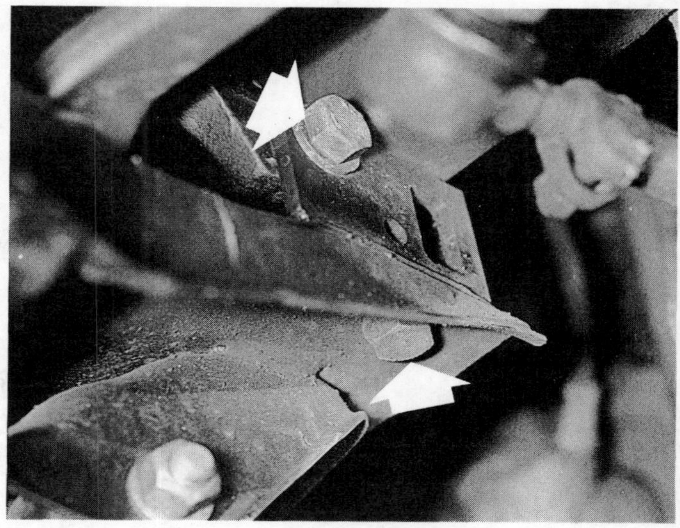

6.16 Front crossmember mounting bolts (arrowed)

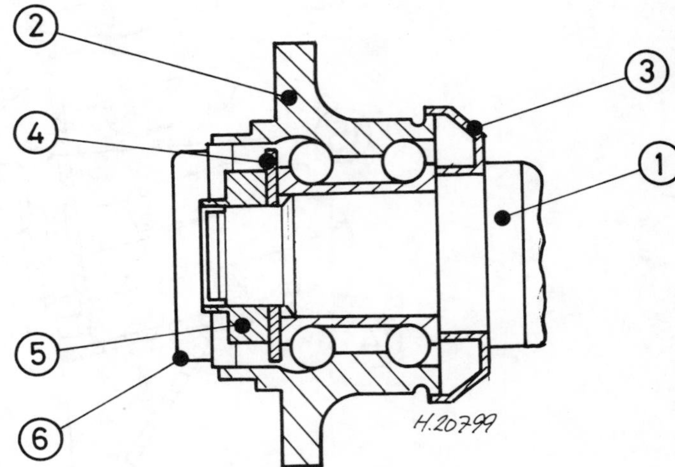

Fig. 10.9 Cross-section of the front hub and bearings (Sec 7)

1 *Stub axle*
2 *Hub*
3 *Dust cover*
4 *Washer*
5 *Hub nut*
6 *Hub grease cap*

4 Prise out the hub grease cap with a screwdriver (photos).
5 Punch the locking edge of the hub nut out of the groove, then unscrew and remove the nut (photo). Also remove the washer.
6 Pull off the hub/bearing assembly with a suitable puller. The dust guard may also be pulled off at the same time if necessary.
7 Remove the dust guard from the stub axle if not already removed. If the inner bearing track has remained on the stub axle it will be necessary to remove this first.
8 Check the hub nut and dust guard for condition and renew if necessary.
9 The hub itself incorporates the outer track of the bearings, so if the bearings are worn it is only possible to renew the complete hub as an assembly.
10 Locate the dust guard on the stub axle shoulder.
11 Position the hub/bearing assembly on the stub axle, then using a metal tube on the inner track only, drive the assembly onto the stub axle. The dust guard will be forced on the shoulder at the same time.
12 Fit the washer and nut, then tighten the nut to the specified torque. Lock the nut by staking it into the stub axle groove.
13 Tap the grease cap into the hub.
14 Refit the brake disc and tighten the socket-headed screw.

7.4A Prise off ...

7.4B ... and remove the front hub grease cap

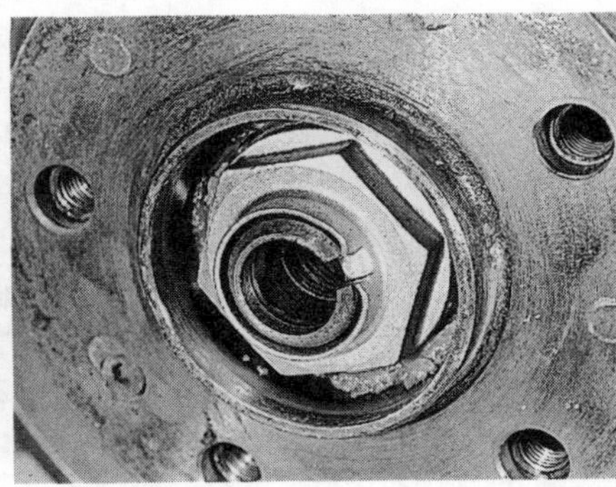
7.5 Front hub nut

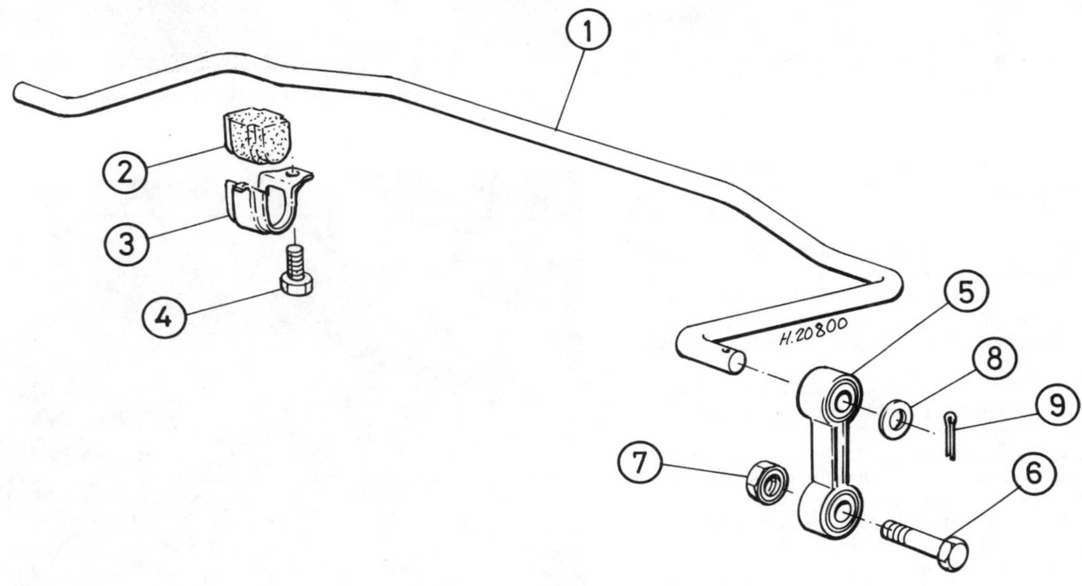

Fig. 10.10 Rear anti-roll bar components (Sec 8)

1 Anti-roll bar
2 Rubber mounting
3 Clamp
4 Bolt
5 Link
6 Bolt
7 Self-locking nut
8 Washers
9 Split pin

15 Refit the brake caliper with reference to Chapter 9.
16 Refit the roadwheel and lower the car to the ground.

8 Rear anti-roll bar – removal and refitting

1 Chock the front wheels, then jack up the rear of the car and support on axle stands. Remove both rear roadwheels.
2 Unscrew the bolts and disconnect the anti-roll bar links from the semi-trailing arms on both sides.
3 Unscrew the bolts, release the mounting clamps and withdraw the anti-roll bar from the underbody (photo).
4 Prise off the mounting rubbers.
5 Remove the links from the ends of the anti-roll bar by extracting the split pins and removing the washers.
6 Examine the anti-roll bar, links and mounting rubbers for damage and deterioration and renew them if necessary. Check that the bonded rubbers in the links are not perished.
7 Refitting is a reversal of removal, but delay fully tightening the mounting bolts to the specified torque until the weight of the car is on the rear suspension. Fit new split pins to secure the links.

8.3 Rear anti-roll bar mounting bolt and clamp

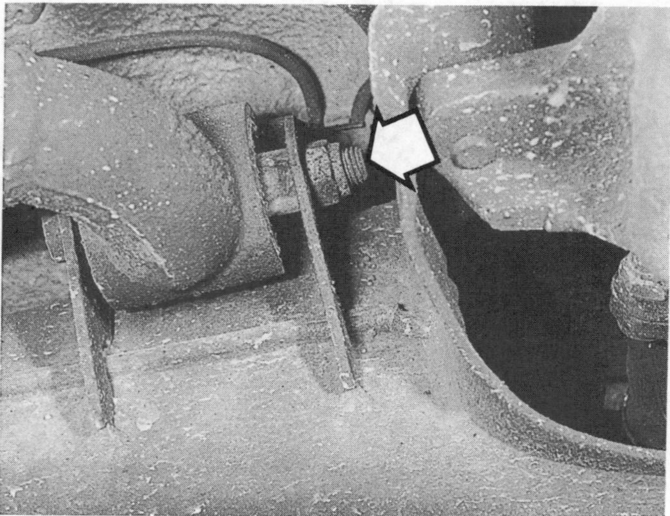

9.7A Rear semi-trailing arm pivot bolt (arrowed)

9.7B Pitman arm (arrowed) connecting the semi-trailing arm and crossmember

9 Rear semi-trailing arm – removal and refitting

1 Chock the front wheels, then jack up the rear of the car and support on axle stands. Remove the appropriate roadwheel.
2 Remove the driveshaft completely as described in Chapter 7, or alternatively, disconnect it from the hub flange and tie it to one side.
3 Disconnect the handbrake cable from the semi-trailing arm with reference to Chapter 9.
4 Fit a brake hose clamp on the flexible hose leading to the semi-trailing arm. Alternatively, syphon the brake fluid from the brake fluid reservoir in the engine compartment.
5 Disconnect the flexible hose from the rigid brake line by unscrewing the rigid line union nut then unscrewing the nut from the flexible hose.
6 Support the semi-trailing arm on a trolley jack.
7 Unscrew and remove the pivot bolts noting their fitted position. Also where applicable unscrew the two bolts securing the small Pitman arm to the semi-trailing arm and crossmember (photos).
8 Unscrew and remove the bolt securing the bottom of the strut to the arm, then withdraw the arm from the car.
9 If necessary, remove the rear hub with reference to Section 12.
10 The flexible bushes may be renewed by using a press or using a bolt, nut, washer and distance piece. Coat the new bushes with soapy water before fitting them. Note that the rear wheel alignment may be corrected by fitting special eccentric bushes which are calibrated so that they can be aligned with a horizontal line drawn on the semi-trailing arm. Normally adjustment can be made by fitting the outer bushes only, however if necessary the inner bushes may be fitted as well to obtain the correct setting. Do not attempt to correct misalignment caused by accident damage by using these bushes.
11 Refitting is a reversal of removal, but note the following additional points:

(a) When fitting the pivot bolts insert the inner one first
(b) Delay fully tightening the pivot bolts and strut lower mounting bolt until the weight of the car is on the rear suspension
(c) Tighten all nuts and bolts to the specified torque
(d) Bleed the brake hydraulic system as described in Chapter 9
(e) Adjust the handbrake as described in Chapter 9

10 Rear suspension strut – checking, removal, overhaul and refitting

Warning: *Before attempting to dismantle the rear suspension strut, a suitable tool to hold the coil spring in compression must be obtained. Adjustable coil spring compressors are readily available and are recommended for this operation. Any attempt to dismantle the strut without such a tool is likely to result in damage or personal injury.*

10.4 Rear suspension strut lower mounting bolt

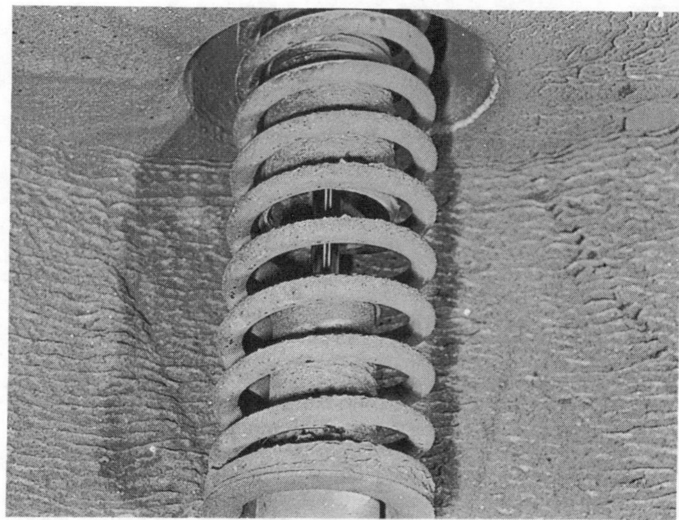

10.5 Removing the rear suspension strut from under the car

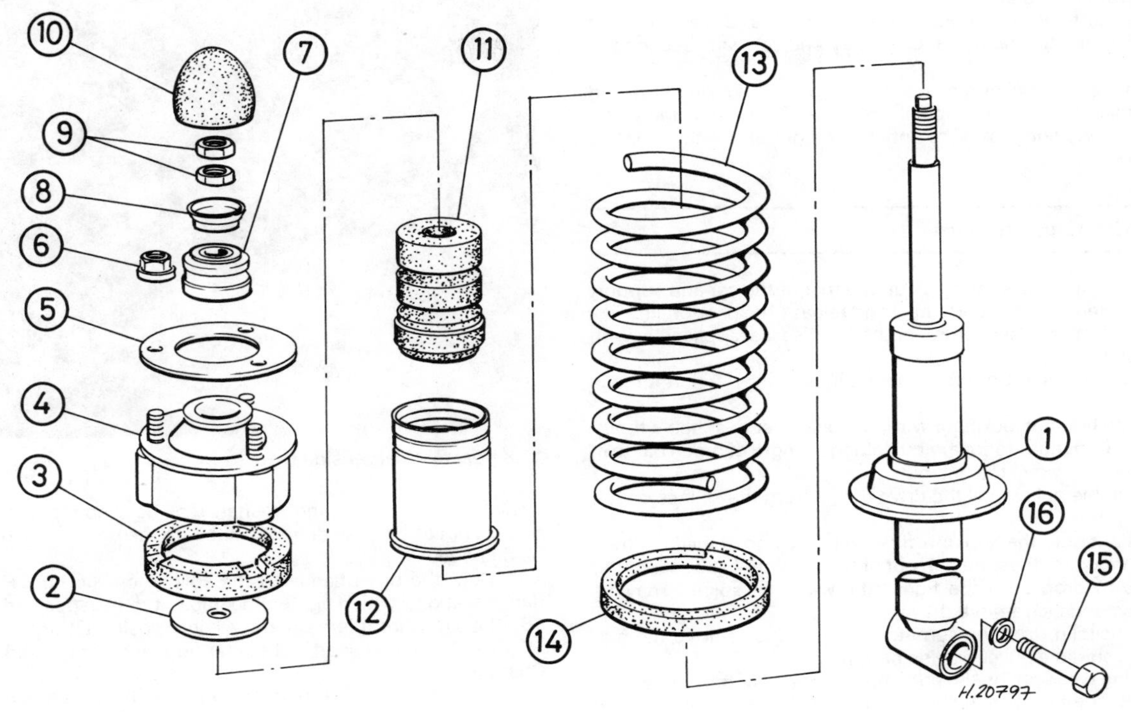

Fig. 10.11 Exploded view of the rear suspension strut (Sec 10)

1 Strut and shock absorber
2 Supporting cup
3 Upper spring pad
4 Upper mounting
5 Gasket
6 Mounting nut
7 Rubber mounting
8 Cup
9 Locking nuts
10 Cap
11 Bump rubber
12 Protection tube
13 Coil spring
14 Lower spring pad
15 Mounting bolt
16 Washer

1 To check the rear shock absorber before removing it, press down on the appropriate corner of the car then release it quickly. If the shock absorber is in good condition the corner of the car should rise then stabilize on the downstroke. If it oscillates more than this the shock absorber is worn excessively.
2 Chock the front wheels, then jack up the rear of the car and support on axle stands. Remove the appropriate roadwheel.
3 Support the semi-trailing arm on a trolley jack.
4 Unscrew and remove the bolt securing the bottom of the strut to the semi-trailing arm (photo).
5 Working inside the boot compartment, remove the trim as necessary in order to gain access to the rear suspension strut upper mounting nuts. Unscrew the nuts and lower the strut downwards from underneath the car (photo). Recover the gasket.
6 If the strut is to be stored for some time it should be kept in an upright position, otherwise the shock absorber may be noisy when refitted.
7 To dismantle the strut first pull off the cap.
8 Compress the coil spring using a coil spring compressor. Do not attempt to use any other method to compress the coil.
9 Unscrew the locknuts from the top of the shock absorber piston rod and lift off the top mounting, rubber, and spring upper pad.
10 Remove the coil spring and release the compressor carefully.
11 Pull the rubber buffer and tube from the piston rod.
12 Remove the lower coil spring pad.
13 If necessary the shock absorber may be checked by gripping it in a vice at its lower end, then fully extending and contracting the piston rod several times. If there is any loss of damping action, jerkiness or seizure the shock absorber/strut must be renewed.
14 If a new unit has been stored horizontally it must be positioned vertically, fully extended, for 24 hours before fitting to the car.
15 Examine the spring pads, top mounting and mounting rubbers for condition and renew them if necessary. If possible compare the free length of the coil spring with a new one and renew it if necessary.
16 Refitting is a reversal of removal, but renew the top mounting gasket and mounting nuts, and tighten all nuts and bolts to the specified torque.

11 Rear axle carrier assembly – removal and refitting

1 Chock the front wheels, then jack up the rear of the car and support on axle stands.
2 Remove the exhaust system as described in Chapter 3.
3 Remove the propeller shaft complete as described in Chapter 7.
4 Remove the handbrake lever as described in Chapter 9.
5 Syphon the brake fluid from the reservoir on the master cylinder in order to reduce the amount of fluid lost in the subsequent procedure.
6 Unscrew the union nuts from the brake lines on both sides of the carrier.
7 Support the rear axle carrier assembly on a trolley jack.
8 Unbolt the side struts from the underbody on both sides, then unscrew the nuts securing the struts to the carrier and remove the struts (photo).
9 Disconnect the wires from the speed pulse transmitter on the final drive unit.
10 Unscrew the mounting bolt located on the rear of the final drive unit.

11 Unscrew and remove the bolts securing the bottom of the struts to the semi-trailing arms.
12 Lower the rear axle carrier assembly and disconnect the handbrake cables from the guide tubes.
13 Remove the final drive unit, semi-trailing arms, driveshafts and hubs with reference to Chapter 8, Chapter 7 and relevant Sections of this Chapter.
14 Refitting is a reversal of removal, but renew self-locking nuts and tighten all nuts and bolts to the specified torque. Delay fully tightening the strut-to-semi-trailing arm bolts until the weight of the car is on the rear suspension.

12 Rear hub bearings – renewal

1 Chock the front wheels then jack up the rear of the car and support on axle stands. Remove the roadwheel and release the handbrake.
2 Remove the rear brake drum or brake disc as applicable with reference to Chapter 9.
3 Detach the driveshaft from the rear hub inner flange with reference to Chapter 7.
4 Prise out the hub nut lockplate with a screwdriver or suitable tool.
5 Hold the drive flange stationary by bolting a length of metal bar to it, then unscrew and remove the hub nut.
6 Using a suitable puller, pull the drive flange from the splines on the hub.
7 Screw the nut onto the hub until flush with the end of the hub, then use a block of wood to drive the hub out of the bearing. Take care not to allow the hub to drop onto the floor otherwise the splines may be damaged. Unscrew and remove the nut.
8 Extract the circlip from the semi-trailing arm and remove the hub bearing using a suitable puller or slide hammer.
9 If the bearing was tight on the hub, the bearing inner track may have been pulled off together with the hub. If this was the case, pull the inner track off the hub using a puller.
10 Clean the components and obtain a new lockplate.
11 Drive the new bearing into the semi-trailing arm using a metal tube on the inner track only.
12 Fit the circlip to the groove in the arm.
13 Fit the hub into the bearing. To do this BMW technicians use the special pullers 231300, 334070 and 334020 which support the inner track while the hub is drawn into it. If these tools or similar tools are not available, a metal tube and washers may be used together with the hub nut. Do not attempt to drive the hub into the bearing as the bearing will be damaged.
14 Refit the drive flange to the splines on the hub. Hold the drive flange stationary then tighten the hub nut to the specified torque.
15 Fit a new lockplate and drive it into position using a metal tube.
16 Refit the driveshaft to the rear hub inner flange with reference to Chapter 7.
17 Refit the brake drum or disc and roadwheel, and lower the car to the ground.

11.8 Rear axle carrier side strut

13 Steering wheel – removal and refitting

1 Set the steering in the straight-ahead position.
2 Prise the motif from the centre of the steering wheel (photo).
3 Unscrew the retaining nut and remove the washer (photos).

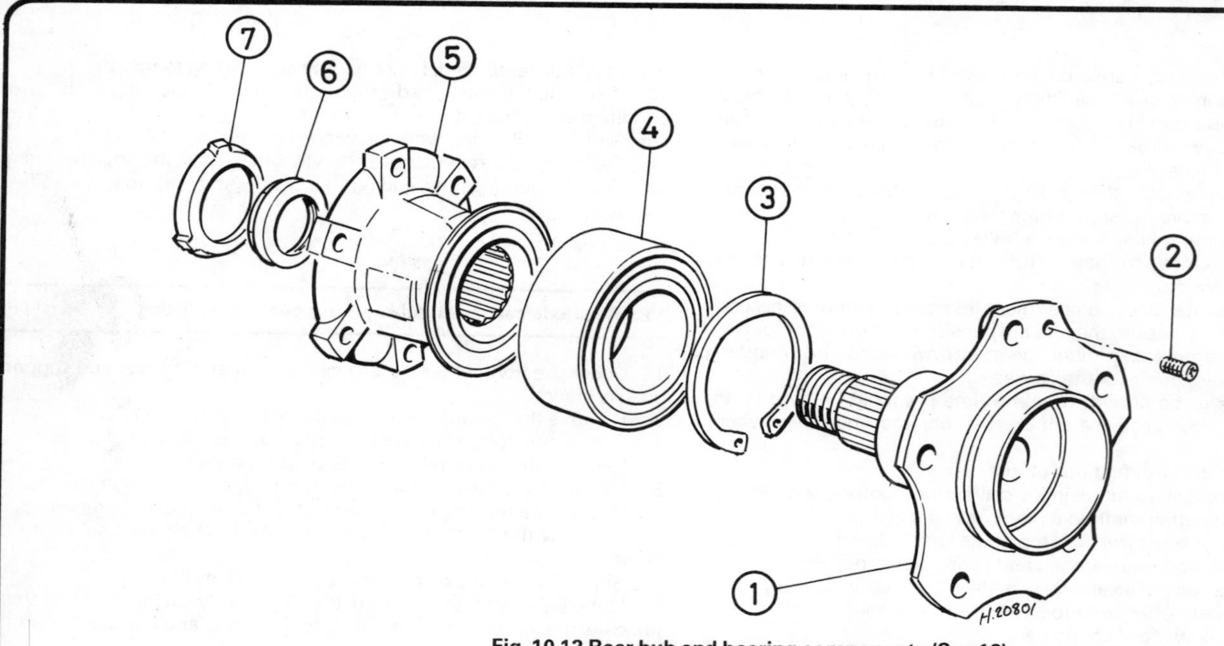

Fig. 10.12 Rear hub and bearing components (Sec 12)

1 Hub
2 Screw (for drum or disc)
3 Circlip
4 Ball-bearing
5 Drive flange
6 Hub nut
7 Lockplate

13.2 Prise out the motif ...

13.3A ... then unscrew ...

13.3B ... and remove the steering wheel retaining nut and washer

14.5 Steering inner column-to-lower coupling pinch-bolt (arrowed)

14.6A Steering column upper mounting bolt (arrowed)

14.6B Steering column lower mounting bolt

4 Mark the steering wheel in relation to the spindle.
5 Remove the steering wheel from the spindle by rocking it from side to side until it is released from the splines. Do not exert excessive force otherwise the safety steering column may be damaged. If difficulty is experienced, a puller must be obtained.
6 If necessary the horn buttons may be prised from the steering wheel with a screwdriver.
7 Refitting is a reversal of removal, but make sure that the curved surfaces of the horn spring contacts are facing upwards before pressing the buttons into position. Check that the turn signal cancelling cams are aligned correctly before refitting the steering wheel, and tighten the retaining nut to the specified torque.

14 Steering column – removal and refitting

1 Disconnect the battery negative lead.
2 Remove the steering wheel as described in the previous Section.
3 Remove the lower facia panel and the steering column lower shroud.
4 Disconnect the multiplugs for the column switches.
5 Unscrew and remove the pinch-bolt securing the inner column to the lower coupling and pull off the coupling (photo).
6 Unscrew the mounting nuts and bolts, and withdraw the steering column complete from inside the car (photos).
7 Refitting is a reversal of removal, but tighten all nuts and bolts to the specified torque. All self-locking nuts should be renewed. When refitting the upper mounting bolt, make sure that it is in the locking groove.

15 Steering column – overhaul

1 Unscrew the four cross-head screws and remove the combination switches.
2 Remove the collar.
3 Remove the flasher relay together with its holder.
4 Disconnect the horn contact wires.
5 Unscrew the column-to-bracket bolt.
6 Drill out or chisel off the shear bolts securing the outer column to the upper bracket.
7 Remove the steering lock plate.
8 Remove the screws and press the casing upper section away from the outer column.
9 Unscrew the screw, then with the ignition key in the 'start' position pull out the steering lock complete.
10 Remove the ignition switch.
11 Unscrew the bolts and withdraw the outer column from the upper casing section.
12 Extract the circlip from the top of the inner column and remove the washer, spring and ring.
13 Pull the inner column and lower bearing out of the outer column.
14 From the inner column, remove the circlip, collar ring, ring and bearing.
15 Using a screwdriver, remove the upper bearing from the outer column.
16 Loosen the clamp bolt.
17 On adjustable steering models, bend open the lockplates and unscrew the bolts from the lower mounting. Note that the bottom bolt has a left-hand thread.
18 Clean all the components and examine them for wear and damage.
19 On adjustable steering models, reassemble the lower mounting as follows. With the lever in the centre of the clamp in the 'Off' position, screw in the lower bolt with the lockplate and tighten to the specified torque.
20 Screw in the bolt with the left-hand thread and tighten.
21 Refit and tighten the upper bolt, then fit the lockplate and bend it over to lock.
22 Refit the clamp to the end of the outer column making sure that the distance to the end of the tube is between 42 and 45 mm. Delay tightening the clamp bolt until after screwing the outer column onto the upper section.
23 Fit the upper bearing to the outer column using a metal tube on the inner track.
24 Insert the inner column into the outer column and through the upper bearing.

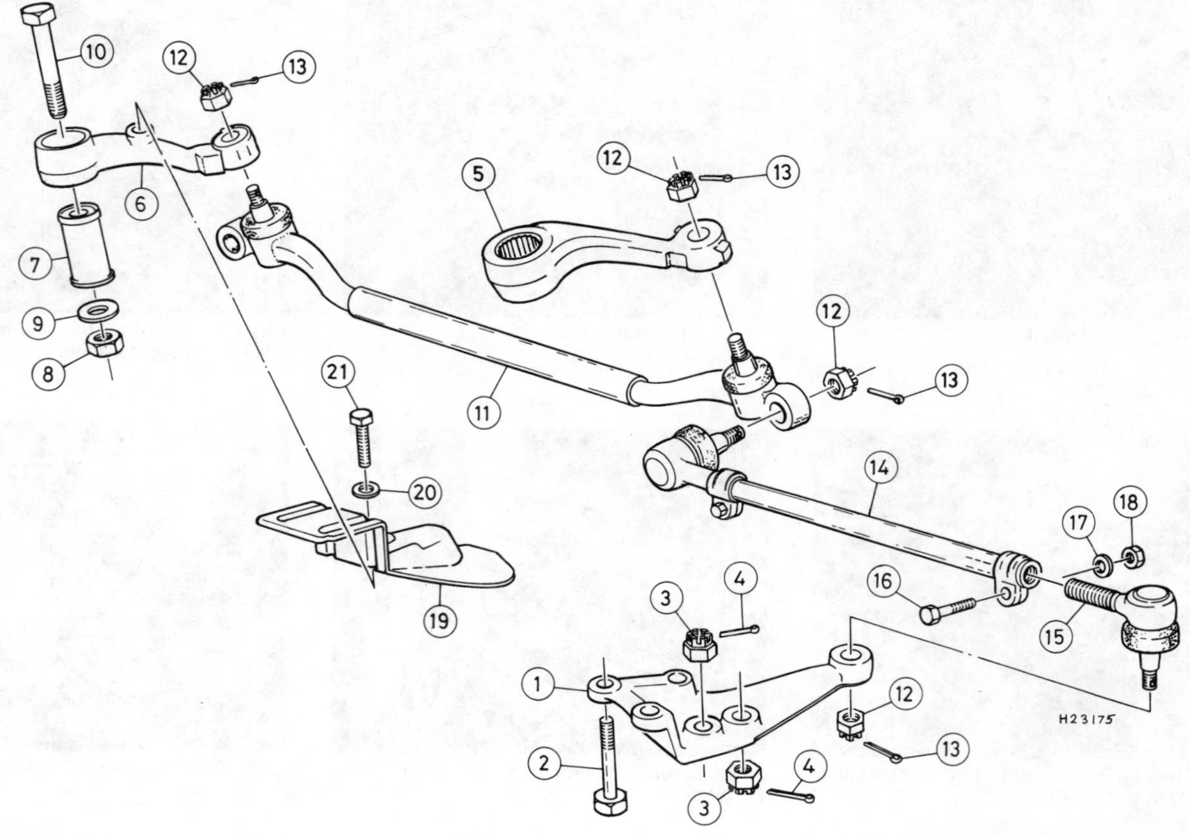

Fig. 10.13 Steering tie-rod components (Secs 16, 17, 18 and 19)

1 Steering arm bracket
2 Bolt
3 Self-locking nut
4 Split pin
5 Steering drop arm (Pitman arm)
6 Idler arm
7 Bush
8 Self-locking nut
9 Washer
10 Bolt
11 Centre tie-rod
12 Nut
13 Split pin
14 Steering tie-rod
15 Tie-rod end
16 Pinch-bolt
17 Washer
18 Nut
19 Heat resistant plate (520i only)
20 Washer (520i only)
21 Bolt (520i only)

25 Refit the lower bearing using a metal tube, then refit the ring, collar ring, and circlip.
26 Refit the ring, spring, and washer to the top of the inner column then refit the circlip to its groove. Make sure that the stem of the ring is facing the bearing.
27 Refit the outer column to the upper casing section and tighten the bolts.
28 Refit the ignition switch.
29 Refit the steering lock.
30 Refit the casing upper section to the outer column. Tighten the screws and lock them by painting with clear lacquer.
31 Refit the steering lock plate.
32 Fit the new shear bolts securing the outer column to the upper bracket but do not tighten them at this stage.
33 Refit the bolt and reconnect the horn contact wires.
34 Refit the flasher relay together with its holder.
35 Refit the collar making sure that it locks onto the circlip.
36 Refit the combination switch and tighten the cross-head screws.
37 Tighten the shear bolts until their heads shear off.

16 Tie-rod end – renewal

1 Apply the handbrake then jack up the front of the car and support on axle stands. Remove the appropriate roadwheel.
2 Loosen the clamp bolt on the inner or outer end of the tie-rod as applicable.
3 Extract the split pin (where applicable) and unscrew the nut from the tie-rod end (photos).
4 Using a balljoint removal tool, separate the tie-rod end from the steering arm or centre tie-rod.
5 Measure the length of the exposed threads on the tie-rod end and note them. Unscrew the tie-rod end, noting the number of turns necessary to remove it. Note that the tie-rod ends on each end of a tie-rod have opposite threads.
6 Screw on the new tie-rod end until the same length of threads is exposed as noted on the old unit.
7 Fit the tie-rod end ball-stud to the steering arm or centre tie-rod, screw on the nut and tighten to the specified torque. Align the nut serrations with the hole in the ball-stud and fit a new split pin. Bend the split pin to secure.
8 Tighten the clamp bolt on the end of the tie-rod while holding the rod in its central position on the ball-stud.
9 Refit the roadwheel and lower the car to the ground.
10 Check the front wheel alignment as described in Section 22.

17 Tie-rod arm – removal and refitting

1 Apply the handbrake then jack up the front of the car and support on axle stands. Remove the appropriate roadwheel.
2 Extract the split pins and unscrew the nuts from the tie-rod ends.
3 Using a balljoint removal tool, separate the tie-rod ends from the steering arm and centre tie-rod.

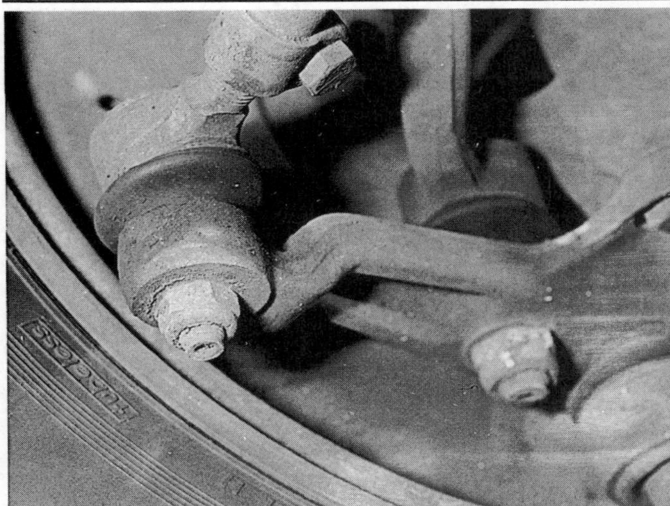
16.3A Steering tie-rod end on the steering bracket

16.3B Left-hand tie-rod end connection to the centre tie-rod and idler arm

4 Refitting is a reversal of removal, but tighten the nuts to the specified torque, fit new split pins, and on completion check the front wheel alignment as described in Section 22.

18 Centre tie-rod – removal and refitting

1 Apply the handbrake then jack up the front of the car and support on axle stands.
2 Extract the split pins and unscrew the nuts from the four balljoints securing the centre tie-rod to the tie-rod arms, steering gear drop arm and idler arm.
3 Using a balljoint removal tool, separate the balljoints then withdraw the centre tie-rod.
4 Check the centre tie-rod for damage and for wear of the balljoints. The distance between the balljoint stud centres should be 500 ± 1 mm (Fig. 10.14).
5 Refitting is a reversal of removal, but tighten the nuts to the specified torque and fit new split pins. On completion check the front wheel alignment as described in Section 22.

19 Idler arm – removal, overhaul and refitting

1 Apply the handbrake then jack up the front of the car and support on axle stands.
2 Extract the split pin and unscrew the nut securing the centre tie-rod to the idler arm.
3 Using a balljoint removal tool, separate the centre tie-rod balljoint from the idler arm.

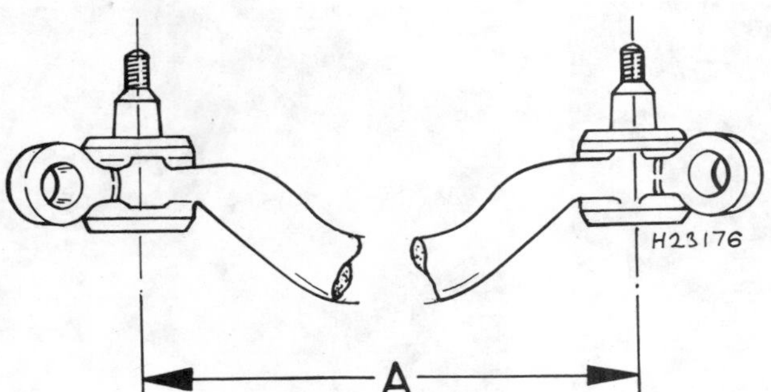

Fig. 10.14 Centre tie-rod checking dimension (Sec 18)

A = 500 ± 1 mm

4 Unscrew the through-bolt and remove the idler arm.
5 If necessary the rubber bush may be renewed by pressing it out with a bench press or alternatively using a metal tube, spacers and a long bolt as a removal tool.
6 Clean the components and examine them for damage.
7 Press the new bush fully into the arm.
8 Refitting is a reversal of removal, but tighten all nuts and bolts to the specified torque and fit a new split pin to the balljoint nut.

20 Power steering gear – removal and refitting

1 Apply the handbrake then jack up the front of the car and support on axle stands.
2 Unscrew the filler cap from the power steering fluid reservoir and syphon out the fluid.
3 Position a container beneath the steering gear then disconnect the hoses from the reservoir.
4 Extract the split pin from the balljoint connecting the centre tie-rod to the steering gear drop arm (photo). Unscrew the nut and use a balljoint removal tool to separate the tie-rod from the drop arm.
5 Unscrew and remove the pinch-bolts from the steering shaft lower coupling and push the coupling from the steering gear (photo). Mark the

20.4 Drop arm located on the steering gear (arrowed)

20.5 Steering shaft lower coupling

20.6 Hydraulic line connections to the power steering gear

20.8 Hydraulic line mounting on the crossmember

coupling and steering gear shaft in relation to each other to ensure correct reassembly.

6 Unscrew the union nuts and disconnect the hydraulic lines from the steering gear (photo). Recover the sealing washers. Cover the ends of the hydraulic lines with masking tape to prevent dust and dirt entering them.

7 Unscrew the mounting bolts noting the location of the washers, and withdraw the steering gear from below.

8 If necessary the hydraulic fluid lines may be unbolted from the crossmember (photo).

9 Refitting is a reversal of removal, but note the following additional points:

- (a) *Renew all self-locking nuts*
- (b) *Renew the sealing washers on the hydraulic lines*
- (c) *Make sure that the pinch-bolts in the coupling are correctly located in the shaft grooves*
- (d) *Fit a new split pin to the centre tie-rod balljoint*
- (e) *Fill the hydraulic fluid reservoir with new fluid and bleed as follows. First top up the reservoir to the 'Max' mark on the dipstick. Start the engine and turn the steering wheel two times to the left and right stops. Stop the engine and recheck the fluid level, adding fluid if necessary to bring the level to the 'Max' mark. Refit the reservoir filler cap.*

21 Power steering pump – removal and refitting

1 Unscrew the filler cap from the power steering fluid reservoir and syphon out the fluid (photo).

2 Unscrew the two union nuts and disconnect the hydraulic lines from the pump (photo).

3 Release the drivebelt tension by loosening the tensioner bolt and turning the adjustment gear. Remove the drivebelt (photo).

4 Unscrew and remove the adjustment bolt, then unbolt the adjustment link from the pump (photos).

5 Unscrew and remove the two pivot bolts and withdraw the pump from the engine (photo).

6 If the pump is unserviceable it should be overhauled by a specialist. It is not recommended that the home mechanic attempt to dismantle the pump.

7 Refitting is a reversal of removal, but tighten all nuts and bolts to the specified torque and adjust the drivebelt tension as described in Section 2. Bleed the hydraulic system as described in Section 20.

22 Wheel alignment – checking and adjustment

1 Accurate wheel alignment is essential for good steering and to prevent excessive tyre wear. Before checking it, make sure that the car is only loaded to kerbside weight and that the tyre pressures are correct.

2 Camber and castor angles and rear wheel alignment are best checked by a garage using specialized equipment. The castor angle and rear wheel alignment are not adjustable but the camber angle is.

3 The front wheel toe-in setting may be checked as follows. Place the car on level ground with the wheels in the straight-ahead position, then roll the car backwards 4 metres (13 feet) and forwards again.

4 Using an accurate wheel alignment gauge, check that the front wheels are aligned as given in the Specifications.

5 If adjustment is necessary, loosen the clamp bolts and turn the tie-rods by equal amounts. Both tie-rods must be equal in length. Always turn both tie-rods in the same direction.

6 After making an adjustment, centralize the balljoints and tighten the clamp bolts.

23 Wheels and tyres – general care and maintenance

Wheels and tyres should give no real problems in use provided that a close eye is kept on them with regard to excessive wear or damage. To this end, the following points should be noted.

21.1 Power steering fluid reservoir

21.2 Hydraulic line connections to the power steering pump

21.3 Removing the power steering pump drivebelt

21.4A Remove the adjustment bolt ...

21.4B ... and unbolt the adjustment link from the power steering pump

21.5 Power steering pump pivot bolts (arrowed)

Ensure that tyre pressures are checked regularly and maintained correctly. Checking should be carried out with the tyres cold and not immediately after the vehicle has been in use. If the pressures are checked with the tyres hot, an apparently high reading will be obtained owing to heat expansion. Under no circumstances should an attempt be made to reduce the pressures to the quoted cold reading in this instance, or effective underinflation will result.

Underinflation will cause overheating of the tyre owing to excessive flexing of the casing, and the thread will not sit correctly on the road surface. This will cause a consequent loss of adhesion and excessive wear, not to mention the danger of sudden tyre failure due to heat build-up.

Overinflation will cause rapid wear of the centre part of the tyre tread coupled with reduced adhesion, harsher ride, and the danger of shock damage occurring in the tyre casing.

Regularly check the tyres for damage in the form of cuts or bulges, especially in the sidewalls. Remove any nails or stones embedded in the tread before they penetrate the tyre to cause deflation. If removal of a nail *does* reveal that the tyre has been punctured, refit the nail so that its point of penetration is marked. Then immediately change the wheel and have the tyre repaired by a tyre dealer. **Do not** drive on a tyre in such a condition. In many cases a punctured can be simply repaired by the use of an inner tube of the correct size and type. If in any doubt as to the possible consequences of any damage found, consult your local tyre dealer for advice.

Periodically remove the wheels and clean any dirt or mud from the inside and outside surfaces. Examine the wheel rims for signs of rusting, corrosion or other damage. Light alloy wheels are easily damaged by 'kerbing' whilst parking, and similarly steel wheels may become dented or buckled. Renewal of the wheel is very often the only course of remedial action possible.

The balance of each wheel and tyre assembly should be maintained to avoid excessive wear, not only to the tyres but also to the steering and suspension components. Wheel imbalance is normally signified by vibration through the vehicle's bodyshell, although in many cases it is particularly noticeable through the steering wheel. Conversely, it should be noted that wear or damage in suspension or steering components may cause excessive tyre wear. Out-of-round or out-of-true tyres, damaged wheels and wheel bearing wear/maladjustment also fall into this category. Balancing will not usually cure vibration caused by such wear.

Wheel balancing may be carried out with the wheel either on or off the vehicle. If balanced on the vehicle, ensure that the wheel-to-hub relationship is marked in some way prior to subsequent wheel removal so that it may be refitted in its original position.

General tyre wear is influenced to a large degree by driving style – harsh braking and acceleration or fast cornering will all produce more rapid tyre wear. Interchanging of tyres may result in more even wear, but this should only be carried out where there is no mix of tyre types on the vehicle. However, it is worth bearing in mind that if this is completely effective, the added expense of replacing a complete set of tyres simultaneously is incurred, which may prove financially restrictive for many owners.

Front tyres may wear unevenly as a result of wheel misalignment. The front wheels should always be correctly aligned according to the settings specified by the vehicle manufacturer.

Legal restrictions apply to the mixing of tyre types on a vehicle. Basically this means that a vehicle must not have tyres of differing construction on the same axle. Although it is not recommended to mix tyre types between front axle and rear axle, the only legally permissible combination is crossply at the front and radial at the rear. When mixing radial ply tyres, textile braced radials must always go on the front axle, with steel braced radials at the rear. An obvious disadvantage of such mixing is the necessity to carry two spare tyres to avoid contravening the law in the event of a puncture.

In the UK, the Motor Vehicles Construction and Use Regulations apply to many aspects of tyre fitting and usage. It is suggested that a copy of these regulations is obtained from your local police if in doubt as to the current legal requirements with regard to tyre condition, minimum tread depth, etc.

24 Fault diagnosis – suspension and steering

Symptom	Reason(s)
Excessive play in steering	Worn tie-rod balljoints Worn track control arm balljoints Worn steering gear
Wanders or pulls to one side	Incorrect wheel alignment Worn tie-rod balljoints Worn track control arm balljoints Uneven tyre pressures Faulty shock absorbers
Heavy or stiff steering	Seized tie-rod or suspension balljoint Incorrect wheel alignment Low tyre pressures Faulty power steering system

Symptom	Reason(s)
Wheel wobble and vibration	Roadwheels out of balance or damaged Faulty shock absorbers Worn hub bearings Worn tie-rod or suspension balljoint
Excessive tyre wear	Incorrect wheel alignment Faulty shock absorbers Incorrect tyre pressures Roadwheels out of balance

Chapter 11 Bodywork and fittings

Contents

Specifications

Torque wrench settings

	Nm	lbf ft
Front bumper bracket to engine carrier	43	31
Front bumper to side panel	6 to 9	4.5 to 6.5
Rear bumper bracket to body	22 to 25	16 to 18
Rear bumper to side panel	6 to 9	4.5 to 6.5
Seat belt mounting bolts	43 to 48	31 to 35
Seat belt height control mounting screw	24	17

1 General description

The body is of all-steel unitary construction with an integrated rollbar and energy-absorbing front and rear zones. The entire body shell is protected against corrosion by an electrocataphoretic dip, and is given a six-year warranty against perforation by rust. Computer technology is used extensively in the design and construction of the body.

2 Routine maintenance

Carry out the following at the intervals given in *Routine maintenance* at the front of this manual.

Check seat belts

1 Thoroughly examine the full length of all the seat belts for signs of fraying and damage, and for security of the mountings. Check that the seat belts function correctly and that they lock when pulled sharply.

Lubricate locks and sunroof

2 Check that all door locks function correctly and that the mounting screws are secure. Tighten if necessary and lubricate the locks with a little oil or grease.

3 Similarly check and lubricate the bonnet and boot lid locks.

4 Lightly grease the sunroof guide rails.

Check the underbody

5 Raise the front and rear of the car and check the underbody for damage and corrosion. Also check the condition of the underseal.

Check the air conditioning compressor drivebelt condition and tension

6 The procedure is similar to that for the water pump/alternator drivebelt described in Chapter 2 Section 2.

3 Maintenance – bodywork and underframe

The general condition of a vehicle's bodywork is the one thing that significantly affects its value. Maintenance is easy but needs to be regular. Neglect, particularly after minor damage, can lead quickly to further deterioration and costly repair bills. It is important also to keep watch on those parts of the vehicle not immediately visible, for instance the underside, inside all the wheel arches and the lower part of the engine compartment.

The basic maintenance routine for the bodywork is washing – preferably with a lot of water, from a hose. This will remove all the loose solids which may have stuck to the vehicle. It is important to flush these off in such a way as to prevent grit from scratching the finish. The wheel arches and underframe need washing in the same way to remove any accumulated mud which will retain moisture and tend to encourage rust. Paradoxically enough, the best time to clean the underframe and wheel arches is in wet weather when the mud is thoroughly wet and soft. In very wet weather the underframe is usually cleaned of large accumulations automatically and this is a good time for inspection.

Periodically, except on vehicles with a wax-based underbody protective coating, it is a good idea to have the whole of the underframe of the vehicle steam-cleaned, engine compartment included, so that a thorough inspection can be carried out to see what minor repairs and renovations are necessary. Steam cleaning is available at many garages and is necessary for removal of the accumulation of oily grime which sometimes is allowed to become thick in certain areas. If steam cleaning facilities are not available, there are one or two excellent grease solvents available, such as Holts Engine Cleaner or Holts Foambrite, which can be brush applied. The dirt can then be simply hosed off. Note that these methods should not be used on vehicles with wax-based underbody protective coating or the coating will be removed. Such vehicles should be inspected annually, preferably just prior to winter, when the underbody should be washed down and any damage to the wax coating repaired using Holts Undershield. Ideally, a completely fresh coat should be applied. It would also be worth considering the use of such wax-based protection for injection into door panels, sills, box sections, etc, as an additional safeguard against rust damage where such protection is not provided by the vehicle manufacturer.

After washing paintwork, wipe off with a chamois leather to give an unspotted clear finish. A coat of clear protective wax polish, like the many excellent Turtle Wax polishes, will give added protection against chemical pollutants in the air. If the paintwork sheen has dulled or oxidised, use a cleaner/polisher combination such as Turtle Extra to restore the brilliance of the shine. This requires a little effort, but such dulling is usually caused because regular washing has been neglected. Care needs to be taken with metallic paintwork, as special non-abrasive cleaner/polisher is required to avoid damage to the finish. Always check that the door and ventilator opening drain holes and pipes are completely clear so that water can be drained out. Bright work should be treated in the same way as paint work. Windscreens and windows can be kept clear of the smeary film which often appears by the use of a proprietary glass cleaner like Holts Mixra. Never use any form of wax or other body or chromium polish on glass.

4 Maintenance – upholstery and carpets

Mats and carpets should be brushed or vacuum cleaned regularly to keep them free of grit. If they are badly stained remove them from the vehicle for scrubbing or sponging and make quite sure they are dry before refitting. Seats and interior trim panels can be kept clean by wiping with a damp cloth. If they do become stained (which can be more apparent on light coloured upholstery) use a little liquid detergent and a soft nail brush to scour the grime out of the grain of the material. Do not forget to keep the headlining clean in the same way as the upholstery. When using liquid cleaners inside the vehicle do not over-wet the surfaces being cleaned. Excessive damp could get into the seams and padded interior causing stains, offensive odours or even rot. If the inside of the vehicle gets wet accidentally it is worthwhile taking some trouble to dry it out properly, particularly where carpets are involved. *Do not leave oil or electric heaters inside the vehicle for this purpose.*

5 Minor body damage – repair

The photographic sequences on pages 206 and 207 illustrate the operations detailed in the following sub-sections.

Note: *For more detailed information about bodywork repair, the Haynes Publishing Group publish a book by Lindsay Porter called The Car Bodywork Repair Manual. This incorporates information on such aspects as rust treatment, painting and glass fibre repairs, as well as details on more ambitious repairs involving welding and panel beating.*

Repair of minor scratches in bodywork

If the scratch is very superficial, and does not penetrate to the metal of the bodywork, repair is very simple. Lightly rub the area of the scratch with a paintwork renovator like Turtle Wax New Color Back, or a very fine cutting paste like Holts Body + Plus Rubbing Compound to remove loose paint from the scratch and to clear the surrounding bodywork of wax polish. Rinse the area with clean water.

Apply touch-up paint, such as Holts Dupli-Color Color Touch or a paint film like Holts Autofilm, to the scratch using a fine paint brush; continue to apply fine layers of paint until the surface of the paint in the scratch is level with the surrounding paintwork. Allow the new paint at least two weeks to harden: then blend it into the surrounding paintwork by rubbing the scratch area with a paintwork renovator or a very fine cutting paste, such as Holts Body + Plus Rubbing Compound or Turtle Wax New Color Back. Finally, apply wax polish from one of the Turtle Wax range of wax polishes.

Where the scratch has penetrated right through to the metal of the bodywork, causing the metal to rust, a different repair technique is required. Remove any loose rust from the bottom of the scratch with a penknife, then apply rust inhibiting paint, such as Turtle Wax Rust Master, to prevent the formation of rust in the future. Using a rubber or nylon applicator fill the scratch with bodystopper paste such as Holts Body + Plus Knifing Putty. If required, this paste can be mixed with cellulose thinners, such as Holts Body + Plus Cellulose Thinners, to provide a very thin paste which is ideal for filling narrow scratches. Before the stopper-paste in the scratch hardens, wrap a piece of smooth cotton rag around the top of a finger. Dip the finger in cellulose thinners, such as Holts Body + Plus Cellulose Thinners, and then quickly sweep it across the surface of the stopper-paste in the scratch; this will ensure that the surface of the stopper-paste is slightly hollowed. The scratch can now be painted over as described earlier in this Section.

Repair of dents in bodywork

When deep denting of the vehicle's bodywork has taken place, the first task is to pull the dent out, until the affected bodywork almost attains its original shape. There is little point in trying to restore the original shape completely, as the metal in the damaged area will have stretched on impact and cannot be reshaped fully to its original contour. It is better to bring the level of the dent up to a point which is about 3 mm ($\frac{1}{8}$ in) below the level of the surrounding bodywork. In cases where the dent is very shallow anyway, it is not worth trying to pull it out at all. If the underside of the dent is accessible, it can be hammered out gently from behind, using a mallet with a wooden or plastic head. Whilst doing this, hold a suitable block of wood firmly against the outside of the panel to absorb the impact from the hammer blows and thus prevent a large area of the bodywork from being 'belled-out'.

Should the dent be in a section of the bodywork which has a double skin or some other factor making it inaccessible from behind, a different technique is called for. Drill several small holes through the metal inside the area – particularly in the deeper section. Then screw long self-tapping screws into the holes just sufficiently for them to gain a good purchase in the metal. Now the dent can be pulled out by pulling on the protruding heads of the screws with a pair of pliers.

The next stage of the repair is the removal of the paint from the damaged area, and from an inch or so of the surrounding 'sound' bodywork. This is accomplished most easily by using a wire brush or abrasive pad on a power drill, although it can be done just as effectively by hand using sheets of abrasive paper. To complete the preparation for filling, score the surface of the bare metal with a screwdriver or the tang of a file, or alternatively, drill small holes in the affected area. This will provide a really good 'key' for the filler paste.

To complete the repair see the sub-section on filling and re-spraying.

Repair of rust holes or gashes in bodywork

Remove all paint from the affected area and from an inch or so of the surrounding 'sound' bodywork, using an abrasive pad or a wire brush on a power drill. If these are not available a few sheets of abrasive paper will do the job just as effectively. With the paint removed you will be able to gauge the severity of the corrosion and therefore decide whether to renew the whole panel (if this is possible) or to repair the affected area. New body panels are not as expensive as most people think and it is often quicker and more satisfactory to fit a new panel than to attempt to repair large areas of corrosion.

Remove all fittings from the affected area except those which will act as a guide to the original shape of the damaged bodywork (eg headlamp shells etc). Then, using tin snips or a hacksaw blade, remove all loose metal and any other metal badly affected by corrosion. Hammer the edges of the hole inwards in order to create a slight depression for the filler paste.

Wire brush the affected area to remove the powdery rust from the surface of the remaining metal. Paint the affected area with rust inhibiting paint like Turtle Wax Rust Master; if the back of the rusted area is accessible treat this also.

Before filling can take place it will be necessary to block the hole in some way. This can be achieved by the use of aluminium or plastic mesh, or aluminium tape.

Aluminium or plastic mesh or glass fibre matting, such as the Holts Body + Plus Glass Fibre Matting, is probably the best material to use for a large hole. Cut a piece to the approximate size and shape of the hole to be filled, then position it in the hole so that its edges are below the level of the surrounding bodywork. It can be retained in position by several blobs of filler paste around its periphery.

Aluminium tape should be used for small or very narrow holes. Pull a piece off the roll and trim it to the approximate size and shape required, then pull off the backing paper (if used) and stick the tape over the hole; it can be overlapped if the thickness of one piece is insufficient. Burnish down the edges of the tape with the handle of a screwdriver or similar, to ensure that the tape is securely attached to the metal underneath.

Bodywork repairs – filling and re-spraying

Before using this Section, see the Sections on dent, deep scratch, rust holes and gash repairs.

Many types of bodyfiller are available, but generally speaking those proprietary kits which contain a tin of filler paste and a tube of resin hardener are best for this type of repair, like Holts Body + Plus or Holts No Mix which can be used directly from the tube. A wide, flexible plastic or nylon applicator will be found invaluable for imparting a smooth and well contoured finish to the surface of the filler.

Mix up a little filler on a clean piece of card or board – measure the hardener carefully (follow the maker's instructions on the pack) otherwise the filler will set too rapidly or too slowly. Alternatively, Holts No Mix can be used straight from the tube without mixing, but daylight is required to cure it. Using the applicator apply the filler paste to the prepared area; draw the applicator across the surface of the filler to achieve the correct contour and to level the filler surface. As soon as a contour that approximates to the correct one is achieved, stop working the paste – if you carry on too long the paste will become sticky and begin to 'pick up' on the applicator. Continue to add thin layers of filler paste at twenty-minute intervals until the level of the filler is just proud of the surrounding bodywork.

Once the filler has hardened, excess can be removed using a metal plane or file. From then on, progressively finer grades of abrasive paper should be used, starting with a 40 grade production paper and finishing with 400 grade wet-and-dry paper. Always wrap the abrasive paper around a flat rubber, cork, or wooden block – otherwise the surface of the filler will not be completely flat. During the smoothing of the filler surface the wet-and-dry paper should be periodically rinsed in water. This will ensure that a very smooth finish is imparted to the filler at the final stage.

At this stage the 'dent' should be surrounded by a ring of bare metal, which in turn should be encircled by the finely 'feathered' edge of the good paintwork. Rinse the repair area with clean water, until all of the dust produced by the rubbing-down operation has gone.

Spray the whole repair area with a light coat of primer, either Holts Body + Plus Grey or Red Oxide Primer – this will show up any imperfections in the surface of the filler. Repair these imperfections with fresh filler paste or bodystopper, and once more smooth the surface with abrasive paper. If bodystopper is used, it can be mixed with cellulose thinners to form a really thin paste which is ideal for filling small holes. Repeat this spray and repair procedure until you are satisfied that the surface of the filler, and the feathered edge of the paintwork are perfect. Clean the repair area with clean water and allow to dry fully.

The repair area is now ready for final spraying. Paint spraying must be carried out in a warm, dry, windless and dust-free atmosphere. This condition can be created artificially if you have access to a large indoor working area, but if you are forced to work in the open, you will have to pick your day very carefully. If you are working indoors, dousing the floor in the work area with water will help to settle the dust which would otherwise be in the atmosphere. If the repair area is confined to one body panel, mask off the surrounding panels; this will help to minimise the effects of a slight mis-match in paint colours. Bodywork fittings (eg chrome strips, door handles etc) will also need to be masked off. Use genuine masking tape and several thicknesses of newspaper for the masking operations.

Before commencing to spray, agitate the aerosol can thoroughly, then spray a test area (an old tin, or similar) until the technique is mastered. Cover the repair area with a thick coat of primer; the thickness should be built up using several thin layers of paint rather than one thick one. Using 400 grade wet-and-dry paper, rub down the surface of the primer until it is really smooth. While doing this, the work area should be thoroughly doused with water, and the wet-and-dry paper periodically rinsed in water. Allow to dry before spraying on more paint.

Spray on the top coat using Holts Dupli-Color Autospray, again building up the thickness by using several thin layers of paint. Start spraying in the centre of the repair area and then, with a side-to-side motion, work outwards until the whole repair area and about 50 mm of the surrounding original paintwork is covered. Remove all masking material 10 to 15 minutes after spraying on the final coat of paint.

Allow the new paint at least two weeks to harden, then, using a paintwork renovator or a very fine cutting paste such as Turtle Wax New Color Back or Holts Body + Plus Rubbing Compound, blend the edges of the paint into the existing paintwork. Finally, apply wax polish.

Plastic components

With the use of more and more plastic body components by the vehicle manufacturers (eg bumpers, spoilers, and in some cases major body panels), rectification of more serious damage to such items has become a matter of either entrusting repair work to a specialist in this field, or renewing complete components. Repair of such damage by the DIY owner is not really feasible owing to the cost of the equipment and materials required for effecting such repairs. The basic technique involves making a groove along the line of the crack in the plastic using a rotary burr in a power drill. The damaged part is then welded back together by using a hot air gun to heat up and fuse a plastic filler rod into the groove. Any excess plastic is then removed and the area rubbed down to a smooth finish. It is important that a filler rod of the correct plastic is used, as body components can be made of a variety of different types (eg polycarbonate, ABS, polypropylene).

Damage of a less serious nature (abrasions, minor cracks etc) can be repaired by the DIY owner using a two-part epoxy filler repair material like Holts Body + Plus or Holts No Mix which can be used directly from the tube. Once mixed in equal proportions (or applied direct from the tube in the case of Holts No Mix), this is used in similar fashion to the bodywork filler used on metal panels. The filler is usually cured in 20 to 30 minutes, ready for sanding and painting.

If the owner is renewing a complete component himself, or if he has repaired it with epoxy filler, he will be left with the problem of finding a suitable paint for finishing which is compatible with the type of plastic used. At one time the use of a universal paint was not possible owing to the complex range of plastics encountered in body component applications. Standard paints, generally speaking, will not bond to plastic or rubber satisfactorily, but Holts Professional Spraymatch paints to match any plastic or rubber finish can be obtained from dealers. However, it is now possible to obtain a plastic body parts finishing kit which consists of a pre-primer treatment, a primer and coloured top coat. Full instructions are normally supplied with a kit, but basically the

7.2 Bonnet hinge

7.4 Gas strut connection to the bonnet

7.8 Gas strut connection to the body

method of use is to first apply the pre-primer to the component concerned and allow it to dry for up to 30 minutes. Then the primer is applied and left to dry for about an hour before finally applying the special coloured top coat. The result is a correctly coloured component where the paint will flex with the plastic or rubber, a property that standard paint does not normally possess.

6 Major body damage – repair

Where serious damage has occurred or large areas need renewal due to neglect, it means that completely new sections or panels will need welding in, and this is best left to professionals. If the damage is due to impact, it will also be necessary to completely check the alignment of the bodyshell structure. Due to the principle of construction, the strength and shape of the whole car can be affected by damage to one part. In such instances the services of a BMW dealer with specialist checking jigs are essential. If a body is left misaligned it is first of all dangerous as the car will not handle properly, and secondly uneven stress will be imposed on the steering, engine and transmission, causing abnormal wear or complete failure. Tyre wear may also be excessive.

7 Bonnet – removal, refitting and adjustment

1 Open the bonnet, release the safety catch and raise it to its fully open position.
2 Mark the position of both hinges on the bonnet with a pencil (photo).
3 Support the bonnet in its fully open position with a length of wood.
4 Extract the spring clips and disconnect the gas struts from the bonnet (photo). Lower them onto the inner body panel.
5 Position cloth rags beneath the rear corners of the bonnet to prevent damage to the body.
6 With the help of an assistant, support each side of the bonnet and remove the support length of wood.
7 Unscrew the bolts securing the bonnet to the hinges and lift the bonnet away. Position it in a safe place with the rear corners on cloth rags or pieces of cardboard.
8 If necessary the hinges may be unbolted from the body and the gas struts also removed (photo).
9 Refitting is a reversal of removal, but do not fully tighten the hinge bolts until the bonnet has been closed and the alignment checked. The gap between the bonnet and the surrounding panels should be uniform all the way round, and in addition the top of the bonnet should also be level with the panels. If adjustment is required, move the bonnet while the bolts are loose then fully tighten them afterwards. The height of the front of the bonnet is adjusted by turning the rubber buffers at each corner. If an appreciable adjustment on the hinges has been made, it will also be necessary to adjust the strikers as follows. First screw the rubber buffers fully into the bonnet so that the strikers will easily enter the catches. Slightly loosen the striker mounting bolts, then shut the bonnet. This will centralize the strikers but also check that the safety catch enters the left-hand lock correctly. Open the bonnet then tighten the mounting bolts. Finally adjust the rubber buffers so that the front edge of the bonnet is level with the front wings.

8 Bonnet release cable – removal and refitting

1 Open the bonnet fully, then remove the covers and release the cable from the levers on the locks by loosening the pinch-bolts.
2 Working inside the car, remove the glovebox and panel from the left-hand side of the facia.
3 Unhook the inner cable from the release lever and unclip the outer cable from the bracket (photo).
4 Release the cables from the clips both inside the engine compartment and beneath the facia, then withdraw the complete cable through the rubber grommet in the bulkhead. The outer cable is in two sections to supply both front locks.
5 Refitting is a reversal of removal, but eliminate all slack before tightening the pinch-bolts.

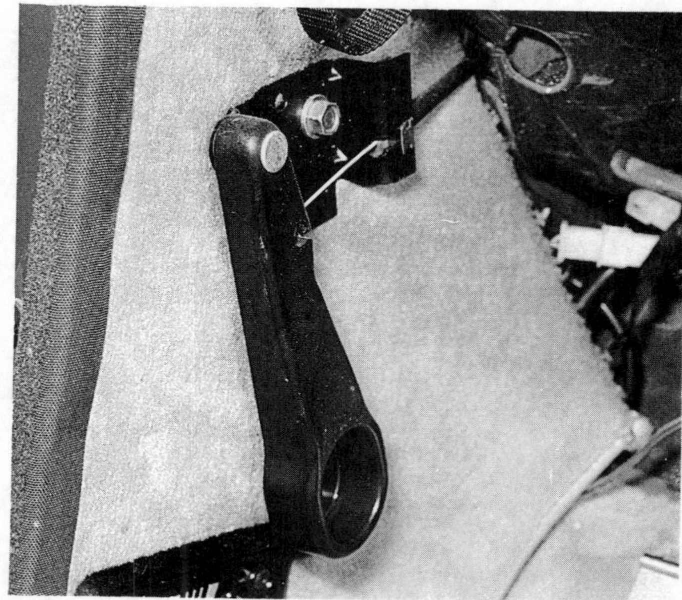
8.3 Bonnet release lever and cable

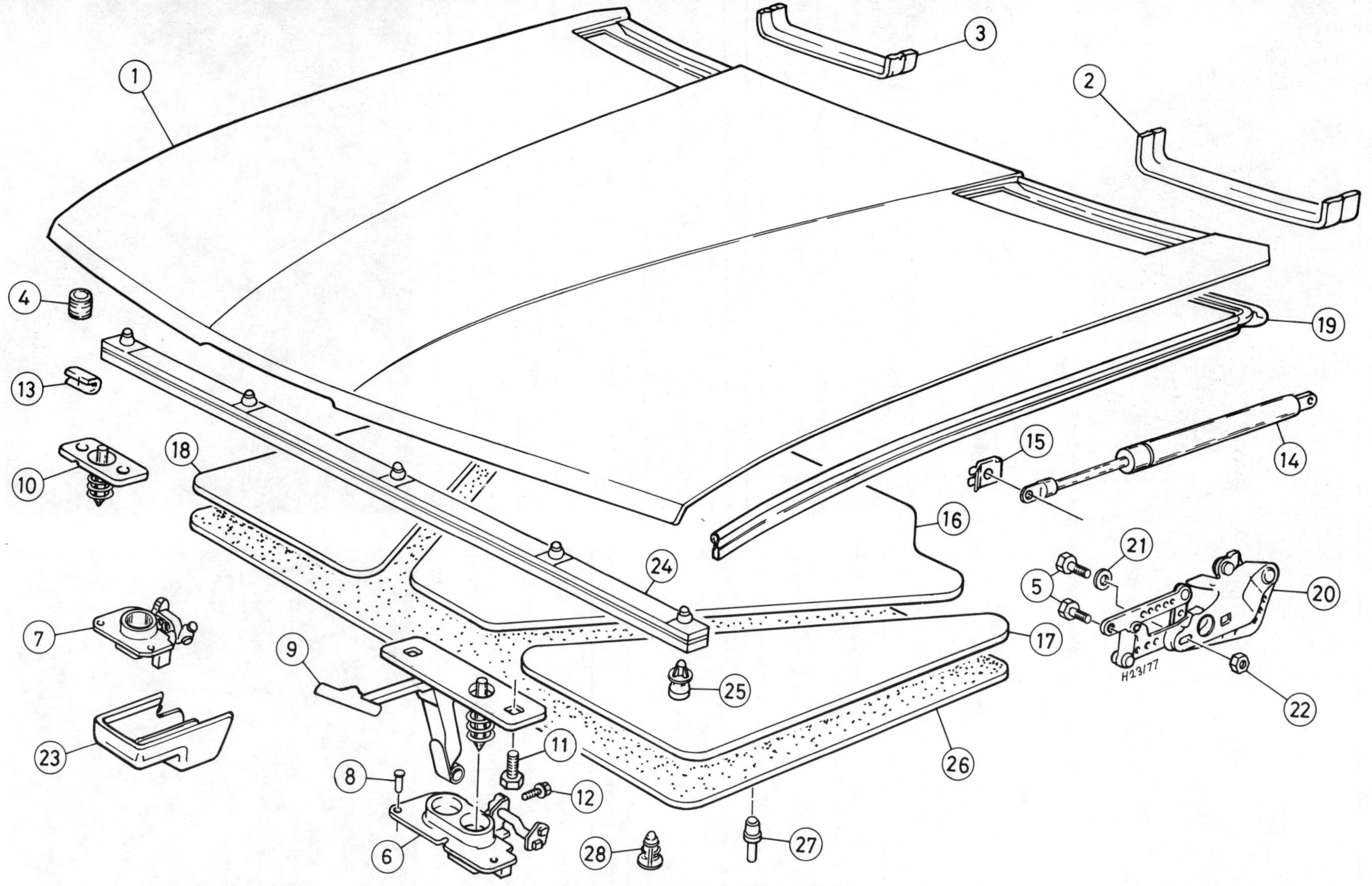

Fig. 11.1 Bonnet components (Sec 7)

1 Bonnet panel
2 Left-hand seal
3 Right-hand seal
4 Rubber buffer
5 Bolts
6 Lock/catch (left-hand side)
7 Lock/catch (right-hand side)
8 Rivet
9 Safety catch
10 Striker
11 Bolt
12 Screw
13 Bump stop
14 Strut
15 Bracket
16 Sound deadening panel (centre)
17 Sound deadening panel (left)
18 Sound deadening panel (right)
19 Weather strip
20 Hinge
21 Spring washer
22 Nut
23 Cover
24 Seal
25 Clip
26 Sound deadening panel
27 Rivet
28 Clip

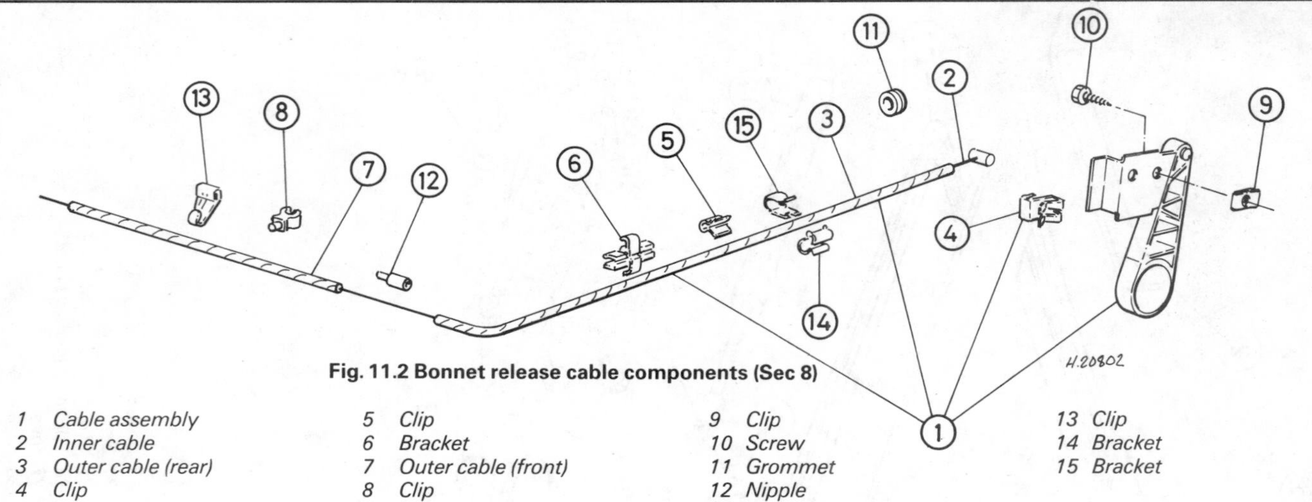

Fig. 11.2 Bonnet release cable components (Sec 8)

1 *Cable assembly*
2 *Inner cable*
3 *Outer cable (rear)*
4 *Clip*
5 *Clip*
6 *Bracket*
7 *Outer cable (front)*
8 *Clip*
9 *Clip*
10 *Screw*
11 *Grommet*
12 *Nipple*
13 *Clip*
14 *Bracket*
15 *Bracket*

9 Bonnet lock – removal and refitting

Note: *The two bonnet locks are riveted to the engine compartment front crossmember, and a suitable pop-riveter will be required to refit a lock.*

1 Open the bonnet fully, then remove the plastic cover (two screws) and release the cable from the lever on the relevant lock by loosening the pinch-bolt.
2 Drill out the rivets and remove the lock from the front crossmember (photos).
3 Refitting is a reversal of removal, but use new rivets to secure the locks to the crossmember and eliminate all slack before tightening the pinch-bolt.

10 Boot lid – removal, refitting and adjustment

1 Open the boot lid and mark the position of the hinges with a pencil (photo).
2 Position cloth rags beneath the front corners of the boot lid to prevent damage to the body.
3 With the help of an assistant, support the lid then unscrew the bolts and lift it from the hinges. Recover the foil strips fitted between the boot lid and hinges.
4 Refitting is a reversal of removal, but do not fully tighten the bolts until the lid has been closed and its alignment checked. Move the lid as necessary to achieve an even gap all round, then tighten the bolts. To adjust the striker, loosen the two bolts on the inside of the boot lid slightly then close the boot lid. This will centralize the striker and the bolts can then be tightened after opening the boot lid again. If there is insufficient adjustment, the lock must be adjusted as well. The boot lid height is also adjusted by repositioning the lock on the rear panel. Adjust the side buffers to support the corners of the boot lid (photos).

11 Boot lid lock – removal, refitting and adjustment

1 Open the boot lid and remove the trim and cover as necessary for access to the lock on the rear panel (photo).
2 Unscrew the two mounting bolts and remove the lock, intermediate plate, gasket and escutcheon.
3 Refitting is a reversal of removal, but adjust the lock with reference to Section 10.

12 Boot lid torsion springs – removal and refitting

1 Support the boot lid in its open position with a length of wood.
2 Release the spring ends from the slots in the mountings. Do this with care, using a cranked lever or large adjustable spanner, as there is considerable tension in the torsion rod.

9.2A Right-hand bonnet lock

9.2B Left-hand bonnet lock

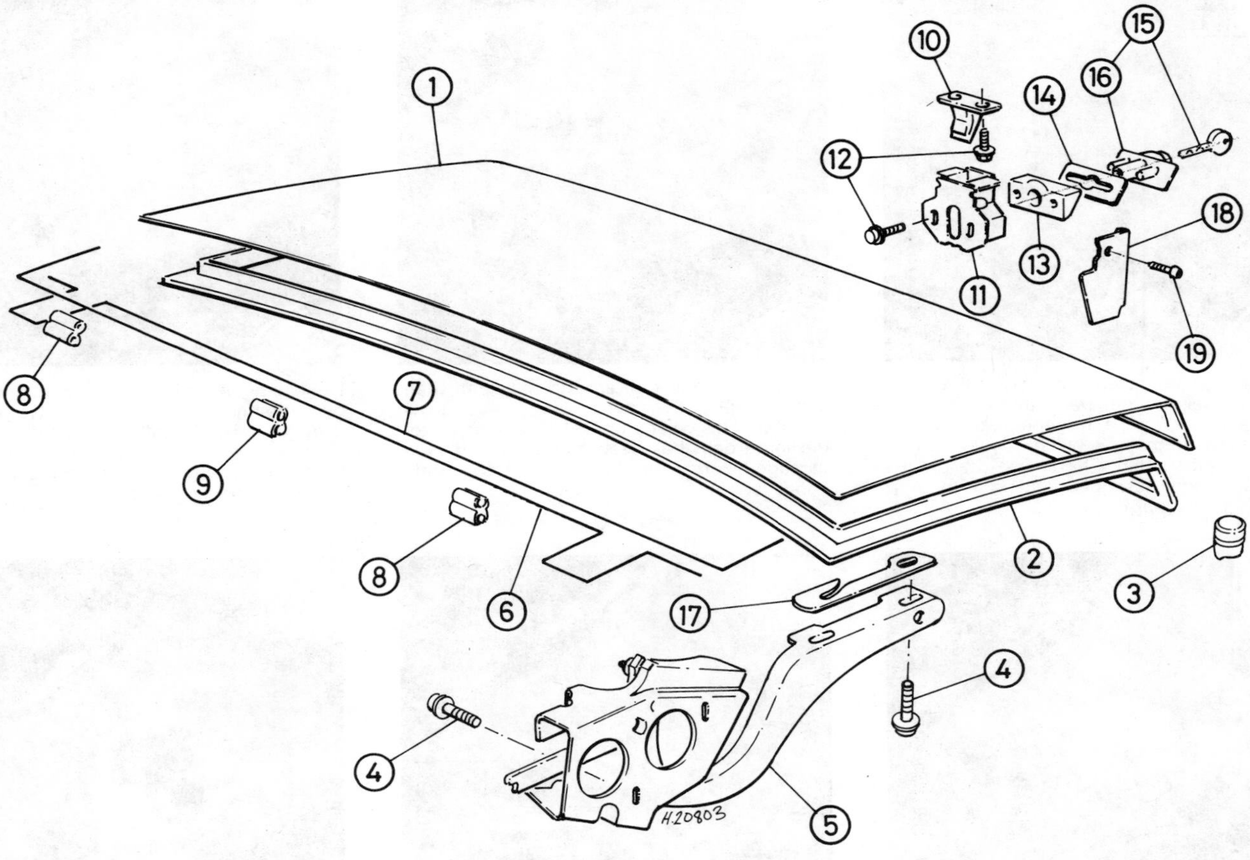

Fig. 11.3 Boot lid components (Sec 10)

1 Boot lid
2 Weatherseal
3 Rubber buffer
4 Bolt
5 Hinge
6 Torsion spring (left)
7 Torsion spring (right)
8 Mounting
9 Mounting
10 Striker
11 Lock
12 Bolts
13 Intermediate plate
14 Gasket
15 Lock and key assembly
16 Lock
17 Foil
18 Cover
19 Screw

3 Withdraw the torsion springs from the clips in the luggage compartment.
4 Refitting is a reversal of removal.

13 Bumpers – removal and refitting

Front bumpers

1 Apply the handbrake then jack up the front of the car and support on axle stands.
2 Unscrew the bolts securing the ends of the bumper to the right and left-hand side panels.
3 Pull off the covers from each end of the bumper.
4 Unscrew the bumper mounting bolts using an extension socket through the right and left towing eyes.
5 Withdraw the bumper from the front of the car.
6 If necessary, unbolt the right and left brackets, the number plate holder, and the rubber guard. Unscrew the nuts and separate the sections.
7 Refitting is a reversal of removal, but make sure that the bumper is aligned with the front of the car, and tighten all nuts and bolts to the

10.1 Boot lid hinge

10.4A Boot lid striker

10.4B Boot lid side buffer

This photographic sequence shows the steps taken to repair the dent and paintwork damage shown above. In general, the procedure for repairing a hole will be similar; where there are substantial differences, the procedure is clearly described and shown in a separate photograph.

First remove any trim around the dent, then hammer out the dent where access is possible. This will minimise filling. Here, after the large dent has been hammered out, the damaged area is being made slightly concave.

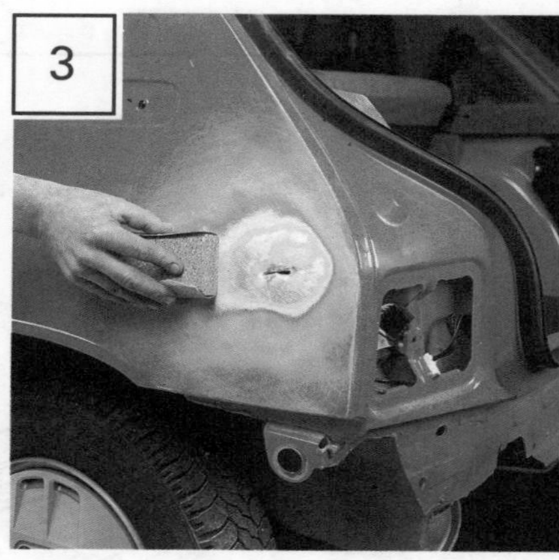

Next, remove all paint from the damaged area by rubbing with coarse abrasive paper or using a power drill fitted with a wire brush or abrasive pad. 'Feather' the edge of the boundary with good paintwork using a finer grade of abrasive paper.

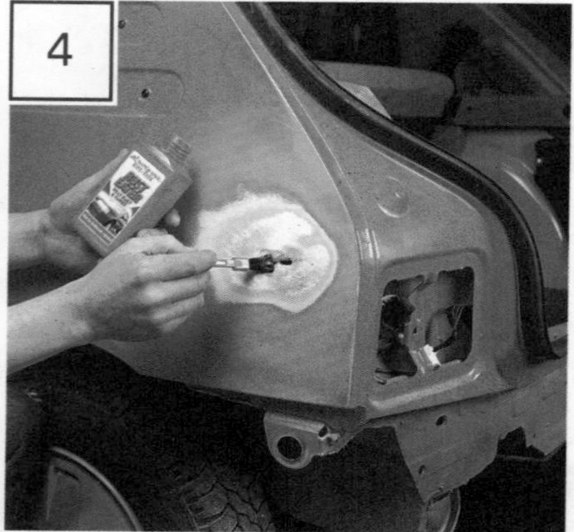

Where there are holes or other damage, the sheet metal should be cut away before proceeding further. The damaged area and any signs of rust should be treated with Turtle Wax Hi-Tech Rust Eater, which will also inhibit further rust formation.

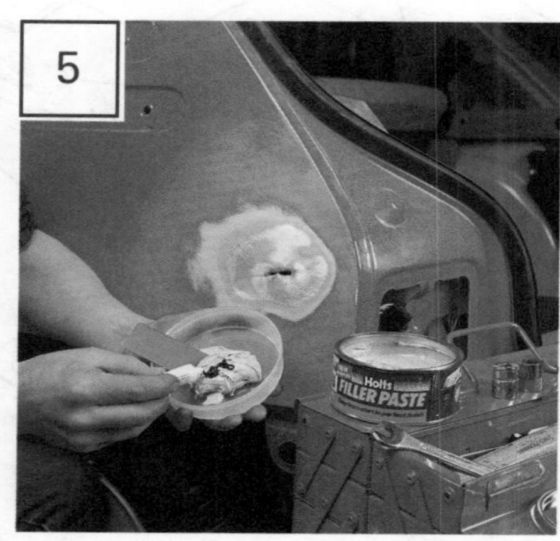

For a large dent or hole mix Holts Body Plus Resin and Hardener according to the manufacturer's instructions and apply around the edge of the repair. Press Glass Fibre Matting over the repair area and leave for 20-30 minutes to harden. Then ...

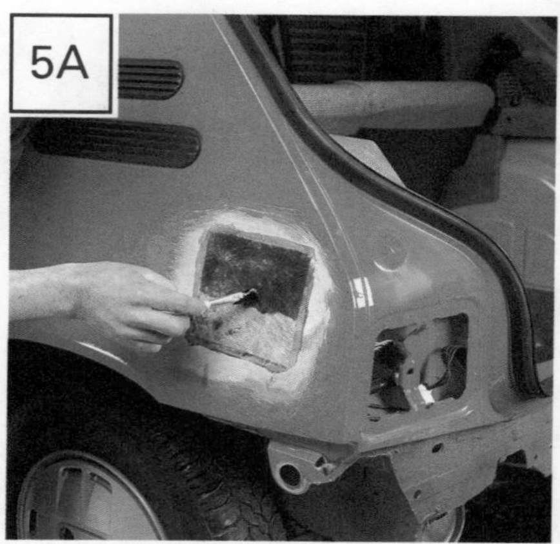

... brush more Holts Body Plus Resin and Hardener onto the matting and leave to harden. Repeat the sequence with two or three layers of matting, checking that the final layer is lower than the surrounding area. Apply Holts Body Plus Filler Paste as shown in Step 5B.

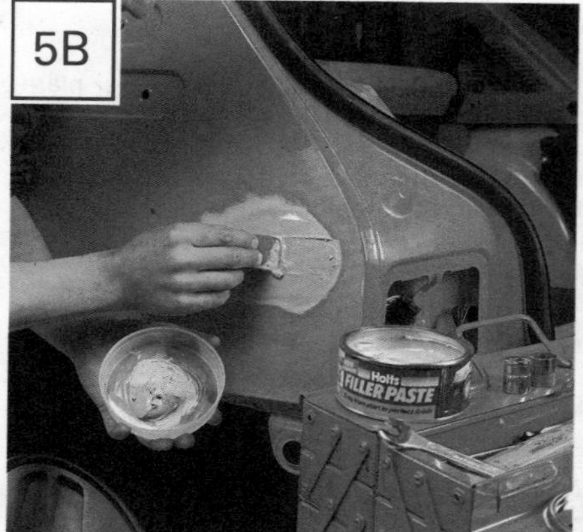

For a medium dent, mix Holts Body Plus Filler Paste and Hardener according to the manufacturer's instructions and apply it with a flexible applicator. Apply thin layers of filler at 20-minute intervals, until the filler surface is slightly proud of the surrounding bodywork.

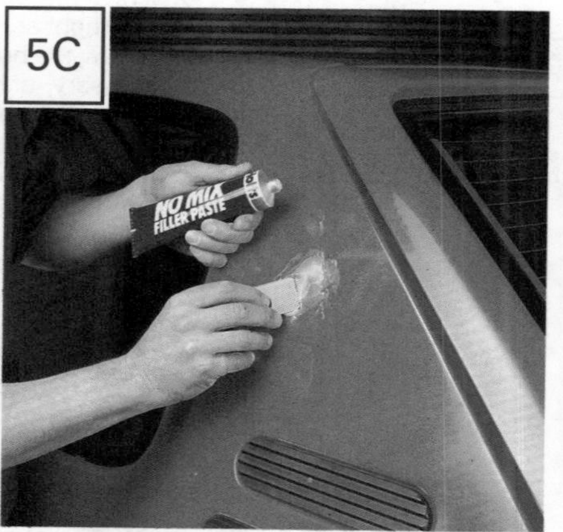

For small dents and scratches use Holts No Mix Filler Paste straight from the tube. Apply it according to the instructions in thin layers, using the spatula provided. It will harden in minutes if applied outdoors and may then be used as its own knifing putty.

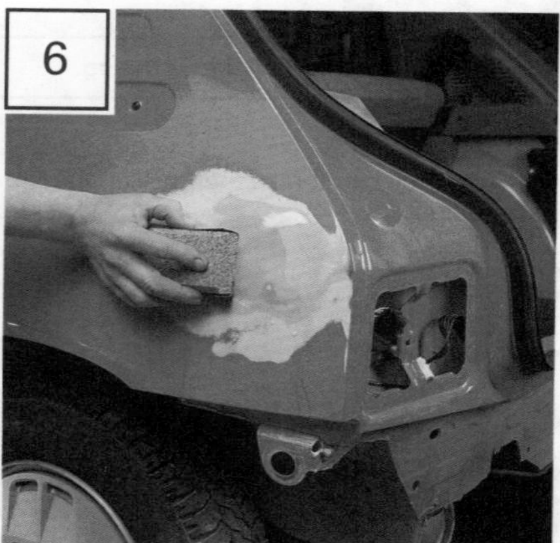

Use a plane or file for initial shaping. Then, using progressively finer grades of wet-and-dry paper, wrapped round a sanding block, and copious amounts of clean water, rub down the filler until glass smooth. 'Feather' the edges of adjoining paintwork.

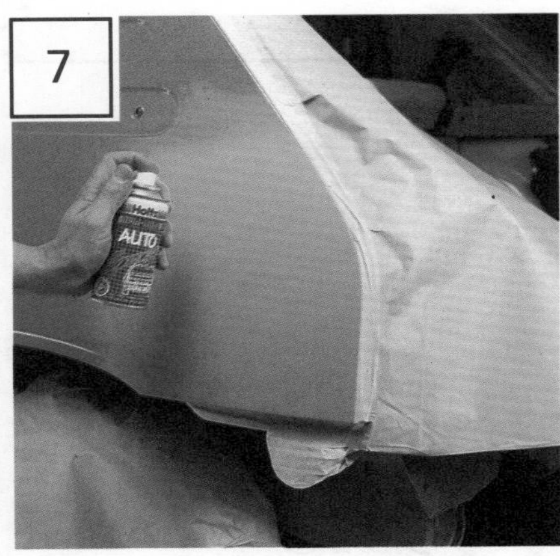

Protect adjoining areas before spraying the whole repair area and at least one inch of the surrounding sound paintwork with Holts Dupli-Color primer.

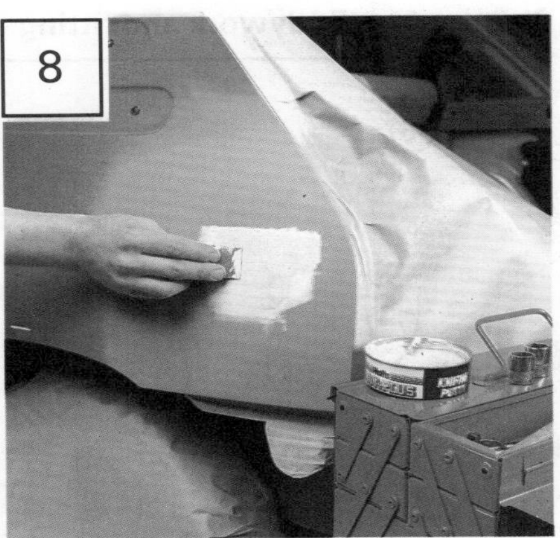

Fill any imperfections in the filler surface with a small amount of Holts Body Plus Knifing Putty. Using plenty of clean water, rub down the surface with a fine grade wet-and-dry paper – 400 grade is recommended – until it is really smooth.

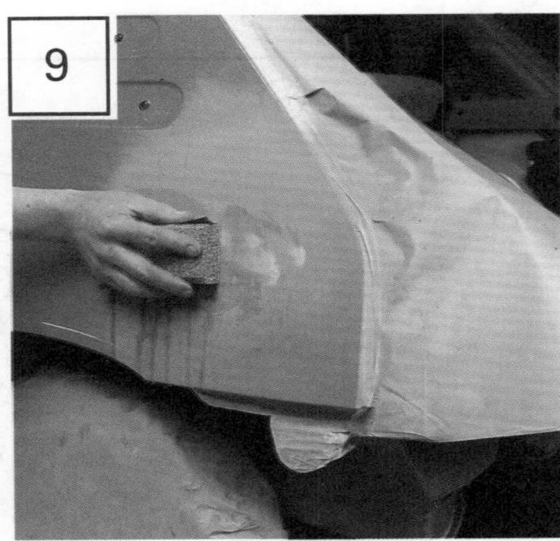

Carefully fill any remaining imperfections with knifing putty before applying the last coat of primer. Then rub down the surface with Holts Body Plus Rubbing Compound to ensure a really smooth surface.

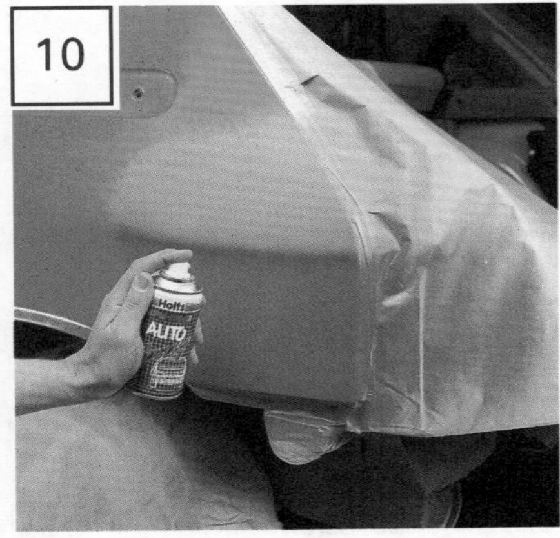

Protect surrounding areas from overspray before applying the topcoat in several thin layers. Agitate Holts Dupli-Color aerosol thoroughly. Start at the repair centre, spraying outwards with a side-to-side motion.

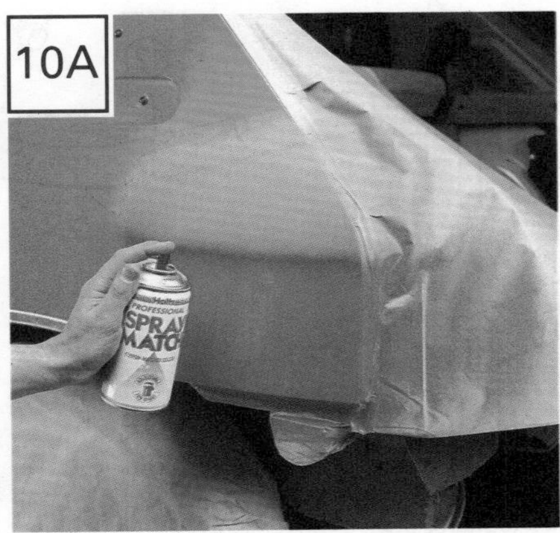

If the exact colour is not available off the shelf, local Holts Professional Spraymatch Centres will custom fill an aerosol to match perfectly.

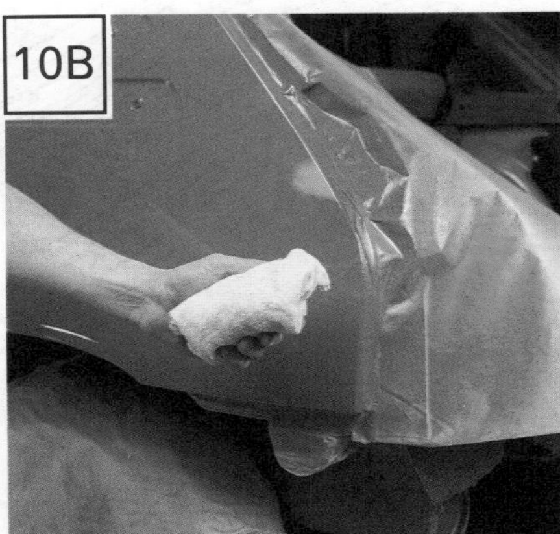

To identify whether a lacquer finish is required, rub a painted unrepaired part of the body with wax and a clean cloth.

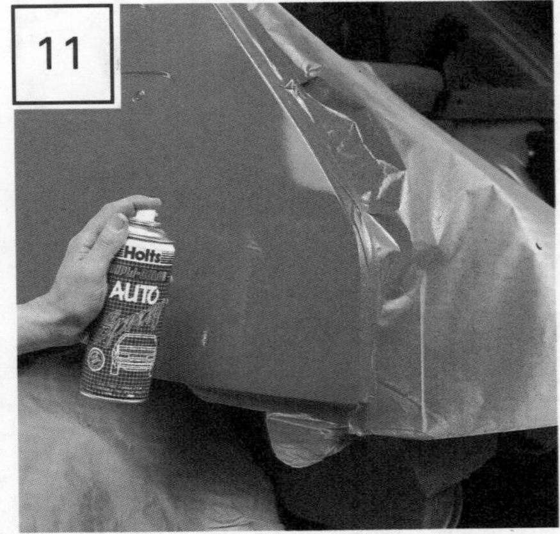

If *no* traces of paint appear on the cloth, spray Holts Dupli-Color clear lacquer over the repaired area to achieve the correct gloss level.

The paint will take about two weeks to harden fully. After this time it can be 'cut' with a mild cutting compound such as Turtle Wax Minute Cut prior to polishing with a final coating of Turtle Wax Extra.

When carrying out bodywork repairs, remember that the quality of the finished job is proportional to the time and effort expended.

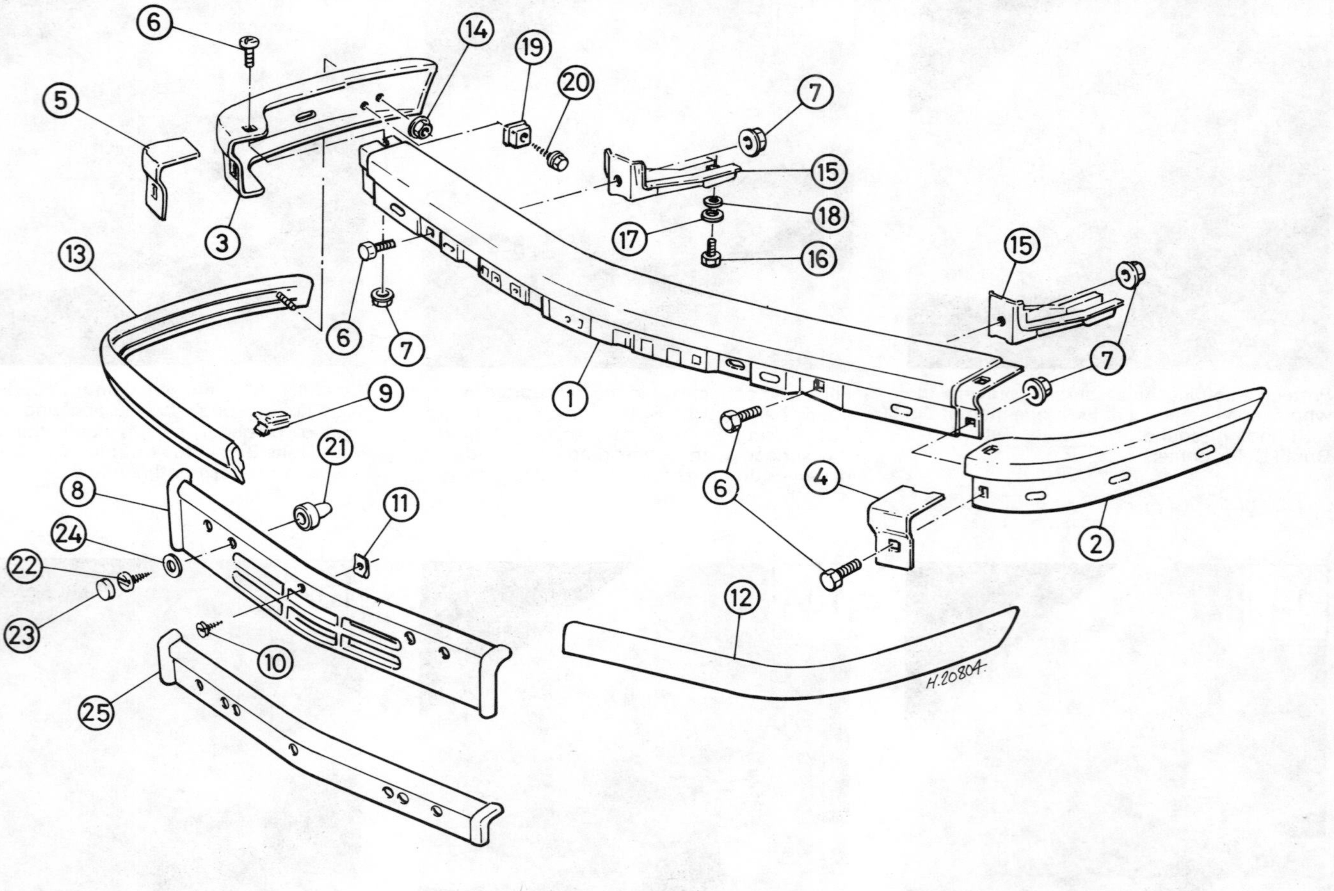

Fig. 11.4 Front bumper components (Sec 13)

1 Centre section
2 Left quarter section
3 Right quarter section
4 Bracket
5 Bracket
6 Bolt
7 Nut
8 Centre moulding
9 Clip
10 Screw
11 Clip
12 Rubber strip (left)
13 Rubber strip (right)
14 Nut
15 Bracket
16 Bolt
17 Flat washer
18 Wave washer
19 Nut
20 Screw
21 Nut
22 Screw
23 Cap
24 Flat washer
25 Base

11.1 Boot lid lock on the rear panel

13.11 Rear bumper mounting bolts

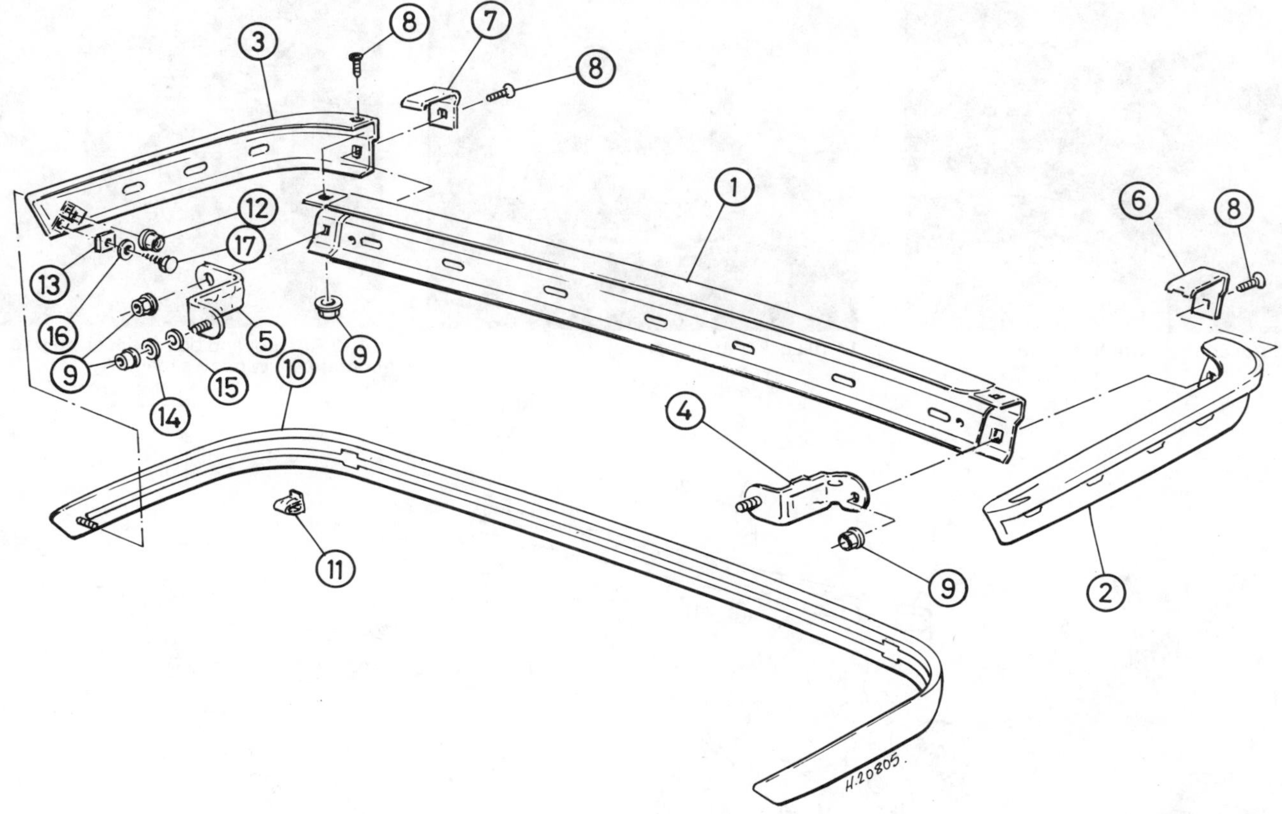

Fig. 11.5 Rear bumper components (Sec 13)

1 Centre section
2 Left quarter section
3 Right quarter section
4 Left bracket
5 Right bracket
6 Left cover
7 Right cover
8 Bolt
9 Nut
10 Moulding
11 Clip
12 Nut
13 Nut
14 Rubber washer
15 Flat washer
16 Rubber washer
17 Screw

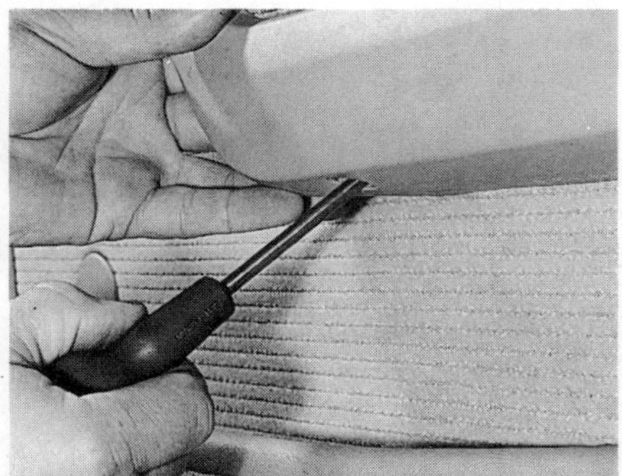
14.2 Removing the front door armrest

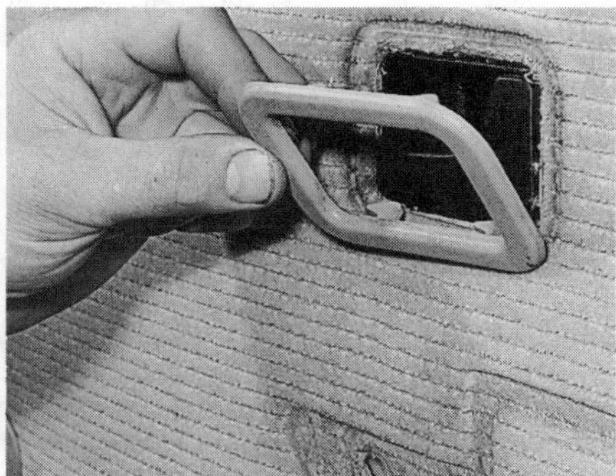
14.5 Removing the inner door handle surround

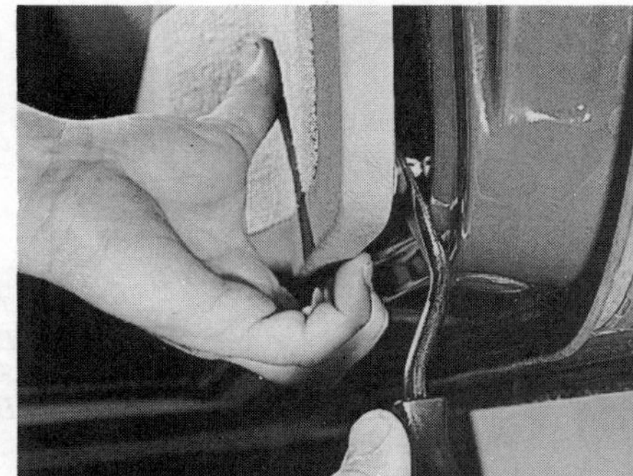
14.6 Removing the front door inner trim panel

specified torque. BMW technicians use a special tool to insert the rubber guard, but a screwdriver may be used instead.

Rear bumper

8 Chock the front wheels then jack up the rear of the car and support on axle stands.

9 Unscrew the bolts securing the ends of the bumper to the right and left-hand rear wing panels.

10 Working inside the luggage compartment, pull back the carpet and remove the trim panel from the inside of the rear panel.

11 Unscrew the bumper mounting bolts from the outer corners of the rear panel, and withdraw the rear bumper (photo).

12 If necessary, unscrew the nuts and unclip the rubber guard. Unscrew the nuts and separate the sections.

13 Refitting is a reversal of removal, but tighten all nuts and bolts to the specified torque. BMW technicians use a special tool to insert the rubber guard, but a screwdriver may be used instead.

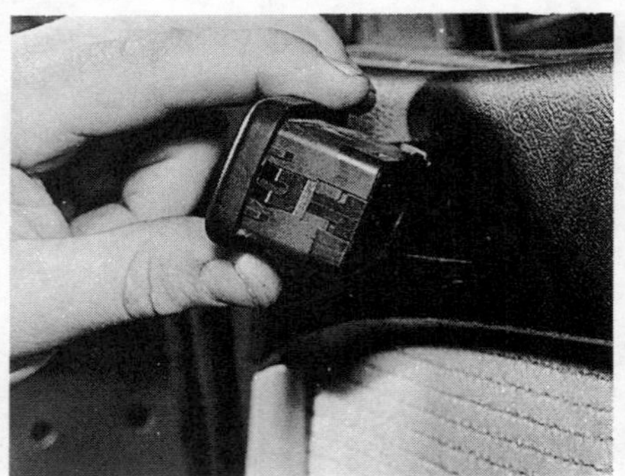
14.8 Mirror control switch removal

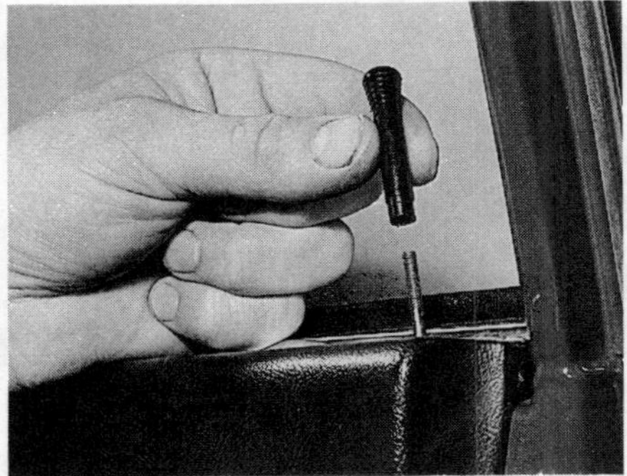
14.10 Lock button removal

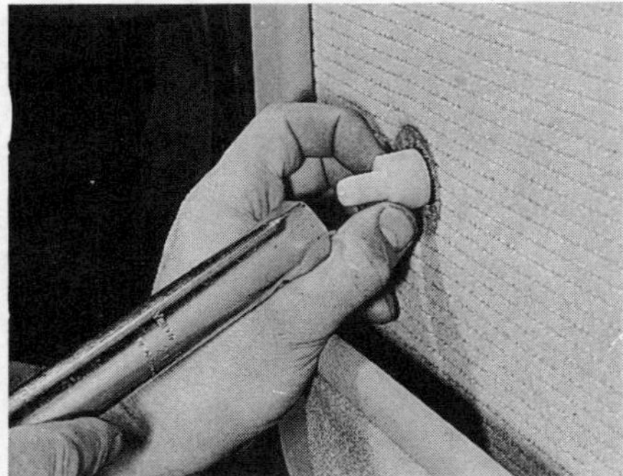
14.12 Adaptor and box spanner used to operate the windows manually

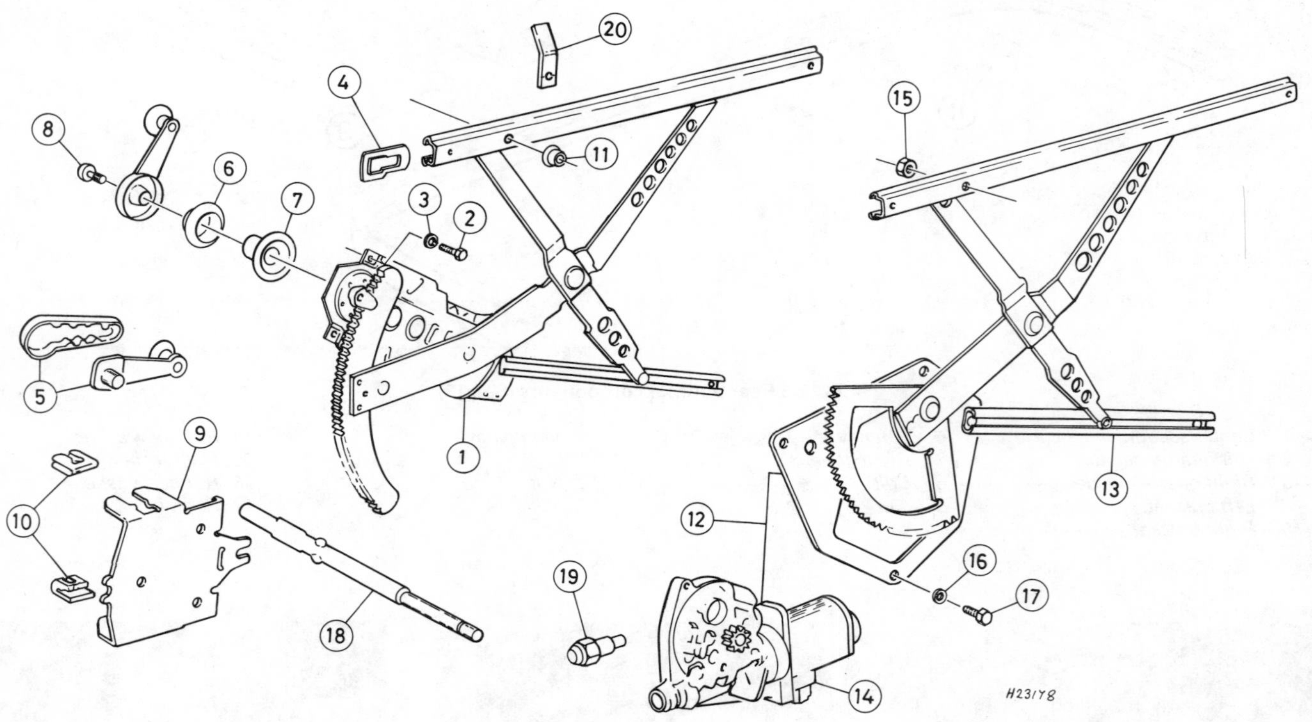

Fig. 11.6 Front door window regulator components (Sec 16)

1 Regulator
2 Bolt
3 Flat washer
4 Sliding piece
5 Regulator handle
6 Thrustwasher
7 Bush
8 Screw
9 Bracket
10 Sliding piece
11 Locknut
12 Electric window regulator assembly
13 Electric window regulator
14 Electric motor
15 Nut
16 Flat washer
17 Bolt
18 Emergency tool for operating window
19 Spigot for emergency tool
20 Bracket

14 Front door inner trim panel – removal and refitting

1 Disconnect the battery negative lead.

2 Unscrew and remove the armrest screws, then turn the armrest approximately 45° and withdraw it from the trim panel (photo).

3 Close the window and note the position of the regulator handle to ensure correct refitting. It should be horizontal and face forwards.

4 Where applicable, carefully prise the plastic cover from the window regulator handle from the end which enters the trim, then unscrew the cross-head screw and pull the handle from the splined shaft. On some models a Torx screw may be fitted instead of a cross-head screw. Remove the washer.

5 Remove the inner door handle surround from the trim panel by pushing it to the rear (photo).

6 Insert the fingers or a wide-bladed screwdriver under the trim panel and pull the panel clips from their holes in the door inner panel (photo). Prise out the trim panel as near to the clips as possible otherwise the clips may break the trim panel.

7 Where applicable, remove the inner spacer and spring from the window regulator, noting that the large end of the spring faces the trim panel.

8 Prise out the mirror control switch and disconnect it from the wiring (photo).

16.2 Front door window glass channel and regulator

9 Peel away the waterproof sheet.
10 Unscrew and remove the lock button (photo).
11 Unscrew the two screws and lift off the trim upper section in an upwards direction.
12 Refitting is a reversal of removal, but renew any broken clips. Where a Torx bolt is fitted to the window regulator handle, it is recommended that it is renewed and its threads coated with thread-locking fluid. Note that where the front windows are electrically-operated, in the event of a fault the windows may be operated by using the adaptor and box spanner provided in the vehicle tool kit (photo).

15 Front door window glass – removal and refitting

1 Remove the front door inner trim panel as described in Section 14.
2 Unscrew the screws and remove the moulding from the inner side of the window opening.
3 Pull off the window seal from the outer side of the window opening.
4 Remove the exterior mirror as described in Section 24.
5 Unscrew the screw from the front upper edge of the door frame.
6 Tap the outer moulding and front triangular plate from the door using a wedged block of wood.
7 Pull off the window opening moulding and remove the clips.
8 Reposition the window as necessary, then unscrew the nuts securing the window glass channel to the regulator.
9 Tilt the rear upper corner of the glass forward and withdraw upwards from the door.
10 If necessary, pull the window glass guide from the upper door frame. Also unbolt and remove the glass channel.
11 Refitting is a reversal of removal, but renew any broken clips.

16 Front door window regulator – removal and refitting

1 Remove the front door inner trim panel as described in Section 14.
2 Reposition the window as necessary then unscrew the nuts securing the window glass channel to the regulator (photo). Support the glass.
3 Where applicable disconnect the wiring for the electric front windows.
4 Unscrew the mounting screws and withdraw the regulator from within the door (photo).
5 Refitting is a reversal of removal but apply a little grease to the

16.4 Electrically-operated window regulator

window channel. Before tightening the regulator vertical adjustment screw, press down on the window glass channel to set the lower stop.

17 Front door lock – removal and refitting

1 Remove the front door inner trim panel as described in Section 14.
2 Unscrew the screws securing the inner door handle and push the controls forward (photo).
3 Prise the connecting rod out of the clips on the lock, then slide the clip forward and remove the lock cylinder together with the seal (photo).
4 Turn up the locking plate on the outside of the lock then unscrew the five lock mounting screws (photo) and withdraw the lock from inside the door.
5 To remove the exterior door handle, unscrew the handle plate screws and lock control nuts. On models equipped with door lock heating it will be necessary to disconnect the heater wiring from the switch on the exterior door handle.
6 Refitting is a reversal of removal.

18 Front door – removal and refitting

1 Remove the front door inner trim panel as described in Section 14.
2 Open the door to its fullest extent and support it on wooden blocks and cloth rags to prevent damage to the paintwork.
3 Disconnect the check strap by extracting the spring clip from the bottom of the pin and driving the pin upwards (photo). If necessary the check strap may be removed by unscrewing the two bolts and withdrawing it from inside the door.
4 Unplug the wiring from the door mirror, electric window and central locking as applicable, and draw the wires through the flexible duct which runs between the door hinged edge and the body pillar.
5 Prise the caps from the door hinge bolts (photo).
6 Unscrew the hinge bolts and lift the door from the car.
7 Transfer all internal components to the new door as required.
8 Refitting is a reversal of removal but tighten the mounting bolts to the specified torque. Before fully tightening the bolts make sure that the door is correctly aligned. The outer surface should be flush with the front wing and sill panel, and this is adjusted by shims added beneath the hinges. The gaps between the door and front wing, and door and rear door should be the same, and adjustment is made by repositioning the hinge. The door beading should also be in correct alignment. On

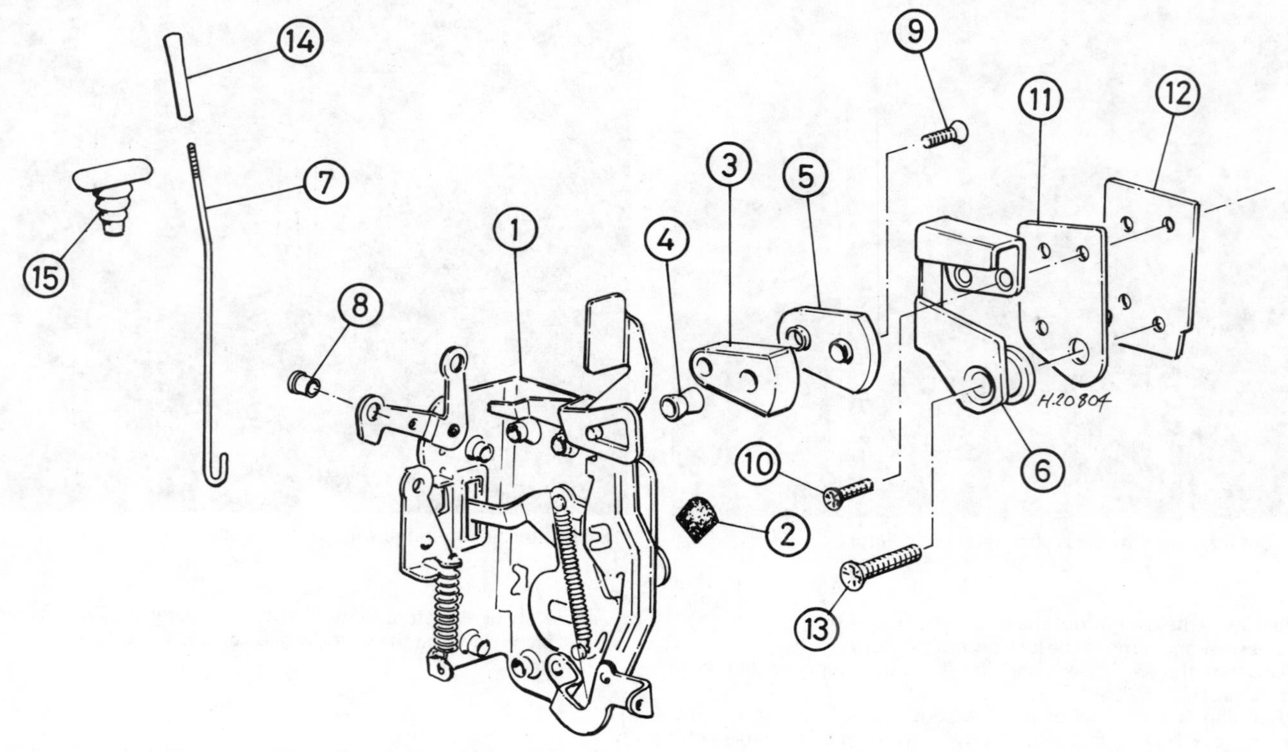

Fig. 11.7 Front door lock (Sec 17)

1 *Lock assembly*
2 *Bump stop*
3 *Stop*
4 *Bush*
5 *Plate*
6 *Striker plate*
7 *Operating rod*
8 *Grommet*
9 *Screw*
10 *Screw*
11 *Spacer*
12 *Lockplate*
13 *Screw*
14 *Button*
15 *Rubber boot*

17.2 Front door inner door handle

17.3 Front door lock cylinder and lock

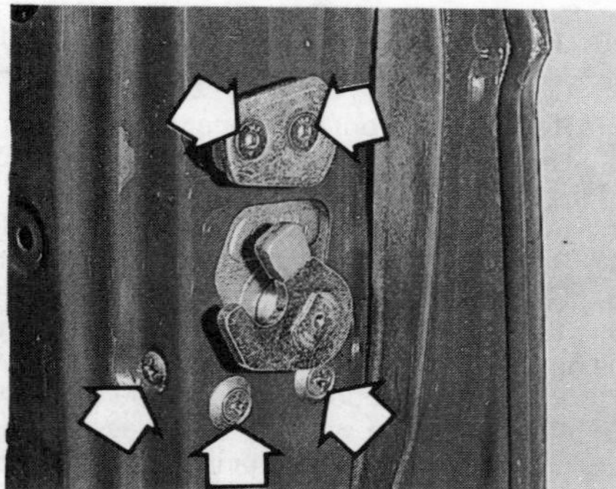
17.4 Front door lock mounting screws (arrowed)

completion, adjust the door lock striker so that it enters the locking plate correctly.

19 Rear door inner trim panel – removal and refitting

1 Unscrew and remove the armrest screws, then turn the armrest approximately 45° and withdraw it from the trim panel (photos).
2 Close the window and, on manually operated windows, note the position of the regulator handle to ensure correct refitting. It should be horizontal and face forwards.
3 Where applicable, carefully prise the plastic cover from the window regulator handle from the end which enters the trim, then unscrew the cross-head screw and pull the handle from the splined shaft. On some models a Torx screw may be fitted instead of a cross-head screw. Remove the washer. Remove the plastic washer (photos).
4 Remove the inner door handle surround from the trim panel by pushing it to the rear (photo).
5 Where applicable, remove the electric window switch and disconnect the wiring.
6 Insert the fingers or a wide-bladed screwdriver under the trim panel and pull the panel clips from their holes in the door inner panel. Prise out the trim panel as near to the clips as possible otherwise the clips may break the trim panel.
7 Where applicable, remove the inner spacer and spring from the window regulator, noting that the large end of the spring faces the trim panel.
8 Peel away the waterproof sheet.
9 Unscrew and remove the lock button and remove the ashtray.
10 Unscrew the two screws and lift off the trim upper section in an upwards direction.
11 Refitting is a reversal of removal, but renew any broken clips.

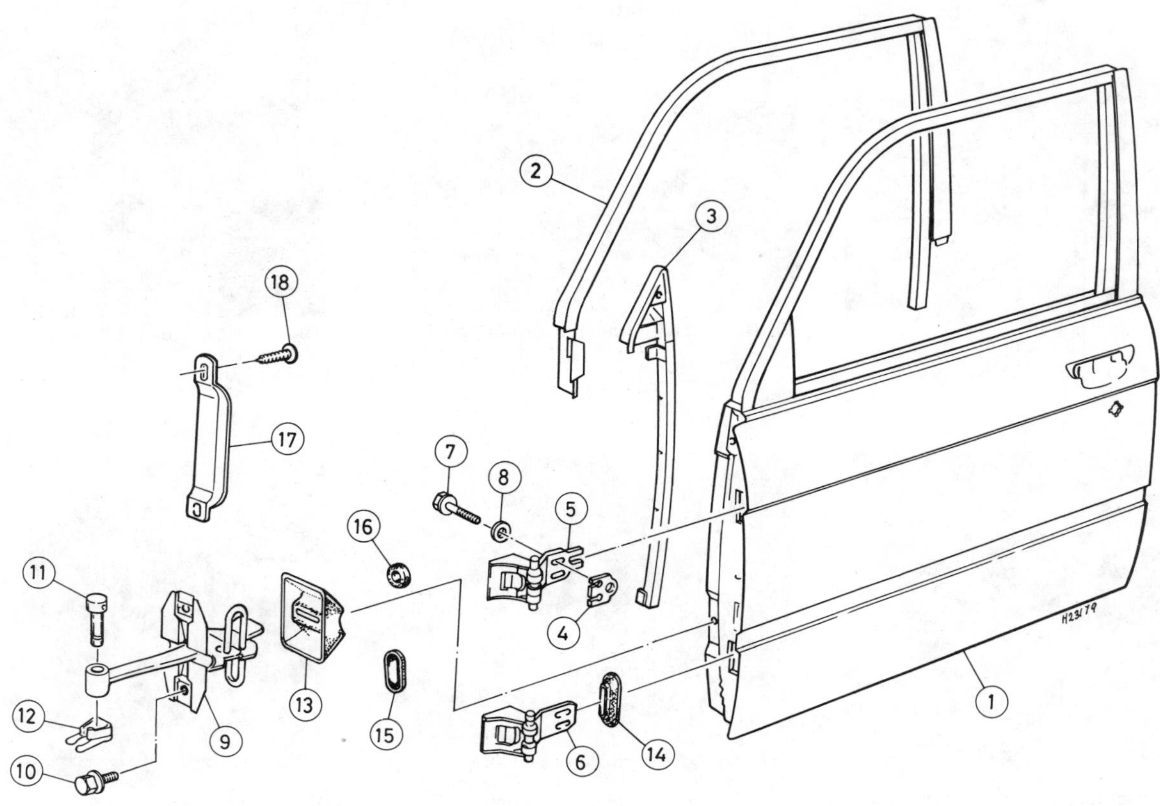

Fig. 11.8 Front door components (Sec 18)

1 Door
2 Window frame
3 Guide rail
4 Spacer
5 Hinge (upper)
6 Hinge (lower)
7 Bolt
8 Flat washer
9 Check strap
10 Bolt
11 Pin
12 Circlip
13 Gasket
14 Gasket
15 Plug
16 Plug
17 Cover
18 Screw

18.3 Front door check strap

18.5 Front door hinge

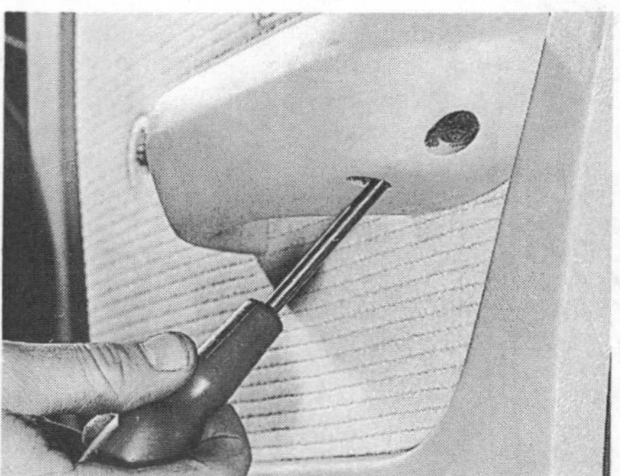
19.1A Remove the screw ...

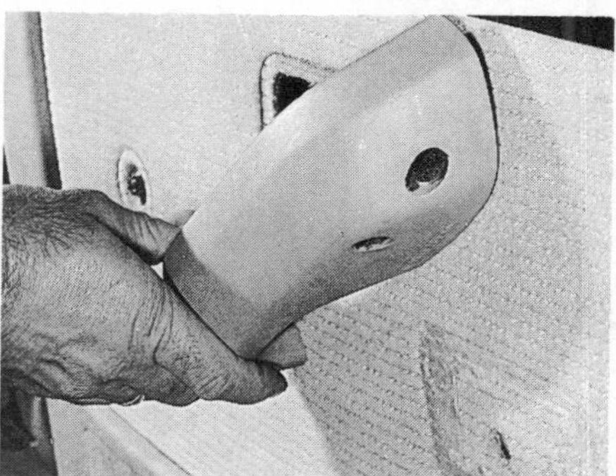
19.1B ... and withdraw the armrest

19.3A Prise off the plastic cover ...

19.3B ... and unscrew the rear door window regulator screw

19.3C Remove the plastic washer

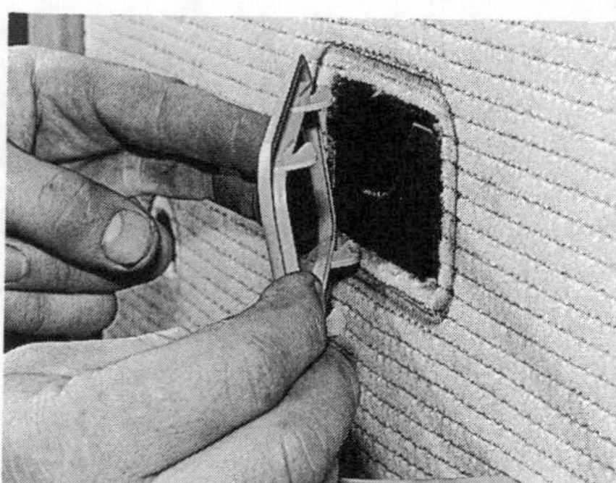
19.4 Removing the rear door inner door handle surround

Where a Torx bolt is fitted to the window regulator handle, it is recommended that it is renewed and its threads coated with thread-locking fluid.

20 Rear door window glass – removal and refitting

1 Remove the rear door inner trim panel as described in Section 19.
2 Pull off the window seal from the inner side of the window opening.
3 Tap the outer moulding from the door using a wedged block of wood.
4 Pull off the window opening moulding and remove the clips.
5 Reposition the window as necessary then unscrew the bolts securing the window glass guide to the regulator. Remove the holder and support the glass with a piece of wood.
6 Unbolt and remove the centre guide rail.
7 Disconnect the regulator arm from the lifting rail.
8 Unscrew the bolts and remove the rear window channel (photo).
9 Pull the rubber weatherstrip from the upper rear corner of the door frame then use pliers to bend the tab on the vertical rail and push the rail down.
10 Pull out the rear quarter glass.
11 Remove the guide rails and window glass upwards.
12 Refitting is a reversal of removal, but apply a little grease to the lifting rail and guides. Renew any broken clips.

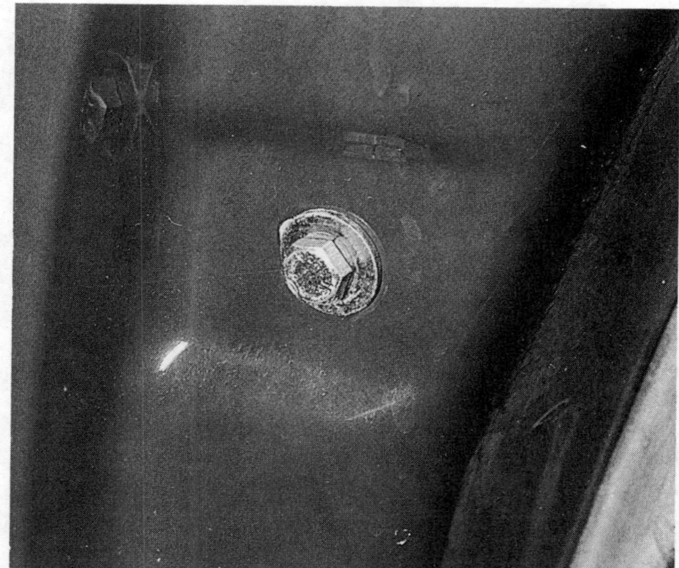
20.8 Rear door window channel bolt

21 Rear door window regulator – removal and refitting

1 Remove the rear door inner trim panel as described in Section 19.
2 Reposition the window as necessary then unscrew the bolts securing the window glass to the regulator. Remove the holder and support the glass with a piece of wood.
3 Disconnect the regulator arm from the lifting rail.
4 Unscrew the regulator mounting bolts, then disconnect the lifting rail from the window channel and withdraw the regulator from within the door (photo).
5 Refitting is a reversal of removal, but apply a little grease to the lifting rail and guides.

21.4 Rear door window regulator mounting bolts

22 Rear door lock – removal and refitting

1 Remove the rear door inner trim panel as described in Section 19.
2 Release the inner door handle connecting rod out of the clips on the door.
3 Unscrew the screws securing the inner door handle and push the controls rearwards (photo).
4 Turn up the locking plate on the outside of the lock then unscrew the five lock mounting screws and withdraw the lock from inside the door (photos).
5 To remove the exterior door handle, unscrew the handle grip plate screws from inside the door.
6 Refitting is a reversal of removal, but make sure that the exterior door handle grip plate rests on the rubber pad.

23 Rear door – removal and refitting

1 Remove the rear door inner trim panel as described in Section 19.
2 Open the door to its fullest extent and support it on wooden blocks and cloth rags to prevent damage to the paintwork.
3 Disconnect the check strap by extracting the spring clip from the bottom of the pin and driving the pin upwards. If necessary the check strap may be removed by unscrewing the two bolts and withdrawing it from inside the door. Recover the rubber weather guard.
4 Unplug the wiring from the electric window and central locking as applicable, and draw the wires through the flexible duct which runs between the door hinged edge and the body pillar.
5 Prise the caps from the door hinge bolts.
6 Unscrew the hinge bolts and lift the door from the car. Note the location of any shims under the hinges.
7 Transfer all internal components to the new door as required.
8 Refitting is a reversal of removal, but tighten the mounting bolts to the specified torque. Before fully tightening the bolts make sure that the door is correctly aligned. The outer surface should be flush with the front door and sill panel, and this is adjusted by moving the hinges either in or out within the elongated bolt holes. The gaps between the rear door and front door, and rear door and rear wing should be the same,

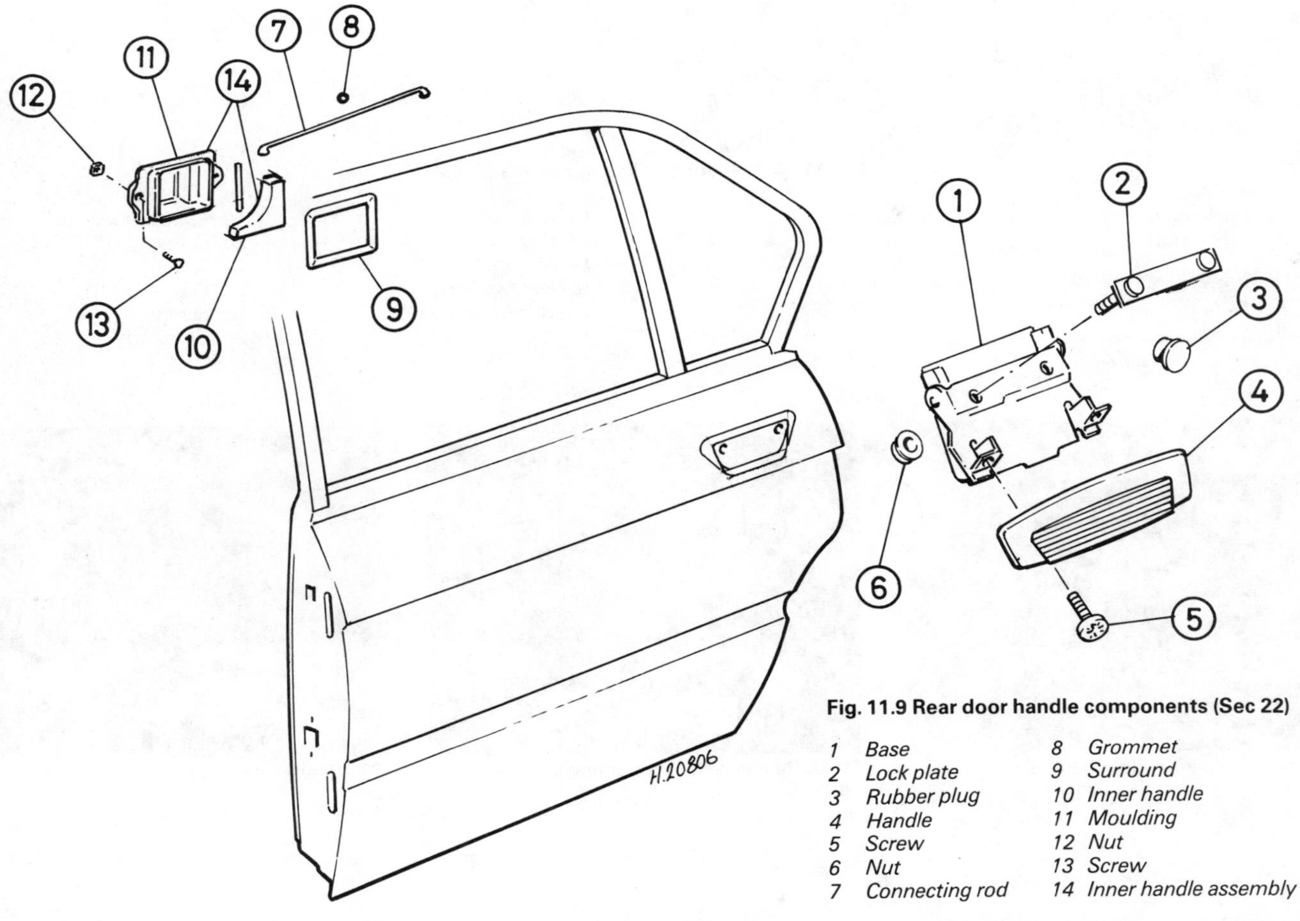

Fig. 11.9 Rear door handle components (Sec 22)

1	*Base*	8	*Grommet*
2	*Lock plate*	9	*Surround*
3	*Rubber plug*	10	*Inner handle*
4	*Handle*	11	*Moulding*
5	*Screw*	12	*Nut*
6	*Nut*	13	*Screw*
7	*Connecting rod*	14	*Inner handle assembly*

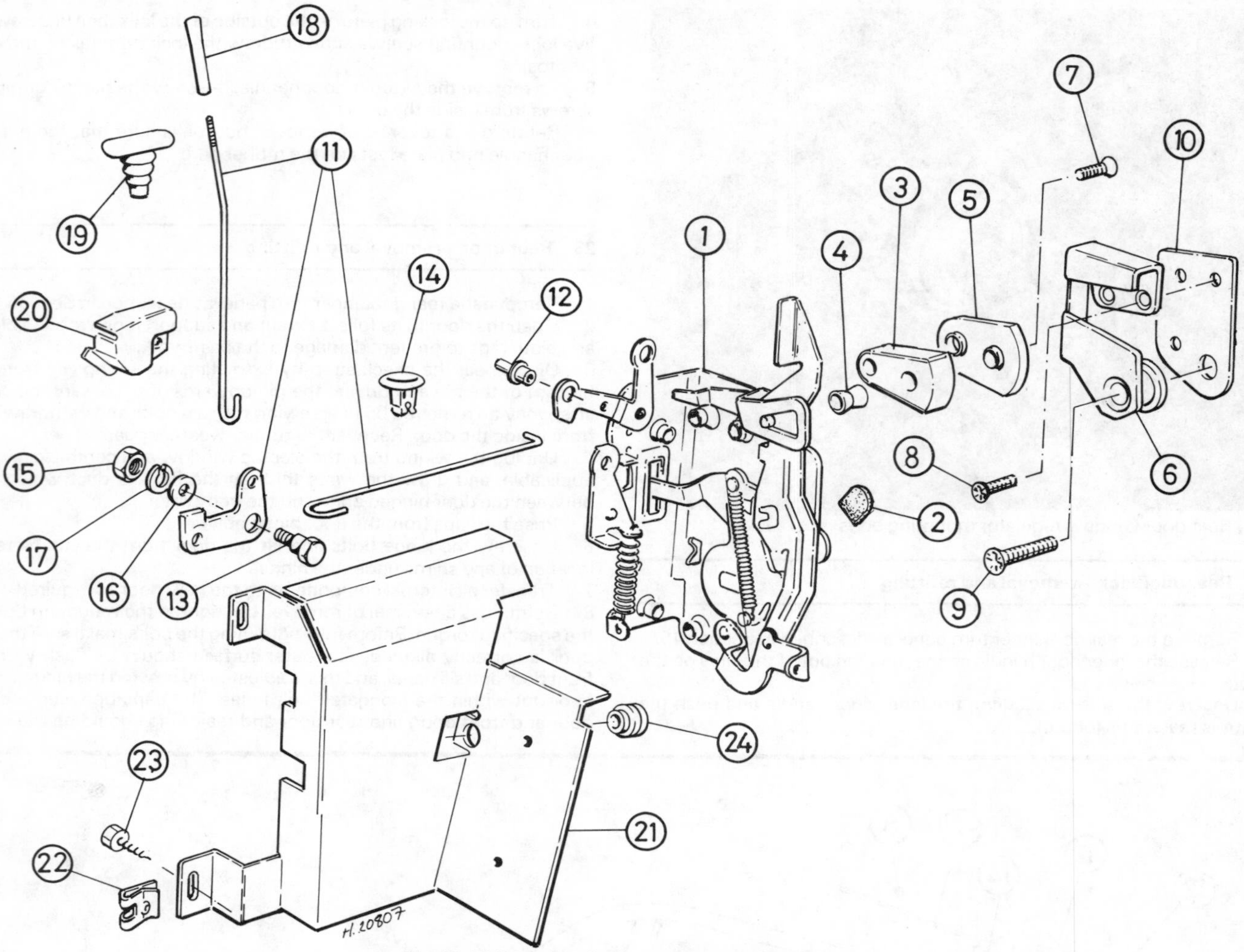

Fig. 11.10 Rear door lock components (Sec 22)

1 *Lock assembly*
2 *Bump stop*
3 *Stop*
4 *Bush*
5 *Plate*
6 *Striker*
7 *Screw*
8 *Screw*
9 *Screw*
10 *Spacer*
11 *Lever*
12 *Circlip*
13 *Bolt*
14 *Clip*
15 *Nut*
16 *Flat washer*
17 *Wave washer*
18 *Button*
19 *Rubber boot*
20 *Cover*
21 *Cover*
22 *Clip*
23 *Screw*
24 *Grommet*

22.3 Rear door inner door handle

22.4A Rear door lock mounting screws (arrowed)

22.4B Inner view of the rear door lock

23.8 Rear door lock striker

and adjustment is made by adding shims under the hinges. The door beading should also be in correct alignment. On completion adjust the door lock striker so that it enters the locking plate correctly (photo).

24 Exterior mirror – removal and refitting

1 Open the front door then prise off the triangular plastic cover and remove the felt pad to expose the mirror mounting bolts (photos).
2 Support the outside of the mirror, and unscrew the bolts.
3 Disconnect the wiring plug and withdraw the exterior mirror (photo). Remove the rubber gasket.
4 If necessary remove the clips from the door panel.
5 Refitting is a reversal of removal.

25 Radiator grille – removal and refitting

1 With the bonnet open, unscrew the centre grille upper mounting screws and lift the grille from the clips.
2 To remove a side grille, unscrew the three upper and two lower mounting screws and withdraw the grille from the front panel (photos).
3 Refitting is a reversal of removal, but renew any broken clips first.

26 Windscreen and rear window – removal and refitting

Note: *There are two types of windscreen fitted, one has a rubber moulding without bracing, whereas the other has bracing. Although the following procedure is given, it is recommended that the work is preferably carried out by a specialist who will have the experience necessary to make a first class job.*

Windscreen (moulding without bracing)

1 Remove the front roof liner plate.
2 Pull off the A-pillar trim at the top and remove it from above.
3 Remove both wiper arms and blades as described in Chapter 12.
4 Pull out the top and sidè moulding insert.
5 Carefully free the rubber from the outside of the body by prising it away with a non-metallic instrument.
6 Starting at a top corner inside the car, press out the windscreen while easing the rubber moulding over the window opening using a wooden wedge.
7 Scrape away all old sealant from the opening.
8 Fit the rubber moulding on the new windscreen, then fit the lower ornamental moulding and coat the exterior of the rubber moulding with glycerine.
9 Locate a length of cord in the rubber moulding groove so that the ends of the cord overlap at the bottom of the windscreen.
10 Offer up the windscreen to the body aperture, engaging the bottom of the groove. Push the glass downwards and inwards and have your assistant pull the ends of the cords evenly which will have the effect of pulling the lip of the rubber moulding over the body flange.
11 Using a mastic gun, apply sealant between the rubber moulding and windscreen, and between the rubber moulding and body. Clean off any surplus sealant.
12 Refit the top and side moulding insert. This is best achieved by using a special tool obtainable from a motor accessory shop (Fig. 11.11).
13 Refit both wiper arms and blades as described in Chapter 12.
14 Refit the A-pillar trim.
15 Refit the front roof liner plate.

Windscreen (moulding with bracing)

16 Prise out the moulding insert strips from the top and sides.
17 Prise out the bottom moulding insert strip and the corners.
18 Starting at a top corner, press out the windscreen noting that the rubber moulding remains in the body.
19 Remove the rubber moulding from the body opening and clean away all traces of sealant.
20 Locate the new rubber moulding on the body opening and press it firmly into position.
21 Using a small brush, apply soapy water to the inner groove of the rubber moulding.
22 Locate the bottom of the windscreen in the bottom groove of the rubber moulding and press it firmly into position.
23 Using a flat length of plastic, ease the outer lip of the rubber moulding onto the windscreen starting with the sides then the top. Lightly tap the perimeter of the windscreen with the palm of the hand to settle the moulding.
24 Refit the bottom moulding insert strip and the corners. Cover the ends of the strip with plastic bags to prevent them damaging the paintwork as they are sharp.
25 Refit the top and side insert strips. This is best achieved by using a special tool obtainable from a motor accessory shop.

24.1A Removing the exterior door mirror plastic cover

24.1B Exterior door mirror mounting bolts (arrowed)

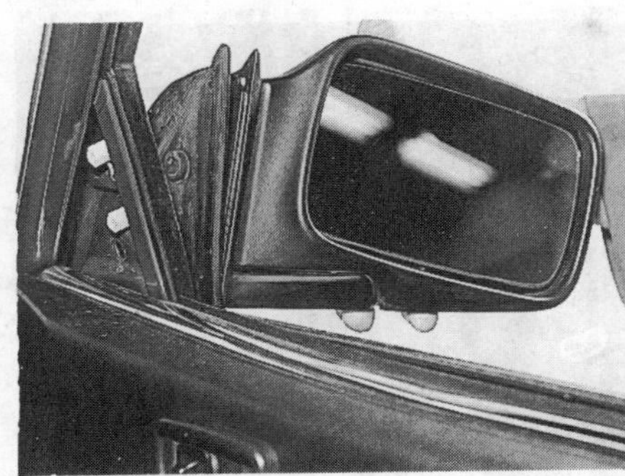

24.3 Removing the exterior mirror

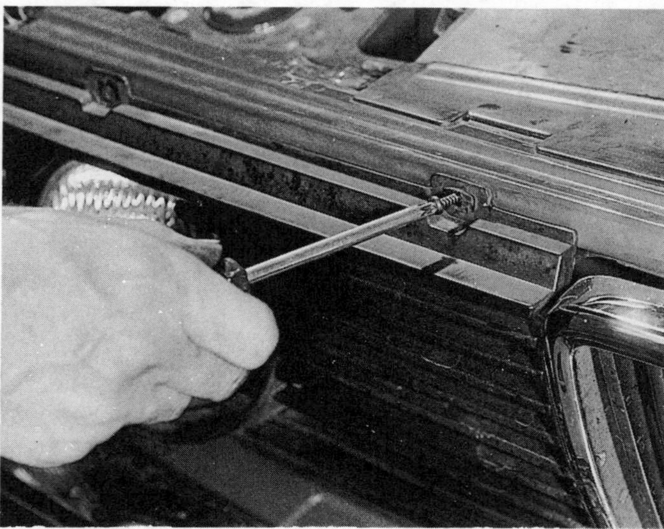

25.2A Extract the mounting screws ...

25.2B ... and remove the side radiator grille

Rear window

26 Disconnect the wiring for the heating elements.

27 The remaining procedure is similar to that for the windscreen described in paragraphs 1 to 15.

28 If the rear window was broken, remove the rear seat cushion and clean away any glass splinters. Also clean the automatic seat belt reels.

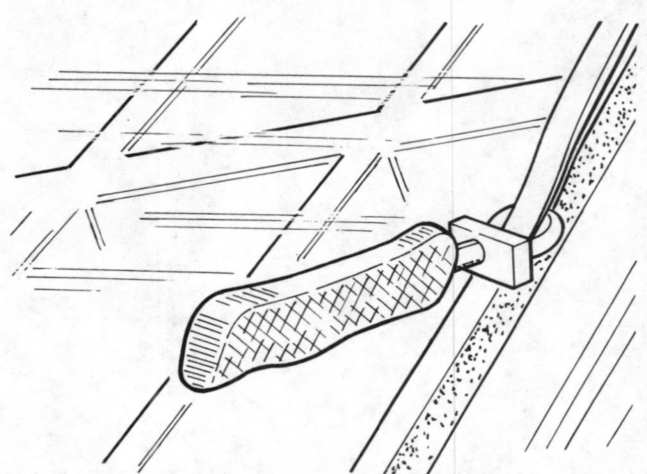

Fig. 11.11 Tool for fitting inserts to the windscreen rubber (Sec 26)

27 Centre console – removal and refitting

1 Disconnect the battery negative lead.

2 Remove the lower facia panel from under the steering wheel by unscrewing the screws.

3 On models with electric windows, disconnect the wiring from the automatic cut-outs.

4 On models with electronic heating control, pull off the vacuum line and the plug on the passenger compartment temperature sensor.

5 Remove the trim panel.

6 Remove the handbrake lever cover by first compressing it inwards then withdrawing it upwards (photo).

7 Prise out the cover or switch as applicable from the centre console and disconnect the wiring as applicable.

8 Prise out the rear covers, unscrew the two screws and push back the rear section (photos).

9 Where applicable pull off the gear lever knob.

10 Where applicable remove the gear lever gaiter.

11 On models with automatic transmission, prise out the front cover, unscrew the screws and remove the surround (photos).

12 Remove the insulation sheet from around the gear lever.

13 Lift out the ashtray, then unscrew the screws, pull out the holder and disconnect the wiring to the cigar lighter and ashtray light (photos).

14 On models with electric windows, prise out the control switches and disconnect the wiring (photo).

15 Open the glovebox then unscrew the two screws located on either side of the heater control panel (photo).

16 On early models without air conditioning, push back the centre console, disconnect the radio wiring and remove the centre console.

17 On early models with air conditioning, and all later models, push back the centre console and unscrew the screws on top of the panel. Disconnect the radio wiring and remove the centre console (photos).

18 Refitting is a reversal of removal.

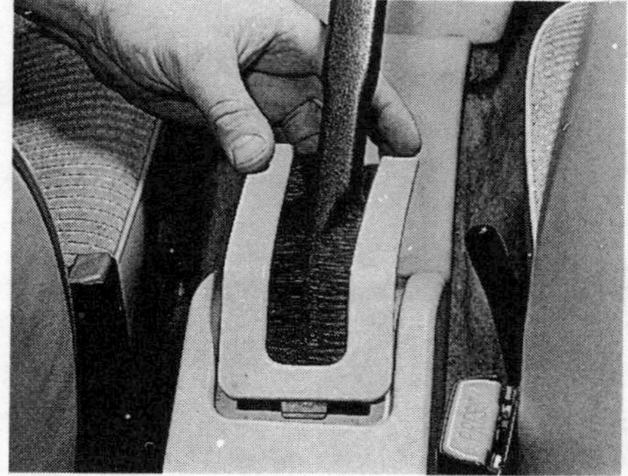

27.6 Handbrake lever cover removal

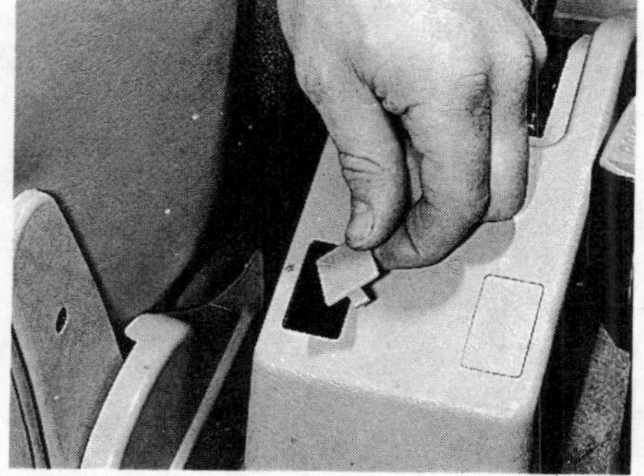

27.8A Prise out the rear covers ...

27.8B ... for access to the centre console mounting screws

27.11A Prise out the cover...

27.11B ... unscrew the screws ...

27.11C ... and remove the surround

27.13A Ashtray holder mounting screws (arrowed)

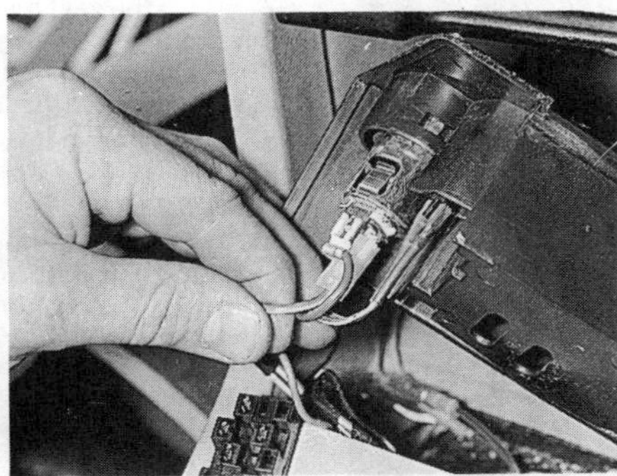
27.13B Disconnecting the cigar lighter wiring

27.14 Disconnecting the electric window control switch wiring

27.15 Centre console mounting screws located on either side of the heater control panel

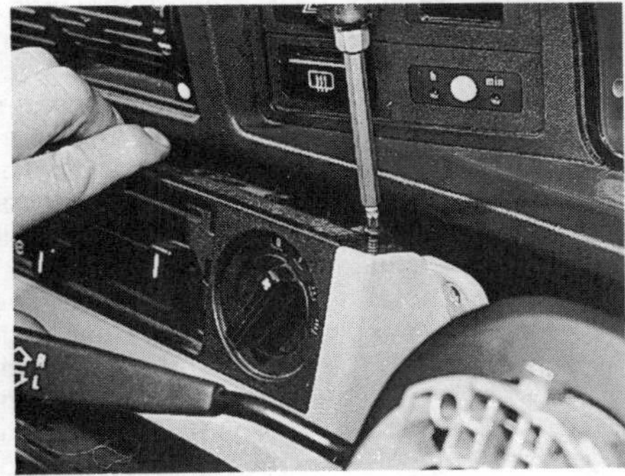
27.17A Unscrew the upper panel screws ...

27.17B ... and remove the centre console

28 Facia – removal and refitting

1 Disconnect the battery earth lead.
2 Remove the steering wheel as described in Chapter 10.
3 Remove the centre console as described in Section 27.
4 Remove the switch plate from under the instrument panel.
5 Remove the instrument panel as described in Chapter 12.
6 Prise out the hazard light and rear window heater switches and disconnect the wiring.
7 Remove the glovebox by disconnecting the joints.
8 Unbolt and disconnect the air ducts, grilles, switch support and brackets. Also release the retaining clamps.
9 Partially remove the front door weatherstrip from the top corners, then remove the A-pillar trim on both sides by unscrewing the screws.
10 Unscrew the mounting bolts on either side of the facia.
11 Withdraw the facia from one side of the car.
12 Refitting is a reversal of removal, but align the facia so that it is central between the left and right-hand doors when shut. Refit the steering wheel as described in Chapter 10.

29 Lower facia panel – removal and refitting

1 Disconnect the battery negative lead.
2 Unscrew the screws and remove the lower facia panel from under

29.2A Lower facia panel inner screw ...

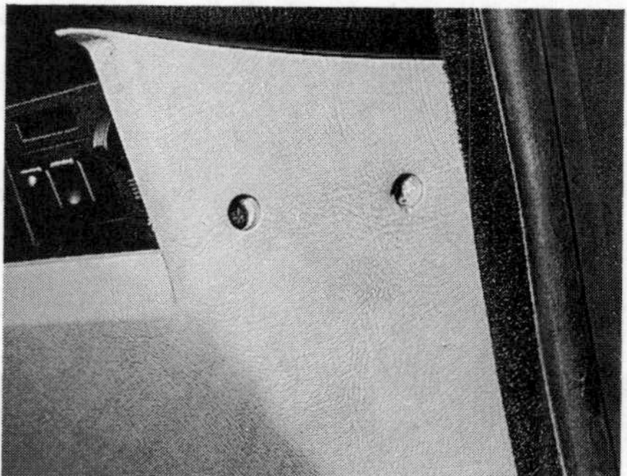
29.2B ... and outer screws

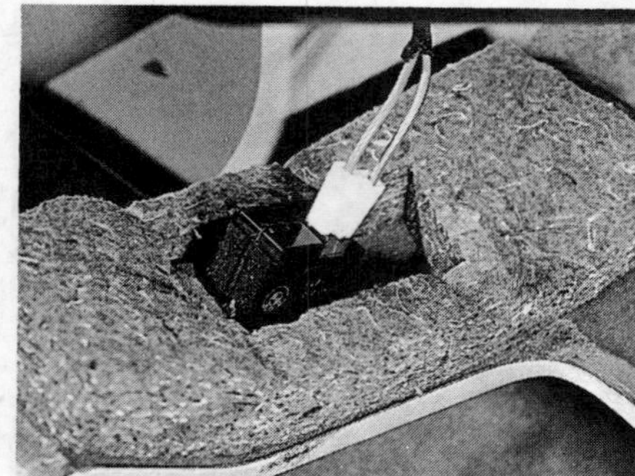
29.3 Electric window automatic cut-out and wiring plug

29.4 Passenger compartment temperature sensor and wiring plug

the steering column and lower it to the floor (photos).

3 On models with electric windows, disconnect the wiring for the automatic cut-out (photo).

4 Disconnect the vacuum line and wiring plug from the passenger compartment temperature sensor, and remove the facia panel (photo).

5 Refitting is a reversal of removal.

30 Glovebox – removal and refitting

1 Open the glovebox and press out the pins from the bottom of the joint links (photo).

2 Unbolt the hinge and rear cover and withdraw the glovebox (photos).

3 If necessary unscrew the screws and remove the catch from the facia.

4 The lock may be unbolted from the glovebox and the joint links removed from the upper plate.

5 Refitting is a reversal of removal, but align the catch so that the lock enters it correctly.

31 Seats – removal and refitting

Front seat

1 Detach the seat belt from the front seat with reference to Section 32.

2 Push the seat fully rearwards then unscrew the front mounting bolts (photo).

3 Push the seat fully forwards then unscrew the rear mounting bolts (photo).

4 Refitting is a reversal of removal.

Rear seat

5 Unscrew the bolt located just below the middle of the rear seat cushion, then lift the cushion and disconnect it from the holders (photo). Withdraw the cushion.

6 Unscrew the lower mounting bolts for the backrest on both sides and in the middle.

7 Push the backrest upwards and remove it from the car.

8 Refitting is a reversal of removal.

32 Seat belts – removal and refitting

Front seat belts

1 Pull off forwards the cover from the front seat belt mounting on the front seat, then unscrew the bolt and disconnect the belt from the seat (photo).

2 Unbolt the centre stalk from the floor.

3 Pull off the cap from the B-pillar anchorage, then unscrew the belt bolt (photo) and the bolt located higher on the B-pillar. Note the location of the plastic washers, belt holder and lock washer.

4 Unscrew the bolts and remove the trim from the bottom of the B-pillar.

5 Unscrew the lower mounting bolt and withdraw the automatic reel. If necessary, unbolt the bracket from the reel.

6 Refitting is a reversal of removal, but tighten all bolts to the specified torque. Make sure that the upper belt holder on the B-pillar is not trapped when tightening the bolt. Similarly check that the stalk is free to move after tightening the lower bolt.

Rear seat belt

7 Remove the rear seat as described in Section 31.

8 Unscrew the bolt for the centre straps, then unscrew the lower anchorage point bolt (photos). Note the location of the lock washer and paper washer.

9 Lift the trim cover from the upper belt holder then unscrew the bolts from the bolt holder and automatic reel (photo).

10 Refitting is a reversal of removal, but tighten all bolts to the specified torque. Make sure that the belt holder can still be moved after tightening the bolt.

33 Central door locking system – description

Central door locking is fitted to some models. The system locks all doors, the boot lid and the fuel filler cap whenever a door lock or the boot lid lock is operated or the safety catch button is pressed down on the driver's door.

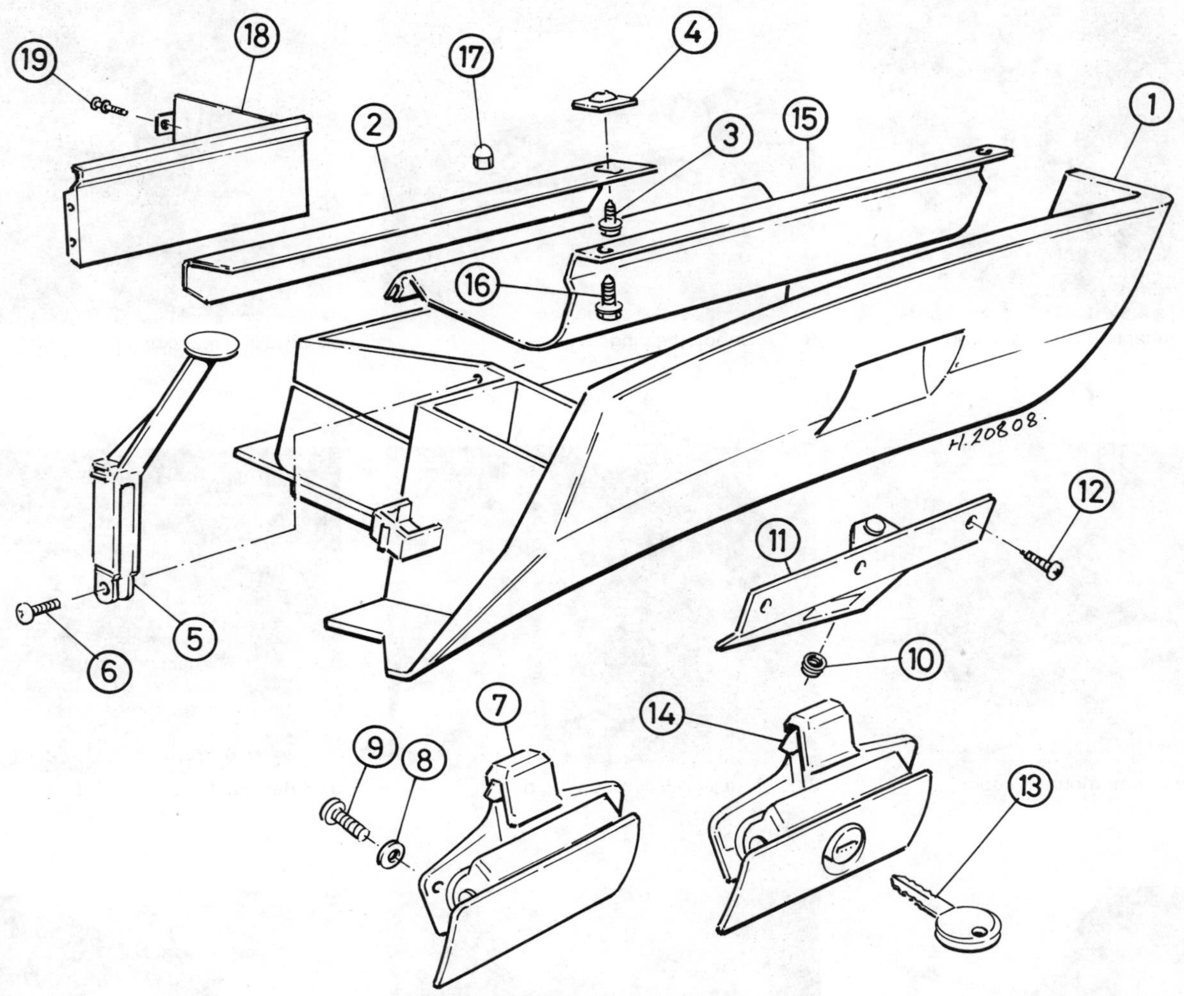

Fig. 11.12 Glovebox components (Sec 30)

1 Glovebox
2 Hinge
3 Screw
4 Nut
5 Joint link
6 Pin
7 Catch
8 Wave washer
9 Screw
10 Nut
11 Catch
12 Lock
13 Key
14 Catch with lock
15 Cover
16 Bolt
17 Nut
18 Cover
19 Rivet

Fig. 11.13 Front seat belt B-pillar anchorage bolt components (Sec 32)

1 Bolt
2 Plastic washer
3 Belt holder
4 Plastic washer
5 Washer
6 Lock washer

The system operates by solenoids (photo) which move the lock plungers into position and also includes control switches and the necessary wiring.

A central inhibit feature is also included whereby the central locking system can be disarmed by turning the key in the driver's door lock fully clockwise. This function must not be used with someone inside the car since it is not possible to release the locks normally.

In the event of a collision or violent impact all locks are released automatically.

34 Sunroof - adjustment

1 The sunroof should be adjusted so that the front edge is 1.0 mm lower than the roof panel, and the rear edge 1.0 mm higher than the roof panel. The gap between the sunroof and roof panel should be approximately 0.2 mm at the front and rear.

2 Open the sunroof about 50 mm and press off the roof liner frame.

3 Close the sunroof and push back the liner frame fully.

Type without plastic gate (up to January 1983)

4 Adjust the front height by unscrewing the two bracket bolts, then turning the height adjusting screw as necessary. Retighten the bolts after making the adjustment.

5 Adjust the rear height by unscrewing the bolts on the gate holder, then move the sunroof within the elongated slot and retighten the bolts.

6 Check that the dimension shown in Fig. 11.16 is 2.0 mm. In the lift

30.1 Strap connection to the glovebox

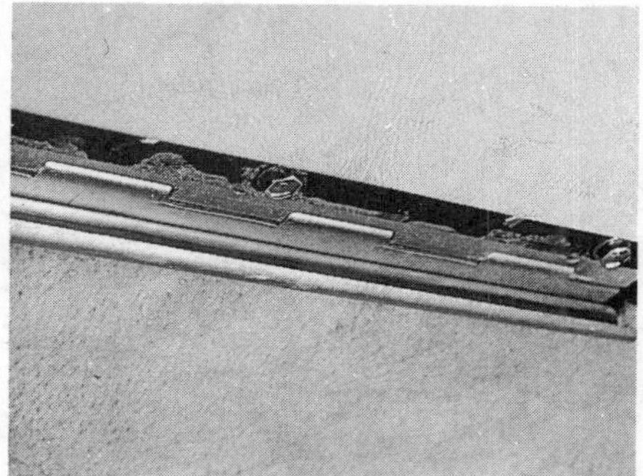
30.2A Unbolt the hinge ...

30.2B ... and rear cover (arrowed)

31.2 Front seat front mounting bolt

31.3 Front seat rear mounting bolt

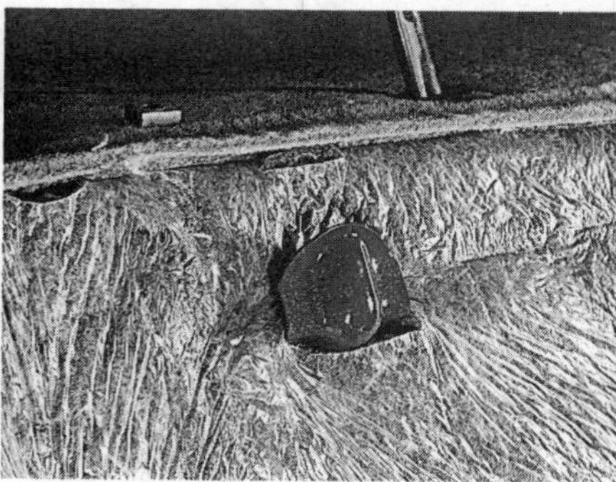
31.5 Rear seat cushion holder

32.1 Front seat belt location on the front seat

32.3 Front seat belt location on the B-pillar

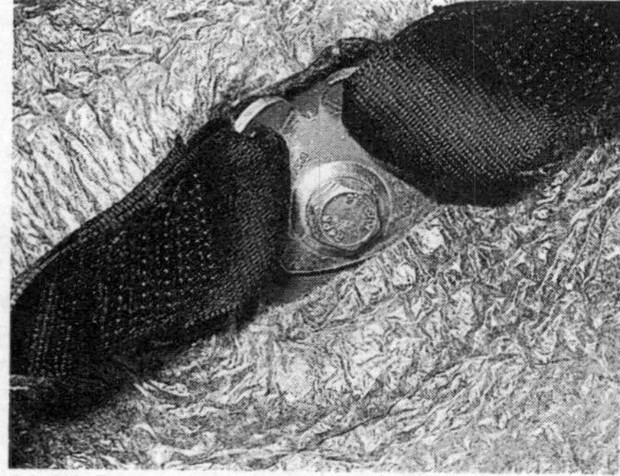
32.8A Rear seat belt centre strap mounting

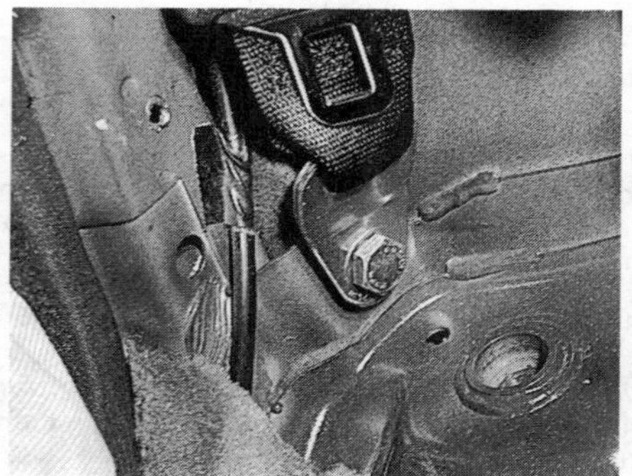
32.8B Rear seat belt side anchorage point

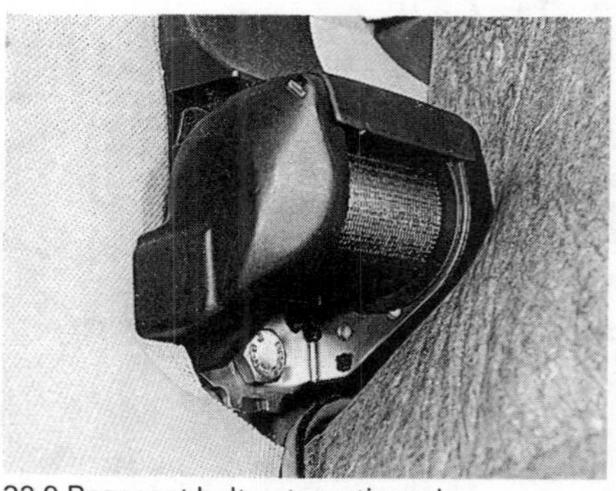
32.9 Rear seat belt automatic reel

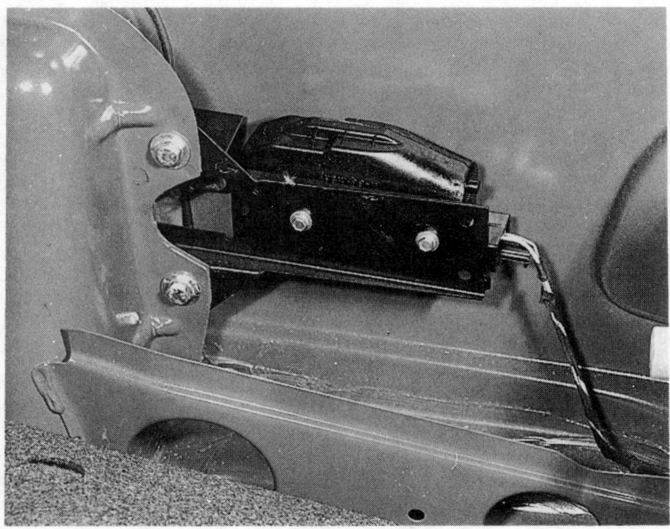

33.0 Central locking solenoid for the fuel filler cap

position the sunroof should rest on the front opening edge, and if necessary the guide pins and guide plates should be adjusted.

Type with plastic gate (up to January 1983)

7 Fully close the sunroof and lock it in this position using a 4 mm Allen key on the left and right sides. The key should be inserted through the guide pin holder into the bores of the opening lever and gate.

8 Loosen the bolts on the left and right sides and adjust the sunroof with the elongated slots. A T25 Torx key will be required to loosen and tighten the bolts.

All types (January 1983 on)

9 A new guide pin is fitted and no adjustment is necessary.

35 Sunroof lid – removal and refitting

Type with plastic gate

1 Open the sunroof fully then unbolt the left and right upper guide rails.

2 Close the sunroof until it is open about 50 mm then press off the front roof liner frame.

3 Close the sunroof and push back the roof liner frame fully.

4 Unscrew the mounting bolts and lift the sunroof from the car.

5 Refitting is a reversal of removal, but lubricate the guide rails with vaseline and adjust the sunroof as described in Section 34.

Type without plastic gate

6 Position the sunroof until it is open about 50 mm then press off the front roof liner frame.

7 Fully close the sunroof then push back the roof liner frame fully.

8 Using a Torx key unscrew the left and right mounting bolts and lift off the sunroof lid.

9 Refitting is a reversal of removal, but renew all self-locking bolts and adjust the sunroof as described in Section 34.

H.20810

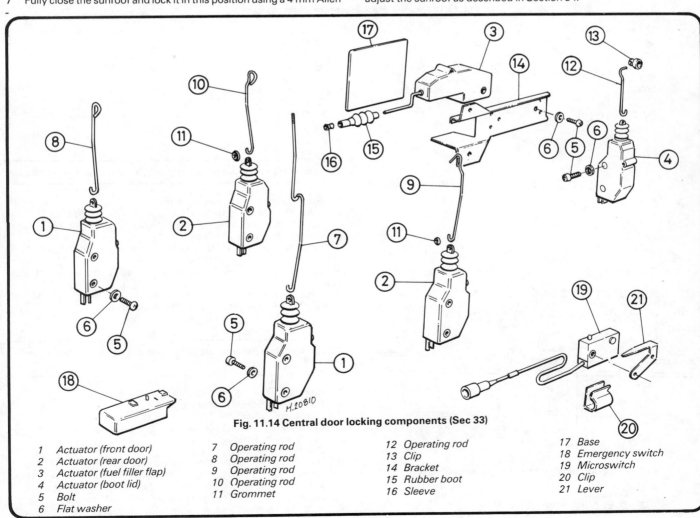

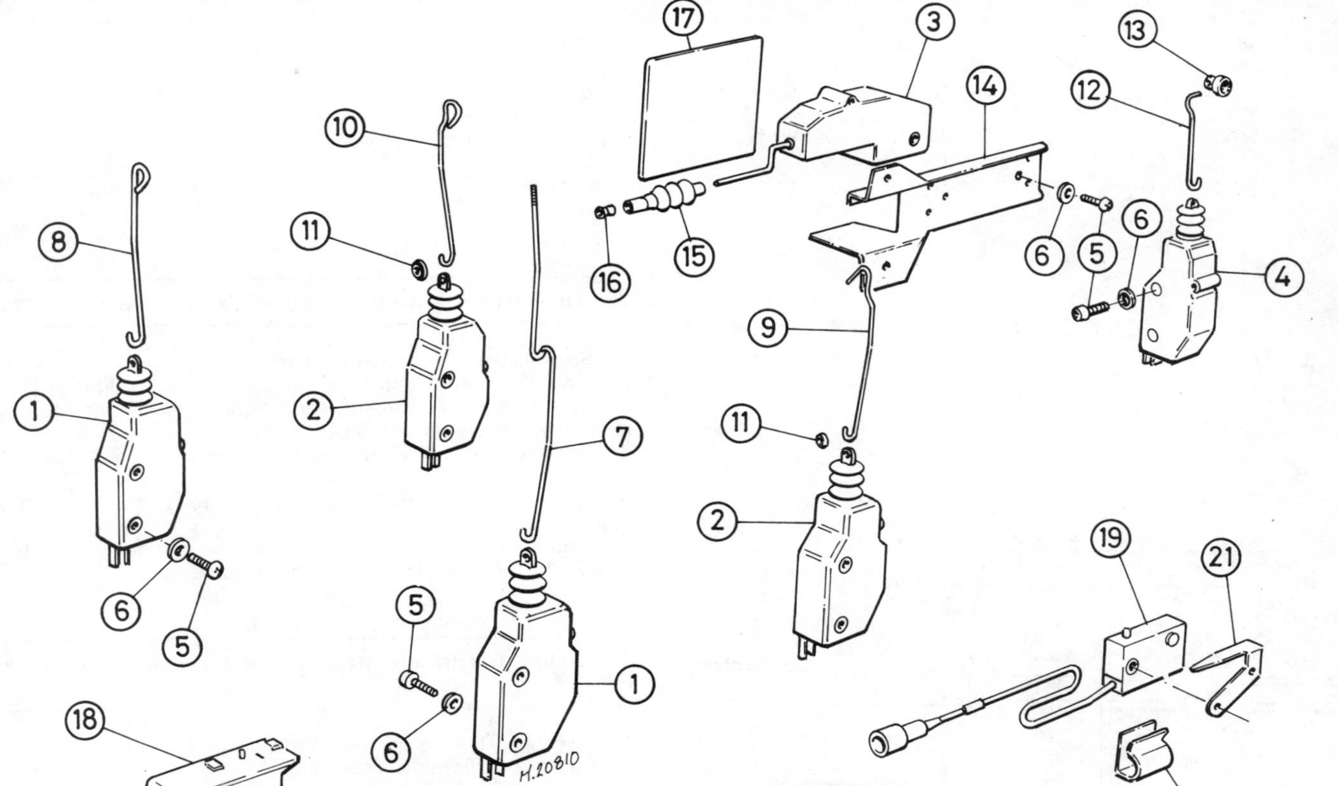

Fig. 11.14 Central door locking components (Sec 33)

1 Actuator (front door)
2 Actuator (rear door)
3 Actuator (fuel filler flap)
4 Actuator (boot lid)
5 Bolt
6 Flat washer
7 Operating rod
8 Operating rod
9 Operating rod
10 Operating rod
11 Grommet
12 Operating rod
13 Clip
14 Bracket
15 Rubber boot
16 Sleeve
17 Base
18 Emergency switch
19 Microswitch
20 Clip
21 Lever

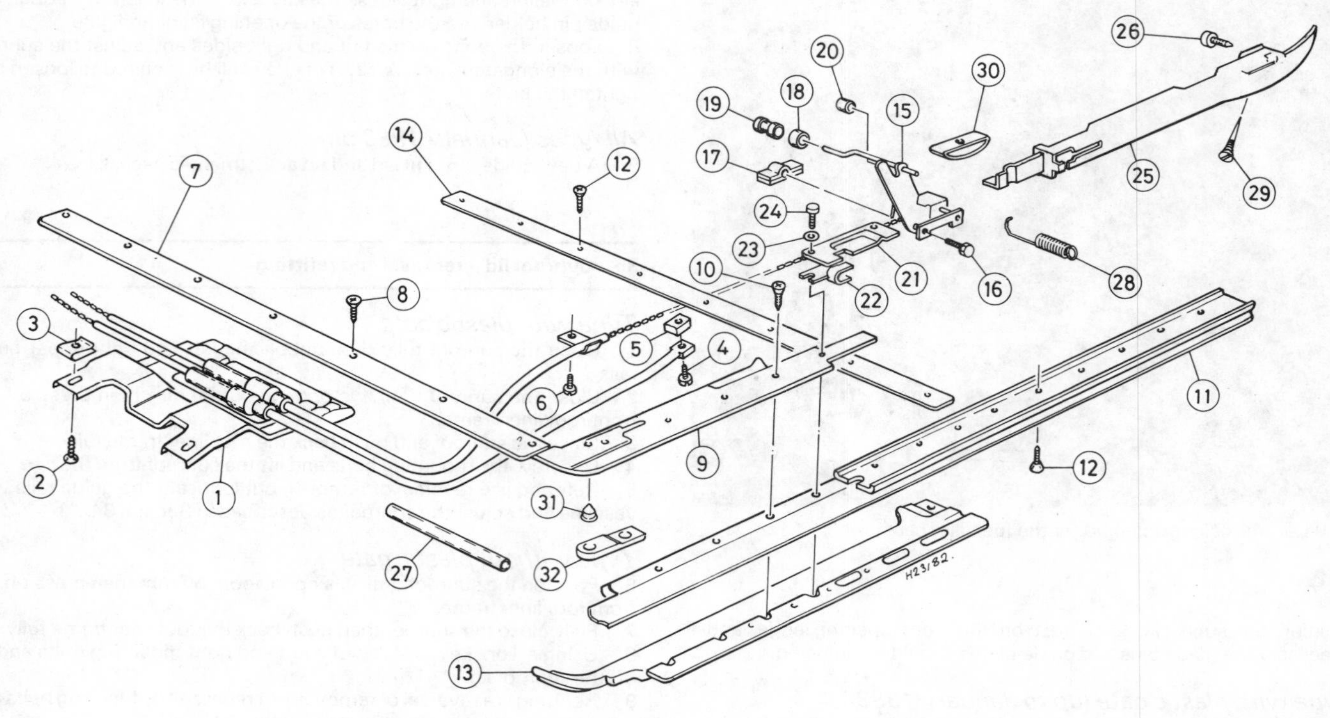

Fig. 11.15 Sunroof mechanism components (Sec 34)

1 Mounting plate
2 Screw
3 Nut
4 Screw
5 Nut
6 Screw
7 Front cover rail
8 Screw
9 Slide rail
10 Screw
11 Guide rail
12 Screw
13 Slide rail
14 Clamping strip
15 Drive cable
16 Pin
17 Sliding piece
18 Roller
19 Bush
20 Roller
21 Guide
22 Guide plate
23 Wave washer
24 Screw
25 Gate
26 Screw
27 Hose
28 Spring
29 Rubber buffer
30 Sliding jaw
31 Rubber buffer
32 Intermediate piece

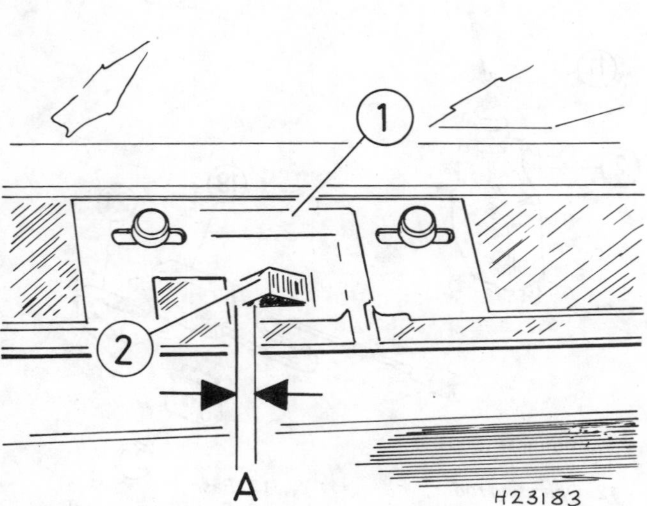

Fig. 11.16 Sunroof adjustment dimension (Sec 34)

1 Guide pin
2 Guide plate
A = 2.0 mm

36 Sunroof (manually-operated) gearbox – removal and refitting

1 Remove the sunroof check control.
2 Close the sunroof to the pressure point but do not lift the lid.
3 Remove the escutcheon (1 screw), then unscrew the screws and remove the recess plate (photos).
4 Unscrew the screws and remove the winder (photo). The larger side of the winder base faces to the rear.
5 Fully close the sunroof then unbolt and remove the sunroof gearbox.
6 Refitting is a reversal of removal but set the gearbox to its zero position by turning it clockwise to the pressure point.

37 Sunroof (electrically-operated) motor/gearbox – removal and refitting

1 Disconnect the battery negative lead.
2 Remove the front roof liner plate.
3 Fully close the sunroof.
4 Unscrew the nut and turn the gearbox drive shaft with a socket-headed spanner to close it.
5 Disconnect the wiring plugs.
6 Unbolt and remove the motor/gearbox assembly.
7 Before refitting the assembly remove the cover and check that the mark on the switching gear is opposite the mark on the control gear. If necessary add grease to the gears before refitting the cover.
8 Refitting is a reversal of removal.

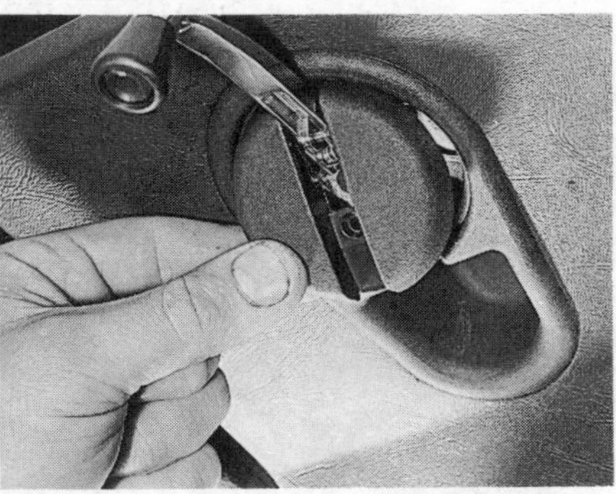

36.3A Removing the escutcheon from the sunroof winder

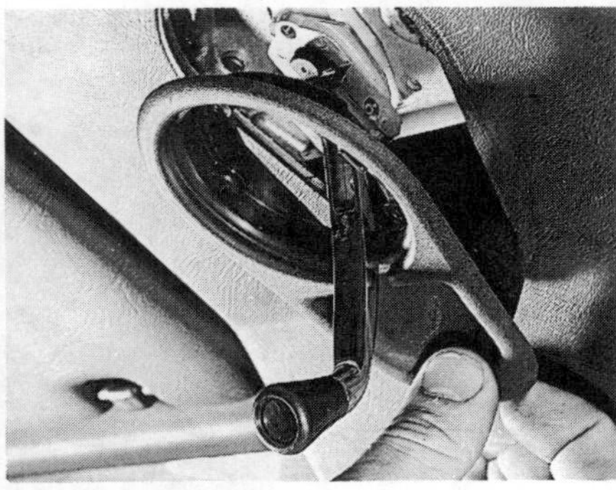

36.3B Removing the recess plate from the sunroof winder

36.4 Sunroof winder

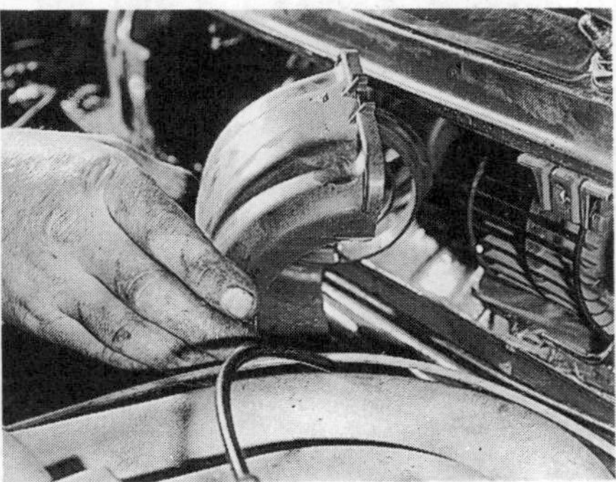

39.4 Removing the heater motor covers

39.6A Disconnect the retaining strap ...

39.6B ... and remove the heater motor

38 Sunroof lid seals – renewal

1 Remove the sunroof lid as described in Section 35.

2 Pull the seals off the lid noting which way round the lips are positioned. The front seal has an extra lip on its front side.

3 Refitting is a reversal of removal, but apply suitable cement to the seals before fitting them.

39 Heater motor – removal and refitting

1 Disconnect the battery negative lead. On 520i models only, disconnect the wiring from the ignition amplifier module on the bulkhead.

2 Pull off the rubber strip from the upper edge of the heater plenum chamber.

3 Unscrew the bolts from the front of the plenum chamber and remove the rubber cover.

4 Bend back the retaining tabs and remove the heater blower covers (photo). Note that the flat surfaces on the covers face the body.

5 Disconnect the wiring plug.

6 Disconnect the retaining strap and remove the heater motor together with the fan (photos).

7 Do not attempt to remove the fan from the motor shaft as the assembly is balanced at the factory.

8 Refitting is a reversal of removal.

40 Heater unit (non-air conditioning) – removal and refitting

1 Disconnect the battery negative lead.

2 Disconnect the wiring plug from the heater motor.

3 Pull off the rubber strip from the edge of the heater plenum chamber.

4 Unscrew the bolts from the front of the plenum chamber.

5 Unscrew the mounting nuts from each side of the motor.

6 Drain the cooling system as described in Chapter 2.

7 Disconnect both heater hoses at the bulkhead.

8 Working inside the car, remove the lower facia panel from under the steering column, as described in Section 29.

9 On models with electric windows, pull off the wiring plugs from the automatic cut-out.

10 Disconnect the vacuum line and wiring plug on the passenger compartment temperature sensor, and remove the trim.

11 Remove the centre console as described in Section 27.

12 Unbolt the heater cover, remove the insulation sheet and disconnect the wiring plugs.

13 Remove the left and right vents.

14 Remove the foam wedge and lift out the air guides.

15 Unscrew the mounting bolts and withdraw the heater unit from inside the car.

16 Refitting is a reversal of removal, but refit the centre console with reference to Section 27, and refill the cooling system with reference to Chapter 2.

41 Heater unit (air conditioning) – removal and refitting

The procedure is similar to that described in Section 40, though it will be necessary to have the air conditioning system evacuated before disconnecting the system hoses, and on completion it will be necessary to have it recharged again. This work should be left to a suitably-qualified specialist.

42 Heater matrix – removal and refitting

1 Remove the heater unit as described in Sections 40 or 41.

2 Pull off the four air guides.

3 Bend back the retaining tabs and remove the heater blower covers. Note that the flat surfaces on the covers face the body.
4 Prise open all of the spring clips and separate the two heater sections.
5 Lift out the heater matrix and remove the foam surround.
6 Refitting is a reversal of removal, but use adhesive to attach a new foam surround to the matrix. Make sure that the air control flaps are correctly located in their bearing bores.

3 Heating temperature control unit – renewal

1 Disconnect the battery negative lead.
2 Working inside the car, remove the lower facia panel from under the steering column as described in Section 29.
3 On models with electric windows, pull off the wiring plugs from the automatic cut-out.
4 Disconnect the vacuum line and wiring plug on the passenger compartment temperature sensor, and remove the trim.
5 Remove the centre console as described in Section 27.
6 Pull off the temperature control knob.
7 Disconnect the wiring plugs from the control unit, then unscrew the bolts and remove the unit.
8 Refitting is a reversal of removal.

44 Heater water valve – removal and refitting

1 Disconnect the wiring plug from the valve (photo).
2 Drain the cooling system as described in Chapter 2.
3 Disconnect the hoses from the valve (photo).
4 Unscrew the mounting bolts and remove the valve.
5 To check the valve, connect a water supply to the small side inlet stub. Without any voltage applied to the terminals the valve should be open and water should flow out of the main stub, but with 12 volts applied to the terminals the flow should cease. Note that the flow of water must only be from the side stub to the main stub and not the reverse way.
6 The water valve contains a filter screen which can become clogged with sediment from the cooling system. If this occurs the valve should be dismantled and the filter cleaned thoroughly. Also clean the cooling system.
7 Refitting is a reversal of removal.

44.1 Disconnecting the heater water valve wiring plug

44.3 Hose to the heater water valve

45 Heater fresh air flap cable – removal and refitting

1 Disconnect the battery negative lead.
2 Remove the lower facia panel as described in Section 29.
3 Remove the centre console as described in Section 27.
4 Disconnect the clips from the fresh air flap cable (centre one). Disconnect the cable from the slide control.
5 Remove the cover from the side of the heater, then disconnect the clip from the cable. Withdraw the cable from the car.
6 Refitting is a reversal of removal, but adjust the cable on the slide control end by first connecting it to the slide control, then pushing the control against the stop. Turn the ring until it can be positioned in the opening then refit the clip.

46 Heater footwell and windscreen vent control cables – removal and refitting

1 Remove the heater as described in Sections 40 or 41.
2 On air conditioned models remove the evaporator as described in Section 51.
3 Remove the control unit.
4 Unbolt the cover from the heater unit.
5 Disconnect the cable from the heater unit.
6 Refitting is a reversal of removal, but adjust the cable on the slide control end by first connecting it to the slide control, then pushing the control against the stop. Turn the ring until it can be positioned in the opening then refit the clip.

47 Air conditioner – description and precautions

Air conditioning can be a factory-fitted option on some models. It is incorporated into the heating system to comprise a complete ventilation, heating and air conditioning system.

The main components include a belt-driven compressor, a condenser and an evaporator.

Always ensure that at least one air outlet grille is open when the air conditioner is switched on, otherwise the evaporator may ice up.

The air conditioner must be operated at least once a month to prevent the compressor shaft seals from drying out and allowing the refrigerant to escape. This is particularly important in the winter months.

Do not attempt to disconnect any of the air conditioning hoses as

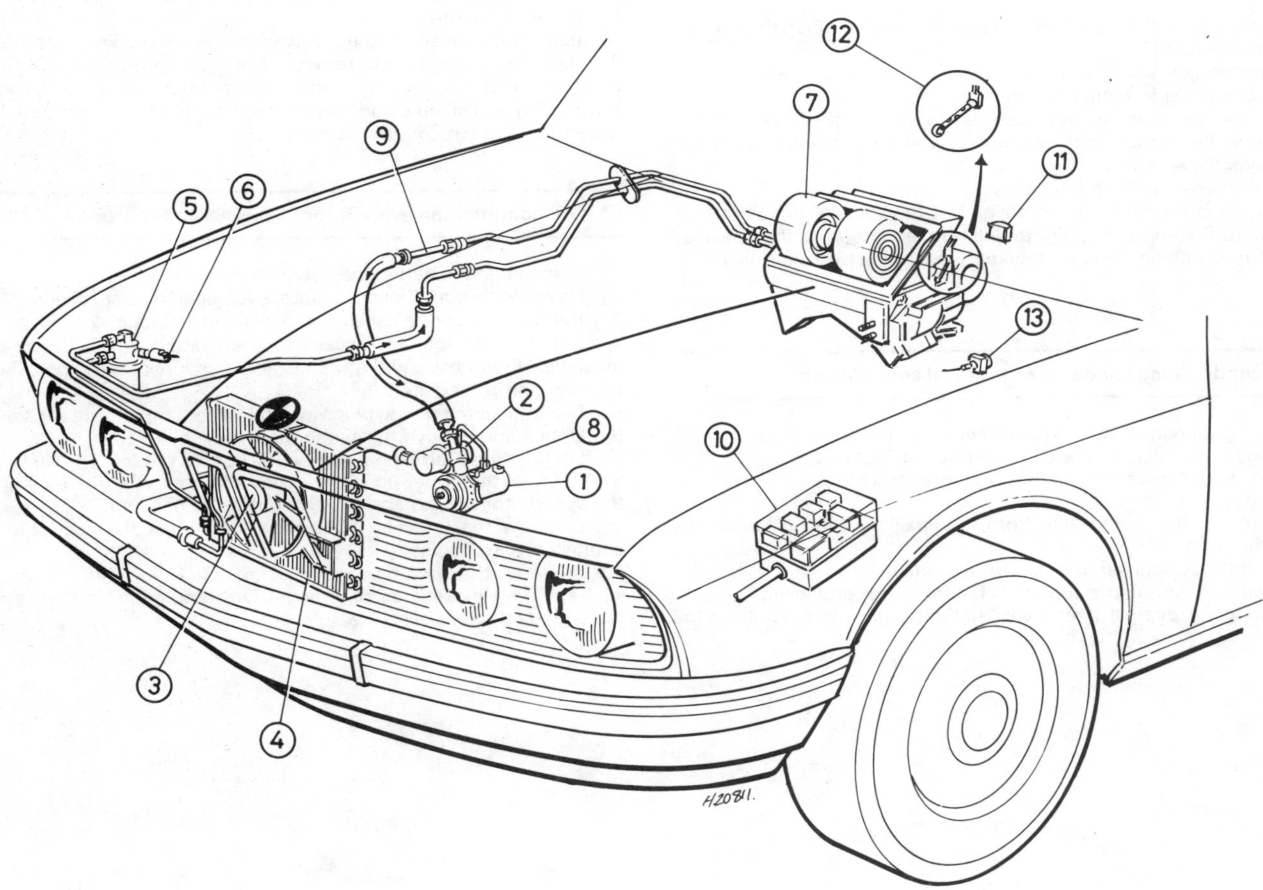

Fig. 11.17 Air conditioning system components (Sec 47)

1 *Compressor*
2 *Relaxer*
3 *Additional fan*
4 *Condenser*
5 *Drier*
6 *Safety pressure switch*
7 *Blower*
8 *Oil inspection bolt*
9 *Schrader valve*
10 *Fuse/relay board*
11 *Evaporator temperature regulator*
12 *Heater temperature sensor*
13 *Passenger compartment temperature sensor*

this may cause personal injury. Before working on individual components the system must be evacuated by a specialist, then recharged after the work has been finished.

48 Air conditioning compressor – removal and refitting

1 Have the air conditioning system evacuated by a specialist.
2 Disconnect the wiring plugs from the solenoid coupling on the pulley.
3 Unscrew the union nuts and disconnect the hoses. Plug the connections immediately.
4 Unbolt and remove the stabilizer.
5 Remove the splash guard.
6 Unscrew and remove the adjustment bolts from the links.
7 Support the compressor then unscrew and remove the pivot bolt and recover the spacer.
8 Slip the drivebelt from the pulley.
9 Refitting is a reversal of removal, but tension the drivebelt with reference to Section 2, and tighten all nuts and bolts to the specified torque. On completion, have the system recharged by a specialist.

49 Air conditioning condenser – removal and refitting

1 Have the air conditioning system evacuated by a specialist.
2 Remove the radiator grilles as described in Section 25.
3 Unscrew the union nuts on the condenser and plug the connections immediately.
4 Disconnect the wiring plug from the auxiliary cooling fan on the front of the condenser.
5 Unbolt the condenser from the front of the radiator.
6 If necessary unbolt the additional fan from the condenser.
7 Refitting is a reversal of removal, but tighten all nuts and bolts to the specified torque. On completion have the system recharged by a specialist.

50 Air conditioning drier – removal and refitting

1 Have the air conditioning system evacuated by a specialist.
2 Unscrew the mounting bracket nut located in the right-hand corner of the engine compartment.
3 Disconnect the wiring plug.
4 Unscrew the unions while holding the nuts with a spanner and disconnect the lines from the drier. Plug all connections immediately.
5 Remove the drier.
6 If necessary unscrew the safety switch while holding the hexagon.
7 Refitting is a reversal of removal, but coat the threads of the safety switch with thread-locking fluid before tightening it to the specified torque. Tighten all nuts and bolts to the correct torque. On completion have the system recharged by a specialist.

51 Air conditioning evaporator – removal and refitting

1 Disconnect the battery negative lead.
2 Have the air conditioning system evacuated by a specialist.
3 Remove the centre console as described in Section 27.
4 Remove the trim for access to the system pipes. Remove the insulation then unscrew the unions and disconnect the pipes. Plug all connections immediately.
5 Disconnect the wiring plugs including the temperature sensor.
6 Unbolt and remove the evaporator housing.
7 Lift out the seven clips, unscrew the bolt and cut off the plastic rivet.
8 Remove the upper housing section together with the blower. Pull the evaporator and expansion valve out of the housing.
9 Unscrew the retaining bolts then disconnect the hose. Plug the connections immediately.
10 Remove the insulation and disconnect the clip.
11 Refitting is a reversal of removal. On completion have the system recharged by a specialist.

Chapter 12 Electrical system

Contents

Specifications

System type ... 12 volt, negative earth, with alternator and pre-engaged starter

Battery

Type ... 12 volt
Capacity:
  520i ... 55 or 66 Ah
  525e ... 66 Ah

Alternator

Output ... 65 to 80 amps
Regulated voltage at 1500 engine rpm with no load ... 13.5 to 14.2 volts
Minimum brush length ... 13 mm
Maximum slip ring out-of-round ... 0.03 mm
Slip ring resistance:
  65 amps ... 2.6 to 2.8 ohms
  80 amps ... 2.8 to 3.0 ohms
Stator winding resistance:
  65 amps ... 0.08 to 0.12 ohms
  80 amps ... 0.05 to 0.09 ohms

Starter motor

Type ... Pre-engaged
Rating ... 1.1 kW
Armature endfloat ... 0.1 to 0.2 mm
Minimum brush length ... 13 mm

Fuses

No	Rating (amps)	Circuit(s) protected
1	16	Electric fuel pump, automatic choke
2	8	Right-hand dipped headlight
3	8	Left-hand dipped headlight, rear foglamp
4	25	Cigar lighter, electric aerial, self-levelling suspension, seat heating, electric seat adjustment
5	8	Hazard warning lights, interior light, glovebox light, luggage compartment light, handlamp, clock, central locking system, on-board computer, thief-proofing system, service indicator, door lock heating, check control component interrogation, sound system
6	8	Warning lamps, rev-counter, mirror, on-board computer, central warning light, check control component interrogation, energy control, service indicator, cruise control, electric windows, self-levelling suspension control, reversing lights, automatic transmission selector lever indicator
7	16	Left and right-hand headlight main beams
8	8	Instrument panel illumination, number plate lights, front and rear foglamps, radio, programmable seat adjustment control, check control component interrogation
9	8	Right-hand front sidelamp, right-hand rear taillamp, engine compartment
10	8	Left-hand front sidelamp, left-hand rear taillamp
11	16	Direction indicators, windscreen wash/wipe system, horn, headlight wash/wipe
12	8	Stop lights, check control component interrogation
13	16	Heated rear window
13	25	Heated rear window, electric sunroof
14	25	Auxiliary fan control, heater blower, air conditioning evaporator
15	8	Front right-hand foglamp
16	8	Front left-hand foglamp
17	25	Auxiliary fan

Bulbs

	Wattage
Headlamps:	
Outer	60/55
Inner	55
Sidelights	4
Headlight control illumination	1.2
Direction indicators	21
Front foglamps	55
Stoplamp	21
Tail light	5
Rear foglamp	21
Reversing light	21
Number plate light	5
Interior light	10
Luggage compartment light	5
Glovebox light	4
Engine compartment light	5
Heater control light	1.2
Main light switch light	1.2
Foglamp warning switch illumination	1.2
Digital clock illumination	1.2
Control unit illumination	1.2
Instrument panel illumination	3
Warning lamps	1.2
Battery charge light	3

Radio/cassette

Output power:	
Bavaria and Bavaria S	1 x 5 watt 2 x 9 watt
Bavaria cassette	2 x 5 watt 2 x 9 watt
Bavaria cassette 3 and CR	2 x 6 watt
Bavaria Electronic	2 x 9 watt 2 x 12 watt
Mexico	2 x 3 watt 2 x 4 watt

Wiper blades

Type	Champion 45 cm (18 in)

Torque wrench setting

	Nm	lbf ft
Starter motor	47 to 50	34 to 36

1 General description

Warning: *Before carrying out any work on the electrical system, read through the precautions given in* Safety first! *at the beginning of this manual and in Section 3 of this Chapter*

The electrical system is of 12 volt negative earth type, incorporating a lead-acid battery and a belt-driven alternator with an integral voltage regulator. The starter is of pre-engaged type.

When working on the electrical system, the battery leads should always be disconnected, as a safety precaution against accidentally short-circuiting wires or terminals to earth. The system contains several computerized components, which can be damaged by incorrect voltages or excessive heat.

Before using electric-arc welding equipment on the car, disconnect the battery leads and the alternator leads. Never run the engine with a battery lead or alternator lead disconnected.

2 Routine maintenance

Carry out the following at the intervals given in *Routine maintenance* at the front of this manual.

Check the water pump/alternator drivebelt

1 Refer to Chapter 2, Section 2.

Check the lights

2 Check the function of all the lights, both interior and exterior, and repair as necessary. Check that the headlight flasher functions correctly.

Check headlight beam alignment

3 Refer to Section 18 and check and adjust the headlight beam alignment as required.

Check the horn

4 Check that the horn functions correctly.

Check the battery

5 Where applicable check the battery electrolyte level and replenish with distilled water as required.

Check the washer system

6 Check the windscreen and headlight washer system for function and jet adjustment. Top up the fluid reservoir if necessary.

Check the wipers

7 Check that the wipers function correctly.

8 Examine the wiper rubbers for damage and if necessary renew them.

3 Electrical system – precautions

1 It is necessary to take extra care when working on the electrical system to avoid damage to semi-conductor devices (diodes and transistors), and to avoid the risk of personal injury. In addition to the precautions given in *Safety first!* at the beginning of this manual, observe the following when working on the system.

2 *Always remove rings, watches, etc before working on the electrical system*. Even with the battery disconnected, capacitive discharge could occur if a component live terminal is earthed through a metal object. This could cause a shock or nasty burn.

3 *Do not reverse the battery connections*. Components such as the alternator, fuel and ignition control units, or any other parts having semi-conductor circuitry could be irreparably damaged.

4 If the engine is being started using jump leads and a slave battery, connect the batteries *positive-to-positive* and *negative-to-negative*. This also applies when connecting a battery charger.

5 Never disconnect the battery terminals, any electrical wiring or any test instruments, when the engine is running.

6 Always ensure that the battery negative lead is disconnected when working on the electrical system.

4 Battery – testing and charging

1 Where a conventional battery is fitted, the electrolyte level of each cell should be checked every month and, if necessary, topped up with distilled or de-ionized water until the separators are just covered. On some batteries the case is translucent, and incorporates minimum and maximum level marks. The check should be made more often if the car is operated in high ambient temperature conditions.

2 Where a low-maintenance battery is fitted, it is not possible to check the electrolyte level.

3 Periodically disconnect and clean the battery terminals and leads. After refitting them, smear the exposed metal with petroleum jelly.

4 At the same time, inspect the battery clamp and platform for corrosion. If evident, remove the battery and clean the deposits away, then treat the affected metal with a proprietary anti-rust liquid, and paint with the original colour.

5 When the battery is removed for whatever reason, it is worthwhile checking it for cracks and leakage.

6 If topping-up the battery becomes excessive, and the battery case is not fractured, the battery is being over-charged, and the voltage regulator will have to be checked.

7 If the car covers a very small annual mileage, it is worthwhile checking the specific gravity of the electrolyte every three months to determine the state of charge of the battery. Use a hydrometer to make the check, and compare the results with the following table.

	Normal climates	**Tropics**
Discharged	*1.120*	*1.080*
Half charged	*1.200*	*1.160*
Fully charged	*1.280*	*1.230*

8 If the battery condition is suspect, first check the specific gravity of electrolyte in each cell. A variation of 0.040 or more between any cells indicates loss of electrolyte or deterioration of the internal plates.

9 A further test can be made using a battery heavy discharge meter. The battery should be discharged for a maximum of 15 seconds at a load of three times the ampere-hour capacity (at the 20 hour discharge rate). Alternatively, connect a voltmeter across the battery terminals and operate the starter motor with the ignition disconnected (see Chapter 4), and the headlamps, heated rear window and heater blower switched on. If the voltmeter reading remains above 9.6 volts, the battery condition is satisfactory. If the voltmeter reading drops below 9.6 volts, and the battery has already been charged, it is faulty.

10 In winter when a heavy demand is placed on the battery (starting from cold and using more electrical equipment), it is a good idea to have the battery fully charged from an external source occasionally at a rate of 10% of the battery capacity (ie 6.6 amps for a 66 Ah battery).

11 The battery leads should be disconnected before connecting the charger leads. Continue to charge the battery until no further rise in specific gravity is noted over a four-hour period.

12 Alternatively, a trickle charger, charging at a rate of 1.5 amps can safely be used overnight.

5 Battery – removal and refitting

1 With the ignition switched off, loosen the clamps and disconnect the battery negative lead followed by the positive lead, in that order. A hinged plastic cover may be fitted over the positive lead clamp (photos).

5.1A Negative battery lead

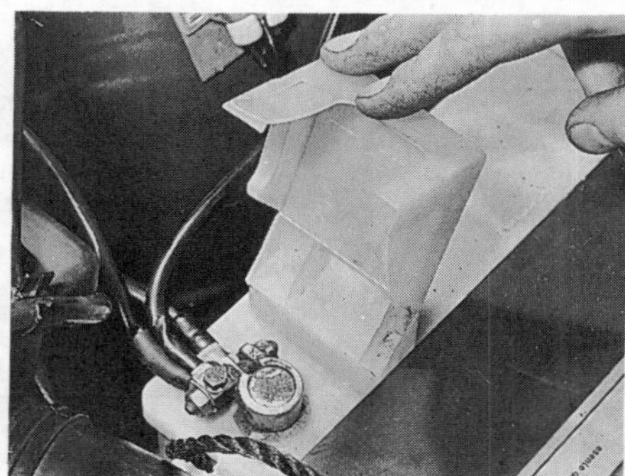
5.1B Positive battery lead

5.2 Battery clamp bolt (arrowed)

2 Unscrew the battery clamp bolt, remove the clamp and lift the battery from the platform (photo).
3 Refitting is a reversal of removal, but on completion smear the terminals with petroleum jelly to prevent corrosion.

6 Alternator drivebelt – removal, refitting and adjustment

Refer to Chapter 2, Section 13.

7 Alternator – fault tracing and rectification

1 Should it appear that the alternator is not charging the battery, check first that the drivebelt is intact and in good condition and that its tension is correct (Chapter 2). Also check the condition and security of the alternator electrical connections and the battery leads.
2 A rough idea of whether the alternator output is adequate can be gained by using a voltmeter (range 0 to 15 or 0 to 20 volts) as follows. Connect the voltmeter across the battery terminals and check that the reading is between 12 and 13 volts. Start the engine and run it at a fast idle, then check that the voltmeter reads between 13 and 14 volts. With the engine still running at a fast idle, switch on as many electrical consumers as possible (heated rear window, heater blower etc). The voltage at the battery should be maintained at between 13 and 14 volts, indicating that the alternator is functioning correctly.
3 For a comprehensive test of the alternator it will be necessary to take the car to an electrical specialist who will be equipped with an oscillograph to check the phased output of the unit and locate any fault in the rectifier diodes.
4 If the output is proved faulty from the check described in paragraph 2, remove the voltage regulator and brushes as described in Section 9 and check the brushes. Renew the brushes if necessary, or if these are in good order, suspect the voltage regulator.

8 Alternator – removal and refitting

1 With the ignition switched off, loosen the clamps and disconnect the battery negative lead followed by the positive lead, in that order. A hinged plastic cover may be fitted over the positive lead clamp.
2 Remove the air cleaner and airflow sensor (Chapter 3).
3 Disconnect the wires from the rear of the alternator. The main cable is retained by a nut. Do not forget the earth wire (photo).
4 Loosen the nut from the adjuster link and the main alternator pivot bolt (photo), then swivel the alternator in towards the engine and remove the drivebelt from the pulley. On the B27 engine it may be necessary to turn the engine over in order to pull the drivebelt up over the pulley as there is insufficient adjustment to allow the alternator to fully release the drivebelt.
5 Unscrew and remove the pivot and adjustment bolts and withdraw the alternator from the engine (photo).
6 Refitting is a reversal of removal, but tension the drivebelt as described in Chapter 2 Section 13.

9 Alternator brushes and voltage regulator – renewal

1 With the alternator removed, unscrew the two screws and remove the voltage regulator and brushes from the alternator. Turn the unit slightly to allow the brushes to clear the housing.
2 Check the length of the brushes and compare with that given in the Specifications. Worn brushes should be unsoldered and new ones soldered in position. Do not allow the solder to run down the leads otherwise their flexibility will be ruined.

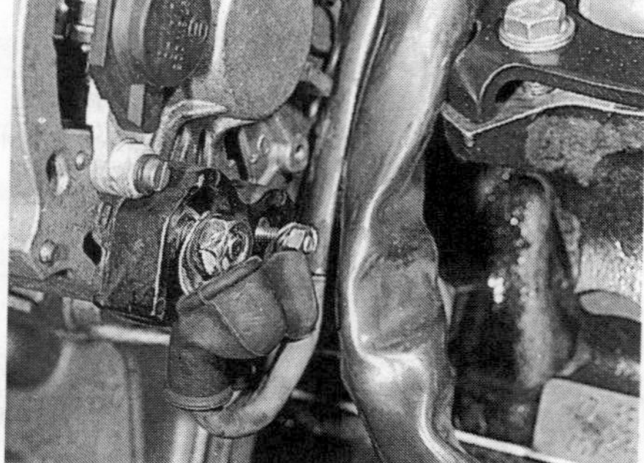
8.3 Disconnecting the wiring from the rear of the alternator

8.4 Loosening the alternator adjuster bolt

8.5 Alternator mounting bolts

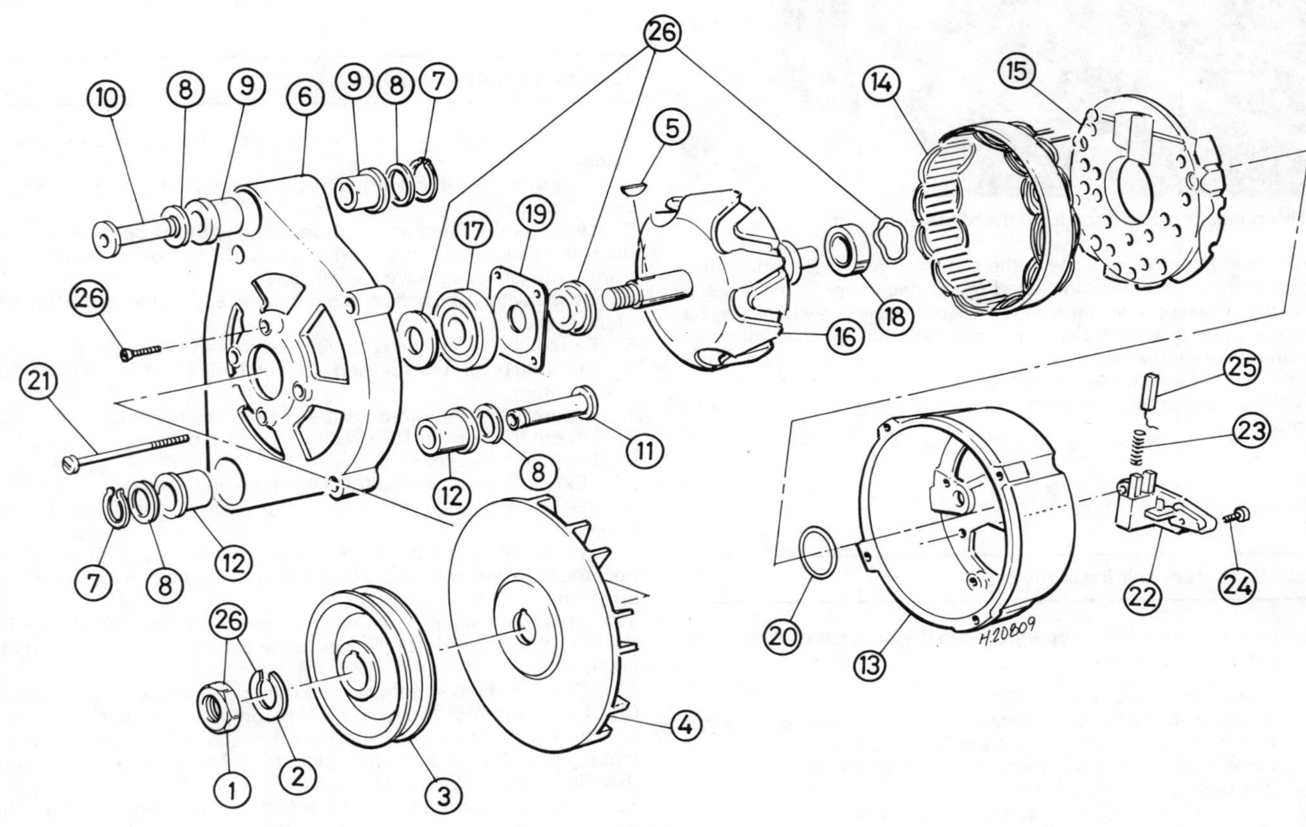

Fig. 12.1 Exploded diagram of the alternator (Sec 9)

1 *Nut*
2 *Spring washer*
3 *Pulley*
4 *Fan*
5 *Woodruff key*
6 *Front housing*
7 *Circlip*
8 *Flat washer*
9 *Bush*
10 *Bush*
11 *Bush*
12 *Bush*
13 *Rear housing*
14 *Stator*
15 *Rectifier assembly*
16 *Rotor*
17 *Ball-bearing*
18 *Ball-bearing*
19 *Retaining plate*
20 *O-ring*
21 *Through-bolt*
22 *Voltage regulator*
23 *Spring*
24 *Screw*
25 *Brush set*
26 *Rotor repair kit*

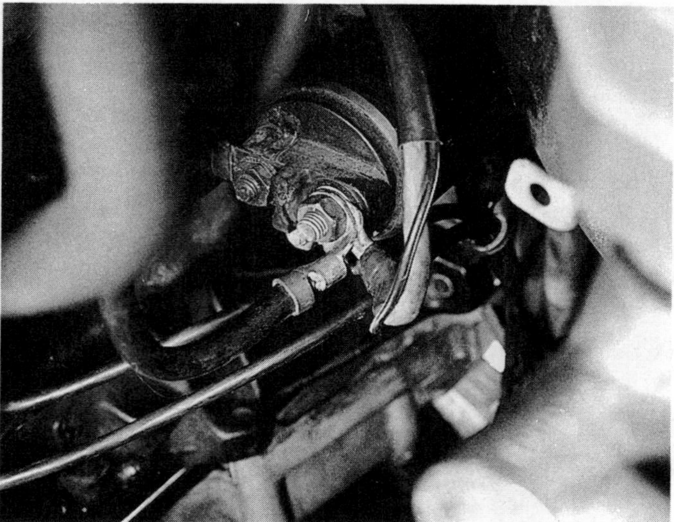

11.3 Disconnecting the wiring from the starter solenoid

3 With the unit removed, check the condition of the slip rings after cleaning them with a fuel-moistened rag. If necessary, clean the slip rings with fine glass paper. If the rings are worn excessively they may be fine ground and polished by an auto electrician, though this will mean dismantling the alternator.
4 Refit the voltage regulator and brushes using a reversal of the removal procedure, then refit the alternator to the engine as described in Section 8.

10 Starter motor – testing in the car

1 If the starter motor fails to operate when the switch is operated, the following may be the cause:

- *(a) The battery is faulty*
- *(b) The electrical connections between the switch, solenoid, battery and starter motor are somewhere failing to pass the necessary current from the battery through the starter to earth*
- *(c) The solenoid switch is faulty*
- *(d) The starter motor is mechanically or electrically defective*
- *(e) On automatic transmission models the starter inhibitor switch may be defective or maladjusted (see Chapter 6)*

2 To check the battery, switch on the headlights. If they dim after a few seconds the battery is in a discharged state. If the lights glow brightly, operate the starter switch and see what happens to the lights. If they dim then you know that power is reaching the starter motor but failing to turn it. If the starter turns slowly when switched on, proceed to the next check.
3 If, when the starter switch is operated, the lights stay bright, then insufficient power is reaching the motor. Remove the battery connections, starter/solenoid power connections and the engine earth strap and thoroughly clean them and refit them. Smear petroleum jelly around the battery connections to prevent corrosion. Corroded connections are the most frequent cause of electric system malfunctions.
4 When the above checks and cleaning tasks have been carried out, but without success, you will possibly have heard a clicking noise each time the starter switch was operated. This was the solenoid switch closing properly (if no clicking has been heard from the solenoid, it may be defective). The solenoid contact can be checked by putting a voltmeter or bulb across the main cable connection on the starter side of the solenoid and earth. When the switch is operated, there should be a reading or lighted bulb. If there is no reading or lighted bulb, the solenoid is faulty and should be renewed.
5 Finally, if it is established that the solenoid is not faulty and 12 volts are getting to the starter, then the motor is faulty and should be removed for inspection.

11 Starter motor – removal and refitting

1 Drain the cooling system as described in Chapter 2, then disconnect the coolant hose located in front of the starter motor.
2 Unscrew the upper starter mounting nut.
3 Unscrew the nuts and disconnect the wires from the starter solenoid (photo). Identify them for position if necessary.
4 Unscrew the bolt from the starter motor front mounting.
5 Unscrew the lower starter mounting nut, and withdraw the unit from the car.
6 Refitting is a reversal of removal, but tighten the nuts and bolt to the specified torque.

12 Starter motor – overhaul

1 With the starter motor removed, clean the motor's exterior surfaces.
2 Unscrew the nut and disconnect the motor cable from the solenoid lower terminal.
3 Unscrew the three screws from the end of the solenoid and withdraw the solenoid from the drive housing. Unhook the solenoid arm from the lever and remove the solenoid.
4 Unscrew the two bolts and remove the end cap from the brush end of the starter motor.
5 Extract the circlip and remove the shims and O-ring seal.
6 Mark the brush-end housing, yoke and drive-end housing in relation to each other.
7 Unscrew the through-bolts then pull off the brush-end housing.
8 Lift out the brushes followed by the brush holder.
9 Remove the yoke.
10 Extract the rubber pad from the drive-end housing.
11 Unscrew the bolt securing the engagement lever to the drive-end housing.
12 Withdraw the armature from the drive-end housing and disconnect the engagement lever noting how it is attached to the collar on the armature.
13 To remove the pinion, first use a metal tube to drive it back from the circlip. Extract the circlip then slide the pinion from the armature shaft.
14 Clean all the components and check them for wear and damage. Check the length of the brushes and compare with that given in the Specifications. If necessary unsolder the brushes and solder new ones into position. Do not allow the solder to run down the leads otherwise their flexibility will be ruined.
15 Clean the commutator with a fuel-moistened rag, or if it is very dirty use fine glass paper. Check that the insulators between the segments are 0.5 mm lower than the segments, otherwise cut them back squarely using a hacksaw.
16 Reassembly is a reversal of dismantling, but check that the armature endplay is between 0.10 and 0.15 mm and if necessary alter the shims to bring it within that tolerance. The groove in the yoke must face the rubber pad. Check that the brush holder is positioned correctly so that the through-bolts enter the special slots.

13 Fuses and relays – general

1 The fusebox and relays are located on the left-hand side of the engine compartment.
2 A blown fuse can be identified by the metal strip between the two blades being melted. Pull out the old fuse and press in the new one, making sure that it is the same rating as the old one. Never use a fuse with a different rating from the original or substitute it for anything else. If a new fuse blows immediately, find the cause before renewing it again. A short to earth as a result of faulty insulation is the most likely cause.
3 The relays located in the fusebox are identified as shown in the photo. To renew them disconnect the battery then simply pull direct from the socket and press in the new ones. Reconnect the battery on completion (photos).

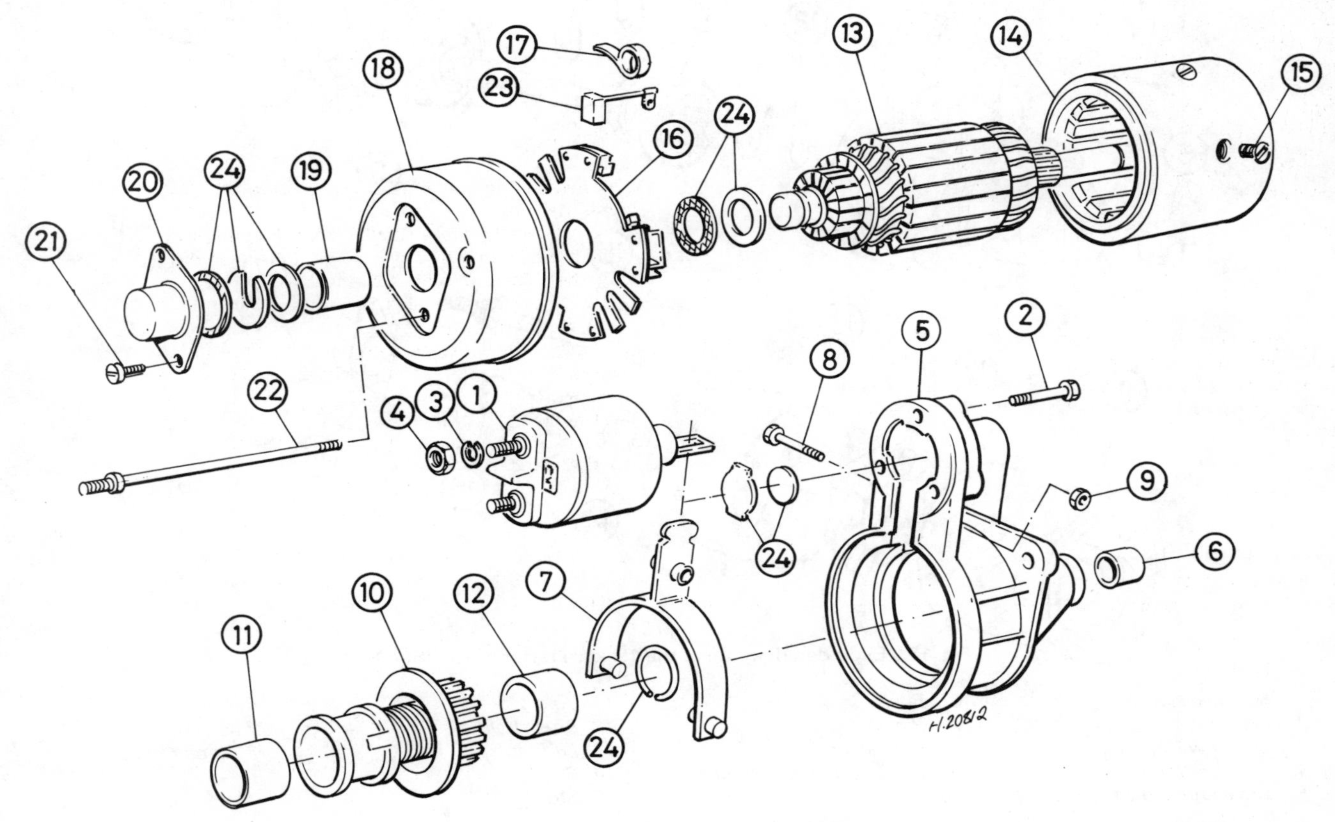

Fig. 12.2 Exploded diagram of the 1.1 kW starter motor (Sec 12)

1 Solenoid switch
2 Screw
3 Spring washer
4 Nut
5 Drive-end housing
6 Bush
7 Shift lever
8 Bolt
9 Nut
10 Pinion
11 Bush
12 Bush
13 Armature
14 Yoke
15 Screw
16 Brush holder plate
17 Spring
18 End cap
19 Bush
20 Cap
21 Screw
22 Stud
23 Carbon brush set
24 Repair kit

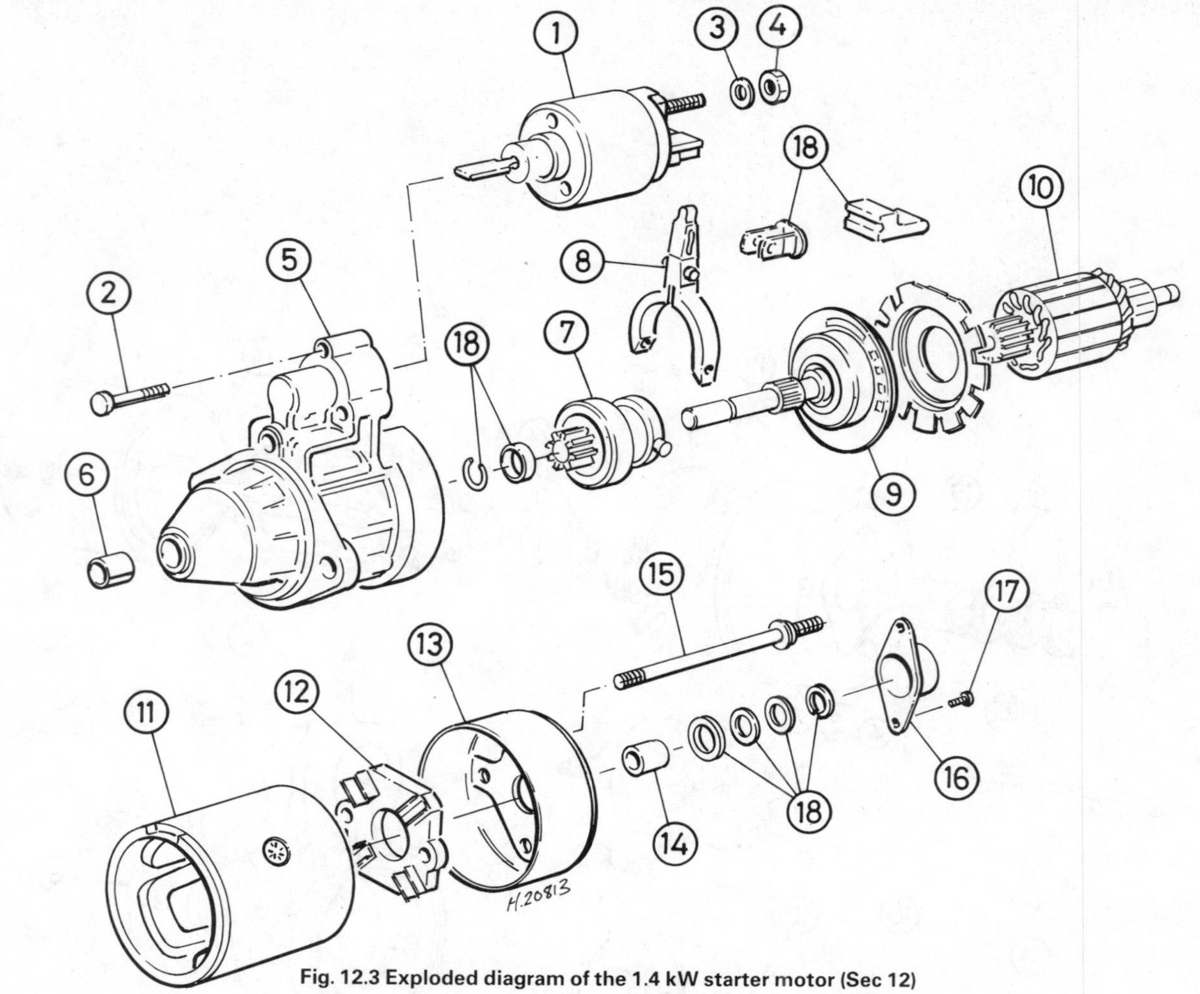

Fig. 12.3 Exploded diagram of the 1.4 kW starter motor (Sec 12)

1 Solenoid switch
2 Bolt
3 Spring washer
4 Nut
5 Drive end housing
6 Bush
7 Pinion
8 Shift lever
9 Reduction gear assembly
10 Armature
11 Yoke
12 Brush holder
13 End cap
14 Bush
15 Stud
16 Cap
17 Screw
18 Repair kit

13.3A Relay positions on the fusebox

1 Wipe/wash intermittent action control unit
2 Dip beam relay
3 Front fog lights relay
4 Power saving relay
5 Main beam relay
6 Two-tone horns

13.3B Removing a relay

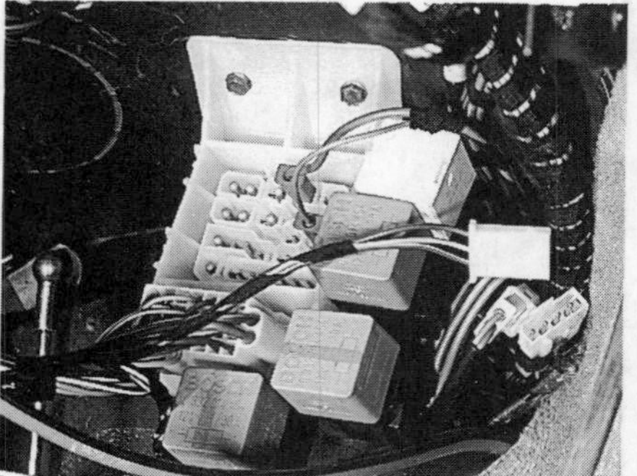
13.3C Additional relays located beneath the facia

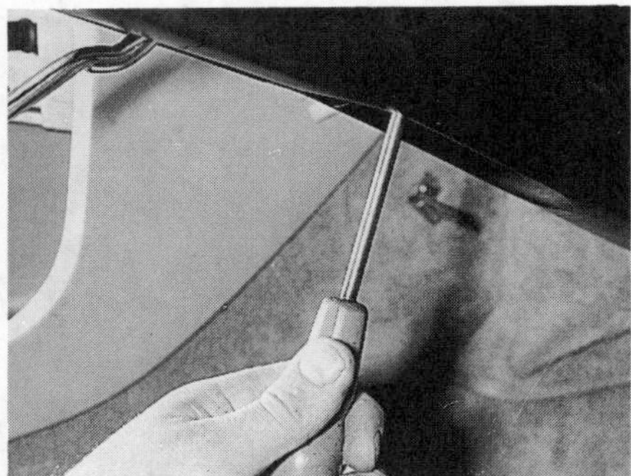
14.6A Unscrew the screws ...

14.6B ... and remove the steering column shrouds

14.21 Removing the hazard light switch

4 To remove the fuse/relay carrier first disconnect the battery negative lead. Remove the cover and pull out all the relays and fuses. Unscrew the two mounting bolts, raise the carrier, then disconnect all the wires and remove the carrier.
5 Refitting is a reversal of removal.

14 Switches – removal and refitting

Note: *Disconnect the battery negative lead before removing any switch and reconnect the lead after refitting the switch.*

Lighting switch
1 Remove the lower facia panel from under the steering wheel.
2 Unscrew the nut and disconnect the multi-plugs from the lighting switch.
3 Refitting is a reversal of removal.

Direction indicator/headlight dip switch
4 Remove the steering wheel as described in Chapter 10.
5 Remove the lower facia panel from under the steering wheel.
6 Unscrew the screws and remove the steering column shrouds (photos).
7 Disconnect the wiring plugs for the direction indicator/headlight dip switch.
8 Unscrew the mounting screws, withdraw the switch, then pull the relay from the holder and disconnect the multi-plug.
9 Refitting is a reversal of removal.

Wiper switch
10 Remove the steering wheel as described in Chapter 10.
11 Remove the lower facia panel from under the steering wheel.
12 Unscrew the screws and remove the steering column shrouds.
13 Disconnect the wiring plug for the wiper switch.
14 Unscrew the two crosshead screws and remove the switch from the steering column.
15 Refitting is a reversal of removal.

Heater blower switch
16 Pull off the heater control knob.
17 Unscrew the centre nut and pull the switch out of the facia panel. Disconnect the wiring plug.
18 Refitting is a reversal of removal, but make sure that the switch is engaged correctly in its surround.

Heated rear window switch
19 Carefully prise the switch out of the facia and disconnect the wiring plug.
20 Refitting is a reversal of removal.

Hazard light switch
21 Carefully prise the switch out of the facia and disconnect the wiring plug (photo).
22 Refitting is a reversal of removal.

Reversing light switch (manual transmission models)
23 Chock the front wheels then jack up the rear of the car and support on axle stands.
24 The switch is located on the right-hand rear of the transmission. Disconnect the wiring then unscrew the switch from the housing.
25 Refitting is a reversal of removal.

Ignition switch
26 Remove the steering column shrouds.
27 Remove the switch retaining screw, then insert the ignition key and turn it to the 'start' position. Pull out the steering lock complete and remove the ignition switch.
28 Refitting is a reversal of removal.

Courtesy light switch
29 Open the door, then unscrew the screw and ease the switch out from the door pillar (photo).

14.29 Courtesy light switch removal

14.32 Removing the electrically-operated windows circuit breaker

14.34 Headlight switch removal

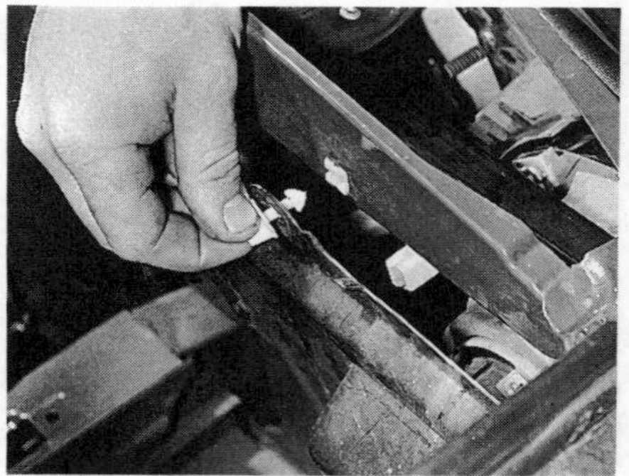
15.1A Unclip the cover ...

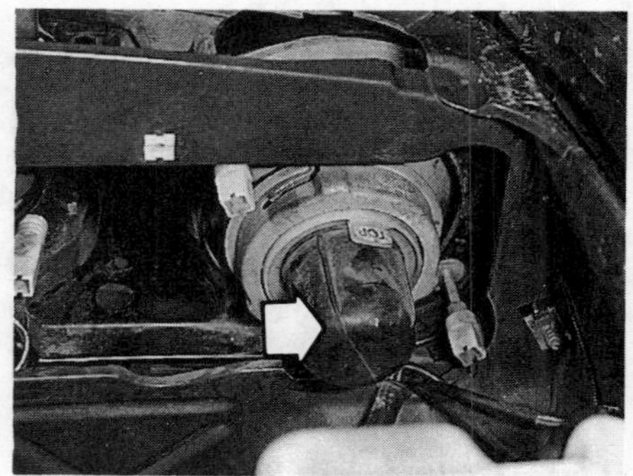
15.1B ... and remove the rubber covers (arrowed)

15.1C Disconnecting the wiring plug from the inner headlight unit ...

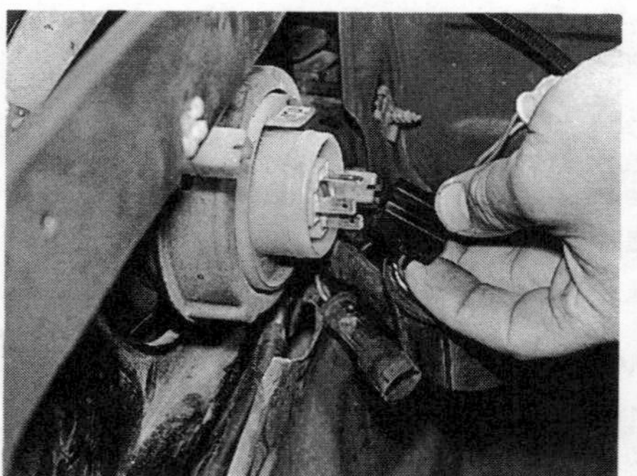
15.1D ... and from the outer headlight unit

15.2A Removing the metal cap from the inner headlight unit ...

15.2B ... and from the outer headlight unit

15.3A Disconnecting the wiring from the inner headlight bulb

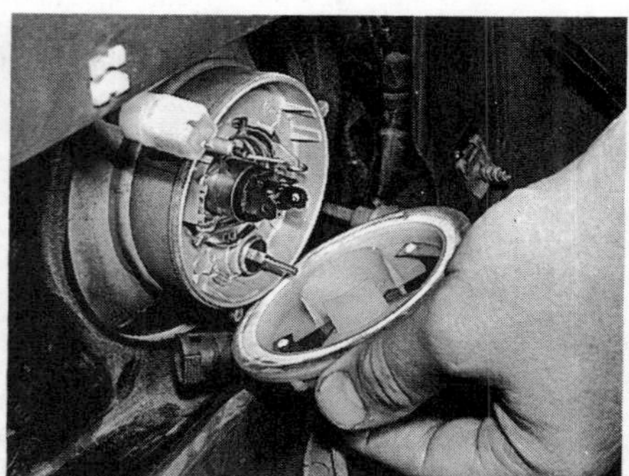
15.3B Disconnecting the adaptor plug from the outer headlight bulb

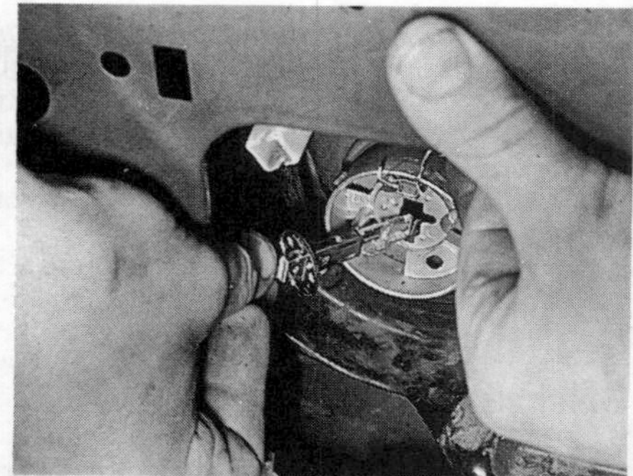
15.4A Removing the inner headlight bulb ...

15.4B ... and outer headlight bulb

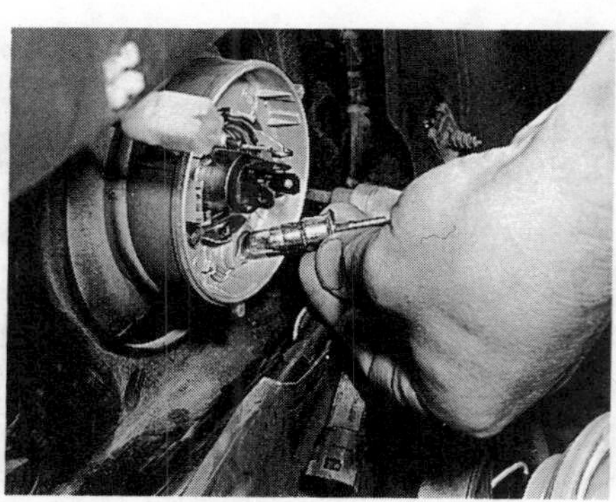
15.8 Front sidelight bulb removal

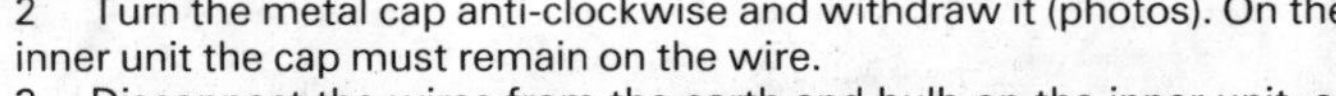

30 Disconnect the wire, taking care not to allow it to drop back into the pillar.
31 Refitting is a reversal of removal.

Electrically-operated windows circuit breaker

32 Prise the unit from the facia and disconnect the wiring (photo).
33 Refitting is a reversal of removal.

Headlight switch

34 Prise the unit from the facia and disconnect the wiring (photo).
35 Refitting is a reversal of removal.

15 Bulbs (exterior lights) – renewal

Headlight

1 Unclip the plastic cover, then remove the rubber cover from the rear of the relevant headlight and disconnect the wiring plug (photos).
2 Turn the metal cap anti-clockwise and withdraw it (photos). On the inner unit the cap must remain on the wire.
3 Disconnect the wires from the earth and bulb on the inner unit, or disconnect the adaptor plug on the outer unit (photos).
4 Release the spring clip and extract the bulb, taking care not to touch the glass (photos).
5 Refitting is a reversal of removal.

Front sidelight

6 Remove the rubber cover from the rear of the outer headlight.
7 Turn the metal cap anti-clockwise and withdraw it, then disconnect the adaptor plug.
8 Pull the bulb holder from the headlight reflector, then pull the bulb from the bulb holder (photo).
9 Refitting is a reversal of removal.

Front foglight

10 Unscrew the cross-head screws on the surround and remove the

15.10A Removing the front foglight

15.10B Disengaging the front foglight from the direction indicator (mounting point arrowed)

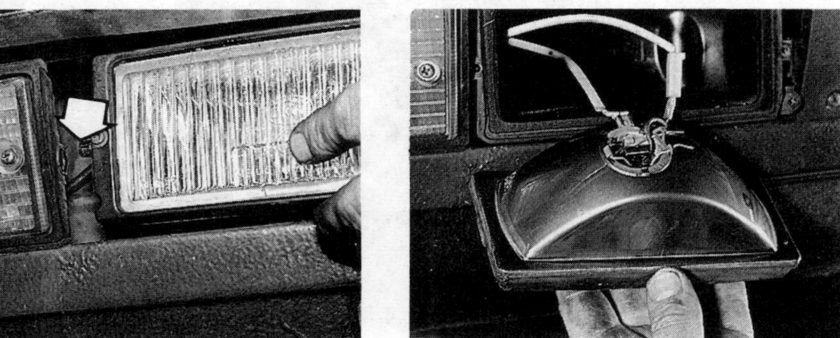

15.10C Front foglight removed from its body

15.11 Front foglight bulb removal

15.12A Remove the plastic trim ...

15.12B ... for access to the front foglight body mounting screw

15.13 Adjusting the front foglight beam

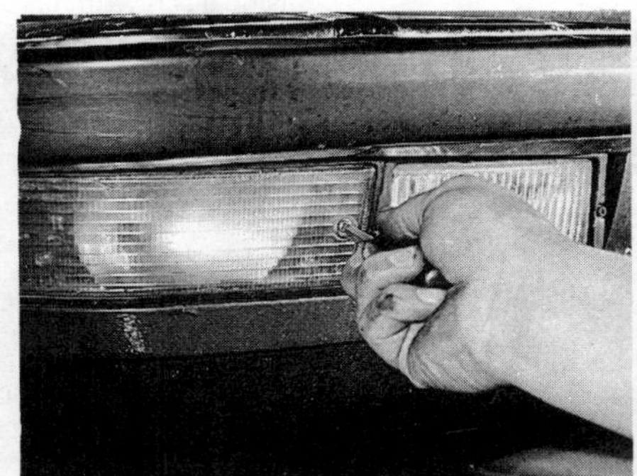

15.14 Removing the front direction indicator lens

15.15 Front direction indicator bulb removal

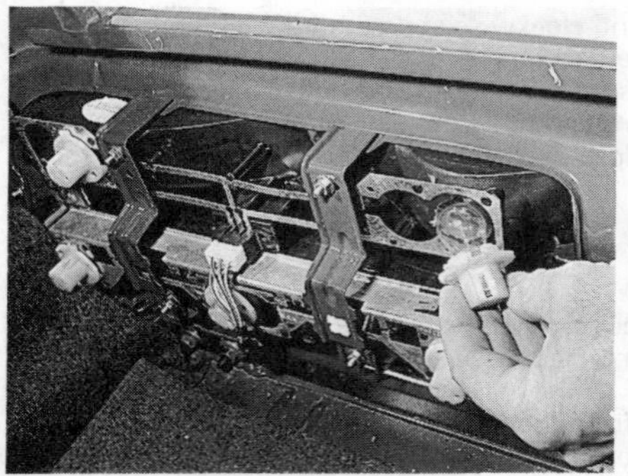
15.18A Pull out the bulb holder ...

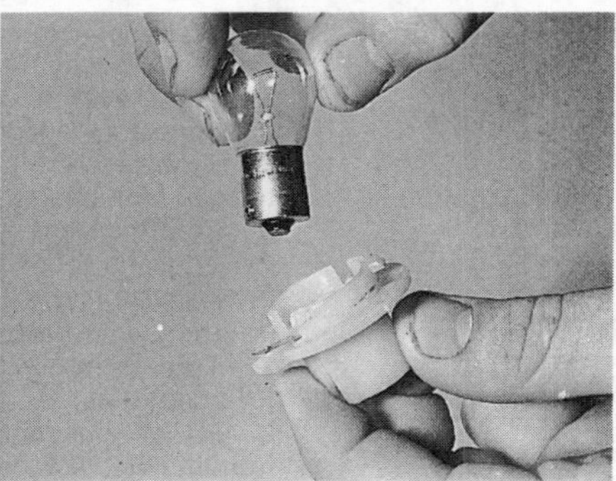
15.18B ... and remove the bulb

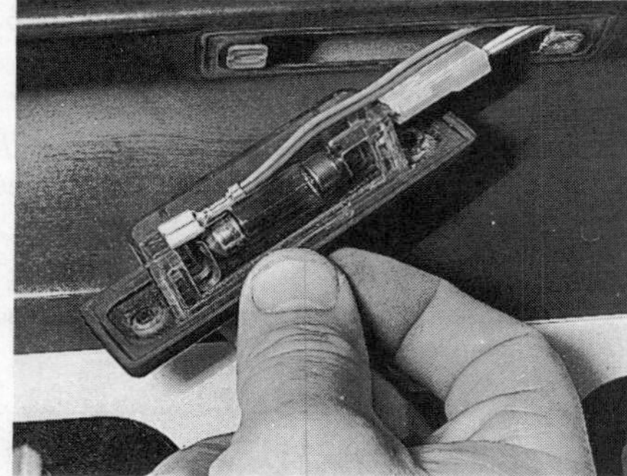
15.21 Rear number plate light removal

15.24 Removing the side marker light ...

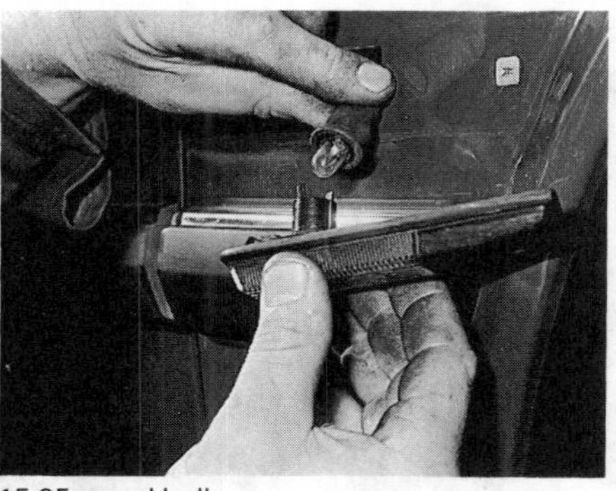
15.25 ... and bulb

foglight unit from its mounting body by disengaging the outer end from the direction indicator (photos).

11 Release the spring clips and withdraw the bulb. Disconnect the wiring (photo).

12 If necessary the body may be removed by unscrewing the mounting screw located behind the plastic trim (photos).

13 Refitting is a reversal of removal, but adjust the light if necessary by turning the screws located through the cut-outs on the bottom of the unit (photo).

Front direction indicator

14 Unscrew the cross-head screws and remove the front direction indicator lens (photo).

15 Push in and twist the bayonet type bulb to remove it (photo).

16 Refitting is a reversal of removal.

Rear light cluster

17 Working in the rear luggage compartment, release the rear panel trim.

18 Pull out the relevant bulb holder, then push in and twist the bayonet type bulb to remove it (photos).

19 Refitting is a reversal of removal.

Number plate light

20 The number plate lights are located on the rear underside of the bootlid. Open the bootlid for better access.

21 Unscrew the two screws and remove the lens together with the rubber seal (photo).

22 Pull out the wedge-type bulb from the bulb holder.

23 Refitting is a reversal of removal.

Side marker light

24 Remove the screw then ease out the front of the light unit and disengage it at the rear (photo).

25 Separate the light from the bulb holder then extract the bulb (photo).

26 Refitting is a reversal of removal.

16 Bulbs (interior lights) – renewal

Luggage compartment light

1 With the bootlid open prise out the luggage compartment light using a screwdriver (photo).

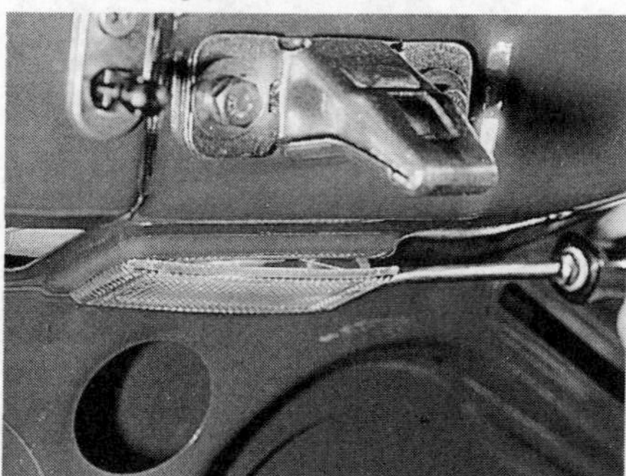
16.1 Prising off the luggage compartment light lens ...

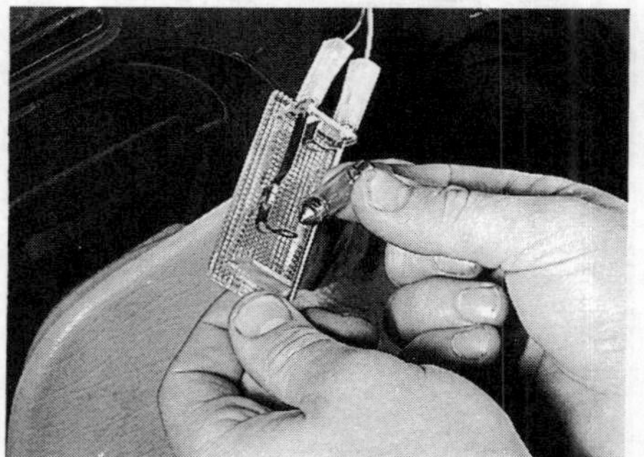
16.2 ... and removing the bulb

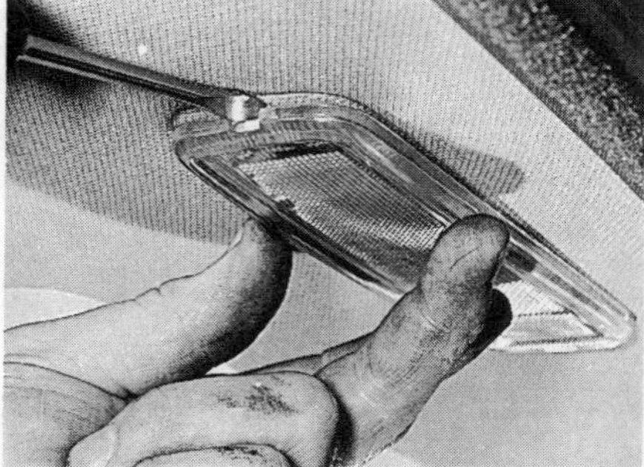
16.4 Prising off the interior light lens ...

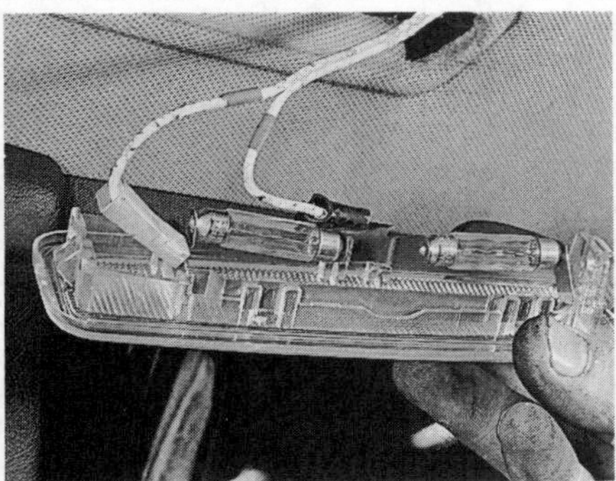
16.5 ... and removing the bulbs

16.8 Removing the glovebox light bulb holder

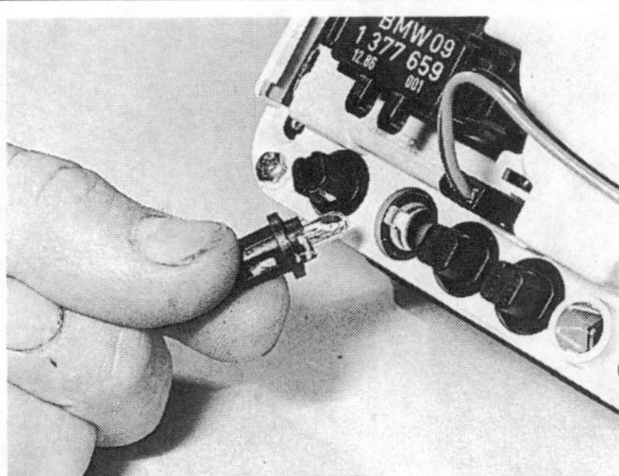

16.11A Removing a warning light bulb from the instrument panel

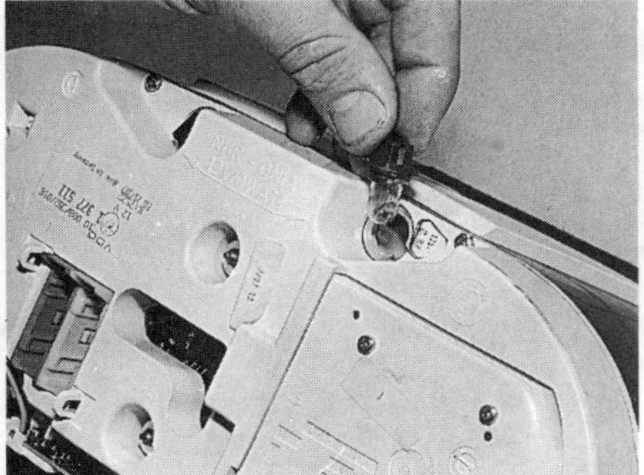
16.11B Removing an illumination light bulb from the instrument panel

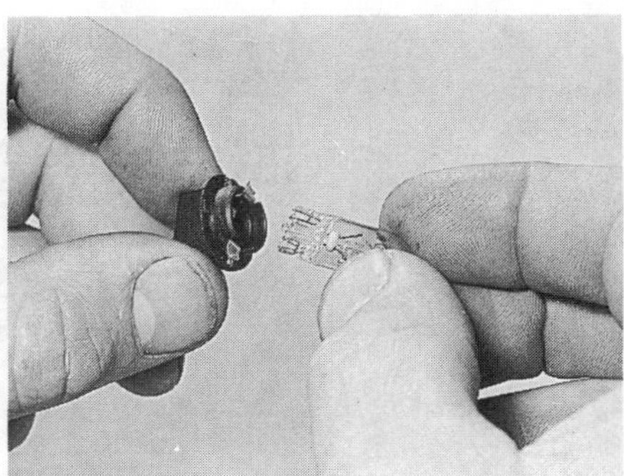
16.12 Separating bulb from its holder

16.13A Prise out ...

16.13B ... and remove the digital clock surround

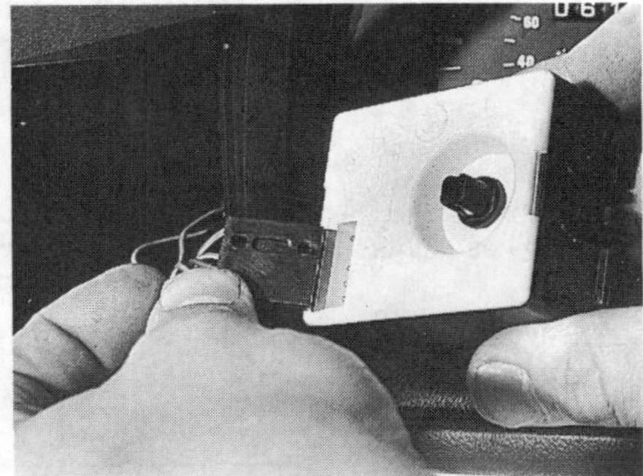
16.14 Disconnecting the digital clock wiring

16.15 Removing the bulb holder from the rear of the digital clock

2 Remove the festoon-type bulb from the contacts (photo).
3 Refitting is a reversal of removal, but make sure that the contacts are sufficiently tensioned to hold the bulb firmly.

Interior light

4 Using a screwdriver, prise out the interior light from the headlining (photo).
5 Remove the festoon-type bulb from the contacts (photo).
6 Refitting is a reversal of removal, but make sure that the contacts are sufficiently tensioned to hold the bulb firmly.

Glovebox light

7 Open the glovebox, then press the bulb holder and switch from the bracket.
8 Depress and twist the bulb to remove it from the bulb holder (photo).
9 Refitting is a reversal of removal.

Instrument panel illumination and warning lights

10 Remove the instrument panel as described in Section 19.
11 Twist the bulb holder from the rear of the instrument panel (photos).
12 Remove the bulb from the bulb holder (photo).

Digital clock illumination

13 Prise the surround from the front of the digital clock (photos).
14 Remove the clock and disconnect the wiring plug (photo).
15 Twist the bulb holder from the rear of the clock and remove the bulb (photo).
16 Refitting is a reversal of removal.

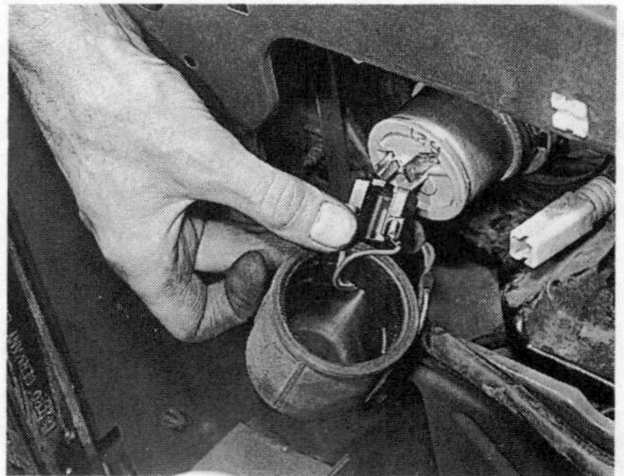
17.3 Disconnecting the headlight unit wiring

17.4 Unscrewing the headlight unit mounting screw

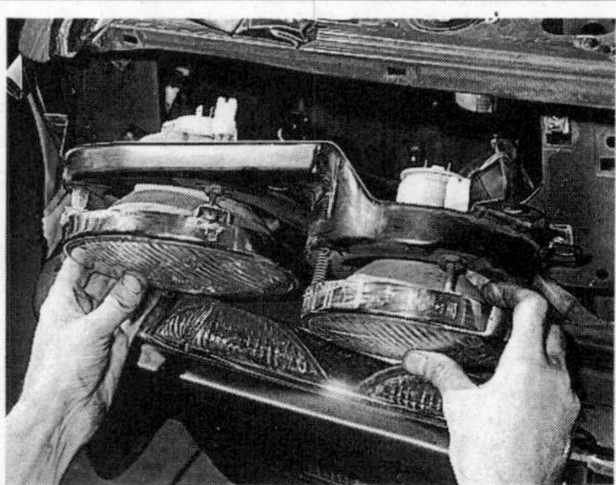
17.5A Removing the headlight unit

17.5B Front view of the headlight unit

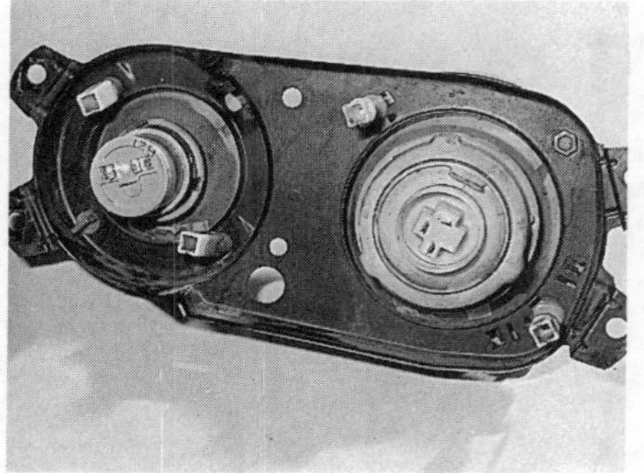
17.5C Rear view of the headlight unit

17 Exterior light units – removal and refitting

Headlight unit (double)

1 Remove the side grille as described in Chapter 11.
2 Working inside the engine compartment, twist the fastener anti-clockwise and remove the headlight rear cover.
3 Disconnect the wiring plugs from the rear of the headlights (photo).
4 Unscrew the four mounting screws from the front of the headlights (photo).
5 Note how the range control is fitted to the headlight unit then turn the bayonet fastener and pull out the ballsocket joint. Remove the headlight unit (photos).
6 Refitting is a reversal of removal, but make sure that the line on the ballsocket joint aligns with the mark on the headlight. Adjust the beam alignment as described in Section 18.

Front direction indicator

7 Working inside the engine compartment, disconnect the plug for the front direction indicator wiring.
8 Unscrew the screws and remove the lens.
9 Unscrew the three screws and withdraw the front direction indicator unit from the bumper together with the wiring (photos).
10 Refitting is a reversal of removal.

Rear light cluster

11 Open the bootlid and release the rear panel trim.
12 Disconnect the wiring plug for the rear light cluster (photo).
13 Unscrew the mounting nuts and withdraw the unit from the rear panel (photos).
14 Refitting is a reversal of removal.

18 Headlight and front foglight beam alignment – general

1 Correct alignment of the headlight and foglight beams is most

17.9A Unscrew the three screws ...

17.9B ... and withdraw the front direction indicator unit

17.12 Disconnecting the rear light cluster wiring

17.13A Unscrew the mounting nuts (arrowed) ...

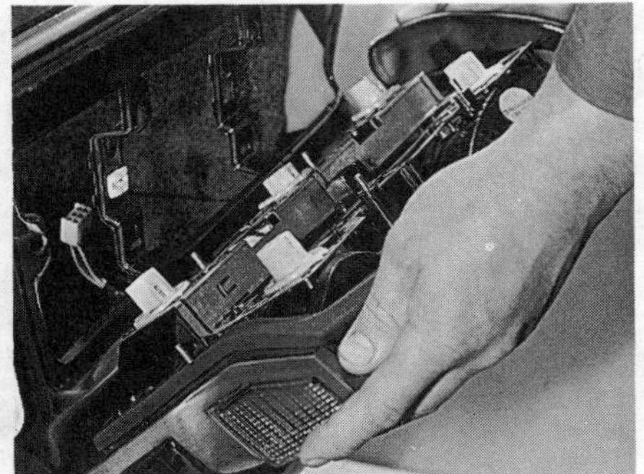

17.13B ... and withdraw the rear light unit

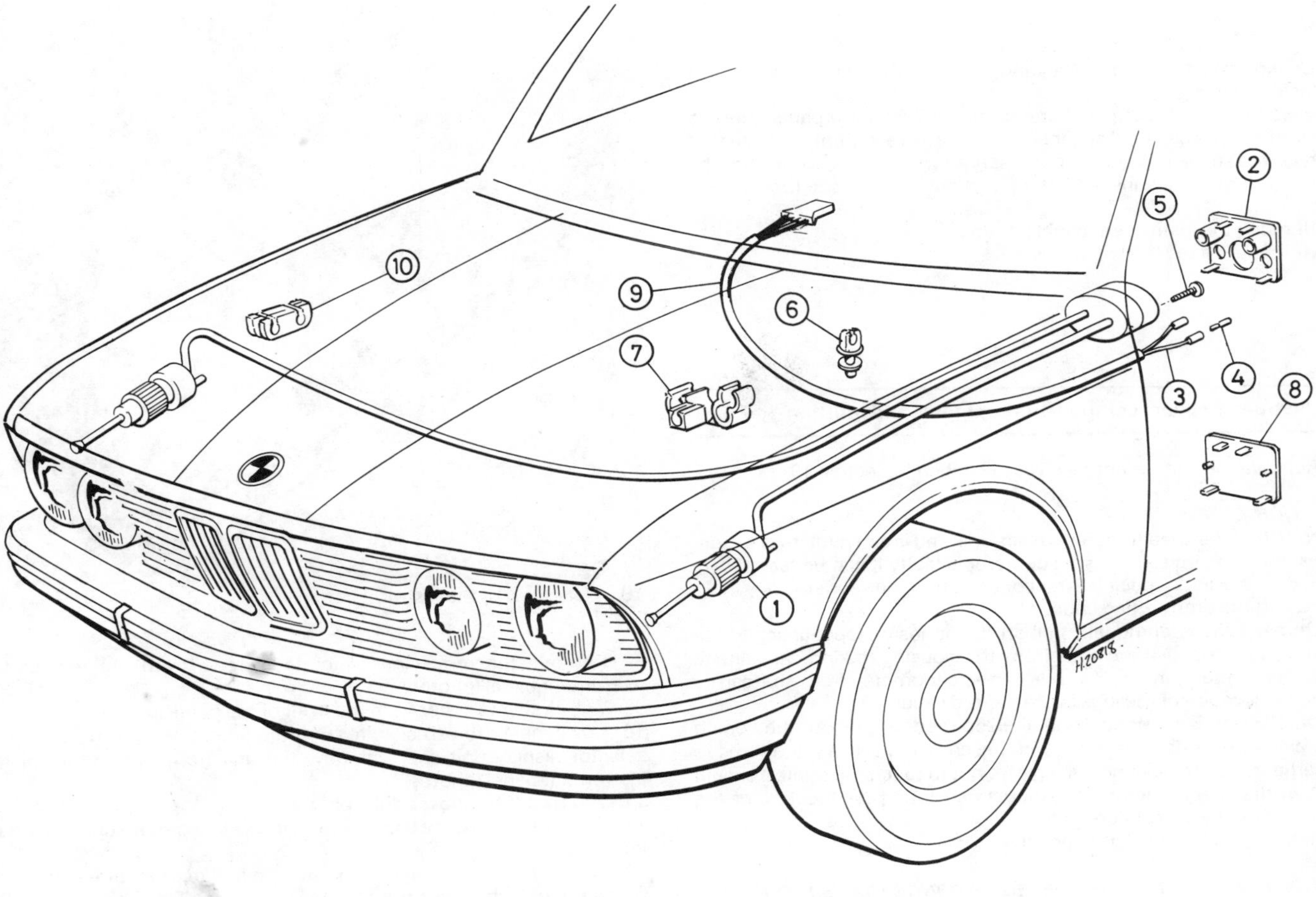

Fig. 12.4 Headlight beam adjustment system (Sec 18)

1 *Control unit*
2 *Plate*
3 *Bulb socket*
4 *Bulb*
5 *Screw*
6 *Bracket*
7 *Bracket*
8 *Surround*
9 *Warning light regulator*
10 *Guide*

important, not only to ensure good vision for the driver but also to protect other drivers from being dazzled. Accurate alignment should be carried out by a BMW dealer using special optical setting equipment.

2 On some models the headlights may be adjusted to compensate for the load being carried by turning a knob on the facia. The hydraulically-operated system is shown in Fig. 12.4.

3 In an emergency, adjustment of the headlights may be made by turning the adjustment knobs on the rear of the headlights (where applicable make sure that the adjustment knob on the facia is on the zero mark). The upper knobs are for vertical adjustment and the lower knobs for lateral adjustment. It will be necessary to remove the rear covers first. The adjustment screw for the front foglights is located in the right-hand front lower corner of the light. However it is important to have accurate adjustments made at the earliest opportunity.

19 Instrument panel – removal and refitting

1 Disconnect the battery negative lead.

2 Remove the steering wheel as described in Chapter 10. Note that it is possible to remove the instrument panel with the steering wheel in position provided that the steering column is adjusted to its highest point, but it is preferable to remove the steering wheel.

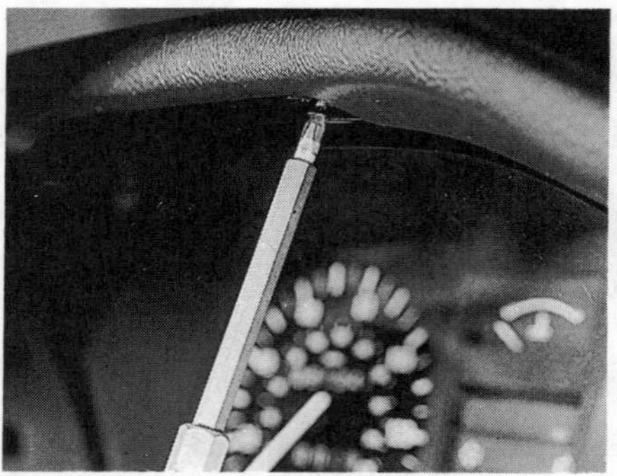
19.3 Removing the instrument panel mounting screws

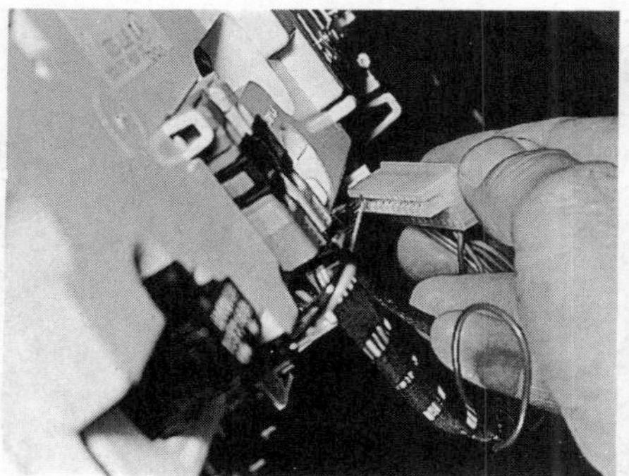
19.4A Disconnecting the multi-plug for the automatic transmission gear selection indicator

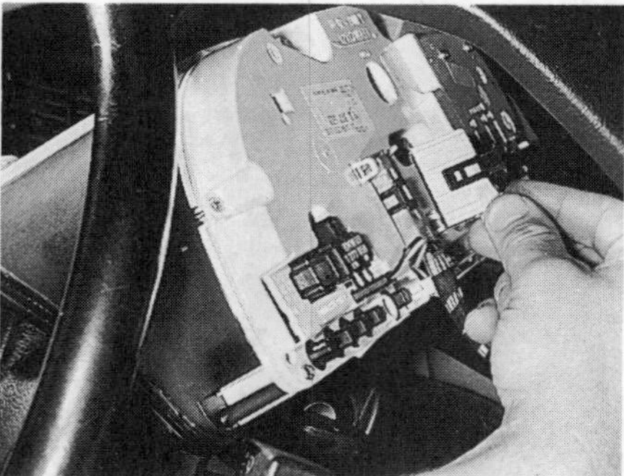
19.4B Disconnecting the upper multi-plugs

3 Unscrew the two screws securing the top of the instrument panel to the facia panel (photo).
4 Ease the instrument panel outwards from the facia panel until the four wiring plugs can be disconnected from the rear (photos). Note that on the three smaller plugs it is necessary to pull out the slider from the plug in order to disconnect it. The plugs are colour-coded for correct refitment.
5 Remove the instrument panel (photo).
6 Refitting is a reversal of removal.

20 Instrument panel components – removal and refitting

1 Remove the instrument panel as described in Section 19.

Speedometer

2 Note that the speedometer is electronic and is activated by a sender unit on the final drive. If the speedometer is faulty it can be tested by a BMW dealer using a special tester connected to the sender unit.
3 Pull off the time setting knob.
4 On pre-1983 520i models, pull off the adhesive tape, unscrew the screws and remove the carrier from the housing, taking care not to touch the printed circuit. Remove the speedometer from the carrier noting the location of the lugs in the printed circuit.
5 On 1983-on 520i models and all 525e models, pull out the coding plug, pull off the adhesive tape, then unscrew the screws and remove the carrier from the housing, taking care not to touch the printed circuit. Remove the speedometer from the carrier noting the location of the lugs in the printed circuit (photos).
6 Refitting is a reversal of removal.

Tachometer and fuel/temperature gauge (525e models)

7 Remove the speedometer as previously described.

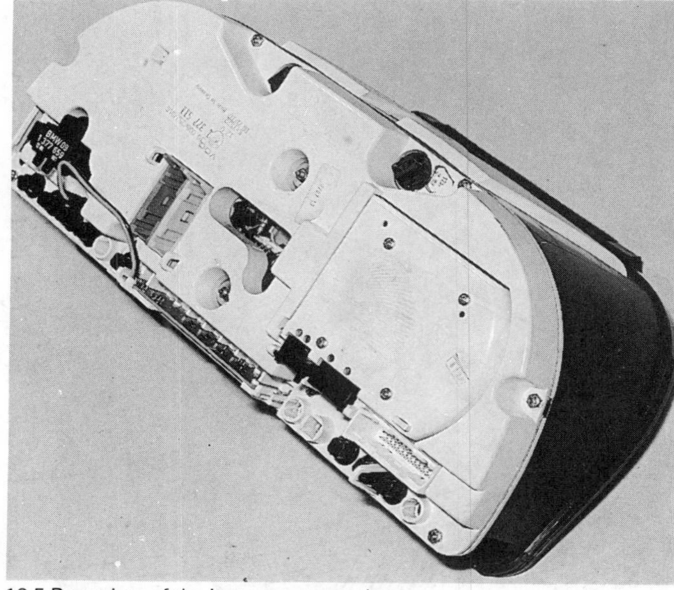
19.5 Rear view of the instrument panel

8 Remove the remaining perimeter screws from the rear of the instrument panel (photo).
9 Withdraw the cover from the front of the panel (photo).
10 Disconnect the small wire from the automatic transmission gear selector display unit and withdraw the unit from the bottom of the instrument panel (photos).
11 Pull out the code module (photo).
12 Unscrew the screws and withdraw the tachometer unit and housing (photos).
13 Unscrew the nuts and withdraw the fuel/temperature gauge unit by pressing on the studs from the rear. Do not pull the unit out from the front otherwise the plastic lands will be broken. The printed circuit

20.5A Pull out the coding plug ...

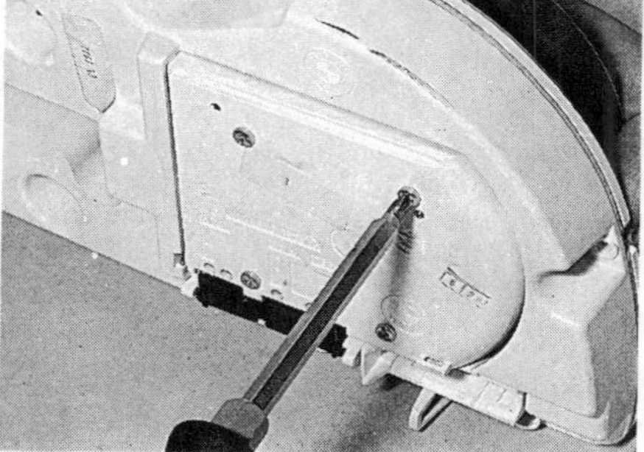
20.5B ... and remove the screws ...

20.5C ... and withdraw the speedometer

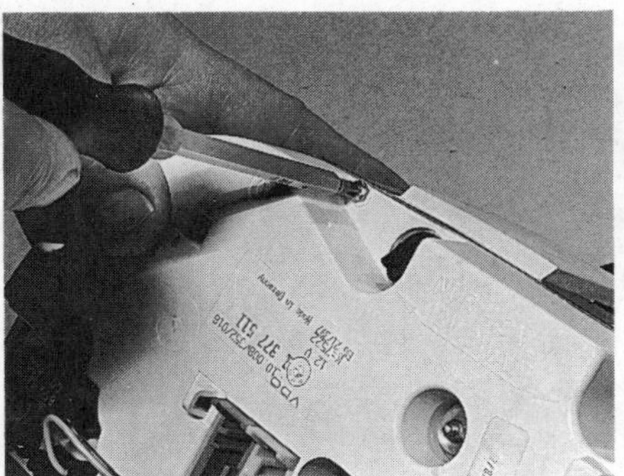
20.8 Remove the screws ...

20.9 ... and withdraw the front cover

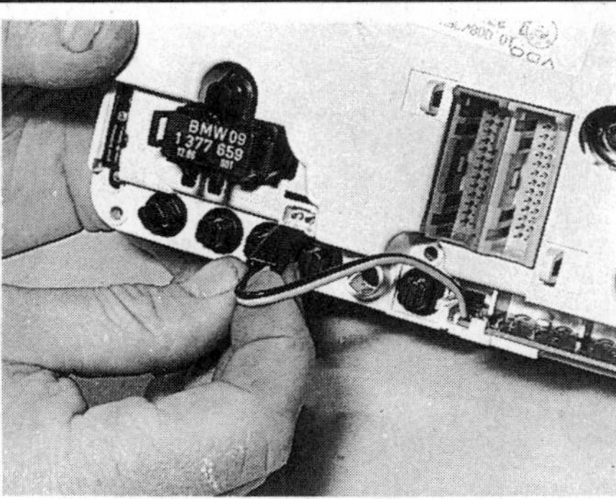

20.10A Disconnect the small wire ...

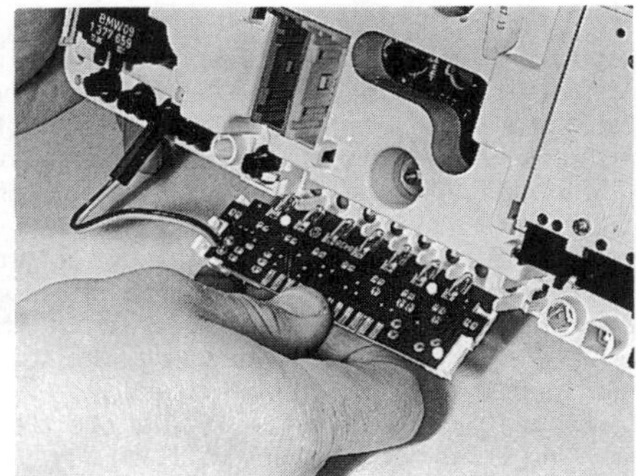
20.10B ... and withdraw the automatic transmission gear selector display unit

20.11 Code module removal

board and service indicator unit may also be separated from the gauge unit (photos).

14 Refitting is a reversal of removal.

Clock (analogue)

15 The procedure is the same as that for the speedometer described in paragraphs 3 to 6.

Instrument cluster (520i models up to 1983)

16 Pull off the time setting knob.

17 Pull off the adhesive tape.

18 Extract the perimeter screws and remove the entire instrument carrier from the housing, taking care not to touch the printed circuit.

19 Pull off the plug and unscrew both nuts.

20 Refitting is a reversal of removal.

Instrument cluster (520i models from 1983 on and all 525e models)

21 Pull off the time setting knob where applicable.

22 Pull out the coding plug.

23 Pull off the adhesive tape.

24 Unscrew the screws and remove the carrier housing taking care not to touch the printed circuit.

25 Remove the speedometer (and clock where applicable) together with the fuel consumption indicator.

26 Disconnect the wiring plugs and unscrew the printed circuit board nuts.

27 Refitting is a reversal of removal.

21 Service indicator – general

1 The service indicator is in the centre of the instrument panel and it alerts the driver when a service is due. The system operates through a

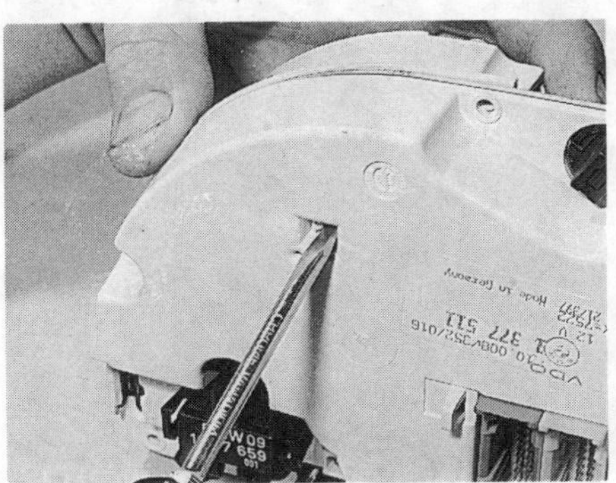
20.12A Remove the screws ...

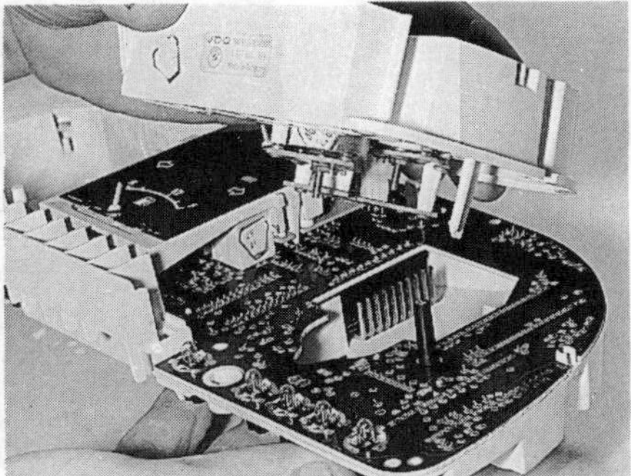
20.12B ... and withdraw the tachometer unit and housing

20.13A Unscrew the nuts ...

20.13B ... and withdraw the fuel/temperature gauge unit

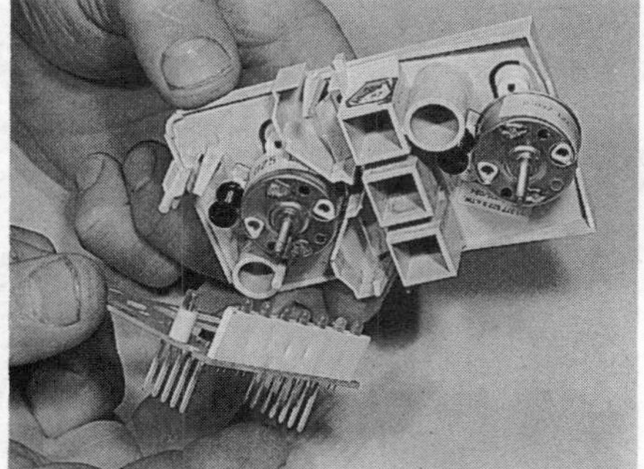

20.13C Separating the service indicator PCB from the fuel/temperature gauge unit

range of sensors which measure ten service-related items on the car as follows:

- *(a) Spark plugs*
- *(b) Engine oil*
- *(c) Transmission oil*
- *(d) Air filter*
- *(e) Clutch*
- *(f) Shock absorbers*
- *(g) Brake linings*
- *(h) Headlight reflectors*
- *(i) Battery*
- *(j) Cylinder compression*

2 The indicator incorporates green, yellow and red LEDs. When the ignition is initially switched on, the green LEDs are lit. After the engine is started some of the green lights may go out depending on how soon the next service is due. The fewer number of green LEDs, the nearer the next service. The yellow LEDs come on when the next service is due, and may operate as the car is being driven along. The red LED comes on when the service is overdue. The clock symbol in the centre of the display shows that an annual inspection is due.

3 The service indicator is reset by using a special BMW plug-in instrument after the appropriate service has been carried out. It is possible to purchase a resetting instrument (such as Sykes-Pickavant tool 300690) from a motor factor (photo).

4 When a service is due the car can be taken to a BMW dealer who will plug in a service tester (not the resetting tool). This shows a visual display of all of the service items given in paragraph 1. Items requiring immediate attention will be 'flagged' and the remaining time and distance will also be given for all items. The 'flagged' items are also priced so that the customer will know the cost of the service.

5 Should an illogical display occur (ie both green and red LEDs) the system should be checked by a BMW dealer.

6 If the speedometer, rev-counter or coolant temperature gauge is faulty then the Service Indicator will no longer operate correctly since it relies on these components for its own input. The system also uses the signal from the starter motor to operate the LEDs so if the car is push-started it will not function correctly.

7 Should the system be faulty, first check all the associated wiring including plugs for condition and security. If the fault persists the system should be checked by a BMW dealer.

22 Horn – removal and refitting

1 Open the bonnet then unscrew the two screws and remove the plastic cover from the engine compartment front crossmember.

2 Disconnect the battery negative lead.

3 Disconnect the wiring from the horn (photo).

4 Unscrew the mounting bolt and withdraw the horn.

5 Refitting is a reversal of removal.

21.3 Typical service indicator resetting instrument

22.3 Disconnecting the horn wiring

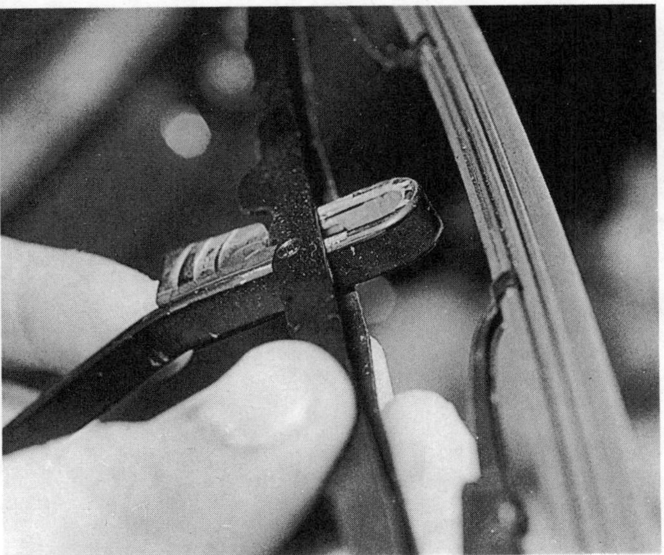

23.2 Removing a wiper blade from the arm

23.4 Wiper arm/spindle nut

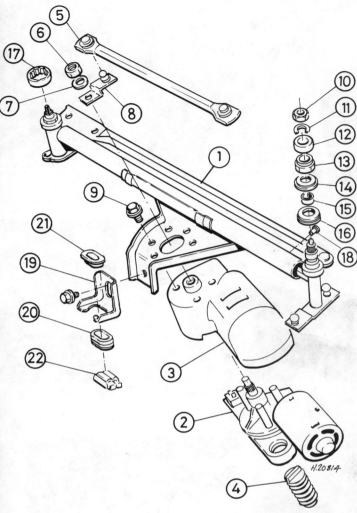

Fig. 12.5 Windscreen wiper motor and linkage (Sec 24)

1 Windscreen wiper assembly
2 Wiper motor
3 Cover
4 Buffer stop
5 Drive rod
6 Nut
7 Wave washer
8 Crank
9 Bolt
10 Nut
11 Wave washer
12 Spacer
13 Nut
14 Washer
15 Ring
16 Spacer
17 Spacer
18 Rivet
19 Bracket
20 Grommet
21 Bearing
22 Nut

23 Windscreen wiper blades and arms – removal and refitting

1 To remove a wiper blade, pull the arm fully away from the glass until it locks.
2 Swivel the blade through 90°, press the locking tab with the finger nail and slide the plastic block and blade out of the hooked end of the wiper arm (photo).
3 Before removing the wiper arm, stick a piece of masking tape along the blade on the glass. This will facilitate alignment of the arm when refitting.
4 Flip up the cover, unscrew the nut and pull the arm from the splined drive spindle (photo). If necessary use a large screwdriver blade to prise off the arm.
5 Refitting of the blade and arm is a reversal of removal, but do not overtighten the arm retaining nut.

24 Windscreen wiper motor and linkage – removal and refitting

1 Disconnect the battery negative lead.
2 Disconnect the accelerator cable from the front of the bulkhead, then unbolt the rubber cover for access to the wiper motor (photos).
3 Remove the heater blower (Chapter 11), then unscrew the lower wiper mounting bolt from the bulkhead.
4 Mark the crank in relation to the wiper motor spindle, then unscrew the nut and pull the crank from the spindle.
5 Disconnect the wiper wiring multi-plug (photo).
6 Unscrew the three mounting bolts and withdraw the wiper motor from the linkage assembly. If necessary the motor may be removed together with the linkage.

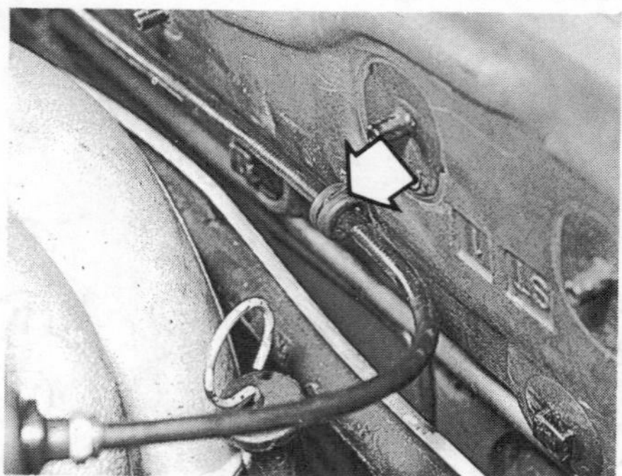
24.2A Unclip the accelerator cable (clip arrowed) ...

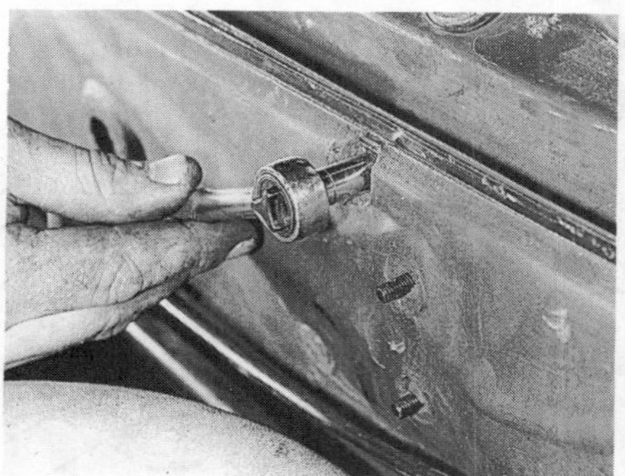
24.2B ... and unbolt the rubber cover from the bulkhead

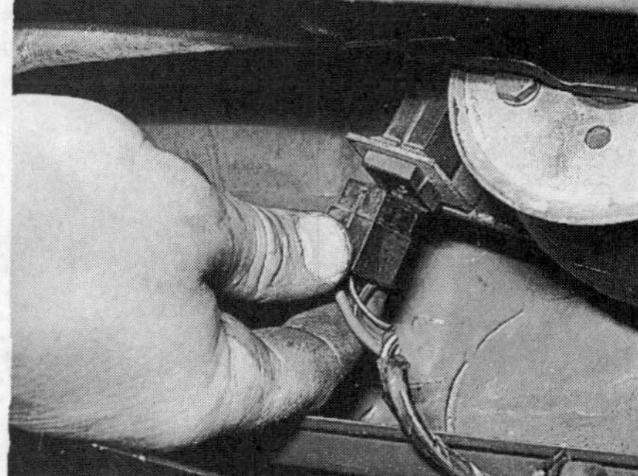
24.5 Disconnecting the multi-plug from the wiper motor

24.7 Removing the rubber cover from the wiper spindle nut

24.8A Removing the wiper spindle spacer ...

24.8B ... and washer

24.10A Removing the windscreen wiper linkage and motor

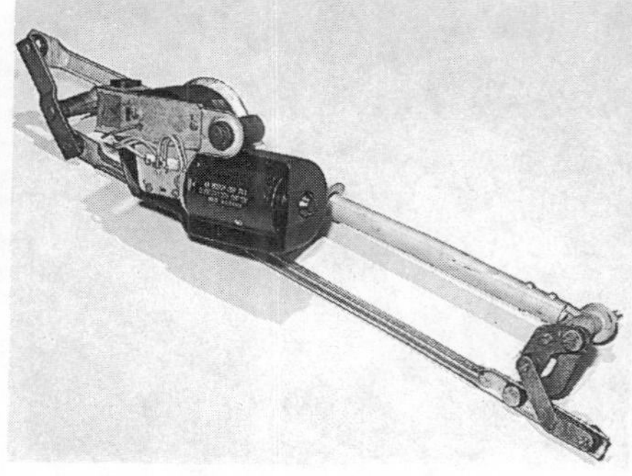
24.10B Windscreen wiper linkage and motor assembly

7 To remove the linkage first remove the wiper arms as described in Section 23. Also remove the rubber covers (photo).

8 Unscrew the spindle housing nuts and remove the washers and spacers, noting their locations (photos).

9 Unscrew the bolt securing the front of the linkage to the bulkhead. The bracket may also be removed.

10 Remove the linkage from the bulkhead (photos).

11 Refitting is a reversal of removal, but adjust the wiper arms and blades as described in Section 23.

25 Windscreen washer system – general

1 The windscreen washer system consists of a fluid reservoir located on the right-hand side of the engine compartment, a pump located on the side of the reservoir (photo), tubing from the reservoir to the jets, and one-way valves fitted in the tubing.

2 The pump may be removed by disconnecting the wiring and pulling the unit direct from the reservoir.

3 The jets may be adjusted by inserting a pin into the spray nozzles and aiming the spray to a point slightly above the centre of the windscreen.

26 Headlight washer system – general

1 The headlight washer system is fitted to some models. The fluid reservoir is combined with the windscreen washer reservoir and the system includes wiper motors on each headlight, with wipers located on a twin arm unit.

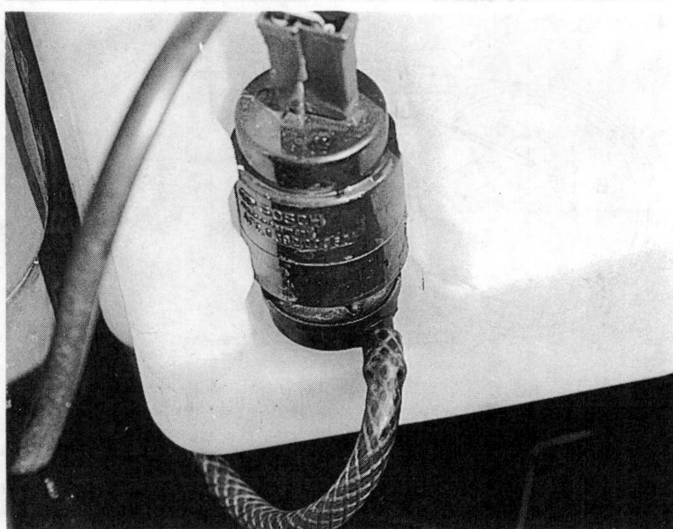

25.1 Pump located on the side of the windscreen washer fluid reservoir

2 The headlight washer system is activated when the windscreen washers are operated with the headlights on.
3 Access to the wiper motors is obtained by removing the radiator air intake side grilles as described in Chapter 11.
4 The jets should be adjusted so that the spray is aimed at the points indicated in Fig. 12.7.

27 On-board computer – general

1 The on-board computer provides the following information:

(a) *Time or date*
(b) *Average speed*
(c) *Speed limit warning*
(d) *Average fuel consumption*
(e) *Range on remaining fuel*
(f) *Ambient temperature*
(g) *Immobilisation of the car*

2 Note that if the battery is disconnected or if the power supply to the computer is interrupted, all stored data in the computer is erased. After reconnecting the battery the data must be input again.
3 The immobilisation function allows the driver to enter a four figure code on leaving the car in order to prevent the engine from being started. On re-entry the identical code is entered so that the engine can be started. Note that if a total of three incorrect codes are entered consecutively or if three attempts are made to start the engine, an alarm will sound for 30 seconds.
4 If the system incurs a fault the car should be taken to a BMW dealer for checking.

28 Radio and radio/cassette – removal and refitting

BMW Bavaria, Bavaria S and Bavaria cassette

1 Pull off the control knobs and rings or tone control as applicable.

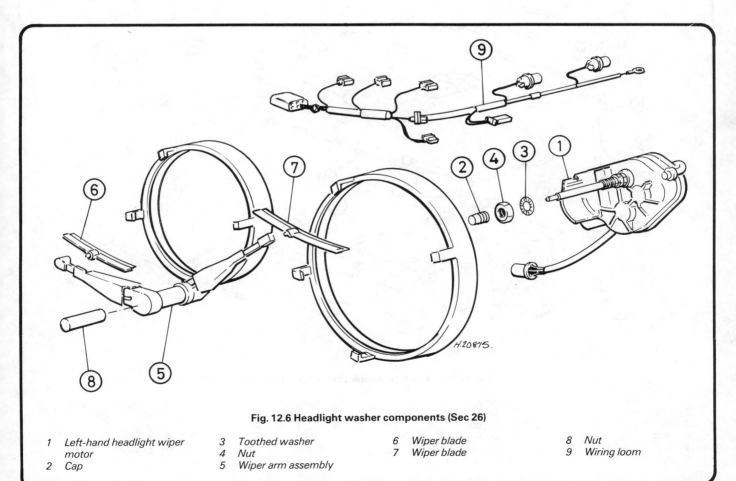

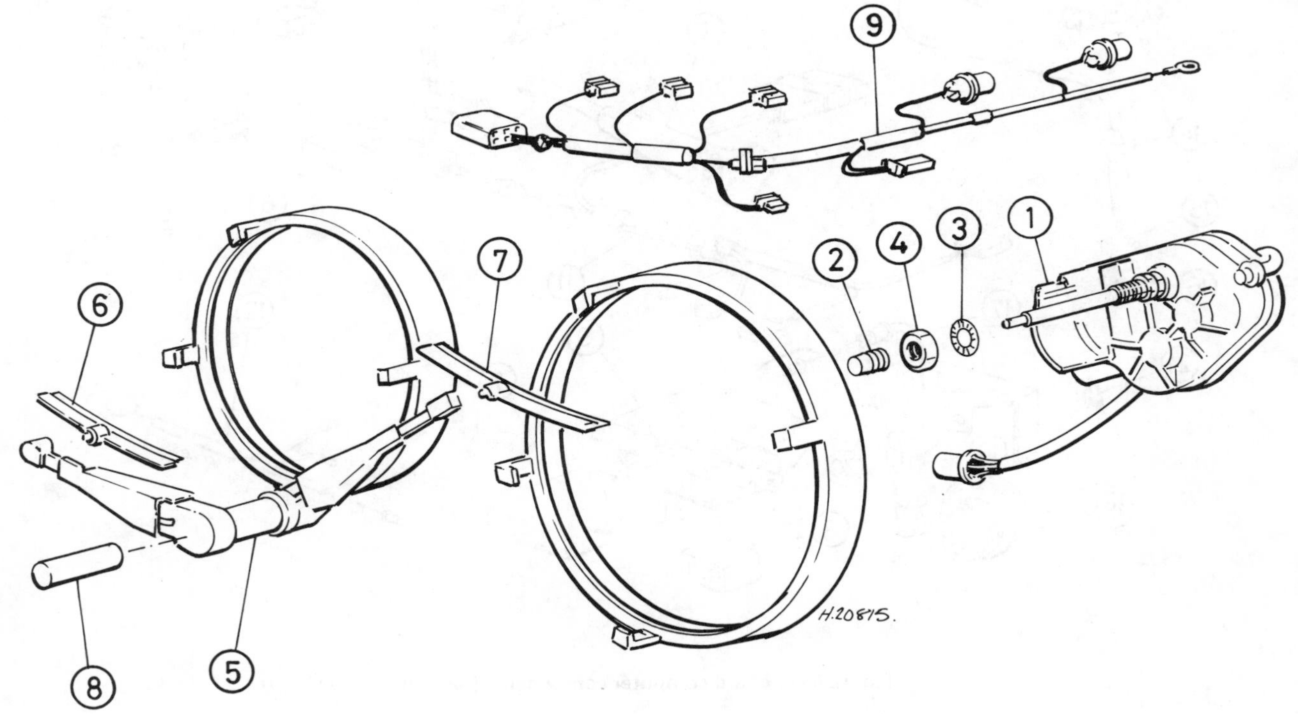

Fig. 12.6 Headlight washer components (Sec 26)

1 *Left-hand headlight wiper motor*
2 *Cap*
3 *Toothed washer*
4 *Nut*
5 *Wiper arm assembly*
6 *Wiper blade*
7 *Wiper blade*
8 *Nut*
9 *Wiring loom*

2 Push back the spring catches and remove the surround.
3 Extract the side screws and lift out the holders.
4 Withdraw the radio and disconnect all the wiring plugs and aerial.
5 Refitting is a reversal of removal.

BMW Bavaria Electronic or similar

6 Pull off the left-hand control knob.
7 Two rods are now required in order to unlock the surround and radio. The correct rods may possibly be obtained from a BMW dealer but otherwise similar rods can be made out of metal dowel rod (photo).
8 Remove the surround.
9 Using the rods, push back the clamps on the left and right-hand sides.
10 Withdraw the radio and disconnect all the wiring plugs and aerial.
11 Refitting is a reversal of removal.

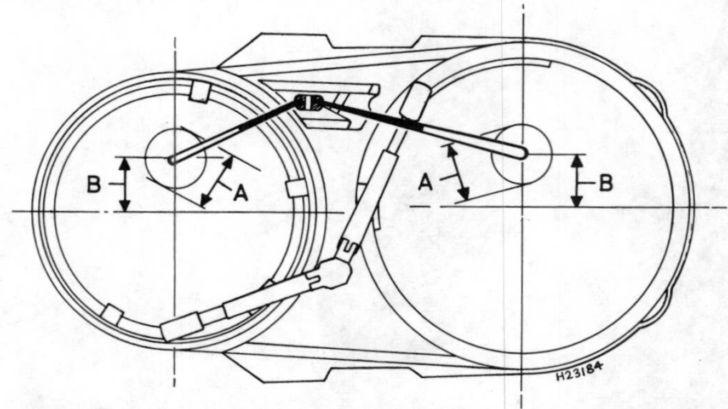

Fig. 12.7 Headlamp washer jet adjustment dimensions (Sec 26)

A = 30 mm *B = 30 mm*

29 Speakers – removal and refitting

1 Unscrew the screws and remove the speaker grille.
2 Withdraw the speaker and disconnect the wiring plugs.
3 Refitting is a reversal of removal.

30 Radio aerial and lead – removal and refitting

Retractable aerial at the front of the car

1 Remove the radio as described in Section 28, and disconnect the

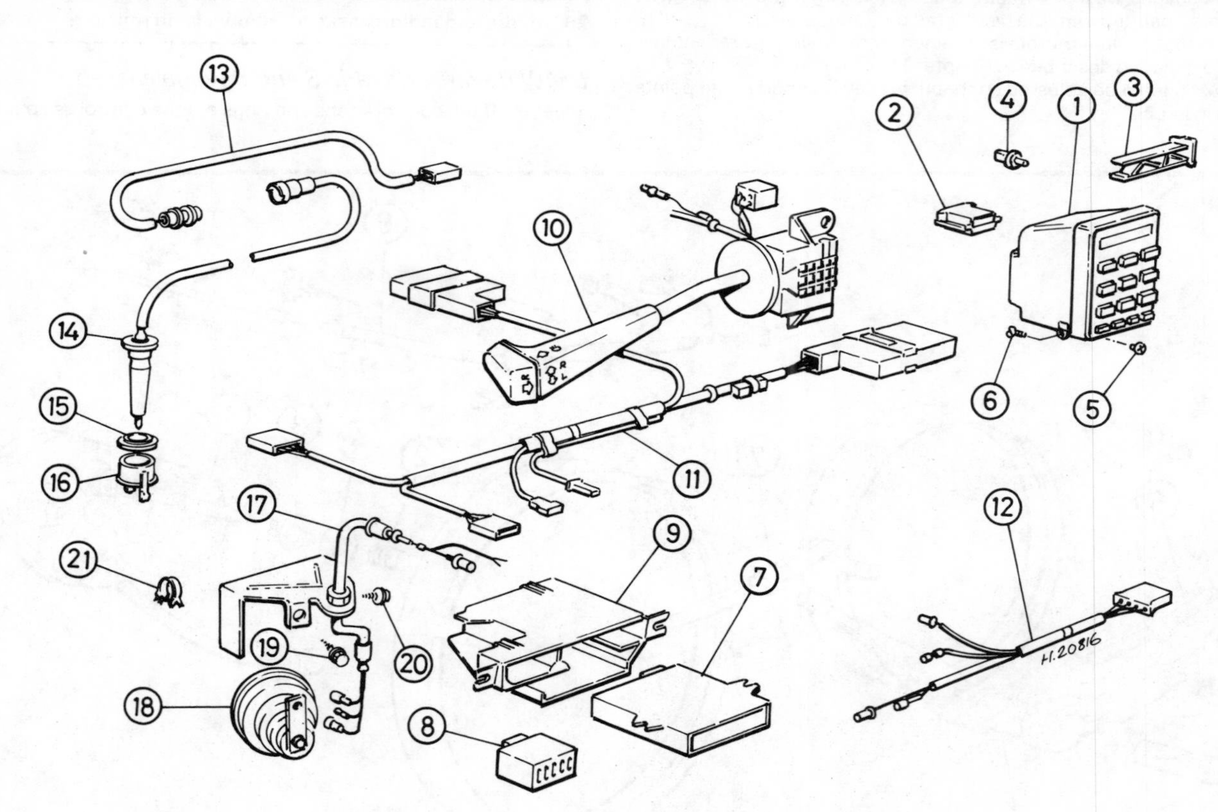

Fig. 12.8 On-board computer components (Sec 27)

1 Computer
2 Coding plug
3 Housing
4 Bulb
5 Cap
6 Screw
7 Relay
8 Gong
9 Holder
10 Direction indicator and dim-dip switch
11 Wiring loom
12 Wiring loom
13 Fuse link
14 Ambient temperature sensor
15 Gasket
16 Bracket
17 Theft alarm wiring
18 Klaxon horn
19 Bolt
20 Screw
21 Clamp

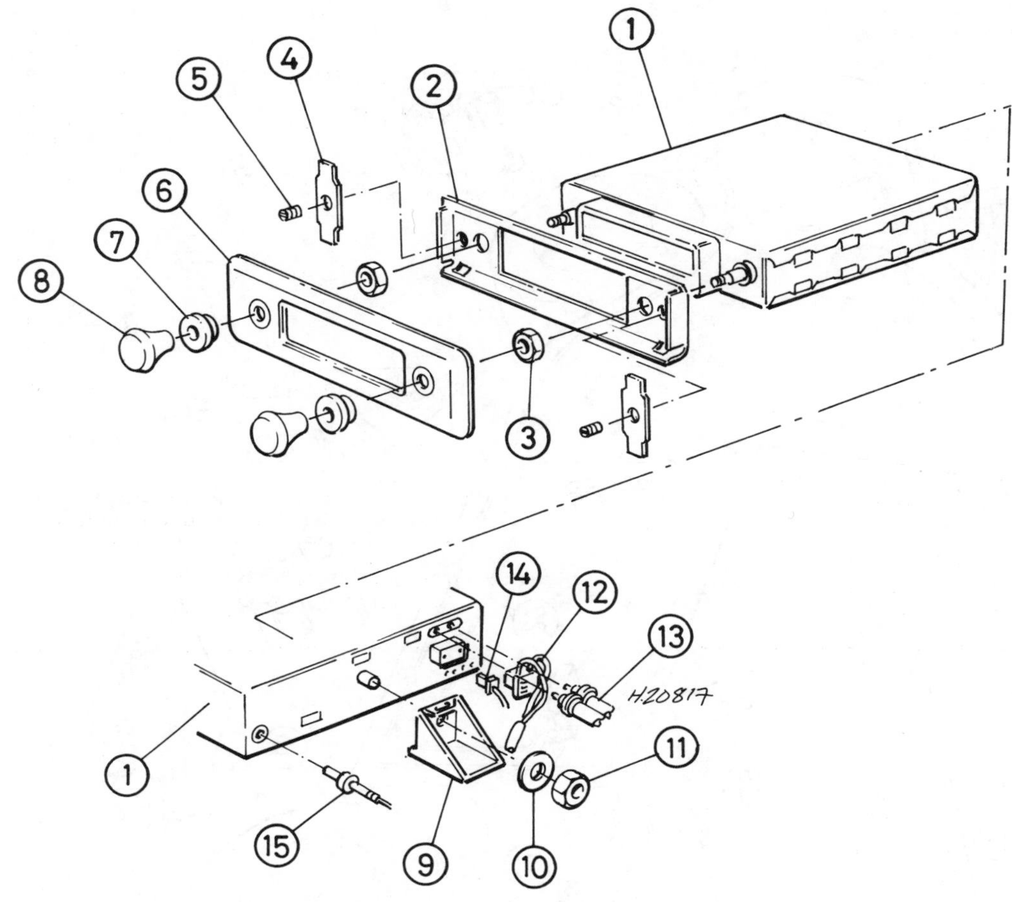

Fig. 12.9 Exploded view of the Bavaria type radio (Sec 28)

1 Radio	*5 Screw*	*9 Support*	*13 Connector (speakers)*
2 Carrier	*6 Surround*	*10 Washer*	*14 Connector (automatic aerial)*
3 Nut	*7 Collar*	*11 Nut*	*15 Aerial*
4 Holder	*8 Knob*	*12 Connector (B + and earth)*	

28.7 Removing the radio

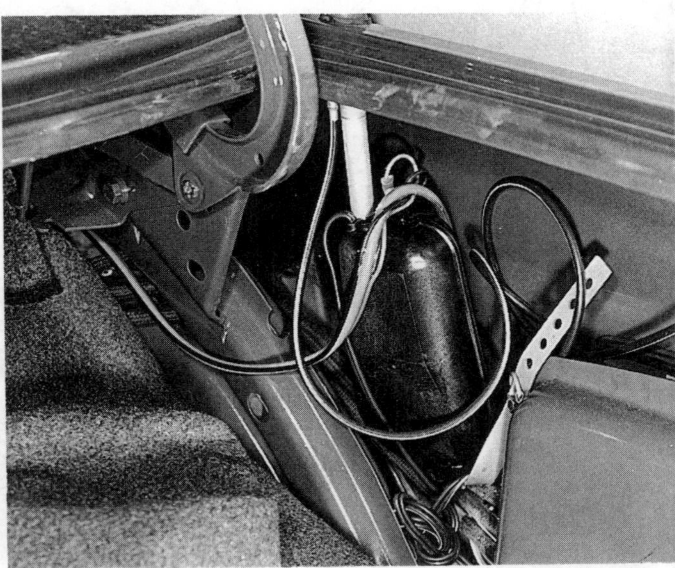

30.7 Automatic aerial at the rear of the car (luggage compartment trim removed)

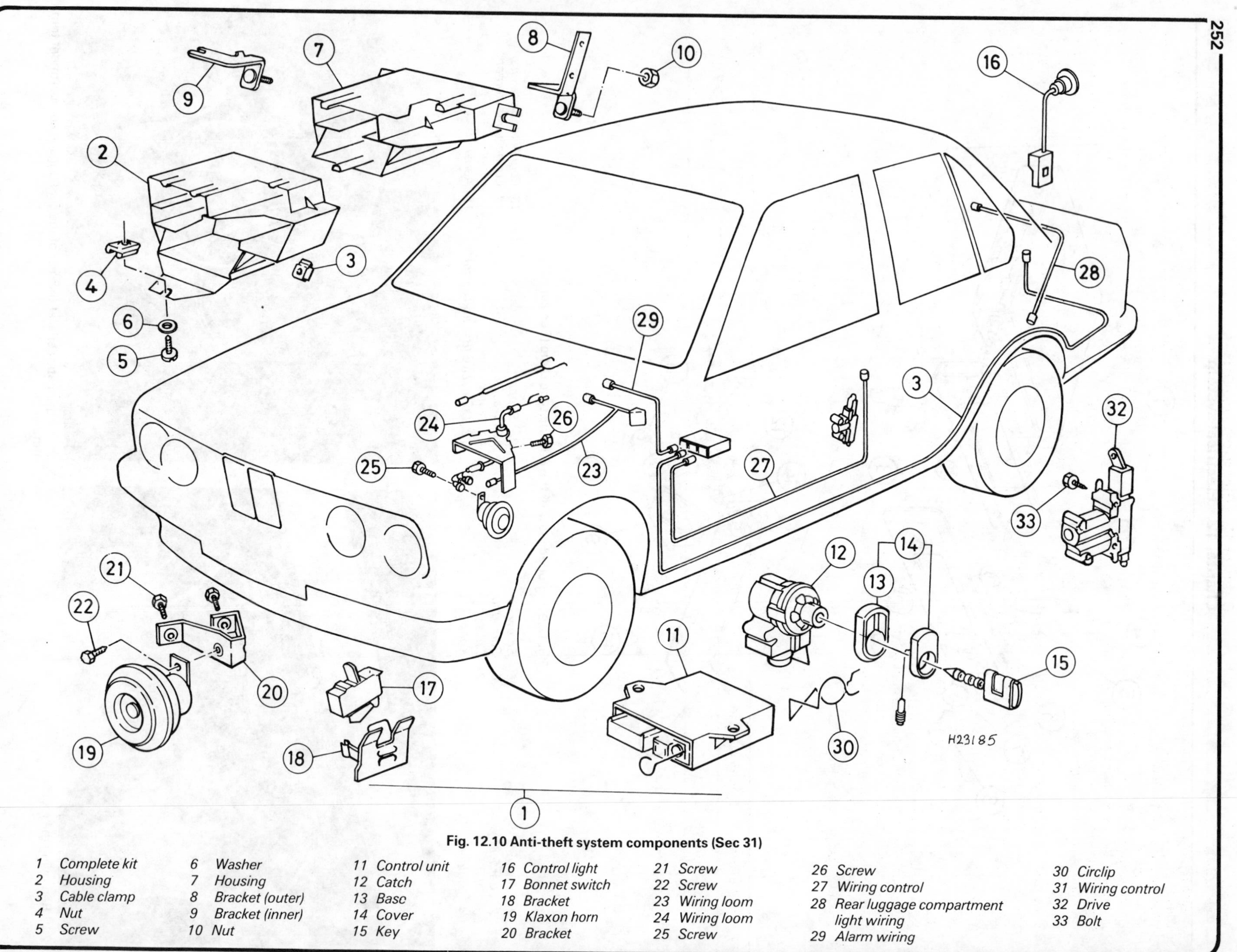

Fig. 12.10 Anti-theft system components (Sec 31)

1 *Complete kit*
2 *Housing*
3 *Cable clamp*
4 *Nut*
5 *Screw*
6 *Washer*
7 *Housing*
8 *Bracket (outer)*
9 *Bracket (inner)*
10 *Nut*
11 *Control unit*
12 *Catch*
13 *Basc*
14 *Cover*
15 *Key*
16 *Control light*
17 *Bonnet switch*
18 *Bracket*
19 *Klaxon horn*
20 *Bracket*
21 *Screw*
22 *Screw*
23 *Wiring loom*
24 *Wiring loom*
25 *Screw*
26 *Screw*
27 *Wiring control*
28 *Rear luggage compartment light wiring*
29 *Alarm wiring*
30 *Circlip*
31 *Wiring control*
32 *Drive*
33 *Bolt*

aerial. Also remove the lower facia panel (Chapter 11) for access to the aerial lead.
2 Working under the front wing, unscrew the bolt holding the bracket to the inner panel.
3 Unscrew the nut securing the aerial to the front wing.
4 Withdraw the aerial from the front wing and remove the lead through the bulkhead.
5 Refitting is a reversal of removal.

Retractable or automatic aerial at the rear of the car

6 Remove the radio as described in Section 28, and disconnect the aerial lead. Also remove the lower facia panel (Chapter 11) for access to the aerial lead.
7 Working in the rear compartment, remove the jack and wheel bolt wrench, then remove the side panel trim (photo).
8 Remove the rear seat cushion and backrest as described in Chapter 11.
9 Remove the right door kickplates and pull up the carpet.
10 Unscrew the nut securing the aerial to the rear wing.
11 On automatic aerials disconnect the wiring from the aerial.
12 Withdraw the aerial from the rear wing and remove the lead through the right-hand side of the car.
13 Refitting is a reversal of removal.

31 Anti-theft system – general

1 The anti-theft system is fitted to some models and consists of a control unit and wiring which sounds an alarm in the event of a thief attempting to enter the car. The system is set by turning a key in the alarm lock. LEDs indicate the state of the system for a maximum of 24 hours, and they will flash if all the doors, bonnet and bootlid are not properly closed when setting the lock.
2 The alarm will sound for 30 seconds each time the door, bonnet or bootlid is opened with the system switched on, and in addition the engine will be prevented from starting.
3 The code is set by turning discs on the system key so that the owner can input his/her own code.

32 Wiring diagrams – explanatory notes

The wiring diagrams included at the end of the Chapter are of both conventional type and the current flow type where each wire is shown in the simplest line form without crossing over other wires.

In the case of current flow diagrams all circuit paths are shown numerically on the earth plate and run vertically from positive at the top to negative at the bottom. Where circuit paths would cross each other, a boxed number is provided for cross reference to a separate circuit.

33 Fault diagnosis – electrical system

Symptom	Reason(s)
Starter fails to turn engine	Battery discharged Battery leads loose Starter motor connections loose Starter motor brushes loose, or dirty commutator
Starter turns engine slowly	Battery discharged Starter motor connections loose
Battery will not hold charge	Electrolyte level too low Alternator drivebelt slipping Alternator or regulator faulty Short in electrical circuit
Ignition light stays on	Alternator drivebelt broken Alternator or voltage regulator faulty
Ignition light fails to come on	Warning bulb blown Warning light open-circuit Alternator or voltage regulator faulty
Instrument readings increase with engine speed	Voltage stabilizer faulty
Fuel or temperature gauge readings incorrect	Voltage stabilizer faulty Sender unit faulty Wiring faulty
Lights inoperative	Bulb blown Fuse blown Wiring faulty Switch faulty
Failure of component motor	Commutator dirty Brushes sticking or worn Armature or field coils faulty Wiring faulty Relay faulty Earth return faulty

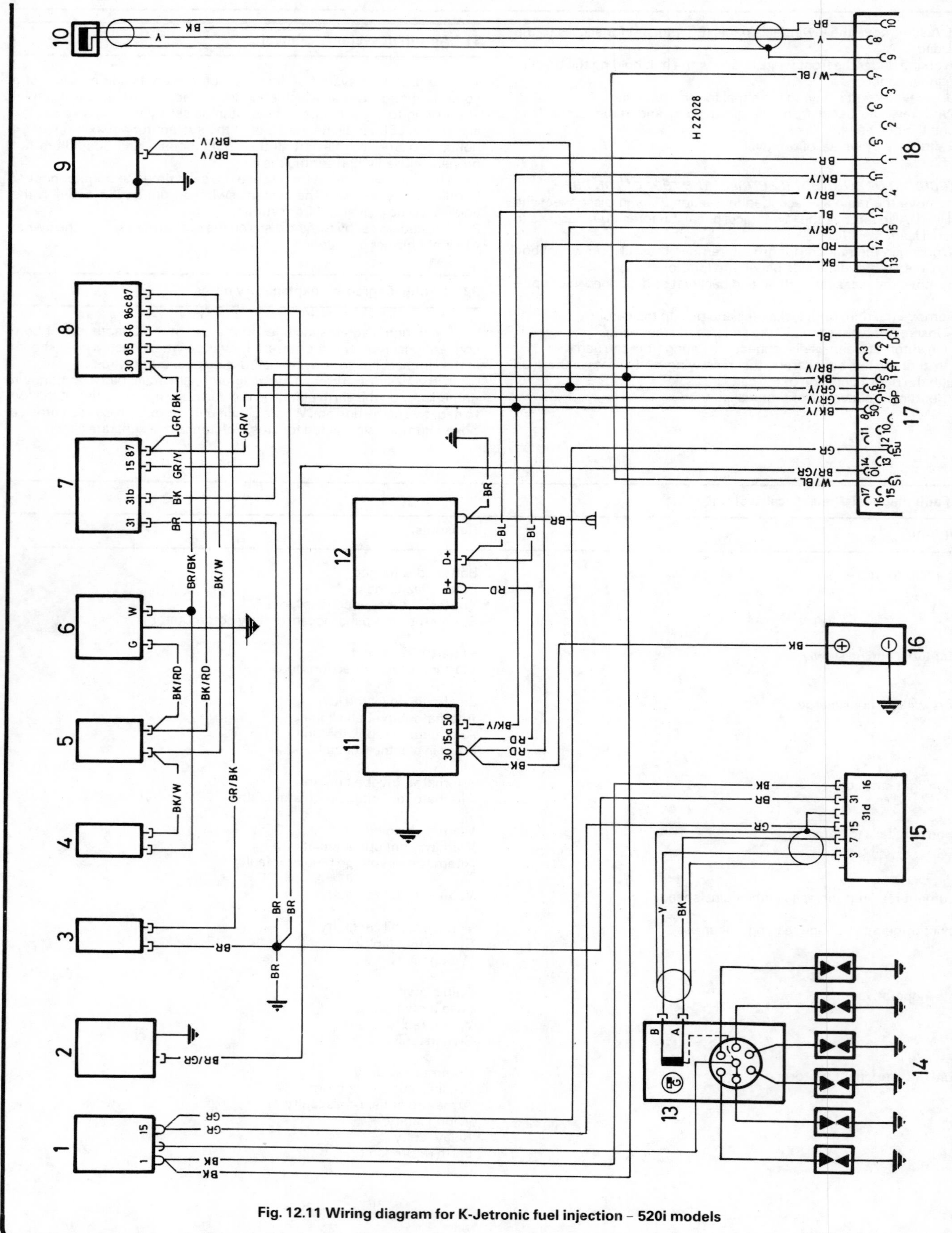

Fig. 12.11 Wiring diagram for K-Jetronic fuel injection – 520i models

Key to Fig. 12.11

No	Description
1	Ignition coil
2	Oil pressure switch
3	Warm-up regulator
4	Cold start valve
5	Temperature switch 0°C
6	Temperature time switch
7	Fuel pump relay
8	Diode relay
9	Temperature transmitter
10	Position transmitter
11	Starter
12	Alternator
13	Distributor
14	Spark plugs
15	Control unit for TCI
16	Battery
17	Engine socket
18	Diagnosis connection

Key to Fig. 12.12

No	Description
1	Injection control unit
2	Connection for injection control unit
3	Throttle switch
4	Airflow sensor
5	Fuel pump relay
6	Battery
7	Temperature sensor
8	Coolant temperature sensor
9	Fuel injector
10	Cold start valve
11	Temperature time switch
12	Distributor
13	Position sensor
14	Diagnosis connection
15	Oil pressure switch
16	Ignition coil
17	Starter
18	Alternator
19	Spark plugs
20	Transistor ignition control unit
21	Engine plug
22	Service indicator
23	Oil pressure
24	Central electric board
25	Electric fuel pump
26	Temperature gauge

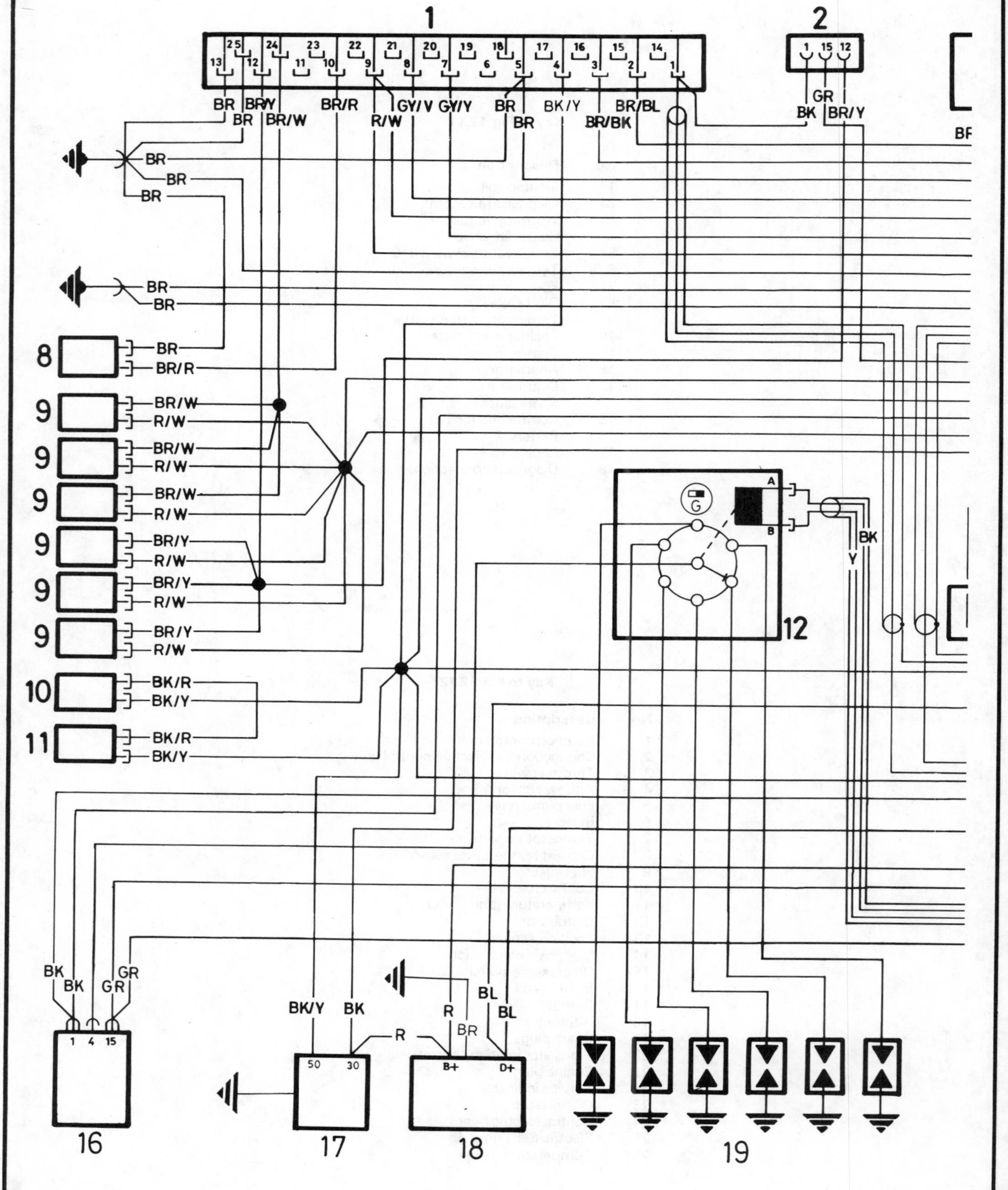

1 2 8 9 10 11 12 16 17 18 19

13 25 12 24 11 23 10 22 9 21 8 20 7 19 6 18 5 17 4 16 3 15 2 14 1

BR BR/Y BR BR/W BR/R R/W GY/V GY/Y BR BR BK/Y BR/BK BR/BL

1 15 12 BK GR BR/Y

BK/R BK/Y A B G BK Y

BK BK G R GR 1 4 15 BK/Y BK R BR BL BL 50 30 B+ D+

Fig. 12.12 Wiring diagram for fuel injection – 1983 520i models

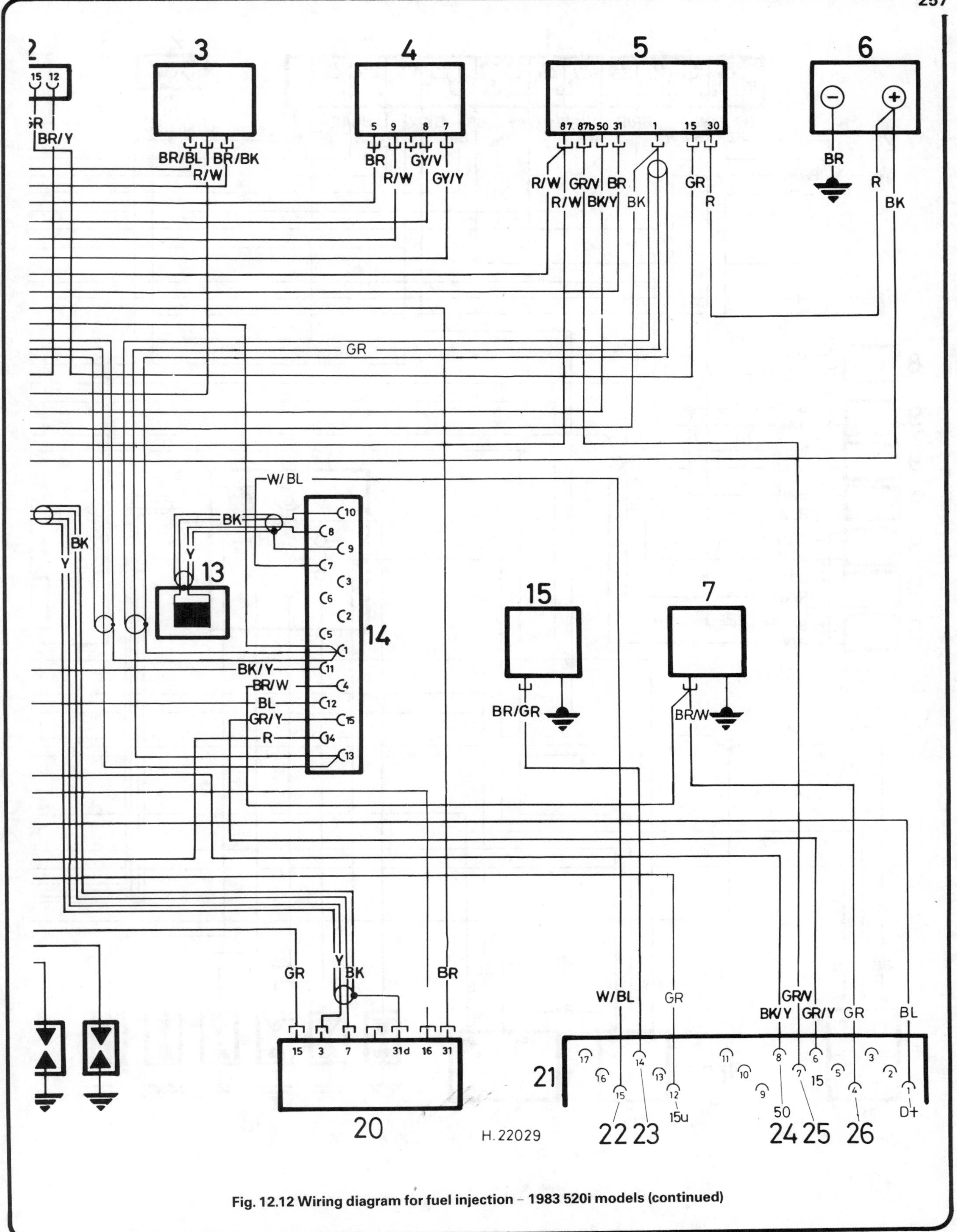

Fig. 12.12 Wiring diagram for fuel injection – 1983 520i models (continued)

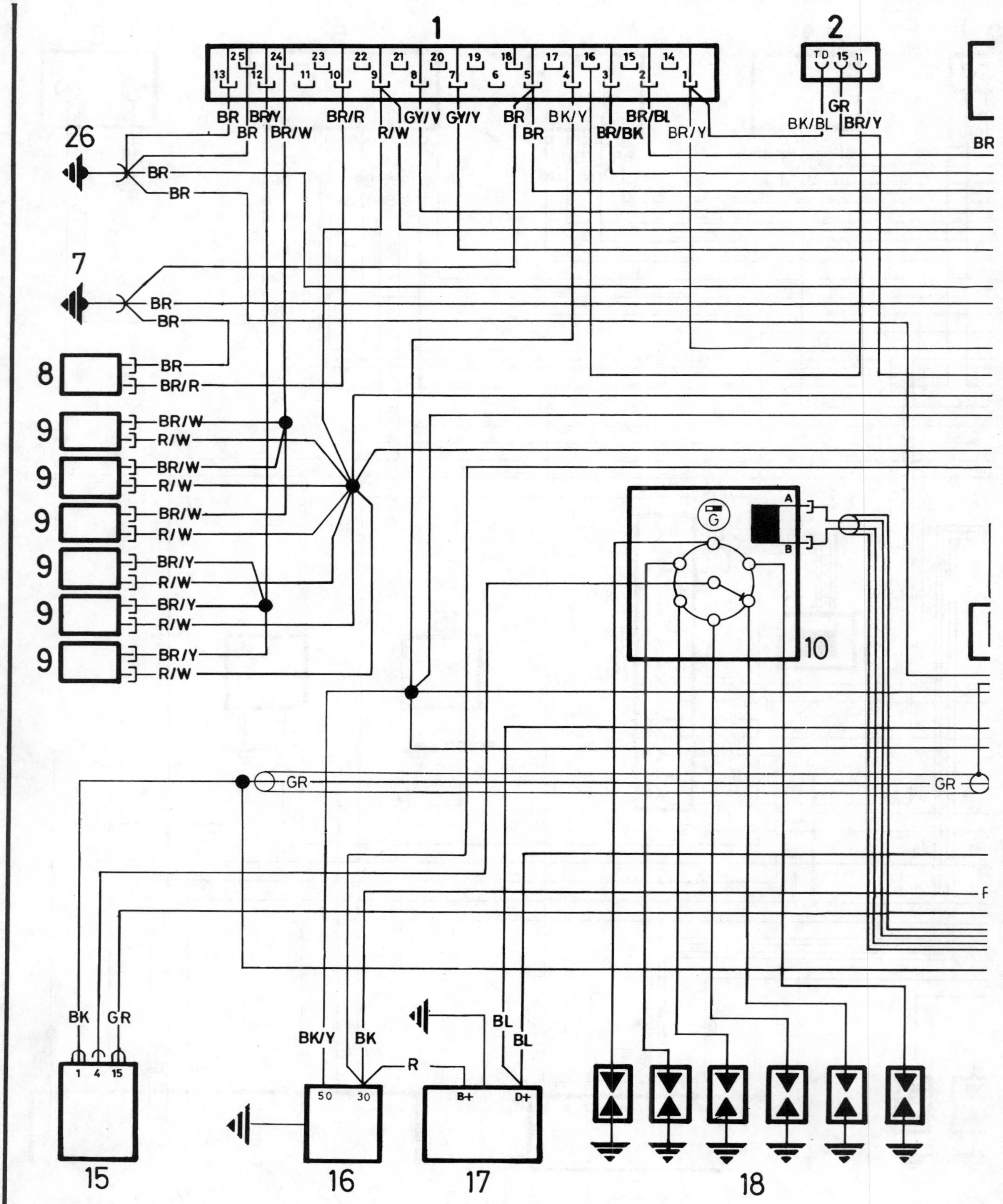

Fig. 12.13 Wiring diagram for LE-Jetronic fuel injection – 520i models

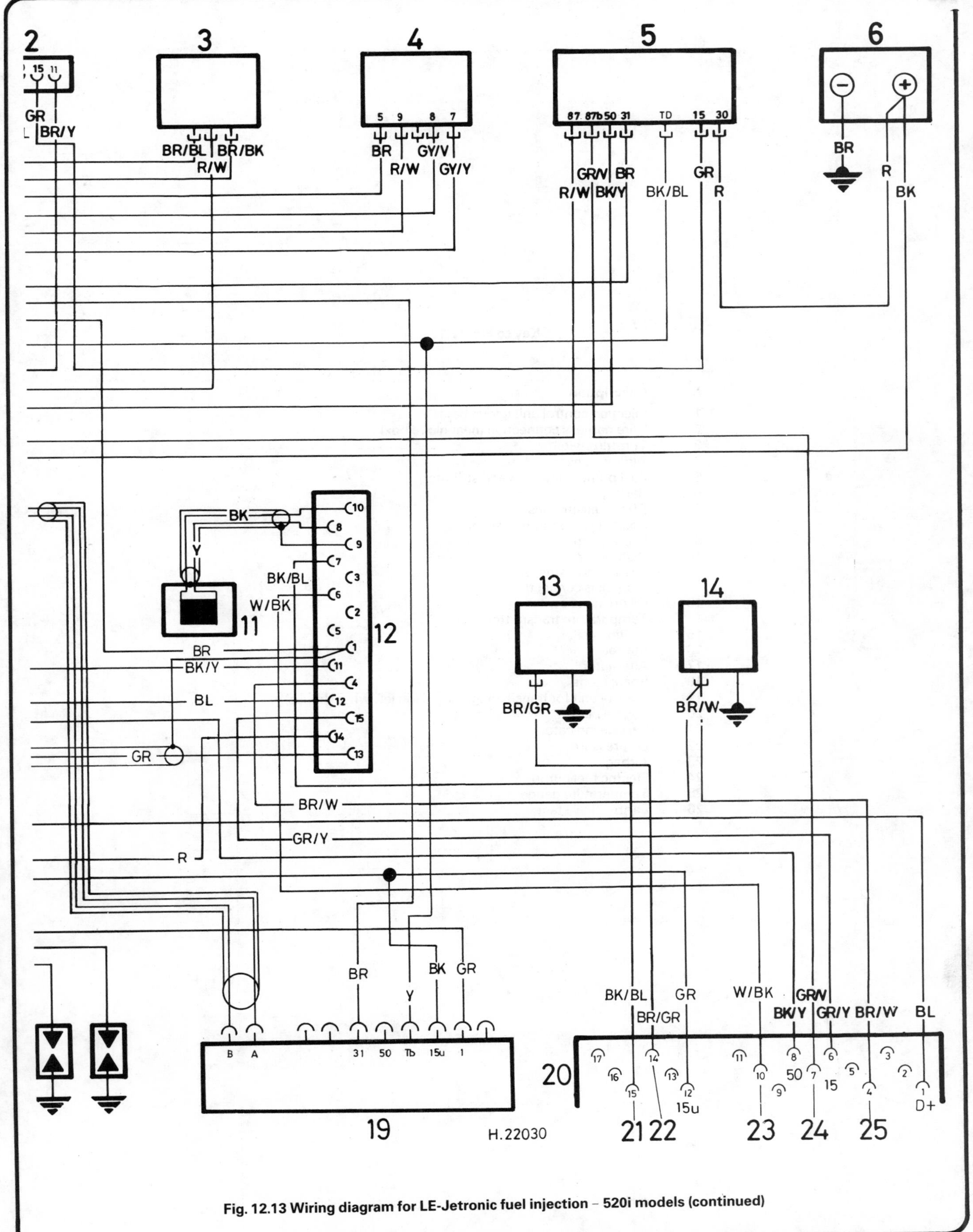

Fig. 12.13 Wiring diagram for LE-Jetronic fuel injection – 520i models (continued)

Key to Fig. 12.13

No	Description
1	Injection control unit (glove box)
2	Wire harness connection (near glove box)
3	Throttle switch
4	Airflow sensor
5	Fuel pump relay (power distributor)
6	Battery
7	Earth – electronics
8	Coolant temperature sensor
9	Fuel injector
10	Distributor
11	Position transmitter
12	Diagnosis connection
13	Oil pressure switch
14	Temperature transmitter
15	Ignition coil
16	Starter
17	Alternator
18	Spark plugs
19	Control unit for transistor ignition S (on left wheel house)
20	Engine plug
21	Service indicator
22	Oil pressure
23	Airbag
24	Electric fuel pump
25	Temperature gauge
26	Earth – final stage

Key to Fig. 12.14

No	Description
1	Digital motor electronic control unit (in glove box)
2	Speed control relay
3	Temperature switch
4	Air conditioner
5	Car wire harness connection
6	Throttle switch
7	Airflow sensor
8	Speed sensor
9	Reference mark sensor
10	Relay 1
11	Relay 2
12	Oil pressure switch
13	Temperature transmitter
14	Diagnosis connection
15	Engine plug
16	Battery
17	Spark plugs
18	Distributor
19	Ignition coil
20	Starter
21	Alternator
22	Position transmitter
23	Plug disconnected for automatic transmission
24	Coolant temperature sensor
25	Fuel injector
26	Solenoid
27	Electric power distributor
28	Oil pressure
29	Temperature gauge
30	Electric fuel pump
31	Service indicator
32	Drive motor
33	Temperature switch 45°C

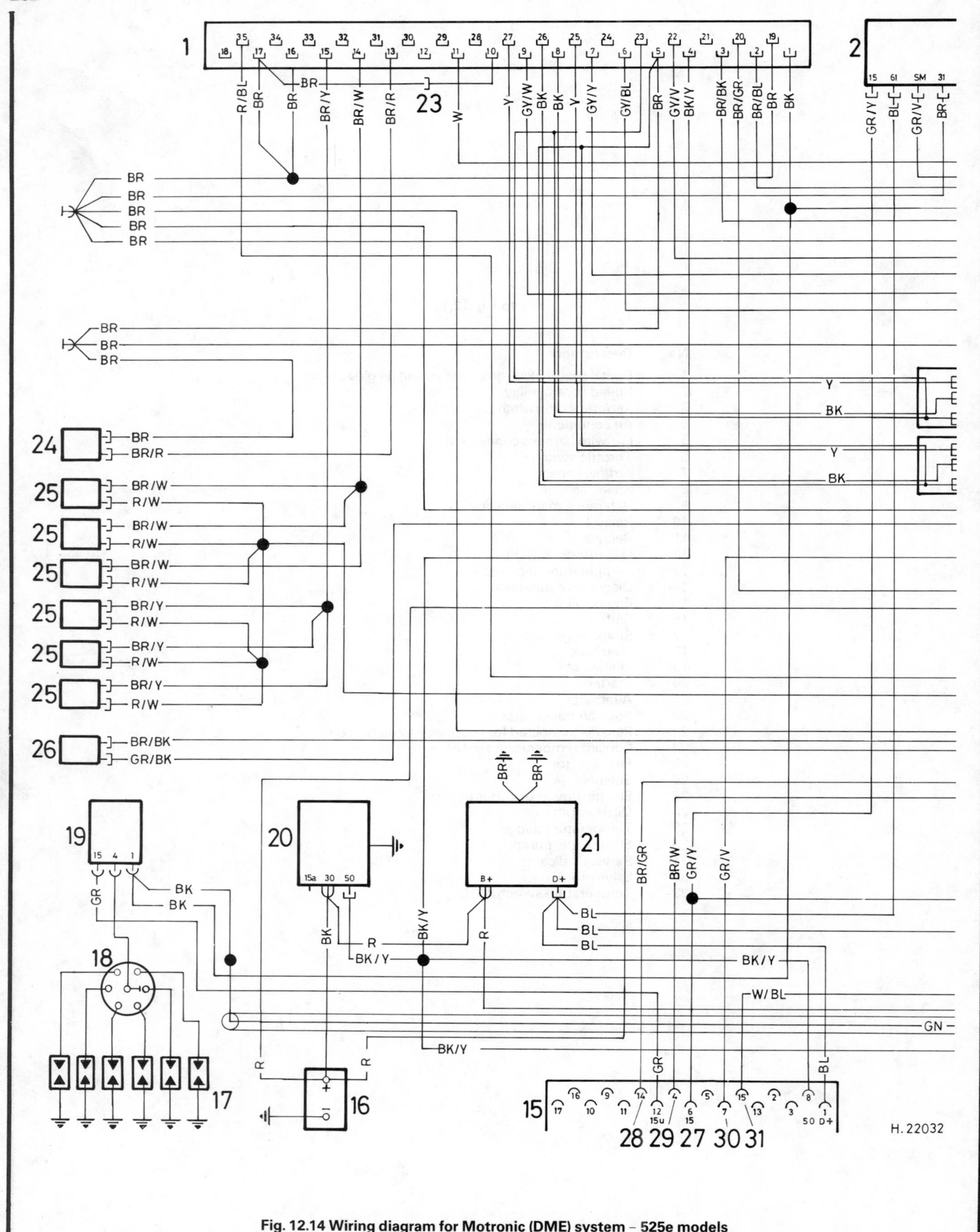

Fig. 12.14 Wiring diagram for Motronic (DME) system – 525e models

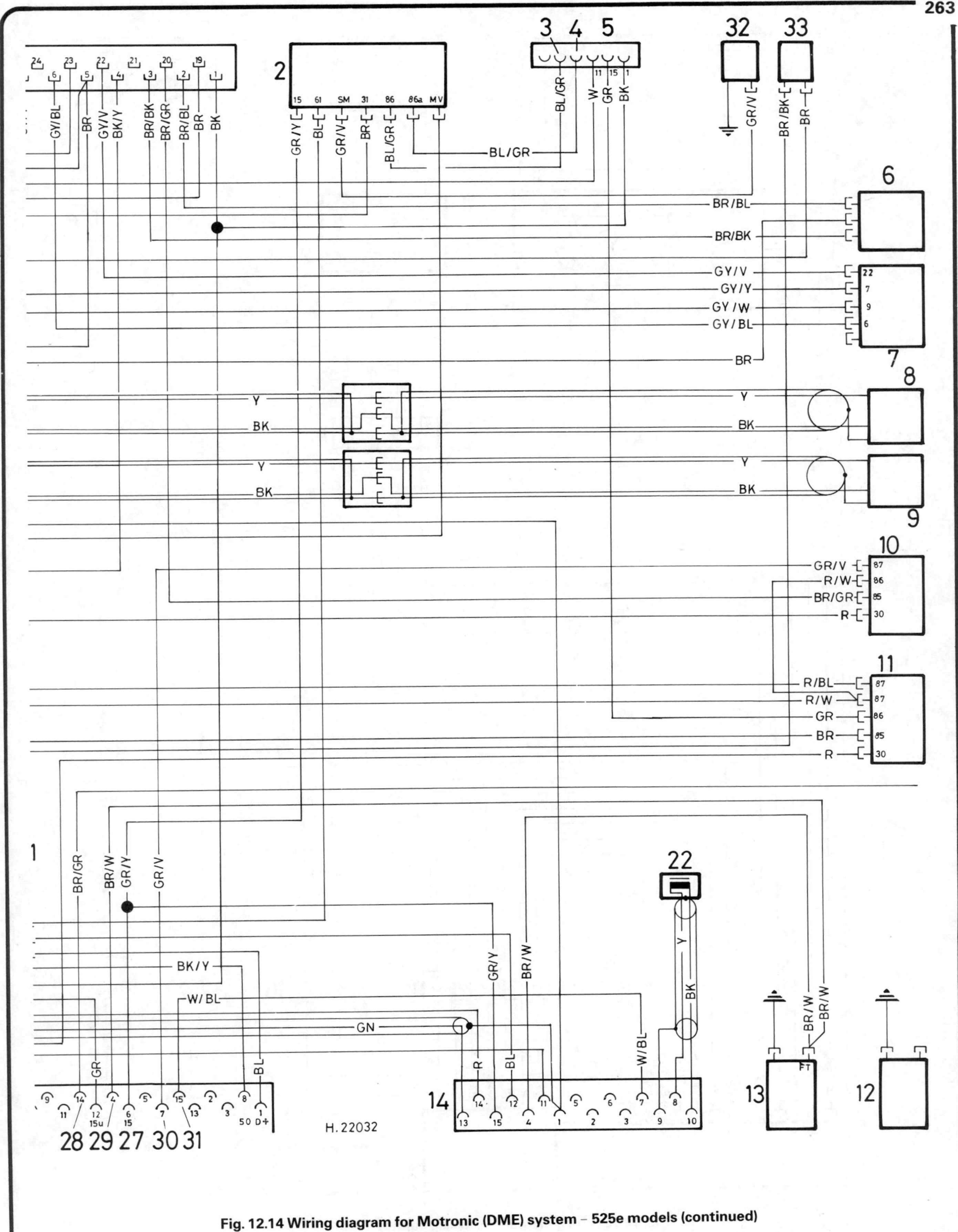

Fig. 12.14 Wiring diagram for Motronic (DME) system – 525e models (continued)

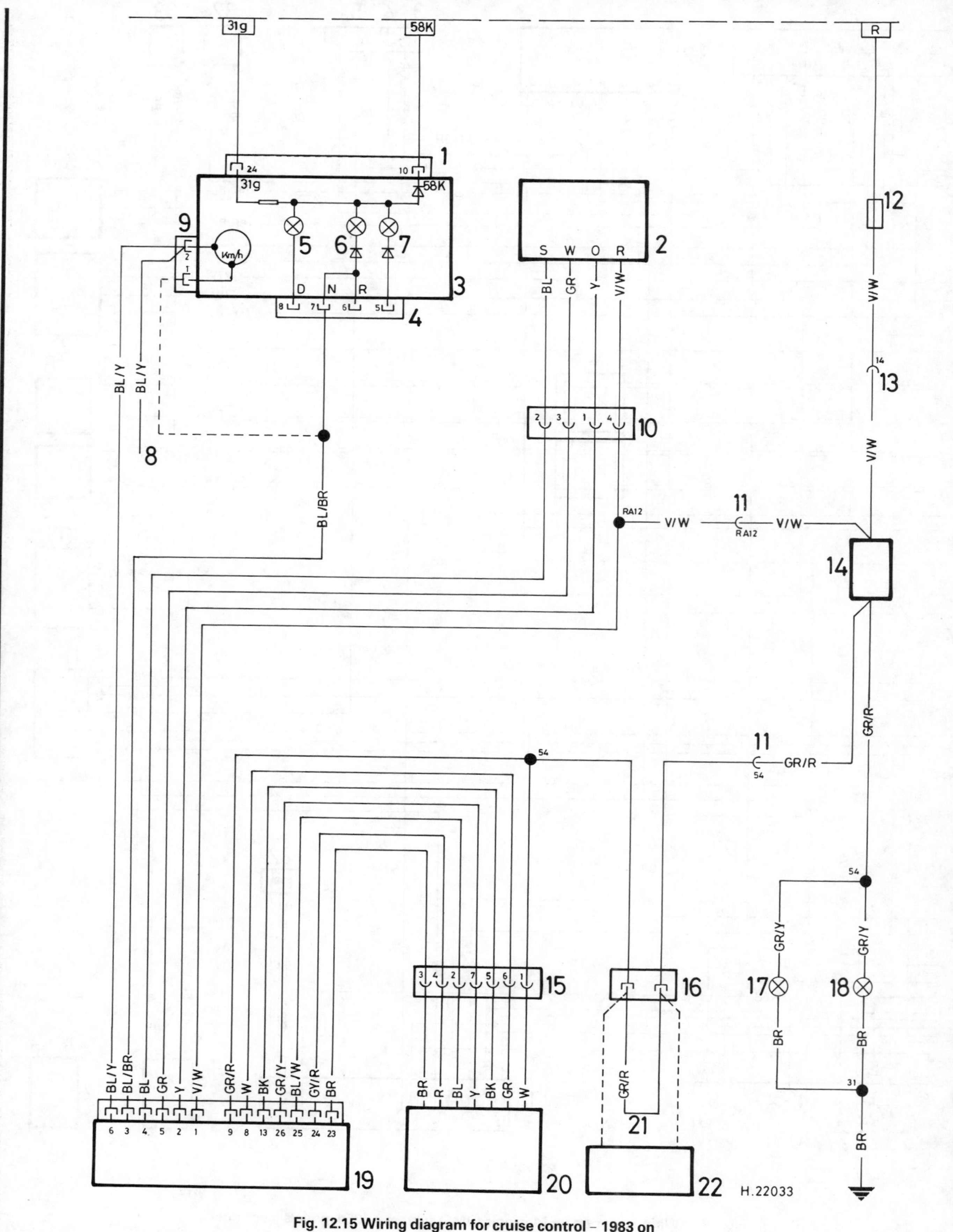

Fig. 12.15 Wiring diagram for cruise control – 1983 on

Key to Fig. 12.15

No	Description
1	Plug connection – centre section to instrument cluster (26-pin)
2	Steering column switch
3	Instrument cluster
4	Plug connection – range indicator
5	Range indicator D
6	Range indicator N
7	Range indicator R
8	Plug connection – speedometer outlet
9	Connection – instrument cluster (2-pin)
10	Plug connection – steering column switch
11	Plug connection – special equipment
12	Steering column switch
13	Plug connection – rear section to centre section (29-pin)
14	Stoplight switch
15	Plug connection – drive motor
16	Connection – clutch switch to bridge
17	Stoplight left
18	Stoplight right
19	Electronic control – cruise control
20	Drive motor – cruise control
21	Bridge (only for automatic transmission)
22	Clutch switch

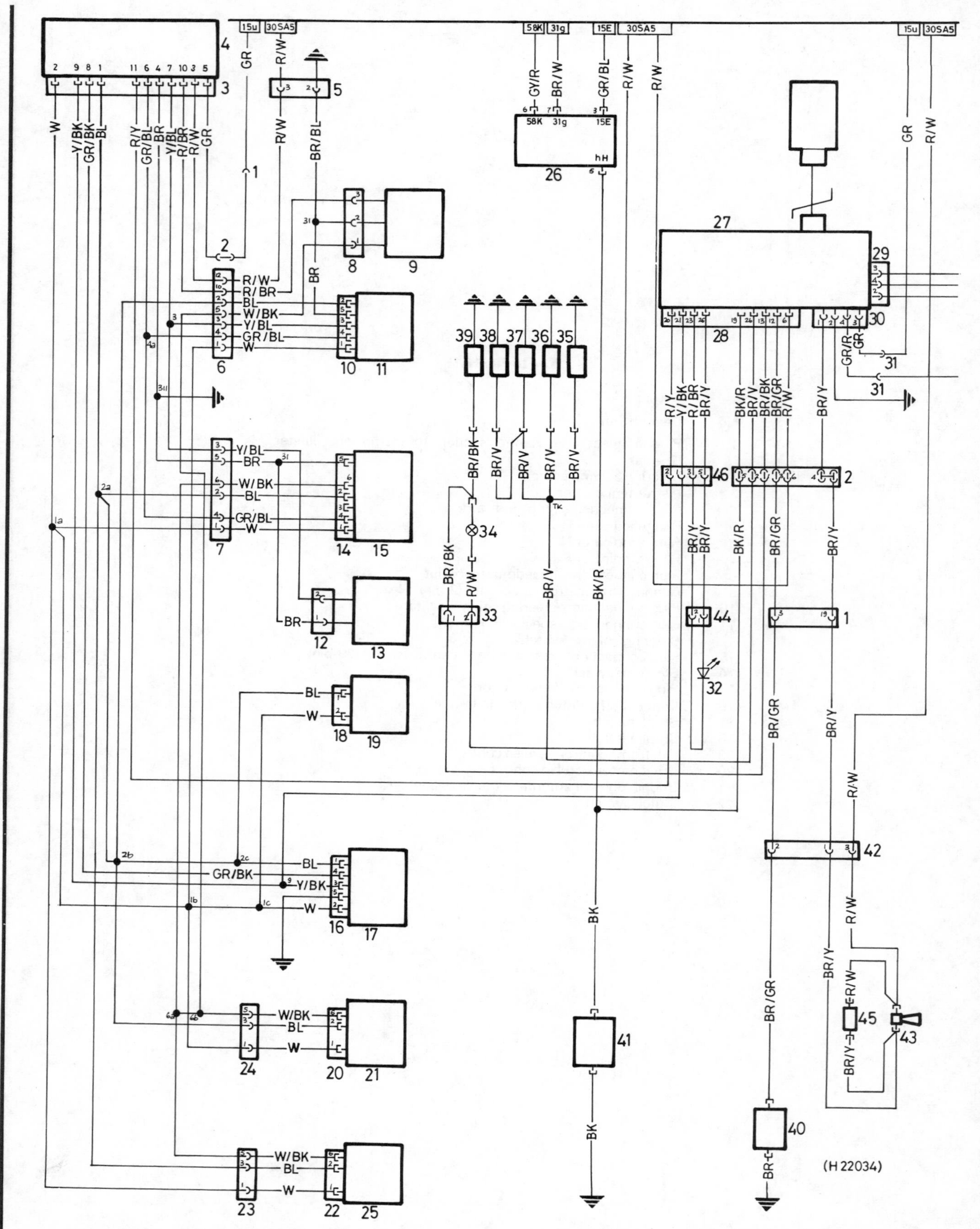

Fig. 12.16 Wiring diagram for central locking, burglar alarm, on-board computer, additional heater and digital clock – 1986 on

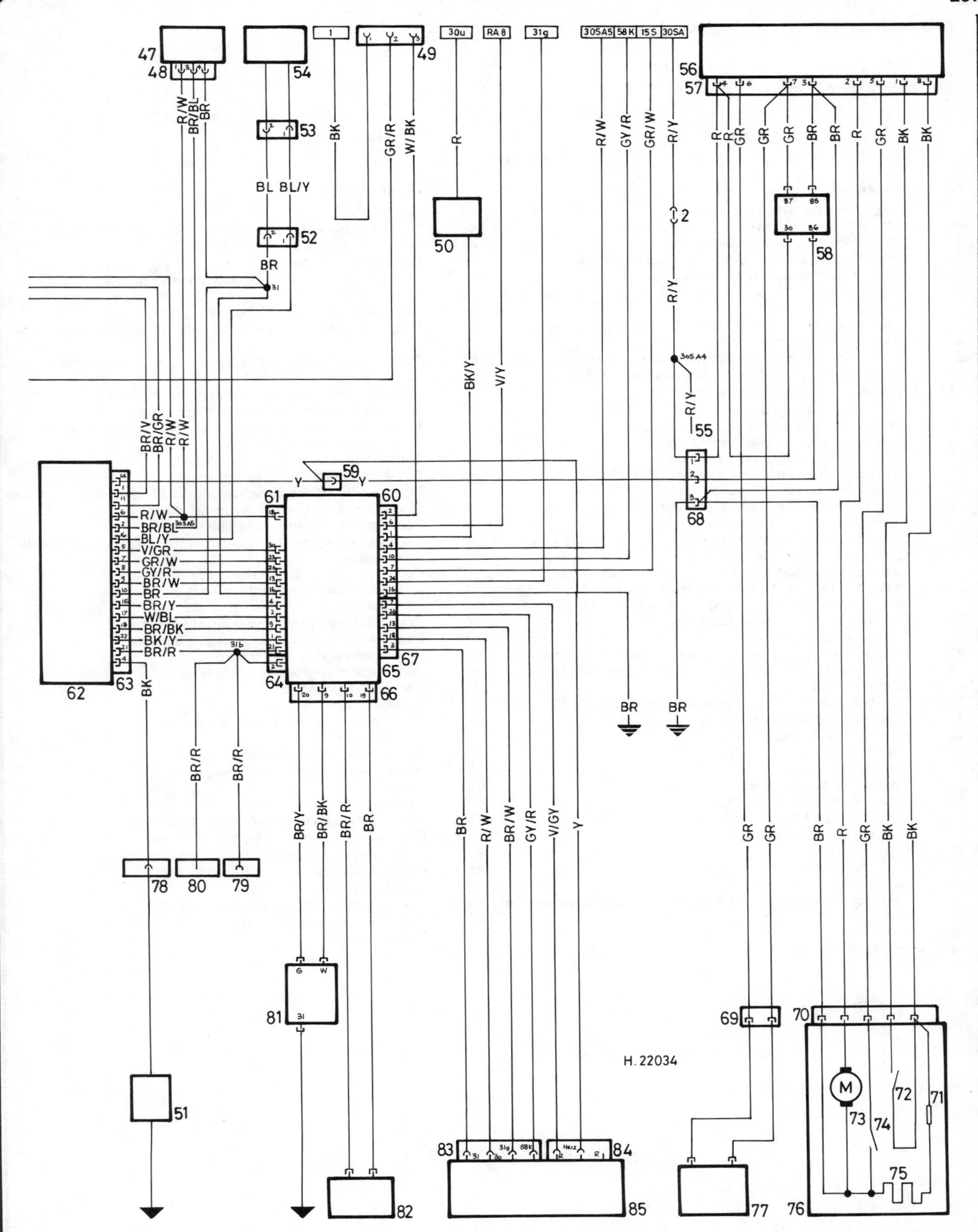

Fig. 12.16 Wiring diagram for central locking, burglar alarm, on-board computer, additional heater and digital clock – 1986 on (continued)

Key to Fig. 12.16

No	Description
1	Plug – rear section to centre section
2	Connection for special equipment plug
3	Connection for central lock control unit
4	Central lock electronic control unit (A pillar end plate)
5	Plug – driver's door wire to rear section
6	Plug – central lock connecting wire to driver's door wire (13-pin)
7	Plug – central lock connecting wire to passenger's door wire
8	Plug – driver's door central lock wire to switch
9	Central lock switch/unblocking arrest (driver's door, on lock)
10	Connection for central lock motor to driver's door (6-pin)
11	Central lock motor – driver's door
12	Plug – passenger's door wire to microswitch
13	Microswitch (passenger's door, on lock)
14	Central lock motor – passenger's door
15	Central lock motor – passenger's door
16	Connection for central lock motor to boot lid (6-pin)
17	Central lock motor – boot lid
18	Connection for central lock motor to fuel tank flap (6-pin)
19	Central lock motor –fuel tank flap
20	Connection for central lock motor to left rear door (6-pin)
21	Central lock motor – left rear door
22	Connection for central lock motor to right door (6-pin)
23	Plug – central lock connecting wire to right rear door (7-pin)
24	Plug – central lock connecting wire to left rear door (7-pin)
25	Central lock motor – right rear door
26	Rear window heater switch
27	Burglar alarm electronic control unit (left of steering column)
28	Connection for burglar alarm electronic control unit I (26-pin)
29	Connection for relay box (4-pin)
30	Connection for burglar alarm electronic control unit II (4-pin)
31	Plug 150 (in main wire harness)
32	Light diode for burglar alarm
33	Plug for boot light
34	Boot light
35	Door contact switch front left
36	Door contact switch front right
37	Door contact switch rear left
38	Door contact switch rear right
39	Boot lid contact
40	Bonnet contact
41	Rear window heater
42	Plug – centre section to wire for on-board computer/burglar alarm
43	Horn
44	Plug for light diode
45	Diode
46	Plug – burglar alarm wire to central lock connecting wire
47	Gong (left of steering column)
48	Connection for gong
49	Plug – centre section to LE-Jetronic wire harness
50	Ignition switch
51	Remote control switch for on-board computer
52	Plug – on-board computer to outside temperature sensor wire
53	Plug – outside temperature sensor wire to outside temperature sensor
54	Outside temperature sensor (lower front panel)
55	Plug – extra heater wire to automatic aerial
56	Parked car heating electronic control unit (on parked car heater underneath right seat)
57	Connection for electronic control unit
58	Relay for parked car heater (on heater)
59	Plug – on-board computer wire to extra heater wire
60	Plug – centre section to instrument cluster
61	Connection for instrument cluster
62	On-board computer electronic control unit (right of instrument cluster)
63	Connection for on-board computer
64	Connection for instrument cluster II
65	Instrument cluster
66	Plug – rear section to instrument cluster
67	Plug – digital clock wire to instrument cluster
68	Plug – extra wire to heater wire
69	Plug – heater wire to fuel pump wire
70	Connection for heater
71	Ballast resistor in heater
72	Thermoswitch (parked car heater)
73	Heater motor
74	Overheating switch (parked car heater)
75	Heater plug for parked car heater
76	Heater
77	Fuel metering pump
78	Plug – on-board computer to remote control
79	Plug – speed dependent loudness control
80	Plug – wire for cruise control
81	Fuel level transmitter
82	Speed transmitter
83	Plug – digital clock wire to digital clock (4-pin)
84	Plug – digital clock wire to digital clock (2-pin)
85	Digital clock

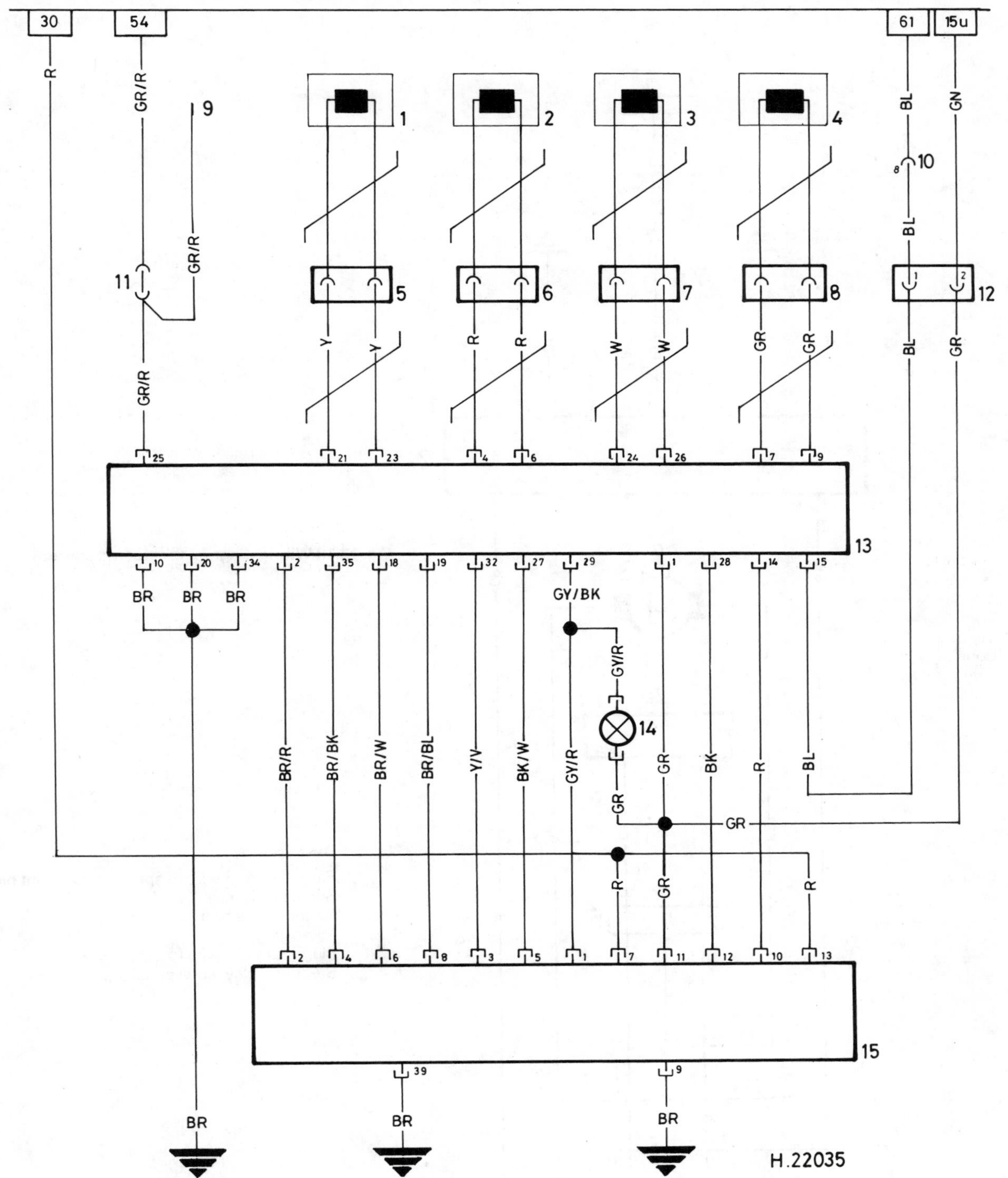

Fig. 12.17 Wiring diagram for ABS braking system – February 1984 on

No	Description
1	Sensor front right
2	Sensor front left
3	Sensor rear right
4	Sensor rear left
5	Plug – right front sensor to electronic control unit
6	Plug – left front sensor to electronic control unit
7	Plug – right rear sensor to electronic control unit
8	Plug – left rear sensor to electronic control unit
9	Plug – ABS wire harness to cruise control
10	Plug – rear section to centre section
11	Plug – ABS wire harness to special equipment plug (54)
12	Plug – ABS wire harness to special equipment plug (15u, 61)
13	ABS electronic control unit (glove box)
14	ABS lamp

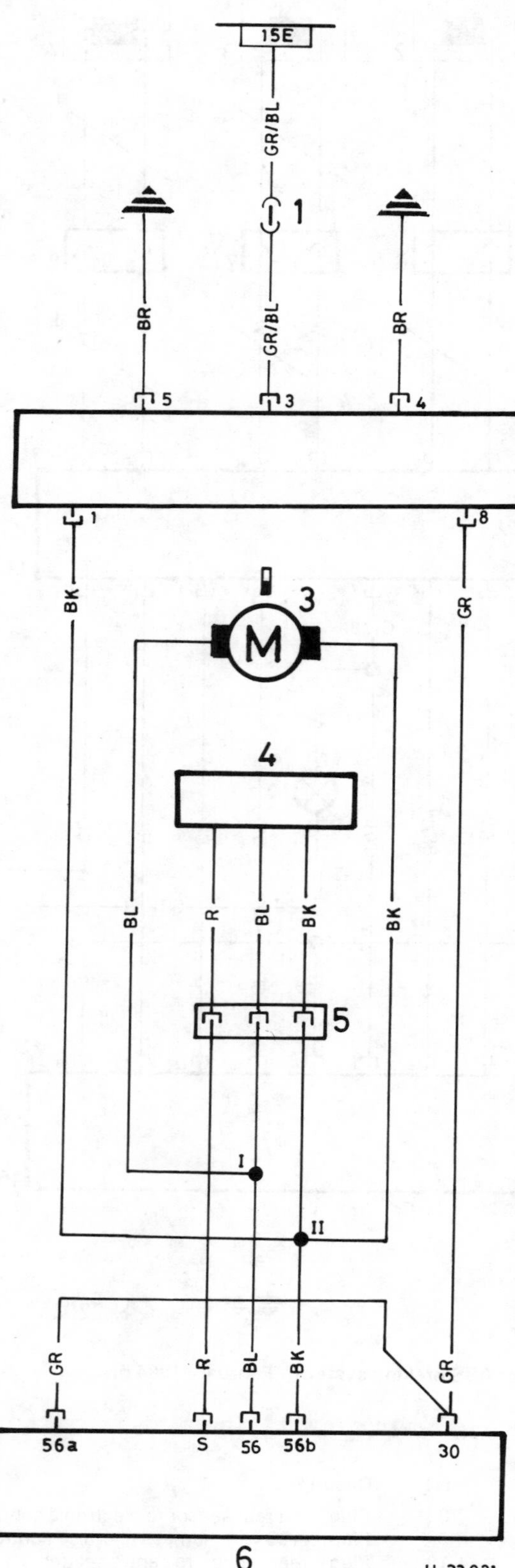

Fig. 12.18 Wiring diagram for electric sunroof

No	Description
1	Plug – sunroof wire to special equipment plug
2	Switch for sunroof
3	Motor for sunroof
4	Microswitch
5	Plug – sunroof wire to microswitch
6	Stepping relay (cowl panel top)

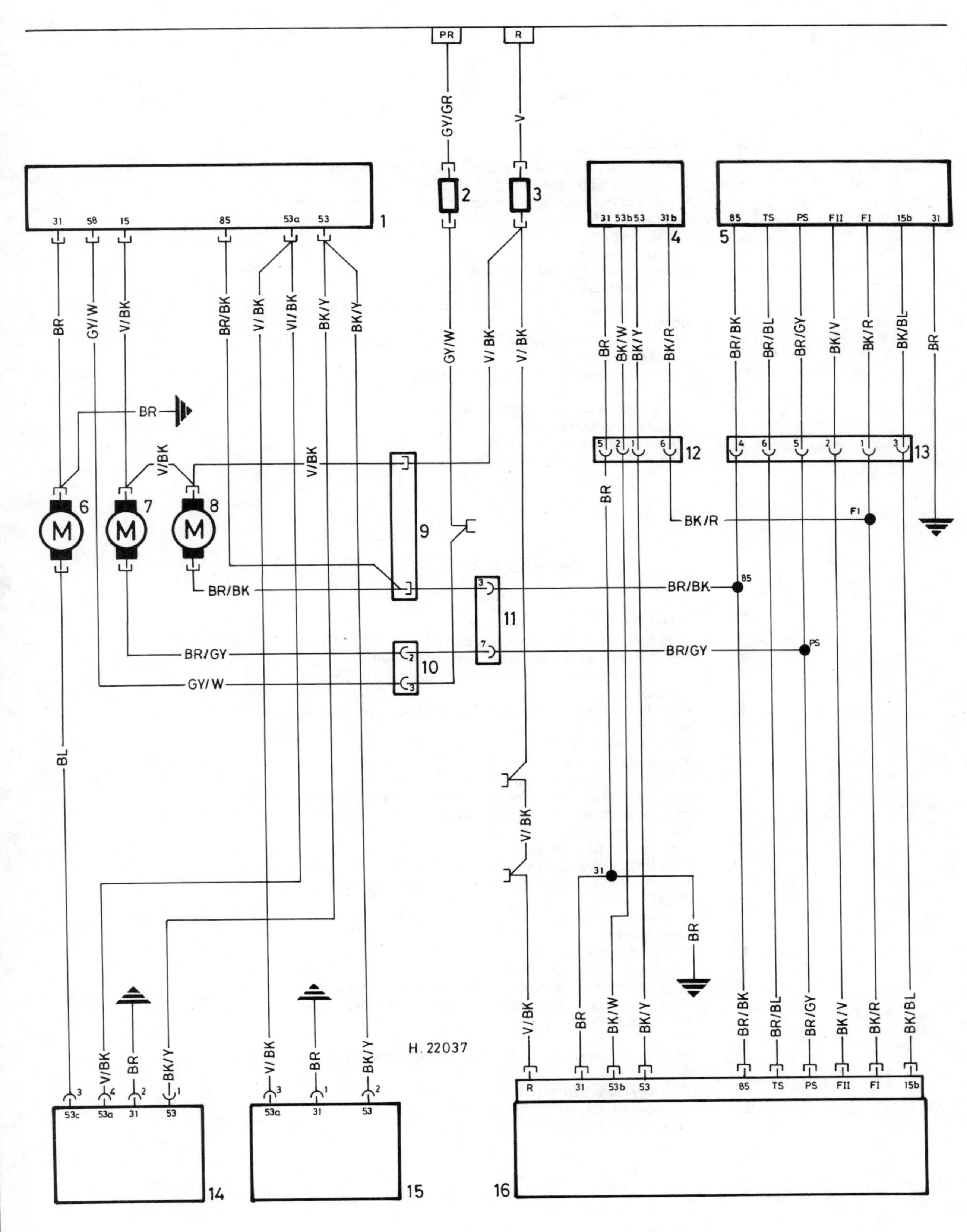

Fig. 12.19 Wiring diagram for headlight washer system

Key to Fig. 12.19

No	Description
1	Control unit for headlight cleaners (on fluid reservoir)
2	Fuse – overnight, tail and parking lights
3	Fuse – horns, wash/wipe control unit and headlight cleaners
4	Motor – windscreen wipers
5	Wiper switch
6	Pump – headlight cleaning system
7	Pump – intensive cleaning fluid
8	Pump – windscreen washing system
9	Plug – headlight cleaner wire to front section I (washer fluid pump)
10	Plug – Headlight cleaner wire to front section II (plug for headlight cleaners)
11	Plug – centre section to front section (7-pin)
12	Plug for wiper motor
13	Plug – centre section to wiper switch
14	Motor – windscreen wipers
15	Motor – left headlight wiper
16	Wash/wipe interval control unit

Key to Fig. 12.20

No	Description
1	Plug for rear section to driver's door (6-pin)
2	Plug for rear section to centre section (27-pin)
3	Plug for window control and central lock wire to driver's door (13-pin)
4	Plug for window control and central lock wire to special equipment plug
5	Window switch rear left
6	Window switch rear left
7	Window switch rear right
8	Plug for left rear door wire to window motor rear left
9	Plug for right door wire to window motor rear right
10	Window motor rear left
11	Window motor rear right
12	Plug for window control and central lock wire to left rear door
13	Plug for window control and central lock wire to right rear door (7-pin)
14	Power safety switch
15	Child safety switch
16	Window motor front left
17	Window motor front right
18	Plug for driver's door wire to window motor front left
19	Plug for passenger's door wire to window motor of passenger's door
20	Relay
21	Plug for window control and central lock wire to passenger's door (13-pin)
22	Window switch front left
23	Window switch rear right
24	Window switch front right

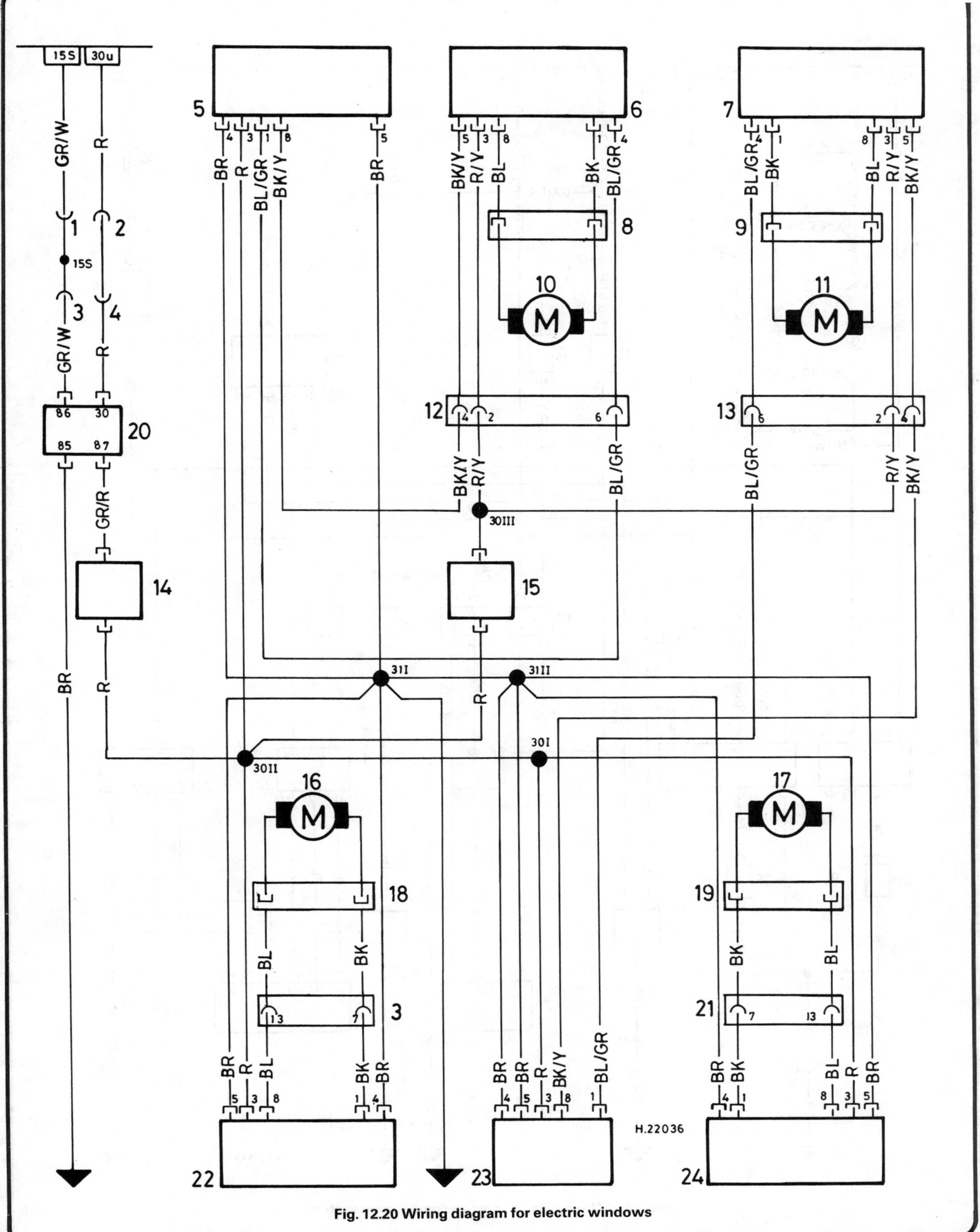

Fig. 12.20 Wiring diagram for electric windows

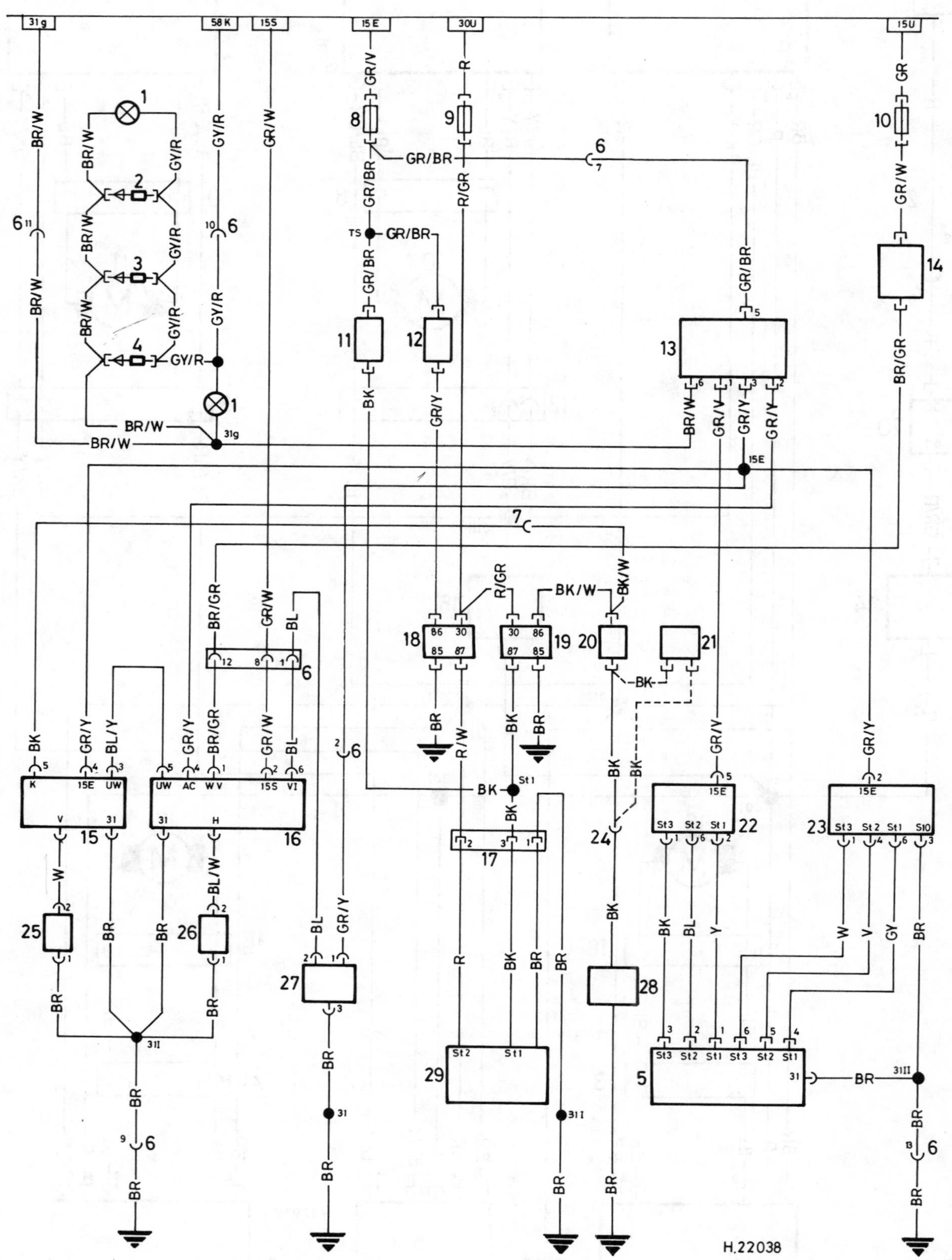

Fig. 12.21 Wiring diagram for air conditioning system

Key to Fig. 12.21

No	Description
1	Light for heater controls
2	Light diode III
3	Light diode II
4	Light diode I
5	Switch – heater/evaporator blower
6	Plug – heater control wire harness to centre wire harness (13-pin)
7	Plug – front wire harness section to heater controls
8	Fuse – heater blower
9	Fuse – extra fan stage II
10	Fuse – ind. lamp, reversing lights, tachometer and mirrors (power distributor)
11	Temperature switch 91°C – stage I
12	Temperature switch 99°C – stage II
13	Switch – air conditioner
14	Water valve
15	Evaporator temperature regulator
16	Air conditioner control unit (heater controls)
17	Plug – extra fan motor (on extra fan motor)
18	Relay – extra fan stage II (on power distributor)
19	Relay – extra fan stage I (on power distributor)
20	Switch – high pressure pressostat (drier)
21	Switch – temperature 110°C (only for 524 td)
22	Motor – heater blower
23	Motor – evaporator blower
24	Plug – high pressure pressostat to electromagnetic coupling
25	Evaporator temperature sensor (in evaporator)
26	Heater temperature sensor (in heater)
27	Inside temperature sensor (lower trim panel left)
28	Electromagnetic coupling for compressor
29	Motor – extra fan

Key to Fig. 12.22

No	Description
1	Heating – passenger's seat
2	Seat heating connection – passenger's side
3	Seat heating switch – passenger's side
4	Plug for heated seat wire (driver's side) to special equipment plug (58K)
5	Plug for heated seat wire (driver's side) to passenger's side
6	Plug for heated seat wire (driver's side) to special equipment plug (15E and 30SA4)
7	Seat heating relay
8	Seat heating switch – driver's side
9	Heating – driver's seat
10	Seat heating connection – driver's side

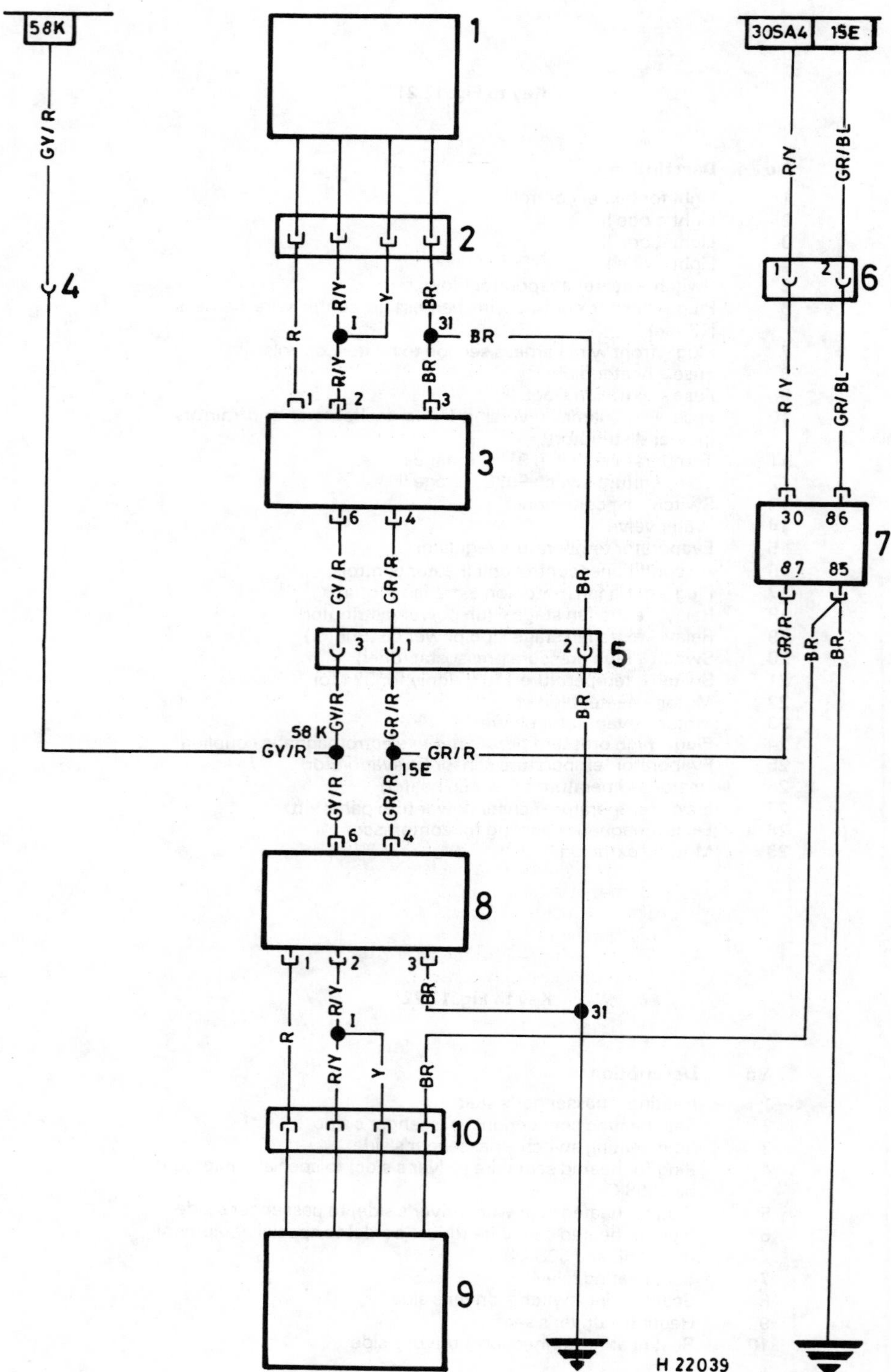

Fig. 12.22 Wiring diagram for heated seats

Key to Fig. 12.23

No	Description
1	Plug connection for special equipment plug
2	Plug connection of wire for passenger's seat
3	Plug connection of wire for seat control with memory
4	Connection of wire for seat control with memory
5	Seat control switch
6	Backrest
7	Slide
8	Headrest
9	Height front
10	Height rear
11	Plug connection for seat backrest/slide control
12	Plug connection for seat headrest control
13	Plug connection for seat height control
14	Electronic control unit (underneath seat)
15	Plug connection of wire for seat control with memory
16	Plug connection of wire for seat with memory
17	Plug connection for seat control drive
18	Plug connection for memory switch
19	Plug connection for slide potentiometer
20	Plug connection for front height potentiometer
21	Plug connection for rear height potentiometer
22	Plug connection for headrest motor
23	Plug connection for backrest potentiometer
24	Plug connection for backrest motor
25	Memory switch
26	Motor – seat backrest control
27	Motor – headrest control
28	Motor – height control rear
29	Motor – height control front
30	Motor – slide

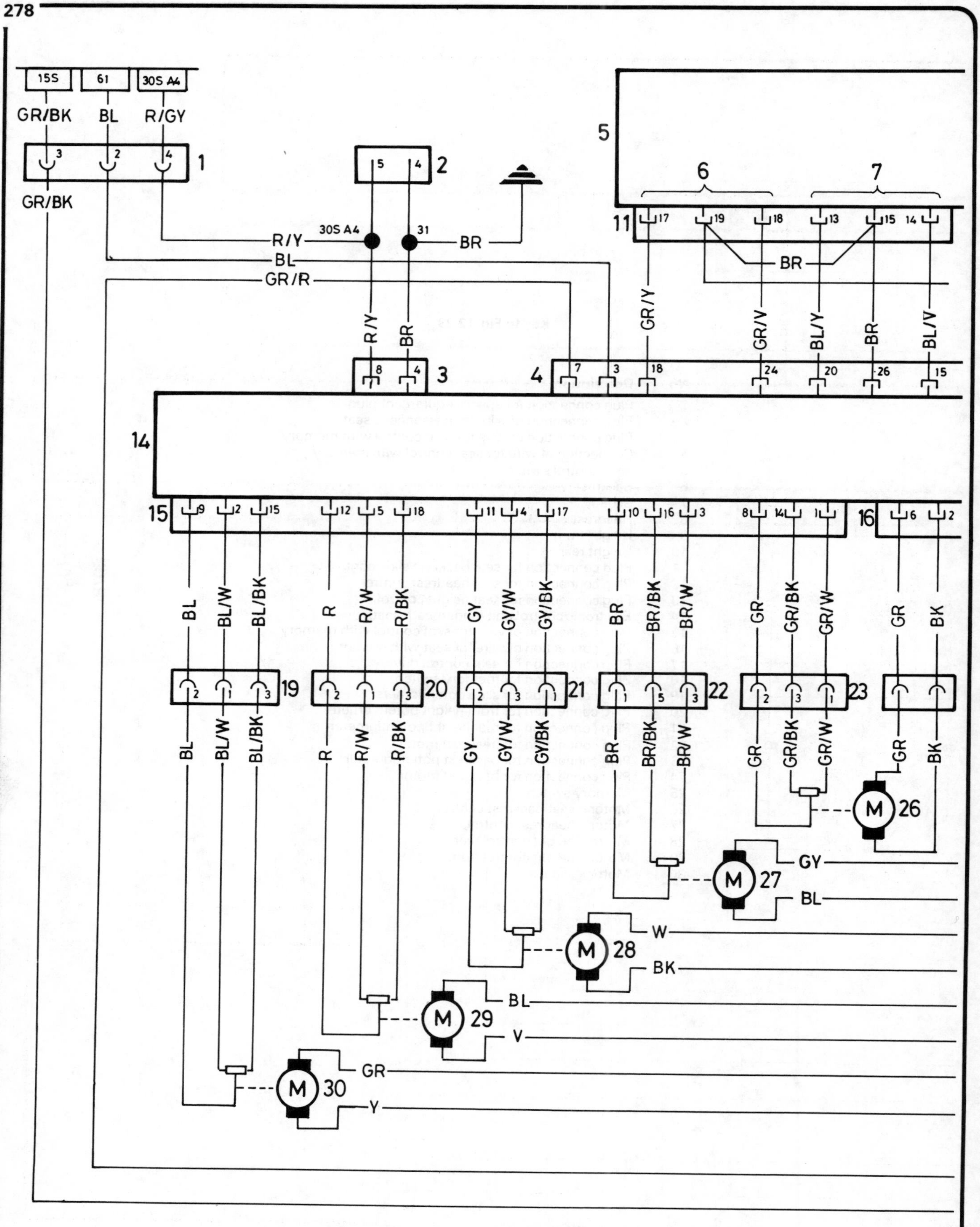

Fig. 12.23 Wiring diagram for power seat control with memory

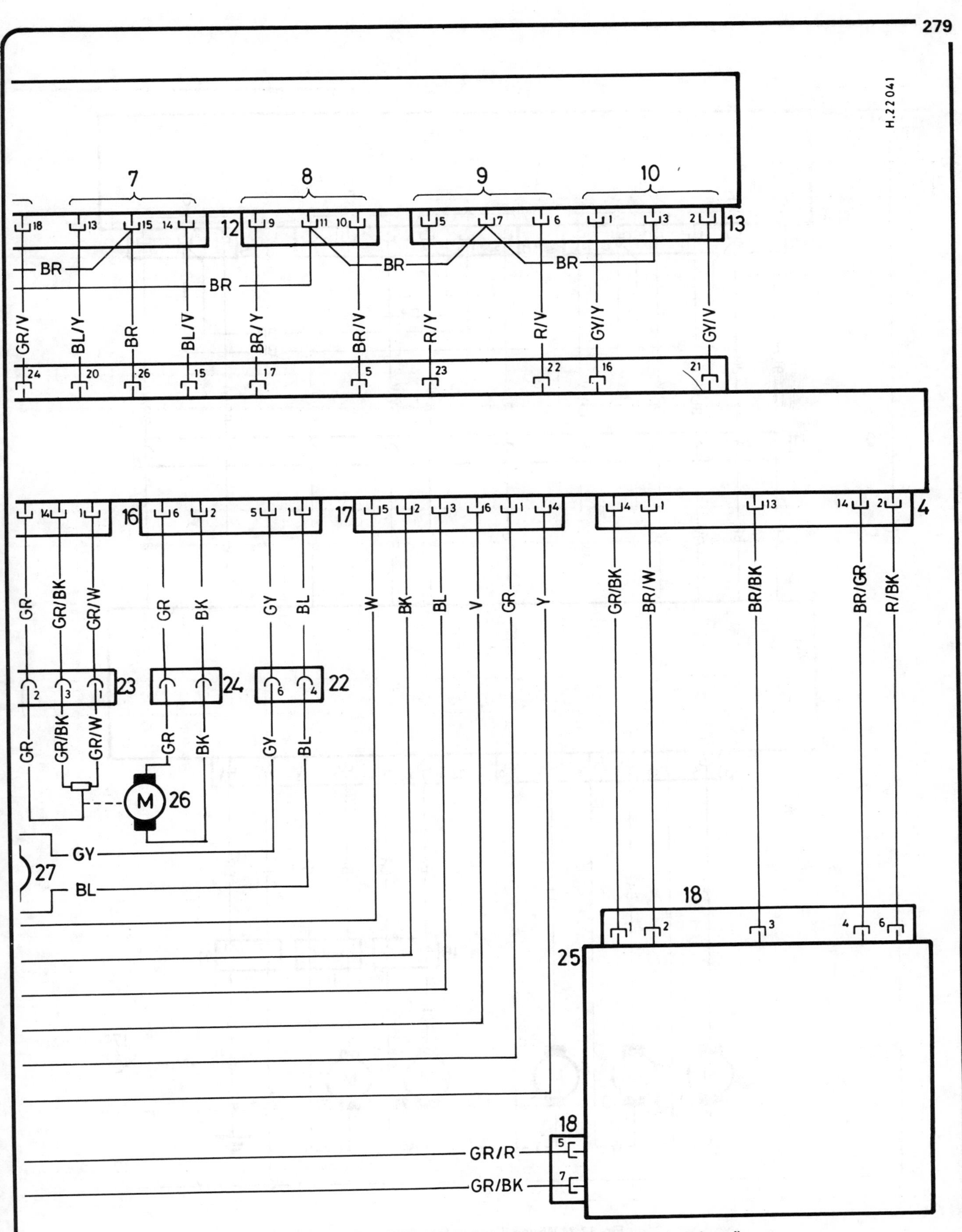

Fig. 12.23 Wiring diagram for power seat control with memory (continued)

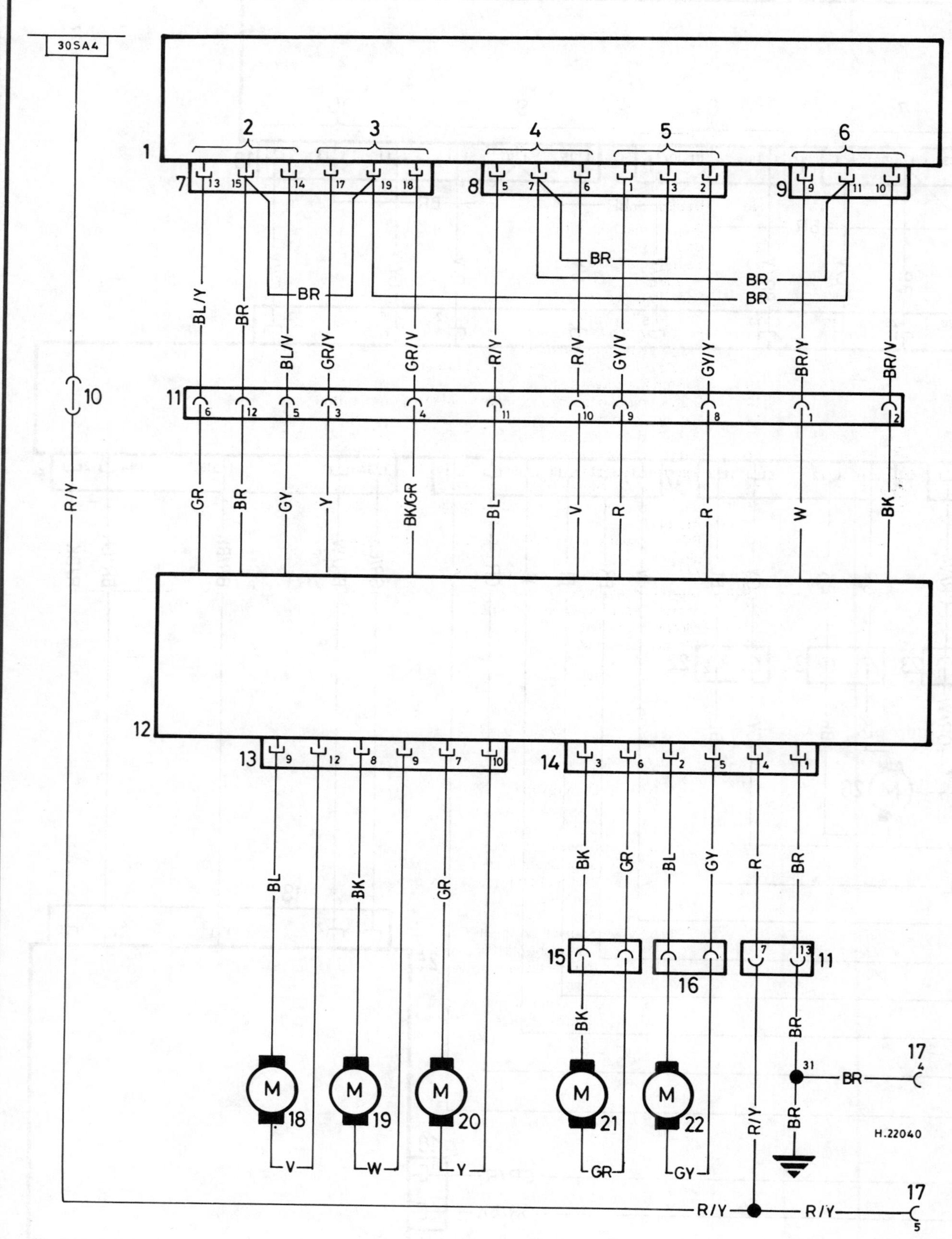

Fig. 12.24 Wiring diagram for power seats

Key to Fig. 12.24

No	Description
1	Plug connection with special equipment plug
2	Backrest
3	Seat forward/backward
4	Headrest
5	Seat up/down front
6	Seat up/down rear
7	Plug – switch for backrest/seat control
8	Plug – switch for headrest control
9	Plug – switch for front/rear seat up/down control
10	Switch for power seats
11	Plug – power seat wire to power seat electronic control unit
12	Electronic control unit for power seats (below seats)
13	Plug – power seat drive to power seat electronic control unit
14	Plug – power backrest and headrest wire to power seat electronic control unit
15	Plug – power backrest and headrest wire to backrest motor
16	Plug – power backrest and headrest wire to the headrest motor
17	Plug – power seat wire on driver's side to wire on passenger's side
18	Motor – seat up/down front
19	Motor – seat up/down rear
20	Motor – seat forward/backward
21	Motor – backrest
22	Motor – headrest

Key to Fig. 12.25

No	Description
1	Speaker door right
2	Speaker front right
3	Speaker rear right
4	Special equipment plug RA12
5	Connection for power windows
6	Amplifier
7	Speaker front left
8	Speaker door left
9	Connection for power supply lead
10	Connection for power aerial
11	Radio
12	Speaker balance control
13	Speaker rear left

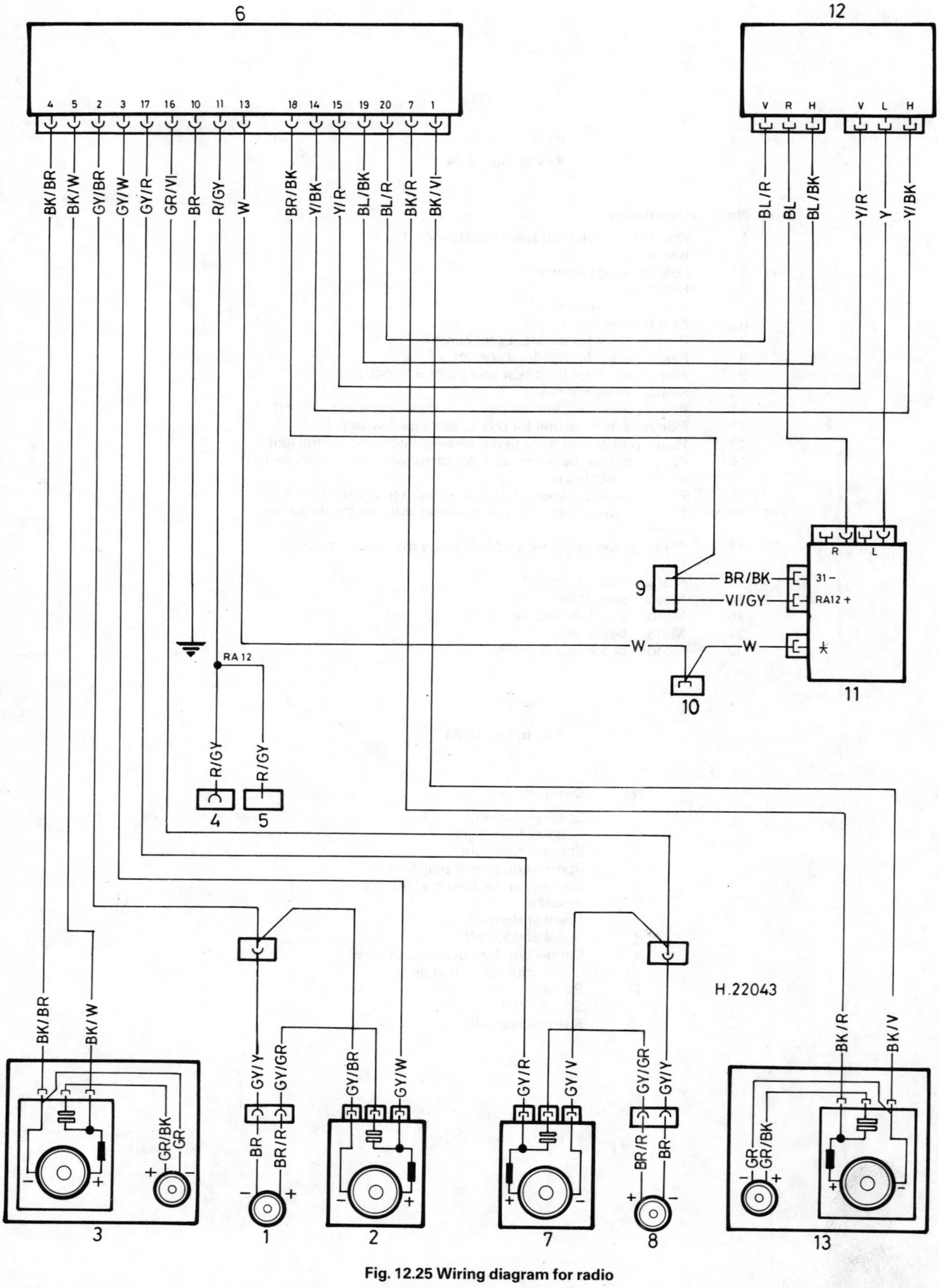

H.22043

Fig. 12.25 Wiring diagram for radio

Key to Fig. 12.26

No	Description
1	White pin rail
2	Yellow pin rail
3	Blue pin rail
4	Temperature warning lamp
5	Front fog lamps
6	Rear fog lamps
7	High beam
8	Diesel
9	Trailer turn signals
10	Disc pad wear indicator
11	ABS
12	Brakes
13	Parking brake
14	Oil
15	Battery charge lamp
16	On-board computer
17	Fuel warning lamp
18	Turn signal left
19	Central warning lamp
20	Turn signal right
21	Instrument light
22	To range indicator
23	To electronic speedometer (for US)

White pin rail
Connection for rear wire harness

Plug No.	Designation
1	Temp. warning lamp
2	not occupied
3	Front fog lamp
4	not occupied
5	56a/high beam
6	31/ground
7	Turn signal left
8	Brake pad wear indicator
9	Fuel warning lamp
10	31b speed transmitter
11	31b speed transmitter
12	31b speed transmitter
13	31b speed transmitter
14	not occupied
15	not occupied
16	Front fog lamp
17	Rear fog light
18	56a/high beam
19	31/ground
20	Fuel level transmitter
21	not occupied
22	not occupied
23	Parking brake
24	not occupied
25	not occupied
26	not occupied

Yellow pin rail
Connection for on-board computer/digital clock

Plug No.	Designation
1	50 starter control
2	Terminal 11 (injec. sign.)
3	31/ground
4	fuel level transmitter
5	30s
6	parking brake
7	Terminal R
8	31b speed transmitter
9	Fuel warning lamp
10	15s
11	Terminal 1
12	Central warning lamp
13	31g instrument light
14	50 starter control
15	Terminal 11 (injec. sign.)
16	31/ground
17	not occupied
18	30s
19	Parking brake
20	Terminal R
21	not occupied
22	not occupied
23	15s
24	Terminal 1
25	Central warning lamp
26	58K instrument light

Blue pin rail
Connection for front wire harness

Plug No.	Designation
1	50 starter control
2	Terminal (injec. sign.)
3	31/ground
4	30s
5	Parking brake
6	Terminal R
7	15s
8	Terminal 1
9	Central warning lamp
10	58K instrument light
11	31g instrument light
12	Temperature transmitter
13	Turn signal right
14	Diagnosis/51
15	Brake pad wear ind.
16	31/ground
17	Brakes
18	Parking brake
19	Oil pressure
20	15s
21	Terminal 61 charge ind.
22	15u charge ind. lamp
23	58k instrument light
24	31g instrument light
25	Front fog lamp
26	56a high beam

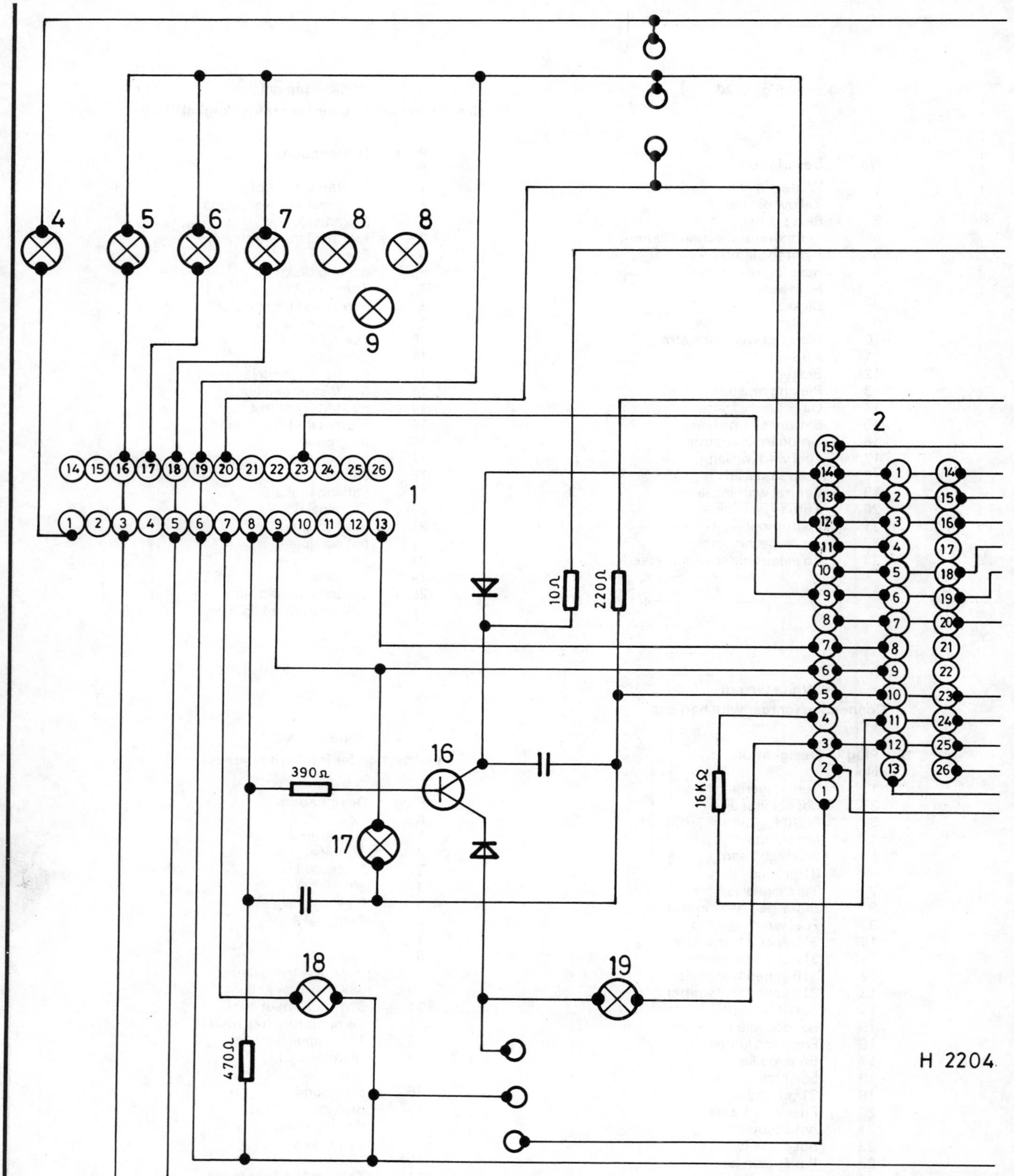

H 2204

Fig. 12.26 Wiring diagram for instrument panel

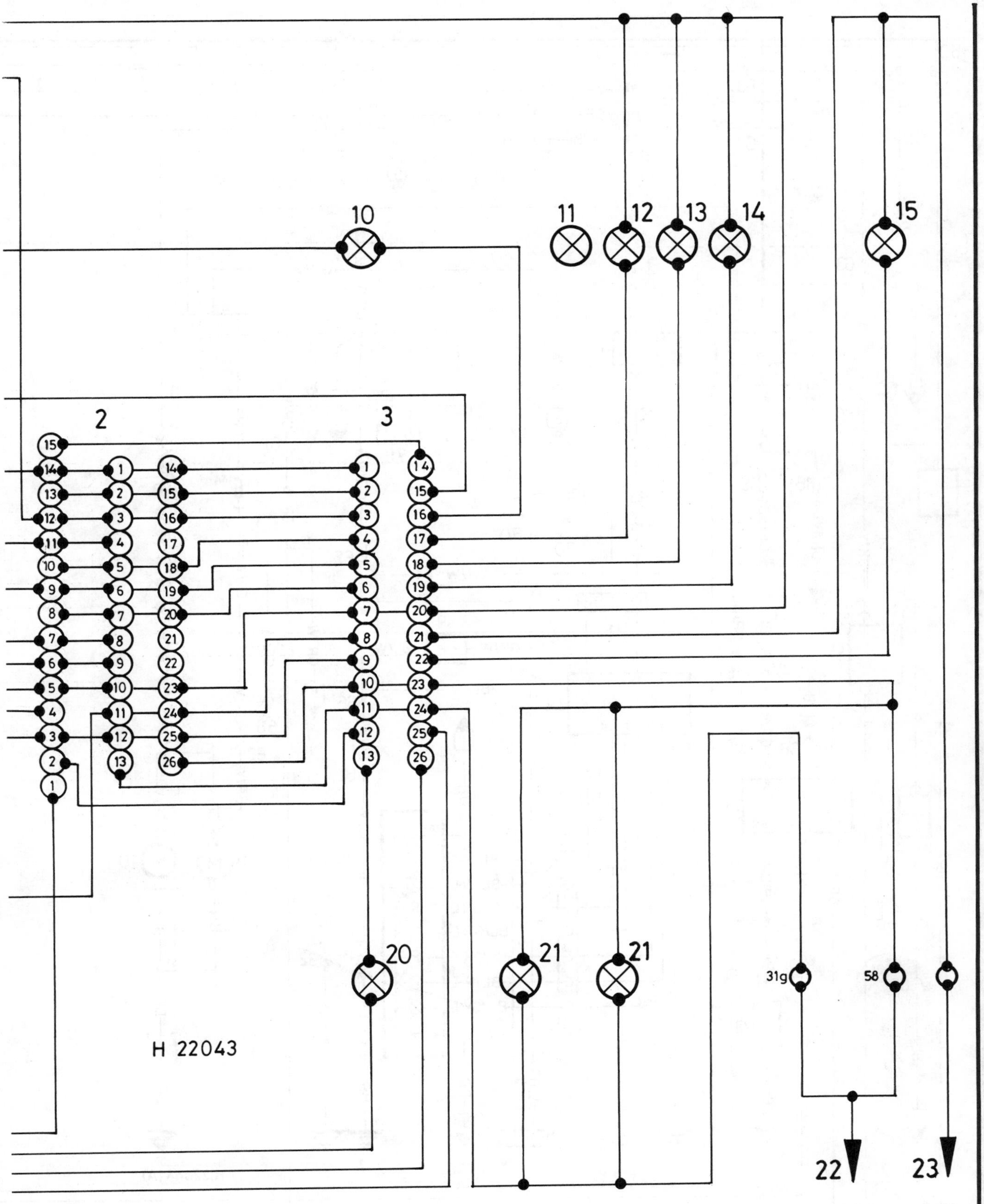

Fig. 12.26 Wiring diagram for instrument panel (continued)

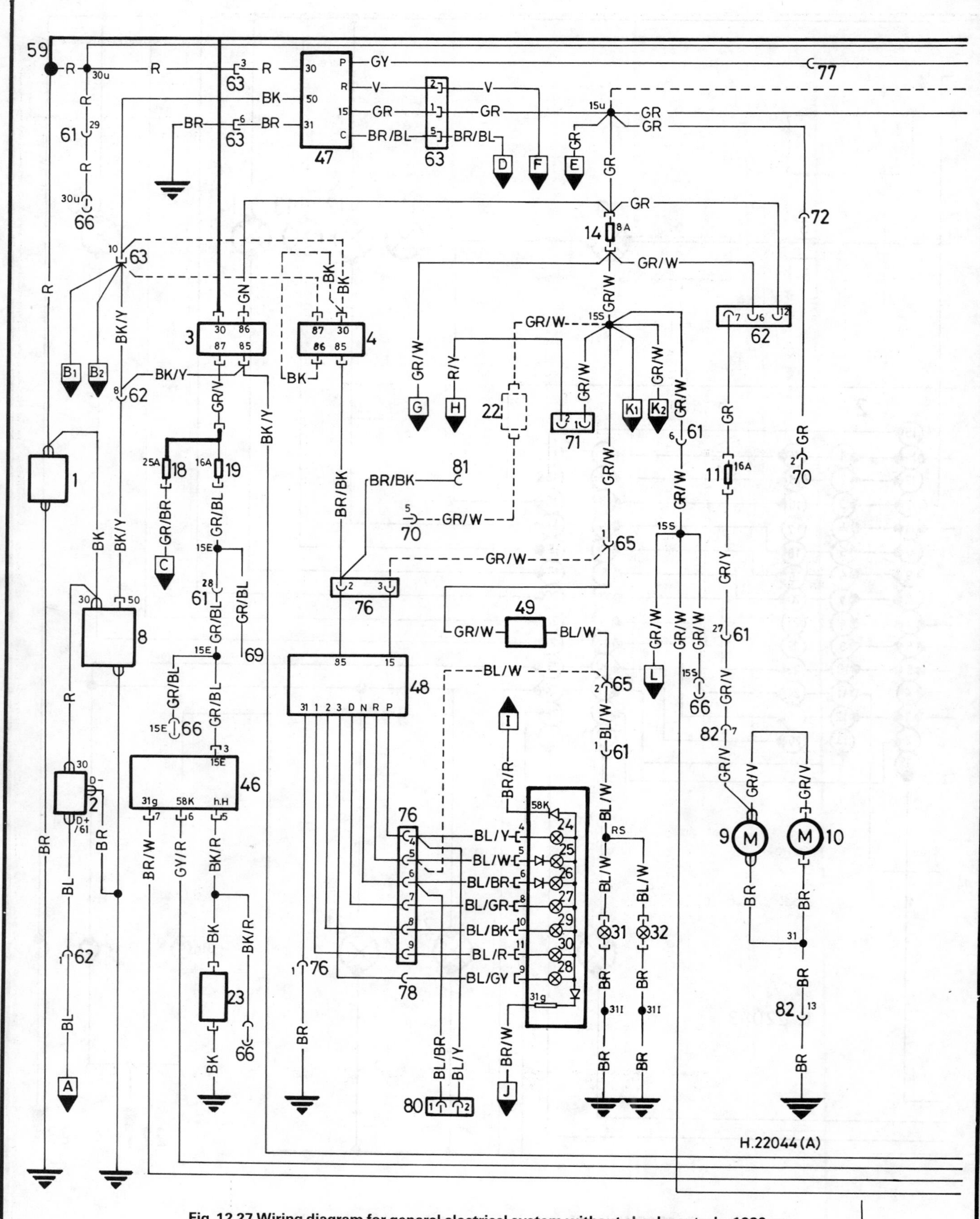

Fig. 12.27 Wiring diagram for general electrical system without check control – 1986 on

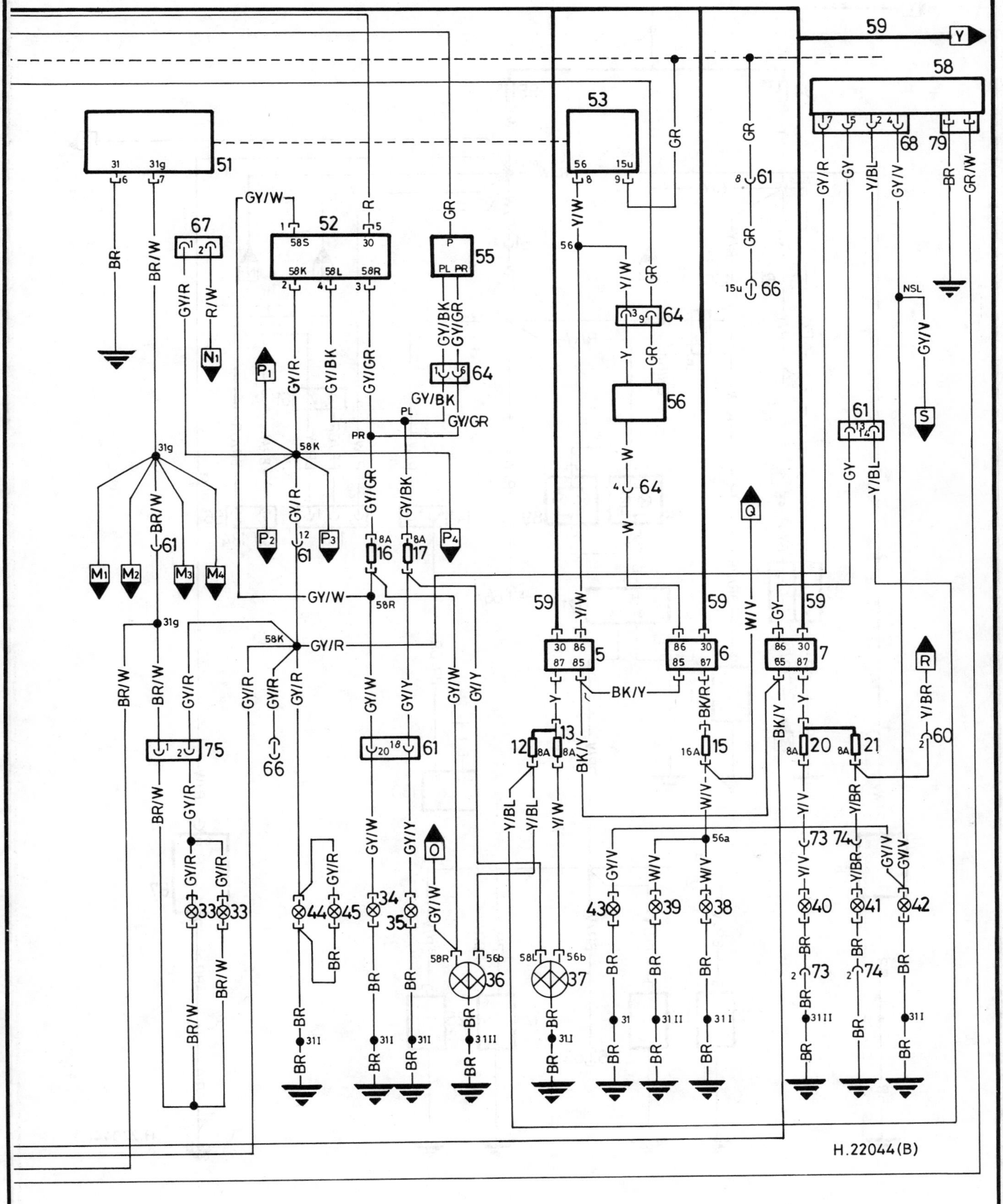

H.22044(B)

Fig. 12.27 Wiring diagram for general electrical system without check control – 1986 on (continued)

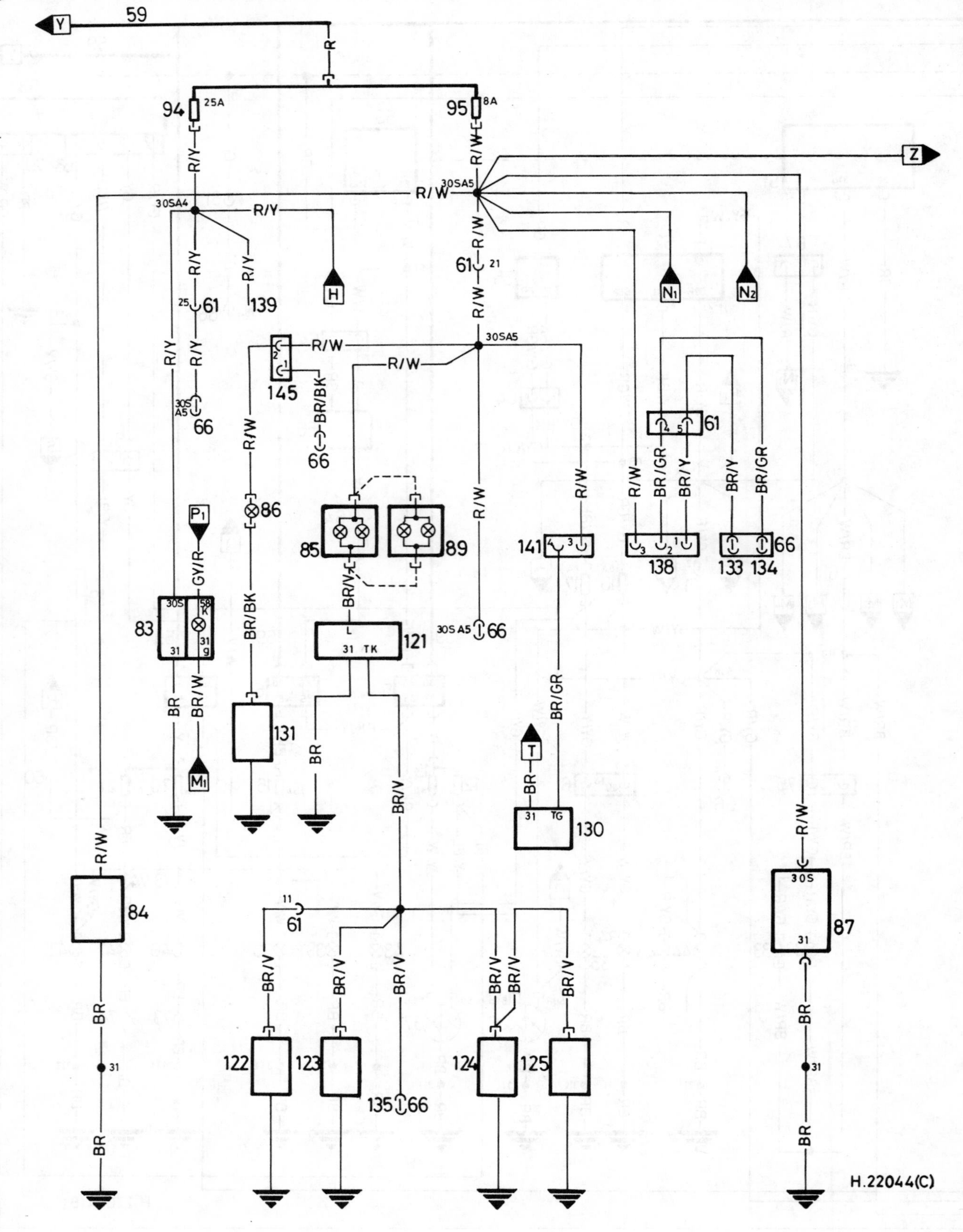

Fig. 12.27 Wiring diagram for general electrical system without check control – 1986 on (continued)

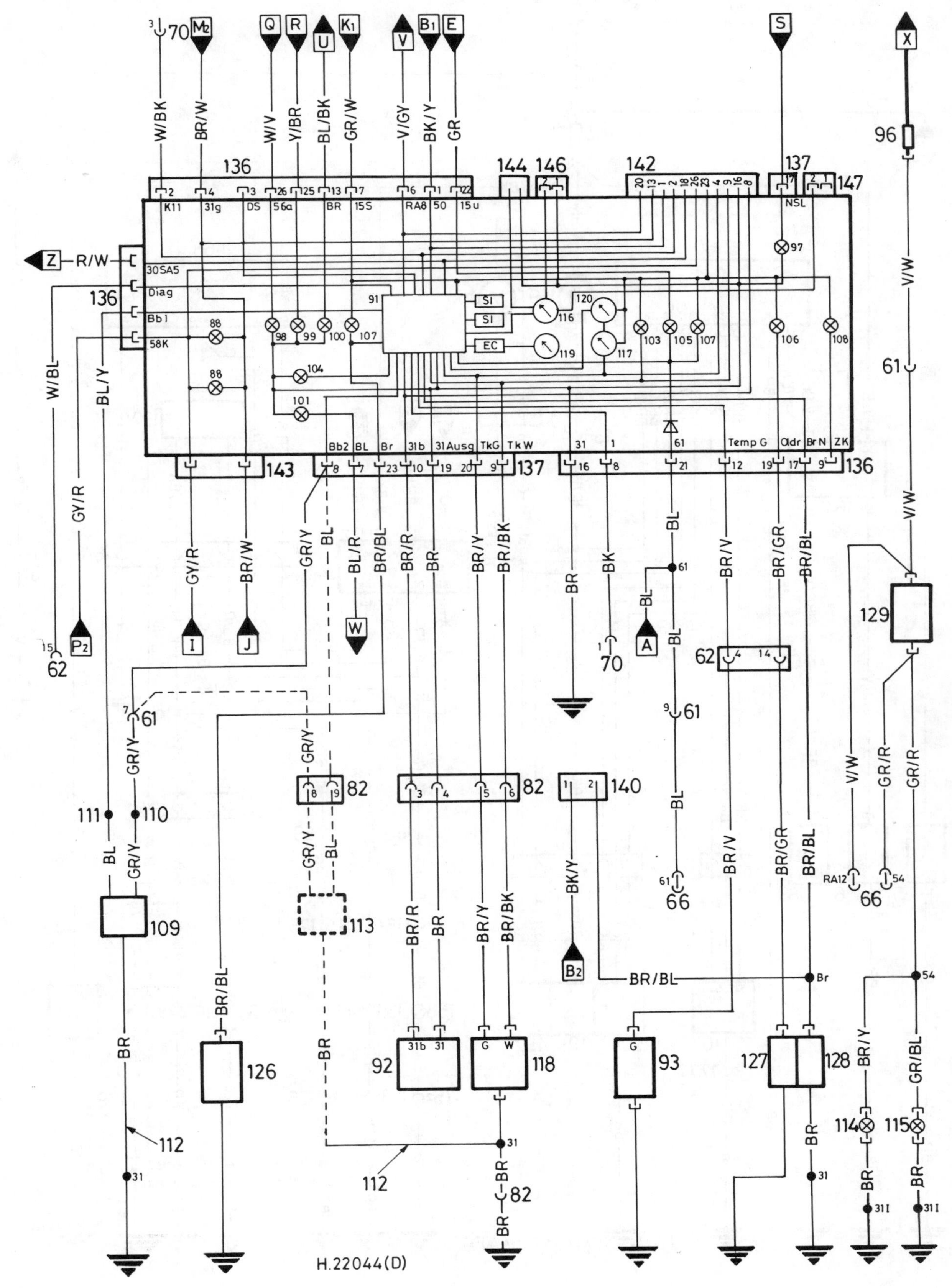

Fig. 12.27 Wiring diagram for general electrical system without check control – 1986 on (continued)

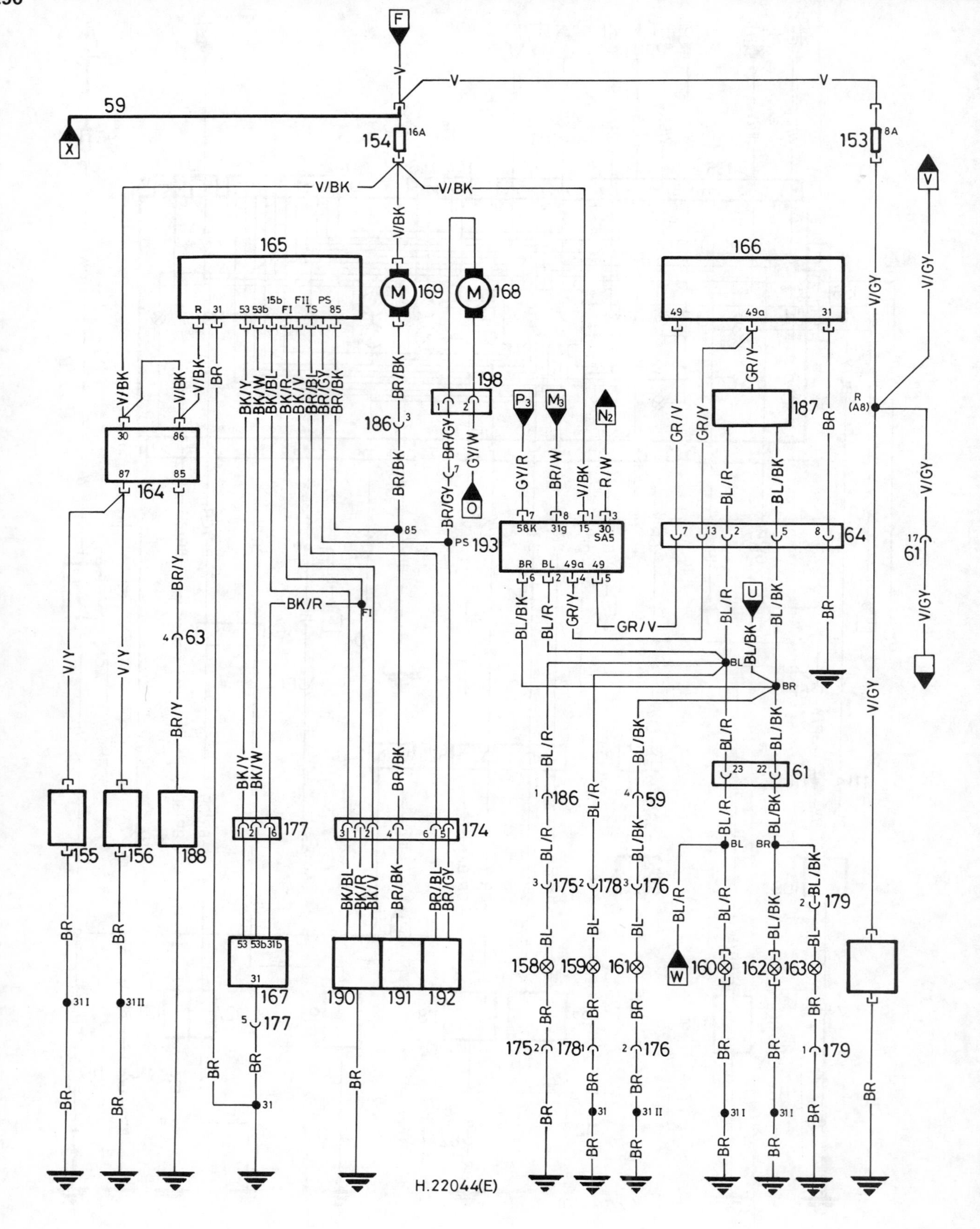

Fig. 12.27 Wiring diagram for general electrical system without check control – 1986 on (continued)

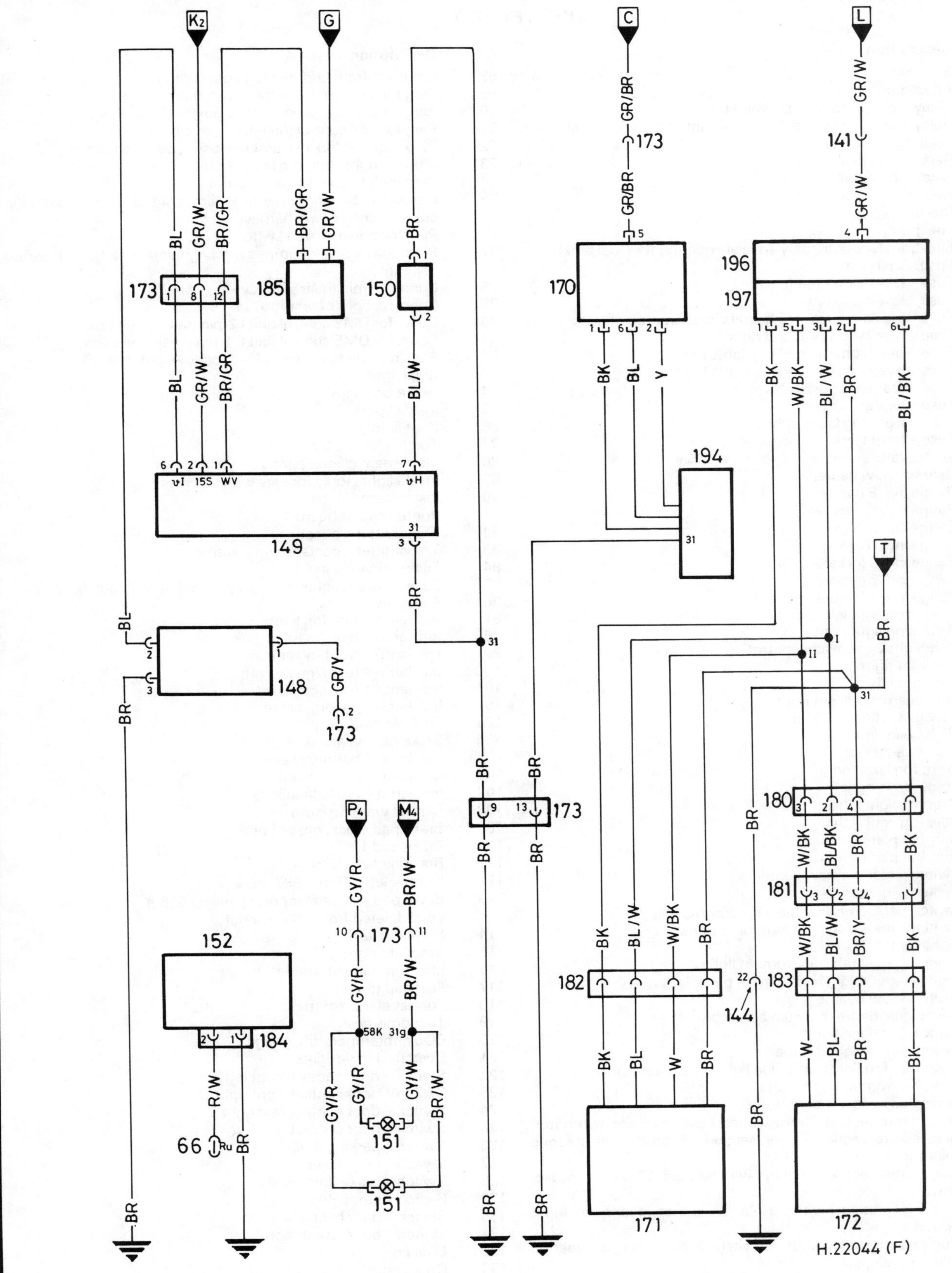

Fig. 12.27 Wiring diagram for general electrical system without check control – 1986 on (continued)

Key to Fig. 12.27

No	Description
1	Battery
2	Alternator
3	Relay – power saving (power distr.)
4	Relay – starting interlock (only for automatics/left of steering column)
5	Relay – low beams
6	Relay – high beams
7	Relay – front fog lamps
8	Starter
9	Fuel pump
10	Fuel transfer pump (only special equipment/in fuel tank)
11	Fuse – fuel pump
12	Fuse – low beam right
13	Fuse – low beam left
14	Fuse – ind. lamp, reversing lights, tachometer, mirrors
15	Fuse – high beams left and right
16	Fuse – overnight/tail/parking lights right
17	Fuse – overnight/tail/parking lights left
18	Fuse – rear window heater
19	Fuse – heater blower
20	Fuse – front fog lamp right
21	Fuse – front fog lamp left
22	Temperature sensor 0°C (only on 525e)
23	Rear window heater
24	Range ind. P (white)
25	Range ind. R (yellow)
26	Range ind. N (white)
27	Range ind. D (green)
28	Range ind. 3 (green)
29	Range ind. 2 (green)
30	Range ind. 1 (green)
31	Reversing light left
32	Reversing light right
33	Headlight vertical aim control
34	Tail light right
35	Tail light left
36	Low beam headlight right
37	Low beam headlight left
38	High beam left
39	High beam right
40	Front fog lamp right
41	Front fog lamp left
42	Rear fog light left
43	Rear fog light right
44	Number plate light left
45	Number plate light right
46	Switch – rear window heater
47	Switch – ignition
48	Switch – transmission (only for automatics)
49	Switch – reversing light (not for automatics)
50	Light switch assembly
51	Switch – adjustable instrument light
52	Switch – overnight and number plate lights
53	Switch – low beams
54	Turn signal/dimmer switch assembly
55	Switch – parking lights
56	Switch – headlight dimmer
57	Front/rear fog light and inside light switch assembly
58	Switch – front/rear fog lights
59	Power rail in power distributor
60	Plug, centre section – front section 7-pin (in power distributor)
61	Plug, centre section – rear section 29-pin (left of steering column)
62	Plug centre section – engine wire harness 17-pin (on power distr.)
63	Plug for ignition switch 9-pin (on upper steering column casing)
64	Plug for turn signal/dimmer switch 13-pin (on upper steering column casing)
65	Conn. for backup light switch 2-pin (below centre console)
66	Conn. for special equipment 26-pin (left of steering column) rear window heater
67	Conn. for digital radio 2-pin (centre console/heater controls)
68	Conn. for front and rear fog light switch
69	Plug for sun roof (on left in glove box)
70	Plug for LE control unit (glove box)
71	Plug for ride control (on left in glove box)
72	Plug 15u (behind instrument cluster, on wire harness)
73	Plug for right front fog lamp 2-pin
74	Plug for left front fog lamp 2-pin
75	Conn. for headlight vertical aim control (left of steering column, centre wire harness section)
76	Plug for transmission switch
77	Plug, turn signal/dimmer switch/ignition switch (on steering column)
78	Conn. 3, 1-pin (near shift lever)
79	Conn. for light of rear fog lamp switch
80	Conn. for DME control unit I 2-pin (near glove box)
81	Conn. for DME control unit II 1-pin (near glove box)
82	Plug, rear section – extra lead (below right rear seat)
83	Cigar lighter
84	Glove box light
85	Inside lights
86	Boot light
87	Torch (chargeable)
88	Instrument cluster light
89	Inside lights (only for cars with sun roof)
90	Instrument cluster
91	Printed circuit board
92	Transmitter – speed
93	Transmitter – coolant temperature
94	Fuse – cigar lighter
95	Fuse – hazard lights, inside lights, glove box light, flashlight
96	Fuse – stoplights
97	Ind. lamp – rear fog lights
98	Ind. lamp – high beams
99	Ind. lamp – front fog lamps
100	Ind. lamp – turn signals right
101	Ind. lamp – turn signals left
102	Ind. lamp – parking brake
103	Fuel warning lamp
104	Brake pad wear indicator
105	Ind. lamp – battery charge
106	Ind. lamp – oil pressure
107	Ind. lamp – brake fluid level
108	Central warning lamp
109	Brake pad wear sensor front
110	Brake pad 1
111	Brake pad 2
112	Lead deleted from 1987 model
113	Brake pad wear sensor rear (only on 525e) Lead deleted from 1987 model
114	Stoplight left
115	Stoplight right
116	Electronic speedometer
117	Fuel gauge
118	Fuel level transmitter
119	Tachometer
120	COolant temperature gauge
121	Switch – inside lights
122	Switch – door contact front left
123	Switch – door contact front right
124	Switch – door contact rear right
125	Switch – door contact rear left
126	Switch – parking brake
127	Switch – oil pressure
128	Switch – brake fluid level
129	Switch – stoplights
130	Switch – door handle
131	Switch – boot lid contact
132	Boot lid
133	Door contact
134	Engine hood
135	Horns
136	Plug, centre section – instrument cluster 26-pin (on instrument cluster)

Key to Fig. 12.27 (continued)

No	Description
137	Plug, rear section – instrument cluster 26-pin (on instrument cluster)
138	Plug for burglar alarm 3-pin (in engine compartment, left wheel house)
139	Plug for automatic antenna
140	Plug for LA Australia (right of steering column)
141	Plug, rear section – driver's door 6-pin (A pillar end plate)
142	Plug for on-board computer 26-pin (only special equipment/on instrument cluster)
143	Plug for range indicator
144	Plug for cruise control (instrument cluster)
145	Plug for boot light (support for boot lid hinge)
146	Plug for 0_2 (white) (not on 525e)
147	Plug for 65 km/h output (not on 525e) (instrument cluster)
148	Temp. sensor – inside (lower steering column casing)
149	Control unit (heater controls)
150	Temp. sensor – heater (on heater)
151	Light for heater controls
152	Conn. for map reading lamp (only special equipment)
153	Fuse – radio, instrument, check control
154	Fuse – horns, wipe/wash system
155	Horn left
156	Horn right
157	Radio
158	Turn signal front left
159	Additional turn signal left
160	Turn signal rear left
161	Turn signal front right
162	Turn signal rear right
163	Additional turn signal right
164	Relay – two-tone horns (power distr.)
165	Wipe/wash intermittent control unit (on power distributor)
166	Relay – hazard lights (in steering column)
167	Motor – wipers

No	Description
168	Pump – headlight cleaning
169	Pump – washing fluid
170	Motor – heater blower
171	Motor – power mirror
172	Motor – extra power mirror (only special equipment)
173	Plug, centre section – heater controls 13-pin (on heater left)
174	Plug for wiper switch 6-pin (on upper steering column casing)
175	Plug for left front turn signal (near headlight)
176	Plug for right front turn signal (near headlight)
177	Plug for wiper motor 6-pin (on wiper motor)
178	Conn. for left additional turn signal 2-pin (left of steering column)
179	Conn. for right additional turn signal 2-pin (A pillar end plate)
180	Plug, driver's door – mirror connecting lead (A pillar end plate, below radio speaker)
181	Plug, passenger's door – mirror connecting lead (A pillar end plate, below radio speaker)
182	Conn. for power mirror
183	Conn. for additional power mirror
184	Conn. for map reading lamp
185	Water valve
186	Plug, front section – centre section 7-pin (in power distributor)
187	Switch – turn signals
188	Switch – horns
189	Wiper switch assembly
190	Switch – wipers
191	Switch – washing fluid pump
192	Switch – headlight cleaning pump
193	Switch – hazard lights
194	Switch – blower
195	Mirror switch assembly
196	Mirror switch – driver's door
197	Mirror switch – passenger's door (only special equipment)
109	Conn. for headlight cleaners (near wall right)

Index

A

B

T

V

W